War Letters of

Henry Cronbach Lowenhaupt

(1943 – 1944)

Library of Congress Control Number: 2024913081
ISBN (hardback): 978-1-963271-27-0

ARMINLEAR

Armin Lear Press Inc.
215 W Riverside Drive, #4362
Estes Park, CO 80517

War Letters of

Henry Cronbach Lowenhaupt

(1943 – 1944)

Compiled by Charles A. Lowenhaupt

ARMINLEAR

CONTENTS

Appendix
Historical Research
Prepared by Alessandro Lavopa of Storie di Famiglia
Including observations by Henry Cronbach Lowenhaupt from the Letters

Introduction

Henry Cronbach Lowenhaupt was born in St. Louis, Missouri on April 3, 1913. His parents were Abraham Lowenhaupt and Bessie Cronbach Lowenhaupt. After attending Soldan High School in St. Louis, he was admitted to Harvard College when he was sixteen years old and graduated in 1933. He went directly to Harvard Law School, graduating from that institution in 1936. He then joined the law firm founded by his father, the first lawyer in the United States to concentrate in federal tax law.

In December of 1941, Japan bombed Pearl Harbor and Germany and its Axis partners declared war on the United States. With that the United States was at war with Nazi Germany, Fascist Italy and Japan as it entered World War II.

Many years later during an interview, Henry recalled that "in about 1937 or '38" it looked to be obvious that we were going to be at war and I didn't see how I could stay out of it." He was practicing law in his father's law firm, but he went to a program in Leavenworth, Kansas, when the United States was expanding the Army.

> My purpose was to conclude whether or not I could tolerate being in the Army and I concluded that maybe I could and maybe I couldn't but it wouldn't be any better to volunteer for something than to sit tight and wait so see what happened. So I sat tight and waited to see what happened, and in due time I got notice. The induction doctor … asked me "how are you doing Mr. Lowenhaupt?" I said, "Very well, thank you" and he said "That's all I wanted to know," so in I went.

He recollected:

> I stayed at Jefferson Barracks at first and learned to type because I figured that was something scarce in the Army that wouldn't matter too much. I was filing and typing and learned to do it sufficiently that I could leave every day about 3:00 and not get back until the next day until about 2:30; I signed my own pass provided it was for less than 24 hours.

He remembered that he "just loafed." "Bored" with that Henry applied to Army Officer Candidate School and was sent to adjutant general school in Washington. There he studied administration as a lawyer, ultimately to serve as a lawyer overseas.

> When they said who wants to go overseas, I was bored stiff, I looked to Bill Clark [his best friend there] and he looked bored stiff and I said let's volunteer, and we raised our hands. So off we went. We spent about a month on the way.

The letters to his mother started on March 7, 1943, while he was still stateside, but he writes of his volunteering to go overseas on March 9. After waiting for orders, he goes to North Africa, Algiers and from there to Sicily, somewhere near Naples and Bari.

The letters, most to his mother but some to his father, his sisters and others, were saved by his mother and given to my mother (his wife, Cecile Koven Lowenhaupt) who gave them to me. Many were v-mails (shrunken letters making carrying them from overseas to the United States easier) and most were handwritten. I saved them and recognizing that I would never read them in their handwritten form but wanting to read them, I found a transcriber, Lauren Reed, who expertly transcribed them all.

Once I could read them, I found that they so reflected Henry's personality that those of us who knew him might like to read the letters. I was convinced that they, including his children and grandchildren, would enjoy the letters and that others too young to have known him, would learn about him reading the letters. So, I decided to publish this volume.

The letters themselves tell so much about Henry and the personality that stayed with him throughout his life. This 30 year old lawyer, who had bicycled in Germany with his sister when Germany was trying to extract itself from the Weimar Republic but before Hitler's control, had already come to appreciate the evils he saw in Germany but remained open-minded about Italy. He never lost his distrust of Germany and his love of Italy.

We see in his letters how he found friends wherever he went, his love of the classics and Latin and St. Augustine, his passion for music and piano, his attraction to fine crafts and craftsmen, his obsession with food and particularly local food. His sense of humor also comes through these letters. Finally, we see the dedication and love he had for his mother and the others in his family. You will find names of friends – both from St. Louis and newly found friends he made among local people and military. Some friendships lasted throughout his life. Others are lost in history.

Little is said about the war and its battles. Yet Henry was actually in the war's Southern arena and would have known about many of the most important events in the war. He does not talk about those; however, throughout his letters is an undercurrent of what is not discussed probably because he could not discuss such matters on account of the Army's censorship of them.

For example, he would have arrived in Bari just several months after the bombing of the Bari harbor on December 2, 1943. That attack, often described as "little Pearl Harbor" was one of the most destructive attacks on naval vessels by the enemy during the war, and the fact that one of the ships was carrying mustard gas resulted in its existence and details being covered up for many years. Yet Henry would have known about the attack, would have seen the damage, and would have recognized in his role after he was placed in the Army Airforce the significance of that attack. He says nothing about that at all.

Henry went on his holiday in Rome just one month after Hitler left Rome. He makes reference to the destruction by US bombers of a famous abbey but does not put it in the chronicle of the war. We never seem to meet enemy soldiers and his description of several legal engagements are relatively bland and say nothing to place the soldiers accused into the arena of war.

Henry used to explain that he was never sure he could tolerate his Army service. He asked himself what he would do if he wanted to desert? So, before he left the states, he purchased a bar of platinum, then a precious metal. That seemed to make sense but how would he keep it from being stolen during his months overseas? His solution was to cover it with oil and grease and use it as a paperweight on his desks over the months overseas. The bar was never stolen and he never felt the need to desert. That safeguard is referred to once or twice in the letters, but Henry would not have said anything directly. Over many years after his return home he used that bar to buy jewelry for his wife and to pay for other luxuries – cutting pieces off to trade for whatever he wanted.

In his recollections Henry talks about Madelena, the daughter of his friend Dr. Petrono. He says she was beautiful.

But the Italian custom was such that you couldn't possibly make it big with a respectable girl. If you made a date with a girl, she was a prostitute, so I have dates with Madelena and always sitting the parlor with her mother and father.... I think I liked Madelena. I think if I had had more confidence and everything else, I might have married her, but I was afraid to. Too many problems.

His letters mention Madelena, but nowhere does he suggest that the relationship might have been romantic – and we have no idea what Madelena thought.

His letters were intended to reassure those at home that he was well and pursuing many of the activities he would have at home – shopping, eating, piano, and enjoying dinners and parties with locals. He mentions a head cold but never mentions that he had malaria. From his recollections:

I was with the Adjutant General's Corps in the front lines, I came down with malaria there someplace in the middle of Italy, and I remember when my fingernails turned yellow and my eyes turned yellow, I decided I'd either cure it or kill myself. Then I drank a half a bottle of Italian brandy. The next day I couldn't get up so he carried me to the hospital and I was unconscious for at least a week or two; I had no idea what was happening to me.

When Henry returns to the States, the letters stop, and we can only surmise what happened next. We remember Henry's stories about his work in Texas as he was assigned to destroy various files. He emptied file cabinets into trash barrels which were picked up and sent to shredding when his commanding officer pointed out that he was leaving paper clips on documents and by regulation they were to be removed. To which Henry replied: "Yes, I am sorry but we must remember War is Hell."

Then he ended up in Virginia near Washington, DC still in service but with nothing to do. As he told it, he spent every afternoon at the capitol going in to see various representatives and senators. Each he visited assumed he had a favor to ask, but he asked nothing and stayed only for a "social visit" during which he remarked on how he enjoyed Washington, DC spending afternoons in the parks feeding popcorn to the squirrels and peanuts to the pigeons. After several weeks of those visits, there appear statements in the Congressional Records of various members saying that it was time to let the soldiers go and they had nothing to do but feed popcorn to the squirrels and peanuts to the pigeons. Of course, one should feed popcorn to pigeons and peanuts to squirrels and Henry would explain that this was how he knew he was succeeding.

He remembered his discharge in his 1986 interview:

I remember the last question they asked was "What do you want out of the Army?" and I said "Yes" and I thought that was the correct answer. They meant what did I want the Army to do for me. My answer was yes. At any rate, they let me out. This was 1945.

Henry's letters are the contemporary record of what he was living, and their accuracy would seem close to perfect. His subsequent recollections and his many stories are delightful but his letters are unquestionably as close to accurate as any we can imagine.

Once he was free of the military, he returned to St. Louis to continue to practice law with his father. There he married Cecile Koven in 1946, raised two children, Charles and Alice, and led a productive life before he died in 1990 at the age of 77 years.

He never lost his love of travel, food, fine crafts, and the piano. And he always surrounded himself with interesting people. Indeed, once I had read the letters, I was motivated to visit Bari with my wife. There in early 2024 and with the help of a historian, Alessandro Lavopa, a guide, Vincenza Pavia, and an organizer, Dario Pacini (from PlacenPeople) we found so many of the places my father describes in Bari and even saw a production of *Madam Butterfly* in the same Opera House where he had seen it 80 years earlier. We spent as remarkable a two days as I have ever spent anywhere, roaming the old city, finding his piano teacher's house, seeing the balcony from which he heard the announcement of the opening of Rome. I am including in this volume Alessandro's piece prepared for us tying the letters to the sights we saw.

This book has been produced primarily for family. My sister, Alice, graciously consented to the publication of the letters. The volume itself was produced with the expertise of Lauren Reed, who transcribed; Maryann Karinch, who published; Judith Bailey, who formatted the letters; and Vincent dePaul Lupiano, who advised. I am most grateful to all of them.

My wife, Rosalyn, and my daughters, Elizabeth and Rebecca, were, like my sister, her children and me fortunate to know Henry Lowenhaupt. They will recognize him in these letters. However, it is to my grandchildren, Ella, Hanna, Theo and Isabel, who never got to know their great grandfather that I dedicate this book hoping that reading these letters will help them understand what an interesting great grandfather they had.

March 7

Dear mama -

I am now, for the moment, in Washington. I arrived at Fort Washington yesterday in due time, and got settled, with a place to eat, and sleep, and stayed there last night. Today, Sunday, having nothing to do, and deciding it would be silly to loaf around the camp all day, I came into Washington – walking a good part of the way, so that it was noon before I got here. I had a slow leisurely dinner, and now am at Union Station waiting for the time to go to a bus, which I hope will run back there.

That brings me to the present.

Tomorrow, I am to start to work on the Restatements as they call it, which means rewriting army regulations. I can do it, but rather hope it does not last too long. It is only temporary, and I still have no idea whatsoever of how long I shall be here. I may learn something more definitive next week.

I have rather more comfortable living quarters than previously. Also better food so far, although it is unsafe to judge in the basis of the two meals I have eaten at the Camp. My understanding is that my working hours are from 8 AM to 5 PM every day, and that I may leave camp any day after working hours. But it is too long a trip to come into Washington for an evening.

I send my love

Henry

My address is
A G Pool
Barracks 124, Room 20
Fort Washington, MD

March 8

Dear Marian[1],

I am writing to wish you a very happy birthday – and intend to send you a present when I can find something. But I have decided that it is silly to go out and look for something, and at best I should find a thing which, if you wanted it, you would buy for yourself. So I am going to wait and hope that I see something I enjoy, and then send it to you – I hope that will be soon.

I wish I could give you more good advice on your 21st birthday – in the style of Polonius - but I have only a few minutes in which to write. I'll use my few minutes to write about myself.

I am here, more or less waiting to be assigned someplace else, which I hope may come soon. Meanwhile, I am spending time at odd jobs – yesterday typing. I find the ability to type a great boon, for it seems to get me out of very many things. It is much easier than other work, as grading examination papers, and rewriting regulations (a project undertaken, I believe, to keep people busy. It will never be finished, and, as far as I can see, no one ever wants it to be finished) I enjoy typing – it is just enjoyable to keep my mind off of other things.

---

[1] Marian is Henry's sister.

So I have to be here from 8 AM to 5 PM – and it hardly seems worthwhile to go into Washington for an evening – I shall go over the week ends.

I have a room here – the place looks like a cottage type summer resort – on a hill over the Potomac. There is a very good dining room, serving abundances of food. The rooms are well heated (too well, most of the time) My room is shared by me with a mousey little man – who distresses me by lack of enthusiasm and perfect indifference. I think he should go to exformer*[?]* and use a few superlatives one way or another – but no – all he does is lie quietly on his bed, write long letters, read detective stories, and grunt*[?]* yes and no *[unclear]* theatrically. I think he must have all the virtues. He is quite colorless – but I hardly ever see him.

There is much the same around here *[unclear]* I knew previously. They will begin being sent elsewhere soon, and I hope devoutly that I shall be sent among the first – although it is conventional to consider staying here an advantage. The proposition is the Holmes *Last Leaf Upon the Tree*[2] thought. I suppose a leaf wants to stay on the tree long, but it does not want to stay there till it is the last.

I send my love – again my congratulations and purest felicitations.

Henry

March 9

Dear mama

I am hesitant to write the way my thoughts have been running today, and where it has got me so far. But I suppose I might as well do so very frankly – partly to see how it looks in writing, partly to know it.

Since I have been here, I have watched as closely as I could what assignments were being given to other people. Some were being sent to the so-called office of dependency benefits in Newark, N.J., where they will clerk. I thought I should not like that, for the advantages listed were that it was close to New York. But one spends most of one's time working anyway. That was considered a good assignment. Some were being sent to teach in new schools for WAAC[3] – to my mind abominable, because, while teaching is alright if one has something to teach, it seems to me it would be intolerable just to teach nothingness like the margins of letters. Others – similar things.

Then today they called for names of people who were willing to go overseas. I gave them my name for diverse reasons. First, it seems that there is not much here that is not terrible piddling. In that respect nothing elsewhere can be worse – Second, I think that if I were selecting men who should be sent, I should select myself about first – therefore, that whether I suggested it or not, I should be sent – and it might be preferable that I suggest it voluntarily. That it makes no difference whether I go sooner or later – I am as ready now as I shall ever be. Thirdly, I am curious to know what will happen. . I

So, along the lines of the conclusion which I have reached over the past several weeks, I asked for it. About an hour later, I was told to get ready to go – which means nothing, and I may go at any time, either one day or six months, and of course I do not know where. I shall let you know when I do know -

---

[2] "I know it is a sin For me to sit and grin At him here; But the old three-cornered hat, And the breeches, and all that, Are so queer! And if I should live to be The last leaf upon the tree In the spring, Let them smile, as I do now, At the old forsaken bough Where I cling." *The Last Leaf* by Oliver Wendell Holmes

[3] Women's Army Auxiliary Corps

Meanwhile, I am to do such things as get an identification card etc. I went into Washington for that purpose this afternoon. And spent the afternoon there.

I sent Marian a slightly belated birthday – which I hope she likes. It is one I enjoyed getting, because I have been tempted by it before.

I shall, I think, go into Washington again tomorrow – there is no use doing everything in one trip – if possibly I can get more.

Love –

Henry

March 10

Dear mama -

A note to supplement my letter of yesterday – I am to go to the New York (Brooklyn) Port of Embarkation at a time not specified – to go to a <u>temperate</u> climate.

My address will be AO 4015 New York, N. Y., but as yet is not that. It may not be that for six months, for all I know.

I am well – and happy as if I were about to begin a journey.

Love –

Henry

March 14

Dear mama -

I have decided to telephone home this morning and so have little to write. As you see, I am in Washington – stayed here over night. I am well.

I expect to leave here either Tuesday evening or Wednesday morning, going to New York. I do not know how long I shall be there, but it is very likely that I shall not be able to write. So I think you may not hear from me for a while. However, I shall write if I can.

I am going to send a footlocker home, for we have instructions not to bring them along. I shall put in it what I think I do not need. With this letter, I am sending a key to it.

Of course, I do not yet know where I am going, but across the Atlantic (and it would seem silly to leave from New York to cross the Pacific) the choice is England, Ireland and North Africa. I wrote a letter to H asking him for the addresses of certain bookstores, and books being heavy, expect to send most of those I have home. The English bookstores will be much closer, and I shall bring any I want. I

Whenever I write about going, I think of very numerous pleasant details and possibilities, and gradually I am learning to overlook the unpleasant parts, like lugging baggage around (it can't take more than a day or so such of total time) and so forth.

The men who are going on the same shipment from Ft. Washington, include one William P. Clarke[4]– of New York – a boy named Darling, one named Clerist, and one named O' Brien. The selection makes it seem overwhelmingly probable that we are going to do some kind of office work, which is alright with me.

I send my love – shall telephone in a few hours.

Henry

March 17

Dear mama -

I am now in New York not knowing how long I shall be here nor what I shall be doing, nor whether I shall have opportunity to call or write. If I have I shall.

I arrived here last evening – with the four others – and we got a room here at the Pennsylvania – *[unclear]* – they gave us a *[unclear]* of display for salesman's samples – with four beds set up temporarily.

Upon arrival we cleaned up – I called up Robert[5] who recommended a restaurant where he said we could get the best steaks in New York. We walked down there and finding that it was a 'meatless Tuesday' We *[I]* had the best roast duck in New York instead.

Then walking up 5th Ave – across 42nd through Times Square and back to the hotel. New York is strange – even Times Square completely dark, and no lights on 5th Ave.

I wanted to report to Fort Hamilton today – and may know more of my status hereafter. I think it is likely that I shall be here about two weeks, but do not know. The basis of my *[unclear]* is that I have to get some inoculations which take two weeks. But of all that I shall know more, maybe, later.

I do not think I shall get around the New York much – being with these other men, I prefer to stay with them somewhat, and compromise or abandon my *[unclear]*.

Love -

Henry

P.S. I mailed you a receipt for a footlocker which I expressed yesterday from Washington.

---

[4] This is Bill Clark (maybe Clarke) who became a close friend of Henry. Whenever Henry visited New York he would look up Bill and spend a lunch or time with him over the years.
[5] Probably Bob Cronbach, Henry's first cousin

March 18

Dear mama -

I write to let you know that I am well and truly rather enjoying myself in a humorsome way.

Of course, I do not know when I am leaving -

I shall write at greater length when I can.

Henry

March 19

Dear mama -

I write to let you know I am well – and more or less enjoying myself – of which more details later.

Love

Henry

March 19

Dear mama -

I received your letter address to me here – and of course was sad to learn of Aunt Lore's death. I wrote to Uncle Jesse[6].

I am well – and still here – not knowing of course, whether I shall leave within a day, a week or a month.

Meanwhile, I am not working much – and have evening free, until I am put on the so called alert. After I am "alert," I think that I shall not be permitted to write, so that my cards and letters sometimes will just stop. If I am in town over Sunday, I shall very likely telephone.

I had a pleasant time last night – went up into Brooklyn, walking about ten or twelve blocks – in the course of it having my clothes pressed, my shoes shined, eating supper, and shopping for about an hour at a very superior French pastry shop, where I spent about half an hour sampling petits fours and Turkish paste. Then I paid my way out for a dime – I think I had a bargain in very excellent cookies and intend to go again.

This place is at the very end of the subway line – about an hour by subway from New York.

I have found also a very excellent restaurant in Brooklyn – called Gage & Tollner – which I understand is famous.

---

[6] This is the brother of Abraham Lowenhaupt and the Uncle of Henry. He was a lawyer and dlived in Chicago and Abraham clerked for him to earn his credentials as a lawyer. His wife was Laura Loeb we think.

I am living here in barracks – quite crowded, but comfortable enough, and spending days wandering around deciding whether or not to get a pair of shoes or another towel – extra weight vs. security. I have about concluded to get no more, because once you start, if one pair of shoes is good, two are better, and three is no limit.

You mention that daddy or you might come to New York. If you would enjoy it, I may or may not be here – I cannot know. After I am put on the so-called "alert" I shall not be permitted even to telephone and no one outside will be permitted to communicate with me at all.

There is a hotel in Brooklyn called the Granada, which is a good hotel, I think.

But my own recommendation is that the chances of my leaving soon are such that it would hardly be worth your while to come now.

If I am free to do so, I shall telephone Sunday.

Love -

Henry

March 20

Dear mama -

I wrote you a postcard about an hour ago, just to be sure that I mailed something today. I shall write a letter too.

I have received only one letter since I came here – yours telling of Aunt Lore's death – and imagine that mail is being delayed or lost someplace on the way. I shall possibly receive a bunch sometime.

Last night I went into New York – I got there at about 6:00 o'clock – in time to wander through Gimbel's galleries for ten minutes before it closed – which I enjoyed. They have some very beautiful things. Then over to Fifth Avenue and up to Longchamps[7] at about 34th. There is something about New York which kind of wakes me up, and I have to remind myself of it now and then lest some evening I remain here out of sheer inertia. Longchamps at 34th & 5th Ave. Is excitingly modern in decoration, and it is fun to walk in. I ate dinner there – and believe that, while many places may serve more exotic foods, there is no place I have ever eaten where such standard restaurant food can be got – no attempt at atmosphere and hominess. I had a kind of hot lobster salad, broccoli with excellent sauce, and potatoes, and my favorite dessert there – baba au rhums[8] enjoying all of it. Then I walked up Fifth Avenue to 42nd St., where I telephoned Robert (Maxine[9] was at home), and I went out there by the Fifth Avenue Bus.

New York looks very brilliant to me. I should like to recommend that you & daddy take advantage of Marcau's*[?]* first opportunity to spend a week there.

---

[7] https://en.wikipedia.org/wiki/Longchamps (restaurant chain)
[8] https://en.wikipedia.org/wiki/Rum_baba
[9] Wife of Bob Cronbach

I spent the evening with Robert and Maxine – who are very pleasant and interesting company – talking about nothing in particular. They have a big, comfortable apartment, and Robert asks to be remembered to you.

That brings me to today – I plan to go into the City again, leaving here at about five, and shall possibly be able to stay over Sunday. There is much made entertainment available – as teas and dances – but I intend to seek more independent amusement. Possibly theatre tonight, if I can get tickets, and tomorrow – I may go to the Frick Museum, Metropolitan and what else is available.

I do not know why, but New York looks to me more beautiful and exciting than ever before.

I shall try to telephone tomorrow.

Love

Henry

March 23 - Monday

Dear mama -

My daily letter – again with a visit to New York. I went in with William Clark, whose company I enjoy, and had dinner with his father and brother (who had to work during the evening) at Gramercy Park[10]. Then walked up to Pennsylvania station, where Mr. Clark, Sr., took a train home (the suburbs) and I went with William Clark, walking up through Times Square and across to Third Avenue, and back to Times Square where we ate a light supper at Longchamps. (Eggs benedict on toasted English muffins – very delicious).

It was late when we got back – it always is – and then to bed.

I am going into town again tonight, I believe.

I am well, and send my love.

Henry.

Bill Clark's brother – a commercial artist – is a good friend of Graves Gladney[11] – whom I knew – slightly at one time – and of whom I used to hear much from ~~Ed~~ Howard Ridgeway.

March 24 – Wednesday

Dear mama -

My daily letter – which must be brief -

---

[10] https://en.wikipedia.org/wiki/Gramercy_Park
[11] https://en.wikipedia.org/wiki/Graves_Gladney

I was tired last night and so went only to Brooklyn, when I had an excellent dinner at a place called Gage & Tollner – oysters, lamb kidneys (a <u>meatless</u> Tuesday) baked potatoes & pie – and a bottle of cider as good as any I've tasted since I was in France.

Then I got lost on the subway, coming back, but arrived nevertheless -

I rather expect that I shall not be here much longer, but of course still know nothing – and when I do know it, I shall not write it.

Called Alice[12] last night – who asked me to come out there Saturday. I did not promise to, because I don't know whether or not I can.

I send my love

Henry

I am not getting any mail – I supposed I shall get it all in a bunch. You might try addressing a letter to me at APO 4016.

March 25

Dear mama -

I have your letter and daddy's – and it was a pleasure to receive mail.

As far as my free time – I am free every evening from *[this portion is cut out]* which means I can be in *[this portion is cut out]* – about 5:30 – and must be back here by 7:30 the next morning. That is contingent upon my not being "Alerted." I may or may not be Alerted – if I am, I shall not be told of it in advance. There is no way of knowing whether I shall leave in a day, a week or a month. When I am told I am about to leave – I may have an hour's notice or a day's or a week – I shall not be able to communicate with you all. So presently, I cannot possibly say that I shall or shall not be free next Sunday. I have no reason to believe either way.

If I am free, I shall look for you.

I send my love -

[This portion is cut out.]

March 26

Dear mama -

I am glad I reached daddy last evening, and hope I shall be able to see him – although it is doubtful.

I called early but reached no one – and kept on trying to call.

---

[12] Alice Uchitelle, his first cousin

I am well – and enjoying ~~m~~ myself.

Love

Henry

March 29

Dear mama -

I am sad that I am unable to respond to your messages. But other than that – I am well and still curious about what will come. I am now what is called "alert," which means that I may leave soon, or may be un-alerted. So that, while there is tenseness in me, there is still nothing known.

Love -

Henry

I hope you enjoy New York – I am sure I did last week.

March 31

Dear mama -

This is to let you know that I am well – looking forward to a voyage which promises to be pleasant – well accommodated – well fed, and so forth. My duties? "supercargo" *[sic]* and I have yet to find what a supercargo does. If supernumerary is one beyond the requisite ~~eou~~ number – a super~~numerary~~ cargo I suppose, therefore one beyond the requisite cargo.

I do not know yet where I shall sail, but do not intend to write again before I do.

I hope you enjoyed New York – it grieved me that I could not be with you.

Love – Henry

March (Not Dated) - Saturday

Dear mama -

I am in ~~tw~~ New York, having decided to stay overnight rather than go back to Camp. Maybe *[unclear]* way – but easier.

This evening I came in arriving at about six; I had a good dinner and went to see *Three Sisters*, by Chekov, which I enjoyed. I never understand these Russian plays, what they are driving at, but this one was very beautifully acted – so well that it made me think of Shakespeare. Also, the settings were interesting, and the whole surprisingly lively and light – although it almost had me weeping toward the end.

I shall continue this letter tomorrow.

Henry.

Now I am about to give up the room here – Sunday evening – and I have had a very delightful day – this morning, after breakfast, I walked out Madison Ave – the shop windows are interesting, as far as the Frick Galleries, and through Central Park, and back down Fifth a way, and then a bus for a while. Finally, some lunch (asparagus and chocolate cake) and then a bus back to Frick Galleries – which are completely wonderful, even though they have their finest pictures in storage.

I then wandered back – mostly walking – to Grand Central Station, and thence the Subway here. I must now get ready to go. I intend to eat dinner here and then go back to Camp.

Love,

Henry.

P.S. I am writing a note to Inv.*[?]* Bates to let me know at what hotel he makes reservations, and the date of them. I shall keep in touch, as long as I can, with that hotel.

April 19

Mrs. A. Lowenhaupt
6237 McPherson Ave.
Saint Louis,
Missouri, U.S.

Dear mama –

I write to let you know that I have arrived in North Africa, and am now in harbor, on the ship, awaiting wharf space. I do not yet know where I shall be, what I shall do, what my address will be. I write as my address *[unclear]* the last I have known; but I think it may be changed soon, if it has not already been changed. You will probably receive, even before the letter reaches you, a so-called "safe arrival card," giving my address.

I am awfully sorry that I could not see you and daddy when you were in New York – but like other things I regret, I am forgetting it. I was on the so-called "alert," and therefore forbidden to communicate with anyone.

I have had a beautiful crossing, having the good fortune to be placed on a cargo ship where I had private cabin, easily accessible showers, and every comfort. The journey was substantially without incident. I built myself a deck chair out of a cargo chamber, and spent the voyage sitting on deck, reading and in idleness. Pleasant company – a Mr. Kennedy, of the Navy, in charge of the gun crew on this ship, and others.

You know how beautiful any harbor is, after a sea voyage – this one is also lovely in appearance. The pleasure of a double discovery of land – once at the Straits and once here.

I just broke my watch crystal – could you send me two or three, taking a chance on breakage? If or when you get downtown. The watch is Patek Philippe. The crystal is square side straight and the length of the size, of the letters (with spaces) "Print the complete" on the top of this paper – full size, of which I think you have some. By the time you get this, the letter, you know, will be reduced in size. I think I shall be unable to get a crystal here, for some of the crew tell me all jewelry stores are sold out of all repair parts. But go to no trouble about this and do not worry for it.

Love, Henry

April 21

Mrs. A. Lowenhaupt
6237 McPherson Ave.
Saint Louis,
Missouri, U.S.

Dear mama -

Today I went to the City – and was enormously surprised, for I had been told that it was so filthy and everything else. Quite the contrary – it is a beautiful city – and reminds me of San Francisco. The buildings are lovely – stucco, for the most part, but fine buildings. The streets crowded, which I always find exciting, with soldiers and civilians, in narrow streets and some broad streets, and all kinds of civilians. Many of them are Arabs, dressed in blankets and turbans; the women veiled (some of them). Many of them look fairly clean. Mostly French civilians, and it quite surprised me that I can still understand some French, and make myself understood in it. I left my watch to be repaired – and may never see it again – it is worth about as much to me broken as if I did not have it at all so that is alright. I drank wine in sidewalk cafes, and walked a great deal, and ended up at a Red Cross Dance, where I ate sandwiches, and danced a little.

The city is full of shops, but there is no merchandise, except here and there a shop handling ladies' hats, or indigenous goods – mostly tooled leather, and some of it very beautiful; here and there a little *[unclear]*, but I intend to look around further and see what I find. The prices of everything are high. The rest of the shops are empty, as the book shops, which have left only a few contemporary pamphlets and *[unclear]* books. The only liquor available is wine, and a little beer. Food is not sold in restaurants.

I admire the Arabs' blankets – many of them beautifully woven. Also, the many quite delicate horses pulling carriages and gigs, and other kinds of vehicles. Streets lined with palms, and a tree which looks like lemon, but I don't know. *[Unclear]* franc. What is a centime?

Love, Henry

April 22

Lowenhaupt, Waite & Stolar[13]
408 Pine St.
St. Louis,
Missouri, U.S.

Gentlemen -

Here I am in North Africa – awaiting assignment to some particular work. I am living on ship board still, but yesterday afternoon walked into the city – which is thoroughly beautiful and to me very interesting. I drank a few glasses of wine, walked the streets, looking around, tried to buy a dictionary, but was told they were all sold, and that's about all. The shops are amazing – they have nothing whatsoever on their shelves, except a little dust – with a few exceptions, and I enjoy speculating. The usual statement made is that there is nothing here to be sold. But a few places – one I saw – have windows full of leathers; some have tooled leather – and I guess that this may be the of reappearance of goods which have been hidden. It is said that the Germans took everything when they were here – which may be so. I doubt it, and am speculating whether what I see is the evidence of a complete money pause – that no one wanted the German money, and they hid their goods to avoid selling them; that there is no confidence in the present money, and people are cautious about bringing more out than they must sell to live. For example, a local newspaper publishes an editorial urging people to bring out their metal coins, now that "the solvent United States!" is back *[unclear]* the paper money. Presently, metal money – I have seen only the 50 centimes piece. The fixed exchange is 50 frs. to the dollar.

I saw one shop with beautiful leather at prices such as 2500 fr. ($50.00) for a small cloth. So I rather suspect that they have goods, but will not sell at the price of the franc. I am going to try to negotiate just out of curiosity – maybe trying to barter, say an old *[unclear]* school ring I have with me (for which I

---

[13] His father's law firm. One in which he practiced before the war. Hy Stolar was married to Ruth, his sister, and together had a child Heymer to whom he refers from time to time

originally paid $3.50) and see if I can get something for it which is said to be unavailable. This is just speculation, and I do not of course, know how to go about my negotiations. But I shall watch for the opportunity.

Is there anything new? ….I send my regards.

Henry

April 23

Mrs. A. Lowenhaupt
6237 McPherson Ave.
Saint Louis,
Missouri, U.S.

Dear mama -

I had my watch repaired, and got it today – really some-what to my surprise. For I did not expect to be able to do it. But I conclude that, simply, customs differ. If at home, a man should tell me "impossible" I should believe him. Here, the impossible can be done. The jeweler said it would take ten days, but he finished in two. It appears that all the watchmakers are very busy – this one overcharged me, and I was willing to be overcharged. I think he was surprised.

I have spent most of today in the city, first getting my watch (which entails a little visit, with thumbs and handshakes); then a long walk down one of the main streets, which was lovely, interesting and, crowded. It may be partly my imagination, but it seems to me there is an easily perceptible increase in the commodities shown for sale – unless commodities, for the necessities are, I am sure, rationed. But I saw today shops full of bread, and charcuteries full of sausages. I have found no restaurants open to the public, and so have used the Red Cross several times, they have a sandwich place and two restaurants.

I bought myself a wallet to carry this money, in all sizes of bills. I cannot appreciate that it is money, for it feels so different from that to which I am accustomed.

I drank coffee, wine and orange juice on a sidewalk. Bought three books, jointly with Bill Clark, no novels were available, and I have now a little Treatise on French law, which is rather interesting – a kind of Law of the Layman book. I send my love. I do not yet know what I shall be doing.

Henry

April 28

Mrs. A. Lowenhaupt
6237 McPherson Ave.
Saint Louis,
Missouri, U.S.

Dear mama -

Here I am – stationed permanently for the present (which means, I think, a month or more) and so bound by censorship that I cannot, as far as I know, tell you where I am, further than North Africa. I am to begin tomorrow learning the organization of the office, and do not know in what kind of work I shall end.

I am billeted with ~~five~~ four other men, with whom I came hither, in an apartment, which is entirely satisfactory – fifth étage or sixth floor, with an elevator for which they charge 2 sous (10 centimes) a ride. The exchange being 50 fr. to the dollar, that is 2 mills. And La Concierge! Hew – she will do anything upon the slightest indication – but her French is terrible; so bad I can hardly understand it! A very crowded city, and apparently flourishing, except that, again, the shops are empty. But food seems ample, and everywhere I have received charming French courtesy. The landlady (concierge) falls over herself to have our laundry done and our cleaning; the neighbors talk in the halls, and we all agree it is very funny. I have had no time to see much of the city – but it is beautiful – again like San Francisco – with white buildings beautiful flowers, and great gardens.

There are numerous messes, where I eat abundant, plain food. Dates, figs, almonds are sold on the street, and I plan to seek out an artichoke, if I can find one cooked. I see many on the streets in wagons.

I send my love.

Henry

April 30

Mrs. A. Lowenhaupt
6237 McPherson Ave.
Saint Louis,
Missouri, U.S.

Dear mama:

I have come to the point where I really never expect to receive any mail – so that if I do, I shall be pleasantly surprised.

I have had all my time occupied since I have been here, trying to leave the routine of this office, the Allied Force Headquarters, and its various divisions and ramifications, so that, much as I should like to, I have not seen any of this city. Bus to and from the offices, and all I see, is very beautiful gardens, flowers and trees on walls.

I eat at a mess in what was formerly a public school, and am surprised at the adequacy of it. The concierge oversees us all to the office, and is taking care of laundry, presently, cleaning (if gasoline is available to the cleaners) and everything else. I think she will charge for her "commissions," to which, of course, she is entitled.

I bought my Post Exchange rations today, although I did not need them – soap, and so forth. I think a week's rations of laundry soap will last at least a month.

All my love -

Henry L

May 3

Mrs. A. Lowenhaupt
6237 McPherson Ave.
Saint Louis,
Missouri, U.S.

Dear mama –

There is really little or nothing to write – except that I am somewhat enjoying myself, am well, and may be working hard soon. Presently, my hours are long, and, since there are no street lights, I have seen nothing of the City. I think it might be interesting, and perhaps shall have opportunity to look around at some future time.

Last night, I saw a movie – my last, I am resolved, for a very long time. It was an American one – but given in a tiny, dingy, theatre, built in the French style, with ushers equipped with coal oil lanterns. That looked funny. The audience was mostly civilians, some French, some Arabs, the ladies veiled ~~over~~ from their chins to the tops of their noses.

It was pitch dark going back to the apartment – one stumbles over curbs and into trees.

This is a substantial city – it would be easier to see and get around in if it were smaller. The buildings are fine and big; it has residential sections and retail sections and everything else.

I send my love.

Henry

May 3

Dear mama –

I just received your letter – dated March 14, addressed to me at Fort ~~Hamilton~~ Washington (it seems that letters come in in about the inverse order to that in which mailed). I enjoyed receiving it, and it made me recall my then state of mind, what I feared, hoped and so forth. I know I then hoped to be in England, where I am not, and feared I might be in Australia or in the middle of a field. So, altogether, I consider myself very lucky so far. Nothing lasts forever.

Yesterday afternoon off – I spent it with Lt. Clark. First we walked down to the native part of town, where a guide came up (he said he was a guide) and we let him take us into ~~the~~ a Mosque – which was quite interesting. I am satisfied that there is something about the European climate or people ~~which~~ or tradition which makes Europeans build beautifully – this building, although quite curious could not be called very beautiful by any standard I know. Maybe just two different for me to appreciate. For example – one room just filled with crystal chandeliers, I don't know why. The guide, then, since we let him, undertook to show us around – and so he brought us to a museum with wax figures dressed in all military costumes and the gun that so and so shot such and such with – reminded me exactly of Jefferson Memorial. We did not go into the heart of the native quarter, because it is not permitted, but from the outside, it looked interesting – in a way of its own – narrow streets, with buildings arched over them, closing them to the sky entirely. The guide was, of course, somewhat of a fraud, and after the mosque, to keep us longer, brought us to the public museums, as places we could not enter by ourselves. But that was alright. He was overpaid for his efforts.

Then we walked back, stopping in a store where we saw some kind of tiles – painted by a man who, the salesman said, was famous. His name was associated with a place Casa Velasquez. Of course, Velasquez is famous.

There I bought myself a wrist watch – partly because it was said that a watch could not be bought, partly because I do not like to wear a particularly good watch when it is hot and I perspire. This is a watch of a make called Movado, a Series watch, unguaranteed, and second hand. I could have bought a new one of a well known make, by paying a very high price. I ascertained that to satisfy my curiosity. I then walked back to the apartment, stopping on the way for a glace and wandering through beautiful department stores which are pitiful because they have so little goods on display. A whole counter devoted to one lace or crocheted shirt waist or a few buttons? Thence, up to a bookstore, but, unfortunately, it was closed, and I got no books. The store hours are desperately inconvenient – closed whenever I get there.

So back to the apartment, where I washed my face and hands, and then to supper at the mess.

Tonight, I intend to eat elsewhere, for variety. Although I probably shall not get much. I have enough this noon to last.

I received some letters today, very old – the oldest come f last and enjoyed them.

I send my love -

Henry

May 5

Mrs. A. Lowenhaupt
6237 McPherson Ave.
Saint Louis,
Missouri, U.S.

Dear mama -

I keep postponing writing to you, hoping for something to develop about which to write. But nothing does, and I shall therefore write with small talk.

I took a walk after lunch today – and am enormously impressed with the beauty of the vegetation of this place – trees, flowers, in clear blue air over the hills. It is lovely.

Last night, I visited with Bill Clark our neighbor, Mrs. Peyrus, and her son, on invitation that she would give us practice in speaking French and we would give her practice in English. She speaks English very well, and I had a delightful visit. Her son does not speak English so well – he is studying it at school, and not doing very well, I judge. I hope to visit again.

The landlady (concièrge) stopped us yesterday on the way in – what a talker, a blue streak, including all the gossip of the neighbors . She told us about a leaking pipe – that the landlord wanted to us pay for its repair – and we told her to refer him to the Army, who would repair it if they wanted to; and so it still leaks. She showed us pictures of all her grandchildren, and lamented the times and the price of soap. I send my love -

Henry

May 8

Messrs. Lowenhaupt, Waite & Stolar
408 Pine Street
Saint Louis,
Missouri.

Gentlemen:

I now find myself with a few minutes of enforced holding down of a room with a typewriter, and already having written home once today, I take advantage of the opportunity of time and typewriter to write to you. I am, in general, quite busy with routine and work, and get much less time than I should like to have for wandering around the very interesting city in which I find myself. But yesterday afternoon, I was free and did wander around, and attempted to say a little about what I saw in mt letter home of today. I will not repeat it.

I am very comfortably billeted in an apartment (with four other men, of whom at least one will leave at some time, I am told) We have two rooms and a bathroom (without bath) and a kitchen, which is very convenient for heating water for washing. An elevator, to bring us up to our cinquieme etage, and a loquacious xx concierge to tell us all the gossip about our neighbors, do our laundry, keep the apartment clear and so forth.

I read in the army newspaper published here (called the *Stars and Stripes*[14]) that Congress had passed a bill about no income tax for the year 1942. If that is so, I shall send you a case, or you may consider that you have one, if in your opinion I have any. But that depends upon how much time you have, how busy you are and divers other circumstances which I cannot know where. I am curious about what goes on there, but it seems so very far away. I have, to the present, received no mail, but rather expect that all at once, I shall receive enough to keep me reading for months to come. That will be alright too.

I find that we have very pleasant neighbors where we are living. Last night I visited the family La Bonne, an old man, his daughter and her husband, and three children. They own a farm about 100 kilometers away, and Mr. LaBonne is interested in farming. So I tell him about the price of milk in the United States, the crops which are raised, the grapes and such other details as I can give him. His is, I think, a modern, competent farmer – his mother in law stays on the farm, while he works, for the most part, for a railroad in some managerial capacity, I think. Madame has a piano, and she encourages me to read her music, much of which I know.

Then there is Madame Peyrus and her son, whose husband (I mean Madame P's) is still in France. She speaks English excellently (has a brother who teachers French at Exeter, N.H.) and desires that her son learn English. He has just begun to study it, and does not do well; but she urges us to come down and speak English for his benefit, in exchange for which they speak French for ours. It is a very pleasant way to spend a free evening. It is not well to be out because it is very hard to find the way back after dark.

---

[14] https://en.wikipedia.org/wiki/Stars_and_Stripes (newspaper)

But two nights ago, Bill Clark and I wandered into a building – very impressive halls – and nobody stopping us we came to a theatre, and sat down as everybody else was doing. It turned out to be the broadcasting station of Radio France, having amateur night that night. It was the funniest proposition I have ever seen. Of course, the singing was poor, but the manners and incidents and excitement when the manager made a performer stop, although the performer thought she was outsinging Lily Pons, were uproarious. One really could not hear anything, so it really did not matter that it was all in French.

I have been looking for ways to spend money – to buy something; but this city is too big to find one's way around very easily, and I have seen nothing in shop windows. My idea is, you know, that durable commodities have gone into hiding, and will come out upon offer of a high enough price. They would also come out, I think, if one offered American dollars, but this is illegal – the currency being the franc of a designated bank – and so I buy nothing. If I found anything I wanted, I should attempt barter of commodity for commodity.

My sincerest regards,

Henry

May 9

Mrs. A. Lowenhaupt
6237 McPherson Ave.
Saint Louis,
Missouri, U.S.

Dear Mama -

Again I have time, and a typewriter, and want to write, not because I have anything to say, but just to talk a little, without saying much I am really thinking about. I cannot write about the work I am doing, except that it is much more interesting than I expected, and is taking just about all of my time. I am well.

Last night, I called on Mme. Peyrus again, and enjoyed talking French to her, for she is quite a learned and cultivated woman – and quite ambitious for her son. She lamented, among other things, that she could no longer sew because she had no needles either for her sewing machine or for her hand sewing. So I gave her half of my package of needles, and said that I should see if it was convenient for me to be sent a package of Singer sewing machine needles, and if it was, I should give her some. It seems so completely incomprehensible to be unable to get needles – such a tiny item – so that one cannot even sew on a button. She collects pins, and has a supply. She has quite a beautiful apartment, and she showed me her collection of rugs and Arabian or Moorish copper and brass – not large, but well selected, consisting of very exquisite oriental rugs – about ten of them – and six or eight brass receptacles. I enjoyed seeing them.

It is somewhat amazing to see very fine people continuing to live apparently quite comfortably, but getting on without things I have never thought of before, as soap. Mrs. Peyrus was prizing a little cake of home made soap – mostly air bubbles, which she intended to use. It looked more like a sugar cookie than like soap. Txxx *[sic]* But there is apparently enough to eat, especially of fresh vegetables and fruits, and I was served lemonade without sugar. I enjoyed the visit. We talked mostly of Gone With The Wind, which she is reading in French, and a few other books.

There has been great elation, as far as I can see, over the Liberation of Tunis and Bizerte, especially since, as it remarked, it came on Joan of Arc Day, the anniversary of the fall of Orleans to Joan of Arc. The streets are hung with bunting, and children walk through the streets with their teachers leading them singing. Of course there are also parades. The newspapers write of the end of the war in North Africa, and General Giraud, who has a genius for epithets, makes statements which are thrilling to read – masterpieces of brevity and idealism.

You see what a Pollyanna I have become.

Today, the busses were not running in the morning when I came up here, and I walked – about a mile and a half, but all up hill and fast. A beautiful walk, nevertheless, for the street was crowded all the way with people already joyous and celebrating, although it was only seven thirty. Bands were playing, and people singing in groups on the street, that is, the Frenchmen. I think they feel that the war is over for them, and that as far as lights at night, food and other things are concerned, they can soon return to normal. I hope they are right.

Love, Henry

May 9

Mrs. A. Lowenhaupt
6237 McPherson Ave.
Saint Louis,
Missouri, U.S.

Dear mama -

I had yesterday afternoon free, and spent the time walking through the city, which I found interesting. Into the native part of town – where there was small market in progress, with abundance of country produce – vegetables – and to my surprise, almost every farmer was carrying a sheep or a goat or a lamb. What a racket they made! The crowds were dense. The permanent shops all had their proprietors sitting out in front. I was apparently in the district which sells cloth, for they all had silk, wool and linen written above their doors, but little merchandise. The names mostly written in Arabic, but frequently one saw "A. Cohen Et Cie" and "A. Goldberg Et Cie."

Then through places, on steep hills with only little walks and steps between the stucco buildings, four and five storeys high. I always find such alleys exciting – the doorways opening onto them, and halls inside, usually of fancy tile, and spotlessly clean, although the streets were dirty.

Then last night, we visited the family La Bonne, upstairs – they always give us a glass of wine when we visit – and talked lamely about everything.

That is all – I have very little time free, and spend most of ~~it here~~ my time here at my desk. There is an olive tree in the window, and I am watching a heavy crop of olives mature.

Love – Henry

May 11

Mrs. A. Lowenhaupt
6237 McPherson Ave.
Saint Louis,
Missouri, U.S.

Dear mama -

I had the afternoon off yesterday, and again spent my time walking, which I enjoyed. This is a very beautiful city.

I am well, really with nothing to write about, and curious to know what is going on at home. But I really expect never to receive a letter again. So if one comes, I shall be especially pleased – and if a hundred come at once – maybe they will.

Everyone here (I mean the civilians) seems to think that war for them is just about over. Maybe it is – I hope so. To me it seems that it can still go on about indefinitely.

In walking yesterday, I saw many sail boats – pleasure boats – lying at anchor and up on the shore. They surely looked tantalizing and tempting. But of course it is not worth trying to make arrangements for the sake of one afternoon a week.

I send my love -

Henry.

May 11

Dear mama -

I have been sending a few letters V-mail and now shall try this ordinary mail, for I am not a bit sure but that it may be faster. Not that I have anything particular to say in a hurry.

I had yesterday afternoon free – and first came back to the apartment and boiled some underwear, socks, etc., to see if they got clean – they did, and the underwear brown and the socks white. That is nice, too.

Then I walked – up hills and down, through the City, and it is still very beautiful. I walked to the native quarter – but did not go in for there were signs all over, saying it was forbidden. So I walked around it, through markets again, and crowds. Then I walked along the waterfront, with its wharves and many small boats – sail boats and the like for sport. My! They were tempting. Then back to the apartment, where there was Glenwood B. Darling, with whom I went out again – we walked through stores, which have short hours and almost nothing to sell. We had a glace (frozen grape juices, with a little white of egg) and looked around. That is all. Then to dinner, back home, and being tired, to bed.

I am well – and becoming impatient to hear – not really impatient for I really never expect a letter – but I am sometimes curious to know what is going on at home.

I am again or still indulging in wishful thinking. General Giraud says (the newspapers here publish every word he speaks I think) that the fighting will be over by the end of June. I am afraid he means only in North Africa – but I take it to mean all over. Would not that be nice?

Nothing to write about. I must now go to the office,

Henry.

May 12 [Written in the same letter]

I continue this letter – we asked Mme. Peyrus, her son and her cousin, who is visiting her from the country about 100 km. away, to come to dinner with us this evening. It may be very funny – and can be pleasant.

I am well, and send my love.

Henry

May 13

Dear mama -

Last night, just for fun, we (Lt. Clark, Capt. Branley and I) brought guests to dinner, namely Mme. Peyrus, our neighbors , her son, Jacques, and her cousin, M. Martin, who was in the city for a few days. I enjoyed it, for although the dinner was standard, the company was new. Mme. Peyrus is a cheerful talker – and pleasant; Jacques is a boy of about 16, old for his age, who goes to school in the afternoon and studies in the morning. His English improves as he gets over some bashfulness, and he now speaks well. M. Martin is a Swiss *[word crossed out]*, of a good order of intelligence, who came to *[word crossed out]* the city to see, he says, an air raid. He is a farmer – he also came to the city, I think, to get a little apartment, as a milk pail, and seed and to determine what to plant. His farm is about 100 km. to the south. Apparently, farming is a very gentlemanly occupation here for he does not appear to do hard physical work. He can speak Arabic, and I suppose, therefore, has natives to do most of the work. It sounds like a very delightful farming life. I think that M. Martin is probably a modern, progressive farmer – is trying a few cows now, which is a good idea, if they thrive, for there is no milk here – Even before the war, they say, all milk, butter and meat were imported from France.

These people are sentimental – they desire the *[word crossed out]* surrender of Germans in Tunisia, and say that the division which surrendered to the French is that which led the attack into France. "Chaqu'un à son tour.[15]" And there is no end of delight in the fact that Tunis "was liberated" on the anniversary of the "liberation" of Orleans by Joan of Arc. I do not think the joy in that fact should be very pleasing to the English, from whom Orleans was liberated.

I am watching the olives on a tree almost in reach of the window at which I work, as they ripen. They are now a faint brown, and I hope I shall be able to *[unclear]* one or two when they are ripe. I am overoptimistic when I say they are a faint brown – they are just not quite as lividly green as they were when I first noticed them. The tree is different from my expectation. I hardly see how Noah's dove could carry a branch of it, for it is a heavy, woody tree.

---

[15] Each his turn.

I am well, and send all my love -

Henry

May 14

Dear mama -

I am well, doing nothing in particular outside of work, at which I spend substantially all of my time. With that, walking sometimes to and fro, my days are about used up, and I am ready for bed.

Last night we decided that the key to the bathroom door fitted the door of a vacant room, with a day bed and comfortable chairs. Possession is nine tenths*[?]* of the law, we agree.

I had my hair cut yesterday, and the barber gossiped – all about the rooms available and so forth. I took mental note, and if I decide to look for an independent room, shall remember, although I think most of his gossip is false.

Will you ask daddy if he can send me *Kiplinger's News Letter*? I think it might be interesting.

Presently, I am reading a French novel – a story of adventure called *La Chatelaine du Liban*

My best address is – Henry C. Lowenhaupt, 2nd Lt. AGD 01001835. AG. See. Force Hq. APO 534, c/o Postmaster, W. Y.

I send my love -

Henry

May 15

Dear mama -

I shall write for a few minutes while waiting for others to get dressed, and ready to go. I slept well last night, and have got up rather early. There is presently a racket of roosters crowing, boys in the street shouting "L'Echo*[?]*," which they pronounce "Les chgo," and "Stars and Stripes," which they call "Staws and Streeps." I think this city has more newspapers (each about one page) than St. Louis - "Le' Echo," "La Depêeche," "Le TAM," and numerous others. They are all the same – and I suppose this morning will still have the same headlines about "Tunis Liberée," and how Pres. Roosevelt or Churchill or somebody expressed his felicitations to Giraud or Juine*[?]* or somebody else. Then the marriage notices are masterful – that, for example, Jean, daughter of Dr. Smith, advocat, *[unclear]* à cour superieur, formerly this and that and such things, for half a page, and – , his *[unclear]* will marry Richard, son of Dr. Jones, physician, *[unclear]*, formerly of the faculté de l' universite, and so forth for the rest of the page.

Last night, I went to see Maj. King – a kind of a siep – and after a while we went to see his concièrge and her family, to ask them to sing. It was the funniest half hour I have ever spent. A kind of dirty concièrge, with a daughter who sings well, if you will make it a factor in your judgment that she has never studied. The father plays the banjo the mother pours wine, and all the time there is chatter loud and fast and furious. One of my favorite occupations is now to tell stories in French – because it is funny to me when I forget the climactical word.

So after that party, I came back and went to bed.

I am well – I hope maybe I shall begin getting letters soon.

Capt. Bryant and Capt. Brainley are dissatisfied with quarters here – saying they are too small. They may move out, and that will leave just three of us rattling loose in luxury. Will the billeting office leave us here? I do not know – nor worry much, because if it becomes necessary, I intend to go out and get rooms upon my own initiative. Maybe it can be done.

I think often of things at home – how people are, and so forth; but it is not sensible to ask questions because answers will come slowly.

This is Saturday already. Day after tomorrow, I have an afternoon off again.

I send my love -

Henry

Censored – Henry C. Lowenhaupt

May 16

Dear mama,

I have this afternoon off. and do not yet know what I shall do. But I am sure I shall enjoy it, as always, if only in the style of *Pippa Passes*[16]. I am well, and hope to receive mail some day, as perhaps I shall.

Last night, the soirée musicale failed to materialize, the singer, being able to sing only by ear, having no notes, and little voice. So she sang alone, and it was funny – would have been horrible if it had lasted longer, but it did not. Promptly at 8:30, she and the whole troupe (a paid troupe of dirty beggars in my estimation) went home.

It was at the apartment of an officer who was at Fort Hamilton, N.Y. with us. He has quite a luxurious apartment, and it is some pleasure to go there, although he is an uninteresting man, a Californian and <u>aller hiinde[?] gleich</u>. The singer is the daughter of his concierge, and my impression is that she comes up there (with her little sister, her little sister's friend (about 10 yrs. old) and her friend, as a kind of thrilling adventure of the Cinderella style. The mama comes up to get them, and at her appearance, they, rush out, leaving a cloud of dust, as it were. I don't think the officer appreciates the customs here at all, that the concierge does not mingle socially with her tenants – any more than the servant woman does at home. But a Californian – what is to be expected?

But the procedure is very funny, because they do not speak English nor he French, and the conversation is limited to single words, or in a confusion, to say to me in English, "Tell them this," and things get all confused, because by the time I understand and am ready to tell them that they sing well, they are telling me or somebody else that there are holes in the roof or that their friend who lives across the street is doing

---

[16] htttps://en.wikipedia.org/wiki/Pippa_Passes

something or other. So the remarks about five minutes late, is a bolt in the blue, and there is no basis of a guess as to what each is going to mean. I remember one, where it because necessary to use the word to the officer "Easter." By that time he was talking about something else, and it took a series of diagrams and calendars to get the word across, even in English.

We have new neighbors moving into our hallway. I intend to call on them and see who they are. I also intend to go to the Red Cross – possibly this afternoon, for I understand that Rabbi *[unclear]* is working there. I think he may not want to see me, but ~~oft~~ I should like to see him.

I send my love -

Henry

Censored – Henry C. Lowenhaupt

May 16

Dear Ruth, Hy, and Haymer[17],

I have been spending most of the very little time I have free at my own disposition wandering around the city, looking for something I could send you; but I have not found anything, for most of the shops are quite empty. Except, leather purses, which, to my judgment are somewhat ordinary, and paintings, every other shop being a gallery. But none of the paintings impress me as much better than ordinary either. That is about all there seems to be for sale here, but I shall continue, for I think still I may find, say, a Majolica plate or some lace or an oriental rug, for in every apartment I've been in, I have seen beautiful oriental rugs, and I have seen fine lace in curtains and native women making lace. I have, I think, tomorrow afternoon off, and shall see what happens and what I can find.

Do you still subscribe to an art magazine? If so, do you ever read any mention of such names as Clos, Montagne, or any other current French? There are always here at least three one-man exhibitions, and I am inclined to believe that numerous refugees from Paris may be here – possibly among them well known painters. If one could buy a painting by any artist who is favorably known; for, say 1000 fr. or 750 fr. (50 fr = $1.00) it would be an interesting venture. So if you can compile a list of current French artists from any magazines, it would be quite interesting to me. My judgement of the painting I see – it usually looks to me like quite clean, craftsmanlike work – that is, definitely professional. It is more conservative, for the most part, than Picasso and other, being definitely pictorial. I see some which has nice, clear colors, and some which have rather good composition – but I am inclined to believe that most of it is of the "over the mantle in a nice apartment" type – a print or a pair of vases would do as well.

But I may go on a lark and buy one anyway – on the principle that there is nothing else to buy, except mediocre wine ~~such as~~ like California wine, and Vieux Marc, a kind of terrible alcohol, like half Prestone and half Listerine.

Tonight I am engaged for a "soirée musicale," which I think will not materialize. The daughter of the concierge of a Major King like to sing – so I am to accompany her. We'll see what comes of it.

---

[17] Ruth is Henry's sister, Hy (Stolar) her husband, and Haymer their child who died.

I have found in the apartment a piano, a volume of Mozart sonatas and a sonata of Beethoven, a Waltz of Goddard, and so forth. I intend to use it, whether the consequences. (It is in a forbidden room.)

I have, as yet, received no letter, but hope that someday I shall. Write if you can. How is Haymer?

If I send any china to you, it will be on leave. I intend to continue looking. My impression is that tangible commodities are coming out of hiding here very slowly and gradually.

I send my love -

Henry

Censored – Henry C. Lowenhaupt

May 18

Dear mama -

Yesterday I had an afternoon free and enjoyed it. I walked into new territory, where natives live, and through a good deal of the City. Although it was dusty, it was very beautiful.

Coming back, I stopped in a music store, and bought a sonata of Beethoven (marked 25 centimes, the 1939 price, and sold at 5 fr., the 1943 price) and a volume of music for piano a quatre *[unclear]*. I hope to be able to find someone with whom to play, and think I shall be able to do so.

Then back to the apartment, and after resting a while, I decided it was too late to go to my regular eating place. I went to a public restaurant, and had a poor dinner – soup, a meatless stew of carrots, peas and potatoes, but for dessert, green almonds, a new delicacy for me.

In the evening, I visited neighbors upstairs, and watched them eat dinner – omelette, some kind of meat, and fruit. It is quite a family – Mr and Mrs, her father, and three children, but I have written of them before. We talked of food, the various kinds of fruit which they have. We talked of native food, and in the end, I was invited to dinner Saturday night, to eat couscous, which they say is a native food. Monsieur likes it with some Piquante, but Madame likes it just plain – and there was long discussion about how it is preferable. I sided with Monsieur, who likes some Piquante. Then we discussed Lily Pons, for some reason, and I asserted she was the greatest singer ever born in America – which met hearty agreement. Was she born in America; I don't know?

The children are very well bred – never a word out of them; but the eldest is getting to the age where she looks bored just listening to other people. They have, apparently been instructed not to accept gifts promiscuously,– the street urchins run along your heels, saying "chewing gum, candy, cigarette, un franc, Joe" – but these refuse anything at least twice – even a green almond, which is very insignificant, and give them away.

I am well; hope eventually to receive mail, as formerly I shall if it ever catches up with me. I send my love, and a faint sample of my work.

Henry C. Lowenhaupt

Censored – Henry C. Lowenhaupt

May 20

Dear mama -

There is no news – I wrote to you of the fur and feathers flying about the extra room, but the matter has not been mentioned again and there are no further developments. So we continue to use the room, keeping it locked all day, and, wait to see what happens. I kind of get the responsibility on my shoulders, because I suppose I speak French a little better than others, but am not sorry, for I do not favor the policy (especially when you're in the wrong and know it) of being impudent, surly and telling people where to go. So the conversation, if it comes, will still be mine, and I intend to apply my maxim – postponement is the first degree of avoidance – and postpone decision and action as long as possible. I think I shall keep a bottle of wine on hand for postponement, so I can change the subject if it gets too hot, by offering a glass of wine. I think it is fine – and it is not fun (although it might be effective) just to throw the friends of the landlady out.

I received my first letter yesterday. It was from Janet Cerf, addressed to me at Fort Washington, and mailed March 29. It was a great pleasure to receive it, and I have replied.

I am well, and wondering intensely whether you have received any letters – I have thought often of taking extraordinary steps to let you know I am well, there being several permissible methods, as ~~sendi~~ cabling money home or something of the kind, but each time have decided that surely you would have a letter by that time – and I now still suppose you have.

I send my love -

Henry

Censored – Henry C. Lowenhaupt

May 21

Dear mama:

There is now a new publication which I understand to state that here-after my mail should be addressed to me somewhat as follows:

Henry C. Lowenhaupt
2d Lt. AGD. 01001835
A.G. Section, Hq. N.A.T.O.U.S.A.
A.P.P 534
c/o Postmaster, New York, N. Y.

At any rate, you might try it for a while, and I shall see if I get any.

I am well, with substantially nothing at all to write about. One day passes after another, and I get used to it, and rather enjoy it - the speaking of French, the climate, the constant expectation of finding interesting things, and now and then a little success in it.

I resume my reading of St. Augustine, having finished my French novel, and in between times my little Cicero, which is particularly interesting in and elliptical passage about the diverse kinds of war which are fought, how they are to be recognized (the declaration or lack of it), what the treaties of peace should contain, and how they should follow the declaration or in absence of the declaration what the terms of peace should be. The passage, very short, in the *De Officiis*, is perfectly obviously right as matter of reason and prudence, and will never, I am sure, be followed or put into execution. I recommend it to your attention – although you will have to read about half of the book to find it. I can't locate it for you, but remember it only as a very short, concise, thought-provoking passage, upon which possibly in my attempted summary I have expanded according to my interpretation.

St. Augustine declines in his *De Civitate* from the heights of his *Confessions*. He devotes pages to minutiae, which are no longer very interesting – the particulars of the psychology of Adam and Eve before the fall, minute discussion of the existence vel on of evil angels, and so forth. My reading of it is too slow, but I shall continue, from time to time. He has a beautiful facility of expression, but it appears best in the ginner generalizations of the Confessions than in the *De Civitate*. He is still always logical, however.

You see how little I have to write about, when I resort to St. Augustine, Cicero, and such. But I send my love

Henry

May 22

Dear mama -

I received my first batch of letters – and was delighted. They make me feel much better – and remember the standards and other delights, and be better satisfied that maybe I can go back to them. You have given me a new name to call myself, and I shall tell you, someday, what exactly the "small cog" is doing, and the catastrophic collapse which would follow if this small cog should fall out.

I ate last night at a public restaurant – since it was full. I sat down with an officer whose face was vaguely familiar, and ate with him. Guffaw! I went through school with him, and for a year, he lived right below me. I urged him to come up to the apartment soon, because it was a pleasure to see him.

I wish it were possible to follow the channels of communication to have Barney[18] find me if he comes here – but I cannot give my address to you to give to him, nor does he know, I suppose, if when or where he is going. Nevertheless, possibly you can ~~wo~~ ask Edith to write him that my address is AG Section, NATOUSA, APO 534, and if he gets into this area, he will doubtless learn where that APO is and what the letters mean. For my part, after about a month, I intend to leave my address at the Red Cross[19] for him, or at least inquire after him there. If, in the event he comes overseas, you will write his address to me, it may mean something to me.

Your description (which you have doubtless forgotten) of Mrs. Friedman's tea pleases me, because I consider her a kind of extra fine salt of the earth – the kind who prevents sudden changes, because she does not know any other way of doing things than as she did them yesterday. And that is so of many

---

[18] Probably Bernard Barenholtz, a friend from St. Louis. He founded Creative Playthings (a toy company) with his wife Edith Friedman Barenholtz.
[19] Bernard was Supervisor and Field Director of the American Red Cross in Italy.

people – as here – demonstrating that the most violent external concessions do not change people. The landlady still argues about her rent, doubtless as she always has; Mme. Peyrus returns social obligations, and carries on a pleasant light conversation, and educates her son, because in the conventions these things are de rigueur . As a theoretical proposition, if her world has collapsed around her, her husband being, I understand, a prisoner someplace, (gossip, for she never speaks of him) and her ice box needing a part from Paris, and her income and support being gone, so she *[word crossed out]* must work, she should just abandon it all and set on the kerbstone , let her son shift for himself, and starve or live as providence provided. But she doesn't know how to abandon even the petty social amenities. Neither do I, for that matter – and I think I am probably in that respect more drastic than Mrs. Friedman.

Tonight, d. v., we go to the neighbors upstairs to eat <u>couscous</u>, manufactured by Ricci – signs everywhere advertise Couscous Ricci[20], and I am impatient to lean what it is. I have in mind a kind of gruel like cream of wheat.

There is talk here of reopening the butcher shops, and the legal notaries– calling the butchers into convocation etc. – indicate that the talk may be true. Mme. Peyrus' cousin returns from the country for another visit, and we are invited to dine there next week. That sounds like quite a social calendar. Add to it the "bonjours" about three times a day, so thick and fast that I hardly dare walk up the stairs, and it sounds as if I were talking all the time. But there are periods of silence, and some neighbors who seem self contented and unanxious to expand acquaintances.

For Marian[21] – that I enjoyed her letter enormously, and she must write again. With her at Woods Hole, what a correspondence you will have! You ought to get a secretary to whom to dictate .

I send my love -

Henry

Censored – Henry C. Lowenhaupt, 2nd Lt. AGD

May 23

Dear mama -

I had a feast last night – which I enjoyed immensely. Unfortunately, being a conservative, before I went to dinner at the neighbor's , I ate dinner at the regular mess, to be on the safe side. Then to dinner, at which we were to try Couscous. We had it – and I thought it was going to be the only course. Couscous is ground wheat – ground course, like corn meal, and it was deliciously cooked, dry and flakey. Served with a sauce of some kind of large, round bean in a juice of meat bones, tomatoes, and other things, and with a little of a vegetable which resembles and tastes something like stewed egg plant, but is green instead of purple. The equivalent of hominy grits and gravy at its best.

There were present, besides Bill Clark and me, Monsieur and Madame and their three children, Madame's father and her sister and brother-in-law, who were in from the farm. Hence, I suppose, the feast, as it was.

---

[20] "...couscous became semiindustrial for the first time in Algeria with the introduction of milling industries by the Ricci establishment in Blida in 1853 or Ferrero in Algiers." From Loucif Chemache et al, "Couscous: Ethnic making and consumption patterns in the Northeast of Algeria." https://doi.org/10.1016/j.jef.2018.08.002

[21] Henry's sister Marian

I ate a lot of couscous – and then there appeared a baked chicken – a beautiful meaty bird which quite defies description.

Next course – from string beans from the farm, I suppose, cooked for lack of butter with meat juices (from the couscous gravy) and garlic, and about the best string beans I can remember. You can imagine that my eyes were beginning to pop.

Next, a beautiful floating island pudding, made, I understand, of powdered milk, but fresh eggs from the farm again, with a cake far better than fair – I don't know how to describe a good solid cake.

This, followed by a big bowl of fresh cherries – black ones and red ones, which are just coming into season.

With each course, its wine – local wine, which, while it is not as good as the named French wines, is as good as the usual vin ordinaire, and much like the California wines.

Well, everything tasted so good that I ate until I was on the point of bursting. I am well, however.

Of course, I am very grateful to the neighbors [for so abundant and good and well prepared a dinner, and wish enormously that I could repay their hospitality. I doubt that I can – it would be embarrassing to try to bring the crowd to the mess here, and they would not enjoy it – There is nothing to be bought in this city which would make a satisfactory present. I ~~may~~ hate to give a cake of laundry soap, which I could get. But I understand that it is possible now to mail packages here, and if at any time you see any odds or ends which you would like to get, if you desire to send them to me, I shall give them away. Presently, such things as household commodities are not obtainable, but an established household has enough of things which last. For my part, I should like much more to have things which I could give to these people who are being so hospitable to me than such things as candy or everything else I don't need. What do you think of that line of thought?

I send my love -

Henry

Censored – Henry C. Lowenhaupt, 2d Lt. AGD

May 25

Dear mama -

Life becomes very boring – day in and day out – as I suppose is to be expected, with long working days, and short evening and nights. But I am still enjoying myself in leisure which comes from time to time.

Yesterday afternoon, for example, I had free, and ~~expee~~ spent it, again, walking. I first walked in a very beautiful park, filled with blooming trees and flowers, and with a few Roman tombstones and such on exhibition. Then I walked down to the crowded part of the city – a wholesale cloth district, where I was amazed to see bolts of cloth in stock. Also, a small market was going on, where Arab women were crowding to get white linen. I suppose for their dress, which is, substantially, a sheet.

Also, the butcher shops reopened yesterday – and women were crowding them to buy meat. I think they are open only three days a week, but don't know, nor do I know what the rations are.

So, it appears in principle, that "Tout va bien" ("all goes well") in just about every respect – except bathing suits, which I think cannot be found here. Maybe George could mail me mine – and if I don't get it, it will still be alright. I cannot use it more than one afternoon a week, if that much.

Would it not be nice to be out of the army – if it could only be accomplished with legality? I seriously consider filing a petition for discharge, but am having trouble thinking of any grounds I could allege. But maybe I shall find some authority for it, as there ought to be, for I am fully aware that the army would be just as well off, if not better off, without me – and I should be much better off out of the army. That looks to me like the basis of an agreement, if formalities could be dispensed with – as they probably cannot. I shall think about it for, say, a month, and then forget it unless I can reach a constructive conclusion.

I have no way of knowing whether or not I receive all your letters – I have received some, and expect more. I should like very much to hear from daddy – to whom I have written once or twice. Would suggest that if he writes, he might make a carbon copy of the letter – and mail it twice, that is, if he dictates the letter or writes at the office.

I send my love -

Henry

How is Haymer? Can he talk? Tell him I send my kindest regards, and am anxious to hear from him.

Censored – Henry C. Lowenhaupt, 2d Lt. AGD.

May 26

Dear mama –

What shall I write about? For I want to write, but have little to say. Well, let's try the neighbor's chickens and rabbits – the rooster is my alarm clock. She keeps them on the balcony opposite our window, each in a separate box. Her rabbits are multiplying rapidly – she had only one when I first observed, and now has about six – all pets, and she fondles them as she feeds them every morning. Then she also has one hen, which she picks up and pets, and feeds every morning. She scatters crumbs of some kind on the floor of the balcony, and then pushes the hen around after the crumbs – apparently concerned about the hen's appetite. She pushes its head down to each crumb, and surprisingly, the hen responds and eats the crumb indicated. It is quite a process, which takes about an hour every morning and evening. She brushes the rabbits to keep them clean, and brushes the hen. I have not seen her brush the rooster. For which, I think, her affection is not so great. She appeared yesterday to be washing the hen's feet, which taxed my faith in my own observation.

Chickens are abundant – every window seems to have a rooster in it – between the inside and outside of the wall, kept in by double screens, and about dawn, it is a marvel, how every window begins crowing so loud and steady that it is like an animated cartoon – the sound is almost visible in a brilliant yellow-scarlet. I prefer rabbits.

I am still reading my book <u>La Chatelaine du Liban</u>, which is exciting, and easy reading. I should have finished it long ago, except that I read for such short periods. Yesterday I saw French-English and

English-French dictionaries in a book store here, which might be satisfactory. I shall look at them if I can find a time when the store is open and I am free.

I received two letters today, of an early date. I also received your letter telling me of Marian and Al Klein, which, I suppose, is not announced in any way or generally published. I am happy to hear of this, remembering Al Klein.

I should surely like to tell you exactly what I am doing, knowing you would like to hear. But I am forbidden to do so, and only say, by way of correlation rather than information, that if I told you, it would not mean anything, and would occupy only a few lines and, would be promptly forgotten, as of no great significance to you.

I frequently reflect – the days are so long, and the nights so short – and send my love.

Henry.

Censored – Henry C. Lowenhaupt, 2d Lt. AGD.

May 26

Dear mama –

I just received a big batch of letters – dating from the first part of April – which have caught up with me, and hasten to tell you what a pleasure it was to hear from you. Also one from daddy – one from Miss Thompson, and one from Bill Charles – which I shall answer. The questions in your letters, as to where I am, etc., are, I suppose, now as fully answered as I can answer them – that I am in French North Africa, working in a headquarters, S called N.A.T.O.U.S.A, in the AG section.

I hope your chickens are thriving – I see so many here, and hear so many, too – all roosters. So I could summarize with the exclamation I use now that I've sworn off profanity – "Pitch, Pine and Turpentine."

That is about all I can answer as to what, in general I am doing.

As to Betty's proposed thesis of my thoughts upon seeing the Evening Star – I do not like the subject, for anything so pale and pastelle *[sic]* and lovely always inspires me with a useless laughing, ~~be~~ resembling sorrow "as a mist resembles the rain" – and that soon becomes homesickness and discontent. So I do not look at the S Evening Star. It is too much to me like a flower bud, which wither before it blooms, or an effort which looks as if it can accomplish something, but is interrupted. ~~Some~~ Like following an arrow – but the wrong way. It is an inspiration which does not last; exhaling instead of inhaling; all frustration; no accomplishment. All this because it sets so soon.

There are so many things that are so. One so often starts out, all prepared, to do something which is accomplishment – and finds the effort misdirected – one would have done as well to stay in bed. Maybe the solution is to keep bouncing – again and, again and again – contrary to the rolling stone doctrine. Maybe the solution is to "hope no more for things that will not come --" and simply wait out the denouement of predestination. I don't know.

Daddy writes a short letter – tell him I enjoyed it and he should write more. I shall write to him some – a treatise on some subject other than the Evening Star.
I enclose a letter to Mr. & Mrs. Schlesinger – will you forward it for me?

I send all my love -

Henry

Censored – Henry C. Lowenhaupt

May 26

Dear Abe[22] -

I received your letter about my account and your purchase of bonds for me, of which I approve. I have been writing to mama, and of course you read these letters, so that there is no occasion for me to repeat.

That leaves me little to write – except of my resolve to go ahead more boldly, and less conscientiously as I have resolved from the beginning, and never executed, because I do not know how. That is habit. I should like to write you exactly where I am, what I am doing, etc. Maybe some day I shall, and not censor my own letter, so that the censor can use his own judgment. For my part, I cannot resist leaning over backward against my own interest and desires.

What is your present thought on investments? I am inclined to believe I have enough U. S. bonds for a while, and should be inclined to do something like increase my little City Ice] and Fuel Co. or Mississippi Valley Barge Lines or some other stock of which I have a little. Anheuser Busch etc. There is a list of what I have someplace around there.

You also know, possibly, that I have in my safe deposit box some bonds belonging to others – I am not sure, but I think there are some of Betty's, some of Ben's[23] and some of Marian's. There is one in my own name, with Marian as survivor as owner. That is Marian's. So if you decide that Marian's should be in her own name, you can have that one changed.

I also recall that my direction that dividends of International Nickel of Canada be deposited in my account in Toronto[24] may expire in August. If you think it not unwise to do so, you might renew that direction. I plan that fund presently as my grand spree fund – and intend to have it least a week of solid *[unclear]* when I can get to Toronto. That, however, is in the indefinite future – and meanwhile, if, as I have heard proposed, you or mama or Marian goes to Canada, you may spend the fund for any luxuries for sale on Marian which would not otherwise be purchased. That would include china, silver, wool, fur, or any nonsense. I do not know what is available – but suggest that if you go to Canada, ~~you~~ (Newfoundland) you go by way of Toronto – see Mr. Moore, Bank of Montreal, Toronto (on Younge St., as I remember) He will be technical, at first, but will get over it.

I have a nice note from Miss Thompson – sorry I'm not in England to see her cousin. Express my thanks and regards to her.

Affectionately

---

[22] Is this his father?
[23] Henry's brother Ben.
[24] Henry maintained this account for many years and would draw on it whenever he went to Canada with his family. He often told the story that Canada had asked Americans to spend money in Canada to help Canada and so he bought a Canadian company and set up that account at Bank of Montreal.

Henry

My wild spree fund is especially available to Marian – only she must not be conservative if she spends it. She knows the principle.

May 27 1943

Dear mama -

Well – I have been receiving mail now, and hope that you too have been receiving it of me. I write notwithstanding that I have little to say, to inform you that I intend to use this V-Mail primarily when I want to tell you something promptly – it does reach its destination a little sooner than other mail, I think. My objection to it is that it deprives letters of style, and, always, looking at the bottom of the page, the temptation is to get panicky– like writing a ten worded telegram. It makes a letter as impersonal as a printed letter from a corporation to its stockholders. Are you of the same opinion? It may be that the objection is just natural conservation – as I think walking is more pleasant and personal than driving, visiting more personal than telegraphing, and writing better than telephoning. "Pure prejudice!" Betty would say; "a word is a word." Forrest Campbell would agree with Betty.

So I send my love, this time impersonally – and shall write again -

Henry

Censored – Henry C. Lowenhaupt , 2d Lt. AGD. 01001835

May 28

Dear mama -

I enjoy receiving your letters, which for several days now have come abundantly. As I open each, the "ayenbite of inwyt "overwhelms me, for it seems prodigal – the seven fat years for the past few days; I ought to save some letters for the lean ones which are bound to come.

I have been doing nothing out of my routine recently – shall have to stir up my energy to push around a little more – it is too early to sit in the room and read and always so much more fun just to go out any place and see any one at all – just to look for ideas. Presently, I have none. I have been arising every morning early, taking a bus to the place I eat breakfast (this morning, grape fruit juice, oatmeal, pancakes and a meat cake, roll, coffee – a far cry from the "petit dejeuner" of convention) then walking thence to the place where I work. There I stay all day – with an hour out for lunch and a short walk – and then back to the room, usually walking. I am well.

I keep my Chatelaine du Liban in the room and read in the evening a little. I am about to finish it, and shall have to seek another book. My St. Augustin I keep here in the office, and read little snatches. Now and then, one finds a nice sentence for imagination – something one may desire to quote – although not as often as in the Confessions. He is still discussing Adam and Eve –whether or not eating the apple was a sin; and concluding in the negative – the disobedience was the ultimate expression of the sin, and, the pride the real sin – ~~"superative, [unclear]," he says.~~ "Initium enim" he says "omnis pecatti suberbia est." – "For the beginning of all sin is pride." He has a genius for concordance of various parts of the Bible, and correlates this with Jesus' expansion of the Ten Commandments – that one who desires to violate them has already violated them.

But I suppose you say "So what?"

La Chatelaine du Liban does not offer much for discussion, a mere romantic story which is now unrolling for a happy ending in the Deus ex machina style – the hero is prevented by a fever from fulfilling his evil intentions, so that his paramour leaves him, and I have no doubt he is about to marry the innocent heroine, as was contemplated in the beginning.

I send my love –

Henry

May 29 -

Dear mama -

I have written a letter to daddy, and write this, which I might just as well enclose with the other. I am well, and without needs. Your V-mail letter of May 11 just arrived – it is unnecessary to write so large, as I have a good reading glass, which I use, principally, to light cigarettes in the sun. For my part, I should like, again to encourage you to go to Newfoundland this summer; but I do not appreciate the details. Or Macatawa – you, Ruth, Marian and Haymer, with daddy and Hy coming if they could. It seems to me that Macatawa is so easy, with its abundant fresh vegetables and milk and so forth. But these are real, long distant suggestions.

So you speculate on where I am! I hope you enjoy speculating – I should like to tell you, and simply do not see the substantial reason why I shouldn't. It is, I suppose, the argument the serpent made to Eve – and if there is no reason why I should not write it, then – well, I suppose if I had been here, I ~~hav~~ should have tested the apple, on the principle of forbidden fruits.

How are Mr. And Mrs. Schlesinger? Please give them my regards, if you see them.

I suppose by the time you get this, about 48 of your 50 chickens will be beginning to crow, if that many survive – but I hope you have luck.

Tell Marian to write me another letter -

Love -

Henry

P.S. Did the principle of forbidden fruits exist before Eve ate the apple?

Censored – Henry C. Lowenhaupt, 2d Lt. AGD

May 29

Dear mama -

Well, I am somewhat tired today, having been up late last night, visiting Mme. Peyrus, her son and her cousin – Her cousin got onto the subject of politics, on which he is a violent conservative, such as I have never seen, and which leads back primarily to the beginning of Ecclesiastes (am I right?) "'Vanity, vanity,' sayeth the preacher, son of David being in Jerusalem, 'vanity of vanities, all is vanity.'" He has things figured out far in advance – how France does not want to be communistic, and after its liberation, will have to fight with Russia; teh teh! It reminds me of the good old days – it I so long since I have heard talk of those things. But I was quite engaged at the conversation. It even went into the Jewish question (he's against it) with condemnation of Blum, and restation of property, and all kinds of things. I kind of shook my head and avowed ignorance of the European situation. I feel for Isserman[25] – if he speaks French, he will surely get into a squabble and come out second best. But Mme.'s cousin, I think, loves to talk politics, and finds very few who will listen to him – a farmer, farming with Arabs – He speaks of the English as being in nature so conservative, with jealousy, I think, and contempt at the same time.

When I went in, although it was late, they were just sitting down to dinner, for they had been to a restaurant, had waited for a table. The menu proposed was soup, *[word crossed out]* ravioli, asparagus and fruit, but by the time they came to be served, they were out of soup, ravioli, and asparagus, and had green almonds instead of fruit. They still desired to charge the price of the dinner, so the party left, and Mme. prepared an omelette and string beans and bread and plum preserves – I watched, drinking a glass of wine as they ate.

I have been eating many green almonds, which are really among my favorite foods now – I think maybe they are habit forming, for I like them so well. What are Philippines? Did you ever hear of a game called Philippino, or some such name, played in connection with green almonds? I heard of it the other evening, and have a memory of having heard of it before. Well – that is not serious.

I send my love – Should like to hear from you – letters come in batches.

Henry.

There is little of which to write – my visit last night did not amount to much, but Mme. urges me to go to visit her cousin's parents – her aunt and uncle, who want to practice speaking English, I should enjoy trying, because there are many fine, conservative people around here.

H. C. L.

---

[25] Probably Rabbi Isserman, the family's Rabbi in St. Louis at Temple Israel

Censored – Henry C. Lowenhaupt, 2d Lt. AGD

May 30

Dear daddy -

I derive very great pleasure from your letters, one of which I received this morning. I regret that I cannot tell you exactly where I am, nor exactly what I am doing. The duties of the Adjunct General's Department are clerical; keeping of records, making of reports, writing of orders and so forth – and in this work, I am a very small cog.

I am happy that you like your new offices – and note the new letterhead. With all that set up, I may as well get me some free legal advice:

Please read Const., Art. I, sec. 9, cl. 8.[26]
       [check mark] Act. Jan. 31, 1881, Sec. 3, 5USC115
       Act July 20, 1942, Sec. I.
       [check mark] Act July 8 1918, Sec I. 22U.S.C.246,
and let me know your resolution of the divers questions you will see raised. Are there any decisions? I have only ~~the~~ a summary (unreliable) of these authorities, and conclusions which seem to me nonsensical. But if you are busy, there is no necessity of answering. Or if you just have the citations copied, I shall see what sense they make.

I am well – and hope that you too are. I miss my weekly telephone call, but there is not a possibility of telephoning from here, at least on personal business, and I am not sure whether or not calls can be put through on official business. So I have to be content with writing.

I presently have abundance of French francs (i.e., issued by North African Banks, of course) and do not hold American money here. I like, as you know, to keep enough cash available for whatever good cash may do – but having over $100 in francs, i.e., over 5000 francs., I begin to wonder what they are worth. They will not buy anything here – there choice is to send them home, for which I would convert them into dollars at 2 ₡ a franc or hold them. I am to be paid again in a few days, and then shall have more. Have you any ideas about the value of francs? There is presently some kind of U.S. guarantee , but I do not know the details of it – I think the guarantee is not very firm, but do not know. Money issued in France is, generally, not legal tender now, but I am inclined to wonder if it will not be, after the war, as good as that issued here. Witness action in Tunisia.

I send my love – Henry

---

[26] Clause 8 Titles of Nobility and Emoluments, "No Title of Nobility shall be granted by the United States: And no Person holding any Office of Profit or Trust under them, shall, without the Consent of the Congress, accept of any present, Emolument, Office, or Title, of any kind whatever, from any King, Prince, or foreign State."

May 31 1943

Censored – Henry C. Lowenhaupt, 2d Lt. AGD

Dear mama:

Well, for a change it is almost evening before I have a chance to write today, but nevertheless, there has not much accumulated to write about. My state remains unchanged – impatient to get home, and the prospect of time ahead before that is one I keep out of my mind, with fair success. Last night I paid my dinner call one the LaBonnes – is not a dinner call conventional?– and enjoyed about twenty minutes of animated conversation about the wheat crops and how corn is raised in the United States, but it is generally too dry for corn here What a pleasant walk they had yesterday afternoon, from which they were tired, the whole family. In short, it was a conversation not so different from almost any other, with strong agricultural tendencies. I originally blundered by telling them I was much interested in farming, and since that time, it is very hard to go onto any other subject, and equally hard to speak of farming, for my statements meet with awe as if they were gospel, and I tremble to speak of the *[word crossed out]* crops they do and do not raise in Oregon and Wyoming.

I did not stay long – it seems I always get there just before supper time, and they are about to eat; but I cannot go after their supper, because they eat so late. The baby falls asleep on Mrs. LaBonne's lap before supper, and wakes up to eat with them, it appears.

I am well. We begin wearing cotton uniforms tomorrow morning. I have a few, but could surely stand more. I have a few pairs of trousers at home. If you get this in time to think they would reach me before, say, July 15, *[word crossed out]* or even August 8, or some time around there, you might mail them to me. The shirts I have at home have not the little loops on the shoulders, which are now de rigueur. My size is 16 ½ collar and 34 sleeve. Two more ought to be plenty – although probably if I can get along on what I have until August, I can get along for the rest of the summer. Do as you like. I am sure the pants are worthless to me there, and the shirts can use even in the winter.

If you send anything, send a bathing suit too.

Let me know all about what you do. I received one brief letter from daddy, and should surely like to receive more. He has a genius for phrase making, when it comes to speaking about leprosy, the Germans, the Japanese, the sea and the Good God, which I think is well up to Horace or somebody at his most vitriolic, and in which I find the influence of the psalms. Have you come yet to: "By the Rivers of Babylon, There we sat down, Yea we wept when we remembered Jerusalem! Etc." I do not remember the number.[27]

How this letter rambles. I write that way when I am trying to come to something to write about. But this time, I am not succeeding. My mind is very full of thoughts of home, which I think is good for me. It keeps me conservative and knowing what fine people there are in the world, keeps me from being too proud of myself.

I send my love:

Henry

---

[27] Psalm 137

May 31

Dear mama -

I wrote you another letter just a few minutes ago, which I shall mail at the same time as I mail this one. So it is a race. Let me repeat a little:

We go into summer uniform tomorrow morning. I have possibly enough to get along on. But if you have any reason to believe that if mailed it might reach me before, say, the middle of August, possibly you could mail me the trousers I have at home. Those I have here are somewhat sleezy, and I am not sure they will stand up under laundry. The shirts I have at home have not the shoulder straps, and so I could not wear them. But if shoulder straps could be put on * No, it is not worth while, because the sleeves would still be all messed up. Possibly you could get me about two. 16 ½ neck size and 34 inch sleeves.

And if you mail anything, you might include a bathing suit. Maybe there will be a possibility of swimming here.

That is all *[written in the margin]* :For The Present *[End writing] I* send my love

Henry

Censored – Henry C. Lowenhaupt, 2d Lt. AGD

June 1

I find it quite impossible to appreciate that spring is over, for I have seen more of it this year, that Marian's school will soon be out; that summer is already here; ~~Im~~ still expect to see spring flowers come out; trees bursting in bud, and all these things which mark the time of year. But I missed them, I suppose, and summer is fully arrived. I have tomorrow afternoon off, and look forward to it with pleasure. What shall I do? I don't know.

I have taken over the "forbidden room" of the apartment – to which I carry the key. It has a piano in it, and I have about decided to use it, notwithstanding that it may declenche a dégat[28]as the newspapers say. I do not mind – because I think the worst that can occur is a little sound and fury. As I have some sheets of music – Beethoven's Sonata in Ab, the first part, which is a *[word crossed out]* theme and variations I believe the next part contains the Marche funebre sulla morte d'un eroë, or something like that. I intend tomorrow to get a little more – trying possibly for Saint Saens, Chopin, J B de Lully – French up and down, which is usually light. The piano happens to be a good one – The first I have seen on which a staccato note can be played. Maybe I can get as much as an hour or so a day in which to play. I hope objection does not come too soon. Last night, I used it for fifteen minutes; nothing has happened yet.

I am well. Today I received the April number of Reader's Digest – so things do come in time – as I remember, I read it before I left New York, so I think I'll give it to a barber or dentist – my barber's supply is antediluvian – Paris fashion magazines of 1938.

I send my love -

Henry

June 2

Dear mama -

I have, d. v.[29], the afternoon off, (it is morning now) and am getting into my usual *Pippa Passes*[30] state of mind. I do not yet know what I shall do, but since by prearrangement Lt. Clark also has the afternoon, I think I shall spend at least a part of it with him. I am thinking of recovering the book situation. I have finished my novel, *La Chatelaine du Liban*, and conclude that I should prefer something a little heavier – I may look for a medical treatise – there is a medical school here – or a good legal treatise, say about Justinian, although I am afraid most of the books will be on little subjects like the conveyancing of easements or excises in ___ Parish, if there are Parishes here. I saw one on "Le Droit Douanier d'Algerie et Maroc."[31] The religious and philosophical books come down to *Tears of the Wicked* and *Daily Thoughts* in paper covers, which, bound, would make nice presents for First Communion or Confirmation or whatever it may be.

Then I may go on an antique hunt, though I doubt I can find anything. Last week, I saw one handsome Lowestoft cup and saucer at a price comparable to that which would be paid in New York, and did not get

---

[28] Possible French translation: "déclenche a dégât." In English: trigger damage.
[29] "Deo Volente" or God willing
[30] Browning, *Pippa's Song*. "All is right in the world."
[31] "Customs Law of Algeria and Morocco"

it, because, shipping added, it would be too expensive. I am going to buy something, because sometimes things look different after they are at home, and *[word crossed out]* after returning, I kind of like tangible things of a place. The pictures I see are no good. Maybe I can find a book; maybe something else. The most common thing is leather purses and silver jewelry of a very low order.

I shall write again – and now send my love. There is a terrible dearth of things to write about -

Henry

Censored – Henry C. Lowenhaupt, 2d Lt. AGD

June 4

Dear mama -

Here is another day beginning – yesterday I tried to write – was constantly interrupted – this morning I shall be too. There is nothing new of which to write.

Last night I took a long walk – it stays light until about 10 o'clock, with changes of time and all those factor – along the harbor, and then back through the city, which was lovely – especially the native parts, crowded with people getting around, running, walking, selling junk, and some push carts with cherries and vegetables and a few apricots which now come into season.

I am well – I tried Wednesday to buy some Chopin, but the store was sold out – it looks as if they are sold out of all but German composers now – but German composers can still make quite an array – It reminds me of Benjamin Franklin story of having a different language from the English.[32]

My mind is quite empty – I shall have to do something to cure that – If I am not busy today (remark the similarity in meaning of "if" and "when") I shall go off under the name of going to the barber shop, and get a book while I am gone.

Last night, after my walk, I read a letter of Gertrude Stein's Paris, France, translated from "the American." It is desperately funny, I think because it is silly.

I send my love – I have a purse which I bought intending to send to daddy, although I know he never uses them. He can give it to you or Marian or somebody if he does not want it. Maybe it will get there.

Henry

---

[32] Debating what should be the language of the new US now that British are beaten and hated, Continental Conference was talking of Greek (Democracy), Latin (Republic), German (Philosophy). Franklin said "We won the war so we should speak English (with which we are comfortable) and make the British speak Greek, Latin or German." A favorite story of Henry through his lifetime.

Censored - Henry C. Lowenhaupt, 2d Lt AGD

June 5

Dear mama -

I left early enough yesterday afternoon to do two things I did not want to postpone to my next afternoon off – I got me some books and a hair cut. Not much of a hair cut – and the books – the shop was about to close and I did not have time to look over the situation completely. I bought the First year course on the Roman Law, which may be interesting. In French, I much doubt that I shall ever finish it, but I have started. It begins, as most such treatises begin, with the development of the family as a social, economic and political unit – the force of necessity for protection to make larger units, and so forth.

Then I also bought a few little booklets of Latin extracts to see what they offered.

Thence back to the barracks where I washed, and went out to dinner at the mess. From there I walked the usual promenade, which was crowded.

I am well – regret that I have so little to write about. You may begin getting letters about Roman Law, which, I have no doubt, will not be very interesting. But, as always, things go on from day to day, and it is hardly worth repeating that the sun rises and sets – as it does –.

My principal purpose in writing is to let you know that I am well, and send my love -

Henry

Censored – Henry C. Lowenhaupt, 2d Lt. AGD

June 6

North African Theatre of Operations
APO 534
New York, N.Y.

Sir[33]:

I have to keep up the volume of your mail, so that you will have something to do when you come down town in the morning. And this is hard to do – there is so little of which to write. Things go on – day in and day out – the season progresses, and I find myself lazier and lazier.

So to try to cure that, I got myself the first year course on Roman Law – and shall see if I can read it with any understanding. So far, I have read two or three observations, which are both obvious and interesting.

---

[33] This letter may be to Jacob Chasnoff, Henry's father's law partner (or law partner to be) relating to the last question about Jane. Jacob was a quite scholarly lawyer. I believe he joined the firm after 1944 though not certain. Eventually he and his son Jules were both members of the firm.

1) Law is closely related to history – economic, political and social. Hence it is necessary, in studying each period of Roman law, to have in mind the social conditions at the time. The earliest period of Roman law - - - etc.

2) The great contribution of Rome to the world was a system of laws – Greece gave art and philosophy, etc - - -. (It reminds me of the bright saying that Christianity was the last and greatest creation of the Pagan world.)

3) Now, that annoys me! I was reserving the most interesting for the third and last and have forgotten it. So let me reserve third, and if I recall it, I shall write it. Oh yes – as related to Holmes' statement that the law is a seamless web – This doctrine is expressed (I expand it) that the law, taken statistically at any time, consists of ~~about 49.999 % principles which are becoming obsolete and~~ three kinds of principles – those growing obsolete, those growing to maturity, not yet mature, and those which are at the moment, in perfection. That the great body of law, as of any growing things, is imperfect – as a flower garden, which, to last any time, must have plants in bud, plants withering, and a minority in perfection, or as the human race, the majority of ~~whie~~ the members of which cannot be at their prime together, because that would make such a hiatus a little hence.

There are very broad generalizations – which allow imagination to run. Maybe it will not be so easy when it gets down to specific detail.

My book is in French, which, at any rate, is easier than Latin, and I come to read French about as fluently as English – almost. However, without a dictionary, there are still many words I have to skip.

Funny train of thought just now – when I write of reading and speaking French, I think of Jane and Jerry Olmer[34] – what are they doing; where and how are they?

I am well -

Henry

Censored – Henry C. Lowenhaupt, 2d Lt. AGD

June 6

Dear mama -

There is still little or nothing to write – and I suppose there never will be – except to repeat the routine of being in this office, eating, sleeping and walking – a routine to which I become accustomed. Last night, against my better judgement, I went to a Red Cross show, in the opera house. It was better than I expected it to be and consisted of a series of vaudeville acts and skits – a few good dances. Mostly amateurs, and my idea is that one must love an amateur very much to appreciate any performance he can give. I intend not to go to any more amateur shows – and no more professional ones, either, if they are movies, especially. For leisure always seems so valuable – and so rare.

Maybe this love of leisure of mine is laziness, because really I never do much or anything constructive – but I always enjoy it so much more without professional entertainment. Walking, talking, lying in bed,

---

[34] Jane Chasnoff Olmer, Jacob's daughter. So maybe this letter is to Jacob Chasnoff.

even, reading – and it seem to me that to go to theatre here is like going to Sile[35] to shop and to New York to spend a quiet weekend. There is much very beautiful here – which I do not tire of seeing – the streets and crowded and buildings. But the superimposition of Army crowds and practices of course is heavy upon the indigenous and is not particularly interesting here, because it is no part of this place, but a continuation of the habits of Indianapolis, Flatbush and Kansas City.

Which reminds me, of course, of the doctrines of Epicureans (much misunderstood by others if Cicero and Augustine have understood them correctly) that the happiness of men lies in being a part of nature – rather than struggling against it and striking out from it like a sore thumb. I do not take this to mean that one should like according to <u>one's own</u> nature, but as a part of the surroundings in which one is – like eating local strawberries instead of California oranges on the Gaspé.

I send my love -

Henry

P. S. What Nonsense!

June 7

Dear mama -

I visited the Peyruses last evening, downstairs, and had a very pleasant visit – They asked me to dinner next Thursday, June 10, and I expect to go – to meet the aunts of M. Martine, although just why I am not clear. I am willing – even anxious – to meet them, because I think they are likely to be lovely, quick minded people. The conversation concerned swimming, sail boats and such things – and I may go swimming with Jacques someday soon – they warn against rented bathing suits "because a Spaniard or a Jew might have used it." And I reply about the miracle of modern medicine. It is presently proposed that a sweater, worn upside down might do as a bathing suit. I am inclined to doubt it.

The conversation rambled on. It was remarked that Jacques was out of socks. It would make a very worthy use of some of my old ones – wool or cotton – if you would care to ~~send it~~ send them to me – four or five or six pairs. While I could buy some here, I should have to sign a certificate that they were for my own use. Therefore, I could not give them away. My understanding is that I am allowed to receive packages. So do as you like – I do not need anything myself – I cannot clothe the population of North Africa – it is pleasant to do personal favors for individuals who go out of their way in courtesy and kindness to one – conflicting cautions you see.

I am well – this afternoon off, and I must make a list of things I must want to do. Otherwise, when the afternoon is over, I shall find none of them done.

I send my love -

Henry -

---

[35] Silex MO, where Copperwood is located, a small town then with a General Store - The Enterprise - and little else.

Mme. Peyrus lent me her husband's Code Civile de France, and a commentary on it – so I have much reading accumulated.

Censored – Henry C. Lowenhaupt, 2d Lt. AGD

June 10

Dear mama -

Well – I had dinner last night with Mme. Peyrus and Jacques, and the aunt (I discovered the relationship is not so remote as I thought – she is the mother of the cousin of the husband) and the aunt's daughter, and the aunt's grand-daughter. They had to leave right after dinner, because they had far to go home – and caught the last street car. Mme. Martine – a regular old war horse, who talks in a deep voice, has a squint in one eye – would be considered a matron of character anyplace. Her daughter will be like her in time – a woman of determination, and the granddaughter, now a lively but exceptionally well bred child, even for a French child, of about 10 or 11 years, will doubtless grow up with firm resolution. How she must be managed! The old lady, I am sure, could be a character of Dickens – what is the name of the woman who takes David Copperfield in hand? – How she hates dirt! It is like warfare, and the Arabs are dirty, she says. That is enough to say about the Arabs. When she has to go, she even gets up ~~whe~~ with firm determination – she does not propose – she states and, commands. What a Captain!

The dinner was good – a kind of thick soup – a combination of porridge and soup, well flavored; a meat pie, mostly pie, but the crust dry and good (they say a dish from Lorraine of which I do not know the name) Potatoes, browned with onions; lettuce salad, pineapple and cherries – with a white wine.

After the aunt left, with daughter and granddaughter in train, we played bridge. That is impossible – I have all I can do to remember that a carreau is a diamond, a pique a spade, a trefle a club and a coeur a heart, (without a sous a tout – no trump*[?]*) and just give up trying to remember what any one else has bid. Add to that that the cards are marked differently – and I always forget that a I is higher than a Roi, Same ou Valleé – and I am utterly confused before the first card is played. Maybe I could do it if I kept notes.

Then Mme. Peyrusse left to wash dishes and press clothes for the morrow, and Mlle. Paulette Alibert came up to continue the game. These people have energetic character, to say the least, and Paulette rages over her cards, and gets *[word unclear]*. Her mother is like her I guess – for she seems to get into trouble. She went to dive on a ship the other evening, and in going aboard, fell off the gang plank or ladder into the water, whence she was fished. The sailors, who were standing at the rail to bring her to the dinning salon laughed, and, as I hear, when she got up to the deck, drenched, of course, she went through the row of them and slapped each one's face. It makes quite a picture – because, I know how mad one gets after having water. The fishing out is such an anti-climax. Her daughter tells the story. I do not know the Mme, but understand it was somewhat of a formal honor paid her – the invitation to dinner, and she was on her dignity, until she fell from the ladder.

Well – we shall, I hope, be invited to Mme. Martine's sometime – which I shall enjoy. She reminds me a little of Mrs. Charles – the old lady – and I think her standards of housekeeping will know no compromise. Mme. Peyrusse is a little on the modern side – would use napkins instead of a table cloth, and might say as Helene Friedman[36], that just a salad and ice tea would be so nice. I am glad she did not say so last night.

I am well. I send all my love.

Henry

P.S. Will you ask daddy if he could conveniently send me a copy of The Revenue Act of 1943 – I am curious.

June 12

Dear mama -

I have not had an opportunity to write today, but now, as it is evening, and I am under duty to wait around, with a typewriter available. Therefore I write.

I was engaged to play bridge with the Alberta, neighbors, but this coming on suddenly, I am not a bit sure that I shall get there. However, my bridge, especially when I must call the suite in French and read the little signs on the cards – for *[word unclear]* French cards have much smaller symbols, in addition to having the Ace marked only with a one, so that it looks very inconspicous *[sic]* - does not amount to much. I sympathize with your difficulty in leaving the honor count, and I do not even try such technical methods. All I can do to remember the names of the suits. But I was anxious to meet Mme. Albert, for she is the one of whom I wrote that when she was going to an honor dinner she fell from the ship's ladder into the water, and upon rescue, slapped all the sailors for laughing.

I received a letter from you yesterday, dated May 27, which I enjoyed very much. Your air mail letters get here more promptly than your V Mail, but I do not know that experience is general enough to make a rule. You say in your letter that you cannot picture my surroundings as well as I can yours, and I wish I could describe in full the details of this place. But even if I tried, I probably should not succeed in giving a very real picture, and I must not try. So I won't. If you imagine San Francisco, you will not be far wrong in atmosphere.

How pleasant it sounds to have Betty at home for a while – and how pleasant for Betty! But I suppose that by this time, or surely by the time you receive this letter, she will already have left. In fact, I hope you will be in Macatawa, though to express an opinion on this is surely long distance thinking. The very word "thinking" makes me quake, for there are so many things for which one seeks solutions, and none exist, and one does not abandon the subject but keeps trying to find a solution. This is worry; but often as I resolve to be completely indifferent to the future – as indifferent as I am to the *[word unclear]* I can't quite get over the hump and actually forget the numerous things I hope for and want and wish. Maybe there is a method of accomplishing the particular desires which come with such persistence and recurrence! I can't quite abandon hope.

I am well. I am thinking still of seeing if it is possible to rent some kind of small sailboat here, just for the pleasure of the one afternoon a week I usually have or the evenings now and then when it is possible to get away, for it stays light very late.

---

[36] A St. Louisan married to Stix Friedman.

There is no news of which to write – possibly I shall have some tomorrow, although I doubt it. I send my love

Henry

Censored – Henry C. Lowenhaupt, 2d Lt AGD 01001835

June 14

Dear mama -

A very brief note – to let you know that I am well, and that I expect to be assigned to a new station in the very near future. I shall let you know a new address if and when I know it. Meanwhile, there may be days where I have no opportunity to write.

I shall be glad to move – if I do.

All my love -

Henry

Censored – Henry C. Lowenhaupt, 2d Lt AGD

June 18

Dear mama -

I think that henceforward I shall not write as often as I have for the facilities are not so good. Note my new address -

Hq II Corps – APO 302, c/o Postmaster – New York -

It was day before yesterday that I arrived here, after a very interesting drive through country becoming progressively barren – through mountains, etc. It reminds me of Western Kansas, except that it is quite crowded, comparatively, with Arabs, donkeys and what not.

I am well – hope you are also so.

Now I am in a small town, which I have not yet seen to amount to anything. Probably not much to see.

Love

Henry

Censored – Henry C. Lowenhaupt, 2d Lt AGD

June 18

Dear mama -

Having moved again, I am somewhat unsettled, and have difficulty writing. I am now in the Adjunct General's Section of II Corps, and do not know what the work will be. I have an idea that the place will be moving frequently – and rather hope so, for at present we are in a small town pretty well on the borders of the desert – a rambling, Arab town, with hot days and cool nights and no rain. There is, however, a swimming pool, which I have already enjoyed once.

We live in tents – and I have quite abandoned any attempt to keep clean – am becoming accustomed to be, rather.

I am well – you see with absolutely nothing to write.

I send my love -

Henry

Am thinking of getting a room in the town for my comfort – hesitate to do so because nobody else does – further, do not know whether or not it is possible to do so, but would suspect that it would be, by overpaying.

This town is almost pure Arab – with a few French – full of mosques which people (Arabs) attend

Censored – Henry C. Lowenhaupt, 2d Lt AGD

June 20

Dear mama -

Still nothing to write – that I am bored is not news, nor right. I am frequently interested, although days are very long. I am now at Hq. II Corps, AG Section, APO 302 – and, gradually, I hope, learning what is to be done.

I am in a small town, mostly Arab, quite dirty and dusty, but with a beauty not unlike the beauty of Western Kansas – somewhat more picturesque, but similarly colored, with mountains in the distance.

I hope tomorrow to have opportunity to call on a M. Esclas, who operates a preserving plant here – and I would call on him just for fun, to see what came of it. Maybe I shall.

I am well – nothing whatsoever of which to write. It is hot as hades during the day, but cold at night.

All my love -

Henry

Censored - Henry C. Lowenhaupt, 2d Lt AGD 01001835

June 22

Dear mama,

Another day – and nothing to write. It is hot – but that is not news. I am well – neither is that. My mind has been extremely empty for the past few days – I am just not thinking of anything interesting, but only worrying around a little bit, in selfish channels. Well – that leads nowhere either.
I suppose that things will change – For the present, I am reconciled to receiving no mail for a long time. For after every move, it seems to take a long time for mail to catch up. But I received a letter from Marian – which drifted in, I believe, by chance or mistake yesterday, and which I have mentioned.

Golly, I am homesick! But that is to be expected, and I shall never get over it, I suppose.

My work presently consists principally of initialing papers – sorting them somewhat – this one to that person and that one to this – answering letters in routine, and when one gets tired, one thinks that it would all work out just as well if none were written or answered – that writing just tangles things up, and if all the writing were abolished, things would work out beautifully by the Grace of God. Maybe – It gets to be a kind of a farce when there are so many, and such complicated administration of so many things is attempted. To the extent that it works, I am sure my initials and all the papers are far less responsible than divine mercy on little children – but God might not intervene to see that some soldiers got his insurance beneficiary changed, even though Congress has said he has the right to get it done.

You see what nonsense is running through my head – and I am just writing in idleness now.

I wonder how many of my letters you receive – and what percentage of yours I receive. I have been writing about five times a week, not that I shall continue. I think my letters are likely to become very irregular in arrival.

I send my love -

Henry.

Censored – Henry C. Lowenhaupt, 2d Lt AGD

June 24

Dear mama -

My intentions are of the best to write – but every time I do, I find I have nothing to say. Well, I must reconfirm my resolution to be Polyanna, and go on.

Yesterday, I had the pleasure of a trip to Oran[37] by truck, being a messenger boy, designated by the fancy name of courier. A very beautiful drive, through dry country – but with quite a few irrigation ditches filled from I know not what source – hot sun, high colors of yellow and pink, so that the little green lines and, spots looked almost black. The mountains of sand color more like a veil than anything so tangible. Crowds of Arabs in all the villages.

---

[37] A coastal city in northern Algeria.

In Oran, after my work was done, I wandered around for a few hours. Unfortunately, everything closes through the heat of the day – about noon till three or four or five – but I enjoyed the town. I found one thing I wanted – and bought it, telling the shop keeper to send it to you when she could. She may embezzle to price – or may be honest and fulfill the agreement. The item is an inlaid writing box. For my records – the name: Porcher, Decorateur, Ensemblier – 23-25 Rue D'Arzew, Oran[38]. I said it was satisfactory if they had to, to delay sending it. The worst that can happen is that I may lose some money on the deal.

Love -

Henry

Censored - Henry C. Lowenhaupt, 2d Lt AGD

June 24

Dear mama -

This is my last sheet of paper of this kind. What more I have is in the bottom of my suitcase and therefore it is likely to be long before I write again. All things are somewhat in a turmoil as far as baggage is concerned – and I am just going to begin abandoning right and left now. I have too much – and nothing I want. I think of "Poor Alice," and may well try to emulate her – should if I had anything I valued for beauty, carry that in preference to something I need. In that line, I can get thinking of buying a rug – and if I can get a pretty one, carry it instead of, say, an overcoat or a blanket.

---

[38] map of the city from 1942-1943 which includes Rue D'Arzew (from the University of Texas Perry-Castañeda Library Map Collection, map of the city from 1942-1943 which includes Rue D'Arzew (from the University of Texas Perry-Castañeda Library Map Collection, https://maps.lib.utexas.edu/maps/ams/algeria_city_plans/). The map follows the text of this letter.

I am in good health – and this evening also in good spirits, having swum for a few minutes this afternoon. I resolved the other day not to holler until some thing hurts – and somewhat to my surprise, much as I dislike many things, nothing ever hurts yet.

Mail dribbles in in a most unaccountable way – today I got a card mailed to me at APO 4015, on March 20, which has been wandering all over creation. "I wish I was a postal card" – it worries neither about oriental rugs or blankets or overcoats!

Nothing new of which to write. I shall leave this open until tomorrow – and see if anything cataclysmic develops in the meantime.
I send my love -

Henry

[Written in the margin] Over

June 25

Nothing cataclysmic or otherwise happened between the time or the completion of the forgoing and now. I stopped in an Arab shop – he showed me the rugs he has woven and is weaving – they are not particularly fine, but I may get one anyway. They are rather gaudy. I should gamble on the shop keeper's integrity and let him send it, for I do not want to be bothered.

I send my love -

Henry

June 25

Dear mama -

Another warm day, as all are to be expected to be, I suppose, with some work, which is more pleasant than none. I must seize opportunity to become better acquainted with this town – the talk of never speaking to Arabs must be so much nonsense, because they seem so friendly, and the children are all over you most of the time with friendly offers – as to dust your shoes free. The men seem anxious to say "Bonjour," even though their French is poor. I think in Arabic one says something very like "Sholom Alechoom," or whatever you spell it, as a greeting.

Well, I have not had time to get my rug shop today – maybe tomorrow.

No news – nothing of moment to write. I am beginning to see very genuine beauty in this town – and the buildings intrigue me – no windows on the streets, mostly, but big court yards.

I send my love

Henry

June 27

Dear mama –

I just received three letters from you – a V mail and two air mail – and it was awfully pleasant to hear. I have been getting quite a little mail, and enjoying all of it. True, it makes me homesick and I think of home with much longing. I am well. I wish I could make a suggestion about Ben[39], but I cannot – he could ask for a transfer, but I think there would be a good chance of his not getting it.

I walked up the street a few minutes ago, and looked at rugs and decided it isn't worth sending home poor ones – loosely woven, mediocre design. So I bought none. Maybe I shall get someplace where there is something I want.

Then I walked some more around the town – a dusty village, but it begins to wake up toward the cool of the evening and the streets become crowded. Maybe I shall find another rug shop – they do have pretty woven caps, and beautifully big straw hats, which I admire greatly.

One gets conservative – to hate change and being dirty and so forth – but I shall get used to that too, I think.

I send all my love – at times the future looks awfully long – that is when I'm homesick, as this evening – but it will have to pass, a day at a time, and I am still abiding my resolution not to holler before it hurts.

Ask daddy to write now – and then – I should like to know what goes on in the office and anything else. I wrote a check for $15.00 today – on a plain sheet of paper – and mailed it. A note should be made of it in my check book.

Love Henry

June (Not Dated)

Mrs. A. Lowenhaupt
623 McPherson Ave.
Saint Louis,
Missouri, U.S.

Dear mama -

I am writing this V mail letter to tell you that I am informed that air mail service is being suspended for a while – possibly a month – and therefore there may well be quite a gap in letters from me. That is, the surface mail takes about six weeks, I suppose, to get there; the air mail, about three, and therefore with the change over, there ought to be about three weeks without mail. But I shall write V mail now and then, much as I prefer to write ordinary letters.

It is very warm today – not as hot as St. Louis, though. We are now in an area among the hills, and the breeze is not as constant as it was in previous places on tops of hills and with broader vistas.

---

[39] Ben is Henry's brother

Last evening, I took a walk of about two hundred yards (a lazy walker's measure) down a little path, past an old, big well, where I intend to do my laundry, if I get any before we move again, and past numerous almond trees. The nuts are now too nearly ripe to be called green almonds, but they are very delicious, and I ate two big pocketfuls of them. I should have eaten more, but it was too dark to find them.

The cattle here are magnificent – mostly bulls, which are more or less between real bulls and oxen. They are used as beasts of burden, and are enormous, red beasts. I have not been close to any of them, and do not intend to go, for I am afraid of them. Then a great many goats and sheep, donkeys and horses, chickens, and to my surprise turkeys.

I have not yet been to the neighboring town here, and very much fear that I shall not have opportunity to go there, much as I should like to. It is a town with some stores, which I have seen driving through, and a very cosmopolitan appearance, as flowering trees bordering the main streets, for a town which is quite small. It too is on a hilltop – but not so precipitous a hill as the hills on which most of the towns are situated.

There is no news. I suppose you know a good deal more about the big events of the world than I do, for I see only the world on donkey back, while you see it on busses and street cars. So I feel inclined to ask the questions the Irishmen used to ask, according to John Synge, in the Western Isles of the stray Englishmen who came from London – about what wars there were in the World, and what events were passing among men.

I have been receiving mail fairly regularly and enjoying it. I send my love.

I am well – suppose that by the time this comes you will be back from Macatawa.

Henry

Censored - Henry C. Lowenhaupt

July 3

Dear mama -

The purpose of this letter is to tell you that I am well – and rather enjoying myself – now staying in an olive grove – and do not expect to write often any more. I have had a very interesting drive for the past few days – and some other time shall write of it.

Mail comes irregularly – I suppose mine comes to you much the same -

Love -

Henry

July 5

Mrs. A. Lowenhaupt
623 McPherson Ave.
Saint Louis,
Missouri, U.S.

Dear mama -

I have not written for a few days, being in the process of moving – and still have nothing to write – except that I have seen much of interest – a few cities and much country – mountains, desert, and farm lands. I shall not write the details.

I am well – presently living in a very old olive grove, which is hot during the day, but cool at night. Not working very hard, except at wondering, which I have now about given up.

At the last town where I stayed, I finally succumbed and decided I might as well send some kind of a souvenir – so I bought a rug; but not desiring to rush around looking for wrapping paper and so forth, I agreed with the merchant that he should wrap it, hold it, and when it became permissible to send it, to send it to you. I told him I was relying upon the "Reputation of the House" that it would be sent – he assured me my reliance was well placed – and maybe it will be sent. "The House" is a little corner room, with straw mats on the floor, and an Arab sitting there. Maybe the reliance is well placed – I am inclined to doubt it.

Again I repeat – I do not expect to write often for a while – but I send all my love -

Henry

Mail is slow in catching up with me – maybe I shall receive some soon.

Censored – Henry C. Lowenhaupt, 2d Lt. AGD

July 6

I am now required to be in a set place for a few hours – and shall write, even though I have nothing to say. It is a beautiful, starlight night. I am well, and hope that everyone else is the same – somewhat homesick, as always -

Being unable to write facts of location, details of travel to this place, hopes or expectations, I shall, of necessity, write a little sentimentality   or maybe something in general of how things pass – I am living presently in an olive grove – one that is too old to bear, I think, but olives would not be ripe at present in any case. Amongst the olive trees are scattered here and there St. John's bread trees – or I take them to be such because they have St. John's bread on them. The place is dry, without rain in this season, although the night air is usually damp. Water for washing and drinking is hauled in by truck.

I have a tent under a spreading bread fruit tree – a small tent, and in it my bedding roll – stuffed much too full for any carrying, but not too full for softness, with blankets, underwear, coats, pants, all kinds of things. On this I am able to sleep very comfortably at night.

The days I spend in another tent – doing miscellaneous "work" – inclined to consider it "small cog piddling" – but that is alright.

Meals are served – entirely ample – usual breakfast being fruit juice, cereal, hot cakes and coffee. Dinner – usually meat (corned beef, or a kind of sausage called "Spam,") with vegetable, sometimes fresh tomatoes, cucumbers, green peppers, onions, etc., and dessert, as canned fruit, and supper the same.

It was permitted me recently to visit a city nearby – I enjoyed it for variety, although the city offered almost nothing I could find. It was a Sunday – and everything closed – if there was anything to open – and it seemed no one but soldiers on the streets. The native quarters were all off limits, and I did not see them. The shopping district – mostly boarded up.

I am, as usual, homesick, and I suppose I shall stay so – impatient to get home and wishing always that some method could be devised to get there – which of course it can't.

I have received no mail recently – for the reason that, moving around, it will take some time for it to catch up, if it ever does. Maybe my mail reaches you as irregularly as yours reaches me. My experience in the past – in Oran and Algiers and Relizane[40] – has been that I receive air mail faster than V-mail. But that may or may not be consistent.

This part of the world surely seems to be a melting pot – more so than New York – except that I do not think the elements melt so readily. The small towns mostly Arab – and I have no understanding of Arabs – they seem very gentle, and mild, but I have had no opportunity to talk to them. Many are very poor. Others are dressed beautifully. Their houses are always blank and closed off to the streets, so that from the streets one can get no indication of how they live inside. There are many Frenchmen in the cities. And here, also, in the cities, Italians, Greeks, Spaniards and others – Moors of all shades from white to pitch black.

---

[40] A city in northwest Algeria

Of course, the army carries with it its Americanisse– which makes everyplace likes mid-western Kansas in atmosphere, or like Arkansas, and no milieu could tune us to a new pitch or circumstance and spirit, so to speak.

But as you see, my mind wanders – the light is becoming poor – and I send all my love -

Henry

Censored – Henry C. Lowenhaupt, 2d Lt. AGD

July 7

Dear Betty -

I just received your letter dated March 23 (?) Tuesday, and enjoyed receiving it. Mail comes here very sporadically, and I am sure there are many letters written which I have not received – and equally many I have written not yet received. So you might pass this one along to mama – notwithstanding that I have absolutely nothing new to write.

I am well – living what is called "in the field" with a unit which will move quite frequently. The "field" presently is a very old olive grove – too old to bear, I think, for I see no olives on the trees, green or otherwise. Fresh olives are terrible tasting things, since they require soaking in brine to be palatable. Also some breadfruit trees, again the fruit not yet ripe.

This country reminds me, in climate, of the Valley of California – cool nights, but days so hot that even in the shade things become untouchable in temperature.

You would be interested in the natives here – in the first place, as a mixture, I suppose, of about every people in existence. They vary in color from black as night to very fair – I think their languages also vary, but they all sound alike to me – a guttural language, full of ch (as in ich) and ks. Then there are many French and Italians and Spanish – but French is the legal language. Strangely enough, I see very many natives who look exactly like your uncles – and if Uncle Haymer or Ike or Jesse[41] were dressed in a turban or fez or whatever it is called, and a white robe – and sandals – a perfect Arab in appearance. I do not know how they think – but those to whom I have spoken (in French) are very gentle – full of gentle handshakes, which are no more than finger touchings. I wonder if they are honest – or what their business standards are – I bought a rug from one, and told him he should hold it until after the war, or so, and then send it. I relied upon "the reputation of the house," a little corner shop with straw mats on the floor, and the proprietor sitting cross-legged on the floor drinking warm mint tea – the most horrible concoction ever brewed.

I find it difficult to become attuned to the milieu in which I find myself – and develop a kind of shell of indifference which reminds me of my boy-scout days. Time continues to pass – for which I am constantly thankful, and I postpone radical action of all kinds from day to day, with my motto that the first degree of avoidance is postponement. But I suppose my sense is mysterious in this, and I cannot specify.

The work I am doing is clerical and, under present ideology and sociological state of development, I suppose, necessary. As I do it (initials everywhere, papers flying, dust and all) I think of Tacitus' descriptions of the Germans and their methods, about what kind of rear echelons Hannibal and Caesar had

---

[41] Brothers of Henry's father, Abe

and how Genghis Khan got along without Personnel System and Machine Records. I suppose the answer is easy – that they also had a homogenous population, in which individualism was not cultured, and in which all mean were substantially alike – so it was neither necessary nor possible to select men adaptable for jobs, because they were all equally adaptable, and all did and could do the same jobs – almost equally well. But now things are complicated, and we have theories about differing adaptabilies and capacities – so that some (ipsi dixerunt) must do this and others that. It makes it appear that many are laboring very hard to produce very little, but it may all be necessary. At any rate, it is not my function to determine whether or not it is.

I am frequently reminded of the Federal Reserve Bank publications – they used to publish a proclaimed list of enemy nations, with whom one should not trade, as being enemy sympathizers – and the list grew and grew until, with all its additions, it filled a room with stacks of paper. And I felt that each name was a kind of personal triumph of some investigator – even if it was only the name of a dealer in mouse traps who unfortunately made some political remarks which were imprudent. So his mouse traps would become agencies of the enemy – and the line between punishing protecting one's self against harm and attacking the enemy, between those and punishing people with imprudent academic opinions became utterly obscured. Well – my mind is wandering again. The "lunatic fringe" of activities makes me furious, and there is much of it to be seen – all justifiable on flowing language in terms of psychology, economy and so forth. It is a nice vocabulary.

By this time, I suppose you have been home – my, what longing consumes me when I think of it. ~~Time passes, as I said, and~~

Write again -

Henry

You see how little I have to write – that I am tempted to play the picaresque – while waiting -

I send my love -

July 8

Dear mama -

This is the third letter I have started today – and each previous one I have destroyed, realizing after a very few lines that I had absolutely nothing to say. Well, I still have nothing to say, except that I am well, a little homesick, and send my love. Mail comes very irregularly – I am sure I have not received most of the letters you have written, and very likely you do not get many which I write. But with my recent change of address, I really expect no mail for a month or so, and the stray letters that dribble in – as yesterday, a delightful letter from Betty, dated March 23 – came, I think, more or less by mistake or accident. Future time seems very long, and it is extremely difficult to acquire the necessary indifference to it.

Are you at Macatawa? Marian at Wood's Hole? I received a letter of those plans – It would be awfully pleasant to receive a letter from daddy, but I suppose he doesn't get much time, and doesn't like to sit down to it. Or maybe he has written.

The thought passed through my mind – there are many potsherds in this grove (if such it may be called) They correspond, I suppose, to rusting tin cans and Hershey wrappers in an American road side orchard. But, presently, I think tin cans and candy wrappers are prettier.

That is all -

Henry

July 10

Dear mama -

The old time again, but I'll try to vary it. There is no news, and things go on from day to day with a little variety in the weather, and each day passing. I am well, and hope that you are also so. It is not too hot this day, but still early morning, but the present coolness – like a Michigan day – lends me to fervently hope it will continue so.

Yesterday I had opportunity to go into a city in the afternoon – a substantial city, but not comparable in beauty to Algiers. Very little for sale, and I bought nothing, but wandered through the streets. The city was very dirty and dusty – all dug up – but has the appearance of having been a fine city – although with an extremely heterogenous population.

I went into one little shop, which had little pieces of silk for sale, and some rugs and odds and ends – the nice things (about two) which they had, they said were not for sale – explained by the proprietor as that they were for sale only at a price I wouldn't pay – as a small ~~carpet~~ rug – at ~~$2~~ 48000 fr. – about $1000, which I took to be worth about $30.00 at most. I told him that I wanted it, but it was not worth talking about, because I wouldn't pay him even one fourth of his price – and asked why he put such a price on it? He said he did not know what it was worth – that after the war it might be worth more, or it might be worth less. This meant he did not know what a franc was worth.

And that question perplexes me very much too. Prices seems to make no difference. The streets are crowded with sandwich vendors – a sandwich consists only of a piece of bread with a slice of tomato and a slice of onion – sometimes a piece of green pepper. But the prices vary from 2 f. 50 to 7 f 50 – right next to each other, and as many are sold at 7 f 50 as at 2 f 50. So also iced fruit juice – the price makes no difference – people would as soon pay 10 f. as 2, and wine – 5 f or 15 f. a glass for identical wine.

I do not know the source of value in a franc. If France is liberated, will she honor these paper francs? How? The north African countries are already to an extent autonomous– what is their relation to currency. It is printed by Bank of Morocco, Bank of Algeria, Bank of Tunis, etc. By fit, the exchange is fixed at 50 f. to the dollar – and I do not know what basis this exchange has. So far as I know, the whole thing may be a gigantic bubble – but there may also be some kind of Treasury Department order or authority about which I know nothing. It may be a kind of child's game, as where one uses pins for money in a toy grocery store.

I just hear a snatch of broadcast about the invasion of Sicily having begun. You probably hear about read more of it than I do. I suppose it is an initiation of more to come. I am well – and send all my love -

Henry

P.S. I received letters from Mme. le Jack Peyrus yesterday – I think I'll send them to you herewith for their humour. Mme. Peyrus is working in General Geraud's headquarters – Jack is going to school. Jack is a dumb boy – for all the English he has studied, he writes it very poorly.

Hope to receive letters soon -

H

July 10

Dear mama:

This is the second letter I have written today – both in idleness and with nothing to say. But the other one was not V mail, nor air mail, so that this can be considered, if you like, a race.

I am still in my olive grove in North Africa, and am used to it, I plucked a bread fruit a few minutes ago, but it was no place near ripe, and was puckery as a green persimmon. What is the name of the fruit? Is it bread fruit, or St. John's bread – like an overgrown string bean, and as I remember it, even at best quite tasteless. Most of the famous old biblical fruits are disappointing – olives, figs, pomegranates, all the them sound nice, but when it comes to eating them, an orange or an apple or a cherry is infinitely superior – there is nothing biblical to compare with peaches and apricots.

Well, I suppose an olive grove sounds pleasant. From far away, I should imagine it as moist and cool and green. But Pan is dead, if I may speak figuratively, and by present intentions, I shall cogitate that thought for about two weeks, and then tell all those interested that that great god is so. It is his presence, primarily, which olive groves lack, as I see them, for here would permit one to see the cool shade of the tree of peace even in those fastnesses of the opposite, and to imagine the delicious olives (even stuffed with pimento) from the mere knowledge that the trees were if the proper genus. But maybe I shall not find those who are interested in Pan's being dead.

That subject is now exhausted. I have nothing to write, as it already very apparent.

I am well, and send my love. I hope that someday soon some mail will catch up with me. I expect a package of at least 50 or 60 – and a day's reading. I look forward to arranging them all in chronological order, and going through them. There is no use asking questions.

The weather has been pleasant today – not a bit hot. Let me know if and when you receive (1) a little writing box from Oran, and (2) a rug from Relizane. Both of them were ordered by me to be sent to you when it becomes possible etc. to do so, and I am wondering if the merchants will do it, or will consider it a good opportunity to just ignore it all.

Write soon. It looks so impossibly long before I shall get home – but "Spe endim salvi facti sumus" sayeth the preachers, St. Augustine, "For in hope lies our salvation." I don't believe it, but sometimes am inclined to believe that if one could just despair altogether and give up, it would be the best thing to do. But one can't. It is not a matter of volition.

P.S. To fill up the page.

Love

Henry

July 13

Dear daddy -

It would be very nice to hear from you – but I imagine you have written frequently. Mail has not caught up with me, and I have received none for about a month. I imagine a big package of it will come all at once – I hope so, anyway, for I figure I have at least fifty or sixty letters on the way some place.

I am well – have been writing to mama about every day, a practice I shall not continue. So there is little, in fact nothing, to write.

I write principally because my mind is full of questions as to what is going on there, and wonder and curiosity. You see, I have heard nothing about whether or not you have moved to new offices, as you intended, what work is being done, how anything is, what is happening – and I am curious about it all. But I suppose letters are on the way, and I'll receive them all at once.

I am still hopeful – and rather enjoying myself from moment to moment.

Love -

Henry

July 13

Dear mama -

I regret that my letters have been very unsatisfactory in the past – as I know they have been. I am going to try to do a little better. The resolution is good – now for the execution.

I suppose you know all of the facts I can tell you – that I am living in a tent in a dry olive grove – and being reconciled to not being very clean and so forth, find it very pleasant in each moment. The disagreeable part, is the reflection of how long – for that extends absolutely indefinitely. The agreeable part – one gets to appreciate the sort of natural beauty of the place – in the distant mountains, the gray, dusty trees. The nights are clear and cool, with such abundance of stars as you know from Copperwood[42], presently a half moon, which is bright enough to cast very definite shadow.

The ground gives one the impression of having been walked on by men since time immemorial – it is covered for layers with pieces of pottery – many buried, many on the surface; th I cannot judge the age of the pieces – some look new, other very old. Fragments of design can be imagined to remain on some – they look more like strange letters – Greek or Arabic – Than like any intended pictures – I found one yesterday with a very definite epsilon.

The people I speak with most frequently are Bill Clark, who with whom I still am, and whom I have mentioned – and a Claude Morris – with whose family I believe daddy is acquainted – his father is (or was) a lawyer in Salt Lake City – his uncle is with Hugh Satterlee's(?) firm in Washington – formerly a member of the Board of Tax Appeals – Logan B. Morris, I believe his name is. I enjoy his company, because he talks a good deal – rambling, and one does not have to pay much attention to what he says.

---

[42] The family's country house in Silex, Missouri

Sometimes I am able to talk a lot – at other times – a question of mood – I am not able to open my mouth.

I wonder if I missed an opportunity yesterday – I chose not to act because I questioned the propriety of what I had in mind, and maybe it would not have worked anyway.

A soldier of the French colonial forces wandered in, and by chance came to me. ~~and said~~ He said he was hungry, and asked if he could get something to eat. I asked him about his unit, and he named it; I asked him what he was doing, and he told me he was, in a vague way, guarding prisoners. Why hadn't he had anything to eat for two days? There just was nothing. How about the prisoners? Oh, they were well fed, with cigarettes and everything. His story may have been in part or in whole true, I don't know. The prisoners were just "over there," pointing vaguely. At any rate, with permission, because he looked hungry, I brought him over to the mess truck, and he got supper. He was a nice, mild mannered boy, looked clean, and was courteous. I think that if I had asked him to stay here – promised him three meals a day – some cigarettes and maybe two, three or five dollars a month, he would have stayed, and I would have had a good orderly, to keep me provided with water, wash my clothes, make my beds and so forth. He would have been well off – and would never have been found – and I too should have been well off. But, as I say, I didn't do it. Next time (if there is a next time) I shall not be so scrupulous. It is not, I suppose, an offense to induce detention from the French army, although I really do not know, and I think it would be funny. But I shall have to make up my mind quickly if the opportunity presents itself again and if I know my own character, shall again hesitate and decide to do nothing. But I should like to try – I might catch holy hell for it, and on the other hands, it might be considered only a joke. If I once got the man far enough away from his unit (if he had any) he couldn't get back. On the other hand, if he was any good, he would probably be taken away from me – if it be permissible – unless I treated him so well that he would not leave. So I should see to it that he wanted to stay. You see, my plans are complete, and if opportunity arises, I shall make up my mind whether or not to try to acquire me an "ordinance"

I send my love -

Henry

July 14

Dear mama -

I am well – not working hard at present, nor do I know when if ever I shall be.

I have had opportunity in the past days to drive on errands over substantial country – and have enjoyed it – although in many instances it is depressing. One sees cities and villages completely wrecked – not a whole window or a complete building – roofs gone, walls collapsed, and the rooms standing exposed as in a doll-house. One very substantial city I saw so – bank buildings a mass of rubble, with twisted brass rails and bits of teller's cages left – that's all. The streets empty – and at one point, hearing a vague whistling, I looked closely at the ruins – there was an Arab sitting in the shade of a crumbling wall, playing his shepherd's pipe. I thought of "willow, willow" or whatever it is Ophelia sings. I do not know where all the people of the city could have gone.

There, of course, it is also very terrible to see at evening a long avenue of trees leading to a farm house – of a magnificent mansion or chateau – with a herd of cattle being driven to the barns, windings its way among wrecked vehicles. It doesn't make sense, you know. Do you remember your quotation about peace makes even the rocks fertile, and war the most fertile valleys barren? Will you write it to me? I remember only one or two words of it, and not their order.

I see a little threshing going on – not as much as I should expect from the size of the fields – the primitive methods – a horse or a team of horses or cows or oxen is tied to a pole and they are driven around on way, wrapping the tether around the pole until they are pulled close, and then around the other way, back and forth. Or sometimes a man will stand at the center, and turn as they go around. Then they toss it all tall grain into the air – a little at a time, and the chaff blows away in clouds. It is a slow process – but I imagine machinery or gasoline is not now available for the purpose.

I see, abundance of tomatoes, onion, apples, melons, squash and other fruits and vegetables coming into season – even pumpkins. I do not understand prices – for tomatoes will vary from three francs to thirty francs a kilo, and melons – they ask sixty, seventy francs a piece – I suppose whatever it is thought the trade will bear.

The roads are dusty. So are the fields. I see abundance of vineyards – but not many grapes – maybe the season is passed or the fruit still inconspicuous among the leaves. Almost all wine grapes – on small bushes rather than on climbing vines.

I still hope someday to receive a letter – but it is nice to have a pleasure to look forward to. So write often, please, and maybe I'll get something. I really don't expect to get any for a long time – possibly the first of August, giving it something over a month to catch up with me from my last address.

Did you ever receive a canned telegram from me? My purpose in sending it was that I thought it would show a return address, as changed. Did it?

I send my love -

Henry

July 15

Dear daddy -

Business is slack – I hope you have periods when yours is as slack as this is now, and when you have opportunity and desire to go out and enjoy yourself. This afternoon, I stay here, as most of the time I must, but possibly tomorrow shall go swimming in the sea – although according to report the drive there is very dusty.

So I get out my *Précis Élémentaire de Droit Romain* and have read thirty or forty pages on the history of Roman Law – which is interesting even in French. It would, I can see, be more interesting to one who knew something more of continental law, because there are a number of words, cast about freely with the assumption that the reader knows exactly what they mean – as "mainmise," which I know has some relation to seizure, and "pegneur"*[?]* which has something to do with distraint.

But my book, generally, is very simple and clear, and even if there may be conflicting theories about many if the propositions, the theories presented have there every pleasant verisimilitude and sound indisputable. The extra legal beginnings of law – as the remedy <u>manus</u> infectio, which, I gather was not much more than a fight, until it was brought "in juire," that is required to be in public, and then before a magistrate. The propositions of appearances of the defendants, the strict separation, as the common law, of the formulation of the cause of action – in juire – and its decision – in judicio – and finally its execution – with assignment by the author of reasons for each phenomenon, rather, I think imagination than strict history. But having read only about 50 pages on the subject, I am hardly prepared to set up as an authority on the origins of Roman Law.

I am well – really, as you see, with nothing whatsoever to write. Hope to hear from home soon, and maybe I shall. Behave yourself, write often, and write me about the pleasantness you find, too. My thoughts are always at home – and no detail is so small that I am not interested. Do you take the streetcar down town? How long does it take? Whom do you see – on the streetcar, down town and at home? What do they say? What do you say? Now, that ought to furnish the basis of a letter –

Henry

It is about time for me to go and shave and take a sponge bath – a truck comes around daily with water – I get a five gallon can full, ~~and hav~~ (sometimes) and a canteen full. I have established this priority with one gallon – first I shave in it; then I bathe in it; then I wash underwear in it, and last I wash socks in it. What is left, I use to water the olive trees -

And that reminds me (when I want to think of how well off I am) of the priorities established by a Captain Campbell (if I remember his name) in his journey across the Sahara, after being shipwrecked on the west coast of Africa. First he drank it; then the Camels drank it – then he washed in it – then the camels drank it again – and so forth – so he stretched a couple of gallons for weeks. At least, I have no animals in the chain of priorities. I write this principally to get a sheet of which to make an envelope.

Henry

July 16

Dear mama -

I am so happy to have received two letters from you – which I feel is a promise of more to come – that I am celebrating by beginning what I intend to be a long letter – so long that I am writing it in book form – and will give you the pleasure – if the censor doesn't beat you to it – of even cutting the pages.

I enjoyed your letters immensely – that you are going to Macatawa sounds very grand – and I am sure you will enjoy it.

You mention packages – any I receive I shall enjoy. Even though I have left Algiers, and am living under circumstances where I do not meet civilians, it will be a very genuine pleasure to give away things I don't need. Even, or especially to Arabs – who are currently and I think thoughtlessly condemned as being beggars. But what should men do but beg if they are hungry and naked? It seems that that is the last explanation for being a beggar that people think of – they just explain it by saying that they are "just beggars" and that they are "dirty," and so forth. Well – I should like to teach some of them to recite in English: "Who feeds the hungry beggar feeds three – Himself, the hungry beggar and me."

I may also now write you my former address, which is also that of Mrs. Peyrus – being the same apartment – It is 8 Rue Lys du Pae, Algiers, Algeria[43].

---

[43] I was, unfortunately, unable to locate this street in present-day Algiers.

I agree with everything you say about Betty – that she is just about the finest and most intelligent person I have ever known – even, in some respects – ahead of daddy. That is why I even envy you the pleasure of seeing her. Your advice too, is consoling, and gives me new patience –

I sometimes think it would be very good for me if I did not have such a fine family – with such admirable people in it. Then, I would not think of them so much, and could be a straight bum – go out and sit in the gutters with the Arabs.

The pages go so slowly in this long letter I have undertaken to write. And the page order is so confused that I don't know when I am coming to the end.

I have resumed the reading of the history of Roman Law – a subject which I think daddy would find very interesting – it is one on which there are many texts – some in English, many in French and German. The English ones exist partly because it is still studied in the Catholic schools, and also it was the only law taught at the English universities until very recently. Is daddy looking for recreational study? I should like to wage on him this – Roman law – and also English constitutional history – especially ancient, because in addition to being interesting in themselves, these subjects are sufficiently related to the subjects with which he works that each will make the other more interesting.

In my opinion, it is necessary to keep a philosophy of a business or profession – one which shows its relationship to the activity of the whole world and all men to keep it from being routine – a proposition which applies to business and law and everything else. Consider, for example, banking, which for most people could be just writing figures – But it would become vital and interesting if one saw its relationships – its development from Florentine and Venetian methods. Merchandising – one should study the history and reasons of markets – a whole subject by itself. And so forth.

But at present I am indulging in pure theory. What can one study in the way of the philosophy of doing nothing? I suppose there is none.

I am well – and hope you are also *[sic]*. Write me about Haymer – even his "cute tricks." Is he saying anything yet? Walking?

What cottage do you have at Macatawa? Is the beach still there? And Perch fishing? The pier? Holland, I suppose, is an industrial town – with its furnace company making tanks or something other than furnaces, and its pickle plant making shells or grenades or bullets – at least they are about the same shape.

I am so much interested in everything there that there is no end to the questions I could ask, and feel so happy that mails have begun to catch up with me, that nothing can disturb me.

What you should send me? I need nothing at present, but am vastly overstocked on clothes of most kinds – uniform ones, which I do not feel free to give away, because I feel that I have only the right to use them. Edibles for my own use are not worth sending – they go too fast. So there is nothing I need. I may eventually have to get rid of some weight of clothing – but hate to give away my over coat (the heaviest) and it seems silly to send it home, because if I should need it, I would need it just while it was on the way there. So I feel that it is foolish to send any clothes home. Abundance of shoes, I have and shall discard them as they wear out.

The weather is lovely – clear (constantly clear and sunny) with a good breeze – sometimes dusty, to which, however, I become accustomed.

I have been noticing the Arab carts go by, bringing produce to market – vegetables and fruits – and carrying water or wood or anything else – they are quire handsome, heavy carts, drawn sometimes by horses, sometimes by oxen, with big, heavy wheels and the tongues (I mean the carts') painted in fancy floral designs.

Then, between the carts and among the military vehicles, lots of donkeys, loaded high with straw or hay or anything else. They are such funny little beasts, and carry loads so entirely disproportionate in size to their own size – you see just a big load of hay with little legs wriggling underneath it.

The donkeys frequently have saddle bags, of a kind, of very beautiful woven material – like rugs.

There is no news of which to write -

Maybe I have letter cut the pages of this letter. Possibly censor will not want to take the time, or will think the letter is all sealed up to conceal something. Well, I wish I knew something which had to be concealed from someone. In my present state of knowledge I can be naive as a baby.

All my love -

Henry

PS. I am writing to daddy at the office.

July 18

Dear mama -

Again yesterday I had reason to go on errands wandering over the countryside – and enjoyed it – driving. Everyplace is hard to find, and nobody knows exactly where anything is, so in looking for it, one goes the wrong way several times at least. The county is not without beauty – although extremely dry and shadeless – the towns offer kind of little havens of shade – and whenever there is a tree or a wall people gather and sit or t and talk. I think of the arguments and discussions St. Augustine describes, which must have taken place in some little patch of shade someplace, so that a fig tree or a wall is responsible for his error into homoousion heresy. And I think I understand how this geography could encourage that like of thought – *[word crossed out]* vast spaces of terrific sun all around – but a nice little shady spot, under a tree or a wall, or inside a room and one does not like to think in big terms of allegory and generalization – so one comes down to very matter of fact thinking – where apple means apple, and has no allegorical meaning about knowledge – and to eat means to put into one's mouth and chew up and swallow – not to appreciate or assimilate. Night thinking would be different – but the nights are short, and the days so long.

I spent a few hours in another town, and went to mass in a very beautiful church – the conventional shape of a cross, with priests in red robes and particularly beautiful singing – Wandered around the town for a while, had a glass of wine and a glass of soda – "anis" which is strange, nasty tasting stuff. Bought a newspaper – quite newsless – and walked a little. The towns do not offer much. I saw an exhibition of water colors, of French Indo-Chinese subjects – gates, rivers and so forth – all conspicuously signed by a man named Gaullet[44], well framed, but to my taste uninteresting, merely illustrative painting, and not very

---

[44] I was unable to find any records of this painter.

decorative. They were for sale at 2500 fr. – 3500 fr. each, which is $50 to $70. I think that people who have fine things do not offer them for sale now – and I am of the opinion that they would be foolish to.

I got a haircut shave and shampoo – an Italian barber who told me about his mother and brothers who live in Chicago – asked me if I knew them. Of course, I didn't but he told me their address and I went so far as to say it was a very comfortable place to live. That is the truth – anyplace in Chicago would be. Also his cousins in Baltimore, who, I told him, must also be living very comfortably.

Then the other barbers came up one at a time and greet me with "Peace be with you" in Hebrew and I suppose I appeared to understand, because there was handshaking all around – as cordial as if I were a long lost brother. Kind of silly, I think. I was at the shop once before – about ten days ago – on the occasion the Spanish counsel (so they told me) had treated me to a soft drink. I told them "au revoir" and shall not see them again.

I am well, and hope that all of you are so. I send my love -

Henry

I am sending some letters to you at Macatawa and some at home, and guess that the ones to you at Macatawa will get there when you are in St. Louis and the ones to you in St. Louis will get there when you are in Macatawa.

Write often – I received two letters from you a few days ago, which encouraged me to hope for more.

Nothing is new -

H

July 19

Dear mama -

Things remain the same – hot, and dry, without any news whatsoever. It is now the heat of the day, and I have not enthusiasm, energy or initiative. But if I did, I do not know what I should do with them. I am well, and hope that you are also – I am still reading my History of Roman Law – it continues fairly interesting, although I do not remember much of what I read.

Mail appears to be interrupted again – see the pile of letters to me growing – a stack hundreds high someplace, which I shall receive and arrange in chronological order and read, over a period of two weeks.

Well, well! What a surprise – now I have something to write about, which may take about three sentences – I went swimming this afternoon in the sea – quite a long drive, and about two other men. To a low lying beach, between high rock promontories just within sight on either side. The water was lovely – quite warm, and barely enough surf – enough to keep it from being stale – a shallow beach – with a sand bar out a piece, to which one could swim – a sand bar not above the surface, but with water only about two feet over it. I swam a while, and lay on the beach – a wide, fine sandy one, for a while, digging little shellfish – like small clams, and watching them rebury themselves in the sand.

To reach the beach, one drives over a wide, flat field, dry, dusty and hot – although it borders the sea – a field or plain, I suppose three miles wide and many miles long. In the midst of this plain are a few palm trees and an Arab village – low mud huts with thatched roofs, and Arabs lying in the shade, or pitching grain to separate the chaff. In the shade of one hut was sitting a red headed, jovial looking, fat white Irishman or Dutchman to all appearances, dressed however, like an Arab. What a surprise – reminded me of a Conrad story, although I can't remember which one – is it *Almayer's Folly?*, or *Lord Jim*? Arabs are generally rather frail looking, and when they are fat, have an oriental look, rather than the jovial look of a fat Dutchman or Irishman. They are usually dark skinned, dark haired. This man, except for this clothes and squatting posture had everything as different from an Arab as could he – but was sitting there in the doorway of an Arab hut – I should have liked to have spoken to him, but it was not practicable to stop the truck.

Then on the way back we stopped and had an ice cream cone – a good cone, and good ice cream – but very little of it – of the watery French vanilla type – An example of prices – 10 f. for one teaspoonful of ice cream and a cone. But if the woman had asked fifty francs, she would have sold as many.

These cities of this country are fine – and you would admire the architecture for summer climates. They look as if they were very prosperous and wealthy – still quite a few fine carriages and horses – and many garages. There are also many fine looking people – but you don't see them often – a glimpse in an office or a carriage -

All my love

Henry

July 20

Dear mama -

Nothing had occurred overnight – since I closed my last letter about going swimming to give material for a new letter. I nevertheless begin one, even without expectation of more material before I end it. After my last letter, I went to bed, slept well, and got up – a little reading before bed, and a little talking – to breakfast, consisting of tomato juice, oatmeal and hot cakes with bacon and syrup. (Breakfast is still my favorite meal.) Then back, and I begin writing this letter. If I desired to write complete details, I should go on: "I have written so far as follows: 'Nothing has occurred overnight – since I closed my last letter about going swimming to give material for a new letter – I nevertheless begin one - - - etc.'" and I think I should never get up to the last minute. So this letter will be out of date before it is sent.

I am well and hope that all of you are also.

There is a hot, dry south wind today – which makes everything which is by any miracle wet dry out in no time – as my pajamas, which by a miracle I rinsed out today.

Ojvah*[?]* – its *[sic]* hard to write a letter – my thoughts are all on what you are doing – and I think of Macatawa – the beach – is Kim[45] with you – will he go into the water? And Haymer – does he enjoy the beach? Is there any fishing? Do perch still bite? How is Ruth? What does one do? Is Holland accessible and what kind of town is it? Is the place crowded this year? Did you drive up there? What cottage have you? Are vegetables still so plentiful there? Do you have any kind of boat available? I suppose not, because there is really no one to use it – or is there? Is the pier still there? And the beach? Any storms?

---

[45] Maybe their dog but I am not sure.

Any surf? All those questions – Is old man Miller still living? What is at Ottawa now? But I suppose by the time I hear of it, it will be past – but that is alright, too.

My book of Roman Law is turning out to be only about 150 pages of history – and then it goes into the substantive law – which may be interesting too – I shall see. It goes slowly, because my mind frequently wanders onto personal things, and daydreaming.

Maybe I shall have opportunity to go swimming again – I hope so, because I enjoyed it yesterday.

There is a constant stream of carts passing   ox drawn, horse drawn, donkey drawn, mule drawn – everything. They are loaded with anything – but mostly bags of grain, and building materials – stone – and straw and dirt, almost everything.

Well, at any rate, I have said that I am in the best of health and spirits – so I might as well mail this letter as not.

I send my love -

Henry.

July 21

Dear mama -

I have neither table nor chair – and writing is somewhat difficult – so this letter will be short – indeed, there is nothing I can think of to say to make it long, anyway.

I have been quite idle today – having really done nothing. I have done laundry little by little – on my principle of saving water – first shave in it, then bathe in it, and then wash clothes – so I wash clothes daily, almost, in a rinsing way, and get along on one pair of socks, one suit of underwear and one shirt – which I shall throw away when they get too dirty or wear out. But if a shirt was clean enough to wear up to five minutes ago, and I dup it, and some dirt comes out, then it is cleaner than it was five minutes ago, and therefore clean enough. The same applies to all clothes, does it not?

So I have spent my day under my St. John's Bread tree, having a blanket above me from a limb. The wind waves the blanket, which drives the flies away – I am proud of the invention.

Then I have read a good deal of my Elementary Roman Law – getting into the more substantive parts, about property, the *[word unclear]*, the methods of acquisition, disposition and so forth. The similarity to English law is great, even in in theory – very likely because the English theorists knew the Roman law.

I am well – and send my love.

Henry -

July 22

Dear mama -

I still have on hand a brief letter I wrote you yesterday. However, it is deal, and I have not made up my mind whether I shall enclose this letter with it, putting both in a new envelope, or send them separately. A hard decision, for I shall have to destroy yesterday's envelope, and somehow that seems much more wasteful than using a new one. I shall decide.

I have nothing to write, except maybe this vignette: yesterday evening, about the time of sunset, I walked to the edge of the camp, and stood looking at the vineyard . An Arab came up, and I said "Good Evening." He did not understand much French, but I tried to ask him if one raises melons in this country, and if he could get me one. He did not understand the word Melon, and I tried to show him, making a round size with my hands – not grapes, but bigger. Well, he became all smiles, and ran off. He rushed back in a few minutes will the biggest bunch of grapes I have ever seen, and gave them to me. I could do nothing but accept – even though they were quite green, and I gave him a package of cigarettes. They are fairly good. I have them hanging in a tree now, hoping they will ripen a little bit. It is true that they are wine grapes, which means that each grape is small, but the flavor is quite good. Maybe they will ripen in the sun – they will either ripen, I think, or turn to raisins.

Well, I still] want a melon, and I believe that they are raised in this country. Maybe I shall try again. I went over this morning, and *[word crossed out]* there was a Frenchman walking through the vineyard]. I tried to speak with him, thinking he might be the manager or proprietor of the farm; but I could not even get a Bon Jour out of him, that is addressed to me. He was talking and mumbling to himself – maybe provoked (as I think he might be) that so many of his grapes are being stolen, as they are, and so many given away, as they are by his Arab farm labour. Fortunately, I can survive very nicely without a melon, as I shall probably have to.

I said before that there is really nothing of which to write, and I still find nothing – that I am well, that I hope you to are so; that I wish with all my power that I could devise a method of accomplishing my desires – wish it so hard that I now make wishes on every hay wagon and every first star I see – I even make wishes on straw wagons, which are far more numerous than hay wagons. That, I suppose, is silly, but I do not utterly abandon superstition. My logical analyses, to attempt by exclusion to determine the possible and practice method, which Hope says must exist, lead to no conclusion, because when I get to one, it must be abandoned as too radical or too villainous. So I'll wait, and I suppose, whether I want to or not, keep on wishing on hay wagons, straw carts and stars.

It would be nice to receive mail – and maybe in a few days or weeks I shall; it will catch up with me.

The weather continues seasonable- hot, dry and clear, but with steady breezes, so that if one finds shade, it is not uncomfortable. I continue to read a little, and wander around in circles. Write often. I send my love -

Henry

You know how curious I am about everything which goes on there. Write all of it – I shall get your letters in time – ask daddy to write now and then too.

H

July 22

Dear mama –

THIS IS THE SECOND LETTER I HAVE WRITTEN TODAY, NOT BECAUSE I HAVE NOTHING *[word unclear]* OR OLD *[word unclear]* FOR *[sic]* THAT MATTER, BUT I AM IN IDLENESS, AND SOMEWHAT TIRED OF WAITING *[word unclear]* THEREFORE HAVE DECIDED TO WRITE A LITTLE *[word unclear]*. I have spent most of the day reading my book of Roman Law, of which I have now read more than half. It is going *[words unclear]* going to meals. That is really all I have done. A hard life? Not so hard. *[word unclear]*

As I remember, my letter of this morning was in a *[word unclear]* vein. *[words unclear]* But as you know from experience, these periods wear themselves out, and give way to *[word unclear]* of content and even happiness. So it is now. The one is just as unreasonable as the *[word unclear]* and it would be nicest if one could attain the spirit of a bump on a log. But that is not possible.

Now is the cool of the evening.

[The rest of this V-mail is largely unreadable.]

July 25

Dear mama –

Now I haven't written a letter for about three days – having nothing I could say, anyway, nor opportunity to write. I have now much I should like to describe, in the way of country side, painted wagons, cities – very ancient – on the tops of hills, which look in color and character exactly like the mediaeval paintings of Jerusalem.

This evening, I am hot and dusty – and intend to go to bed soon – inside an elaborate building, built, apparently, as a city hall. Elaborate paintings – as Aubusson rugs, and oriental, on some floors, and the whole in the most splendid, pillared courtyard style.

Villages, which make me think of Crusaders and Robert the Uorinan*[?]* – but, if I can remember them, I shall describe them more at another time –

My greatest pleasure! I received a good batch of letters from you here – and read them and shall reread them. They were mostly older then the latest I have had.

Also the pictures of you and daddy – I enjoy them. I wish I could send you a picture of me – ~~bu~~ I tried to from Algiers, but all the photographers were closed for lack of film. I shall continue to watch for an opportunity. Your pictures are nice, and a very great pleasure to have.

I am well.

I feel that I have much to write still. But I shall not. It would be description – my conversations in Latin, which seems to be understood, but I can rarely understand the answers.

I also received watch crystals from Stix Baer & Fuller[46], and hold them as insurance.

It is getting too dark now to write.

All my love -

Henry

July 26

Dear mama -

Well – I am now, I am told, in Sicily, and believe it, for everything I have seen so far is exactly as I imagined it should be – towns on the hill tops, very ancient, each with its ruins of a mediaeval castle – The people are surprisingly nice looking – clean, to all appearances – but the city people appear hungry – (which it hard to look at) and there are other things disagreeable to see. On must ignore them.

I wish I could speak Italian but it is not worth beginning to try to learn it now. I find I can read it – at least the sign boards – without difficulty. Most of them say only Duce Duce Duce – some enlarge upon the same theme.

I hear rumors today that Mussolini has (1) resigned (2) been imprisoned (3) fled, (4) etc. I believe them, because the usual news broadcast channels (the English broadcasting ~~conf~~ stations) are all filled up with Italian, German and other broadcasts, and the reception consequently so poor that one can't understand anything of any of them. Just now and then the name "Mussolini" or "Badoglio" comes through.[47]

I am well – in my peripatetic existence – enjoying it sometimes and between times having periods of boredom and depression, which I suppose are my nature rather than any external circumstances.

I have rejoined Captain Morris and Lieutenant Clark, whose company I enjoy, and upon whom I become somewhat dependent.

Now the day is about finished. I have taken a walk through the town – a beautiful city, with fine buildings – alas, many in ruins – and people just learning to come out

[Letter is incomplete. Additional pages missing.]

July 28

Dear mama -

I have now spent a day in a Sicilian town – had about two hours, in which I walked around – up and down steep hills, through very narrow alleys – beautiful doorways of carved oak, iron balconies and iron protection for the windows above the doors – beautiful grill-work. Streets crowded with people sitting in

---

[46] A St. Louis department store
[47] On July 25, 1943 (the previous day) Mussolini was dismissed as head of government (a consequence of the Allied invasion of Sicily) and placed in custody. Pietro Badoglio was selected to replace Mussolini as Prime Minister.

the streets, talking, playing cards – and other similar things. In the wider, main streets, painted wagons, but not crowded. Many of the buildings in ruins. That was a few days ago.

I am now writing on captured stationary, having removed the letterhead which discloses too much. Maybe in a few weeks, I shall be able to leave it on – although it is not particularly interesting.

Now, I am living in a grove of almond trees, near a town which I have not yet had opportunity to visit. Perhaps I shall. These towns are thoroughly mediaeval. As are the roads, with shrines, painted, carved wagons, and so forth. I am having difficulty with the almonds – a little too green to be eaten as green almonds, for the shells are hardened. They are too hard to cut open with a knife, and if hit with a hammer, most of them squash, and very little meat is recovered. They are too wet to be hit with an axe, because, unless hit square, they just shift away, and I am not accurate enough to hut them square. What problems overwhelm me! But I do not require suggestions, because, by the time they arrive, the almonds will be completely ripe, and can be cracked as any nut.

As I was walking through a town, I had a roll of mints in my pocket. The children have learned to ask for things – cigarettes and candy – They say "Caramela, Caramela," which I take to mean any kind of candy – although their acceptance of a mint as a caramel proves nothing, because they will accept a stick of sealing wax, after asking for caramel. I gave my mints away, one at a time, and was mobbed with children climbing all over. I emptied my pockets and turned them inside out, and began trying to tell them to go away – I had no more. I tried Latin on them – "Se dissipate," "Andate," and they thought it was funny, I believe understanding, ~~There~~ but certainly not obeying. Musical terms did the trick – and when I combined the one of my Latin terms "Andate" with the musical "vivacissamente," it got results. I don't know what I said, but some of them ran away, and the most persistent hung back. I wonder if possibly I cursed them – I intended to tell them to get out and step lively.

Italian seems to be a funny language. If I speak French, German or English to the children, it just doesn't make an impression. But when I get a good Latin phrase all prepared, and say it to them, a peculiar half understanding, perplexed expression comes over their faces – ~~I imag~~ as if possibly they almost understand. I imagine an English child might look about the same if you spoke to him in Chaucerian English or Anglo Saxon. They don't quite understand, but almost do – and they understand enough to make it worth trying.

The towns here are tremendously interesting – I hope to have opportunity to see more of them.

I send my love. I have been receiving mail, now and then, and now that it has caught up with me, as I hope it has, may receive letters promptly sometimes. Triumph of hope over experience.

I am living very comfortably – in a tent, with a cot, and a water jug and an orderly. So maybe it is just as well that I didn't pick up my French "ordinance."

Henry

July 28

Gentlemen[48]:

I have a box of candy[49] for which I wish to thank you. It arrives in good condition and delightful flavor.

Two days ago, I was walking in a town here in Sicily, up steep hills, through narrow alleys, overhung with balconies, crowded with people. The children were all crying "Caramela, Caramela," which means candy in general, I gather. I had in my pocket a roll of life savers – my week's ration of candy, and gave one to a child. What a mob came up! I was swamped with hordes of children crying for "Caramela." Well, my roll of life savers was gone in no time – and I was then put to it to try to get rid of the mob, who refused to appreciate that I had no more. I turned my pockets inside out – the demonstration was not convincing. I tried all the musical phrases in Italian I know – and could understand the children saying "See! He speaks Italian." I still do not know what phrase ultimately made them go, but finally they did.

But I am no longer in a town – and I shall make more enjoyable use of the candy I now have in abundance. It is hard to refuse a plea of "Candy for the baby," if one has candy in one's pocket, and these people are so friendly, so open in the expression of emotion that it is quite impossible to bear in mind and remember that they are our enemies.Our ee

Thank you again for the box of "thrills" and "Change Bank" candies.

Henry C. Lowenhaupt

July 29

Dear Daddy -

I have been thinking recently, of course, about Ben, and trying to inquire about the possibilities offered. I labor under the fundamental difficulty of not knowing whether or not he is satisfied with what he has, whether he knows of anything he would rather have; what he wants to do, and exactly what he is doing. So I write in considerable ignorance, and am not able to inquire (I have limited facilities for inquiry in any event) about anything in particular. Further I know that policies and practices differ considerably in different places, and what may be true or a consistent practice in one place may not be so in another. That is administration.

Nevertheless, I have decided to write a few thoughts rather to you than directly to Ben, because, being thoroughly out of touch with sentiment, with knowledge of right conduct and everything else, I should prefer that you determine which of my thoughts should be passed on to Ben, if any.
I have presently the good fortune of being in close friendship with a man, the nephew of a respected friend of yours, a Captain Claude B. Morris (nephew of Logan B. Morris, of the B. T. A, formerly, now of

---

[48] This letter is addressed
National Candy Co.
Gravois At Bingham
Saint Louis, Missouri
ATT. Mr. Gay
[49] The National Candy Co. building, located at 4230 Gravois Ave. is currently occupied by U-Haul Moving & Storage of Dutchtown. The building is on the National Register of Historic Places. https://npgallery.nps.gov/AssetDetail/NRIS/09000889

the Washington Law Firm) who is in charge of personnel work at Two Corps. He is very well informed on placement questions and generally, on personnel questions (as related to placing a man in a job for which fitted.) He also knows the practices, and to what extent it is true, and how far up one must go, to get big-minded consideration of the placement problems necessarily presented, and action upon them in line with a big-minded conclusion. So if I know what Ben wants, if he is satisfied, what he would like to get, and so forth, I think I can get fairly good advice on whether or not he can get it, and how to ask for it. Captain Morris has had about three years experience, on top of a civilian, human background, in this type of requests and placements.

The proposition might even go so far as to enable Ben to get a discharge, although this is surely far from certain. The proposition would be that agriculture is an essential industry. That if Ben could get a letter from some authority of say Shaw's Garden that his services might contribute in experimental agriculture to the increase of agricultural production, that his work could help relieve food shortages, in short that his services in experimental agriculture would be very valuable, a statement which I think would be true, and that they would employ him if discharged, he might be able to be discharged "for the benefit of the Service."

This I would consider very desirable. But I do not know the existing attitudes and thoughts upon these subjects, and so forth. That is my reason for writing to you rather than directly to Ben.

Then as to transfer, I wish Ben would write me frankly what he wants, what branch of the service he would consider more desirable than that in which he finds himself, what schools he might consider interesting, and so forth. I might be able to get him advice on how to go after it.

As for schools – Ben is a good mathematician, which would indicate such a school as Ordnance or Coast Artillery Anti Aircraft (Both schools considered [desirable because immediately upon the termination of the war, there will be no further need for officers of these branches) He is sufficient chemist I believe, to be interesting to Chemical Warfare Service (A service in which there is likely to be nothing to do except to be prepared)

I do not know that I can give Ben any advice which is worth having. But it would be interesting if he would write and let me know what his interests and desires are.

I received a letter from you today – one of which I am proud, and which makes me very happy. I am addressing some of my letter to mama at Macatawa Park, and some at home, just to take care of unforeseen possibilities. I am glad that business is thriving – and may remark incidentally that I am far less of an idealist than you – at least in expression – maybe in what I should do I should be about the same, because I am tempted to agree with you – that in addition to the fact that it is socially undesirable to do acts which reduce the amount of income taxes or other taxes it is probably legally true that any act done with that purpose would not succeed. But that is too harsh.

Write again soon. Remember that my curiosity is insatiable, and that I should like to give advice to Ben, although I do not know that I can give any which will be of worth to him.

For the past two days we have been having exceptionally good meals – fresh fruit and eggs, wine for dinner (which I have just finished) Sicily is a very beautiful country, and I only hope I have some opportunity to see the town, truly mediaeval, and some more of it than I have seen today. But you read my letter to mama.

Here's all my esteem -

Henry

July 29

Dear mama -

Another day begins in routine – except that we had a far better breakfast than usual – being fresh honeydew melon, dry cereal, and fresh eggs and bacon, and coffee – yesterday some men bought eggs from a native (I think about every Sicilian either used to live in New York or has a cousin or brother or something who lives in New York, and when they talk English, they talk it like New York boot blacks) and I watched them making an omelet over a gasoline lamp. They also bought a chicken, and intend, I think, to fry it over the same lamp. It is a smoky proposition – which they insist on concealing, because, they say, there is a colonel who if he discovers they have a lamp which cooks so well (?) will take it from them to heat water for shaving. I suppose they know, and I shall not mention their lamp.

The climate here is far damper than in Tunis. Last night, I rinsed out my regular pants and shirt – to get the soluble alien materials out, and some of the dust – They did not dry over night, so I was forced into my reserve supply, which is clean. Well, they will be dry by the time the sun is high, and I shall put my reserve away again.

I am well. I have not yet had opportunity to go into the town, which I desire to visit. It is a village, and there will be no shops or other things there – only the buildings and streets, which are alleys, overhung with iron balconies. The houses are all of gray stone – and the living quarters seem to open right onto the streets. This town is built in a valley – instead of on a hilltop.

Around the area where we are is apparently very fertile land. It is tangled thick with grape vines, fruit trees (apples, figs, pears, and so forth) and almond and walnut trees, and vegetables between – very intensively cultivated. The only large fields seem to be wheat fields – now with nothing in them, for the wheat is harvested. But frequently, the orchards are also planted in wheat. I am still eating green almonds – when I can get them open.

It may be that I am writing too often – my letters surely have nothing in them, and are probably repetitious, over and over again. But then, also, it maybe that all of them do not arrive – and I enjoy writing – partly because it builds up my hope of receiving letters – which I enjoy so very much – and partly because it concentrates my attention for a few minutes on things which are pleasant to think of.

I send my love – ask daddy to write now and then -

Henry

July 30

Dear mama -

Here is another day almost spent with keeping papers flying – a beautiful cool pleasant-weathered day. I have eaten many green almonds, which I enjoy – am becoming almost a fiend at it – and have received several letters – which come quite without regard to chronology – but always with much pleasure. I received one from Phillip[50], and one from Paul Weil[51], as well as one from Mr. Gay of National Candy Co. Mr. Gay's is the hardest to answer, because he tells me that he can no longer mail candy without a request from me. I think I shall ultimately determine to request it.

July 31

I walked to town yesterday evening – with an Englishman whose English is more difficult to understand than an Italian's Italian. It was a very beautiful walk – we cut off the road – which is dusty – along an old cobblestone road which runs up the hill to the town, which clings upon a steep slope. It is a beautiful village   only one street wide enough for a vehicle to pass – for the rest the hill is paved with stones between the buildings, which makes ways and alleys, cutting in and out, close together, all of old gray rocks, with oak doors carved beautifully and old iron works in fans above the doors and balconies. There is a little place in front of the church, overlooking the valley and the hills, with towns in the distance, and straight down into other streets or alleys. Everyone sitting at windows, or doors or on the streets, which are alive with children, checkers, guineas, ducks, pigs and every other kind of animal. Women sit in the doorways spinning wool – by a *[word unclear]* I have never seen before – a spindle or bobbin of a kind, which they spin. It hung by the thread, and as it whirled, they let *[word crossed out]* wool out of a part, possibly a distaff, and the whirling spindle twisted it – then wound the spin thread on the spindle, whirl it again and spin a little more. Quite interesting – and these little household tools, carved and decorated, with the top pieces, a kind of bell on a staff, filled with fluffy white wool, look very beautiful to me – they suggest conversation. I suppose the method antedates the spinning wheel.

The village has no shops apparent. The people – well, the women look content, and go on with their spinning, combing children's hair, cooking, scrubbing, everything which has to be done. The men look to me rather bitter and perplexed. Who could blame them for being so? The children point to their bare feet or ragged clothes, and say "Mussolini."

Then the place, and the countryside where I am happens to be so beautiful that it almost makes me weep. Great hills around – rock farm houses, with lacy trees overtowering them – this is gentle, kind looking country

I am well.

I received letters yesterday – and enjoyed them. I shall reread them – now I must leave -

Love -

Henry

July 31

Dear daddy -

I received a letter from you yesterday, which I enjoyed very much. Except that I think when you apologize for devoting your whole mind to business you show a lack of appreciation of your business. It

---

[50] Probably Phillip Moss at Moss and Lowenhaupt. He was Henry's first cousin.
[51] I believe a St. Louis lawyer

would be a valid objection if you devoted your whole mind to the business of being a clerk in a ten cent store. But, now, you ought to stop for three minutes and appreciate what your business really it – a thing I believe you have not done recently.

As the general practice of law, it is a very profound study of the relationship of men to each other in a refined community. You have passed beyond the elemental study of the Ten Commandments and direct relationships of individuals – which are fundamental and within your knowledge – to the more intricate concepts, where social policies beyond the animal desires enter – associations of men; the obligations inter se and the permissible extent of association <u>under</u> the State and among other associations. That is corporation law. The attempt of men to perpetrate their interests – according to natural desires – which conflicts with the interests of others, who desire the advantage of others follies to aid their acquisitions. That is wills and trusts – and the policies and conditions which affect the substantive law are always changing – for example the existence of large unclaimed properties in the public domain (unsettled land; possibilities of new industries and inventions) permit a closer and longer hold on property.

Then as a specialist in taxation, you study a particular refinement of the ethics of communal living – the rights of one man against all other men, and the relationship of government to its citizens.

Surely these studies are interesting enough to be worth all your time – they are the modern applied philosophy, and to regret lack of other interests is the same as to regret that Socrates had no interests in ping-pong and dancing. (His wife, wasn't it Xantippe?, scolded him – and you have the advantage, for mama does not try to urge you to dance)

So, if you think for a minute that you ought to be interested in politics or parties or what not – that is silly – like a desire of Des Cartes to go back and be interested in the multiplication tables, even though, doubtless, there many arithmeticians who could add, subtract, multiply and divide much faster than he.

Well, that is enough of didacticism.

You mentioned the proposition of investing money – that is alright with me. I am a gambler, in a way, and my idea of conservation is breweries, tobacco and chewing gum and the like.

I am being paid here – a good deal more than I can spend – of which I now have about $500 or more. But I believe in keeping it. Partly because I may desire to spend it; partly because next month I think we shall be apud in little fiat Italian Lire – printed in the United States, and all they say on them is "1 lira." Well, the presently planned exchange is 100 lire to the dollar. Italians remember the lire as being worth about five to the dollar, and there is no possible guess as to what these little scraps of paper will be worth, what acceptance they will receive, or anything concerning them. So it may be that in continental European countries dollars (if I am permitted to keep them) will be worth something – will buy something, when, perhaps these little lire will not. So I intend, possibly, if I receive lira to send them home at the same rate as that at which I receive them.

I have no news – I should surely like to be free to wander around in Sicily at will for a little while, for I think it would be in a charming island.

I send my love – write again soon.

Yours,

Henry

August 3

Dear mama -

I suppose I have not written for a day or so, but time squeezes out of the tube so grudgingly – and nevertheless in spurts at times – that I really cannot remember how long ago anything will be. I am now in mountainous country – quite high on a hill, with a view over miles, to mountain ridges. The most unbelievable thing is, that, with a pair of glasses, one can see villages on the very tops of the mountains, and we are near one which perches so precariously on the rocks at the very top that it just can't be understood how it stays there.

Yesterday, again, I had occasion to drive some distance – and enjoyed it, although my conscience and width of the roads did not permit me to stop and wander around as I should have liked to do. We drove though mountains – quite dusty and dry, but with many groves of almonds and fruit. There was one village, the name of which I can't remember, built mostly in caves – that is, holes in the mountains – just doorways out on them. Of course, in such a mountain-top villages, there was not much room, and the pigs, chickens, goats and so forth were kept inside. Even on the caves, they put very beautiful doorways.

Another town on a little broader mountain top was quite spectacular – with stone buildings suggesting a very fine city – streets, of course, such towns have only one street, and the rest are little alley-ways. The one street winds and twists over the peak of the mountain. This town has even a few shops, although, I could not see that any of them had any merchandise for sale. But the doorways and iron grill work over them are always very beautiful, and the closeness of the buildings.

The fine houses, I believe, are in the country – and there are many fine villas scattered around. Also many peasant farm homes – always of stone, and usually hidden among large trees.

Nearby, there is a village I should like to visit – except, although it is only two miles away, I think it would be a long walk, because it is all up hill – steep mountain climbing. Near the bottom of the mountain, from which one has about a mile straight climbing to get to the town, there is a place which rents donkeys – and maybe (but I doubt) I shall rent one and ride up. I have never ridden a donkey, and think I should just feel so sorry for the little beast I should carry him. They are not bigger than large dogs. But there is one road up – very steep, with hairpin turns and switchbacks – by which the village is about six miles away.

The climate here is delightful – the days have not been hot – the shade cool and a good breeze – and the nights are cold. I have been freely occupied with keeping quite a volume of papers flying across my table.

I send my love – am well, and hope you too are so.

Henry

August 5

Dear mama -

I received two letters from you this morning – both of which I enjoyed very much. I kind of regret your sending me a package of clothes – for I am now moved from the place from which I requested them, and am wearing wool. But there was nothing I could do about it, and if they come, I shall use them if I can, or send them back or do something else with them.

I am well. Last night, having a choice of walking to town (two miles straight up hill) and staying here, I stayed here and washed every item of clothing I had on – so this morning I start fresh in clean clothes. It is quite difficult to wash a pair of wool trousers in a helmet – but I get them wet through, and that makes them feel a little cleaner.

This afternoon, I expect to drive to a place about fifteen miles away – I have been there before – and know I shall have a very beautiful drive – although dusty. So maybe tomorrow night I shall be able to walk to the nearby town.

You see I have no news – that I am now content, being in a very beautiful place – these mountains of Sicily – it is all mountainous – that I am now being fed well – with lots of cantaloupe, eggs, tomatoes, onions, and other things which are now seasonable.

Macatawa sounds very delightful – the foggy days – the hill tops – is the beach still there? Swimming? Fishing?

I also have a letter from daddy, in which he says he is very busy – glad to hear it, and hope daddy writes often -

All my love -

Henry

August 6

Dear mama -

I received a package from you – and shall be able to use most of the contents. The rest, I shall send to someone who possibly can. I can use especially the bathing suit. The shirts also, possibly. So I shall keep them.

Yesterday I had another occasion to drive about fifteen miles, over a road I have once before travelled and described, through the speluncal town (do you like that word) and hilltop villages. Again I enjoyed it, but there is no occasion to redescribe it – for observed nothing new.

I rode with a Chaplain – and am always impressed with the inadequacy of clerical education – a subject I shall not enlarge upon now.

In fact, I have really nothing to write – weather beautiful; I am well – and send my love

Henry

(over)

In view of the privileges of sending packages – upon request – I enclose a few requests – do as you like with them – you know, I do not need the things requested.

August 6

Dear mama -

I should like very much to receive some candy. What would you think of sending about as much as possible – or a mélange of candy and cigarettes.

This would serve as a request.

I am well, and send my love -

Henry

Hq. II Corps, APO 302
c/o Postmaster, N.Y.

August 7

To Phillip Moss[52]
Moss & Lowenhaupt Cigar Co.
723 Olive St.
ST. Louis, Missouri

Dear Phillip:

I received a letter from you yesterday – one which I enjoyed very much and I thank you for it.

I am presently in Sicily – and have had a little time to drive around through two or three very beautiful towns. In fact, if one could forget what is going on, one could enjoy sitting in one's tent (mine) overlooking an enormous valley beautifully planted in square plots – rocky mountains with villages of gray stone on the peaks – old stone farm houses – as lovely and peaceful looking as anything to be seen.

But the towns are deserted, as far as any business is concerned. Only the barber shops seem to be thriving.

I should like to ask for some cigarettes – of which I am presently out – if you would like to send some – but only on that condition. And this request is intended rather to enable you to send a package, if you would like, than to beg for it. Or some tobacco, if they will give you a pipe of mine.

Yours truly,

Henry

---

[52] Phillip Moss was Henry's first cousin and one of the principals at Moss and Lowenhaupt.

August 8

To Mrs. A Lowenhaupt
Macatawa Park
Near Holland
Michigan
USA

I.

Dear mama,

I received letters yesterday – and enjoyed them very much. Also a package, containing shirts and trousers. It grieves me that they were sent now, for we are now wearing wool clothes, and I cannot use them. I shall, however, carry them for a while and maybe can use them. Well – I shall forget that with other requests.

Last evening I walked to the edge of the area, and stood by a dirt path, which runs up to the town. It was surprising to see the amount of traffic passing – on horses, mules, donkeys, and on foot. Some returning to town for the night, from farms where they had been working (this is threshing season) some bringing grain or straw or hay to town, some going there to get something – quite a steady procession of people – peasants all, shabbily dressed. One man stopped and talked – he left the United States almost 25 years ago, having worked there long enough to buy himself three farms at home here. He worked in New York, Chicago, St. Louis – I don't know where else. But he was riding a donkey, and it seemed very funny to try to place him in New York or St. Louis. I don't know what kind of work he could have done. Now he is managing his three farms – and barely speaks English.

The road through the fields was again so beautiful. One almost wept.

Love -

Henry

August 8

To Mrs. A Lowenhaupt
Macatawa Park
Near Holland
Michigan

II.

Dear mama -

I have not yet been to the nearby town. Although it is only two miles. The road is all almost straight up a cliff. The horizontal distance I doubt that it is more than one mile. Maybe I shall try to walk there this evening.

I am well. I know nothing new. There is something incongruous in being in so beautiful a place in such surroundings, and in the midst of orders and attitudes which are so extremely wicked and contrary.

I am afraid that autumn is coming – which fills one with fear. It will bring such things as rain, and cold, and other things. But "Consider the lilies of the field" etc.

I am making a practice, I am afraid, of writing requests for things. Well – they will not be sent unless there is a desire to send them. So in this letter, I'll request a bath towel, and that is all I need. But if the package is filled up with candy, cigarettes or anything of the kind …

I send my love -

Henry

August 10

Dear mama -

I have intended throughout the day to write to you – but it has been a day full of interruptions, and I just have not gotten to do it. But the day is without incident, while yesterday still has a bright spot – of which I shall write.

I again drive to my old and usual driving place – but less interestingly, because I was with a man who was in a hurry, and skipped all the towns on new short cuts – dusty. But I still enjoyed the drive, through new country – with caves in hills and quite a few fine country houses – regular, big, square castles.

Then, as I was driving into this area, I met Captain Morris, who was going to town, and I went along. That is the town[53] I was trying to get up courage enough to walk to – and so, I drove, I concluded it would have taken much more than courage – say an auto or a mule or a donkey. It is straight up for about two miles – and the road doubles back and forth up the face of a cliff – finally gets to the top of the mountain. There, it goes along, making a promenade for well dressed villagers, overlooking miles of valleys and mountains, with two or three villages in sight on other mountain tops.

Suddenly, then, the road turns into a little square, and breaks up into narrow streets, too narrow for passage, some going down the other side of the mountain in steps – others running along the ridge – not level, but only relatively so – and backs of buildings. On the either side of the square is a church – or monastery chapels – with very old appearance.

We walked down the main alley – with stores on either side, although without display windows. The grocery stores hang out wire baskets, with samples of their wares – so that overhead was hanging with lemons and eggplants in a beautiful color combination with the gray stone of the buildings. A modern school house and administrative building, clinging to the cliffs.

The one comes upon another little square – with a big church[54], fairly modern, built upon or as part of an ancient tower, with little statuettes, and a Knight of Malta appearance. One side of the square opens over

---

[53] I believe this town is Gangi, Sicily, a small town southeast of Palermo.

[54] After some digging, I am almost certain this church is the Chiesa Madre San Nicolò di Bari in Gangi. Additional information is surprisingly elusive, but there is a TripAdvisor page with pictures. https://www.tripadvisor.com/Attraction_Review-g1127406-d10226564-Reviews-Chiesa_Madre-Gangi_Province_of_Palermo_Sicily.html

the other side of the mountain – over rooftops and streets – and beyond the valley and more mountains with villages in sight.

We stood there – and crowds gathered. Then into the church, and the priests greeted us. There was a baptism, and then the priest showed us through his church – the painting of the universe[55], in an apse [(is that a word?) behind the alter, with heaven at the top and hell at the bottom and the humorous bishop in hell – a fine and careful painting in the style of the masters, but in quite a dark place.

Then it was suggested we go down stairs into the vaults – where the corpses were, or skeletons, and we went with most of the village along, I believe. The basement is mostly out of the mountainside and opens in arched windows over the valley again. Around it, each in his niche, stood the former priests of the church, embalmed somewhat. Quite gruesome, and decaying – teeth loose in shrinking skin – fingers falling off – all propped up with wire by the backs of their necks, and dressed in the finest ceremonial robes of lace and silk. It was impressive, and funny and horrible.

Then back up – and we were again showed carved marble – really lovely, although clearly not great – pedestals for the water basin – the bays over the door – I think the priest was to some extent mystified. None of us crossed himself or prayed at any of the images – although I was severely tempted to do so.

We left – giving the priest money – which hurts a little bit, because money is so utterly worthless here; there is nothing to be bought, as far as I can see. But it is all that can be given. The priest was a lovely, pink, round faced man – gentle, sweet spoken, gracious and full of laughing and humor. Even though conversation was quite impossible (a little Latin passed), I liked him immensely for his kindness and gentleness.

Then walked back up – the streets were quite crowded with people walking – they looked clean and well dressed – maybe because of the contrast to Arabs whom I am used to seeing – One would not leave the town for a walk – it is too steep to come back. Children were following.

We left in time to get back before dark.

I received salt tablets. Thank you very much – I have eaten a few – also a letter which I enjoyed very much. Then too a batch of letters from Janet – all at once – from May 1 on to July 22.

I am well – and I send all my love.

Henry

---

[55] The Chiesa Madre San Nicolò di Bari houses the painting *Final Judgement* by Giuseppe Salerno.

August 10

To Mrs. A Lowenhaupt
Macatawa Park
Near Holland
Michigan, USA

Dear mama –

This is a note to let you know that I am well – and going on in routine. That I have no news of which to write. Am still eating green almonds, and watching pomegranate trees – but the fruit is not ripe – just a faint tinge of red beginning or appear on it.

Today at noon we had watermelon and grapes – which I enjoyed very much, for they have much cool moisture in them.

As I have no complaints.

Macatawa sounds very lovely – and I may write my next letter to Mary – see if she will answer – but should have trouble spelling her last name.

I am afraid I shall have no opportunity to buy you a disstaff and/or spindle, such as I hoped, for the chances of getting into towns are now rare. But maybe I shall have a chance to get something. Well – I always expect that I shall not have opportunity to write again for a while, and these do have the chance. Maybe I shall not write for a while – but I shall try. I send all my love -

Henry

August 11

Dear mama -

Today has been a slow and eventless day – I have worked a little, and watched the mountains, which becomes appallingly beautiful. They contain my favorite combinations of curves and lines – and I have tried to draw a picture, but cannot make it simple enough. It really should be drawn as no more than this:

[Drawing of a mountain range.]

But then, I become tempted to put the foreground of trees, framing it, in, and the shadows. The bottom line represents the top of the first range. I try to represent the patches of fields, and lines of trees and shadows and rugged places. But they are not a part of the overall big effect of lines – although the lines change constantly by virtue of shifting of shadows. There too, the variation of depth are beyond my capacity.

I am well – and without any news whatsoever. I suppose this is a shabby letter.

I received a letter from you – and as always enjoyed it. You must take Macatawa as a vacation for you, too, and let daddy do the housekeeping for a few days at least.

That would be funny.

Write often -

Henry

I hope to be able to get to Palermo someday – but doubt that I shall. Well – I am seeing quite a few towns, and intend now to take a walk over to a road, and watch the world go by on donkeys.

I remember an Alsatian peasant, who said:

"Als ich Soldat in Struszburg war, da hab' ich die Welt wiel kennen gelerut."

"When I was a soldier in a field in Sicily, I learned to know the world very well. They ride donkeys."

August 16

Dear mama -

A warm day today, without news – but I write because it is in my thoughts to do so. I have been doing nothing about which to write – except hoping to get out to some of the towns – and finding no occasion.

But it is very lovely where I am – I gave laundry yesterday to the family who live about 100 yards away – and hope to get it back. Maybe I shall. A peasant family, living in a little stone house, tile roofed. Downstairs is the barn, where the donkeys, chickens, oxen and so forth are kept. Upstairs, the family lives. The laundry is done at a well – a little way off – in the almond grove from which I fill my pockets in the evening. Idyllic? Indeed it is.

Mt. Etna is barely visible – may be anyplace from 50 to 100 kms. away by road, for the roads wind – and on distant hill tops cities are visible.

The neighbor, whose wife is doing the laundry, has been to Messina – when he was a child, and I think has not left his valley since.

Communications with him are difficult. He is not very talkative – but it would not do much good if he were.

I just received a package from you – how I regret that I asked for summer clothes – because now I can't wear them. But there were many contents I am delighted to have – as toothbrush, soap (which I can now use lavishly again) and beautiful ties! How I laughed, when I considered that they were pleasures to me – and what would happen if I were them! So I mailed one, with a pair of socks, to M. Jacques Peyrus, of 8 Rue Lys du Pac, Algiers, and the other I am keeping for the event I may desire to give someone else something -

I am tempted to tear off the tags, and mail it to someone as a Sicilian purchase. But shall not!

I am well, and send my love -

Henry

August 16

Dear Betty -

I just received your letter about atabrine – which I am now taking daily, except when I forget it. It makes me feel so rotten that I think I am getting malaria and quickly take a few more pills – so you see the quantity increases (or should as a theoretical proposition) in a geometric progression. For I am in an area where, I am informed, malaria is, as I should say, hyperendemic. But others just call it rampant. I do not know how they know it is so, because the disease is usually diagnosed as F U O, which means, "fever undetermined origin."

But I have already told you enough about medicine.

The malarially hyperendemic area in which I find myself is Sicily. That is, I suppose, in part the reason why the towns are all on mountain tops – which is strange. That reason and for defense. And they are charming, beautiful, romantic villages. I have described what I have seen of them in letters to mama, which possibly you have read. I haven't seen nearly as much of them as I should like to see – but I am hopeful of seeing more. The Sicilian campaign, however, is now about ended – or ended – the news is not clear – and possibly I shall have leisure here – on the other hand – well the possibilities are still integral and I know not where I shall be from moment to moment.

It makes sending laundry exciting.

I am in magnificent mountainous country now – very dry and quite dusty on roads – but in this particular area, many trees – including almond trees which yield deliciously.

I am glad you are busy – and hope it is interesting.

Write again soon -

If daddy invests your money in a cattle ranch – I should like a share in it. Only why not closer than Colorado – closer to St. Louis, I mean. There is fine range in Lincoln County. Or near San Francisco; either.

My Italian leaves much to be desired. I find I can talk a little Latin to the priests – as thanking them for the privilege of visiting their most beautiful church. But Italian – beyond musical terms, which do not discuss or impinge on the subject of laundry or when Etna erupts, leaves much to be desired. I have learned "good day, "go away," and that is about all.

I am well -

There is a beautiful old well near here (where mosquitoes breed and women are making a fortune doing our laundry. Sicilians – those I have seen are peasants, and about 100% of them have lived in New York, I think. Nearby, the house, of stone, is a barn downstairs, where the oxen, donkeys and chickens are kept. Many goats – but it seems goats milk is all saved for cheese – and the babies go hungry, because they surely look undernourished.

One was sick – I was present when the army doctor was consulted – and when he told the baby needed milk, they looked surprised, and of course they could give milk to the baby, as if they had never thought of it before – and brought out a goat to show him they could.

I send my love -

Henry

August 19

To Mrs. A Lowenhaupt
6237 McPherson Ave
Saint Louis
Missouri

Dear mama -

Hard to write, because I have nothing whatsoever to write about – except that I am well – that the weather is warm – that I have done nothing of interest for the past several days, and have hardly any prospect of doing anything. But I shall take a walk or do something soon, and maybe acquire something to write about.

We have been having reasonably good meals, all things considered, recently -

Mt. Etna is visible at a very great distance – and sometimes one can see smoke rising from it.

I have very interesting letters from daddy – and one from Miss Thompson – I shall write to the soon.

I send my love -

Henry

August 19

Dear daddy -

I received your letter and enjoyed it – the one written just after your return from Macatawa – in which you lament the amount of work accumulated. I agree that there is a legitimate lament if you do not have time to consider things. But I cannot give advice to Saint Louis from Sicily.

I appreciate the favor of your buying United Fruit Co. stock for me –and remind you of my policy, which exists in large part for convenience – to work towards the goal of holding in even lots. So, absent a reason to the contrary, investment is easy for a while – that is, keep buying United Fruit, until I have 100 shares. The determination that it is a desirable stock is made, and it takes an affirmative reason to change the existing conclusion. You will observe, however, that there are numerous instances where my policy has not been accomplished – as in the case of American Chain and Cable, New York Shipbuilding, etc. etc.

Why is the stock marker booming so? Is there any reason?

We are now to begin to use so-called Allied Military Currency[56] – now issued in denominations of lire at 100 lire to the dollar. I enclose a sample for your information, and because you many find it curious. It is a far departure from metal ~~curren~~ money and the notion of negotiable instruments. It does not even contain a statement that it is legal tender. I wonder if there is any prohibition of counterfeiting it. On whom would a fraud be perpetrated – who would be damaged if it were counterfeited?

Well, I don't know. The counterfeiter would not be helped very much.

It is now supper time.

August 19

To Mrs. A Lowenhaupt
c/o Lowenhaupt, Waite, Chasnoff & Stolar
408 Pine Street
Saint Louis Missouri

Dear daddy -

I received your letter yesterday – the one you wrote just after your return from Macatawa, and enjoyed it very much. I should like to be able to answer it with an interesting letter, one as interesting as yours was, but despair of doing any such thing, because I have been sticking very close in the area and doing nothing except sitting at a table, going to and from meals, eating and sleeping. But maybe sometime soon I shall have opportunity to do something about which I can write.

I agree with you in principle that one *[sic]* ought not accept a bit of work, and should let everything just get done as best it can, and have resolved to do so. But it is very difficult to do. I hope to learn, however, and shall let you know my success.

I wish to thank you for buying a stock for me. You know my policy – which was adopted in large part out of laziness , which I support with reason. It is that one ought to hold stocks only in large enough blocks, so that I have set a block at 100 shares. That means that once the conclusion is reached that a particular stock is desirable, one keeps on buying it until one has one hundred shares. That is, unless cogent, affirmative reasons develop to contradict one's original judgment in purchasing the first lot. So, having started on United Fruit, one might as well keep on with it, until a total of 100 shares are owned. As you know, there are several odd parcels on which I have not perfected my policy – as American Chain and Cable, New York Shipbuilding, and so forth. My own idea was, then, whenever I had money to invest, to choose] a stock on which I had started, and, add to it, towards a hundred shares, unless at the moment I thought that there was something else more desirable – as I frequently did with Mr. Gatch and Mr. Arnstein[57]and others around. So the policy comes only to this, that all other things being equal, it is preferable to add to a holding already started than to scatter too broadly, and to obtain diversification over a longer period, rather than substantial quantities over that period. That is, it is true, a little bit riskier, but if one does not add to what one owns, one forgets all about them, and never goes back to them, with a resulting accumulation of too many little bits of odds and ends.

---

[56] The Wikipedia article for this topic includes a picture of these 100 Lira notes.
https://en.wikipedia.org/wiki/Allied_Military_Currency
[57] Two St. Louis stock brokers

I feel presently that I should like to keep cash to the extent of about $1,000. Beyond that, except for saving something with which to pay taxes, it might as well be invested. There is presently, I am sure, no possibility of my drawing a check, for I am accumulating cash in my pockets – more than I know what to do with. I left someplace a list of the securities which I own, which I believe MissThompson[58] could find. There was one in a blue notebook, given by Mississippi Valley Trust Company.

I am well – hope you too are so, and are taking care of yourself. Now that the Sicilian campaign is over, I am very curious as to where we go next – not that it makes much difference, but it is nicer to move around than to stay in the same place, and I have been in Sicily long enough.

I received an interesting letter from Miss Thompson. I wish you would thank her for me, and I shall answer.

I send my love:

Henry

August 21 1943

To Mrs. A Lowenhaupt
6237 McPherson Ave.
Saint Louis, Missouri

Dear mama -

I have not written for a few days – the same story, that I have nothing whatsoever to write about. Still here – and imagine by the time you get this, you will be settled again at home. Well – I hope you enjoyed the summer, and that Haymer[59] is improved and growing up. I received a picture of him and one of him and daddy. Haymer looks cute and devilish.

Last evening I went for a walk down the hill a little way – and came to a small rock house, in a formal Italian garden. The garden dying out for lack of water – it looked very forlorn, but the olive trees struggle on, and fig trees stay green, but the fruit does not mature.

Then, walking back, I met a man with a pail of ripe figs – he gave me five of them – ripe, but of a variety which is green instead of black or purple. They were red inside, and about the most delicious fruit I have ever tasted. He sat down then, on a stone bench by the path, and ate figs with a crowd of old women and men – who talked at a great rate. I wish I could understand them, but I can't.

I am well – and send my love -

Henry

---

[58] Helen Thompson was the office manager at the law firm.
[59] Haymer is the son of Henry's sister, Ruth

August 22

Dear mama:

I have been writing V mail letters for the past day or two – largely because there was nothing whatsoever to write about. Not that that condition has cleared itself, for it hasn't, but I might as well write an ordinary letter. It may be very slow in reaching you, because I understand there is no air mail service for the present. I shall nevertheless try.

I am well, and, when I think of it, really very comfortable. Presently – living on a hillside more or less terraced – well back from the road, so that it is not dusty – above the tent, large oak trees, and around, a number of almond trees, apple trees, pear trees, fig trees. A Farm homes are all around – with oxen, donkeys, geese, chickens, turkeys, roosters – which keep up quite a racket of mooing, braying, quacking, cackling, crowing and gobbling. I prefer the vegetables.

I have a small tent – called an igloo – which is like the covered part of a covered wagon. In it, I have a cot, on which my bedding roll is spread. A mosquito net covers it. I have a larger water can, and two orderlies, who make my bed and keep my water can filled. The flies are numerous, but that is normal.

So my habit is to get up in the morning at about six thirty or a quarter to seven – sunrise is at about six now – to fill my helmet, and first shave, then take a sponge bath, then put on shoes and underwear and then wash a pair of socks, and sometimes a handkerchief and underwear. By that time the helmet of water is too soapy and dirty to use further, and I throw it away. I have been able to have laundry done here, but with my system I really never have anything dirty to have laundered. Shirts – wool – can be rinsed out and then they feel clean.

By the time I am dressed then, it is time for breakfast (7:30) which usually consists of bacon and eggs – sometimes tomato juice or canned grapefruit – and coffee. I usually dawdle over breakfast until about 8:30, the news being broadcast from British Broadcasting Corporation at 8:15. These news broadcasts are all sweetness and light and poppycock, to a good extent, I think.

Then down to the tent where I work – and there I spend my time – wandering away now and then – until lunch time – about noon. After lunch, again to the tent, until dinner time. After dinner, I stay around the area – usually walking up a hill, or down through paths past fruit trees – always thinking of your Greek proverb about π ο λ γ ζ δ ε *[?]*, or whatever it is, until dark. Sometimes, then, there are movies – usually old ones – which I sometimes watch. The Sicilian neighbors come too, and I wonder what they see in them. Then to bed. So you see I am not overworked. On the other hand, I have very little, if any, uninterrupted time of my own.

The days are getting very noticeably shorter. The sun rises later – behind a high peak, which has a thin wisp of smoke or mist rising from it. Yesterday, it clouded up for a while, as if it were going to rain. But it didn't. I haven't seen a drop of rain since April – and I fear it – especially in Sicily, for I believe there is hardly a bridge left on the island, and the roads now just go across the stream beds – sometimes filled in. The first rain will, I think, wash out every road on the island. But – consider the lilies of the field – I can't stop it from raining when the time comes. Maybe I shall be elsewhere, although of course I do not know.

I send all my love -

Henry

August 25

To Mrs. A Lowenhaupt
6237 McPherson Ave.
Saint Louis
Missouri

Dear mama -

I have not written for a few days, because I have had nothing to write, and have been in a confused state of mind. But I shall settle down now, and maybe think of something to write. I am well, have moved to a new area – still in an olive grove, but within sight of the sea, and no fig trees or other edible fruit bearing trees around.

It is very beautiful – last night, I walked to the top of the next hill, and watched the sunset – with clouds clinging to the mountain tops. The landscape is always so very lovely.

Near the coast, the season is farther advanced – figs are about gone – olives are picked (I suppose green). I hope for an opportunity to go swimming soon – and *[word unclear]*. Maybe I shall have it – I surely hope so, for I am somewhat bored again.

I send my love -

Henry

August 26

Dear mama -

It is difficult, again, to write, not only because there is really nothing I enjoy writing again, but, as a matter of mood. I have not received mail for some time – but suppose they will get the ship unloaded someday – and I'll get the whole load.

I am in a new location – and expect to be able to go to a town tomorrow – to which I look with pleasure. Maybe, I shall get there.

Our new location overlooks the sea – and again is unbelievably beautiful – sharp stony mountains, with clouds drifting over the tops. Olive trees on the hills -

And it rains now and then – the showers are delightful, as night before last, when the shower came at about midnight.

But then, the moods of the sun are wonderful too – sunsets up the coast, with mists of all colors along stony cliffs. Towns are in sight, and at their distance, look like fortresses of Jerusalem in mediaeval painting.

The sea always gives me a sense of desire to wander – as the long blast of a ~~railwa~~ train whistle. It makes me think of a sail boat, and the coasts available on the Mediterranean – from Spain to Judea and Port Said or Suez to Gibraltar. But man is only ambulatory – and goes only from one village to another.

I have had most of my time occupied recently, with little bits of things which accumulate and take all time before one has finished. But I am doing my best to follow daddy's advice – and succeeding fairly well – of not taking responsibility or letting anything worry me.

Really the only thing which annoys me is the lost opportunity, being in very interesting and beautiful country and parts of the world, to see so little of it. But it cannot well be helped – Meanwhile the sun and air of Sicily are lovely.

I am well – and send all my love -

Henry

August 30

Dear mama -

I have not yet been to town – maybe I shall still have opportunity to go, as I hope – but that only time can tell.

Last night it rained – hard – as I has forgotten it could rain – and it was very wonderful, for this was the first rain I had seen since about April.

Of course, it had its concordant ridiculous parts. At about 2 o'clock I awoke, to hear Lt. Clark (who shares my tent with me) complaining that the canvas was in his face – the tent pole resting on his neck – so I got up, put on a raincoat and slippers, and stumbled out to see what I could do. By mere coincidence, I found an axe, and put tent pegs in – not very well, because I held a flashlight between my knees, which hinders axe technique.

Then, being soaked, I took off my pajamas, dried and went back to bed. After about twenty minutes, the whole tent came down – the rain having softened the ground so much so that the tent pegs all pulled out. It was really very cold in the rain – I tied the tent to an olive tree at one corner (I have developed a great affection for olive trees, although as yet they've yielded me no edible fruit) and struggled with pegs at the other – and to bed again.

Next time, it came down in toto – falling clear of my bed. Mosquito netting does not offer much protection from the rain – and this time I left Clark under it, like Gandhi, and went up and roused the orderlies. I think the orderlies should be at least Lt. Colonels – I respect them more; they can do anything. They came down and put up the tent – professional like, not attempting a temporary job. But they had clothes on, whereas I was struggling around dressed only in a raincoat.

This morning, things are quite a mess – underwear and socks buried and mingled with the mud. But surprisingly, I still have quite a few things dry.

There are a few things I could use, if you desire to send them. Bath towels (one or two) a hat – but this I mean the uniform hat, called an overseas cap, which is a masking flat hat with braid around the edge (wool – not khaki) wash rags – one or two – a pair of wool pajamas (I have cotton and silk) But there is no urgency. Socks to fill a package -

But last night was not all wild and wooly. I started the evening by drinking a bottle of very good champagne with Clark.

I am well – hope you too are so – and send all my love.

There has been no mail for a long time. Maybe it will come through soon -

Henry

I am staying away from the tent this morning. My lieutenant colonel orderlies are working hard – and I expect that soon they will have it all polished up like the inside of a *[word unclear]*. Maybe they will even have a tile floor or linoleum – they can do wonders.

I wish Betty a happy birthday – can't write long enough in advance of these things.

August (Not Dated)

This evening we had a fine dinner – turkey and cranberry sauce and rice and dressing. After dinner, I told the men who are working with me – and sent one up to the kitchen (anonymously*[?]*) with about half a bottle of rum (very poor). He traded it for four splendid turkey sandwiches, so that I am still surfeited and full. Add to that two oranges and numerous roasted chestnuts, roasted on the top of the oil stove. I cannot make them sell me persimmons which are ripe enough to be good.

I walked to the neighboring town today – and wandered a little – stopped in a carpenter's shop and talked a little – and in a dry goods shop, where I asked for linen. She said she had no more.

It is late. Now it appears that I shall not be able to go for my box tomorrow – but day follows day, and after tomorrow will do as well.

Write often -

Henry

September 2

Dear mama -

Well – I have intended all day to write about Palermo – which I visited day before yesterday – and now shall try – I had the most enjoyable time I have had for a long time. Beginning about noon, I spent the afternoon shopping, more or less, walking the streets. First, a man plucked my sleeve – "beefsteak, spaghetti," he said – and I "è buono?" And he said "yes, yes!" and I went in. So I had lunch, a very small beer steak, but very good – a dish of spaghetti, with stewed peppers and tomatoes, and very sweet, solid grapes. Then walking – bookstores, dry goods shops and miscellaneous ones – but most of the town is closed.

The city is beautiful – much like an American city – but bare mountains at the end of the main street – an old section with narrow streets, fish markets (where people were trying to grab fish) and splendid fine buildings – usually in the finest, newest WPA post office style. I bought a little lace – a little linen – a little pottery which I am sending, as previously written.

For dinner, to the Excelsior Hotel – a big, dark hotel, where we first drank a glass of Vermouth and a glass of cherry brandy. Then into dinner, where I had about the funniest dinner I've ever eaten. The food was good – and a bottle of wine – but the service desperate, plus the fact I cannot say "stop" in Italian. First (after about 20 minutes wait) rice soup, with parsley, carrots, etc.; then, after about half hour, lamb, with very delicious savory gravy, peppers and string beans. Then waiting and waiting. The waiter cleared the table – we became impatient, and began asking, as best we could. For desserti and fruitto – finally he brought soup, and we got the head waiter, who spoke English, and we got our dessert, a very excellent fig and almond tart.

Palermo is a fine city – to my way of thinking, however, not nearly as interesting as, say, Algiers or Oran or Tunis or even the smaller towns around Sicily as Gangi, Nicosia, Caltanissetta, Mistretta, and others. Palermo is too much like an American city and WPA post offices are much the same, whether they are Mussolini's or American. Plush desks, pink marble staircases, spacious rotundas surrounded by little cages –for post office or bank, while they may be fine and beautiful, aren't worth looking at, to my taste, when one can see old streets and alleys, with charming character and color, with a way of living which is independent of time.

"A rude peasantry, a cautious pride,
When once destroyed, can never be supplied."[60]
and similar thoughts.

I shall go to Palermo again, if I have opportunity – but I derive no pleasure from going around to army units – they are all the same and entirely independent of their place, set a little spot of Kansas in the heart of anyplace.

I send my love -

Henry

---

[60] Reference to *The Deserted Village* by Oliver Goldsmith
https://www.poetryfoundation.org/poems/44292/the-deserted-village

September 3

Dear Hy -

I received your very interesting letter of July 27 today – and am casting my bait again where I caught such a big fish – or, if I may mix my metaphors, such a delicious and delightful letter:

I answer it, first under your own headings. Office affairs: give my kindest regards to John Bardenheir, whom I haven't seen or heard of for a long time – except to greet him in Speibs*[?]*.

Personal affairs – postponed.

Oil – Easy come easy go – and oil funds may be considered gambling funds.

Art – I find nothing to buy – except new wine and trash. But I think it is in hiding. My little piece of barter[61], which I have with me, is too big to expose – and I have seen nothing for which to expose it. Nor am I near enough the center of Europe, yet, to expose it. But if you feel like sending me a small piece of some tangible commerciality, I shall see if I can bring something out of hiding, more than wine and cheap linen. Of course, it is hard to find where the things are in hiding. Peasant things – hardly worth shipping home. All I have found is a little linen, which I shall send. Palermo reminds me a little of Indianapolis – it has long been on the periphery of the grande monde. While it has fine buildings, and might normally have good peasant commodities, it is not a place to find things of good value.

I am convinced more than ever that our original plan to charter a boat and stock it with necessary commodities to be bartered for trinkets is sound – even in Italy where the worthless regime dominated for a long time. How much more so in France, where no one has ever wanted Italian or German money! In Italy, I think, and in Sicily, people are hiding their fine things.

And the civilian population is in need of many things – as soap, bread, and so forth. But drugs and medicines (quinine, atabrine, vitamins, and such) would bring a better price in commodities being hoarded. One could deal though doctors – who are very affluent in this milieu – and priests, who have access to fine commodities. I have seen beautiful marble statuary and paintings in churches, and think they, even from the churches, could be purchased for (1) drugs for the flocks, and (2) labor and materials to repair damages to walls and stone. I shall try, if I have opportunity. But now I can pay only in money, which is a worthless commodity, except for the purchase of things of no permanent value.

The churches have textiles, statuary, paintings, silver and other commodities. Individuals who have them – as I learn –from newspaper items, on the rare occasion when I see them, that there was a robbery or a burglary. They list the gory details of what was stolen. Well – maybe I shall still be able to get something.

Philosophy: - "O Israfel, if I could dwell[62] -
Consider the lilies of the field -
Ape enin salvi facti sennes.
Tolerari jubes ea *[sic]* non amari -
        Modieium enim lilies manest
homuiclus. Ambulent, ambulent ne
tenebres comprehendent.

---

[61] This is probably Henry's Platinum bar
[62] Reference to *Israfel* by Edgar Allen Poe.
https://www.poetryfoundation.org/poems/48628/israfel

Investments: You have my full approval to buy a laundry – believe me, I need it, for I have been doing my own in a hat for the past two months – and surprisingly well. But a professional laundry which uses soap! My oh my! In all seriousness, however – go ahead!

You say I ought to have good investment ideas – well, I haven't, except a few observations. For I see, superficially, a good deal of inflation. This one must watch: if the expressed idealizations are practiced, the United States is probably in for a good share of inflation. But they are not being practiced. Take the proposition of the Allied Military Currency in use here – pure fiat money – and now so called. But no policy is announced. If it is left to the Germans and Italians to make it good – fine! but if we are responsible for it, pfah*[?]*! My favorite statement is one I hear about towns – "we found that the people had elected a fascist mayor, so we fired him and established a democratic government." The allied military currency is pretty paper with ~~words~~ the four liberties written on it and nothing more. All talk is about how soldiers mustn't overpay for commodities, because if they do, the poor Sicilians can't buy. It is quite true that the merchants will charge what they can get and can sell anything at any price. But, if they ask too much for merchandise, why not just print more money? Prices are controlled. Of course, it results that people will not sell anything they can keep.

How does this affect investments? Here it is clear, that nothing is of value, except commodities. Prices are attempted to be fixed – with the result that the open and notorious stores have no merchandise – or are closed. Moral #1: price fixing destroys the retail business and even large inventories will not help. Price fixing is to be considered concordant with inflation – not really a remedy, because instead of causing money to have purchasing power, it destroys <u>all</u> the value of money. It will not buy even a little merchandise. I therefore disfavor merchandising stocks, regardless of inventory. One needs rather fixed assets. Inventory is a liquid asset, which, in a big, *[word unclear]* store, is very soon converted to cash in an inflationary period – cash which is worthless.

Price fixing has been tried before. Read the early history of Connecticut and Rhode Island.

Of course, the best investment is a trade. Here, the most flourishing trades are barbers, pressing and laundry – and notwithstanding price fixing these traders ~~to~~ get almost any price – sometimes by telling you to pay whatever you want, sometimes by indicating that all the buttons can be washed off laundry, etc. Then no one objects to overpaying.

Farmers are still well enough off, especially those with varied crops.

This letter has so many interruptions.

I have just been to a nearby town – which is on a hill above the sea. Nobody likes these towns as well as I do, it seems – I find them beautiful. No streets – just alleys going up the hills, paved with stones and houses over-hanging the alleys. Little shops – shoemakers on the alleys, launderesses, etc. The shops have little – but I found that fine things are to be bought. The cost of living having risen enormously, women are offering for sale their old wedding linen – exquisite quality of bedspreads and sheets and pillow cases, with lace and embroidery. I did not buy any – but maybe shall. The sheets and spreads are so enormous, five or six yards each way. Of these, there are many to be found. Of more conventional linens – table clothes and scarves and so forth there are fewer. Pottery must exist, but I have seen none for sale. Have not yet gone on a definite hunt for it – except I found a little mediocre in Palermo. Lace is still being made – quite expensive – but I may get a few small pieces. I have sent one big piece home – hoping it arrives.

I hope you will explain by intentions – I am addressing all packages I send arbitrarily to Marian, Ruth or may another – and intend that whatever I send shall be divided in large part for my own pleasure – and you, Ruth, Marian mama etc. are the *[word unclear]* for distribution. It is impossible to judge of worth or beauty here, because there are no standards of comparison. So I should like to have an estimate of quality or value from the recipient, to deter me from sending more if it is not wanted.

I have a great liking for heavy linen – but no judgment of it, nor do I know the difference between lace and embroidery.

Paintings could be acquired here also. They are of religious subjects mostly, and are treated as little household shrines – without regards to merit – a little lamp kept burning under them. They vary from photographic plates of a crucifix to oil paintings of superior workmanship. Every shop, every house, has one of them.

Yesterday, I bought almonds, which are now ripe, and ate them until I was somewhat sick. They are about my favorite food. Figs are gone, now. Olives, not yet ripe. Lemons are ripening, and prickly pears are abundant.

The day is beautiful – after a little rain, it has cleared – enough around to raise a considerable surg on the sea, which is as intense a blue as I have ever seen. You will find it impossible to imagine the beauty of this coast – towns in night on the promontories and in the mountains. The roads (ignoring military vehicles) crowded with donkeys, horses and carts – the carts elaborately carved and painted with scenes in bright colors – reds, yellows, blues and so forth. I'd really like to send you a donkey and cart, for use in connection with your victory garden – it would be lovely, and all you need.

I am, again, in an olive grove. Green olives, fresh from the trees, are terrible – puckery, sour, bitter, every bad taste at once.

I like Sicily – find the towns enormously interesting – and am trying to cultivate a hard heart, so that I can buy heirlooms and paraphernalia for this money, if I find people driven by hunger or disease to the necessity of selling. I suppose the women this morning hated to sell her bed spread – kept in a trunk, she said, – but was nevertheless disappointed – although only half way so – that we would not buy. There were yards and yards of linen in it, and pretty embroidery and lace.

My kindest regards to all in the office.

Henry

September 4

Dear mama -

I suppose I have not written for a day or two – I have just received a long letter from Hy, which I am answering – I enjoyed the letter very much.

Also, I receive particularly enjoyable letters from you, and one from Ruth – a picture of Haymer – in short, I have fared beautifully.

This morning I went to a nearby town, and really believe I have never enjoyed an hour more than the hour I spent walking there. The town is beautiful – streets paved with little stones in patterns, too narrow for any vehicular traffic, leading up the hill to the church, which backs against a sheer precipice. Quite somber . The balconies of the buildings overhang the streets. The shops – filled with merchandise – mostly fruits, vegetables, a little linen, embroidered.

As we were walking, a man approached us and indicated he had something to show. Out of curiosity, we went along – into a building, and up a flight of stone stairs, open onto a paved courtyards, through a bug unglazed window. Quite a poverty stricken dwelling – with bare rooms and a smell of stewing tomatoes. There, first, we saw pictures of his wife's four brothers who live in Greenville, Mississippi, In the room was a large stretcher, which they uncovered to show us how they were making lace. Then the lace they had for sale. I bought a piece – overpaying enormously, I think. And I do not know lace, but consider this piece strikingly beautiful. It is net work, with a design of thread put in, and quite a big piece . I shall send it to you – it may do as a table cloth, or for curtains, or even a bed spread. I think it is pretty.

I intend to address packages variably – some to Ruth, to you, to Marian, to whom not! By this I intend that you shall do as you please with what is received, having that one keep or use it who most nearly wants it.

I see very lovely kitchen pottery, but can never make up my mind to ship home commodities of so little intrinsic value – plain white clay pottery, but nicely shaped, in baking dishes, and other kitchen pieces.

All my love -

Henry

September 7 1943

To Mrs. A Lowenhaupt
6237 McPherson Ave.
Saint Louis
Missouri

Dear mama -

I have not written for a few days – but wrote a relatively long letter to Hy – in response to one of his – and imagine you will read it. There is nothing new of which to write – except possibly I have mentioned packages so often that you will not knew what I have sent. To date – I have mailed one package, containing lace. I intend to mail another, containing some linen and lace; ~~some~~ one bed spread and one set of mediocre pottery (five small cups, a tea pot, etc). I think Betty might have use for that – but distribution is your problem. I expect to buy more – why not?

I am well, and hope that you too are so. The weather here is beautiful – I have had a few opportunities to visit neighboring towns –so beautiful that they make me heart sick – towns on hills, narrow streets leading up to the church – the square or the quay – houses of old stucco and hewn timbers – wrought iron door guards and supports – shore makers in the doorways, and laundresses and grocery stores – The towns are charming beyond description.

Write me about the linens – judgement of quality, desirability, etc. – families are selling their heirlooms and wedding chests in order to buy necessities – mostly the unused things, as bed spreads, pillow cases and such – but possibly also some table linens. These are not so much in demand, because most people are looking for things of a more conventional souvenir type.

Love

Henry

September 10 1943

To Mrs. A Lowenhaupt
6237 McPherson Ave.
Saint Louis
Missouri

Dear mama -

Yesterday, finally, I got into Palermo, and enjoyed it very much – arrived at about noon, after a very lonely drive along the coast, and spent the afternoon walking in the city – the fish market, which is beautiful, and the streets. Palermo is a fine city – with fine stone buildings, abundance of public buildings surprisingly American, and reminds me, at first sight, of Chicago. Most of the shops, however, are closed – and I searched hard for things to buy. Ultimately I bought some linen, which I shall send to you or Ruth or Marian – really for distribution amongst you where desired, if at all, and some cups – because I was determined to get some pottery. What I got are childish, I think.

I shall write in more detail about Palermo some other time – when I am not writing V mail and have more patience and fewer interruptions.

Love

Henry

September 10

To Mrs. A Lowenhaupt
6237 McPherson Ave.
Saint Louis
Missouri

Dear mama -

Weather continues lovely – Italian surrender is good news – but does not bring to me as much elation as I expected or should expect – that is the world event section of this letter. I now turn to microeconomics – what little there is of it.

Yesterday I took occasion, to the pain of my concussion[63] which, however, heals very readily, to go to a neighboring town for no good reason except to see what is there. The towns are so very lovely that I

---

[63] We don't know anything about this concussion.

cannot describe them – so few automobile streets – mostly steps up the hills and valleys – built solid, with the first floor living quarters on the streets. So people do their living in public – make their spaghetti, comb their hair – the children sleep on door steps – and babies nap, dogs wander in and out, and flies cover everything! I could find beautiful pottery – better if I could talk better Italian – I see none in shops, but the kitchen work bowls, in parts – or water for pressing clothes – the pitchers of wine – you know what I mean by kitchen work bowls.

The town is, of course, crowded with soldiers, and the shops just about bought out. I bought nothing – having determined to wait a while. Then back to the area (I hate certain words – bivouac, camp, and so forth).

I am well – and send my love. The country too is beautiful, and the Mediterranean bluer than its reputation.

Love

Henry

September 12

To Mrs. A Lowenhaupt
6237 McPherson Ave.
Saint Louis
Missouri
U. S. A.

Dear mama,

I am well – with really nothing to write – still in lovely weather and very beautiful place – but doing nothing about it. Maybe I shall go swimming this afternoon – but that is in the future, and therefore unknown.

There is not a bit of news to write here – I have sent a few trinkets home and hope you receive them. I wanted to buy some, if I get a chance – but do not know whether or not I shall. I hope I have the opportunity. I should like to buy, say, handkerchiefs or something of that kind – but little things of such conventional use are about unobtainable.

It frightens me to appreciate that the summer is over – the time in the past having gone so quickly. But I control my thoughts as best I can and don't think of the future. So you see this is one of my blue days – when I ought not write, but do anyway.

I wrote a letter to Ben yesterday – not a good or interesting letter – because, I suppose, it is extremely difficult to write. I received letters from you, too, and enjoyed them very much, as I always do. A letter from John and Walter[64] – which amazed me. It also amazed me that Paul was in the army – I thought of him as too young and too small.

---

[64] John and Walter Gusdorf, twins taken in by Henry's parents as their parents stayed in Germany. Paul was a brother who stayed elsewhere. Their parents arrived in New York on April 8, 1941 and then joined the boys in St. Louis. The two families remained very close over many years.

I send all my love -

Henry

September 12

Dear mama -

I write now, although it is the second time today, because I think I shall be unable to write – amidst the press of interruptions I expect – in the near future. But if I can write, I shall.

I am well – in a beautiful climate – and did not go swimming this afternoon because I have just not gotten at it. Dolce far miute[65] – and procrastination.

I received three letters today – one you wrote on the beach, blotted with sand and it contained still a few grains of sand, quite delightfully! Another was long and interesting. To it not getting to the point where Haymer ought to be taught to talk? He will be three years old by the time this letter reaches you – and a year ago, he was almost talking. I should think a specialist might be able to teach him.

But then three is walking, too.

And a letter from daddy, which I enjoyed very much, as I always do enjoy his letters.

Olives are ripening fast – maybe I shall yet have opportunity to eat a ripe olive fresh from the tree. Green olives fresh taste terrible.

Oh yes – for a long time I have intended to write and ask for a present – and now remember as I write, two things I should like to have.

1. A pocket knife – I lost mine -
2. A pair of slippers of some kind, with hard enough soles so that one can walk on rocky ground in them.

With that I close.

Love,

Henry

---

[65] I believe this is intended to be the Italian saying, "Dolce Far Niente," or "the sweetness of doing nothing."

September 15

To Mrs. A Lowenhaupt
6237 McPherson Ave
Saint Louis
Missouri

Page 1

Dear mama -

I had the pleasure yesterday of again visiting Palermo – and shall write about it V-mail, partly because I have no other paper right here. This is page one.

The drive is very lovely – through towns which I have described. The heavy military traffic makes them dusty – but they are still beautiful.

In Palermo, Lt. Clark and I walked the streets – looking in shop windows for several hours. The shops sell out by shortly after noon every day, and the merchandise is pitiful. I saw one handsome tablecloth – at $90.00. It ought to be handsome, at that price – but maybe someone will think the price is not excessive.

In the afternoon – late – we went up

September 15

To Mrs. A Lowenhaupt
6237 McPherson Ave
Saint Louis
Missouri

This is page 2.

To Monreale – a town near Palermo[66] – where we visited as magnificent a cathedral as I have ever seen. I shall possibly send some picture post cards of it. Mosaics – quite beyond imagination in color and intricacy. Then, the cloister – a square of pillars, with the capitals varied impossibly– possibly also pictures of that.

Then to the Excelsior Hotel for dinner – a few dishes. I met a man named John Kelsey, in the coast guard, and asked him, if he got to New York to telephone you collect and tell you he saw me – I suppose he won't do it. He may be in New York in a matter of months. A good dinner at the Excelsior, ending with a bottle of quite fine champagne .

All beer and skittles. I'll write again.

Love

Henry

---

[66] Monreale is a town slightly south west from Palermo, Italy.

September 15

Dear mama:

I just wrote two V mail letters – but in the last analysis, it seemed utterly impersonal – and I shall write again.

I was in Palermo yesterday – and besides wandering the streets – crowded – and many side streets with furniture factories (hand) and women washing, and cobblers and tinkers and spinsters and ale traders –fish markets – everything. Then to Monreale – one of the world's most magnificent places – a church[67], in marble, and mostly mosaic – stories of the old testament, a huge figure of Christ, whose arms extend around the apse – in gold and red and blue. And a chapel – I almost wept for Ruth to see it – for it is in solid marble, frames of one color around high reliefs in pure white, carved or sculpted so exquisitely – Donatello style, and Michelangelo and all – they are superb, and in the class of masters, which so transcends just plain sculpture that there is nothing left to say. The cherubs – almost flying out of the stone, and the figures with such grace and elegance – you cannot believe that it could be done in marble.

Then to the cloisters – a square of old stone – with arched doorways, now filled in, formerly leading to archbishop's study, and other chambers – a square of pillars – no two alike – some covered in mosaic, others carved, and all the capitals very ornate – with figures – all different – from bible and Christian legend – from there, one walks through the ruins of a more ancient building – onto a terrace, overlooking the city, a great valley, with towns in the distance – a fertile valley, filled with orange groves – and out to sea. The beauty is complete.

Then ~~dow~~ we sat in the car while the driver went in to look around briefly – and a woman tried to sell us handkerchiefs, and finally a tablecloth, snatched from her table, and spotted with spaghetti sauce. We escaped though if we had stayed five minutes longer, I think she would have come down to our price. That would have been a misfortune.

Then to the Hotel Excelsior – Palermo's finest – for dinner – small in quantity, excellent in quality, and we finished the day with a bottle of champagne.

Those are the hardships – the days between are also interesting. I send all my love

Henry

---

[67] This is Monreale Cathedral he is describing. It is a UNESCO World Heritage Site, noted for its mosaics.
https://en.wikipedia.org/wiki/Monreale_Cathedral
https://en.wikipedia.org/wiki/Monreale_Cathedral_mosaicshttps://www.tripadvisor.com/Attraction_Review-g666663-d4470498-Reviews-Duomo_di_Monreale-Monreale_Province_of_Palermo_Sicily.html (This site includes many traveler photos.)

September 18

To Mrs. A Lowenhaupt
6237 McPherson Ave
Saint Louis
Missouri

Dear mama -

I write V mail really when I have nothing to say – so I might as well send you a complete blank sheet of paper. There is no news – I intend to go to *[word blanked out, perhaps by the censor]* again someday – but when I do not know – possibly this afternoon to a town in the vicinity. The future is always unknown. Still on my hilltop over the Tyrrhenian or Mediterranean – where olives are getting bigger. The temptation is to put an olive branch between my toes, and, flapping my arms, say "coo."

You see how much I have to say – I have been thinking of Virgil recently – and wish I had memorized more than the first few lines. But even though I can't quote that as far as I want to I can still say that possibly at some future time it will be a pleasure to remember these things. I send my love -

Henry

September 22

To Mrs. A Lowenhaupt
6237 McPherson Ave.
Saint Louis
Missouri

Dear mama -

I wrote a very brief note last night – intended to go on, but darkness overtook me – and now I still have nothing to add to that note. It is mailed, with a handkerchief, first class mail, because I was too lazy to walk down the hill to the post office. I thought, as I finished my note, about the picture St. Augustine left in my mind – "There remains still for men a small measure of light. Let them walk; let them walk, lest the shadows engulf them."

All I wrote yesterday was that I visited a neighboring town – a gem, to my way of thinking, closely built right on the sea, up the hill, and tacked to a cliff – a big church dominating it all – and colors of stone – tradesmen in the street – old women spinning hemp, men braiding rope (barefoot – they use their toes to hold the reeds of which they are making the rope) a little beach crowded with fishing boats pulled high. The streets crowded. And all the shops filled with fancy sewing.

I got a pair of pants in Palermo – having little choice of size I got them just too big – and had them altered in town yesterday,

Prices are fancy – $50.00 for a lace tablecloth – and the whole business section of town looks like a ladies' bazaar or Women's Exchange. How they embroider "Remember Sicily" on handkerchiefs and doilies! But I feel sorry for the ladies. Some of them – in joint enterprise with a room full of embroidery and lace – are quite genuine ladies in all their mannerisms and speak -

There is no news. I send my love

Henry

September 23

Dear mama -

It is some time since I have written a respectable letter, and I am afraid I am not about to do it now – for I really have nothing to say, am in a little bit of a bored state – not that is to be expected at the beginning of a day when I really expect nothing to happen. Maybe tomorrow I shall go to a town – Palermo or some other – and see what there is to do. I am well, and hope you are also.

I have finished my book on Roman Law - truly I did not read it very thoroughly, but nevertheless found it interesting. Mostly just pure textual. So I have abandoned it. Now I shall go back to Augustine. I should like to reread ~~She~~ *Confessions* – but do not send a copy, because that makes a good quest here – if I can find a bookstore with any stock.

I am still in Sicily – and going on from day to day. My present fancy is speculating on the campaigns of Hannibal – how he held Sicily, Sardinia and Corsica, and how he and his brother cooperated in their attempt to conquer Rome. If you can get the ~~21st, 2~~ 20th, 21st and 22nd books of Livy, you will find the story – with many embellishments, of the bare outline I have in mind, too vaug~~ely~~, however, to write.

It is very hot here – I should be inclined to say unseasonably hot, except that I do not know the seasons. Figs are gone – no longer available. But almonds are ripe and in abundance. I try to keep a helmet full of them on hand – but they are, with me, habit forming, and I eat them too fast.

Do you know the feeling that the forces of ignorance are closing in upon one? I think of that in the evening – when, usually, I walk to the edge of the cliff, and watch it get dark – over the Mediterranean. Then also, one thinks – "There remains for men a small measure of light. Let them walk, let them walk, lest darkness engulf them." But all that is disconcerting

Last night I had a treat – as I was sitting at the top of the cliff the Red Cross representative – a man named Snyder came up, and we talked a while. I think Mr. Snyder is lonesome – and his work is so futile in so many respects. He opened a fancy Red Cross Club in a neighboring town, at great labor getting space, and doughnuts and so forth. Then, one day afterwards, the town was placed off limits, for no stated reason. So Mr. Snyder had a pocket full of chocolate which he had acquired from the British – and we ate it. Nothing has tasted so good since I left New York.

But those are minor things – I suppose these almonds sound good. There is also abundance of hazelnuts – but I've not yet gotten any. I thought they were acorns until I ate one. Walnuts also coming in now. Lemons are ripe, but I haven't seen any oranges yet.

So you see here is nothing to write about. I think I shall buy something when I get an opportunity because I have more money than I know what to do with. So do not be surprised if you get some gaudy table clothes. To date, I have sent, since my last list, two handkerchiefs. Did my rug from Relizane ever arrive?

I send all my love -

Henry

September 24

Dear Ruth and Marian -

I have decided to write to you for variety – although when I think of the months hence it will be before you receive this letter, it hardly seems worthwhile.

Yesterday afternoon I went to my favorite nearby town – a town which looks as if it were quite wealthy recently. The apparent wealth and sign of towns here is directly proportional to the extent of the low fertile land around them. Palermo has the biggest valley. This town has a substantial extent of flat land around it – but the town itself backs right up to the cliff, which over hangs it. It is crowded with fancy sewing – and I bought some doilies and a tablecloth which I shall send home when I get a chance.

Now I have been to Palermo – mostly for the drive, with Lt. Clark who had some things he needed and could get only there. The drive is lovely, although Palermo is not particularly enjoyable to me. It is very dusty, and substantial parts are in ruins. The shops offer only trinkets – but possibly if one could spend a few days looking, one could find something. Trinkets and fancy sewing again! I am surely anxious to hear an opinion on whether that I send is in any wise desirable [because I cannot judge.

For a few moments I had high hopes – for I came upon a china shop. But looking at each thing individually, it was all of the Woolworth type – except some, whose only value was that it was covered with a gold color. It looked so very Italian! as so many things do – that it reminded me of 14ᵗʰ St. in New York.

I have exhausted Palermo's book stores for *Confessions of St. Augustine* – there is none in town. "All sold" they say. So I shall wait until I get someplace else. But I am in need of some of that philosophy – for the temptation gets severe to call these Sicilians a crowd of dirty, lying beggars. But they beg – I suppose because they are in want – and they are dirty because they lack facilities for keeping clean, and idle because they have no materials with which to work. So one ought to feel charitable toward them – and quote:

"Who feeds the hungry beggar feeds three -
Himself, the hungry beggar and me." But Augustine can beat that.

Will you write me the poem (E A Poe) about

"O Israfel, if I could dwell"?

It's in my mind -

I send my love -

Henry

September 25

Dear mama -

I received two letters from you today – and enjoyed both very much. I hope you are keeping active and enjoying yourself – you really ought to – just go out and celebrate say once a week – with champagne or wine or anything.

This afternoon I went swimming – it was really very fine – in the Tyrrhenian [, which seems much saltier than most water. It was very refreshing, as it has been ~~very~~ hot and dusty here on our hilltop.

While I was on the beach, a man and two boys came along – fishing. They had a net, ~~like~~ a flat piece, with a draw string, which they cast into the sea, and pulled in, loaded with little fish – they looked like very small sword fish – and I suppose are sardines or something similar. It was quite amazing – and pleasing to see how abundantly the sea still yields. They must have pulled in about five pounds at a haul – and I saw them cast three times.

Add to that, that it was very picturesque – the distant towns like mediaeval fortresses.

I enjoyed the swimming – how I forget that it is the end of September, and winter will be settling in there soon.

Driving to Palermo yesterday I noticed that lemons are ripe. It is a beautiful crop, for the groves are dark green, spotted with bright yellow – lemons, like jewels. Lemons – about 3¢ a kilo – and lemonade (without sugar) in great abundance. Oranges ought to appear soon.

I dispatched today two packages – one little one, containing embroidered doilies, which, if you or Ruth of Marian or Betty do not want, might make a Christmas present, say, to Heather or Sonya Glassberg: A large package, containing a table cloth, which I thought striking, and therefore sent. The sauce goes for that – I send these things because I enjoy buying them in towns – pure extravagances – and think you may find them different from most things, possibly attractive or pleasant to use or give away. Of course, I am anxious to be told whether you think they are worth sending – or whether you could get the same thing there, and so forth.

I am well, and send all my love. I enjoy hearing from you frequently, as I do.

Henry

September 26

Dear mama -

I wrote you last night – and shall repeat a little for there is nothing new to add – I dispatched two packages, which I hope you receive – one is an orange envelope containing doilies, and one, a brown paper parcel containing a table cloth.

Last night was a wild night – just after I went to bed, the wind came up – and I suppose is the wild, west wind of which Shelley writes. It was a regular hurricane, and I was much surprised with every gust that the tent did not fall. It didn't. But clouds of dust came with each gust of wind – and this morning I am digging out – hair, eyes, ears, nose; blankets, towels; papers covered with about a quarter of an inch. What a mess!

It is a strange wind – not cool, but hot and very dry -

You ask what present you might send the Peyrus family – Well – it is really unnecessary to send any – but I suppose that edibles would be appreciated – but do not suggest you send anything. I have a letter from Madame – she has heard from her family in France – her mother in Paris, her brother, who has been repatriated in France, and others. I have their addresses, and if ever I get near their respective towns shall call on them.

While I was in Algiers, I ordered a French dictionary from England. It arrived yesterday. La! La! But I think I shall get more expeditious service hereafter – I sent some extra, so that I have about enough credit with Blackwell's to buy one or two books. It ought not take more than two weeks to get a book, and Blackwell's is considered the most complete bookstore of the English speaking world.

I received a letter from Mary. So I enclose an answer with this letter, for I do not know her address.

Love, Henry

September 30

Dear mama -

Today has been a hectic day – not really – but with much confusion of papers flying – so much that I have not paused to look at the sky and the sea and the olive groves and the loveliness of the weather. But they are there nevertheless, and as I think of them, I derive some pleasure -

Yesterday I went to a neighboring town with Captain Morris – the town which has gone hog wild on the manufacture of fancy sewing – but which has now discovered that easy cross-stitching can be sold for as good a price and as easily as the finest lace. So the abundance of trash is growing, and the finer things are, as I judge, diminishing.

I enjoyed the afternoon – parked, as always, at the edge of the town, on a square which is in a kind of embankment at the sea – and walked directly into the narrow street which is near the shore – and opens, at a little distance, into another paved, open place on the sea. Then around, up a hill – built fine and solid – the street a little wider – and into the main street – narrow and crowded. Then walked up that, and into a tailor shop to have some clothes pressed (they use beautiful, big, old, slow charcoal irons) The people are learning English faster than I am learning Italian. I left my clothes there – agreeing to return at four o'clock for them – it was then about two – and walked up the main street, looking in every window and going into every shop. New At one shop, we saw a tablecloth which Captain Morris wanted – but did not buy because he wanted to see the rest of town first. Further on, a shop with pastry in the window – what looked like doughnuts, filled with custard – in roll shape. So we bought two. They were rye bread, filled with a kind of custard, and a slightly fried crust. One would have made a complete meal, I am sure, for a heavy laborer – and after about three bites, my eyes were bulging. So I gave the rest to a child – and he devoured it avidly.

Then on to the end of town – up an alley to another street – and back – the street had women sitting out sewing – wood working shops – beauties – making cabinets, chairs and other things, and I wandered into one and watched for a while. At the back – fancy sewing in progress. We came out on an alley by the church – the alley goes steep up to the face of a cliff, against which the church backs – a solid old church, square and solid, matching the cliff in color, with capacious arches, and lovely carved stone pillars – the capitals with little figures – and the stone around the windows carved in wreaths and floral patterns. The whole church has a lovely, simple, spaciousness about it, and overtowers the whole town – and is in turn overtowered by the cliff which dominates it and the town.

Across the square and back to the main street – and up a block to a pastry shop. First, a piece of candy, made principally of figs, which tasted like a laxative – ground figs with an almond on top, but it was very pretty. Then they had cakes in the window – going fast, so there was not time to spend long choosing. We got a beauty – a mess of marshmallow or goo, with a cake inside – with a custard and fig filling – and ate it in our fingers. They provided a napkin, and we washed in the soda fountain. Then we walked back to the end of town, wandering on a few other streets, and back – Captain Morris buying a very beautiful table cloth of white linen – which he calls cut work, and I buying a handkerchief, which is enclosed– I thought of sending it to Irma – but you are my dispenser [of trinkets. I also saw an embroidered tablecloth – which I may buy at another time. It was of linen – brownish – in very beautiful colors, designed. But I did not feel like shipping another package until I learn whether anything arrives. I may change my mind.

Then to the barber shop – where I had a haircut and shampoo – the shampoo being extremely refreshing, in cold water – little soap.

Then back to the tailor shop. On my way, a Red Cross worker gave me two doughnuts – and we carried them along – and I got some more fig candy to bring back. The tailor had not finished – explaining that one shirt I had left there was dirty, so he had washed it. In due time, he finished and we went back to the car, and here – where we came in time for dinner.

The days are getting very much shorter, and it is now dark, although it is still early.

I am well – really no news – except hope – which lies in the prospect of going to town again someday soon – any town, although I really enjoy the smaller ones just as much as Palermo.

I am accumulating more money than I know what to do with. I shall find some way to spend it.

All my love -

Henry

September (Not Dated)

To Mrs. A Lowenhaupt
6237 McPherson Ave
Saint Louis,
Missouri

Dear mama -

This afternoon I went swimming in the Mediterranean – a beautiful beach, sunny, and nice surf. The water was very pleasant. I swam for about half an hour – then watched the town – about two or three miles – on a road which parallels the sea, crowded with military vehicles – but here and there a fancy painted Sicilian wagon, loaded with a ton of grapes. One man – with grapes and two children – offered us a ride. I gave him a cigarette – and tried to explain that we did not want the ride – how it was a pleasure to "andare al pie[68]" – which I think he understood. The town, when we got there, was a rather sprawling village, with nothing. The church was not fine – only a few carved doors, little iron, and the people very dirty. So we did not stay long. On the way back we picked up a crowd of children following – whose English consists of "g-d - s-o-b Mussolini, hell d-." But one showed us he could count in English to 5. Then another man stopped and gave us bunches of grapes – very delicious and sweet, and I enjoyed eating them.

There is another town in the same direction – somewhat larger. Maybe sometime I shall go there.

I wrote, I believe, that I hoped to go to Palermo today – well, I didn't as you see – but perhaps shall still have opportunity to go sometime.

I hoped to be able to buy something in town – but there was nothing for sale except tomatoes and grapes.

Love

Henry

---

[68] Attempting to say "andare a piedi," or "to walk/travel on foot."

October 1

Dear mama -

Today is a quiet day – except that this afternoon the band is practicing for a ceremony to occur tomorrow, when a general will visit. A band playing in a place like this – the diddle diddle doo dap and so forth – makes everything seem like Kansas, and is to me quite depressing. But that does not matter either -

This morning it rained – a thunderstorm which was quite lovely, or is so to remember – I stood in it and took a bath although it was very cold, as all rain remains to be. But also, it made me fear weather to come, and I decided it was much too early for winter to set in. So to some extent I refused to recognize it, decided that it was only rain <u>de facto</u> and not <u>de jure</u>.

I also thought of St. Jerome's expostulation – So a man whom he was urging to leave the luxury of Athens to come to the desert and be a hermit – "O delicate soldier, whom winter under canvas terrifies."

Well, I have much to learn. Tomorrow, if there is occasion and opportunity, I shall see if I can shake hands with the General *[word unclear]*, without it being noticed. It will be a reception without the shrimp cocktail.

You see, I have very little or nothing to write. I mailed yesterday a small lace handkerchief, quite useless as a nose blowing utensil – with a letter – I do not know if it will go first class mail or how.

I am well, and send all my love.

Henry

October 3

Dear mama -

My mind is full of yesterday – which was a long, rainy day – rained all day, very beautifully; the kind of steady drizzle which lasts all day. But it was warm enough, that it was not bothersome to be slightly wet.

Now this morning, the ground and all the brushes are covered with slugs – everything is bright, and the sea shines and sparkles magnificently.

Yesterday afternoon, although it was raining, I went to a town – a real beauty in the rain, for there was not dust, and the streets were washed clean and bright by the floods of water roaring down them – regular streams in every street. The buildings shone in their colors, and the shapes and details stood out beautifully.

I enjoyed wandering around the town very much – the streets empty except for a few people going fast through the rain. I wish I could describe the towns here, to give you an idea of them. They are beautiful quite beyond any possible description – and without seeing them, I couldn't imagine that such things exist. Especially the smaller ones – a city like Palermo is harder to appreciate – it has wide streets, and one must pick out the particular beautiful buildings – of which there are many. But there are also parts with long straight streets and streetcar tracks – like Gary, Indiana.

I am well – I found in town yesterday some chocolate for sale, and bought a bar 0 it was very excellent – German chocolate, not milk, but the chocolat *[sic]* fondant. The price – 35 lire (35¢) a cake – about as big as a 5¢ hershey -

All my love

Henry

October 4

Dear mama -

I was in Palermo today – and enjoyed it – have just about exhausted the town – and have walked all these streets – extremely beautiful. Today it rained – I got wet, but have now dried out. Rain makes everything look much brighter – settles the dust. The facades of Palermo are lovely – and it is an extremely fine city.

I had a native lunch – which tasted good – consisting of what they called minestrone – a big dish of rice, cooked with tomatoes, carrots, chards, onions, and so forth. Really much better than it sounds. Then some candy – about solid sugar, and some consisting of ground up figs in a sugar coat.

The shopping of Palermo is exhausted so far as I am concerned – it offers no pottery or china, except some Bavarian junk, and poorly overdecorated or over simple Italian porcelain. I have seen nothing such as native Sicilian pottery, which should be beautiful.

I bought two handkerchiefs, one of which I sent to Irma and one of which I sent to Miss Thompson – who writes me letters sometimes. I bought some envelopes, the beauty of which you will have seen by the time you read them. I bought some lace – doilies, I suppose, just for fun, and I shall send them to you or Ruth or Marian for disposition – if they are pretty in your judgement, Betty might like them – or anyone can keep them. Same principle. I thought them quite superior – and they were the best I could find in Palermo.

I know where there is (or was) an embroidered tablecloth. I am tempted to get it, but begin to fear you will be so overloaded with poor gaudy linen that you will have to stuff it up the chimney. Maybe I had best wait until I hear whether what I send arrives or is wanted -

There's been no mail recently. I am settled into routine of dolce far niente – and shall be shocked when I have to change and do something. But life is just a series of shocks -

I see Sicilians here – boys discharged from the army now – they look happy.

I send my love

Henry

October 5

Dear mama -

It is again difficult to write – for mail seems to be delayed, and I have received none for a week or two. What is the motto on the New York post office? In addition, I have the feeling again that the forces of ignorance are closing in, like clouds or darkness after sunset – "There remains still for men a small measure of light. Let them walk, let them walk, lest the darkness engulf them." So Augustine thought.

The forces of ignorance manifest themselves in ceremonies – which are like a million little needle voiced devils – and play acting, like dolls' houses – but I cannot say what I mean – the sentiment is really purely introspective and intangible – which I take to be exactly what Augustine meant. The concept of the holy ghost is also applicable – that which hovered over the face of the deep in Genesis – even before light was created.

But the cure is easy – the forces of ignorance are to be combatted by (1) indifference and (2) laughing at them. So I am making up paraphrases of Pope's

"If to her share some faculae follies fall
Look on her face, and you'll forget 'em all."

I am well – of course inpatient to hear from you, but imagine a pack of letters is on the way.

I was in town yesterday – and bought some lace which I considered beautiful – and sent it home. I hope it arrives. I expect in the pack of letters to have some acknowledgement of receipt of parcels – and some indication to guide my future operations. I have more money than is good for me.

Here are three letters! Howard Ridgeway, John Gusdorf, and you -

I have so many – I'll close this and read at leisure

Love -

Henry

October 5

Dear mama -

I have a confused day today, with many things which have withheld my mind from worthy thought and my hand from worthy action – but that passes – and between idleness, the devil's workshop, and confusion, I do not know what alternative lies. Shall I despair? Never! The Mediterranean is still lovely – and I still have olive branches overhead to cast a thought to now and then.

Last night – for some reason – buffet supper – on the hilltop. It gets dark so early now that it was so before we finished eating. I suppose buffet supper was served out of consideration for the kitchen – who had served our ceremonial feast at noon – with steak, and canned peas, and for dessert excellent pie, for Sicily at least, I am sure. The honor of a ceremonial occasion – the dinner, even with the fine pie was not worth the ceremony – even with cherry pie, as it was, and which you know to be my favorite.

Nothing to say – I send my love -

Henry

October 10

To Mrs. A Lowenhaupt
6237 McPherson Ave.
Saint Louis
Missouri
U.S.A

Dear mama -

I write largely to tell you that I shall be unable to write for a while – lacking not only facilities, but material of which to write. I am presently in idleness.

The date reminds me – is it Haymer's birthday – he has much of my thought – but I cannot make up my mind to send him trinkets, although he might like them – as miniature donkey carts. They are not worth the packing.

It also reminds me of your birthday and anniversary coming soon – nothing I can do about it, except wish, as I do.

This morning I took a short walk around the area – came upon a man with a horse loaded with almonds, and bought some, which I now eat. After the recent rains, there are many flowers, strange to me. One in abundance, I think is colchicum – a full blown purple flower, close to the ground, in a flat patch or rosette of plantain-like leaves. Then a little stalk, covered with tiny purple flowers, without leaves; wild roses, and many other flowers.

Olives are ripe. They are not good – full of a bitter, milky juice – and I suppose they must be cured before they are fit to eat. I am disappointed. I fancied eating fresh olives from the tree.

You see there is no news. No mail is coming in – and while I haven't received any for about two weeks, I hardly expect any for another two weeks.

Well, says St. Augustine, "tolerari jubes ea, non amari." Thou orderest these things to be borne, not to be loved -

Love -

Henry

October 10

Dear mama -

I am writing not because I have anything to say, being now in complete idleness and having been so for three days, but because I have not written for a few days, and probably shall not write for a few days. Meanwhile, facilities are disrupted, and I really do not know when this letter will go out.

Well, idleness is somewhat stupefying – and so I have nothing to say, but that I am well – the sea is lovely, and I am curious and impatient.

There had been no mail now for a long time – that builds up my hopes.

All my love -

Henry.

I have no air mail stamps -

October 17

To Mrs. A. Lowenhaupt
6237 McPherson Ave
Saint Louis,
Missouri

Dear mama -

Not having written for some days – I write this note to let you know I am well. We have just completed a journey – and are now in as idyllic an orchard as could be imagined – with wild cyclamen growing and blooming thick, and very delicious apples for the picking.

I am well – and intend to write of the journey at a later time. Presently, all is confused, in getting settled.

Lots of rain – lots of mountains.

All my love -

Henry

Italy

October 17

To Mrs. A. Lowenhaupt
6237 McPherson Ave
Saint Louis
Missouri

Dear mama -

I had much I intended to write you, but now find that there are new censorship regulations[69] (which I've not yet read), which do not permit me to write what country or places I'm in, or anything substantial of

---

[69] While I could not locate specific policy changes around this time, I was able find a few pamphlets of censorship regulations from this period.
U.S. Postal Censorship Regulations (April 13, 1942) https://archive.org/details/USPostalCensorshipReg/mode/2up
U.S. Censorship Regulations (January 30, 1943). https://archive.org/details/USCensorshipReg/mode/2up

what I see. So I can't write – except that I have seen many interesting things and very beautiful country – more beautiful than I could imagine to expect. Women carrying great *[word unclear]* on their heads – beautiful peasant costumes – and oxen, crowds walking on the roads – all these things which make rural roads so very interesting. Magnificent mountains and towns and fruits and gardens.

When I was in Tunisia*[?]* *[word unclear]* once inviting *[words unclear]* were accepting gifts to help rebuild a church. I gave them 10 lire, and they gave me a little religious card – with bright colored pictures of saints, and a prayer on the back – A boy on the road looked nice*[?]* – and I gave him a biscuit – he stood there, and I rummaged through my pockets and happened to find the card. So I gave it to him. What a demonstration it provided! He read it, and wept, and rushed into the house with it. Then his sisters and brothers came and, bringing me a big box of very delicious apples. I have no idea what prompted the deluge – the brother spoke a little French – and stood there talking on non-committal subjects – about school and his work and so forth.

I hope to be able to see some of the towns or cities near here someday soon – but *[word unclear]* I shall miss them.

Love

Henry

October 18

Dear mama -

I wrote to you a note a few days ago, telling you that I was well – knowing that you had not heard from me for a few days – since I had not written.

Even now, however, I am in doubt as to how much I may write about a journey – and so I shall skip it altogether.

I am presently very fortunately situated – physically – in a fruit grove – very moist – and enormously fertile and closely cultivated. Grape vines growing on the fruit trees make it almost jungle-like.

And fruit is in abundance – apples, oranges, lemons, passion-fruit (which I think is about the same as Japanese persimmon) walnuts, hazelnuts (which I do not like), abundance of wine. The neighboring farmhouses are regular mansions – where whole colonies seem to dwell. All stone – no wooden buildings.

There is a town about 150 yards away, into which I walked last night with Lt. Clark – it was dark, and nothing could be seen, except the children, who sang loud and clear about "Over the Summer Sea, with Light Hearts Gay and Free" – in their own language, of course. We bought two pounds (a kilo) of walnuts from them – they wanted to be paid in cigarettes, we went on to a cash basis – and paid them 20¢. What are walnuts worth? I am very fond of them.

Then into a wine shop – which was very beautiful – lit only with small oil lamps, so that figures were dim, and shadows leapt upon the wall a crowd of them drinking wine – and we attempted to talk – with very little success. The men had the grotesque look which a French painter – school of what's his name who painted sunflowers and landscapes – not Gaugin, but Van something, who went crazy. I can't think of his name – no significance – you'll know it. Born in Holland – lived in France, I think.

We had a bottle of wine – vin ordinaire -

My intangible surroundings – I am in a separate echelon, so that I am working alone – with two men to help. I do not know what work there will be to do, but shall find out. The two men – one quiet, the other talkative – one had a good head the other a good back – a city boy and a country.

So I am curious to know what happens – though I hope it does not happen too soon, for I am anxious – in fact aching all over, ~~as I~~ and have been in the last days, to visit neighboring cities. Well – I miss the triumvirate which is, I suppose, formed, of Lt. Clark, Capt. Morris and myself – but still can see the others frequently.

I send all of my love -

Henry

P.S. No mail for a long time – the last day any came being about a month past. I long for it, and expect an accumulation to come piling in soon.

Have you received any packages?

October 19

Dear mama -

I received a little mail yesterday – a package of candy from the National Candy Company; a package of cigarettes from Philip; a letter from Janet Cerf. I cannot understand what is happening to letters, for I have not heard now for about a month. But I can only hope that they will catch up with me – and it is futile to ask questions about what goes on there, since long before an answer can come, I shall surely have heard. Maybe today -

I am in very beautiful surroundings – of which I have written. The climate is so wet that nothing ever dries. For example, I have now had two pairs of socks hanging out to dry for three days – and they are not yet dry. I suppose I shall have to abandon attempts to wash these things.

Well, I just found a child collecting laundry for her mother to do – and gave her pajamas, shirt, underwear and towel. I hope I get it back. Two small cakes of soap into the bargain -

I send some postcards, which I found in my suitcase, having carried them around a long time. Censorship regulations forbade sending picture post cards – I am told they have now been rescinded.

Write often – I send my love -

Henry

October 19

Dear mama -

I just received your letter of September 12 – the first I have had for a very long time, and am so delighted that I write again, to revoke all complaints of lack of mail – it is like the first drop of a rain storm, which breaks a long drought. You wrote about Aunt Sally[70] – and I think I shall write her a letter. I believe she is trying to be nice – just misjudges character so completely, and you have her baffled. She wants to adapt her conversation to your interests and can't decide whether you are interested in sieves and carrots and pot-roast or Shakespeare and the musical glasses – and every woman in the world must be in one class or the other – either you exchange recipes or you decide the fate of the nation and the future of art. There is no middle ground.

I have written everything I have to say – Therefore, acknowledging receipt of your letter, I close. I expect to visit neighboring cities tomorrow – but "the best laid plans of mice and men gang aft a-gley."

The sun has come out – things are drying somewhat.

Love

Henry

I am thinking along these lines – many people are ambitious for promotions, and talk much of them – for a time they infected me somewhat. In my present place there is no possibility of promotion. To get it, I would have to ask for a transfer.

I have concluded not to do so, but rather, not to hope or work for promotion, but merely wait it all out. In my present position, I can get no promotion. Neither can I be demoted. So, if I go along without working much (there is no work I want to do) the worst that can happen is that I may be transferred elsewhere – a leap in the dark – which I should have to take to get the other. Therefore, the worst result of lackadaisy is exactly that for which I should have to ask to get incentive. Hence I am carefree and safe – like a bump on a log, and shall be as much an opportunist for those things which I desire as conscience and my character such as it is will admit of.

Do you agree?

H

October 20

Dear mama -

I enclose a trinket or two, which I got today, and shall write of my day to the extent I may, in another letter, tomorrow -

---

[70] Aunt Sally was Sarah Wiener Lowenhaupt, Mrs. Haymer Lowenhaupt, the sister-in-law of Henry's father Abe. She was a controversial member of the St. Louis School Board and generally remembered as a character (though bright). She moved to California and resigned from the School Board in 1938.

No news – no mail – all my love -

Henry

I am tired this evening and going to bed.

October 21

Dear mama -

Yesterday I visited some neighboring cities, which, I may now say, are in Italy. One, I think, is about the most beautiful I have ever seen – with its fine buildings rising up the hills – its crowds and bay. And many shops open – although there is really nothing worth having offered for sale – unless possibly paintings, for there are many, in the most conservative old school, which look to me quite fine. However – who wants a religious painting of Madonna and Child, or a dark landscape? As I remember them now, they were quite dismal.

I did, however, see some very beautiful pottery – did not buy it because it seems the possibilities of getting it home intact are too slim. Just pottery, with painting on it. Also little pieces of pottery from ruins, which were interesting, but not beautiful.

Then, I got properly cheated at one place – a place which sells gloves of a well-known make – and manufactures them. I decided to get a pair, and started to try one on. No, no It was too small, I said. "No, no," said the sales girl; and pulled hard. The glove ripped, and I said no.

Then the manager came, and told me to come over to the other counter – he has a pair for me. He stretched a pair – and tried on the left hand. They got on, and I took them – at $1.50. When I got them back, I found he had sold me the same pair – the right glove ripped. Well, they are not any good anyway, or they would not have ripped. Clever, these Italians!

Then we went to another city, which was extremely interesting – I wish I could describe it at least in part, but can't – except, possibly, to say that the décor, what could be seen, of the interiors, was lovely – suggested the French period room at the art museum in line and color – the room which, as I recall, is designed as Egyptian. But my memory is weak on these points.

It was dark when we left – or getting dark – and we had some trouble finding the way. But, fortunately, we knew the general direction, and could keep direction by reference to the hills and mountains which showed up against the sky, above the horizon. And there are not so many roads.

It is worth your life to ask these natives roads directions. You never find one alone who knows, and the one asked always goes into consultation with ~~with~~ several others, and they argue whether you should go through St. this or St. that, and whether it is shorter to go over or around this or that hill, and they never do decide. The first difficulty is always to make them understand the name for which you are asking, because, although each letter is pronounced, you must find the right one on which to put the accent – a matter of trial and error, as far as I am concerned. But I have learned to understand the three material words in road directions, which are diritto – straight ahead – a sinestro[71] and a destro[72]. I don't know the

---

[71] "Sinistro," meaning left.
[72] Meaning right.

word for turn around – but you get the effect from a windmill motion of the arms and excitement and confusion.

All the roads are crowded with animal drawn vehicles – ox carts and so forth.

I have hoped to get some picture post cards and other things yesterday – but these are sold out completely.

I was never a great admirer of cameos or intaglios or whatever they are called – and thought that they should be made of coral or stone. Those here are made of shells, which may be as it should. I decided there was no harm in trying two, just to get something – almost anything. It is my estimate that in a very few days there will be nothing even in the nature of junk available for any price, because the soldiers descend upon shops like a swarm of locusts, and buy everything they can find.

The street merchants sell things which remind me of Coney Island – you know this type of shiny, satiny cloth, with figures on it, in bright reds and blues – the kind I imagine in Mrs. Baron's house (and I think there are some) draped over pianos. They look like imitations of something, the genuine one of which might be beautiful. But I have never seen a genuine one.

It is no longer raining – the sun has been out now for several days, and things dry out somewhat.

I am homesick – and would give almost anything – in fact anything – to get home out of the army. It seems hopeless, and the future long. I suppose I think too much of home – and seeing the wonders of the world, as I do, begins to pall. They all start to look alike, and the road backwards, through Algiers and so forth looks so enticing, because it has a definite end. I think a horse may feel much the same when he leaves the stable, and wants to turn back. But how can it be done? No answer.

I am hungry for mail – and hope to receive some soon. It seems just not to be coming through.

I send all my love,

Henry

October 22

To Mrs. A. Lowenhaupt
6237 McPherson Ave
Saint Louis,
Missouri

Dear mama – To acknowledge receipt of a letter today, which I so much enjoy that I am now extremely happy, and desire to rescind all previous complaints about no mail, and every other subject.

"Himmelhoch jauchzend,
Zum Tode betrübt –"[73]

---

[73] Quote from Clärchen's Song in Goethe's *Egmont*. Translates to "heavenly joy, deadly sorrow."
https://en.wikipedia.org/wiki/Egmont_(play)#Quotation
https://www.lieder.net/lieder/get_text.html?TextId=78485

I'll write again -

Henry

October 22

To Mrs. A. Lowenhaupt
6237 McPherson Ave.
Saint Louis, Missouri

Dear mama:

I might as well try a V mail letter, because it is possible that the letters I am writing are coming through as slowly as those you must be writing me. That is to say, not coming at all. Not that I have anything to say, but I *[word marked out]* might as well repeat what I have already said.

I am now in Italy – for the present in an orchard and vineyard – that is they have grape vines growing on the trees. Notwithstanding this, the soil seems so fertile that both fruit trees and grape vines bear heavily, and there is abundance of grapes, apples, pears, peaches, oranges and everything else. I am well; not working hard, and suffer therefore to some extent from boredom and ennui. But that is not of consequence.

I had the opportunity a few days ago to visit a city nearby. It was a very beautiful city – about the finest buildings I have ever seen, mounting up the hill. The city extends over a very great distance. I looked at the shops – which are the same old story, a great deal of junk and all of it being sold like hot cakes. Things which are desirable to have are either sold out or in hiding. So I bought substantially nothing, although I intended to buy everything I could lay hands on. Two cameos, which I have sent to you, and which may or may not be worth having. They are small, and therefore no trouble. Most things are cheap imitations of finer models – like Woolworth's – inlaid boxes, etc.

Then I went to another place and some of the wonders of the world. The country is completely magnificent – has some of the character of France. But wandering through even this beautiful country becomes monotonous. I shall find new interest in it soon, I hope.

I am well. Hope that you too are so. A letter form Myron Glassberg came drifting in yesterday – mailed about September 18 – and he said that we were well which I was glad to hear. But I have no doubt that by the time this reaches you, I shall be receiving mail again.

There is, around here, great profusion and abundance of walnuts, which I am enjoying. I am now out of them, and must seek an opportunity to buy some more. I am thinking of exchanging some of the candy I have from National Candy Co. for walnuts – but cash is easier to get than candy.

It is becoming difficult to write. I have been reading old Saturday Evening Posts and Colliers, which are not very inspiring. I shall go back to my Cicero and Livy, and see if they do better. At least, they will last longer.

I send all my love.

I fear my letters become too dull to be worth writing.

Henry

October 22

Dear mama -

I just received a long letter from you – and enjoyed it so much that I wrote a quick V mail letter to acknowledge it.

I think I have an advantage over you – you hate talk of these matters which are so constantly pressing around – these things which are of all things most hateful – so do I. But I can escape them more easily – as I did for fifteen minutes this evening, walking into the neighboring town. Although it is pitch dark out (the day became very short) it is very, very lovely – outline of a mountain in the sky behind the town; the church steeple shows darker against the mountain – here and there the faint gleam of a candle or oil lamp from a window or door of one of the very solid buildings. The church has an open place or square in front and in back – the center of the town – and around the church, narrow streets. I have not been into the town during daylight, but maybe still shall have an opportunity to go. In front of the church, groups of people stand talking – and many singing – quite beautifully. Then, behind the church, one could hear the church choir practicing or singing.

I thought of St. Augustine – and his statement of the beginning of hymn singing in church. As I remember, it was in Rome, when Justina was debating whether she should tolerate Christianity. All the Christians gathered in the church to pray, until her decision should be reached – a matter of days. To relieve the tension and make the long period of prayer tolerable, St. Ambrosius led the congregation in songs – not so fast as to be too light and frivolous; and not so sad that they would induce despondency or hysteria. Just enough to maintain hope and courage. I suppose singing can do that. The sound of the choir in this church suggested it.

I just walked around the church and back – it is too dark to find one's way on the little side streets. The wine shop was open, and I looked in – the one I have described – a few men sitting at the tables drinking wine – but very quiet. I suppose it was too early for it to be filled – only about 6:30. Their little oil lamps were burning. The town is without electricity.

The road to town is always crowded with pedestrians – women, men, children – and animal traffic. I suppose that is not strange, although it feels strange after dark. I think of it as so much later, because I am in the habit of going to bed about dark, and thinking of it as nine o'clock. But this is winter – and to be out after dark – it is to be expected. I shall have to get used to it.

It is not cold here. The nights are chilly, but the sun is delightfully warm all day.

Many of the horses have great metal pieces – like silver – as part of their harness, rising up over their backs, and little bells attached, so that they jingle merrily as the horse plods down the road. Quite a contradiction – the bells make it sound like a merry trot, and the poor old nag is dragging a load of wood or manure or something else, with a man in back pushing to help the beast along.

All this is quite out of the present world, or I see it as being so, for the externals are strange and beautiful to me, and I have no understanding of the upheaval and turmoil which may or must exist in these people, all of whose ideals are shattered, a greater wreck, I should think, than even bombs could make. The walls are still littered with signs about Duce Duce Duce, and Believe, Obey and Fight, and The more enemies the more Glory, and Live the King Superior, and The Future of the Italian Empire – signs ~~wh~~ and credos which must have become as well accepted and reasonable to these people as a road sign "Keep to the Right" or any slogan we have – thoroughly accepted. Now, all the imagery and implementation which these mottos implied is gone into thin air, and what must previously have seemed an absurd, remote contradiction of the mottos has prevailed. Nevertheless, it cannot be said that the mottos are wrong – one must still believe and obey, and ~~most~~ they cannot believe that glory is in defeat instead of victory or that ignominy is in victory, and so forth. The mottos are still true, but all the implication and interpretation is confused. How can one reconcile it, if the walls on which one has written these creeds, understood patriotically, are in ruins – the mottos still there, among ragged edges of the former buildings? That problem perplexes me, as if a wall with some such motto as Justinian's "Not under men, but under God and law" should be destroyed by those who, I had been taught, believed otherwise. It would be hard to revise the motto – and hard to accept it as having a different meaning than I had always believed. Mussolini has ruled for more than 20 years. Hitler has ruled for 10, as I remember. Consider the profound effect Cromwell and his party had on England – they ruled for only 11 years. Their régime ended bloodlessly – died out. Mussolini's regime is ended over the opposition of his supporters.

Well – that is a far cry from the lovely tangibilities of this Italian countryside, and the rich, heavy beauty of its towns and cities. It does not show in the dwellings – filled with big families, looking self sufficient and placidly appearing to go on as always. But laundry of soldiers is hanging out to dry in palace gardens – Well dressed, charmingly mannered ladies are selling walnuts from their aprons, and asking for laundry, which they do up neatly, as if it were to be scented with lavender.

I send my love -

Henry

October 24

Dear Marian -

I am so late in doing what I am so very anxious to do! I know perfectly well that you were going to graduate this fall – and that you were going to graduate at the top of your class. But time has so slipped by that I still think it is summer – and now, even late, I send you my very heartfelt congratulations. And that you were way up at the top of the class – which it was to be expected, still I think some celebration and congratulations are in order for the fact that you have used your abilities successfully. That is the best that anyone can do; therefore you have done the best possible. The additional fact that you have real ability to do anything you decide you want to do – some people would say you are lucky.

But I am not so sure. If your only ability were to learn mathematics, or write poetry, or learn typing, or any other one thing, it would be so easy to discover the one thing and do it. You find yourself, however, able to do just about anything you want to do – even play the flute – and have the terrific problem of deciding what you want to do, and sticking to it. You have a sister, Betty, who has the same problem, and sometimes I think it makes her pretty unhappy, because she knows she has the ability (but not the time) to do so many things she's not doing. Well, to the extent that your great ability is a misfortune, I feel a little bit sorry for you (but not very, for in many respects it is extreme good fortune.) At least it is interesting to have the freedom of choice – but don't take it too seriously – the fault, or fortune is largely in the stars.

But you merely don't need long distance philosophy of the "This above all, etc." school. Mama is one of the best in those lines – and has the same fortune that you have; that she has the ability to do any thing the world offers. So has Ruth – and you have only to look at mama or Betty or Ruth – see how very well each does what she chooses to do or goes into doing – and you can know that it is just your character that whatever you go into doing, you will do as well – not by reason of any striving to emulate, but just because it is yourself, and your way and ability.

You see, I am not a believer in "aptitudes," except in the lower levels of intelligence – as a person might be able to cook but completely unable to build a fire in a furnace. There would be aptitude for one thing. But most people can do both, if they try.

The occasion deserves a present – and I wish I could find something particularly for you. But choice is never offered here – and I hope you will find something among the items I send home for fun which you like well enough to be particularly for you – whether it is sent before or after this letter.

A great surprise this evening – just at dusk, I decided to take a walk – along the little dirt lane out in front – following the horses and pedestrians, who have been passing all day apparently so purposefully. A most pastoral or ecological lane – under fruit and nut trees, heavy with humidity, leading up to a ⊥ road lined with pine trees which reach the sky. All the lower limbs of the pines are cut, which makes them look even taller. I crossed this road, and went on – a quiet lane, completely idyllic. It was getting dark. Suddenly a great rock wall spung up one side, with fruit trees hanging over – then a wall to my left – and then a building, and, within a half mile of camp, I found myself in a city – just enough light to see arches leading into court yards – crowds on the street – narrow alleys – through a lighted window to vaulted rooms and rooms with old, roughhewn beams showing – little oil lamps, candles for light. Then it got quite completely dark, and I walked back – a little bit scary, in such a small tunnel, under the fruit trees, and across the road, where the tops of the pines showed against the sky – giants!

The most beautiful country! So fertile, it is quite completely unbelievable. Friendly people. The children all say "caramela, caramela," and laugh when I reply "Niente di caramela" – or correct me, saying "Nieute caramela." They laugh, as if they don't believe me; but I really do not walk around with pockets full of candy – as a walking confectionary store. My "good day" and "good evening" are almost perfect, I think, for the people reply, instead of laughing.

I intend to go back to my city, whose name I do not know, completely hidden in the orchards, tomorrow or during daylight soon. I need a haircut, and shall use that as a reason for talking to a barber – ask him if he knows where I can buy linen. It is all I know how to ask for – except chicken (gallina – hen) spaghetti and candy.

Write soon. I repeat my belated congratulations.

With love -

Henry

October 24

Dear father -

Do not expect much of a letter from this – I am sleepy, and impatient for bed time to catch up on sleep. I received your letter – and shall be glad to receive copies of the Internal Revenue Laws. Also I appreciate your buying bonds for me.

My intention, I think, should be to pay whatever income tax I owe for this year next March, filing a return, although it could be postponed. My reason is, that if I can pay them, it may be harder to pay at another time. The alternative would be to buy U.S. bonds up to the amount of the tax, but the interest would hardly be enough to make it worthwhile. So you do as you like, but I can tell you that the possibility of cancellation of the tax by reason of my being killed is non-existent. The only danger around here is that they dig slit trenches – mostly for practice and play, I think – and if one walks around in the dark, one may fall into one and get hurt.

I am well – have moved a few miles since my last letter home, and am now living in a walnut grove, next to an apple orchard. Apples and walnuts!

While it does not seem to rain much here, it is extremely wet – every night the dew drops from the trees like rain and everything is moist.

I am well, with nothing at all to write about. I am accepting your advice for being carefree – and not doing anything I can get out of doing.

All my love -

Henry

P.S. I, too, am sorry I did not see Isserman[74] when he was in Algiers. The first time I went to see him, he was out – expected back in about a week. The next time – about 10 days later, he was not going to be back. I have no doubt Isserman says he did much fine work. Under any circumstances, good or bad, I should not have heard of it.

Write again soon -

Henry

[Not Dated, 1943- The letter mentions the visit "yesterday" to the town in the orchards; I presume the date must be October 24 or 25 1943]

Dear mama -

I happened to run across the following line in *The New Yorker* of August 28, 1943[75], which surprised me:

"Fanny Cronbach, 1166 Lexington Avenue (80th) has a small shop that does work with painstaking care."

The article is about rejuvenation of old clothes. You see what I am reading, sometimes!

I received mail yesterday – a letter from you which I enjoyed very much, and also one from daddy.

---

[74] Possibly Rabbi Ferdinand Isserman, the Rabbi at Temple Israel in St. Louis, the Temple of which the Lowenhaupts were members.
[75] Link to this publication in The New Yorker archive: https://www.newyorker.com/magazine/1943/08/28
As I do not have a New Yorker subscription, I cannot double check to find the article that is mentioned, though.

Yesterday afternoon I walked into town – quite a beauty, with old stone buildings – the town is much larger than one would expect – the way it is hidden in the orchards – and extends over quite an area – Plenty of slums – one looks in the doors from the streets, and sees people living crowded in a small room, cooking over buckets of fire on the door steeps, and so forth. But there are also fine houses, with sunrooms and gardens and all, where people must live luxuriously. The town is strictly agricultural – on the side streets are big rooms, opening on to the street, filled with enormous barrels – *[word unclear]*, I suppose they are called – of wine. Then on the streets, crowded engaged in washing, grading, sorting and packing applies – very painstakingly, putting them in boxes with some leaves on top, so they look like Christmas baskets. I don't know why they pack them so beautifully, but they do – red apples, green leaves, yellow baskets.

So the town offers no formal amusements whatsoever. Its only shops are tobacco shops, without tobacco, grocery stores without groceries, except possibly a few apples, and maybe some squash, a few stands, one with about a dozen stale looking peanuts, one with a lot of raw chestnuts, one with a big pile of passion fruit; one with a kind of assortment, sad looking, of b thread, ribbon, lace frills, and shoe strings (a very few) a few hair pins, and similar stuff.

There is a cabinet maker in the town, who was busily engaged in making something. These cabinet makers are very skilled – too skilled, in fact, for they are able to take as models the worst of Grand Rapids, and polish it up so fine that it looks as if it came straight from the floor of an installment furniture house. I may, if I have a chance, see if he will make me a small, inlaid box. Risk being cheated again, but what the ! I should like to try to get one of divers kinds of wood – say olive and apples and what other there is; maybe he could do it, although most of his work seems to be larger -

Well – that is just an idea – an idle one.

Today it is cloudy – I send my love -

Henry

October 25

Dear daddy -

I received excellent mail today – a letter from you and a letter from mama – both of which I enjoyed very much. I am glad to hear that business if thriving – ten stenographers going at once sounds like an enormous increase! Oil wells thriving also sounds encouraging, and White Rodgers doing phenomenally. I think Joe Newman is, in addition to able, one of the luckiest men in the world. But it cannot all be luck – Mark Steinberg seemed to teach luck. Maybe it is gambling, because, even though every gambler is not lucky, one cannot give luck a chance to come without gambling. I suppose Joe Newman gambled very heavily when he started the business.

I approve of investing money as you have been. But it seems to me that I should avoid temptation and so forth by keeping or saving enough to pay taxes for the current year, in cash. Maybe United States bonds do as well – but when the time comes to pay taxes, if deferment is claimed now, there can be so many things changed – all investments can go out of the picture. Money can be very hard to get. United States bonds may be the only thing left, or there may be nothing left – the possibilities cannot be envisioned. If there is not inflation, then it may be that some kind of moratorium will have to be declared on repayment of the public debt. But a corresponding moratorium could not be declared on taxes – faint possibilities. But it seems not worth building up false quantities by buying bonds and leaving taxes unpaid. The public interest does not so require. The bonds do not pay large interest. I should like, therefore, unless you believe it unwise, to accumulate enough cash to pay the taxes as soon as they become payable.

But there is another possible speculation. There are many war profiteers in the army – more than in business, I should say – who desire to stay in as long as they can, and overseas. They hope to stay in the army of occupation, assuming there will be one, because, as long as they are in an emergency, they will draw high pay – but when they go back to regular army, they will go way down. They are the regular army corporals, say, who are no majors and colonels (exaggerating, possibly, in many cases) They will desire to stay here, and have other do the work for them, while they seek entertainment. Is there a possibility that owing taxes, so that one could represent that one should go home to pay them, would be persuasive to anyone? There may be such a possibility and if there is, it is worth every chance one would take by not keeping cash to pay the taxes. Of course, the solution would seem to be, then, just what you are doing – to buy U.S. bonds instead of paying taxes. The reasoning may be far-fetched; I don't know, and the proposition of getting a discharge to pay taxes might or might not be persuasive. So, on the whole, I cannot decide – and therefore don't. Whatever is done is alright.

Ha ha! I just got asked this question about income taxes – which I could not answer definitely for two reasons: 1) the man doesn't have all the facts, and 2) I don't know the law. An officer here has allotted from his pay a certain sum per month to his wife's bank account. He has no income except his pay; his wife is working, and has some investment income. The bank is withholding an amount which appears to be 22 ½% from the allotments to his wife. Question: is this proper? I suppose the treasury may be ruling that allotted income in such a case is the income of the allottee. I believe it so ruled in the case of an enlisted man under the Dependency Benefit Act[76] – and I thought it was wrong. But I don't know. I suggested that he might discontinue the allotment, and make his wife a gift each month, if he liked – and so resolve the question. But if the action of the bank is right, and they are withholding as from her income, what is happening to Douglas v. Willcuts and Larch v. Helvering and all the cases about attributing the fruit to a different tree from that on which is grown and about discharge of obligation is a benefit to the obligor – here discharge of obligation to support a wife?

So I look forward to receipt of the statute which I understand you sent me. Is an allotment taxable income to the allottee? ~~If not~~ The allottee has no taxable income, because, I believe, his exemption of pay as an officer exempts all of his income.

Today I walked into the neighboring town – but this letter is already too long – so I shall write about that in a letter to mama tomorrow.

Affectionately

Henry

---

[76] Reference to, I believe, the Servicemen's Dependents Allowance Act of 1942
https://www.ssa.gov/policy/docs/ssb/v6n7/v6n7p21.pdf

October 26

To Mrs. A. Lowenhaupt
6237 McPherson Ave.
Saint Louis
Missouri

Dear mama –

Mail has been coming through so irregularly that I assume possibly mine to you is doing likewise. So I intersperse a few V mail letters now and then, in the hope that I may profit by not putting all of my eggs in one basket. But I have little more to say than that I am well, for I have written other mail which will reach you in due time, and there is no pleasure in repeating. That is, assuming that there is something in the other letters to repeat.

I received a letter from you yesterday and one from daddy. It was surely pleasant to hear again, and now I have even higher hopes for more. There is not a bit of news here of which to write. The place is beautiful, as I have said an orchard which is very fertile and lovely. The weather is satisfactory.

I shall be very happy to receive the things you say you are sending – cap, tie, socks and so forth. I can use them all. I hope to get into town some time soon and see what I can find.

So far, the clothing situation, as far as I personally am concerned is excellent. I have concentrated on two pairs of socks at a time, and have worn out only two so far. If wool socks last as well, I have enough to last several years. So also shirts – I have four woolen ones, and have not yet worn any out. Again, I have concentrated on two, and these two are beginning to get little holes, which I darn and sew up. I think they are good for a long time yet, and then shall start on my other two. Underwear is the same, although I have no idea of the total number of suits I have. So also trousers – one pair I decided a long time ago was worn out, but it is always good for another day, and so I am still wearing the pair. Shoes – I have worn out one pair, but have acquired two – one pair of shoes and one of boots. That leaves me with one pair of high shoes almost worn out; one pair of high shoes unworn; one pair of boots unworn; three pairs of low shoes in good condition – as new. My slippers are worn out, but those things I can get along without most satisfactorily. So you see I need nothing, and whatever I receive is for pleasure, not for necessity.

My reading material is not so fortunate – I have misplaced my St. Augustine, and shall have to conduct a search for it. Meanwhile, I intend soon to order some books from England, whence I can receive them sooner than from home. Problem: what books to order. It is hard to get ideas, without seeing any books which look at all attractive. But I shall think of something, and see what I can get.

I wrote a letter to Marian, for congratulations upon her graduation. I repeat those sentiments here, for the possibility that this letter may arrive before the other. Both are late, which I regret.

I send all my love:

Henry

October 27

Dear mama -

I received your letter – with two quotations from Menander[77] – and enjoyed it – the thought has been in my mind so long, and it is a pleasure to see it expressed concisely and well by an ancient.

In exchange, I shall repeat again my favorite – I favor it for a different reason; it is so full of feeling that it can be applied to almost anything:

"Manet enim modicum lueis hominibus; ambulent, ambulent, ne tenebres conprehendant."[78]

(There remains still for men a measure of light. Let them walk; let them walk, lest darkness engulf them.)

That is from Augustine's Confessions. As I remember it, it just springs out at you from the pages – I have ordered Augustine from Blackwell[79], because I want to reread it.

Today I went to a town near-by, ostensibly to buy an oil stove – for the bottom is rusted out of the one I have, and the oil runs out. I got a little alcohol stove – which will do, if it doesn't turn too cold (I think it won't) and a pint of alcohol, under the name of a litre. It doesn't amount to much, but it will fry eggs beautifully, when I get the egg.

The town was interesting, although I looked around very little – a long main street, with church and square. Most of the shops closed, I think for lack of merchandise. I was not alone – and stayed only fifteen minutes to suit the plans of the man with whom I was – an awful dumbbell.

But the country is really the most lovely. The fertility seems infinite, even when the land is not well cared for. The fruit trees so luxurious; nuts in such abundance; the fields are so green – foliage hides the houses and everything.

Yesterday I walked down the road – met a family which looked like grandmother down to grandchild of about 4 years – only the women and children. The children rushed toward me, crying "caramela." I replied "Niente" – but they just about mobbed me – women, children, grandmother and all, pulled at pockets, saying I had some there, grabbing sleeves, in the wildest fashion. I have a little candy from National Candy's lot – hard candy – but it wouldn't last six second in such a mob.

They were farmers – but I suppose one can get pretty hungry living on fruits and nuts, even with vegetables interspersed. And these people, although they are peasants, seem to make no attempt at complete farming. They raise only fruits and nuts, and very few vegetables. I see neither cattle nor chickens in this neighborhood. The fruit is beautiful, and I suppose in peace times all prospered, exporting it – but now without commerce they seem to have nothing else.

I am well – shall be hard up for anything of which to write – as I am now – but keep on trying repetitiously. Maybe all of the letters do not arrive.

From Sicily I sent one large piece of net lace – I saw it being made, and bought it off the frame – which I considered quite beautiful, in and of itself, and wondered how it would appear in one of three ~~places~~ or

---

[77] A Greek Dramatist who was known for his comedies. He lived from 342-291.
[78] From Book 10 of St. Augustine's *Confessions*, Caput 23. https://faculty.georgetown.edu/jod/latinconf/10.html
[79] An English bookstore

four places – the front door; the sun-porch door; the small dining room window (north), Ruth's hall window on the stairs, or as a table cloth. The last, I think, would be unpracticable – and I cannot judge the size. I hope it has arrived by this time. One bed spread I send I consider a mistake – not very consequential. Handkerchiefs were just picked up as insignificant almost every time I saw one not embroidered "Remember Sicily" or "Ricordar Sicilia."

But I suppose it takes packages a long time to get there, if they ever do. The handkerchiefs were sent about last, but possibly went by air.

Write often – your letters delight me - and the prospect of the next keeps me interested and hopeful.

"By hope we are made caused to be saved" – again St. Augustine.

I send my love -

Henry

P.S. – When did Menander live? He is a writer whose name is familiar, but of whom I know nothing. But you need not answer – by the time you do, I shall have forgotten the question. Where did he live – what wars did he know?

October 30

Dear mama -

I haven't written now for a day or two – and in that day or two haven't accumulated anything to write about – I am well – the weather continues beautiful, but damp – a little rain mostly dew. Nuts continue abundant, as do apples and Japanese persimmons. The last, however, are good as a rarity. As a steady diet, not comparable to walnuts and apples.

I was in a town a few days ago – and another town nearby. The smaller towns I find more interesting than the larger, for I never have the time to try to do any serious shopping – and in the beginning one always finds only the shops which are like Woolworths. Better things are not conspicuous. As cameos – which can be bought in abundance, but I think they are probably quite worthless.

I have now a little alcohol stove – on which I heat water for shaving. I shall soon be out of alcohol, when I shall, I suppose, abandon the stove.

I am glad you received a handkerchief I sent – it gives me hope that other packages may come through.

Here is the end of October – time drags, but nevertheless passes, for which I am duly thankful. I have absolutely nothing to write, but as usual, await your letters very eagerly.

The country here, as I have said very often, is beautiful -

Love -

Henry

October 30

To Mrs. A. Lowenhaupt
6237 McPherson Ave.
Saint Louis, (5)
Missouri, U. S. A.

Dear mama: This letter is in pursuance of my policy of writing a V mail letter now and then, although most of my letters are the other kind, just because they seem to arrive so much more promptly. That they are impersonal, and never seen to say anything – well, I have nothing to say anyway.

Right now, in between words, I am eating walnuts – I think they are walnuts, but whenever I realize that walnut is a kind of lumber, I think the name must be different. The nuts with the shell which splits in half very easily, and inside, the nut is full of convolutions and partitions. We have them at Christmas. A big nut, and very delicious – next to almonds, which seem to be no longer available, my favorite. Then I have a bottle of wine – so you see life is quite pleasant. There is abundance of wine here; the shortage is of bottles. So I keep my bottle – new wine in old bottles quite literally, except that I think cat skin bottles were intended, for these glass ones do not wear out. It is good wine, although new, the plain vin ordinaire, very light and dry.

I enjoy your letters – two of them today – one about Abe Cronbach's[80] visit and one about Isserman[81]. I did not give him my address in Algiers, because I was told he would not be back, and I was not sure how long I myself would be there. I do not need books. Fortunately, I found my De Civitate Dei, and shall go on with it. In addition, I have Livy – one book – with Blackwell's Ltd., of Oxford, whence I can order books, and receive them much more expeditiously than from home. So if you come across any which you think are particularly interesting, write me about them, and I shall order them direct.

I am well – and rather enjoying myself much of the time. It sometimes annoys me that I am doing so little work – but I have taken on this job, somewhat extracurricularly: a boy, who has been working as a runner, a table waiter, and so forth, is very ambitious to become a typist. I have him here with me, and am therefore undertaking to teach him typing. It is a good job. In the first place, I believe he genuinely desires to learn; in the second place, he is quite bright – if he will stick to it; he has a kind of Irish versatility, and is red headed. Then further, he is able to spell adequately, and that is a good beginning. So I try to teach him, but of course ninety percent of learning is practicing, which does not take time on my part. And as far as making typing interesting, I think that it just can't be done, any more than the alphabet can be made interesting. That, fortunately, one learns young, when one's imagination is broader. I think that if I did not know the alphabet, I should be completely unable to learn it – witness the Greek alphabet, in which I always stick at just about delta.

I have not been to any town recently. Tomorrow is Sunday, and I suppose therefore a bad day to go to any city, even if I could. Then I never look as far ahead as day after tomorrow. But it might be interesting to walk to a small village, if there is opportunity.

Nothing new. I have begun to believe that packages never reach their destination – either to or from me; but maybe it is just because they come surface mail. I fancy a ship, by this time loaded with boxes like

---

[80] Bessie Lowenhaupt's Uncle (though younger than she and by a second wife). He was a Professor at the Hebrew Union College in Cincinnati. He was a Pacifist and would have been on the faculty in 1943.
https://en.wikipedia.org/wiki/Abraham_Cronbach
[81] Probably Ferdinand Isserman, the Rabbi at Temple Israel, their Temple

shoe boxes, all addressed to me, now in mid Atlantic someplace. What fun to unload it, as I do, in my imagination sometimes. The number of shoe boxes in a ship is infinite.

Love Henry

October 31

Dear mama -

Today is a rainy day – slow, gentle rain – and I suppose winter is upon us – I am postponing wearing wraps, because I do not want to get into the habit of being too warm. As yet, although it is damp, it is not cold, and I am comfortable without a coat.

I have stuck very close to camp for several days now – and as a result have seen nothing of which to write. But I enjoy writing, because when I do, I look up and see the very remarkable beauty of this country. One tends to get used to it, and ignore it – and then everything becomes drab. ~~But~~ However, if one opens one's eyes, the colors are unbelievable – an avenue of great pines in sight, which in the evening are brilliant with blacks and coral reds – persimmon tree grove in sight, and the fruits are like jewels. I cannot remember the name of the painter – a Frenchman[82], who went to the South Seas and painted native under exotic fruit trees – but his fruits trees are dull by comparison with these. The fruits heavy like lanterns on the trees – orange and yellow and red, in a very heavy, night like green.

Then, even though the country is quite level, they have terraced it to make it perfectly so – and the walls on the terraces are covered with ivy and arrowhead, beautiful greenery. Poplars for rows and many avenues of them.

I just discovered, while digging a moment ago, to make a hole in which to burn papers, that this field, under the fruit trees, is planted to potatoes. I shall have a boiled potato, maybe.

It is still raining -

Henry

---

[82] Probably Paul Gaugin

November 1

Dear mama and Ruth -

I suppose it is sometime since I have written a letter long enough to be called one – and now, although I've started out ambitiously, I already realize that anything I write is bound to be a repetition of what I have already said twenty or thirty times before this. There is no use writing again of the oxen passing, and the horses and wagons, and the apples or the town nearby, which I rather intend to walk to again very soon.

But I suppose it is just as hard for you to write to me.

Is it not high time for Haymer to be talking? He is three years old, and ought to be asking questions and everything, I should think. What does Dr. Jahorsky say? Does Haymer even try to talk? Does he walk alone yet?

It seems strange that he does not talk, since he no doubt has plenty to say – as when he indicates he wants to be a solider. One does not require more sense from one his age. I think I shall write him a letter -

Dear Haymer -

I am writing you a letter because I want you to tell your mama and grandma what to say in a letter from you to me. Or you yourself can write it, with pictures. There is a lot you can tell me about.

How is Kim? Does he come when he is called? Do you feed the squirrels this winter? I have many nuts, and just wish I could give you some to feed them. Are your chickens laying any eggs?

Your grandma tells me that you like to take walks to the Campus. What happens there? What do you see?

But I can write you something about the little boys in Italy. There are many of them, just your age. They walk along the streets and roads, with their mamas and other children. They have no shoes, and most of them hardly any clothes. Their feet get very dirty, and often they sit down in the street and get dirty all over. Many boys wear their sister's dresses, or any kind of old rags, and their clothes fall off, or get tangled around their necks, and they just go on wandering on the roads and in the streets, without any clothes on at all.

Also, they do not have very much to eat, no milk, no meat, just apples. So they all run after me, and say "biscuit," "biscuit," "bread, bread," and "candy, candy." They are tired of eating apples. Sometimes, if I have a biscuit or a piece of bread, I give it to them, and they laugh, and try to get more. But they are good children – the bigger ones bring the biscuit or candy home for the baby, and if there are many of them, they divide it, and each gets a little, tiny piece. Their mamas also come out and ask for biscuits and candy and cigarettes for the baby.

They talk a funny language, with words I cannot understand. They call each other bambini, and piccolini, and biscuits are biscotti, and when they say "niente pane" they mean "I have no bread." They have never learned to talk, as you have.

But they have many nice things – horses and wagons, and pretty buckets, in which they build fires. They have nice beds, which rock like a rocking chair. Then also, they go to churches, although they do not seem to like that, because most of them holler and scream and knock chairs over, the whole time they are there.

Please write me a letter about yourself, and tell your mama to do the same.

Affectionately

Henry -

November 3

Dear mama -

I wish you a very happy birthday, and hope that this arrives in due time. I shall reexpress the wish in a V-mail letter.

I know that you object to birthday presents – so I have sent none. But I was in town yesterday, and bought two things, which slightly struck my fancy, and I therefore mailed them to you. I continue optimistic that these things reach you, although as yet I have heard of nothing which has. I sent a cameo, which I considered a little nicer than most, and a tortoise shell box, which can be given away or kept or burned. The color struck my fancy, and it was inexpensive.

Then, besides, I found one shop, where I shall go again if ever I have opportunity, filled with lovely things – small paintings, which I now wish I had bought, because I am sure they were pretty. But I think how tiny they would look in any room I know, and the big ones are expensive beyond my certainty. Also, portraits and religious subjects – a little odd. And tile, which would make Ruth's mouth water something desperate.

So this time, I bought one plate, which I shall send home in time. I considered it the most magnificent I had ever seen, and if and when you get it, you may, if you like, lend it to the art museum. It is finer than anything they have, and was the most beautiful thing in the shop. I bought it this time. Next time, I shall try to decide what is the most beautiful remaining. If they sell nothing, I shall be pressed between

1) three cups and saucers, capo di monti, old, of lovely shape, and an orange, yellow and gold pattern. Fine porcelain, magnificent decoration.

2. A tile, painted in wheat – yellow and blue, predominantly representing a woman riding an ox through a sunny field. A man driving the ox. About one foot square, and bright and clear. That is what would make Ruth's mouth water – other tiles, bewhispered portraits, by comparison, but also lovely.

3) An old plate, painted in a sea scape

4) Small, antique bronzes, relics, but they are trivial.

5) Small paintings, one on wood, about 5" square, showing a medieval battle. The subject of the painting is what really prevented my buying it yesterday. But I was, I concluded, oversensitive. There was Jerusalem in the clouds, a bright spot, which suggested St. Augustine's hope.

Also, a small portrait, about six inches by eight inches.

6) Another plate, I think Majolica, in blue and yellow, but quite coarse by comparison with that I got.

The plate I have is now packed in a wooden box. I shall unpack it to look at it again, to see if it is as lovely as I remember it to be.

The town is full of costume jewelry and junk – as cameos, which always tempt me because the colors are clean, and there are so many of them. I bought three of them yesterday – one much nicer than the other two – have sent the nice one home, and I think I have sold the other two at their cost to me So -

I had lunch in the town. Lunch is found by walking on the street until someone plucks your sleeve and says "spaghetti spaghetti." Then you follow him to the place he indicates. But you must listen closely – he might be saying "calzctta scta" – offering to sell silk stocking, which seem to be in demand – or anything else. One takes a chance – I had ravioli, with tomato paste, and wine, which was really very excellent.

The town I visited was beautiful beyond description. But all these towns are, and I have quite abandoned hope of describing them. I bought some picture postcards, which I may not now send, but shall hold until I may.

I am well. Yesterday's wandering about the city was the most fun I've had for a very long time. How magnificent it would be to travel in this country in peace times – there would be such plenty of everything enjoyable. Now, everything is closed – and the best shops look like a possible cartoon of, say, Lord & Taylor, with one frayed dress on display amid the unlighted spaces.

If one had time, I have no doubt one could find many lovely things, and get them upon trade. The current statement is that the Germans and Mussolini took everything – which may be a way of trying to prevent Americans looking for them. And to say that the retail business thrived, and they made a lot of money which is now nearly worthless. Those who did not desire to sell for Italian lire under Mussolini probably are not now ready to sell for the present lire, although it could not be worth much less without being worthless. The exchange is 100 lire to the dollar – purely nominal. Of course, one does not see metal money, and a one lire note is rather funny.

I am well. I send my love.

Henry

November 3

To Mrs. A. Lowenhaupt
6237 McPherson Ave.
Saint Louis,
Missouri, U. S. A.

Dear mama -

I received your letter yesterday, telling of Betty's walnut picking expedition, and enjoyed it very much. I write principally to wish you a very happy birthday, and to hope that you celebrate it properly. I am sending no particular present as a birthday present, but continue to send home whatever I can lay hand on and like well enough to overcome my hesitancy to buy it and the realization of what an aggregation of junk one can accumulate. But the house at home is big, and can hold an awful lot of junk without showing it. Just think of the cabinets on the third floor!

So yesterday, having the opportunity to be in a town, I acquired a little more to put in the cabinets there. Or to keep out, if you want to. I do not mean that you are to consider these particularly as a birthday present – but just a present to dispose of or keep as you like, in your capacity of distributor. You see I continue hopeful that these things arrive, notwithstanding that the only thing I know to have come is a handkerchief, mailed first class mail. But I have written all of this in an ordinary letter, and this is just to let you know that I am well – that I wish you a very happy birthday, and had a very enjoyable time yesterday in town. How lovely a town, in fact the whole countryside, these would be to visit in peace times, when one could wander around at leisure.

Here's all my love. Write often. How is Marian? What is she doing and what are her plans ?

Henry

November 5

Dear mama -

No news to write – but the usual, that I am well, and am glad to receive your letters, which I enjoy very much. I have now dispatched a box, containing the most beautiful plate in all Italy, and hope it arrives. I insured it for $20.00, just to attempt to get more special handling. It is packed in a wooden box, with paper and a little cloth as packaging. I thought the cloth rather pretty, and am inclined to believe that the man who packed it put the cloth in as of some value because he so over-charged me for the plate. But it was put in as packing.

My memory of the plate is clear of the colors, but not of the exact arrangement – the head of a woman in blue or white as a center; a yellow – almost gold – background for purple-pink-red lead design. As I have said, if you desire to lend it to the art museum – so that all of St Louis can see it – or to the Metropolitan, to confer a substantial benefit on New York – that is alright. I hope you enjoy looking at it as much as I did.

Alas! they have more in the same shop – and I shall not return, and wish I had bought more. But such is life. ~~The~~ Wouldn't it be nice to be able to telephone, and say "Please send - - -" But, one can't. The man who sold it to me was able to speak French – so we got along alright.

Yesterday, I bought some charcoal – got a fruit can, which I punched full of holes, so that I now have a satisfactory tent heater – which is worth having these evenings. Add to that, that I can step out of the tent and dig potatoes or pick up chestnuts, and bake or roast them – it is quite wonderful. I think it is about time to light it, as it is completely unpredictable how long it will take to start it burning.

A flock of goats is now passing on the road. What are goats good for? Milk alone?

I am well – I repeat – I have a letter from Mrs. Max Myer, a very nice letter. She is concerned that she misaddressed a package to me – but it makes no difference, because the AGD is unnecessary. AGD means Adjunct General's Division – AGO (which she used) mean Adjunct General's Office. Same thing.

Is Mrs. Myer getting absent minded? She addresses me: "Dearest Henry," which is alright, but I believe she thought she was writing to Leo[83] I hope her package comes – the contents she mentions are some

---

[83] Leo Drey, her son. I knew her and she was not absent minded.

hotel size cakes of soap, and some shampoo soap. The thought of a shampoo makes me shiver, because it is quite cool – about like St. Louis Octobers. Leaves are falling, but I do not expect frost, because there are palm trees nearby, decorative. But then we may move into the mountains.

I am sure I can trade shampoo ~~for~~ soap for almost anything.

All my love -

Henry

It would be time to send daddy, a birthday present – I intended a pair of gloves for that purpose, but when I discovered how poor they were I kept them. Well - I suppose I shall be unable to send any present for particular occasions. At any rate, I shall not try.

H

November 6

To Mrs. A. Lowenhaupt
6237 McPherson Ave.
Saint Louis,
Missouri

Dear mama -

Here is another V Mail letter written for lack of anything better to do. And I really have nothing whatsoever to say. But it is quite chilly at night, and the days turn delightfully warm and pleasant. But one stays warm at night under an abundance of blankets. Also, as I have said, for the evening, I have a little can, which formerly contained fruit, with holes punched around it and in the bottom. In this, I burn charcoal, which makes a very delightful warmth. And it adds interest to my life, because one can bake potatoes on it. So far I have not had any luck with my potatoes. I think they are not yet ripe, for they are small (I dig them just outside) and very moist. They burn on the outside, but inside the peeling stays just as well and raw as ever. Maybe one cannot bake new potatoes successfully. Then a mushroom this morning – it would have been delicious, I am sure, except that I burned it to a crisp over my charcoal. But chestnuts really come out delicious, and the fire improves hazel nuts, which raw, have some kind of irritating principle to them.

We are just about out of charcoal, but shall try to get some more in town – whither I shall walk if and when opportunity presents. There is not a bit of news of which to write, so I shall repeat what I have already written two or three times in air mail letter. This may be justifiable, because my impression is that just about fifty percent of the things mailed to me arrive at their destination. Maybe it is so with the letters I write to you. I mailed yesterday to you the most beautiful plate that ever existed, and suggested that you might, if you want to, lend it to the Art Museum - it would be beautifully in place either in one of their period rooms or just on display. Or you may lend it to the Metropolitan Museum. Or (and this appears the most probable course) you may keep it, possibly lending it to Ruth for a week or ten days now and then. It is really, in my opinion, the first pretty thing I have found, and I sincerely hope it reaches you in good condition. That is the subject on which I now fear.

I am glad you received handkerchiefs. It gives me hope that you may also receive some other packages I sent from Sicily – one containing a piece of lace which I considered quite pretty – it was the net kind, which I saw being made in Cefalu – of a size which I cannot remember. Then also a table cloth, which kind of made me think of Marian – the colors were striking. I am afraid it is not big enough for your table, or any of your tables, even at their smallest. But my memory of sizes is so vague. Well, also, as far as cameos are concerned, I do not care whether or not you receive them, for they do not amount to anything, and were purchased in desperation to find anything at all to buy. Maybe they are shells, and maybe they are plaster of paris or paste, cast in a mold. I do not know anything about them anyway.

So I wander on writing. I hear from Janet Cerf frequently – and her letters are usually very dull. They are always V Mail, and usually typed. That is enough to make any letter dull. I received a letter from Mrs. Max Myer – and though it was a very funny letter – in which she seems concerned that she addressed a letter to me AGO instead of AGD. It makes no difference, and I suppose the package has equal chances of reaching me, with any other. My understanding is that the principal contents of the package are soap (hotel size bars) and a bottle or cake of fine shampoo. I do not wash my hair – but all things have trade in value, I think, and I should be curious to see what shampoo will bring. Maybe a few haircuts.

Love,

November 9

Dear mama -

Now I am in a new area – in an olive grove again, although it is hard to appreciate as such, because in my former experiences, olive groves were dry and hot – this one is wet, and cold, and the trees are far more luxuriant. Still lovely – stone farm houses, and idyllic country roads – I have not yet left the area but will soon, to see whence the church bells come. Italy is so very beautiful – and one must overlook the ruins now, in hope that the buildings and countryside will keep their charm when they ~~were~~ are restored.

It is very cold – or feels so, in part, I suppose, because I have not yet resolved to put on all my clothes. I shall in time

Presently, I have a little can of glowing charcoal in the tent – and have stood a can of water close enough to it to take the chill off – I shall shave in it – and a bottle of rum by it, because the rum, cold, tastes like vanilla extract. It is improved by heating. So I munch English walnuts and sip rum, as I lean over my charcoal fire.

A pig was bought yesterday and so this evening we had pork chops – very excellent, although they are difficult to eat after watching them grow from a live hog.

In hope, then, this evening, one man here went out to look for a chicken, which he said he knew how to cook over a charcoal pot. But he came back only with a variety of reasons why ~~they~~ a chicken could not be bought – as:

1) The Germans have taken them all.
2) Mussolini took them all.
3)The ~~R~~ English Red Cross took them all to Naples and Rome.
4) They all got sick and died.

And there were several others – but no chicken to be bought. I am inclined to believe that they do exist (because there are some fresh eggs), but that everyone knows they won't last long if they are discovered – as they won't.

I have debated whether or not to send you some very delicious walnuts, and have concluded it would be too silly to do it. As it would. Betty's Last Ditch Farm will have to provide.

Yes – it seems that this horror has gone on a long time – and that really no one wants it to continue – that there really as an abstract justice, sufficiently definite that it ought to be reorganized by all – now that the folly of the mad course attempted against justice has shown itself. But -

"What may conduce
To my most healthful use
Almighty God me grant.
But that or this
That hurtful is
Deny thy suppliant."

Things will go their way, not within intelligent control, but by a force we need not attempt to understand -

"Keep on my feet;
I do not ask to see."

Meanwhile, I am having the best time possible and consistent. Quote again:

"Thou orderest these things to be borne, not to be loved."

Augustine says the obvious very beautifully.

I enjoy your letters, every one, very very much – and always look forward to their receipt.

I am well – not writing as often as I should like to, because I hate to sit down to write without having at least one thing I enjoy saying. I have not been getting around enough recently to see much about which to write. Result – letters get a little stale.

I am about giving up hope of your ever receiving packages I send – but shall continue to send everything I can – what's lost? And after all – it was about the first of September or later when I mailed the first – and three months to get there may be normal.

So let me hear often.

Love -

Henry

November 12

Dear mama -

This will be a short letter – to tell you I am well -

I was in town again yesterday for a very few minutes – and intended to clean up loose ends – but my conscience again would not let me go whole hog and buy everything I wanted – so I bought the following 1 small painting which I am sending to Haymer.

1 small painting and one bowl which are being sent to you. Captain Morris is sending them for me – his is nearer the post office – so when you get a package from Claude B Morris that is the explanation. I shall write again.

All my love

Henry

November 13

Dear mama -

I have been anxious to send Betty some kind of present – something pretty – but am so remote from all of you that I can just buy things which I like and think pretty – and send them home kind of to be distributed. When I think of what I have sent – with reference to Betty – the first pottery I sent – a tea set of 5 cups, etc, in blue – it is not fine enough or pretty enough to be worth mentioning – was bought when, after a long time of seeing nothing, I was desperate to buy anything. If you think Betty would enjoy such a tea set, by all means send it to her, but it won't count.

There was an embroidered table cloth, with six napkins whose colors I considered quite glorious. Does Betty ever serve tea or supper? If so, she might particularly enjoy such a cloth – because I think Betty likes colors as well as I do. Other than that –a few miscellaneous handkerchiefs really don't count.

But then, I sent two little paintings, one to Haymer – the other to you – while the one to Haymer – a village street – is, I think, very nice painting, the other, a mediaeval battle, is more intellectual and I think Betty would enjoy it. Possibly, if you think it worth while, you could have some kind of frame put on it and send it on to Betty. You see – you are my clearing house – to see that Betty does not get loaded up with junk, for she has not much room for it.

Then I have sent two pieces of pottery, and am trying to make arrangements to get a third. If I succeed, I shall send it. These are my real prides and joys. I really do not wish to part with any of them except on a loan basis, at least until I get home & can enjoy them a while. But on such a basis, it would be a delight to Betty to have one to look at – or you could lend it to the San Francisco museum, where she could see it. I surely hope they reach you – you will see I do not exaggerate when I mention lending them to a museum; because the St. Louis museum really has nothing comparable in beauty.

Many paintings, new, are available here. Most of them have some style, quite a little color – but remind me of the photographs of Clark Gable and Myrna Loy at Woolworth – somewhat chromo-ish. But they might be decorative – I have thought of sending one home – but haven't been able to make up my mind to it. They make a bright display, but one selected out, has such an old rag, weak look.

Let me know when something arrives which you would consider for Betty – because I should like to send her a present – maybe the mediaeval battle picture – or, if you think the other more suitable, trade with Haymer – if he won't trade, spank him (or his mama or both) until he will.

Henry

November 17

To Mrs. A. Lowenhaupt
6237 McPherson Ave
Saint Louis
Missouri -

Dear mama -

This is a brief note to let you know I am well – have not written recently, but shall, if I can, think of something to say. Things go on from day to day without change -

The weather has turned cold and rainy – but I have managed to keep warm – what with an oil stove I have acquired (at a fancy price) and my charcoal cans – Maybe this weather will not last – surely it won't, because nothing lasts forever -

So I have taken up Augustine again – and found a very beautiful statement that the punishment for the original sin was proper and the very quintessence of justice. Which I suppose it was, a full explanation.

I received a pipe and some tobacco. I do not know who sent them – whether it was Philip or Hy – but shall write both.

I send my love -

Henry

November 19

To Mrs. A. Lowenhaupt
6237 McPherson Ave
Saint Louis
Missouri
USA

Dear mama -

My mind today is full of wishes for your happy birthday – and that I could be home for just a little while to see you. Maybe someday I shall be – and if I knew of any effort I could make to that end – to get to a termination of all this futility, I should surely hasten to make it.

There is nothing new of which to write – just the same old repetition – that I am well, and always impatient to hear from you – Maybe I shall hear today.

You mention visiting Betty – I hope you do and enjoy it – but by this time, if you were going you will have gone and returned.

I have a letter from Bill Charles – without much news, except that he is still in North Carolina -

Please write often – I enjoy hearing about Haymer, Marian & daddy and everyone else.

I am not trying to send any Christmas presents – it is just impossible -

Today, it is rainy, after three days of rain

I send my love -

Henry

November 19

Dear mama -

I wrote you a V-mail letter today – and really have nothing to add. But shall nevertheless write a few lines – partly to tell you that I really do not expect to write again for about a week – partly to ask you not to hesitate to repeat anything in your letters, for I think many of them miscarry.

The sun has come out at last – I am doing really nothing – except keeping warm – now having an oil stove, a little steadier than my charcoal burners.

I received a pipe and some tobacco and hard candy I think from Hy. I just can't write thanking him for them now, but shall. Meanwhile I wish you would express my thanks to him for me.

No news – I am becoming impatient to get home – to do anything – it seems so long that I have been piddling – but day follows day – and I am thinking – futilely

I send my love

Henry

November 21

To Mrs. A. Lowenhaupt
6237 McPherson Ave.
Saint Louis
Missouri

Dear mama -

It is raining still – I did not know that it could rain so long and steadily – but on this score there is much more proportionate hope than on most others – for it can clear up on a day, and I do not see the prospect of getting other things so much desired. But maybe they will come suddenly – and to that end, I have been gathering up every superstition and prejudice I have – picking olives leaves, and branches, and not so long ago I saw a rainbow for a few minutes. I cannot help believing that there is some significance in that – even though I recall another rainbow, in which I put great faith.

You see I have no news – that I have been doing nothing. Neither have I received mail for a week – but sought to receive a packet soon. My mind wanders – but the few decisions I have to make I shall make in due time.

I send my love – write often. I am going to have to start fresh on better writing to see if I can get something to say.

Henry

November 25

Dear daddy -

It was a very great pleasure to receive your letter – I got quite a pile at once – with packages – and spend the most enjoyable hour I've had for a long time reading letters and opening packages. A letter from Miss Thompson – which I enjoyed and shall answer. Lots of candy, which I am eating abundantly.

Poor, bleeding Italy! It is awfully hard not to feel sorry for a country so wrecked – and the realization that that is the natural and now foreseeable consequence of false ideals does not make one less sympathetic and sorry for these people. Their troubles are economic – with lire at 1¢, and American soldiers having abundance of them to spend, an Italian who has saved lire at 20¢, or who works at a salary now equivalent to $9.00 a month is very poor. Maybe there are Italians rich in commodities – I don't know, but I think so, but they cannot be rich in necessities, because there is no transportation. One place abounds in oranges, another in nuts – and in both places people go hungry for lack of the other. Street vendors sell oranges – about six for 10¢ – but that is $4.00 a dozen to an Italian, and where there are Americans, children beg even for oranges, which are piled high along the streets. A few short stretches of rail are being repaired; electric power and telephones are being restored – maybe there will be improvement.

Then the physical damage. The finest, most beautiful cities in the world, are, especially around the harbors, railroad stations – that is, the industrial and fine parts of the towns – masses of rubble. I thought of Italy as a poor country – the peasantry may be so; but they know finer buildings than anything we have ever conceived. New York may be well built in a few small areas – say 4̶2̶34th to Central Park on 5th Ave, Madison Ave – and other small districts. Chicago has only Michigan boulevard – Saint Louis a few small sections. But imagine a city, which, over centuries, has been built up solid, of fine masonry, entirely comparable to the fine small parts of the American cities – a city, say of the size of St. Louis – of course concentrated in a smaller area – and then imagine all of it, except the new remote suburbs, without a roofed building and all the walls caved in – leaving here and there an interior exposed – still furnished, even with pictures on the wall – like a doll house cut open. The ruin is very terrible. A few towns have escaped – but they are so cut off, that they have nothing either. No bridges left – no transportation, except a few carriages – horses and wagons, oxen and the like, to try to function in a system of distribution physically developed to have the land from hundred to miles contribute to the center of population and the art. The Royal Palaces – with décor and appointments more luxurious than any known in American (Frick, Isabella Stuart Garden, these people were poor peasants by comparison) are deserted, and exposed to every destruction.

But people are starting to rebuild – it is such a hopeless task – what can remain of Italy? Has Italy learned a lesson effectively? I doubt it. A change of heart – wishing to cut Mussolini's throat, welcoming Americans – is only a disappointment. It does not restore buildings or transportation or economy. I am sure you cannot imagine the extent of the physical ruins, even in the villages. I doubt that there is an unbroken pane of glass in all Italy.

A Colonial Exposition[84] was planned, ~~w~~ like the Pair Fair, or the Chicago Fair – and walks tiled and laid out, with palm avenues, and exposition buildings – portraying the beauties of the Italian Empire – a building for Ethiopia – Tripolitania, Eritrea, even for Egypt. The buildings now gape to the skies, and mosaics are scattered in little pieces – admission tickets fly in the wind – What a wreck! The opera houses stand, with the fronts blown out – There is no such things as a bank as far as I can see. There is no fair medium of exchange – and one merchant asks two dollars for a string of beads, another 50¢ for the same string, and I cannot say that either price is unfair. Should they still sell at a mark-up over cost? Or at the cost of fruit (there is no market on most other foods) There is no present cost of identical commodities because either they are not being made or that cost is an incalculable as the retail price. They can get any price – one man buys while another ridicules the price – Should you give a beggar 1 lire? I don't know 5 lire might be like giving him a dollar, but he can't buy anything after he has it.

Well – I do not see how it can be helped – not that any proper moral lesson will be learned. Theories, political philosophies, cannot build railroads or buildings. Maybe the rich landowners will come out alright.

The estates are all marked on the gates – "Proprietà di ---." I have seen some marked "Proprietà di , Rosaand have been inclined to wonder if they belonged to your friend – or a man I've heard you mention – by that name, as I remember.

I am well – hope you are taking care of yourself. I have been considering the proposition: if a man could get out of the army on the basis that was psychologically or temperamentally inapt or unfit, would be he unwise to criminal to do it – I mean, of course, without bribery or any improper influence, but only the necessary contacts with psychologists – taking advantage of their being crack-pots. What is your opinion? The question is purely an abstract one not of immediately contemplated application – a kind of exercise of judgement of right and wrong – ~~an~~ maybe taking advantage of other people's weaknesses.

I send my love -

Henry

November 25
Thanksgiving Day

Dear mama -

What a delight I have had today – I came back to my regular place this morning and found three packages – and a stack of mail. First, I read the mail I wanted to get out of the way – letters from Janet, Myron and Sonja – and a peculiar thing from Philip Moss – purporting to contain fine razor blades. Although the little packets were sealed, they were empty, and I do not know if it was a joke, or if fraud as perpetuated on Philip. I shall write and thank him for his intentions.

Then I came to two packages from you – two pairs of wool pajamas – what I have been longing for, and about to cut up a pair of paints to make some.

---

[84] This could be referring to the Triennale d'Oltremare, an exhibition of Italian colonialism and imperialism which took place in Naples, 1940. https://en.wikipedia.org/wiki/Mostra_d%27Oltremare
This page is in Italian, but includes a few pictures: http://www.archividellascienza.org/it/storia/item/terre-italiane-d-oltremare

Another package – towels, soap and Bissinger candy, with which I shall be very selfish, because good candy is rare – and I am directed to eat sweets. Also, peanuts, hard candies and towels and soap – all delightful to receive.

A package from Ruth, with a drinking cup and good soap – a delight. We are in the rainy season, and I shall not wash many things, because they do not dry – but now and then there is a sunny day.

Then your and daddy's letters. I am glad you received doilies – and hope a few other things eventually come through. I suppose the lace doilies came in messed up condition, because I did not wrap them well – and sent them air mail. But they can be ironed, and I thought they were very superior. Recently, I have had no opportunity to buy anything. But maybe shall.

I cannot begin to say how much I enjoyed your letters, after a long time without them – and how much they encourage me – as pleasure in the present always does – one gets tired of looking forward always to times to come in the indefinite future.

I received a batch of letters – shall reread them, and answer them one by one – for now, I am well – and hope you too are so.

I send all my love -

Henry

November 26

Dear mama -

I wrote yesterday – and have nothing to add – except that I am still enjoying packages immensely and the receipt of them gives me pleasure – as if I have something of my own for a moment – and they restore a little feeling of individuality. One gets to feel so utterly useless to everyone. Letters and packages are the only cure for this – and that is why, primarily, I so enjoy receiving anything - it is a little flattering.

I should like to send a photograph of myself home – they are simply not available – no film. To send an undeveloped film is so complicated I do not wish to start it. Also so uncertain.

The sun is out today – and I have put shoes and so forth out, hoping they will dry before it rains again. Sun is rare this time of year, and mud everywhere is knee deep. Fortunately, it is not cold.

I am well – I wrote a long letter to daddy the other day, and put it aside for the night to decide whether or not I might mail it – or should destroy it. But it got lost, and I do not now know whether someone mailed it. I hate a neat desk or table – things always get off of it before I want them to. Well – it is of no consequence, except I am a little worried whether or not some statements are censorable. If they are, they are only technically so, and nothing will come of it. Besides, it would make life more exciting if something did.

The country is beautiful – trees not yet bare – maybe olive trees are not deciduous, I do not know. It would be pleasant to take a walk – but the roads are knee deep in mud. The natives who walk go bare foot, and are caked up to their thighs. The oxen sink to their bellies. Even the few chickens seem to bog down. Geese and ducks stay fairly well on the surface.

So I stay pretty well in the tent – which is solid, although the ground is damp. An oil stove combats the moisture fairly – and charcoal burners will dry little patches – which however, soon becomes moist again from the surrounding areas.

Yesterday – Thanksgiving – was celebrated with a big dinner, which I enjoyed – tomato juice, olives, turkey, peas, dressing, potatoes, apples, walnuts, apple pie, and wine. It reminded me of Aunt Sadie. And included butter, which is rare – the usual stuff being unmeltable stuff, colored to resemble butter, or having the same color as butter, but greasy and sticky, like w cup grease. The bread, however, is always good. Recently, we have been having fresh eggs for breakfast.

Tell daddy not to take too much stock in powdered egg factories – that in my opinion no one will ever individually, voluntarily, and knowingly have anything to do with a powdered egg. Maybe cheap bakeries – but that's all. If he becomes enthusiastic about the industry, try to procure some powdered eggs, and serve them to him for breakfast – not on Sunday, because he would be hard to live with afterwards – and might blame the scrambling. Or you can get the same taste sensation by stirring sawdust into lumps. But, as I say, we have been having real eggs, and our food is excellent – now and then we have a few days of corned beef hash or stew, but generally – far better meals than one could expect, and in abundance -

What is Marian studying?

I send all my love -

Henry

November 27

Dear mama -

Well – I suppose we should be thankful for one day of sun – as we had yesterday – Last night it started to rain again – and it is still raining. I suppose it will stop in about a month – meanwhile I shall quit writing about weather and mid – until I can say something nice about it. M Now I am mud-bound – just can't walk the mile to town, because it is knee-deep all the way.

I received a grand bunch of letters again last night – four of them. I am glad the lace tablecloth was received – addressed to Marian – and that you think it is somewhat useful. I am not sure I recall it – Is it a tablecloth or just a piece of lace? I remember sending some lace doilies – just for fun – addressed them to Marian as a part of the committee to decide whether to keep them herself or give them away. I intend that things which you like are to be kept to given among you Betty, Ruth and Marian. Other things given away completely.

I am told that there is fine linen available in some towns not very far away – but just have no occasion to get there. Besides, with pottery available, I prefer it – if any arrives home unbroken.

An experiment – I was unable to do it my self – so Captain Morris ordered it for me – telling an Italian cabinet maker to make a box, after his own fancy, the very best he could do. He is going at it very artistically, and if I ever get it, it may be interesting. Not inlaid, but carved, which is, according to his judgement finer – and mine too, for Italian inlay does not amount to much – it has been so commercialized and cheapened. Here's hoping I get a box – I shall support the family of seven for about six months on the price I think – but gave him his head

I received three little volumes of Shakespeare from Ruth a few days ago – and last night read Measure for Measure with great pleasure. I think it shows Shakespeare just beginning – for here and there, a burst of great poetry comes through, and the ideas are beginning to appear tentatively, kind of experimentally, which later make the great passages of *Merchant of Venice* (Quality of Mercy) and *Hamlet* (about death). It is as if Shakespeare is trying a few of these thoughts to see if the audience will take them or fall asleep – and they make the play very interesting.

Other than that, no reading recently – a little of St. Augustine – who discusses a problem I must check in the *King James Version of the Bible*. As a matter of arithmetic, he says the *Hebrew Bible* makes Methuselah survive the flood by 20 years – but says that only Noah and his three sons and their wives survived it. So I shall add up the ages and see how it works out in the *King James*. Do you want to compare your *Bible* – the one said to be a more nearly literal translation?

Well – I might as well make the computation now and see how it works out. If I get to it, I shall write the result as a postscript.

Love -

Henry

PS – here is my computation

(Gensis, 5, 6 & 7)

Name -	Born	Died	
Adam -	0	930	After creation
Seth	130	1042	
Enos	235	1140	
Cainan	325	1235	
Mahalaleel	395	1290	
Jared	460	1422	
Enoch	622	987	
Methuselah	687	1649	
Lamech	867	1624	
Noah	1049	-	

Flood – 1649 *[line drawn connecting this figure to Methuselah's date of death.]*

So it seems a safe guess that Methuselah's life was prematurely cut short in the great flood. What a struggle the old man put up, as his beard went under!

Henry

Which reminds me of a passage in Cicero, which I cannot quote exactly – in praise of old age – He is refuting the proposition that old age is uncomfortable because death is closer. After denying the proposition, he goes on to compare death to quenching a fire. A great, roaring one can hardly be extinguished. And to plucking fruit – "If they are green, they can hardly be pulled from the tree; but when they are mature and ripe, they fall almost of their own weight." Contradicted by the *Bible* – it took the great flood to extinguish old Methuselah – even though at almost a thousand years he must have been mature and ripe.

November 28

Dear mama -

I said I should say nothing about the weather until it improved. Now I can say something, for now for two solid days, it has not rained. The ground is even drying out a little in places where the water is not stirred in. The sun has been lovely and warm, and I have spent some time standing in it, and some sitting in it, reading Augustine – one of the chief pleasures of which is his fervent and sincere expression of hope in faith – a matter never subject to doubt. "In hope," he says, "lies our salvation," or "By hope we are made to be saved." And when he finds indications in Genesis of the coming of Christ, "Hope and faith in the redemption is the way of life, even in the earthly State." It is easy to guffaw at such statements, call them unreasoning[?]. But I think they are factual – in human nature (after God's image) because in smaller things, it is so clearly true that hope and faith alone make it possible to go on. Hope for the end of a long night, if one is sitting awake all night, and faith that it will end – or hope and faith for the end of anything unpleasant can even make the thing somewhat pleasant. But how intolerable it would be now, say, if one had neither hope nor faith. So I think it is sound to put it a little farther – hope and faith in redemption are the only earthly salvation, means of being contented, without which or unselfish, or virtuous in any way. Because, it seems to me, good works without contentedness are no more virtuous than ~~lady's~~ ladies' clubs and the pettiest, ambitious striving for selfish ends through hypothetically virtuous means. I do not know whether or not I have expressed what I mean, but the conclusion seems to follow that hope and faith are essential fundamentals to good works – and all else.

Now down to prunes – we have been having very good food recently – I told you, I believe, of Thanksgiving dinner – a few days or weeks before that, they butchered a hog – and it provided good spareribs, and pork chops. Then tonight, steak, carrots and peas and onions – the onions fresh; for they are abundant here. Blueberry pie -

I watched women picking olives for a day – they walk around, stiff kneed, bent over at an acute angle at the hips, a basket in one hand, sweeping up olives with the other hand. Well, I tried again to eat a fresh olive, and with determination and imagination you can get an olive-like taste. But you can't help spitting it out soon – puckery, and for hours afterwards, you spit a beautiful deep purple. The color of the expectation almost justifies the bitterness of the taste of the ripe olive. Maybe they are preserving olives or something – but I cannot see the basis of the fame of the olive tree. At best, an olive is an appetizer, and one could never make a meal of them. A little oil, for frying or salad dressing – a purely subsidiary fruit, not much better than a lemon, for example.

But persimmons and oranges there are a very matter. I particularly enjoy overripe persimmons, and the trees are so beautiful – like a painting. And oranges are refreshing, even if sour. Apples here – delicious! and I can now, having a pocket knife, eat them pleasurably – quartered and peeled as they should be. To eat a whole apple makes my lips sore – bruises them – and the peelings are usually very dirty.

I am well – grasping at straws always (hope, says St. Augustine - -) as the reports that the Germans asking armies free. Maybe it's true, and I so desire it, that I will believe it as long as I can. The denial of the fact by eight archbishops and a cardinal would not convince me -

I am enjoying abundance of candy – today a box from National Candy Co. Bissinger's – that was really something! soft and luscious, and it arrived in perfect shape. The other (some mailed from Macatawa, some from Maorako[?]) arrived in somewhat damp and syrupy condition - but I have dried it out, and now enjoy it. Today, also we had a store – and I got a tootsie roll and some charms – There are certain things which are ruining their reputation. By virtue of being the only things available of their kind, everyone hates them – these are particularly, Chelsea cigarettes, charms and fruit drops of the life saver variety.

You see how well I am situated – with abundance of candy, many comforts, delicious fruits of the season. I have quit eating walnuts for a while, being tired of them, although they are doubtless the world's finest nut. Ha ha! a boy here got a present from home consisting of about five pounds of walnut meats. Coals to Newcastle! I see neither almonds nor hazel nuts here – I really like almonds as well as walnuts, or better, for they are delicious green, or in any season. I had them fresh from the end of May until the first part of October. That is a wonderful tree, which will feed you for half of the year, fresh from the tree, and where fruit is easily kept for the balance of the year.

But my thoughts seem to be all of food. Really not so – I am just writing along, thinking other things than those of which I write – of coming home, and so forth -

Henry

November 30

Dear mama -

Well, I'll save my thanks for a climax – and first write that I am well – that we have moved to a place where the ground is rocky, so that one does not sink into the mud so deep. That is all of the news, except:

I received yesterday a pair of house slippers, which are a very genuine delight. I can keep them dry, and use them when I am not out in the mud. Thank you very much.

Then also I received a box which also delights me – handkerchiefs, socks, wash rags, and! a box of Bissinger's. The candy is in excellent condition – and, again, I am going to be very selfish with it – giving to other people only hard candies and the like – for soft candy is a very rare treat. I suppose these are all Christmas presents – and it surely makes me wish I could send something which would give as much pleasure. But the choice is so limited, and I have no prospect of getting to any town at any time soon. So I shall just go on – and when opportunity presents itself, shall buy what I can. The villages offer absolutely nothing – except a few oranges and barbers. Maybe with time one could find some fine linen or something of the kind, but I doubt it, for peasants are too busy with food and ploughing to weave much. So it seems – and fine things come from cities

This too is an olive grove – with the olives already picked. Soon one ought to be able to buy cured olives in abundance.

What is Marian studying this winter and what are her plans?

I am now well stocked on candy – but do not let that discourage you – it will not last long.

I am going to try to go up to the village today – just to see what is there – and to buy some oranges, of which I am moderately found. I send my love -

Last night I read *Genesis* – St. Augustine's study and interest in that Book gives it new delight. He insists on the significance of every word and phrase -

Henry

December 1

Dear mama –

There is no use telling you that a new month is beginning. I suppose a new year will be by the time you get this – and the thought raises a lump to my throat.

I wrote a letter to Aunt Sally today – because I feel sorry for her. She is, I suppose, completely ignorant and little – and just does not know any better.

Then I walked into the town nearby – tried to get a shampoo. They had no soap. So I gave the barber half a cake of Palmolive. The water was apparently hard – he did not get any suds – and he did not get the soap out. So I shall wash it again.

Then to the grocery store where I bought six oranges and a pound of chestnuts. I have now boiled a few of the chestnuts, and they are very delicious, although small. I happen to be very fond of chestnuts, boiled or roasted, but raw they are abominable.

The town is quite completely destroyed – the buildings all have gaping holes in them, and many are just piles of stones. So it is not beautiful. It is just a village – a few grocery stores, with fruits and vegetables, a few barber shops, bicycle repair shops, one dry goods store, with a little ribbon for sale, and that it about all. I do not think it ever was a fine town.

The streets now flow with mud – although they are cobbled underneath.

I am well – the sun has come out – and it is now raining only two or three hours a day, which is a considerable improvement. I am enjoying candy, which is lasting very well.

Write often – I enjoy your letters very much.

Henry

December 2

Dear mama –

I had a very exciting time yesterday afternoon – I have already told you of my box gamble – they were to be done yesterday, and I went with Captain Morris to get them. But I found that he wanted four – the fifth was to be mine – and the fifth wasn't done. It will be next Tuesday, and I am anxious to get it – I consider them works of art, and shall send it home (if I can get it) possibly daddy would like to keep it in the office for miscellaneous things, or you would like to keep it at home. But, if I get it, and it is up to what I expect, I believe I shall maintain it as my personal property. I almost wish I had ordered two – but maybe I shall try another kind at another place. It is a museum piece, again.

But we stayed for supper. The whole family works at cabinet making – on the ground floor, in the court yard, and all around, and lives upstairs. One boy is a wood carver; another a joiner, and so forth. Language? One speaks a little French, and the old man a little English. The dinner was a feast – started with noodles, cooked like spaghetti, with tomato sauce and a little cheese – a big soup bowl full, and I thought surely that was the whole dinner. But, alas, then came fish, and I realized my blunder – a good white fish, with olive oil – and then artichoke hearts with oil and vinegar, and roast beef, with the tomato sauce – then walnuts and apples – and wine! If you put your hand over the glass to indicate no more – they poured it through your fingers. I think it was as good a dinner as I have ever eaten. It was lots of fun.

I should like to give them a present – and when I go for my box (if I go) I shall bring some candy or soap of whatever I can get. It would be nice, if you would watch for the opening of the Italian civil post office, and when it opens, send them a few unrationed articles. Flour, which they lack principally (bread, noodles and all, are brown, for lack of white flour) – I suppose is unpractical. Coffee? Is it rationed? Sugar? Would be wet. Canned meat? I don't know. I can't send you the name of the town – but I can send you the address, and when I it becomes permissible, shall send you the name of the town.

Guiseppe D'Alterio
Piazza Mercato[85] – 143

Maybe I am too soft in respect of repayment of hospitality, but these people show me such a good time – maybe they are beggars.

Only men sat down to the table – the women were all too busy cooking and serving – each course on separate plates – each time, the table cleared and reset. Really a feast – it lasted from three to five o'clock, and it was dark before I got back to camp.

The boxes I have seen are very fine – beautifully carved. The woods I do not know, and my dictionary is non-technical. One wood, the man who spoke English called "ash," but when I looked up "ash" in the dictionary, the word was wrong. So he gave me the Italian word – which I found in a French Italian dictionary as "érable," which, I am sure, means maple. But he denied it was maple, and I know it was not. It might be box or birch or beech, or even sycamore. Then the outside – the word we found was "noce," which, although it usually means "walnut" may mean any kind of nut. The man who spoke English vigorously denied it was walnut – and said it was chestnut – (castagna) – He showed us the nut – and it was what I call a walnut – the shell in two halves, with a much involuted meat. "Diamond bread" as I recall it advertised. At any rate, before I was through, walnuts, chestnuts, almonds, all nuts were mixed up, and so far as I was concerned, it could be assorted nut meats wood, fresh from Funston.

The boxes which were finished were very handsome I cannot draw a picture of them – but the wood nicely finished – a good brown – and the carving I considered magnificent. I am not much of a judge of it. They insist that inlay is not "modern," but carving is. What strange ideas people have of modern. Well, I hope to be able to send a box home – and if it is convenient, I shall get a second -

I send my love -

Henry

---

[85] There are several Piazza Mercatos ín Italy. There is one in Naples, which is the same location of the Triennale d'Oltremare and could be the city which he is currently in. If this is the Piazza Meracto in Naples, this street is known for traditional handicrafts. However, the D'Alterio shop is not present.
Piazza Meracto 143, Naples on GoogleMaps:
https://www.google.com/maps/place/Piazza+Mercato,+143,+80133+Napoli+NA,+Italy/@40.847549,14.2652631,18.83z/data=!4m5!3m4!1s0x133b083efdeca2e1:0x604e38fc24e3d590!8m2!3d40.848079!4d14.2658241

December 3

Dear mama -

I saw a rainbow this morning – a double one, extending from the horizon on the left to the hill on the right, a complete and perfect bow. It so delighted me and impressed me, that having Christmas cards at hand, I sent them all, making reference to Genesis 9, 12 – which I beg you to reread – about the covenant of the Lord – which I extend somewhat, hopefully, to include a promise against destruction by other agents than flood. Rainbows lend infinite scope to the imagination – it would be fun to make an anthology of verse or prose or both, according to subject – rainbows, to show the Hebrew, Greek, Latin, English and other reaction to them – only one would have to choose subjects carefully, omitting Spring. Maybe dictionaries of quotations do it.

Besides that, I have been eating oranges and chestnuts. Chestnuts roasted on the oil stove (they burst wildly), boiled, and finally, I boiled some with a few pieces of candy, and have them glace, cinnamon flavored. I got a dozen oranges today – and am eating them with pleasure. Brought a little gunny sack to town, to carry them home in – bought them and fortunately had possession of the sack with a dozen oranges and a pound of chestnuts, when the little boy began insisting on carrying it for me. It appears that they considered it terrible that I should carry it – but I did – over their insistence.

Then I had a shower this afternoon – they have them set up in a tent. I got very clean – but very muddy again in the process of getting dressed. Hot water, soap, everything. So you see, I do still know what hot water is – and I use it every day to shave – heating it on my oil stove.

There is no news. I find really nothing of interest in this small town nearby; it is just about wrecked – little of it left.

I send my love -

Henry.

It is raining again. One needs the reassurance of the rainbow now and then.

December 4

Dear mama -

I received yesterday a very funny package from Miss Thompson – sent by Stix Baer and Fuller[86]. She wrote she was sending me a book – Lin Yu Tang's *Between Tears and Laughter*. That was there. Also, playing cards, candy, and, in the book, a used pencil (eversharp) which I think must have belonged to the packing clerk or sales girl. Enclosed – a card – saying "To Ed," "Merry Xmas Ed. From Aunt Florence, Uncle Gus Gary." I wonder who got the package "Merry Xmas, Henry, from Miss Thompson" The package is wonderful – and I have a guilty feeling as I eat – may be it was intended for Ed. Was the address right on the card?

---

[86] A St. Louis department store

Then today a letter from Walter G. Liebman, which is so funny that I enclose it, without comment. It is a commentary in itself on Darkness and Ignorance. But I answered it, with a letter on the theme which for a few days has been a favorite of mine – about rainbows and Genesis 9, 12.

It has been raining all day and I have done absolutely nothing – a little work – translated a little Italian because there was no one else who could do as well available, and standards are low – Read a little – and now ready for bed. I may go out and walk a while in the dark before I go to bed, just to be out.

So I am hard up for anything about which to write. I do not recommend Lin Yu Tang – so far, it is a little simpish ,and, insofar as it is a discussion of western civilization and politics compared to oriental, based, it seems, on a total lack of appreciation for western civilization. As if one should take Rosalind[87] and Aunt Sally as the ideal of Western Civilization. Maybe he knows as little about Oriental as Occidental – I don't know.

There is no news – rain. Constantly – I tried to buy some persimmons in town yesterday. They returned to self, on the ground that they were not good. But they do sell awfully ♭ sour oranges, and wormy chestnuts on occasion.

The mails have been scant and fruitless – as far as letters are concerned – recently. But maybe they will begin to yield something interesting in the way of letters. I finished Part I of *Henry IV* today – and thank Ruth for the pleasure.

I send my love -

Henry

December 5

Dear mama -

I plan to take a shower today – when the water truck arrives and they get the fire started, for I had my hair cut today and am full of little pieces and the sun is out. Do you like that logic? If I said: "I had my hair cut today; the sun is out," would you say, "Therefore you will take a shower"? I think not. The reasons are incomplete, and maybe I shall not take a shower. The sun is going behind a cloud. If I could find a dandelion, I should pluck petals to decide – shall I? Shall I not?

I was paid a few days ago and have too much money in my pockets. I shall seek a way to spend it – carved boxes – maybe I can find some linen. I have sworn off of cameos, because I really think they are very ugly. Maybe I shall try to get an inlaid box – as a sample. I saw one – of satinwood and rosewood – somewhat Victorian, but quite beautiful. They are not to be bought in shops, for they are turned out very ugly. If I order one, I shall specify the use of varied woods – olive and apple and nut and as many kinds as possible. I think I should like it smaller than my carved box. Well all of that depends a great deal upon my being able to get to a certain town, for the adjacent town has nothing.

You see, there is not a bit of news or excitement – I ought to try to make some, but don't knew where to begin.

Have you ever received an embroidered tablecloth – of a brownish linen, with grapes and oranges – which struck my fancy? You said you received two sets of doilies – one I suppose of lace and one embroidered.

---

[87] Rosalind may be Rosalind Moss, Philip's wife.

You mentioned a lace table cloth – I wonder if that was what I considered just yardage of lace? It would be upside down from one way as a tablecloth. But I do not know why I ask, except that I am curious to know what reaches you – especially two pieces of pottery – one mailed yesterday (I mentioned it before – two is the total number of pieces of pottery from Italy) and one about a month ago. I should like to get more – but it looks like there will be no chance to get to a city.

I am well – I suppose possibly the water truck has arrived and the fire has built. I'll go see -

I send my love -

Henry

Lin Yu Tang's book of *Tears & Laughter* is a very stupid book. It leaves me feeling very dull and uninterested -

What a terrible letter – I have nothing to say.

PS – I took a shower & got my feet muddy. I shall have to take another

December 5 1943

To Mrs A. Lowenhaupt
6237 McPherson Ave.
Saint Louis
Missouri

Dear mama -

I write this V mail note, because, not having received mail for a few days, I think it likely that my recent mail to you may be delayed too – Christmas rush or something – so write this to let you know I am well and have nothing whatsoever to write about.

I walked to town today – it has nothing – a country village, with a few barber shops – beautiful colors of gray and pink – a few grocery stores (oranges, apples, greens, squash, persimmons – and wood.

I send my love.

Henry

December 6

Dear mama -

I'll try to write notwithstanding that I have nothing to say. The relative amount of sun to rain is increasing, and I therefore imagine that the rainy season is coming to an end. I hope so. I begin to long for dust as I longed for mud during the summer. There is no happy medium.

I expect to go to a town tomorrow – and get my box. If I do, I may order another one, because they are very handsome. ~~A~~ It would make a very fine present, say to Mr. Waite[88], if not too beautiful to be given away.

The progress has been very interesting, although I have not seen them as often as I should like. The corners are well made, joined like this *[Hand drawn diagram of the corner of a box.]*

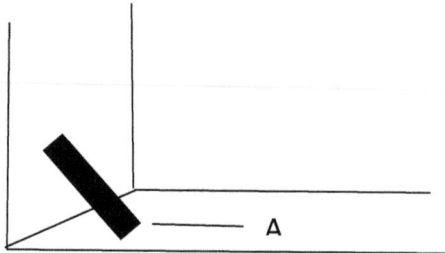

A is an inset, which does not come all the way to the top, and therefore does not show. The box~~es are~~ is heavy – of ½ inch walnut (the high parts of the curving I think are up to 1")

The shape, generally:
[Hand drawn diagram of the side of the box.]

The top:
[Hand drawn diagram of the top of the box.]

Lined with a white wood, ash or birch or something. Those are the names they give, but I am inclined to believe it is sycamore or plane. My dictionary is hopeless on names of trees – it gives none of them, except oak.

I always feel ashamed of myself when I tell people your old standard jokes – and people haven't heard them before. It amazes me. At dinner yesterday I boasted of how fine my tent was, telling that it had two kinds of running water – running in and running out. One is desperate when one indulges in such humor – but since that time every letter I've seen has included that. So I shall have to try, on occasion "Farewell," signed "remarkable poise[89]–" and the other stand bys – to see what happens.

I just received these letters – and enjoyed them. I am glad you received the package – and do not care that a cup & saucer were broken. Those came from Palermo – and were bought in desperation, to buy anything, for there was nothing in town I wanted, and it was depressing that day – the town once so [word unclear], and great building stones scattered through the streets. Better, I think, comes later.

I saw a woman with a shawl today – if I had known Italian should have bought the shawl. But maybe one should be ashamed to buy the clothes off peoples' backs.

I have plenty of reading material – Augustine still, Bible, Cicero, Shakespeare. Please do not send me more. It is unnecessary to send guide books or literature about Italy. I can get an old Baedecker[90] if I want it, but really never have much choice as to where I go. I ~~g~~ can order books from Blackwell's in Oxford and get them in about two weeks – having credit (about $15.00) there. I have a little Italian dictionary –

---

[88] One of Abraham Lowenhaupt's law partners
[89] May be reference to a joke: She has remarkable poise - blueberry, apple, etc.
[90] Guidebooks of the era

and a little grammar, which I never study. I have the Internal Revenue Laws. Old magazines and detective stories abound. I have *Between Tears and Laughter*, & shall give it away.

I send my love -

Henry

December 8

Dear mama -

I went to get my box today – but, alas, it was not done. Will not be, they say, until Saturday. I think they may be getting tired of making the same thing over and over again – so I did not order another, and shall not.

I also went to another town, with a royal palace in it, which was very beautiful. The towns I find so very interesting that I certainly wish I could get to more of them, and more often. I could have bought silk – plain or beaded, at ab $3.50 a yard. Thought it not cheap, and did not know what silk would be good for anyway. No linen. Many places were selling rayon under the name of silk, and I really cannot tell the difference. I bought this stationary – hoping you would enjoy the variety of the colors of the linings of the envelops – there is, surely, little else varied in my letters.

The towns I visited were very crowded and active – as if come back to life – for they are not much damaged – almost all the buildings intact. I should surely like to get back to a city – see what one looks like, and maybe some time shall. By hope we are made to be saved.

In the neighboring village, I found a photographer, and had my picture taken. It was to be done this afternoon, and I have asked a man to get it for me. I now resolve to enclose it, even if it is as bad as I expect it to be.

The camera is set up in the courtyard of a building – most of the building in ruins – and there are potter palms as a background. A camera of vintage circa 1850 – it might be valuable as an antique. I hope the picture is not so bad that it makes you angry – but if I get it, shall enclose it, and make no comment after I have seen it.

I am well – heard just now that Turkey declared war on Germany[91]. To what terrors the world has sunk – But "small measure of light - -" and that news is certainly to be counted on the side of good news.

I send my love -

Henry

---

[91] Turkey at this point was actually a neutral state and was actively providing materials to both sides. It did not declare war on the Axis powers until February 1945.
There were several countries in Latin America and the Middle East (such as Iraq) which joined the Allied powers in late 1943, however.
https://en.wikipedia.org/wiki/World_War_II_by_country#Turkey

December 8

Dear mama -

I have three letters from you – in one of which you suggest buying, if possible, peasant goods. Italy, in recent years, has, I think, been an extremely modern country – manufacturing and so forth. The Fascist regime I think was intended to industrialize the country, to establish fine roads and great public buildings – so that every village, almost has its fascist buildings, like the town post offices in the United States. The peasantry is, at least for the present, in abeyance – and seems to consist, at least around here, of old women only. They are poor – without cattle, without chickens, pigs or anything else, – a few poor greens, and olives and ~~meaegre~~ meager fruit, for the land has not been tended for several years. That is why I have been thinking of your Greek quotation – about war making fertile fields barren – and Goldsmith's "A rude peasantry, a ~~cou~~ nation's pride When destroyed can never be supplied." The dwellings are in large part destroyed – and people live in haystacks, ruins, or anyplace else – in Hooverville, you will see something of the conditions and the difficulty of trying to find anything. I have never seen so much of people trying to use, say, half a jug to carry water – a piece of a plate, rags for clothing – most have, apparently, abandoned pretense of dressing children – the clothes they had a few years ago, with all hems released, still do, and they run around – five, six year old children – in little dresses which reach down only to their bellies. The women wear rags sewed together – and the only cloth I have seen is the pieces they use to protect their heads in carrying hard things – as stones – on their heads. They all want flour – It will take a long time to restore the country – there are no cattle, except oxen and a few goats. I saw the first sheep I have seen just a few days ago – and that was one solitary old one – too tough to eat, I suppose. Here and there a solitary pig. It is not as if the peasants had abundance, and could make things with pleasure. They are too pressed by necessity.

It may be that I exaggerate – the country looks so very beautiful overall – one may consider the ragged peasants or the roads merely picturesque. But I remember other parts, where the peasants on the roads were dressed in abundant, clean clothes, of native costumes, in bright, clear colors, ~~with~~ looked healthy. ~~He~~ There, the destruction was not so extensive.

But I intend to see if I can find anything – and keep on looking. There is some native pottery, in use, mostly broken, which is very pretty – but coarse, and I hesitate to send anything so heavy and fragile and of so little value.

Love -

Henry

December 9

Dear mama -

I have a few minutes in which I may write – and these are delightful minutes.

A crew of three men is in the tree above the tent, beating the olives down, and they pepper the tent, like hail stones – beautiful ripe purple olives – which fall and roll all around. I could not resist eating one – they are terrible tasting – sour, bitter – and stain terribly. My fingers are purple from the olive.

While they work, the men are singing (and they sing well) all the old favorites – La Donna è mobile – Santa Lucia – and others. There is a very beautiful melody they sing, most of it without words, other than aaah,

I am trying to hear it clearly enough to write it to you – but my ear is not keen enough, and each time, although it is obviously the same melody, I write it differently.

They knock down the olives – then women pick them up – They also pick up the broken branches, and carry them in, in enormous bundles on their heads. But I still do not comprehend the fame of olives.

I am well – here is another picture – still without comment. I had six altogether, and send them one by one to expedite. Some letters arrive quickly – others slowly. I am glad my Palermo blunder has arrived. The linen of the bedspread may be of some use.

Love -

Henry

December 9 1943

To Mrs. A. Lowenhaupt
6237 McPherson Ave
Saint Louis,
Missouri
USA

Dear mama -

I haven't written a V-mail letter for a long time – so now. But I have an additional reason. I had a photograph of myself taken – six copies – and am sending them, to you. This is advance warning – 1) that I am not as mad as I look. 2) That the lighting was peculiar – in a courtyard that all light came from directly overhead, making very dark shadows which give a strange appearance. But photographs they are – unquestionably.

I am well – have not a bit to write about – except that I continue enjoying roast chestnuts and oranges and enjoying your letters. All my love -

Henry

P.S. - I'll send you just five pictures – the sixth keep to look at myself when I want to laugh – H

December 10

Dear mama -

I sit down to write with enthusiasm – I have just received quite a batch of mail – two letters from you – which I saved till last – one from Marcy Krausnick – one from Philip Moss - one from National Candy – one from Owenbooks*[?]* – one from Bill Charles – two from Craig Clark, brother of Bill Clark here.

Philips', the Candy Company's, and Owenbooks (at the insistence of Mrs. Schwab) of the "I am sending you "variety." Intentions are so good, I shall write thanking -

Today I went on a spree – illicitly, but covered by poeritically *[sic]*; I went ~~just~~ last to the cabinet makers shop (how much easier it would be if I could name towns!) but my box wasn't done – the top has to be put on. Magnificent – I surely hope I can get it! Had a cup of coffee with them – and am invited to spend Christmas Eve and night at their house. I hope I can do it.

I think of daddy's birthday – I have been trying to get him a present – and am concluding to send him the box – as a belated Christmas and New Year's present.

I went first, however, to the City – always unnamed – and went ~~ju~~ whole hog to the extent I could. First to the second hand book stores, where I got a beautiful *Valgate Bible* and a handsome Valerian. I may send the latter to Chris Peper, but may not. No decision will be made before it is posted. I escaped a Venetian box, covered with divers colors of straw, and a bottle of brandy – as not worth bothering with. Why drink mediocre liquor? Most of it is sterno.

Then to a friend, Ciro Gallo, ~~who~~ with whom I carry on long political discussion in French. He says America is the land of his dreams, and Italy must sever ~~bui~~ its traditions. Have you ever heard of the doctrine of Karma? He even admires American music – and American art as "tentative," which I consider a good word for the best of it. "Tentatif" in French. Literature – Jack London, the Dostoevsky of America – so I am trying to refresh my recollection of Dostoevsky, if I ever had any. He hopes to visit America – and I gave him my address – just because it would be very funny if Signor Ciro Gallo[92] should come to see me, with wife and small daughter, who are in the country.

He runs an antique shop – the best in the city – and I bought more pottery from him – two plates which I am sending home. I shall not comment on them – but I hope you will describe and comment upon receipt. These too you may lend to the museum. I say I went hog wild on them, and paid a fancy price – but a rare opportunity because I do not often have occasion to spend money, and having it in my pocket can spend it, as I intended. Ciro Gallo is a gentleman – and his enthusiasms on abstract subjects and matters of principle, which I enjoy. He had a box made for my plates – while waiting we had our conversation.

Then to a shop, where I bought a pound of chocolates – they were good (Captain Morris and Lieutenant Clark visited me this evening, and we ate them, together with cheese sandwiches from our loaf of bread and Sgt. Lincoln's Christmas cheese)

Then to the centre of town – (it was lunch time) and a man stopped me, asking of I wanted lunch. Gamble! I said yes – and went up secretly to a third floor place where I ate spaghetti (white flour!) and tomato sauce. Quite good. More like noodles than spaghetti. The man I considered of the criminal type -

The city is wonderfully interesting – of course crowded with soldiers – but one sees that it must contain the extremes of the finest people in the world and the worst. Ciro Gallo – a gentleman by every standard, even though a tradesman, the clergy, some fine shops and reliable, sound merchants. Then walk off the main street and onto a side street, where the hawkers are out for illicit trade – and I shall write about it – of every kind – with three words, "Mangiare; Cognac; Signorina –"[93] to get people by any means. The "Mangiare" (eat) is the least they can give you (I wanted some); the cognac is in opened bottles, and worse, doubtless, than the worst bootleg stuff – the pimps follow along urging about how special the girl is. One man was offering vermouth – and I told him I would take Cinzano. He said he had it – I followed

---

[92] Unfortunately, I could not find any further information on Ciro Gallo or his antique shop.
[93] Translates in English to "Eat; Cognac; (young/unmarried) Woman."

him, into a little bar; where he offered me a bottle recorked, and unlabeled, obviously not Cinzano, even if Vermouth. As I stepped in, there was a fat woman, hair ~~died~~ dyed blonde, face thick and caked with powder, as typical a looking prostitute as could be imagined, caressing a big buck N [Black Man] – who was slightly drunk. The scene was beautiful, in a French modernistic sort of way – so low that nothing could go lower – As I came in, the woman moved over, and said "Come in, dearie." The negro reeled a little bit.

Quite a beautiful saloon – like the ideal of toughness. Down a few steps from the street, a narrow side street. A bar, with empty bottles, and dirty glasses; oak tables, quite murky and dark – this bright colored woman in hard pink and yellow, and a big black negro. The prostitute takes the initiative – not sure whether they are being investigated or raided – either deciding that the whole is so clear that is cannot be avoided, or that not knowing how to say anything else. "Come in, dearie," she whimpers, and smiles. Her teeth were yellow.

That is what makes a city, I suppose – the extremes – the magnificent palaces, opera houses, castles, fine buildings – the little dark holes – some with paintings, some with junk. Everyone hawking something, out for the trade; children soliciting, showing menus, offering wine, everything.

It makes the City seem to seethe on the main street. The best merchandise is pitiful. I bought Marian a bracelet, which I thought rather pretty. Merchandise is pitiful – I found no linen. Some silk is available. Then I bought a deck of playing cards for fun – they are not like ours. Intended them for daddy (they are like Haymer's, but big), but decided they amounted to nothing, gave them to Bill Clark.

Then drove back to the carpenter's, as I have said, and had a pleasant visit. He desires that I get word to his brother in New York of his health and so forth, which I shall do, if I decide I may. Presently I think I may. I visited for about half hour – am invited for Christmas – they are very pleasant, plain people – and now and then I laugh as I think how like the New York Italians they are, when they try to talk English, and how funny it is – as if I should be in the Italian quarter of New York – and just wandering around, visiting them. I should probably be afraid to. The lady of the house lived in New York for about a year – met the man who is now her husband, who had been working there and had saved enough to open the shop he now has, married him and returned to Italy with them. They laugh at my Italian, which indicates that it is improving, as I believe it is.

I think that Italians are more liberty-loving than Americans – I do not believe they were ever effectively fascistic. What black markets! I don't think anyone can ever enforce restrictive legislation or communal regulation – they are too profoundly individualistic and out for themselves – and I admire it a little bit. Beef steak for sale – at a price – coffee apparently available.

Well – I must go to bed – for now, my love – I am glad you received a cameo – does it amount to anything? I frequently buy in desperation for anything to buy – and always enjoy acknowledgement of receipt. Marian, I am sure, is well by now. I think she takes many things too seriously – and your letters sound a little blue. Weight of the world and shadows engulfing. Pip, pip! There's something to be said in favor of "fiddling while Rome burns," because it doesn't help much to worry while it burns.

Henry

This is extravagant! My stationary comes one sheet for one envelope. If I write more long letters, I shall be overstocked on envelopes!

December 10

Dear mama -

I walked to the neighboring village today, again, and bought myself the following – two handkerchiefs of mediocre quality. (I think they were used, but well washed and ironed to look like new) The store keeper asked, as all people do, if I was born in the United States – and was disappointed (as they always are) at my "yes." So we compromised, as I normally do, that I am the son of Italians. What does that make you, signora?

Then a funnel, to power oil into my stove, and some wick – could not get the right kind, so I bought strips and have sewed them together into a round one, which works beautifully. "Was I from Rochester?" they asked. "No" – but I know the answers – "from Pittsburgh" – "ah the cousin of my aunt's sister in law, who lives over there, is in Pittsburgh – la la la!"

But I write what I bought to show, partly, how impossible it is to imagine what I want or might need – nor how all wants can be provided. Did you ever think of sending a present of wicks for kerosene stoves, and a funnel? The question is rhetorical.

Tomorrow – I may go to town.

Someday soon I may go through my baggage. In present circumstances, I have absolutely no idea of what I have, Every time I open anything, a cake of soap falls out – or a can of shoe polish, or something surprising – or an odd razor blade. What an unholy mess. I shall reform it.

I now have the feeling that I have so much of necessities – I think I shall look for a luxury in the way of a pretty thing to carry around with me. I ought to be able to find it.

This evening, Sgt. Lincoln received in a Christmas package a can of tongue – so we found a loaf of bread – and we have been eating tongue sandwiches all evening. I am now full and tired. Add to the tongue – some candy (fudge) which was brought in, some roasted chestnuts, some oranges – and you have quite a meal.

I am nevertheless well -

I surely hope I can get to town tomorrow. There are many who go from here to hear an opera, which has now opened. I intend not to go, for grand opera always bores me – and I am not at all in any mood for a hard evening's work of going and coming (a few hours each way) just to hear singing no matter how fine. Notwithstanding all the fame of Italian opera, it surely could not approach the Metropolitan – and even that is beyond my understanding. I think the chief attraction of it is that it is cheap – 10 or 15 (equivalent) for *La Traviata* or *Boheme* , which would cost as many dollars in New York.

I send my love -

Henry

December 13

Dear mama -

My letters have been too long, and I am accumulating a plethora of envelopes – for these packets of paper come with an equal number of sheets and envelopes. So, although I had many envelopes, I walked into the village this afternoon, and bought some more paper. I enjoy these little packets, and the salesman helps me select, so conscientiously. This packet has on the outside a picture of Michelangelo – with his name – and I received a long discussion of him as one of the greatest men, compared to Mussolini. I understood only a very small part of the discussion, for I have progressed in Italian grammar only through the verb "to have." Then of the paper – this is the finest, and to be used only for very special letters. So it is. While in town, I visited the grocery stores – and first bought ~~two~~ one kilos of big oranges (two pounds) at 12¢ a kilo. I do not understand prices, for another place wanted 10¢ for 3 similar oranges. There were about eight in my kilo. Then a kilo of chestnuts to be well supplied – at 20¢ a kilo; and I went to the next place where I found much finer chestnuts – larger and fewer worms – at 12¢ a kilo. So I bought another kilo – and asked about persimmons – It was the finest grocery store – and he sent home for some ripe ones. I bought four beautiful, mushy ones, of which I have now eaten three. Delicious things – Four big persimmons – 6¢. That was my marketing in the town.

Inasmuch as I may not name towns, and it is hard to write about nameless places, I shall henceforth give them purely fanciful names – this village shall be Cinnabaro or Persimmone. I like the village – although there is really nothing in it.

This is indeed fine paper. It is a pleasure to write on it, and I just wish I had something to write worthy of the paper.

I am disturbed to hear of Marian's not being well. I am so far away that I cannot imagine about it, because surely she will be well by the time an answer can arrive.

I am glad you received the table cloth, which was bought in Cefalu[94] – and I just wished I had bought more – for I saw others as pretty, and really intended to get more when I got back. But I didn't get back. But maybe I shall find more elsewhere. Since that time I have seen no linen.

I am well – it has not rained today, for which I am duly grateful, and things begin to dry up just a little bit. I have no news whatsoever to write – and really write for the sake of the paper. I received the news of Kim. Is he still at Ruth's?

I send my love -

Henry.

I also bought some air-mail paper, which I shall show you soon.

---

[94] A municipality within Palermo, Sicily.
https://en.wikipedia.org/wiki/Cefal%C3%B9

13 December

Dear Marian -

I have already written to mama all the external facts I know – and, having received and answered letters from Forrest Campbell, Bill Charles, Mr. Gay, and others, am just about written out – but I am anxious to take the pleasure of writing to you – ought to be a musical letter, because men ate knocking down olives – "put, pit, pit!" on the tent; and singing furiously while they do it; and a band is practicing – "wail, wail, wail," and children are singing a little phrase in the road – altogether like rubbing your head, patting your belly and tapping your feet at the same time.

Mama writes that she received a tablecloth, which I think must be, finally, the one I liked – with oranges and grapes on it. I regret I did not buy another similar one. She also writes that you are not very well – and (happy medicine!) should rest through the winter. What fun you can have doing it! Under the title "resting" should come on vacation – maybe in New Orleans, which should be interesting. And if you should decide to go there – do you remember Henry Louis Cohn's sister, who was at our house once? She now lives in New Orleans, named Mrs. D̶r̶ Gottschalk, if I remember correctly – but you can find it certainly. Her husband is a doctor – I just mention this, trying to find some interest in New Orleans. Henry Louis Cohn could tell you – address Hundred Oaks, Banton Rouge, La.

But there is an awful lot else for which I envy you – as you could, for example, just for fun write a history of St. Louis, say, from 1850 to 1870, or from the building of the old cathedral to the completion of the old courthouse. This would involve, as I see it, first, a little reading, including the WPA works on the subject[95] – (which are not much good) and then, after you know the factual part, and the dates of events, going around and visiting people (whom daddy could name to you) as Mr. Chouteau, O'Neill Ryan's widow, Judge McDonald, maybe some of the Greensfelders, and getting them to tell you the stories they had heard about St. Louis – If you should write such a book, it could be very interesting, and much fun – especially if it did not purport to be 100% accurate, but were based in part upon gossip and stories. It would be most interesting to take a short period, if you could get descriptions of people living then – their oddities, what they did, their feuds with each other – their cows and dogs and horses. Well – it might be drudgery – but it might also be fun.

Or if you could write, say, a little on the history of chemical manufacture in St. Louis – the subject, locally, would be equivalent to the sarcastic*[?]* history of the Du Pont's written not long ago, and might not be publishable. Patent Medicines, or Cure-alls and Chemicals – illustrated with advertisements from the beginnings of NR and Listerine.

You see what fun I have imagining what I would (but should not, in all probability) do with a lot of leisure. Then I should surely raise at least one orchid, or have one orchid plant, whose progress I should watch (from its prime to the ash-pit, probably, in race track time.) By the way, do they still have horse racing in East St. Louis?

I sent you a small bracelet the other day – a trinket – because I thought it was prettier than most of the junk. My present buying is really not that at all, but simply buying anything pretty I can find – and

---

[95] On the subject of WPA publications, I located the following resources:
A Missouri guide-book from the WPA Federal Writers' Project.
https://archive.org/details/missouriguidetos00writrich/page/n5/mode/2up?view=theater
A finding aid for a collection of the WPA's Historical Records Survey for Missouri
https://collections.shsmo.org/manuscripts/columbia/c3551

sending it home for whoever wants it – except for things which I consider special, which are to be kept in familia. The bracelet is not special – and may be given away or kept as you like.

Write soon, Marian – I am sorry you are not well – but hope you feel alright and enjoy yourself.

I am well – and now interrupted – shall continue letter.

Now I continue – rambling on – the sun has come out – there was a strong wind last night, and things dry out a little bit. I just ate lunch – we had fresh butter – that is, unpreserved butter, which is quite a rare treat, so I concentrated on bread, butter, jam, and cocoa – with canned pineapple. It strikes me as a cardinal sin to serve canned fruit when fresh fruit is in season, oranges rotting for the picking, and piled high everywhere – and one eats canned pineapple, which, when fruit is out of season, will be a very rare delicacy. But that's the way it is done – canned tomatoes, when tomatoes are very abundant here. So it goes. It is a detail which makes me desire to attempt a reformation.

The texture of olive trees is lovely. Yesterday, I picked a few handfuls of ripe olives, and put them in a can to dry out over my stove. They turned out fried, and quite good, although the skin is tough, and they are a little bitter – refreshingly bitter, I might say – like quinine. I have thrown most of them away – and give up olives as a bad job.

I sent some (two) very handsome majolica plates yesterday. I hope they arrive – one blue, or striking for its blues; one, a primitive, in yellows, oranges, browns and blues. These, I suppose no one wants as much as I. But if the art museum would like to borrow them, or Ruth (I mean, not that the art M. would like to borrow the plates) either or both is alright. I may get to town again – Hope.

Love

Henry

December 15

Dear mama -

I feel as if I have been writing very often – possibly I have, and possibly that is just a deceptive feeling. At any rate, the conclusion is that I feel that I have nothing to say. And this may be considered a sample of stationary. I wish there were a ~~sample of~~ convention of stationary, as of flowers – blue lining for security; red for choler; purple for something else, etc. etc. But I don't know any.

We are no longer near the town I call Cinnabaro, having moved. I have not yet been out of the area, and do not know what is near – but the country is still lovely. Now on a hillside, a chestnut grove, with many oaks among the chestnut trees – and chestnuts free and abundant for the picking up – finding them among the husks. They are sweet and delicious. Acorns – natives are picking them, to feed to hogs, I suppose. But I tasted one, and they are much sweeter than most acorns. In the distance are snow covered mountains – some with towns on them – like ancient castles. Close by, are some big farmhouses – like whole towns, rambling in and out of courts and wings. A kind of baronial farming, it must be for a hundred people live in each building, apparently.

Yesterday, in walking down to supper, I found a beautiful patch of mushrooms – and picked them. Took from the supper table some grease, colored to resemble butter, and cooked my mushrooms – with a piece of bread, they were very delicious. I suppose I acquire from daddy my love of eating anything I can find. Maybe silly, but fun – and a good mushroom sandwich is really something. I shall watch for more.

Birds are abundant here – all of strange varieties. Every night I hear one, which must be a nightingale – and reflect on the traditional beauty of his song. I suppose when his reputation grew up, they did not have as fine flutes and piccolos as they now have – I prefer a good flute melody. But a nightingale is a natural wonder.

I am well – sitting in the sun which is very warm and lovely. The rainy season may be over -

I send my love. What is Marian's illness?

Henry

December 16

Dear daddy -

I am sending you a belated birthday present – and Christmas present combined – a carved box. It is belated partly because I was slow in ordering it, more because I was slow in getting it. I send it to the office to impress you that it is yours. It probably will not arrive until February or March.

Just to fill the package, I enclose two presents for mama, which I considered also beautiful – one piece of brocade and one of linen. I am not sure just what they are good for – but I enjoyed buying them

You see I was in the City today – going beyond my cabinet maker's shop. Business in the city is done in the street, for the shops cannot keep any good merchandise in stock. One wanders around, and when a person has something to sell, he comes out and grabs a customer. The shops, almost entirely, have junk. On the streets – children solicit – "mangiare; vino; cognac; signorina." These are in abundance – and the mangiare, wino and cognac very bad. Then today a woman came up and asked if we were interested in linens and other materials. We went up with her – and she showed the collection of her sister and herself – partly what they had made, partly what, she said, she had been commissioned to sell for a nobleman who needed money. She used to go onto the ships to sell to tourists, and there learned to tell the truth, because the captains wouldn't let her come back if she didn't. She had about six pieces – I send two. She is working on more. Also two miniatures on ivory, which were not interesting.

I have already told you all about the box.

Since it is likely to be the last time I get into the city, I bought all I could lay hands on. More may follow. But everything I get I like too well to give to anyone outside the family.

I am receiving much for Christmas – food (candy, cookies, etc) – and must write my thanks for all. I shall write again.

Love

Henry

December 17

Dear mama -

Yesterday I wrote to Betty – addressing the letter in your care, hoping that you would read it. But in doubt, I shall not hesitate to repeat. Betty sent me a translation of Tacitus, which is very interesting. Unfortunately, much is lost in translation – for the interest of Tacitus lies in part in the conciseness of his phraseology, so that he reads almost like a series of new, witty proverbs. The narrative, however, and opinion are interesting.

Yesterday I went to the city – but that I remember. While I remember – I sent Mme. Peyrus a present a few days ago, of soap and National Candy Co. Candy. But maybe Algiers has opened up fully now, with soap on every counter. I doubt it, and don't know. How would you like to get a cake of Palmolive for Christmas?

I had an awfully good time in the city yesterday – on the streets wandering around – eating lunch (very poor) buying a bottle of cognac, which is quite good. But I shall not write again in detail, for you will, I hope, read Betty's letter. That is why I sent it in your care.

I have dispatched my box, addressed to daddy. It is a birthday present and Christmas gift combined – and if he does not think it magnificent, he should give it to you. I consider it very, very interesting and lovely – maybe because I've had a good time with it. Now I am invited to Christmas dinner with Signor D'Alterio. His son must go back to the army – and I think it is harder to leave, having thought he was through.

I put inside the box two ot other things which I thought lovely – a piece of linen and lace – I do not know as what it was intended – a large handkerchief, or a small table piece. If you think it nice, you may give it to Betty to Marian or keep it. If you think it worthless, give it to Heather or Janet or st somebody else. I am inclined to take the lady at her word – she said it was a 17th (meaning 18th) century gentleman's handkerchief. But I don't care.

Then a piece of brocade – made into a table scarf. Maybe the edge should be removed – but you decide. I know where I can get another piece – not in as good condition, and the shape more irregular – but larger. Let me know if you want it and I shall see if I can get it. Doubtful – that will be two months hence. The other piece is pink or rose, instead of blue, possibly a little finer – but worse. The piece I sent is said to be 18th Century again – and old. I do not know. I surely hope these arrive safely. They are in daddy's box.

Then (you see I went on a real spree!) I got two table clothes – both rather small, but maybe useful – one embroidered, one white and embroidered in white. They were so much superior to anything I saw, that I sent bought them. Cameo The colored one I consider quite handsome. I've not sent them yet, but shall. Cameos as thick as flies – but I stuck to my resolution – no more cameos. No more costume jewelry unless someone definitely wants it.

I send my love

Henry

December 18 1943

To Mrs. A. Lowenhaupt
6237 McPherson Ave.
Saint Louis, (5)
Missouri, U. S. A.

Dear mama -

This is a note to let you know that I am well, which I write because inasmuch as I am not receiving mail I judge that possibly there are the same lapses of my mail. I have nevertheless been writing just about daily, and have said everything that there is to say – the letters will doubtless reach you in the fullness of time.

I am now in a chestnut grove, with abundance of chestnuts for the picking. And roasted chestnuts are just about my favorite food. Add to that, mushrooms, which I am learning by experience to cook – and I am living in the lap of luxury. Not only that: I have received so much candy that I have been able just to eat all I want. I think the doctor's order to eat a lot of sweets has probably expired – but I enjoy it. Edith Friedman Barenholtz sent me a box of very delicious Christmas cookies, which I have enjoyed. National Candy Company, and others. Now this evening I received a package of candy and cookies from Myron Glassberg – and am commencing on the enjoyment of it. Except that I have resolved (rather weakly) to keep it until Christmas, and then, if I go to dinner at the cabinet maker's, to give it to them. I think they will enjoy it more than I, and I know they will serve a feast on Christmas. Boy, am I subject to disappointment!

This is still very lovely country – and I must open my eyes and see it. I took a walk today, about a mile down the road – lovely cultivated country, now in winter, and the trees (chestnuts, oaks, and fruit trees) are bare. The mountains in the distance are capped with snow. I don't know why that reminds me of the four bottles of Fitch's hair tonic and shampoo, together with a passel of hotel size cakes of soap and a sponge, which Mrs. Alma Myer sent me. She also sent me an Italian grammar and a life of Cicero. Why are all these people sending me presents and so kindly? I am writing and thanking them for them, but I cannot possibly return their generosity, because I will not buy such trash, which they know to be trash; it is silly to send them candy (excellent is available in the one big city I have visited, although expensive, and I rarely get there – such as chocolates filled with whole cherries in brandy, candied fruits, bon-bons, filled with walnuts and pistachios– richer candy than can be sent – but I have only rare opportunity to buy it; when I find something I like, it is too rare an occasion to give it away irretrievably, where I shall not see it again and where it probably will not be appreciated. However, I shall watch for something – say handkerchiefs – but they go in such extremes; the ten cent store variety, and worse, at a silly price, to the finest antique lace ones – I saw one beauty for which they were asking $25. There is nothing in between. So I shall forget it, having already written and expressed the thanks which I sincerely feel.

I have, as I have mentioned in letters which will probably reach you after this, sent home some pet trinkets. First, to daddy, a carved *[word crossed out]* walnut box, which I had made and of which I am extremely fond, partly because I feel that I myself cause it to be made, and therefore it is no stereotyped. A particular affection which may well warp my judgement. I put into it a piece of linen, embroidered and bordered with lace, which I considered beautiful, for no particular purpose, and a piece of brocade, which had much the same attraction. I still have to send two tablecloths. I write about this hoping that you may have the pleasure of anticipation, which I have in anticipation of your getting some pleasure of them. My mind is on Marian. How is she?

All my love

Henry

December 18

Dear mama:

I suppose I had better write small, because I shall, if I continue to write as much as I've been writing, run out of varied stationary soon. I am no longer near a cartoleria or a town – but I shall obtain paper – if necessary using typewriter paper and seeking interest elsewhere.

This morning I wrapped two table clothes and six napkins – in a package addressed to you. I've not yet dispatched it, desiring to roll on my tongue, so to speak; the pleasure I had in buying them. For I did enjoy my few hours in the city very much.

So having nothing to say – except that it is a grey day – like late October or mid November in Missouri – I shall describe them to you, for, being packed out of sight, they already grow in beauty. The one is white linen, of a very nice quality, with the edges embroidered – ~~like~~ making a sheen, rolled hem. Then, there are parts cut out, and the edges secured, to make a leaf design, and from these, embroidered stems, as it were, also in the shiny white. The napkins match it. Unfortunately, it is rather small – and probably would not cover any table you have. So, maybe it should be considered for – Marian or Ruth, unless my judgement of size is wrong, or you like it as a runner, or for Betty if she ever has tea or anything of the kind. But you are the decider in these matters. It could even be given outside, if you have occasion to give what I should consider a very fine present.

The other, though, is, in my memory, a pet and darling for you or Ruth or Betty or Marian – being somewhat larger. Its handicap – no napkins. It is a gray, or natural colored linen, with a ribbon and fruit design embroidered in brilliant colors – purple for grapes, green, pink and pearl grey for peaches, blues and reds – in a very fine thread, which, I think will make it glow magnificently and make any table look even jeweled .It is, I believe, both as fine and as bright as the one I sent from Cefalu, which I believe you have received. Did you determine to let Ruth have it? Why not, if you consider the two equal, lend them, or use them by turns. Both I am anxious to see again when I get home. But that doesn't matter either. My judgement may be so entirely wrong – but one must snap up anything ~~pretty one thinks~~ one sees and thinks pretty. Your letter lent me confidence, because you say you enjoy the Sicilian one.

Now – I just walked about a mile up the road, to see if there was a town – I did not come to any. But the road is interesting – much donkey traffic, old houses, caves (apparently for the cattle, but no cattle in them) The road is mostly between banks – and in the fields above, chestnuts, a few vineyards.

Now we have two bottles of fair, sweet cider. Fifty cents a quart and selling like hot cakes. So what are values? My memory of the price of cider is 50¢, and one bottle for about 10¢ worth of candy and soap.

I am well – and send my love -

Henry

December 19

Dear mama -

I have been writing so often and doing so little that there is absolutely nothing I can write about. So I suppose I should just end this letter here and now. I have received no mail recently – none has been coming in – but I suppose there will be a big batch at once.

I took a shower this afternoon – with Fitch's Shampoo, which Mrs. Myer, Leo and Dr. Myer sent me – and, thinking it was funny, made a very ceremonious bath of it. The shampoo is very good – but my hair is so short that it is quite unnecessary to use more than Palmolive.

Then I sent some laundry out (giving her too much soap, as always.) Everybody here had a relative in the United States – this one, a brother in Providence – when I ask if he is in Providence, Rhode Island, she says, "no, Providence, just Providence," in the United States'. I suppose, because she wants me to send him a message – not having heard of or from him for four years or so. Maybe I shall – I don't know/ But one does not send messages, by Vmail, even, to the only other Providence I know.

The woman works on the land here – spending most of the day picking chestnuts and acorns. The latter, apparently, they gather for the pigs (they have left a hog and a sow only) Just when she does laundry I don't know – but she promised it back tomorrow. So I gave the children, who were traipsing along some candy.

I suppose these people are very deeply religious or something, for they lead hard lives, and keep on going, singing Santa Lucia or some other song. This woman, yesterday, was trying to find someone who would take a picture of her four-month old child, before it was buried, for it had just died. She did not succeed.

Now I am eating roasted chestnuts – with a little sweet cider – it makes one think it is Halloween instead of almost Christmas. But that thought doesn't amount to anything.

It is quite chilly out at night, but this tent is on a hill – one end low – and if one puts the stove down there, the other end is very warm. I am well – I send my love.

I hesitate to ask questions – because by the time my letter reaches you the question may be obsolete. You know that I am eager to know how Marian is -

I send my love -

Henry

December 20

Dear mama -

I have been writing often, it seems to me, and receiving no mail – except inexpensive candy – today a box from Janet – hard candy, life saver rolls, chewing gum – yesterday a box from Myron – strong Scotch biscuits, prunes stuffed with marshmallow, and so forth. It will be mostly for the bambini. Then a letter from Aunt Sally[96]– which I shall try to answer, but it is very senseless. Mostly devoted to the proposition

---

[96] This is Sarah Wiener Lowenhaupt who married Haymer Lowenhaupt and had no children

170

of how she must learn to cook. I have an idea that if she wanted to, she could cook well – but she is kind of boasting that in her busy, social world she has never got down to cooking. Besides, she probably has no one to cook for. Surely one could learn to cook in a month – with a cookbook – unless one wants to make lamb chops out of ground meat.

It is always so – that when mail isn't coming the few that do come in you don't want anyway.

Therefore I felt very dull – quite unable to write – and I sought a remedy in a walk. I walked fast – and accomplished a double purpose – got good and warm and had the most magnificent walk! up the road, after a few yards downhill, it begins to ascend steadily, and winds up a gentle hill, terraced in grapes in some places, planted in apple trees, chestnuts and the like. At frequent intervals, old stone houses. As upon ascent [, the prospect broadens, and ~~open~~ sees villages on the other hills and in the valleys – they look like walled towns, they are so compact. On up, and up – it was a grey day, almost wintery, and pretty soon, I saw wisps of cloud or fog in the valleys.

Then I came upon a village, off to the right. First, a small, old stone chapel, crucifix in front, with a background of the whole valley, and the INRI standing out. The village was tiny – really just a courtyard. But the children swarmed out, asking for candy. I gave one boy a broken cigarette lighter – and a fight ensued. Another boy took it away. So I gave the loser a pocket comb as a consolation.

Women in the windows – watching the traffic on the road – nursing their babies, sewing, knitting, always singing beautifully. They wear a peasant costume – full shirts, bright colors, rather indescribable.

Then, along the road, there were a horse and buggy – the horse's hoof was slightly injured, apparently, and he would not or could not pull the buggy, which was light. About six men were pushing – they could push the buggy but not the horse – while a gentlemanly looking fat priest was whipping the horse. It made a very funny scene – such as Hogarth might draw.

I suppose my whole walk was about four miles. It was very refreshing. The days have become so short that one has really only the middle of the day with bright light. The twilight is long, both morning and evening.

Now it is raining. Maybe it will turn warmer.

I am well and comfortable. Hope you too are so – write often – maybe mail will come through.

All my love -

Henry

I am forgetting Christmas this year, for there is no pleasure in remembering it. It is the 137th Psalm: "How shall we sing the Lord's song in a strange land? If I forget thee, O Jerusalem, let my right hand forget her cunning" – I don't know exactly what the connection is – and "O daughter of Babylon, who art to be destroyed; happy shall he be who rewardeth thee as thon hast served us. Happy shall he be who taketh and dasheth thy little ones against the stones." Not the Christmas spirit!

December 21

Dear mama -

I got my laundry back – damp because the weather is damp, but it will dry as well here as elsewhere. I have no idea of prices, and they always refuse to fix them – saying to pay what you wish – so I paid a dollar, having no change, for my own and Sgt. Lincoln's – and gave her a cake of soap and some candy – much more valuable than the money. She did a good job of laundering.

Then an old woman came through with a donkey, selling new wine. I bought some. She wanted 40 lire, which is much too expensive for vin-ordinaire – but we compromised, and gave her a cake of soap and a little candy instead. A good use for the candy Janet sent me, which is poor. So is the wine – even though it stains the corn cob pipe very purple.

Money is of no value, apparently, especially, in support, here in the country, where one cannot buy anything at any price anyway. The woman could buy more wine with her money, but that is all, and she had more wine than she can use.

The poor laundry woman! She said she spent all day thinking and thinking, for she had laundry for about five men – each had a list, written in English, and she could not get it straight. She got it almost straight – after a day's thought. That's why she did not get the laundry back yesterday.

Well – here is the mail – and for me – one box of Bissinger's candy from Aunt Ruby, Uncle Bud, Ellen and Jack[97]. Another letter to write – the candy is very excellent.

I had a fair shower today – now it is raining – what is the connection? My stove is smoking. I must try to fix it. Not very successful   tomorrow I shall have to try to get a new wick, or do something about it.

I have nothing to write – Still no mail -

I send my love -

Henry.

December 22

Dear daddy, mama and Marian -

Since it is your birthday, daddy, I name you first. I very much wish I had been able to send you a birthday present – to reach you in decent time – but I couldn't get anything. I hope the box I sent reaches you – it is a birthday and Christmas present – which may get there by Easter.

It is a rainy day, and very dull – muddy, wet, gray. But nevertheless I took a short walk a few minutes ago – just up the road, about half a mile – then in the other direction a little way. There I saw some men in a cellar – with a lot of boxes, and went in to see what was there. It was a wine cellar, and I asked if they had wine for sale. Quickly they gave one a glass to drink – and then another – and then I bought a bottle of it.

---

[97] Ruby Lowenhaupt Cronbach and Bud (Lee) Cronbach. Ruby was Abe's sister and Bud was Bessie's brother. Ellen Cronbach was their daughter married to Jack Friedman.

It is pretty fair wine – a red wine, very dry – and quite clear. They drew the first bottle from the spigot of an enormous hogshead – but it was not clear – so they put that aside and drew a bottle from the top – a bring*[?]* – and it was much better. They will never fix a price for anything – "whatever you wish," they say. I ended up paying 40 lire for the wine, which is too much – even with the two big glasses I had.

Now I am back – eating candy – really doing very little. I intend to get away from here more often – maybe go to a town tomorrow and get a list of things I need, if I can. They include writing paper. I am disappointed in now being within walking distance of a town where I can buy some paper. This is my last sheet of regular stationary, and for my next letter I shall have to begin scavenging around for such as I can find.

It is so long since I have received any mail – apparently first class mail is just not coming through – but I have received boxes and copies of *Time*, which I find very uninteresting. It is a present from Dici Schwab[98]– (Mrs. William). All very nice -

You see, I have absolutely nothing of which to write – there is no news; nothing whatsoever is happening – I am inclined to be bored – which is a satisfactory sentiment. This morning I reread the old letters I still had, and thew them away, deciding I had read them often enough.

Write soon -

Love

Henry

December 23

Dear daddy -

I just received a very gratifying letter from you – and one which I know is sound. One gets exasperated at times – and impatient and desperate and gets crazy ideas in desperation. But one does not act on them, and with the confirmation of ~~may be~~ your letter, I shall not.

Reminded of the ancient Germans, according to Tacitus, who deliberated while drunk, to prevent deceit, and postponed decision until they were sober. But that has nothing to do with the situation.

It has been raining all day – so I have been mud bound, and have nothing whatsoever of which to write. Certainly not the weather – nor of expectations, for they are too likely to be disappointed – as my tenuous hope to go to Christmas dinner with the family of a cabinet maker. So I fuel my mind with trivial things, on a day like this, and wonder about things really of no consequence – as whether or not you will receive a box I sent home – of no value, but fine – and what you will think of it – whether mama will get any pleasure of the two pieces of materials in it – and whether one would make a birthday present for Ruth – a table cloth I sent to mama – all those things of the tiniest importance.

There are many sources of disappointment, displeasure, and so forth. I am learning more and more to ignore them all.

---

[98] Not sure how she spelled her first name but it was pronounced "dc"

Also some pleasures – temporary ones – as the purchase of a bottle of wine in a beautiful wine cellar.

I am finally convinced that there is good wine and liquor in this country, not for sale for cash. What would you think of taking a piece of metal, butting it, or having it cut into pieces of one half ounce each – and sending me a few pieces? I should like to try trading on a fancy basis – but all I have is either too valuable or not valuable enough. A cake of soap is alright, but one cannot expect to get a bottle of brandy for it. People who are hiding brandy hide it for the future. One must offer to give them something which can be held in its place. So, if you wish to send me something, of permanent value, in pieces worth, say, $10.00, it would be interesting to see what could be unearthed.

I gave up a small ring I had (for which I paid $3 –) to have a watch repaired. I could not get it repaired for cash, although I offered $10.00.

I am well – and going on still -

My love -

Henry

December 24

Dear mama -

I received a wonderful batch of letters from you yesterday – and was thoroughly delighted. It has been so long, since I had heard anything.

I am particularly pleased that some package or something arrived close to your birthday maybe you can consider it a birthday present.

I finally mailed two tablecloths to you – yesterday – and hope they arrive. I have no doubt that utter confusion exists there as to what I have sent, because I repeat so often. Let me try to list them -

From North Africa:
2 leather purses
1 rug (to be sent by the merchant probably never will be)
1 box – to be sent by the merchant, probably never will be)

From Sicily: miscellaneous handkerchiefs – I believe all received, and laces and linen – I think everything sent from Sicily has been received.

From Italy – various cameos, the best in a tortoiseshell box.
1 embroidered table cloth (brownish linen with colored design)
1 cut-out linen table cloth – white
1 carved walnut box, with a piece of brocade and a piece of linen bordered with lace.
1 bracelet, a trinket, for Marian.
1 plate, primitive
1 plate, pink with a Madonna
1 plate, yellow, green and blue
1 plate, with particularly fine blue coloring on it – sky and clouds -
2 small paintings.

I think that is all – the total is a lot of junk, but it furnishes something remote to think of – and I hope to give you the pleasure of receiving packages – which I have had recently.

Not a bit of news – rain and mud, which is confusing. I shall buy some wine this afternoon, or try to. I like the native vin ordinaire, although it is new and very dry. Maybe the wine merchant will ask me into his home – I shall bring him some candy.

I enjoyed Marian's birthday card to you – and am forwarding it to Ben.

I send my love -

Henry

December 24

Dear Mrs. Gay -

I just received a box of candy from you, for which I desire to thank you very much. It is a real pleasure to receive this candy – even though I am getting so fat that I can hardly make my belt reach around me.

I have been rain and mud bound here for the past several days, and consequently have absolutely nothing of which to write, notwithstanding that the country – with chestnut groves, orchards, vineyards , is as lovely as any I have ever seen.

The date reminds me that this is Christmas eve – but celebrations are not possible. Possibly it comes down to the psalm: "How shall I sing the Lord's song in a strange land?"

I wish you a very prosperous New Year -

Henry C. Lowenhaupt

December 24

Dear mama -

I am so hard up for material of which to write letters that I grab each faint notion and write a note of it. The ideas of vacations intrigue me – and I have one, which now strikes me as perfect – but may be thoroughly unpractical. However, you have the perfect set up for it.

Suppose this as a vacation for you and Ruth, to which the others could fit in – say you want a 10 day vacation. Well, the first 10 days, ~~Ruth~~ you and daddy and Marian would visit Ruth. If her house is not big enough, she and Hyman and Haymer would come over to yours. Ruth would run the entire house hold for ten days – and be responsible for all cleaning, mending, meals, everything else – even entertainment, so that she could give you a party, or do anything else. You and daddy and Marian would be company, as if in a strange city, and you could sight-see, sleep late – do anything you do in another city. Daddy would not go downtown to work, but would show you what he knows around there, and you would be regular tourists. You would live quite as comfortably at home as anyplace else – even the best hotel. You could even have breakfast in bed.

Then the next vacation could be Ruth's and Heyman's in which they would visit you – and you and Marian would entertain them as out of town visitors – even giving them breakfast in bed – taking complete care of Haymer, so that Ruth and Hy could wander off or do anything else.

Or don't you think that would be a real vacation?

My own ideas always are that, especially for a winter vacation, cities are best – and of cities – well, there is just New York, unless Betty could be with you either in San Francisco or halfway between St. Louis and San Francisco. And if Betty could be with you even part of the time, it would make even Salt Lake City or Carson or Tucson or Los Angeles interesting.

I am well. Write on -

Henry

December 25

Is the Golden Eagle[99] still running – to Mardi Gras? if Mardi Gras exists – or Greene Packet[100]?

Last night – just before sunset – I saw a rainbow, and, as I have written, it always encourages me to see one, even though I find no tangible results from the last rainbow. But there is no occasion to be logical about it.

I am still hopeful that I shall go out to Christmas dinner – and that notwithstanding that they are probably serving a feast here. Better a dinner of peace etc.

I think that I shall not be able to go back after another box – the distance becomes too great. But I am flirting with the idea of ordering one – this time inlaid – and asking them to send it when it becomes possible to do so.

I am well – the weather is still wet, grey and cloudy. I hate holidays!

Henry

"Christmas, humbug!"

---

[99] Waterways Journal article about the Golden Eagle
https://www.waterwaysjournal.net/2021/05/24/the-str-golden-eagle-was-a-st-louis-favorite/
Post-Dispatch article about the sinking of the Golden Eagle
https://www.stltoday.com/news/local/history/a-look-back-the-day-the-golden-eagle-steamboat-sank-in-1947/article_e784b0b2-1f05-55d6-a6e8-49a54c66bbb2.html
[100] There is actually a Wikipedia page about this steamboat
https://en.wikipedia.org/wiki/Gordon_C._Greene_(steamboat)

December 25

Dear mama -

I hasten to write while, although it is raining, my memories are so pleasant. I went to Christmas dinner today, and had as delightful a time as I have had in my memory – with the cabinet-maker's family. Arrived about two thirty; they had a pleasant grate fire burning in the room, which is architecturally handsome, but quite shabbily furnished – no rug, the rickety type of furniture, like 20-year old installment plan stuff. I brought them a box of candy, as did Captain Morris – gave it to them – and we sat down to eat. A most interesting meal, and to my taste very good   notwithstanding that I had eaten a plate of turkey, peas, dressing and potatoes and butter beans first (at about 12:30. (you see, I am not lacking calories) Started out with an enormous, heaped bowl of "minestra," which was a cabbage soup, deliciously and delicately flavored – salt, pepper, a little oil, and I think a touch of thyme or marjoram. In quantity! And the broth of cabbage is always very appetizing. The cabbage, green and crisp was delightful, fragrant! Then came beef – which is always inferior quality, but this was well prepared and seasoned, and with a relish to be dreamed of – pickled peppers, mostly green, a few red, excitingly hot and fragrant, with ripe olives in it. Which made it rich. That relish, with a slice of black bread crust – I have not eaten such a delicacy! And good, dry red wine with it, flowing in abundance.

Next – fried chicken (friend in olive oil, a little garlic) almost like broiled, done perfectly – with french fried potatoes. The chicken was most unusual – the drum stick was dry and almost white – and I remembered again what a delicacy chicken should be. The french fried potatoes – soft all the way through, perfect! That dish was a masterpiece, and I can't describe it – only dream of it and remember it as one thing I shall, if I behave, find again in heaven. So chicken is quite an inducement to a virtuous life, and French fried potatoes lead to morality.

Then (and I was full) walnuts and apples, with more wine – and apples and walnuts happen to be a good combination. Add wine – well!

Then, after about an hour, a glass of anisette a cup of coffee, (strong and sweet, demi tasse) and anisette and cookies – little crisp things, like pretzels in short sticks, but not salty, and they were sweet – a little taste of cinnamon – very crisp, hard and dry, and an almond cake – flat, chewy, like a macaroon, but drier, with whole and ground almonds in it.

I cannot describe the feast as it deserves to be described.

In the interludes of dinner – There was quite a crowd there – we sang the old familiars of Italian opera – and even I (wine does it, I think) was asking "Do you know - -" and bursting into my best rendition of "Celeste Aida" and "Caro mio ben" and "L'esperto nocchiero" and Chi vuol innamorarsi." And La Donna é mobilè" in chorus, and "'Ve Marie" – until we even came to something that sounded like "Ippee appee ai ay!" The last I did not sing. No one was drunk, indications to the contrary notwithstanding. I sat next to Matthew (Matteo) D'Alterio, who spoke French, and we got along swimmingly. The child stood behind me, and we discussed his Latin lesson (amo amas amat – rosa, rosae, roseae rosam rosa – the same everywhere it seems) and it apparently pleases them no end to find someone who had heard of, say, Michael Angelo, and Verdi and Puccini, and who recites, in what must be a very drôle accent – "nel mzzo del cammin di nostra vità - -"[101] and they go on – and 'zita zita! Senya parlar'" and "Lasciate igni speranga[102] - " Would it give you personal pleasure, I wonder, if Mr. Gusdorf should, on no provocation, start out "Of Man's First Disobedience and the fruit - - -" and "To be or not to be - - -" and "In the beginning, God created Heaven and Earth."

But anyway, we had an awfully jolly time – and I was invited to come down and dance all night New Year's Eve. I declared – it seems too hard to get there.

Well, for the present, it appears I shall not get to the City again – the horsemen of the Apocalypse come upon it -

Then we took leave of the D'Alterios - I was very soundly kissed on both cheeks by the whole family – children (little boy of about 8, girl of about six) sons – boy of about 20, and boy of about 25 – uncles, aunts, parents, grandparents – my cheeks are getting callused – and I do not know how to be kissed – it is an unnatural gesture of friendship. So I shook hands too.

Looked for our driver – and seeing a store opened, I went in and asked for stove wick (sold out) and paper. They showed me this. "How much." "Ten lire." I saw the woman's husband nudge her. "I'll take three packets." She gave them to me, and I handed her 50 lire, expecting change. "No, she said." And I multiplied then by three on my fingers. But it was 10 for the envelopes, 10 for the paper, and 10 for the wrapper and 10 for something I could not understand – good measure, I suppose. Made 120 lire. So I took only one - and paid her price – 40 lire – because I did not want to spend time there. It was getting dark. Fortunately, the driver had, at my request, bought me three other packets – for a total of 40 lire. Maybe the quality is inferior.

I am well. I enjoyed this afternoon very, very much – even with a constant memory of:

"How shall we sing the Lord's song in a strange land?"

I send my love -

Henry

When I bought the paper, I forgot to see if there was glue on the envelopes. My pet peeve – to have to paste them shut. I've come to the test now -

H

26 December

Dear daddy -

I received your letter – and was very much interested in the financial summary of the firm's business to December 1 of this year. I am happy that it came out so well. I suppose expenses are bound to go up – they are always carefully hard to cut down.

---

[101] Quotation from the opening of Canto 1 from Dante's *Divine Comedy*.
https://digitaldante.columbia.edu/dante/divine-comedy/inferno/inferno-1/
[102] Translates to "Abandon all hope, ye who enter." Quotation from Canto 3 of *Inferno*
https://digitaldante.columbia.edu/dante/divine-comedy/inferno/inferno-3/

The purchase of war bonds is alright with me – more than alright, of course. I have in mind, however, the limitation to $10000 maturity value in any one year of certain bonds. I am inclined to fear I may have exceeded that in 1943, for I purchased a considerable amount before April, 1943. You might be able to check on that.

I read in a newspaper not long ago (the paper was about a month or six weeks old) that distiller's stocks (by which maybe they meant whiskey and maybe they meant shares) were having a boom. I own ten shares of National Distillers – and have held onto it for a while doubting whether to purchase more or sell that. What would you think of selling that? It pays good dividends – as I remember, about 10% on my cost – but if the price has gone up substantially, the dividend is so longer so good – unless increased – and there is no reason for holding it longer.

My cash finances here are in good shape. While I am spending almost fantastically – I mean paying outrageous prices for many things – I am not spending all I get, and have accumulated a sufficient reserve of pocket cash for almost anything. I wrote a check on my account for $10.00 in favor of American Friends Service Committee[103]– it may go through, though not on the printed form.

I have some memory of writing either you or Hy, asking if you could have a piece of metal cut up in small pieces, and sent to me for attempted trading – mostly for fun. I'm not sure I wrote – therefore repeat.

No news – it is cold out – and a heavy wind – I am well -

Affectionately -

Henry

I had a very merry, even jolly, Christmas yesterday – and hope you did too – Happy New Year – I feel confident it will bring me home with peace. "Spe enim salvi facti sumu[104]"

H

December 26

Dear mama -

I wrote everything I have to write last night – and today can add only about the weather – that a howling wind has come up, with a little rain – and it has turned cold. I suppose it is now winter – and I do not know what to do about it.

Today I intend to bring laundry out – a small bundle – but it is better to send it in small bundles, because one may depart and be unable to get it back. I have been intending for a long time to go to a town where there is a sales store, and get some extra pants and shirt – and sooner or later shall get there, although I keep postponing it for no sufficient reason.

---

[103] Throughout his life, Henry gave an annual gift to the American Friends Service Committee. They used to visit him every year to thank him.
[104] Romans 8:24

I am well – regretting extremely that to all appearances I shall not get back to the city I like so well – for I had just begun to discover my way around that city and where to look for things. But maybe the reason will abate, and I shall again go there. ~~Or~~

Just received your letter that Irma[105] is back – and am very glad, because (1) I think probably Irma is better off there – more comfortable living and all else, and (2) I am sure you are – more comfortable eating, especially.

I suppose I have exhausted the subject of Christmas dinner.

I just took a very short walk, up the road, stopping along the way to ask for stove wick. I have a makeshift wick, consisting of tangled string and blotting paper, which works for the present. I was unsuccessful. I think I shall write a V mail letter asking for some to be sent air mail. I may write to Sears Roebuck, direct, asking them to send me one – and see what gets here.

The women – dress in their Sunday best – beautiful red shawls, I think hand woven (not knitted, at any rate) I was tempted to try to buy one – but did not have the courage to try to buy the clothes off a peasant's back. Maybe some other day I shall.

Wine is abundant here – I have two bottles on hand – and my inquiry into stove wicks along the road led me to a glass of wine as a gift in a lovely, dark, deep wine cellar.

I am well. You say in your letter that you think I would not tell you if I were not. Quite mistaken! I delight in complaining about anything – if only I could find something to complain of.

All my love – I am impatient to get home – but when I think of being in the army at home vs. being in it here, I'd rather be here. Do you want to send me things? Trousers and shirts would always be useful (wool) but I can get them here, when I can go about 30 miles after them. The best kind is brown – in contrast to "green." Not green, but brown – not more than one of each.

Henry

27 December

Dear mama -

Today is magnificent! I revoke all my complaints about weather – it is crisp and clear, with a raging north wind, which is drying up the ground, making it solid again. It reminds me of some verses, which are irrelevant, but run in my mind – if you want them correct, you'd better read the original – (Henryson – *Testament of Cresseid*[106]
"A cairful season to a doleful dight
Suld corres pound and be equivalent.
Right sar it was quhen I began to write

---

[105] I think Irma was a cook

[106] The Testament of Cresseid from University of Rochester –
https://d.lib.rochester.edu/teams/text/kindrick-poems-of-robert-henryson-testament-of-cresseid
The Testament of Cresseid from Internet Shakespeare -
https://internetshakespeare.uvic.ca/doc/Henryson_Cresseid/section/The%20Testament%20of%20Cresseid%20by%20Master%20Robert%20Henryson/index.html

The Elegy – The frost freesid, - - -
The northern wind had purified the air
And swept the misty cloude's fra
the sky - -"

You would enjoy the Henryson anyway for his vivid descriptions of weather.

Well – I might as well write what is on my mind – I am sticking my neck out – feeling that the two men who are with me are sticking too close around this place – I sent one of them into town today, on the pretense that he should buy some wick. Not a pretense, because I hope he does buy some, but fear that he can't find any. My real reason was to give him a chance to get out of here for a while, for it is very confining around here. It is hard, though, because he hasn't much sense – talks too much. Well – I may get bawled out – which really does not worry me. The other man is more of a problem – I cannot go with him, because that would leave only one man here. I know if I ~~le~~ send him to town, he will make a bee line for one saloon after another, and while he says he never gets drunk, I believe he gets happy enough to play little practical jokes, in good humor, on passing strangers. No harm – unless someone stops him, and he gets asked why he's there. That would leave me holding the bag for his jolly time – besides, he is red-headed, and conspicuous anyplace. I can't say he's dumb, but he has a one track mind, so that if he were reading a paper, and a fire broke out, he would merely put the fire extinguisher job on the list of his agenda. His mind works in a way I can't comprehend – a little wooly, but quick in some things. A genius for blundering and forgetting – but nice and likeable. He is a very faithful Catholic, when his mind is on that track – but as completely irreligious as anyone could be, when it is on another. But I am gambling – I shall risk getting my neck in a sling some day, and see how it feels.

Long interruption – during which Lt. Clark and Lt. Boone came in to see me – and we talked for about half hour, and drank wine (dry, nutty, quite good) Lt. Clark is going tomorrow to a resort hotel – called a rest – to spend three days. Each takes his turn – I shall go December 29 – to be there the ~~29th, 30th and~~ 30th, 31st, and 1st. I do not like being there over New Years – but the choice is not mine. It is always considered such a privilege that one cannot say one does not want to go. The place is famous – and if I should name it, Aunt Sally or Mrs. Myer or anybody could tell you what kind of place it is.

Then I took a shower – lovely and warm while in – and very cold coming out. There I saw Lt. Masser – whom I haven't seen since Sicily. I asked him to come over here, sometime, for I enjoy his company – an Englishman – kind of shop keeper type.

All my love -

Henry

December 27

Dear mama -

Mail is now coming through again – and I received today your letter of November 28 – one month! You see by this that I got more stationary, and now I am well stocked – at least for a while.

I am very happy that Marian is feeling well. So am I -

As for fabrics – of which I should like to buy some – I have seen a little silk, at $3.50 a yard – and a little wool, which I have not priced, because it has been inferior. Linen is rare – all fabrics seem to be rare, as all commodities. You have no idea how commodity-less this country is – the things they have being those which can be whipped up in a few minutes or hours. As a sample – I wanted to have a shirt sewn – no trouble finding a tailor, but I had to furnish the thread – I gave the tailor a needle, and he apparently considered it a fine gift.

You see things appearing gradually – yesterday I saw a woman spinning flax – I think it was flax – a brownish color – into thread. She had her spindle almost filled – a ball about a big as two fists. My guess is that in about three weeks, she may have a piece of linen. But that is very slow – and she could sell as much as could be made my machinery. But there is no machinery where the raw products are, and no way of getting the products to the machinery. To haul flax, say, fifty miles by donkey just wouldn't work. So the materials available are those which are drawn out by the owner's need for cash – and search out with much tedious labor by people who know the markets very well. But I shall keep on looking – I do not see the use of buying wool – inferior imitations of English suiting – of which I have seen on or two bolts. I somewhat regret not having bought a little silk brocade, but I know where I can get a little, if I ever get back there. Presently, I am not near a town, but next time I see a handsome shawl, I may try to buy it off the woman's back – or if I see the woman spinning, I shall see if I can order a piece of home spun, home woven linen – although I suspect the demand for thread here in the country is such that she may never get it farther than thread. You do not want some very fine linen thread, do you?

I am glad that Haymer received the little picture I sent – I sent another one, in a larger box, with other things – have forgotten the subjects, but considered both quite graceful and charming. Of course, to send a picture to Ruth (or Haymer) is dangerous, because Ruth had definite judgement (I don't). But if Ruth does not want it around the house, she can make a present of it to Betty.

I am well – shall quit this rambling – Love -

Henry

December 28

Dear mama -

I suppose I am writing too often – but I have to show you very good variety of stationary – and so frequently I think – and it just comes to mind that I want to write – and nothing else. So I write – notwithstanding that there is a movie I could go to – Jane Eyre[107] – and that I have written once today and have nothing to say.

But I just received two letters from you, and one dated the 13th of December (good time!) and one the 29th of November (usual time.) How can one calculate the order in which letters will arrive – each letter must be independent and reference must never be made to anything previously written, I suppose. So I write again anyway – and desire to write about the weather and landscape, which have been so exciting today. I wish I could describe them – you must read some of Robert Henryson to see how these big aspects of nature can be first lines of *The Testament of Cresseid*. There are other passages in the same author, about which you would be excited.

Today, there has been a violent north east wind all day, cold, drying out the ground so that one can walk upon it again, and purifying the air, driving the clouds from the sky. So it had been clear – and for the first

---

[107] Jane Eyre (1943) starring Orson Welles and Jane Fontaine.
https://en.wikipedia.org/wiki/Jane_Eyre_(1943_film)

time I have seen the magnificent color of the mountains – it is like a revelation – the sudden realization that this is winter (and I can't help thinking of the hermit St. Jerome: "O delicate soldier (of Christ) whom winter under canvas terrifies!") and then I see all the beauties of winter – the rolling ground, grown up in the ravines and on the steps of the terracing in ferns, now brown and brittle, but comfortable to the tread – the barren trees – grass most places, still green. The wind howls. Then the mountains! They have grown shinning white in places near the tops – a close hill is apastel green – marked with white – and the more remote ridges purple and lavender and grey and blue and black – Then changing constantly with changes in color, and as the sun gets low, they take on a brilliancy such as I have never seen. The villages and houses upon them glisten – some big towns spreading up ravines – some single, isolated houses standing along – all at their distance looking immaculate.

The realization of this dazzling beauty came on me so suddenly today – I suppose it is like being converted to a new religion, to see this sun and color after weeks of gray clouds and mist, and wind and rain.

Today also I called for my laundry, which I had left at a neighboring farm house or village – I am not sure which it is – and was very much interested in going in – such as architectural building – and such mazes and labyrinths – One enters through a great, arched gate, into a court yard, with a big sow running around, and chickens rushing away cackling from under your feet. (Eggs cost 15 to 20 cents each and it is unsafe to let chickens out) a few goats in the courtyard and one sheep – quite lonely looking. Through the courtyard, and to the right, is a little stairway, four heavy, oak stairs, worn round, going right into the wall – and at the top, a heavy, plank oak door, with a forged latch just too high for the child who was leading me to reach. But in one motion, she yells "mama," and scrambles up, raises the latch and pushes the door – quite agilely. I enter – up very steep steps now, with a hole in the wall through which a chicken flies and a pigeon follow, going into a manger which is beyond the hole – a mere peep hole into quite a spacious barn. I cannot imagine where the exit from this barn can be – there is no door from the court – and the building is surrounded on all sides. At the top of the steps, a room about 15 feet long and ten wide, with a great, carved stone fireplace in one side – one big window opening onto a small area way – a kitchen table of oak, and a rush-bottom chair, in which I am invited to sit down. The lady of the house (or at least a lady, clean looking, and surprisingly, fair haired; thin, bony and strong looking, intelligent face) is cooking over the fireplace – most of the smoke is coming out into the room, and not going up the chimney. A big, iron pot, on a little stand. She knows my errand remembering me – and goes up a ladder to the next story , brings back my laundry, neatly done, and counts it out. It is right. "How much?" I ask. "Whatever you wish," she replies, and I gave her 50¢. Too much or too little? I don't know. One shirt, one pair of trousers, one bath towel, one pair of leggings, two pairs of socks, four handkerchiefs. She seems content and I give her a box of candy for the children. She goes over to a corner (I saw no door in the room – no exit, except up the ladder. Was this the dwelling of her family? Two children were there) and pours me a glass of wine – which is good here – dry and nutty in flavor. And I am to come again, as I shall, d. v.

Hospitality even over laundry! I think maybe she makes her profit in the soap – I gave her a whole cake of Palmolive – large size – to wash the clothes, and observed a piece of Lifebuoy stuck in a hole in one legging. So she did not use the soap I gave her. So I felt, having enjoyed the whole transaction very much.

This letter is much longer than I intended -

Love -

Henry

December 30

Dear mama -

I must ignore the season and the years. It would be nice if, they meant some-thing, but they don't. I won't requote the 137th Psalm, although it is in my mind again, with the end of the year.

Yesterday I received three cartons of cigarettes, I suppose from Philip, for which I shall thank him. Conversations with natives are expensive in cigarettes – One gives them one each to smoke – if by chance two protrude from the package, the native takes two and pockets one. That's alright too. But I think I prefer first class mail to packages any day – a sentiment I may overcome when packages are exhausted. Presently I am eating (and enjoying) coffee toffee and salted peanuts. I have lost my appetite for sweets – but expect to regain it soon. Really, roasted chestnuts and wine are much more delicate, but after a time, one comes almost to crave candy – except hard candy life savers and fruit drops.

I am happy that Haymer received the small picture I sent – have forgotten whether I considered it the superior or inferior of two I got. The other is with a plate, and I surely hope it arrives. It should have come by this time, for it was sent back in November – However – maybe it hasn't. Small packages seem to arrive much more promptly than big ones.

I expect to go tomorrow to a resort hotel for two days – do not know what I shall do there – but expect to sleep a good deal, and whatever else there is to do. I shall see. One man here asks me to pick up a painted and inlaid box he has ordered – I shall do so, although I hate to, because I know that it will be a shiny atrocity. The thought makes me impatient to receive a comment from you and daddy on the carved box I sent. I shall try to find some material – cloth – but most of the "tissuti" stores are close for lack of merchandise.

All my love -

Henry

December (Not Dated) [Letters included within the original order of December 1943 letters, but lacking a specific date.]

This letter is like the thrust – If you did not believe the first time that such a picture would exist – here are two more. A nightmare? From the picture, of what crime would you judge me guilty?

Henry

December (Not Dated)

without great fear. We bought a honey-dew melon this afternoon, and ate it – not quite ripe, but otherwise excellent.

We also tried to buy some Italian currency – but the bank is closed. Presently, it is considered that a lire is worth about 1¢. It may be that we shall not use lire; but if we do, I imagine an exchange will be fixed much higher. Well – I suppose I could buy some if I tried hard (although language is a difficulty, and the only business being done is barber shops) but it does not make much difference – one spends so little, and I doubt that I shall find much if anything for sale.

I am now writing on conquered paper – having cut off the heading, least it be taken to disclose my exact location, which may be specified only as in Sicily. Maybe in a few weeks I shall *be [portion missing]* itled to use this paper *[portion missing]* off the top.

What paperwork went on in this building! Folders and folders on foods, individuals; rolls and rolls of paper – I wish I had it at home – case after case of records – the place is almost like the Treasury Department in Washington although only for a small province.

It is a magnificent, fine mansion – and very beautiful – and enormous. I speak now of the building. But I have never much admired wooden Italian furnishings – they look like imitations of Renaissance, with pressed wood instead of carving. All the finery of marble, without the delicate skill necessary to give marble more charm than a tombstone. The best things are tapestry – and I would put some in my bedding roll if (1) They were not too bulky, (2) they were mot rumored to be lousy and (3) it were legal. (Order of importance) I send my love -

Henry

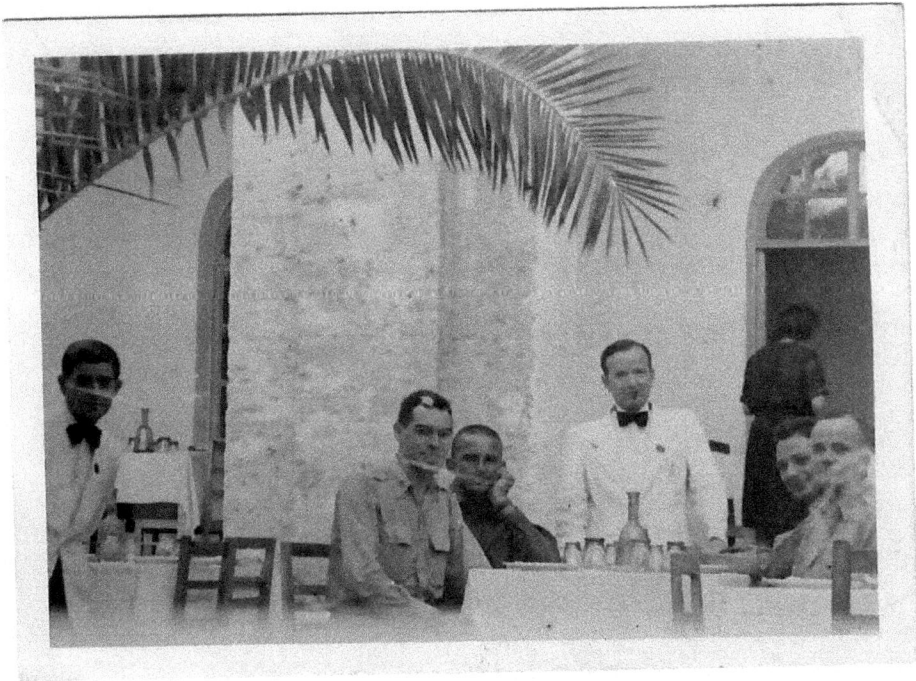

1944
LETTERS

January 1

Dear mama -

This is my first letter of the year but I'll ignore that. I am writing for a few minutes before I go to bed (in a bed with sheets) from a hotel which is being used as a vacation hotel – a beautifully located place, with excellent meals, and in a village lovelier than any you can imagine – tightly built on narrow streets – many arches – little parks, at the top of the cliff, overlooking the sea, far below. Across the bay – which is a blue emerald, with white caps, the mountains are covered in cloud, and now and then one glimpses a patch of thin snow.

I have walked the streets all day – yesterday afternoon I walked also, although it was raining, and found two very beautiful Capodimonte cups – which I have sent home. I sat down in the shop, over a charcoal brazier, and drank anise with the proprietor and his family.

Today, seeing a church with a sign about exhibition of art, I went in – a kind of house next door – and found three nuns selling sewing and inlaid boxes made at the nunnery and monastery. I almost bought an inlaid box there, although I consider them quite hideous – but got onto the subject of what they called "testamenta fidei" (They brought out a folio for me, when I told them I was Catholic, which is so much easier than having a religious discussion, and the monks were around)– Apparently whenever any one takes order, he or she writes, as a work of devotion, one sheet, usually a quotation from the New Testament, in Latin – they make a study of it, apparently, for there was a magnificent collection – Carlovingian, Lombardy (Lamgobardian), Gothic, Classic, etc., designs, with borders – like the medieval illuminations. Must take a year to make one – but they are not for sale – they go into the archives of the church.

They were so beautiful that I abandoned all thought of a silly inlaid box – and instead bought two cards, as suggestion of the illuminations, which I could not get.

They also bind books for the church library – and I saw a magnificently bound set of St. Augustine.

What a confusion of language! One sister spoke a little French, another Latin and a third only Italian – between the three, I got so confused that I did not know what I was doing. Then, at the suggestion of the sisters, I went to see the monks – there were about five of them, enjoying a kind of cookie which is the New Year's cookie – with wine. Not particularly ascetic, for the cookies were excellent. It was funnier than anything imaginable, for (having been looking at their copy of St. Augustine) discussion came to a comparison of Augustine and the Greek philosophers (about which none of us knew much) – with a fundamental recognition that the Greeks lacked inspiration. A discussion in slow, bad Latin, which was quite a handicap to ideas – but all things considered we got along amazingly, over wine and cookies, for about an hour – and the discussion (I understood what I tried to say) seemed to me to indicate that "inspiration" and "sentiment" or "feeling" are about the same. Augustine lacks the clear, concise logic of the Greeks, but if you have the same "feeling," he is just as convincing. Upon the assumption, then, that Augustine was inspired, he was much greater than the Greek Philosophers, because his subjects are broader and his influence bigger.

So I send the two religious cards – which, please, feel free to give away if you know anyone who would like them. They are of no gre value, intrinsically, but too fine to give to local urchins, to see the effect. I had my hypothetical pleasure of buying them – of which I am somewhat ashamed.

I shall write more. Now I am tired.

Love Henry

(over)

P.S. – Since everyone buys inlaid boxes, I bought the cheapest one I could find – it is no better than the usual hard curlicues– and maybe I shall send it home, for the suggestion of color. Maybe I shall destroy it. The Monastery of S. Paolo[108] had quite fine p inlay, or marquetry of holy subjects – if she can stand blood from the cross in trickling mahogany or rose-wood, and similar representations. But inlaying seems to be the local fad – I do not think the natives like it (they don't use it), but they believe Americans do. Maybe so – an ebony and kingwood lectern can be quite striking.

H

January 3

Dear Marian -

I can imagine how pretty your room must be coming to be – and with pretty things in it – (some say they make it hard to dust – if mama is of that school, get John or Walter[109] to build you a glass-doored what-not cabinet) and yesterday I mailed to mama two little cups – representative of Capodimonte second and third periods – did not buy the first period, because it had no color. Take your choice, and keep one of them in your room. They are prides and joys.

You see, I was on a spree yesterday and the two preceding days. I was in a resort – which looks like war never touched it – lights, even across the bay, and great natural splendor – I could write pages about it, it was so lovely. Beds, with sheets, sometimes running water – excellent meals, well served, with music and dancing and singing – a beautiful view from the hotel, across the bay, at the mountains, lightly covered with snow, and the town (with lights! the lights of Europe are coming back on again!)

And what a town! The character of this coast is much of that of the coast of Brittany – remember the Pension Roch Amour[110] *[sic]*? Steep cliffs to the sea – and hills well cultivated. Oranges are magnificent now – and olive trees have a lovely texture – The town has narrow streets, twisting and complicated – with high buildings and many arches. The hotel in a park of orange and lemon trees – I wandered through the town for my few days – into a monastery, of which I have written to mama.

I made a few purchases – the two cups, for whose safe arrival I fervently hope – pets again – one table cloth, quite pretty, but bought for pleasure of buying in large part, and selected partly because I cannot make up my mind to so called cut-work, which is linen with little pieces cut out – like folding a piece of paper and snipping for a design. I sent the table cloth as a gift to mama – and napkins and little finger bowl towels to Ruth – write me about the condition which comes about, if any. I sent it that way as a compromise.

---

[108] San Paolo Convent in Parma, Italy
https://en.wikipedia.org/wiki/San_Paolo,_Parma
[109] The two Gusdorf boys living with the Lowenhaupts
[110] Not sure what this is

The lady who sold it to me said she gave me a special price as her first customer of the New Year. ("How shall we sing the Lord's song in a strange land?") And I did her the favor of helping her in an act of charity to two Catholic sisters, who had brought in a can of bean soup, which they had received to feed their poor. I translated the label into French for them – really having trouble with such terms as "Yankee Bean soup concentrate" and "~~Pr~~ Grade A navy beans," and while ¼ cup of soup to 1 cup of water, was easy, just try "the contents of this can to 1 ¼ gallons of water." What is the French word for "navy bean" – I am sure it is not "haricot de marine" So I called it just an haricot – something like petit pois but yellow.

Which led to a discussion of food prices and "black" (some economists would say "free") market. The lady (Madame Galloni) said she had 12 people to feed, herself and 11 orphans whom she had taken in after the last war, and who, through grown, had just stayed on. (If each of them takes 11, that will make a family of 122 – as I was going to St. Ives!) So every morning, she would think in bed of what to feed them, and finally get up with a headache. One simply had to have a good soup, whatever else one had – but what could one make soup of? With pasti at 70¢ a kilo and eggs at 30¢ a piece – one can't live on oranges and apples – all of which I suppose is true!

In the barber shop, I saw a farmer trying to sell a chicken – he asked $7.00 for it – and came down to $5.50. But the man wouldn't pay the price.

Then, as a de rigeur of the place, I finally bought an inlaid box, which I so disliked after I had it, that I sent it to Janet Cerf – I look forward with my tongue in my cheek to a letter of thanks!

Another day – yesterday afternoon, I took a walk up the hill, beyond the town, through groves covered with mats to protect from frost, past a waterfall, always overlooking the sea and mountains across the bay; saying "buon giorno" to all passers for practice – stopped in a little saloon and had two big glasses of good cider (they call it wine), where a little girl asked for stamps – I had none – but told her I would send her some – Laura Cappuro, Via Capo U. 28[111]. (geographical location, Anonymous, Italy.) Soldiers had taught her that, as she filled glasses, she must say "Drink Up," and so she chirped – a smart child – precocious – and her mother and grandmother sat in the corner and beamed.

Write often, Marian; I enjoy your letters very much.

Affectionately -

Henry

January 5

Dear Ruth and Hy -

I have been anxious to write to you and Hy for a long time – and, of course, never have anything to add to the letters I write home. But now I might as well write to you, and, although I repeat what I have already

---

[111] A street by the name of Via Capo can be found in Sorrento, Italy. This may be the location Henry is in. It is near Naples, where he likely was stationed around. It is also located on a bay with mountains in the distance.
Via Capo U. 28 via GoogleMaps
https://www.google.com/maps/place/Via+Capo,+Sorrento+NA,+Italy/@40.6256592,14.358876,17.46z/data=!4m5!3m4!1s0x133 b9ea2187dfbeb:0x8031120deb4038a5!8m2!3d40.6262843!4d14.3595753
Sorrento, Italy Wikipedia
https://en.wikipedia.org/wiki/Sorrento

written, I at least have the variety of writing it to someone else. And you have the variety of colors of envelope linings.

I have returned now from a kind of two days' vacation at a place you would enjoy loafing in – it is so very beautiful – overlooking the bay – mountains on the other side – steep cliffs on my side. And all the country around the town completely cultivated in beautiful orange groves, lemon groves, olive gloves – except the sheet precipices which abound in waterfalls. It is almost too perfectly idyllic to be true – like trite phraseology from Pope – purling rills and mossy banks.

And the town itself – a gem!

The hotel was kind of fun at night – a dance New Year's Eve – Of course, the men were mostly soldiers – except a few chaperones, to whom I had no occasion to speak. Ladies quite scarce – two classes – 1) nurses, who, if I may venture, are in general, a low crowd. That is, they are quite ignorant, uninspired girls, who put on uniforms. But the uniforms do not make them more interesting or agreeable than plain nurses and servant girls at home. They are still frowsy minded. 2) The native girls, to whom an opportunity to go to this hotel is a privilege, and who are probably the best of the town. So I danced with native girls – and found it very interesting, for there is no one finer than a fine Italian. These girls were educated, I think, to be charming after the French ideal. They were excellent conversationalists, in an easy, agreeable way. Some had studied in France – very cosmopolitan – and they spoke French. They were very delightful people – and, believe me, they come heavily chaperoned – both parents and usually at least one grandparent, who sit at a table, and after each dance come out and get the girl, bow to you, and bring the girl back to their table. So, for another dance, one must go up to the chaperones and ask. The chaperones will not dance – and they abhor the custom of cutting in, which to a considerable extent circumvents their ~~all~~ vigilance. They do not with that custom, meet each dancing partner.

I expected to be able to celebrate with a hot bath – but the power was off most of the time I was there – no running water in the pipes – and I did not have a bath. No loss – I should be dirty by this time anyway.

The merchandising situation in the town is as always – little for sale, and at high prices. Except delicious oranges, apples and nuts. Mostly junk. But what is called "black market" – I was offered fine liquor by the hotel violinist – 30 yr. old Black and White whiskey, at $37.50 a quart. The price seemed excessive. Old cognac – at $25.00 a litre – Champagne at $20 a litre, and so forth. Good liquor is all being hoarded – and comes out in dribbles as the owner needs cash.

I had a good time in a monastery – I always admire and enjoy people who can discuss purely abstract, irrelevant subjects with enthusiasm – as these monks discussed Augustine and Plato – realistically. It seems to me a mark of a trained and interested mind.

I am well – Give Haymer my regards – and tell him to write soon too.

Henry

January 5

Dear mama:

One writes right now under some difficulty, because the lights are out. If one opens the tent for light, one gets much air – and it is very cold. And windy – well – I have nothing to write ~~anyw~~ anyway – and finally soon the lights will be on again anyway. For now I give up.

Now the lights are on – it does not help me to say much – for I feel I have already written about all I can of the resort I visited a few days ago – partly to you and partly to Marian. Still my mind is full of it, and as I remember it, I enjoy it more and more – the beauty of the mountains across the bay – with their thin snow and trailing, smoky clouds. I sent some things home, already mentioned – which I hope you receive – they are -

1) a tablecloth – large, in what the sales woman called "Church" linen – I think you call it handkerchief linen. You will note a defect – a very small hole – which added to its availability and can possibly be mended. I send the napkins to Ruth – leaving it to you and her to make any desired consolidation.

I bought a box, because that seemed to be a standard of the place, but did not like it well enough to send to you – so sent it to Janet Cerf, who may like it – or not.

My pride and joy, though, were first, two cups and saucers – one of which Marian may desire to keep in her room – (or both, of course) and two little religious cards – articles of bigotry and virtue, if you like. But they suggest very fine work which I saw and could not obtain.

The weather is cold now – cloudy and gray – with a strong wind. We are in a new place – again an olive grove, with a great mountain rising sheer on one side – and a road on the other – rather a deserted road, except for a few imbeciles who sell chestnuts. The chestnuts are good. There is a town about two miles away – and I shall try to get there. Although I understand the walk is mostly straight up.

I am well – and send my love – write soon and often.

Henry

January 6

Dear mama -

I am striving for greater variety in my letters – hence this two-toned effect.

Well – now the weather is about all I am thinking of – it is beautiful today, bright and clear but quite cold. This morning all the puddles were frozen – a trace of snow, not falling, because the sky is clear, but blowing down in the heavy wind from the mountains. The olive trees, in which we are, still hold their leaves, which rustle and dance in the wind.

Unfortunately, I see little of it, for I am in a tent – and to keep warm, one closes it.

I intend soon – maybe tomorrow – to take a walk outside of the area – and see what there is – I have heard descriptions of a town about two miles away – which is said to be beautifully situated -

I am well – enjoy your letters, but, unfortunately, mail has not been coming for the past few days. So I have little of which to write -

This evening I expect to have a party – I got two loaves of bread from the kitchen. A man who had no bread, had a few little packages of cheese which he received from home (cheese to Italy should be like coals to Newcastle – but it isn't – there is no cheese here) So we shall divide – I give him bread, he gives me cheese – and we both have sandwiches. Night before last (the cooks are friends of mine) – I procured about a pound of sliced turkey – and I now have on hand a dozen oranges. We are now out of the orange growing country.

The wind is howling – and I have nothing to write.

I think of the first plate I sent home, which should have arrived by now – I hope it had – I have somewhat forgotten it, except that I remember a general, soft, pink color, with the head of a lady. I wish you would describe some of these things, and tell me of them – because I have no standard of comprehension – and may simply be completely off center – I should, I suppose, quit buying table linen, or I shall crowd you out of the house with it. I have not been able to find any fabrics in bolts are or big pieces, but shall continue looking.

I send my love -

Henry

January 6

To Mrs. A. Lowenhaupt
6237 McPherson Ave
Saint Louis
Missouri

Dear mama -

I just completed one V-Mail letter to you – and now continue – The jist of the one just written – I am well. I took a short walk this afternoon down the road a little way, to a main highway, leading someplace – and then back. What a wind in my face! blowing stones and everything – so I cut through the olive groves, where the wind was strong but no stones throwing blowing. (Read Ernie Pyle's book – chapter 7[112] – about a red-headed boy, and you'll what distressed me to write "throwing" when I meant "blowing.") Ahead of me, snow covered mountains, glistening in the sun.

Well – I have been trying awfully hard to think of something to ask you to send me – I suppose the only thing possible is edibles – and I suppose most things which can be sent are rationed. I am now out of chestnuts, and must look for more. I have a pocket full of dried figs given to me today. Nuts and fruit are abundant. The desirables – chocolate, meat, cheese, fish and the like – but God forbid Vienna sausage packed in water! (Armour & Co, I think) and Campbell's meat and vegetable stew. Well – I need nothing, of course, and doubtless if I receive a package shall be situated where I didn't want it.

Love

Henry

(V Mail is *[word unclear]*)

---

[112] Reference to *Here Is Your War* by Ernie Pyle
Via Internet Archive
https://archive.org/details/hereisyourwar0000unse/page/86/mode/2up?view=theater

January 7

To Mrs. A. Lowenhaupt
6237 McPherson Ave
Saint Louis
Missouri

Dear mama -

You are, I am sure, the writer of the finest and most delightful letters ever written – and the greatest pleasure there is – greater than sitting in the sun and seeing the panoramic valley from the ruins of an ancient castle to which I climbed today – is to receive your letters. Even your letter of December 20, in which you urge me, in orders that you may be sure I'm telling you the truth, to tell you I'm sick. I would tell you so, to convince you I am well, but the letter talking of my recovery might miscarry, or be dubious, So I gotta stick to the truth – the best policy. I am well.

Since the letters you mention, just look at the accumulation of circumstances – I have dined with D'Alterios twice. I have been to cities – I have walked miles – I have climbed to this town – of which I wrote today. I recovered my strength quickly -

I just received a couple of pounds of Malty Milkies from National Candy Co. I no longer need sweets – but still enjoy them. I enjoy anything to eat – the tailor did do poorly on my pants I am trying to grow to size 40 *[word unclear]* compensates.

Send my love -

Henry

January 7

Dear mama -

I just returned from a walk with a double purpose. 1) When I was on my 2 day pass, I bought a pair of pants – as close to my size as obtainable, which was 40" waist and about 38" long. I wanted to bring them to a tailor and have them cut down. Then I wanted to stop at the doctor's to see if I needed any inoculations. The latter was quietly concluded, and I need nothing for a month. No more of that – I walked up to the village – about two miles level and about 500 feet straight up. The town is on steps on a cliff – and a narrow cobbled path zigzags up through the town, here and there through vaulted archways, sometimes opening out over the valley, planted in regular rows of olives. It commands a great view. The village is crowded together, along the paths, over the archways – and at the top of the fill, the ruins of an old castle – The buildings open onto the street beautifully – arched doorways, carved doors – here and there a very tiny door – or a simple door leading into a stable. Pigs run through the streets – and some pigs are kept tied up by the hind legs – chickens (beauties!) and dogs.

I looked through one arched doorway into what must have been the single room of a dwelling. A built in fireplace and stove – only small, high windows – stone floor – a work bench, a sewing table (primitive, Ruth would go crazy about this furniture) a cradle made of hewn boards, and painted with pictures of the Virgin (without a child in her arms – I wonder? A suggestion that this might be the child, returned?) I imagine the cradle was very old. The people of the town all look much alike – except some, who seem to have chosen it as a refuge from war – and have chosen well – it is high on the hill, and untouched by bombs and shells. There were some of these in the tailor shop, and they looked like smart alecs and misfits. Many tiny people – almost dwarfs, especially women – and others of normal size – but they all looked much alike. Children playing on the steps – five little girls sewing clothes for their dolls out of bits of rags, salvaging thread from the rags. They were doing nicely – a little boy sitting with them on the steps was petting a pig! and if I understood, begging the girls to make a hat for it. They had the sun and view of the whole valley coming in upon them.

Then there was a woman putting out homespun and home woven wool to bleach – plain, beautiful material, much like Ruth's Peruvian wool. (There were about five sheep pasturing in the ruins of the castle at the hill top). Quite surprising – I asked her if she would sell it, and she said no. She was a clean looking, intelligent woman – her pieces of wool look like blankets, and she had four of them. She spoke a little French, and told me that I did not need it – pointing to my clothes. She was right, and I think maybe one would be ashamed to buy rich material. Also, I saw a number of linen sheets – again apparently hand woven – hanging out to dry. But I made no inquiry of them – The few things which people have they need so badly – and they cannot buy them in the shops.

The tailor shop men wanted to appear to be men of the world – they talked about cities.

I am well – I send my love – it is turning warmer.

Henry

January 8

Dear mama -

I hate this ungenerous small paper – and shall therefore use it up first. Hard to do, because there is little to write.

First, I shall write about my health – it is perfect, and I am well.

Next, the weather – it turns cold at night – water freezes in the water cans – but during the day, as now – it is delightfully sunny and warm – very lovely, clear, beautiful sun.

I have already written about my walk to town yesterday – it is still clear in my mind – the loveliness of the village on the cliff. But alas! I forget to try to buy chestnuts, and am now out of comestibles, except Malty Milkies, which will not last long. I shall look for chestnuts – I have been asking for cured olives, so far without any success, although they ought to be abundant.

Yesterday there was a man around here – returning laundry. He looked like a moron, and I think was, because he has no comprehension of the possibility that anyone could not understand Italian. He told me he would bring me chestnuts today – as I understood him – and that there was going to be a great market Monday (the key words – Lundi and mercato) in a town about 5 miles away. But I could not understand the name of the town – and would hesitate to strike out for a town which I know only vaguely to be about 5 miles to the southwest. So I hoped to see him again, and try again to learn where the market is, for it might be very interesting.

I just spoke to a man who is gleaning olives here – asked him for chestnuts – he says there is a house about 20 minutes walk from here where they have them – maybe I shall go there tomorrow. Did I want a sheep instead? I think a whole sheep would be a lot to undertake on a one-burner kerosene stove. Now, a chicken would be a different proposition.

Chestnuts, however, are cleaner and easier than chickens and sheep.

You mentioned in your letter of December 20 that you had already heard of my box – I mailed it on December 22 – and maybe it will be there by the middle of February. It is addressed, to daddy at the office – but there are enclosed some materials intended for you, as I have previously explained.

I suppose by this time you have received a few additional gew-gaws   as cameos – which, I suppose, should be disposed of as well as possible. I shall never again look at a cameo.

I send my love -

Henry

January 10

Dear mama -

It had turned much warmer – but with that change, it had become damper, so that the day is now filled with a depressing mist.

Yesterday afternoon I took a walk, down this road to the main highway, and down that a piece – these roads are very heavily travelled, so that they are not particularly pleasant or interesting walking. I was in search of chestnuts, but natives cannot travel on these roads, for a donkey or mule doesn't stand much chance along the military vehicles. So after a while, I turned off onto another road across the fields – and left the atmosphere of Gary, Indiana, In the distance, a village on a hill top, but I did not get that far. I asked the pedestrians for chestnuts, and they all said they could have some for me the following day. So I got none on my walk. I hope someday to get up to the village on the hill, although it is quite a distance. It may be the town of which the imbecile spoke, saying there was a great market there today – where he learned the world – but I have asked everyone where the market is today, and no one else seems to know.

This is not a good chestnut buying neighborhood, for one cannot find civilians. Now and then they appear someplace, but they seem just to appear out of the ground, and I cannot find where they live. It is quite mysterious.

We are on a hillside – which goes up to the foot of a sheer precipice. Olive trees grow up to the precipice, and the ground is covered with olives, which have not been gathered. At the bottom of the hill is a stream – just beyond the roads, cut deep in the ground. It is surprisingly clear and swift. On the other side of the stream, fertile looking bottoms. But the whole countryside here now has the dusty, devastated look of northwestern Indiana and Chicago suburbs. The towns – those I have seen, still hold charm – and in season, this country must be lovely too.

When I returned from my walk yesterday my friend the imbecile was sitting by the road here with a little raffia basket of dried figs. They taste good, but look so mangy that I can't eat them without dipping them in boiling water. That, of course, ruins them, making them sluicy and tasteless and un brittle . But a little later he turned up with a sack of chestnuts – selling them at 10 lire for a little basket – something less than a pound, I should judge. So we asked how much for the whole sack – answer 150 lire. We compromised and took the whole sack – I should say about seven or eight of the little baskets – for 100 lire, a few lemon drops, and some cigarettes. So the imbecile cheated us.

So you desire a detailed statement of my health. As an over-all proposition I am well. My complaints are that I have a very slight cold, from which I shall recover soon. I am treating it by drinking abundance of water. My more serious complaint is that the tips of my right thumb and fore-finger are sore. This is caused by picking hot chestnuts off the stove, and peeling them while they are still hot. They will not heal as long as chestnuts are in season because I keep picking up hot chestnuts. However, I treat them with burma shave, which is soothing, and with camphor-ice. In overall summary, however, with only the exceptions mentioned, I am well.

Presently, the band is practicing "hot" music about a hundred feet away. They recently acquired a piano, and I am waiting for them all to go away for a concert and leave the piano. I shall see if I can get at it, although I doubt if I can remember a note.

You see from this rambling that there is not a bit of news. Mail had been slow – and in desperate hope, I threw away all the old letters I had – but new ones have not come in. I look forward to a big batch sometime soon.

Also, sometime soon, I am just going to pick up and go to a town for fun – I do not know what town it will be, or when -

How was Chattanooga –for I suppose daddy will have gone by the time this letter reaches you. I should like very much to read daddy's lecture -

Write often – I hope you are all well – I am somewhat homesick – but can find enough to keep my mind off of it -

All my love -

Henry

January 11

Dear mama -

I received your letter of December 24, which gives me great hope for more on the way – for I've not yet received any about daddy's birthday party. Maybe tomorrow – It pleases me to know that you received the small tortoise shell box, which was sold to me by a man named Bastor, operating a shop with fine fixtures but no merchandise. He spoke English – and said he used to sell shell goods to Tiffany – but he would sell me the box especially cheap because it was the last he had. I was there a week later – and he had more. I wonder if he told such stories to Mr. Tiffany?

You make me remember how beautiful St. Louis is – it is just as beautiful as any of these cities, if not more. But one must find what is near. Ruth writes me that daddy thinks I am homesick – he is 100% right.

You ask me to write about myself – but I have nothing to write on that subject. I get up in the morning – go on through the day, and go to bed at night. I eat chestnuts. I took a shower today, including a shampoo with Mrs. Max Myer's Fitch's shampoo – advertised as dandruff removing, which suggests a caterpillar tractor on a concrete road – it could go through mud – so my shampoo would remove dandruff, if I had it. But I don't. It is still good shampoo – kind of magic, the way it won't make suds until you add water.

Letters suggesting that I request something to be sent to me. There is nothing I need – and, nothing, really, I want. I think maybe I could have some fun with little religious cards – you know the kind, little cards with pictures of saints on them, in bright colors – I would give them to children instead of carameli – and see what might happen. Any cards with a picture of St. Louis, in a saintly pose, with a halo – are they available there? There used to be a store on Broadway between Walnut and Market.

I have nothing of which to write. The little box you have received was sent after the first plate I sent – but little packages seem to be delivered more promptly than bigger ones – Nevertheless, possibly that has now been delivered I am anxious to hear if it arrives unbroken – not only because I have sent more, but also because I may be able to find still others – and I consider them chefs d'oeuvres. Little tortoise shell boxes – cameos – are too trivial and all alike. Good pictures seem unobtainable. But maybe I am too ambitious to find little Tintoretto and Michelangelo and what not.

I am going to go on an expedition sometime soon – I do not yet know where –but someplace, to get away for a while. It cannot be tomorrow, because there is some kind of a show here – Joe E. Brown[113] in person, I think, which I shall not see, and have no desire to see. But most other people seem so anxious to see such a performance – so I shall stay here while they go, and then the next day, possibly I shall be able to go someplace. I'd rather go for a walk any day, I'm sure, than to a professional Hollywood entertainer.

Write often – now I'm going to bed.

I send my love -

Henry

What a surplus of envelopes! This stationery is calculated at one sheet to the envelope – and I *[word unclear]* have left one sheet of paper and eight envelopes. ~~I'll~~ And envelopes are easier to get than paper. I'll have to waste envelopes -

January 12

Dear Ruth and Marian -

I have decided to write you joint birthday letters, because, while your birthdays are not so close together, still I am utterly unable to calculate when this letter will reach you. If it is early – well, I am helpless to do anything about it. But the truth of the matter is simply that I wish both of you very happy birthdays. Because of the incalculability of time required for anything to reach home, I am not sending birthday presents. Besides, I can't deliberately find anything, but must just rely on luck. So I buy everything I can find which I want – and it is up to you to take what you want as a birthday present.

Well – I ought to harp on the subject, because, heaven knows, I have nothing else of which to write – But now I've departed from it.

---

[113] Actor and comedian who toured with the USO
https://en.wikipedia.org/wiki/Joe_E._Brown

The weather here is fine, having turned much warmer, and with quite a little sun, which I enjoy. I had hoped to leave the area this afternoon and go for a walk someplace – but then suddenly it was announced that somebody is going to perform – Al Jolson or Bob Hope or somebody – and everybody gets all excited and wants to go. It is a rare treat (to others) on a particular date – so I sent them – and I shall seek my pleasure elsewhere some other time.

There is a book written by an author named Ernie Pyle – a newspaper reporter – which I do not recommend at all. But in the book, one Thomas F. Doyle (Red)[114] is mentioned. He is now working with me – and it is delightful to see how good it makes him feel to read about himself about a paragraph. The funny part is that what is said about him is as true as most reports – say about 35%. The other 65% is that he is about the dumbest man I've ever come in contact with. Last night I experimented – he was reading (he has no understanding of anything he reads, but has a little book of excerpts from the Bible which he reads with a devout expression on his face). It was getting dark out – the tent was open. One must close the tent, if one turns on the light. So I just waited to see what he would do. He moved his face closer and closer to the book, as the light got dim, and I got quite excited. Will he turn on the light? I waited. His nose was almost rubbing the pages. Finally he quit reading and just sat. I went to supper. When I came back, he was just sitting in the dark. I gave up, and suggested the possibility of turning on lights. "Oh yes," he said, "I didn't think of that."

He is a mooner – and has a genius for taking the most ungodly long time for anything – and that without doing anything else in the meantime.

And are his conversations terrible! I find him very interesting, because I never appreciated a man could be so wooly-minded. He moons that he wanted to be a professional baseball player, but the war prevented it. I think other things prevented it too. He suffers from a Sunday school complex too. He is married and every time he sees a movie he says he liked it because the heroine reminded him of his wife. I think he's going to be terribly disappointed when he does see his wife. I would feel sorry for him, if I did not have such an overwhelming urge to everytime he opens his mouth to put my foot in it.

Ah well – that is not a birthday greeting subject – but what if?

I just took off all my clothes – put on clean ones from the ground up, and gave the old ones to a woman soliciting laundry at the gate. They will be done dopo demanno – day after tomorrow – and I have apparently acquired a reputation as the man who wants to buy chestnuts. I have trouble saying I've already bought 'em, and all the natives of these parts now come with them. Quite funny! I try "Ho gia comprato[115]" which seems to work. Two women and a boy are soliciting laundry – they will bring chestnuts if I will want 'em – but I have five or ten pounds on hand! Walnuts seem to be not indigenous to these parts.

The country – the precise little part here – is quite unlovely – it is shattered and strapped, and one must get back from the roads, out of the dust and confusion to see again the peaceful groves and farms and quiet hills which are so lovely – the kind of places Pan must have inhabited. The mountains are fearsome.

Marian – I have a letter from mama that she is sending Betty a little tortoise shell box I sent home – and that you liked it – Well – if you liked it, I shall try to get another, when I can get to the city – not an immediate prospect. Meanwhile you have a bracelet on the way, which I believe you will like better than

---

[114] *Here is Your War*, Ernie Pyle (Page 86)
Via Internet Archive
https://archive.org/details/hereisyourwar0000unse/page/86/mode/2up?view=theater
[115] Translates to "I've already bought."

a shell box – and prize and gem of all! the <u>use</u> of a Capodimonte cup or two of them. With saucers. Not to mention the privilege of seeing (and taking <u>one</u> as a birthday present if you esteem it highly enough) three plates. Ruth may also take one as a birthday present – but I wanted the privilege of changing my mind. No I don't - if each of you takes one, it's final.

Again – my heartiest wishes for very happy birthdays.

I send my love

Henry

January 12

Dear mama -

I am looking forward to going someplace for pleasure soon – to get away – but all such plans are vague and indefinite. When to go? and where to go. The when – almost any time. But the where – my favorite city, quite far – its dust has been smitten by the rod of Aaron, so to speak. And I'll not go there – although one always hopes for a change. Set out to find another. Until I go, I have nothing to write.

I did hope for a letter this evening, having received one last night telling me you had written of a birthday party for daddy – a letter I've not yet received. It did not come tonight – maybe tomorrow.

I wrote to Marian and Ruth this afternoon – and had trouble filling pages even then. Nothing new has occurred.

I am well – but in line with your request that I write all details of my health, will say that I have lost my voice today. I whispered to the doctor about it – he gave me a pill. "Shall I be able to sing, when the pill had taken effect?" "Yes." "You're a wonderful doctor!" So my voice is now coming back, although I am not using it today or tomorrow.

It helps my Italian enormously to be without voice, for I talk (?) to Italians and Americans in the same manner.

I am still looking for the reference to the Four Horsemen of the Apocalypse. I find some Horsemen in Revelations 10, but thought there was more about them. Do you know the reference? Unfortunately, I abandoned my Latin Bible as too voluminous; it had an index and concordat – Which, if I could select the right Latin word for Horsemen, or Apocalypse might have served my purpose.

I send my love -

Henry

January 13

Dear mama -

I did not get to any town today, as I had hoped I might, nor shall I, as it now appears, tomorrow. But instead, I did take a walk for about forty five minutes – enough to be re-impressed with the fundamental loveliness of the countryside – classic looking olive groves and orchards, covering the knolls of the little hills in the valleys of the great ones. And I saw a man leading a milk-white cow – the first cow I have seen in Italy. She was resisting being led – and balking at every passing truck. Quite a beautiful animal. Again the striking color which appears every time one opens one's eyes in Italy – the cow, with plowed field, and close by, the lovely, intricate texture of olive trees – their color of green is distinctive, partly for the texture – I know no other tree like it, with such intricacy of boughs and such fine leaves – it combined something of the aspen, in delicacy, with the interest of an apple tree in shape. A dark, shady, subdued green – it is the background foliage of, say, El Greco (is he the Spaniard, who painted tall thin people?)

The sun was lovely today – overhead – but there has been a low lying haze which obscures it early. Late, one sees the snow covered mountain tops all around, but the bases of the mountains are concealed in mist.

I have nothing of which to write – but shall not close finally until this evening's mail comes in, for I am hopeful of letters – through the day, the packet grows in my imagination, until by this time of the evening I see a package of six or eight letters, all from you, tied up with a little piece of manila cord. Well – they won't come.

I am well, regaining my voice nicely. It is pleasant to be unable to talk for a while.

I send my love.

You ask what I should like to have sent me. Food, I suppose; not only candy, but any other kind of food which is available. But I do not know the food restrictions there.

Mail just came – a letter from Betty and two from you. You complain that your letters are trivial and you have nothing to say. What complete nonsense! I enjoy your letters very very much, and await them eagerly and have my chief delight in receiving them. They talk about the things in which I am most interested – I might call it Jerusalem, referring to Psalm 137, which is a favorite of mine and I have quite before.

The little roll of prints – I picked them up in ~~the~~ a building with papers piled high to be burned – the preparation for an Italian colonial exposition.

January 13

Dear mama -

Well, well! I suppose I went to bed too early (7 o'clock) because I just couldn't sleep after 5 – so I got up, and washed well and in leisure. Now it is almost breakfast time – and a very beautiful early morning – full moon, just fading with the daylight. Sunrise, by my time, at 6:55 – no – it isn't up yet – just prick in the east. Place it at 7 o'clock.

I am well – feeling chipper and pert – my voice is on the way back, but I can't try out for the local opera yet – or couldn't if there were a local opera. I intend to try to go to a town this morning or this afternoon. Probably shall not make it – but still try.

I was reading Exodus last night – about the plagues – and Aaron smiting the dust. It is very wonderful reading -

I have to look for a new city to visit. The one I was just beginning to know and find my way around in is now forbidden to me. But maybe, still, I shall be able to get there – I'm trying to think of the application of "Let my people go," to some refutation. But drama is in the *Bible* – and justice and purpose are not so apparent here.

I am surely enjoying and thankful for my wool pyjamas and my soft slippers – they are lovely luxuries.

Henry

January 14

To Mrs. A. Lowenhaupt
6237 McPherson Ave.
Saint Louis, (5)
Missouri, U. S. A.

Dear mama:

You see that I am departing from custom and writing a V-Mail letter. My reason, that I really have nothing to say, but would just like to write a word or two before I go to bed – to a large extent that I am a little cross this evening, and feel peeved at people quite without reason. Fortunately, I have known it all day, and have not said anything to anybody to indicate how much I have resented everything which has or has not been done. Nothing has been done or left undone which I should or should not resent. Just that I am tired, and now I am about to go to bed.

I still look forward to the big batch of mail which must be on the way. This evening I retrieved your V-Mail letter of December 27 – in which you say your previous letters were of a worried and nagging nature, and should be ignored. I still hope I receive them, and suppose that I shall. I need a little nagging.

Your last letter impressed me that you let yourself be imposed upon. So do I, but the difference is that I think you remain happy in being imposed upon, whereas I make resolutions that it shall not happen again. Are you not taking things too seriously? Working too steadily? You write that you go over and sit with the baby while Marian goes to the Movies, daddy plays bridge and Ruth goes out to dinner – and that after a whole day of doing chores. Is not that ridiculous? But I do the same thing with two men here – I stay here so that they can go to the movies, which are supposed to be enjoyable, but which I would never enjoy anyway. So I really prefer to stay here – but I expect more appreciation on that account than I get. That is why, principally, I have been mad all day – to see little punks thinking they are playing so shrewd by just plain taking advantage of opportunity – taking four hours to do a fifteen minute job, if I happen to be away someplace, and conniving to get the fifteen minutes job in which they know they can take four hours. So I shall crack down a little bit – but if I should say anything now, I should get an argument of all innocence, like a servant girl puts up, if you find dust under the rug – that she didn't know she was supposed to sweep under the rug, or something. But I am in large part brooding, and really do not care. I should do the same thing (in fact, I think I do) but I believe I should do it both more successfully and more skillfully. So I'll just let it be known that I see what's going on and continue patient and unsympathetic. Now I hate dawdling – I don't mind idleness, but dawdling is neither restful nor pleasant nor anything else. It is just deadly. That one is not in a hurry is no reason for doing something slowly, unless doing it slowly will be doing it better – and it usually is doing it worse.

I am well. I have done nothing of interest all day – and apparently shall not do anything tomorrow. I wrote a letter to Mme. Peyrus, having received one from her. Jacques is graduating from school this June. I shall watch for a book to send him – that will give me an interesting quest, anyway, although I probably shall not find a book, surely none in French or English, and to send an Italian book would be silly. Maybe Latin, but I think Jacques would not appreciate the kind of book I should like to send. I think I wrote you in a fit of honesty after your reprimands about not telling you truly of my state of health that I had lost my voice. Well, I'd better tell you now that I have recovered it, but am peeved at the Doctor. He told me I could sing when I recovered it, and I can't sing any better than I could before he gave me pills.

I send my love

Henry

January 15

Dear mama -

I received your V-mail last night, that you had received a batch of ten letters – I envy you, for mail has really not been coming through except in little dribbles – that some letters mention previous ones is my only indication that there are letters. So I am hopeful.

I must keep on writing often, even though I have nothing to say – and the more deadly-dull I feel, the more often I write. It is like saying "good morning" or something – and is necessary to maintain the illusion that there is still such a place as St. Louis, and that I still belong there more or less – and have some foundation. But my letters must be boring and disappointing to receive. I shall try to find something about which to write.

I intended to go to a village nearby this morning and look around for some project. But Captain Morris called and said he was going to be here – so I shall stay this morning, and possibly go someplace this afternoon – or Monday. Sunday is a bad day for any such purposes, although for the most part, it is just exactly like any other day – right here. Conflict: "Remember the sabbath to keep it holy - - - -" vs. "Every seventh day they spend in idleness and sloth."

I am well – have been sleeping long hours and doing absolutely nothing of interest. A few short little walks. Worrying – I gave my laundry to a woman who was to return it yesterday, and she hasn't shown up yet. Well – the nights have been damp, and maybe it didn't dry. Also, she promised to iron it.

Ironing is a slow process. They use, exclusively, charcoal irons, which are quite pretty. Several times I have been tempted to send you a present of one – until I feel the weight. Then I think that art has more truth. I also almost bought Ruth several little rough-hewn benches – just four legs and a top – of oak, worn and smoked to a beautiful color. Good fire wood! And a painted candle, very primitive. But, don't worry, I shall stick to smaller articles.

I send my love -

Henry

January 16

Dear mama -

I sometimes picture a man swimming in the middle of an ocean – with nothing whatsoever in sight – except a branch of a lowest tree, which is thorny – and he hangs on to that. That is the way I feel now, writing letters. Nothing to say, I cannot possibly make letters interesting or significant – but I dare not stop writing. So I keep on writing my daily letter – without any attempt at what is quite impossibly – at saying what is really in my thoughts. The stream of letters, I hope, is a kind of life-line, which still holds back to the place I desire to be, and may still keep a little of the community of thought and conversation I hope to maintain. A sense of individuality – and the underlying hope each day that the evening will bring mail, and the morning or next day an achievement towards coming home, which lies beyond my power. So you see, I am homesick – and my thoughts run sometimes in largely repetitive quotations from the Book of Psalms – which are particularly delightful. If I forget thee, oh Jerusalem, and "I lift mine eyes unto the hills. From whence cometh my help?" and "How long, oh Lord," and so on and so forth.

But there is a little spark in me which stirs up the notion that maybe one I could throw the whole sentiment overboard – eat lotus, so to speak, – and at the same time (I associate it with eating lotus) let Circe turn me into a swine. Then, I should have a perfectly indifferent and contented time, lying in the sun, and rooting in the gravel for acorns, in complete slovenliness, without memory of the past and hope of the future. The funny picture always comes up, however, of my being asked to explain my conduct in such an event, in term of idealisms, to a bigger, fatter, swine than I would be, who coming from his sty and sitting on a silk cushion with easter lilies around, always gets the words of idealism into his mouth first – and puts me on the impossible defensive by hypocrisy and big, hollow, meaningless words – a swine which always bears a sight resemblance to Emil Mayer, with a touch of Judge Baron – and says: Patriotism, Responsibility, Industry, Loyalty – and ultimately comes to the Boy Scout laws. Quite a nightmare! So I do not eat lotus, or just go off and on and quit, ~~been~~ mostly because I don't know how, partly because I fear those who do it more successfully, and without knowing they do it – maybe because they were born swine. Now, that is a psychopathic notion –and you see how idle my mind is. I must go for a walk this afternoon -

For it is a beautiful, warm sunny day -

I did go for a walk – and am now back – down the road about a mile, then off onto a little travelled road, across fields, up a terraced hill - to a village which crowns the hill, running along its ridge. The hill below is terraced on all sides – vineyards , orchards and olive groves. At one end of the village, a castle – round walls – but the old castle is gone, except a charming little gate house, with tall grass on the roof, and rebuilt in solid buildings. The buildings are surprisingly comfortable looking upstairs – they are mostly three story buildings – with big French windows (all glass broken) but downstairs one sees poor dwellings – with beautiful box-beds, painted and carved, filled with straw. Delightful furniture cradles – The town is quite lovely and charming -

One can see the town from miles away – and when one gets there, one can see five towns on five different hills. They all look somewhat deserted, considering how closely built they are -

I hope for mail -

Love

Henry

P.S. I've just started an experimental campaign – I started it on a man who is very pliable – and my campaign is to urge people to discontinue the sending to them through the mail of ~~second class matter~~ local newspapers and the like. My reasons:

1. They take too much shipping space for their value. *The Van Wert Times* – for example, or the *Troy Free Press*.
2. They delay the first class mail
3. They take too much labor.

So I say no one should receive a publication unless first, he reads it, and second, it is of sufficiently general interest that at least five or six other people want to read it.

My first attack was a success – and the man promises to write this evening asking the publishers to stop sending his local paper. They send it free, and doubtless think they are performing a patriotic service. But they forget that the same space would hold things of much greater value -

I myself am an offender. I must write to National Candy and ask them to stop sending their magazine. My reasons are partly, selfish, partly noble – I'll see if I can write a letter which won't offend

Henry

January 18

Dear mama -

I feel as if I am starting a very long letter, for I feel I have so much to say – we shall see whether or not it comes out long. I just received your letter of December 28 – and feel one hundred per cent in accord with not drinking to "our boys overseas" – because stupidity, can go too far and you don't have to be a party to it. My sentiments are much the same when anyone tells me (as they frequently do) that "we are all one happy family." I do not think I could put up with that statement if I had to do anything – but I just grin. The feeling is not one which can be put into words – it is just that some things are so banal and stupid that it is bestial to say them. And Jack is one of the worst offenders I know on this score.

I laugh at your character analysis of the picture I sent. I enclose another – with another man cut off, because I fear I may look as ugly to him as he does to me. I shall have more pictures taken if there is ever opportunity – or (and) maybe have a picture of myself drawn – although most places draw just quick cartoons which are uninteresting and ugly. My mind will be made up on the spur of the moment.

I am always delighted to receive your letters – and read them and reread them. Leisure to read them! What nonsense – I have leisure to memorize them – and if I had the ambition should have leisure to memorize the whole Bible -

I had a letter from Ben Charles yesterday – and learned, alas, too late, that I was for two days within 100 yards of him. His letter sounds quite dispirited – possibly because he knew this country before war passed over it – I can imagine its former delight – and the suffering can make one quite sick -

As yesterday, I saw a town – the park, with an avenue of small trees, overlooking a great valley, was left, but all the buildings were just piles of stone and rubble, and people, who had come back to the town, just stood around in the park talking. There was nothing else to do. There was not a building left in town – a town of, say, 5000 people, closely built.

But today, at last, I went to another town – I guess about 10000 population – which was only little damaged. Beautiful buildings – quite beyond anything you can imagine – on a steep hill, the bottom part obscured by military use, which makes it confused and dusty – but up the hill, narrow alleys and archways, ancient stone and stone carving – old churches – little shops opening onto the dark alleys – cabinet makers, who move their benches into the streets for light, shoe makers sewing by hand in the doorways – each with a little boy as apprentice, helping him. The women carrying water up the hill in copper vessels (without power, no running water) and carrying laundry down to the river, where there is a laundry-place.

The shops are completely empty – I tried to buy some string – could find only a few little pieces – very expensive – and no stove wick at all.

There were some French nurses or WAAC[116]s in the town, dressed in American soldier's uniforms – leggings and all – I suppose all they could get. The children of the town, ragged in all degrees to nakedness, followed them screaming with mirth "signorina sono signorene[117]!"

I found two ladies sitting in a shop, sewing – and since there was nothing else for sale, I bought some doilies – which I have sent to Ruth, intended as a birthday present. I could find nothing else for sale. The principle of these things is that labor is abundant and inexhaustible – material is rare.

Every shopkeeper, if you ask for anything – stove wicks, string, writing paper, anything at all – tells you that the Germans took it all. I am inclined not to believe it ~~and~~ but that they want to keep everything they have. Of course they do! The Germans have been out of the town for a few weeks only – the money they had from them is worthless, mostly, and they have no confidence in any money.

I saw an intelligent looking old priest standing in a doorway – watched him talk to people for a while, and then mostly just because I wanted to, and because I felt so completely helpless, I gave him $10.00 - and asked him, in English, to use it for the benefit of the poor of the city. "Non copisco" he said – so I tried "Volo hale donare, ut pauperes huius urbis adjuventur" (I wish to give this that the poor of this city may be helped.) He understood – and thanked me – and I think he was having as much of a lark (and a more profitable one) ~~Then~~ as I was – we proceeded to discuss the number and situation of the poor – and whether anything could be done for them with money. There had been, he said, many wealthy men of the town – but they had long ago, brought everything out of the town, and were keeping it - which was just as well, because in the town it would either have been lost to the gentlemen or sold, and nothing could be purchased with money. I asked what kinds of things they had brought, and he listed – bolts of linen, as I understood, silverware, wine in bottles and in kegs (wood, by which I understood kegs or barrels) and other drinks. Herds of sheep and goats – I did not understand all he listed. I said I thought it was time that they could come back safely – and he laughed, saying that people didn't come back in a hurry, having been frightened, and having seen such extensive destruction – that no one would come back to the main roads until he had to – or at least until there were some advantages to be gained from being on a road. I do not know what good my $10.00 will do either him or his poor – but what else can one give? I suppose I had about $3.00 worth of pleasure out of it and do not regret the impulse. ~~for~~ I shall not miss the money, having more than I know what to do with - The priest was quite a thorough gentleman, as most of the clergy seem to be here. It is always surprising that they are not Irish – as of course they are not.

You see, I have been wandering around a little bit – and rather intend to continue - just to keep posted on what the world looks like.

---

[116] Women's Army Auxiliary Corps
[117] Roughly translates to: "Ladies are gentlemen."

This is wild, mountainous, big country – and very beautiful. It does not show intensive cultivation – maybe in summer it does, but now the fields are barren.

I should like to find a special birthday present for Marian – but do not think I possibly can – no prospect of getting back to a substantial town, which has opened up somewhat.

I send my love -

Henry

I watched cabinet makers in town – they were all very busy, but I saw none who looked able to design anything. Some were making tables – chests of drawers, boxes etc. The town is too far away to order anything made anyway!

January 19

To Mrs. A. Lowenhaupt
6237 McPherson Ave.
Saint Louis, (5)
Missouri, U. S. A.

Dear mama -

A V-Mail letter, because I neglected for a day or two to write to you, and, although I wrote last night, after I wrote, I decided I wanted to reply to your very welcome letter more promptly than my air mail letter would reach you. In the first place I am in whole hearted sympathy with your refusal to drink bum egg nog to a banal toast. And I think that if it is mentioned, it is making a mountain out of a mole hill – and there is no occasion to think a second time of it unless one desires to make a Jane Austen novel, in which case it might furnish the theme for chapter on chapter.

Next, I finally got to a town yesterday, about which I have written at some length in my other letter. So I'll not mention it further now. I got some doilies (the only thing there was in the town) and have sent them to Ruth intending them as a birthday present. The linen, what there is of it, is quite fine. I only regret that one cannot buy linen in plain pieces, not all cut up in little shapes and cut-outs.

Further, I laughed at your analysis of the picture *[word crossed out]* I sent you - the science of physiognomy, is it, or phrenology? I shall try to send another for your analysis when I can get it – which may be soon or never or any time between.

I am well – with no news at all. I have already exhausted everything I got to write about in my visit to the town yesterday, and have nothing to write now. The weather is cold and clear, but the sun is warm enough when one is in it. I am very homesick – which is a perpetual state, relieved principally by receiving letters and eating. You suggest that you might send me something to eat, with my next request. Well, I am running low on a few things, and if it is convenient, I should like to receive them. Therefore I write for them.

Please send me a spool of khaki-colored thread, and a few needles. I am not out of needles, but they rust so badly that they are hard to use. I should also like some food of any kind – not necessarily sweet, but in no event hard candies. Any candy included should be soft. You see, I am well enough off to be particular. Fudge? Or is sugar still rationed?

There are divers foods which are served day in and day out. I list them. Fortunately, they are things I liked originally. Spam; vienna sausage; canned corned beef; canned string beans; dehydrated potatoes; dehydrated eggs; Right now, there are a few tangerines available – and I have been eating about a dozen a day. But we are not in citrus fruit country any more. If I get back to it, I intend to lay in a stock of oranges – about six crates at least. This is chestnut country – and I have not even seen apples around here. I do not know what becomes of the olives – the country is full of olive trees. The natives say the Germans took them all, which leads me to believe that they are stored away someplace. Or else Germany is flooded with olives

I send my love

Henry

January 20

Dear mama -

Well – the mail situation is desperate - I have received one V-mail note of about three lines (last night – I didn't count it) and that is about all. So I must have a lot on the way – maybe it will come.

I am well – have absolutely nothing to say – about I suppose there is no use rambling on. So I'll call it a letter – ending here – and maybe continue in the morning.

Love

Henry

P.S. I have changed my mind about the V-mail note – it tells me that you received a plate – I imagine the first one I sent. The first was the best – I think, but the others, which follow, are also excellent – of a different kind. The one you have is the one I said you might lend to a museum, if you desired – but others follow which are also better than anything the museum has.

The little piece of red material was just included as a piece of packaging – I considered it rather pretty, but worthless. Is it not quite dirty? I remember it so, but did not wash it, partly because it was raining and I did not want to wait for it to dry – partly because I thought it might fade and I wanted to keep the color.

But you have two pieces of fine material on the way – in daddy's box – one all served up with gold braid around the edges (which does not hurt it, nor improve it much) and a lining – all can be removed if you like – but I would be inclined to leave them – and one just a trinket of fine linen and lace – which Marian might like particularly. The lace is quite fine, I think.

Materials are very rare and hard to find. I know one place where there was some silk and silk brocade of commercial type – would send some if I could get back there to get it, but now cannot. I think that northern Italy is the textile part – and that cloth if hidden as a tangible thing of value. It is brought out little by little, and since labor is abundant, in proportion to material or which to expend it, especially female labor, it is cut up in little pieces and made as fancy as possible – as doilies. I admit, I like a plain piece of material better, because it had such infinite possibilities – like a clean canvas, which could have the Mona Lisa painted on it – but after the Wolf Boy is painted on it, and it is framed and hung, it is finished and ended and no longer interesting in its possibilities.

Well – I am very hopeful of receiving mail this evening.

January 21

Dear mama -

I received your letter written on daddy's birthday – and it is one I have been waiting for, because you mentioned having written of daddy's birthday in a letter I received long ago. So I hope the drought had been broken – a dearth of mail breaks like a drought – first a V-mail note – like a drop of rain (very welcome, though small) then a single letter, like a shower, and tomorrow I expect a big packet of letters, like a steady rain all through a summer day.

I am anxious to write a letter this evening, before I go to bed, although I have nothing to say. I shall repeat largely what I have already written.

This afternoon I took a shower – and changed all my clothes, from head to toe – for no sufficient reason except that a woman was soliciting laundry and I decided I might as well start fresh. I wish I had some idea of how much soap laundry requires, for I fear I always give too much. My laundry list: one cotton underwear shirt; one underwear trunks, one woolen underwear shirt; one woolen underwear drawers; one wool shirt, one pair wool trousers (you see, I feel like an onion) one pair wool socks, three handkerchiefs, one pair wool pajamas. I gave her one cake of English laundry soap (like yellow American soap, but harder) about three inches by 1 ½ inches by ½ inch, and one small-size cake of imitation Palmolive – about 1 inch by 2 inches by 1 ½ inches. Is that enough? And, while you answer, how long is a piece of string? A little boy with the woman was trying to learn English – He can say "wash" and understand it, but cannot understand either "yes" or "no." So his "wash?" is not very successful.

Well – I feel clean this evening. The weather has been beautiful – frosty, clear nights, lovely, sunny days – and I have quite forgotten what mud is like – except that when I am on a dusty road, I no longer curse at dust – I have an affection for it.

A man here had some tea – so we now have a can of water on the stove, and shall soon be drinking it.

I was in a town the other day – quite a beauty, of which I have already written – and had a good time wandering through the narrow streets, up and down the hill on the side of which it is built – about a ruin, which winds through great bottoms, barren now, but I suppose cultivated in grain in season. Shoemakers in the streets, cabinet makers (I saw no excellent work – none which indicated any ability to design) barbers, and empty shops. I bought some doilies, which I am sending to Ruth. I should very much like to find some materials, but so far have found substantially none – labor is cheap and cannot be stored up – and so for selling, the materials are not sold – they can get more if they put work into it first. So, while the doilies are of nice linen, the fabric is hardly apparent, being much worked.

I am extremely happy that you have received the plate I sent – I presume it is the pink one, with a lady's head – and it is a joy to realize you have it – for you must feel the same excitement I felt when I saw it – I knew I had to have it – and I think Ruth may enjoy seeing it. It is the best I have – the one you may lend to the museum if you like. Two more are on the way – somewhat inferior to it, but not a whole lot. If I ever get into the city again – there is so much I think I know where to find – china from Signor *[sic]* Gallo (and he had a beautiful piece of old fabric) made into a kind of robe – but I don't think I'd buy it. It is not dissimilar to the piece I've sent, with gold braid around it.) Linens and laces from Signore Romano – although they too are all worked into things.

I even think I might be able to buy a few pieces of fabric, although that, being a raw product, so to speak, is the hardest to find.

[Section cut out.]

Tea is ready – the trouble with drinking tea from a metal cup is that the cup gets so hot it burns your lips before the tea gets there. And tea should be drunk hotter than your lips can bear the cup. Ah well! What a grievance!

I have decided that ~~the~~ part of this letter above is censorable – so I have cut it out – it really wasn't interesting anyway.

I hope by this time you have received two additional plates – and enjoy them – the three, with two cups sent later, are my pride and joy.

I am well. I received a letter from Bill Charles this evening, and a Christmas card, with a militarily humorous (?) subject. One shouldn't try to sing the Lord's song in a strange land – it makes a discord.

My – this tea tastes good – hot & wet, and with a little sugar in it! Also, weak – for tea is normally served here black and strong. That is no way to serve tea – well – I fancy you and Ruth and Marian will sit down some afternoon to a cup of perfect tea – just for no reason – and have a tea party – you might celebrate with the little CapodiMonte cups when they come – and have cookies with it. Then write me a letter about your tea party.

~~If the~~ I must get out of the area for a while tomorrow – see if I can find something definite of which to write.

I now send my love -

Henry

January 22

Dear mama -

I feel as if I have enough to write a long letter – as I always feel when I start to write – and we shall see if I have. Preliminarily, I just received your December 24 letter – what topsy turvy order letters come in! I have already received one of December 26. And since you are still doubtful of my health, I'll say again that I am well. I am. The weather is fine now – the days warm – the nights cold. So much is repetitious – I have written it every day, I think.

This will, incidentally interest Mr. Schlesinger on the liquor situation here. Today, finding a man who was going to a town – a rather rich town, though not large, in former times, and desiring to give D. --- an opportunity to get out of the area for a while, I sent him along. Suggested that he bring back fruit, and liquor, if he could find any. (He is an amazingly ignorant boy – He came back – and this is what infuriates me – oranges are very abundant, and very delicious apples – so he brings back six oranges and six apples (will last about 10 minutes) and about one pound of walnuts – excellent – will last half an hour. I should have thought any fool would have the sense to buy eight or ten dozen oranges at least – the greatest luxury the country has to offer, and a very great one.

Then, he got a bottle with Champagne written on the outside. Contents: slightly adulterated and carbonated cider – really quite good, but he paid $4.00, for what should cost 10¢. And that, after being given a sample taste! Then two pint bottle labelled "Cognac" – which contain about three teaspoonfuls of cognac each, filled with water and burnt sugar to color it. Also quite good – but worth a nickel, at most – cost $2.00 a bottle. These bottles are labelled without the name of a manufacturer – which is not a circumstance of suspicion, but indicates nothing. Labels, with well-known names, are easily available, but contents replaced or diluted, so that there is no possibility of knowing what you buy. Price does not indicate anything, either, for the poorest sells at a high price as a representation that it is good. So, one must abandon any attempts to buy liquor – except vin ordinaire, which is so cheap it is not worth adulterating elaborately – they just add water, which doesn't hurt it much. This "cognac" is pure sugar-water.

So I am disappointed – but have learned a lesson – the financial loss is not mine – but I regret not having oranges, apples, nuts and good brandy.

This afternoon, a well-dressed woman (she looked like a city woman) was at the road into the area – with another woman, who was carrying laundry. She asked one where she could find a certain man to return his laundry – and it looked to me as if an intelligent, city woman had come along with her peasant friend or servant to deliver laundry, because she wanted to see what was happening in the world – So I decided she was a good risk and asked her if one could procure any cloth – for Italian materials are so beautiful – I desired to give a little piece to my mama. She said she was from ---, a town about 5 kilometers away, to which I walked not long ago – that there were no shops there – and the only possibility was that some private family might have some to sell. She will let me know Monday – I am hopeful – she was a clear-spoken, intelligent woman – looked like she would be influential in church circles – and look forward to Monday – I asked for linen or wool – am afraid she understands me to mean a piece sewed or cut into something, although I did my best to explain I was interested just in a piece of material, of linen or of wool. I liked her – because she seemed to have a clear, bright, realistic conception of her surroundings. This is Saturday – I must wait till Monday to find out anything.

Well – I feel as if I have requested you to send me so much, that I shall make no request in response to your letter. But I may write V mails making requests – first trying to recollect what I have already requested.

Now – I send my love -

Henry

January 23

Dear mama -

I suppose that I am writing home much too often – and that these letters come all in a bunch – and aren't worth reading and you are busy, and everything else. But I write mostly for my own pleasure – and hope that my numerous letters are not a burden to you. I also hope that by writing frequently, maybe one letter will stray into a mail by which, otherwise, you would get none.

Well – no mail this evening – so I reread the letters I fortunately still had on hand – the V mail acknowledging receipt of a plate – I am not sure which one – the one about daddy's birthday and the one written on Christmas eve about bringing things over for Haymer. So, as I eat chestnuts, I try to recall what I was writing about that time – on the assumption that you are receiving those letters now – I remember Christmas dinner at the d'Alterio's – I must have written on that about December 26 – and the two Christmas dinners I ate – I remember those with pleasure for food is getting monotonous now – I remember thinking about singing the Lord's song in a strange land – then nothing was happening a month ago.

You ask me what my favorite candies are – that is easy   liquor beans (chocolates filled with rum, brandy, etc.) Next, chocolate covered cherries – and generally, chocolates – Then, I suppose, bon-bons and such kinds as Turkish paste and gum drops. But any kind of food would be welcome – although I have plenty to eat.

So you know by this time that I am well – and settled into a philosophy of sitting around, waiting things out – which I regret saying, because I think I shall get a lecture in vague terms. Maybe now -

I look forward with curiosity to tomorrow, when the Signora said she'd be back and let me know if she could find any fabrics. I fear a disappointment – but hope for the best in hand woven linens and other textiles.

We have had beautiful weather – until half a minute ago, when it began to rain. I hope it does not continue too long.

I send my love – write often -

Henry

January 24

Dear mama -

I might as well write a few lines before my mail comes in this evening, which I am happy in the contemplation of the two inch stack I expect – before I am disappointed in getting none.

This evening is a mixture of disappointment and hope – the weather has cleared and is lovely – I hope to have opportunity to go to a town tomorrow – and if I do, shall buy something – anything. That summarizes the + side.

The lady who was going to look for fabrics for me did not show up today, as she said she would. I suppose I shall never see her again – and her relation to Weaving and Fabrics is like that to history of the man Joseph met crossing the fields.

I bought some walnuts today – and having no change paid 50¢ for about two pounds – they are mostly spoiled, but some are good. I really prefer chestnuts to walnuts – anyway.

I shall reserve the remaining space to answer your letters which will come this evening (or complain about the lack if they didn't come.)

Henry

Later

It didn't come – but why complain – maybe it will be here tomorrow -

I indulged today in the game of opening the Bible at random, to see what prophecy I could find in the passage to which I might open. I opened to Isaiah, Chapter 2 – and read about "And he shall judge among the nations and shall rebuke many people; and they shall beat their swords into plowshares and their spears into pruning hooks; nation shall not lift up sword against nation, neither shall they learn want any more."

So my little game was very pleasant. The trouble with the game is that one plays it over and over again – and does not accept the prophecy of the first opening as final and conclusive.

I am well – still hopeful of going to a town tomorrow – and maybe I shall. You see there is not a bit of news – and that I am very impatient to receive mail I had better quiet down and be reconciled to not receiving it.

All my love -

Henry

January 24

To Mrs. A. Lowenhaupt
6237 McPherson Ave.
Saint Louis
Missouri

Dear mama -

I think that maybe my mail to you is as slow coming through as yours to me – so write this letter to let you know that I am well – that there is no incident to ruffle the tranquility of dolce far nente of my existence. So I go on – waiting for mail, buying what of interest I can, and always hoping.

It rained a little last night and this morning, but now has cleared – and is a beautiful starlight night.

I got cheated today on the purchase of walnuts from a native – mostly because I wanted them so badly I was willing to pay any price – had no change for 50 lire – and of course she, desiring the best price obtainable, would not give me change. So my choice was to pay 50 lire for about 2 pounds of nuts – or do without. So I paid 50 lire. And now about 60% of these are rotten. So I have neither walnuts nor 50 lire.

The lady who was going to look for fabrics for me in a nearby town did not show up – another disappointment. Write often -

Love

Henry

January 26

Dear mama -

Now I have not written for a day or so, and ought to have a great deal accumulated to say – but I haven't – it does not work that way.

Yesterday I went to a town – unfortunately it is quite an uninteresting one – perfectly flat, with a great palace in it – but generally dirty and rambling looking. So I searched for fabric – and could not find any, because every time I see a rayon bed spread, in bright yellow with a kind of white damask imitation of a design – and the salesman begins telling me pure silk – I get a little sick at my stomach. A little wool – some silk in plain colors – but at $4.00 a yard I do not think it can be a great enough bargain to send home. So I bought nothing. I also looked for brandy and cognac – there are two kinds "original cognac" and "just cognac," the latter being whatever happens to be put in a cognac bottle. I found one bottle of original cognac – a litre – at $40.00. I did not consider it worth bargaining for, because even if he came down to half or a third it would have been too much. So instead, I got 50 very delicious oranges and a kilo of walnuts. And I shall stick to vin ordinaire for drinking. That is not worth fancy adulteration – and the worst they'll do to it is add water, which really doesn't hurt it much.

My lady, who was going to look for fabrics for me, has never shown up, although I have been watching for her.

No mail yet – boy, what a stack is on its way, to arrive this evening, I am sure. You see, I am somewhat on tender hooks. I received a Vmail note of January 3, saying you received a plate – one which I considered, if I am right in my guess as to which one, the world's most beautiful. You say you are curious as to what ruth would think of it – and so am I – but all the letters I have received since that letter (2 of them) were written long previous to it. So I think I have letters on the way.

It has been raining again – but only showers, as if it were April – and not enough to make mud – besides, we are on rocky ground, which, it is true, gets slippery, but does not get muddy (I hope)

I am well – I send all my love -

Henry

Bought this paper recently – alas, the beautifully colored lining for envelopes seems no longer available.

January 27

Dear mama -

I have tried to save up things to write about – so I could write a somewhat factual letter – and for a day now have treasured two little incidents – oh, so small, but at least something – and I write this prologue to try to spread my two little grains of corn, so to speak, and make them cover more pages.

So just let me tell you about the beautiful weather – lovely, clear and cool, so that now mountain ranges come into view in the sunrise. And that I am well -

And now my incidents – both of which are incomplete, but lead to hope.

1. I stopped a woman yesterday who was soliciting laundry and asked her if she could get me a piece of hand-woven material – not enough to make a dress (as she thought) but just a little piece to look at, because Italian fabrics are beautiful. I indicated about 2 feet square. She said that Italy is very poor after 4 years of war – and that all the material they could get they needed for clothes, even in little pieces (pointing to her shirt, which was patched and repatched – almost a rag – but she said she would look for some. Maybe it is wrong to try to buy material, which is badly needed. If I could give materials in exchange – maybe I shall have some wool from a pair of worn out pants soon. The conversation always starts by their thinking I am offering to sell or give them some material – and I get enthusiastic responses until the misunderstanding is cleared. So I await results.

2. Last night I had some sugar on hand – so I made marrons glacés – shall I give you the recipe? They are not as good as they should be, but I think I know my mistakes – I cooked the chestnuts too long and they turned too hard.

Recipe – bring ounce chestnuts to boil in water – drain them, and shell them. Place them in a pan. Cover them with wine (I had ounce very sour, poor, watered wine on hand) Three tablespoon fulls of sugar. A little orange peel, from the orange you are eating while they cook can be added, to make candied orange peel at the same time. Let them boil down – until sticky – then stand them out on cellophane removed from packages of cigarettes.

My mistake – too much liquid for the sugar – so I boiled the chestnuts too long. I should have boiled the liquid down before I put the chestnuts in – they dried out and got too hard. So I shall try again. The use of wine instead of water makes them marrons glacés à la Bordeaux (my own name)

Now I am boiling 2 birds with one stove – boiling water in the pan I used to get the sugar out – and at the same time boiling handkerchiefs in the water – efficient?

Love -

Henry

January 27

To Mrs. A. Lowenhaupt
6237 McPherson Ave
Saint Louis
Missouri

Dear mama -

This is a note to let you know that I am well – which I write because mail seems not to be reaching me – I have had one V-mail note in a long time – and I think possibly my ordinary letters are similarly delayed in reaching you.

The weather is beautiful – sunny and clear and warm enough that one needs no coat during the day, if one wears woolen underwear. In other words, it is like St. Louis autumn, and I have no appreciation whatsoever that a new year has begun and spring is on the way. Nor do I desire to have any such appreciation -

I hope to receive letters this evening – and shall write again -

Henry

January 27

To Mrs. A. Lowenhaupt
6237 McPherson Ave.
Saint Louis
Missouri

Dear mama -

Still writing V-mail notes – because the mail situation is desperate – but I suppose it will all come in in a great batch – and I shall have a good time reading letters for hours on end – how my fancy grows!

There is not a bit of news of which to write – weather continues lovely – I continue well – it would be nice to have something of interest of which to write. I hope you too are well -

But why dribble on to the end of the page?

Henry -

January 29

Dear mama -

I have been too impatient lately even to write a decent letter – impatient for mail, impatient for something, anything, to happen, impatient for no reason at all. Even now, I suppose, much of the irritability of impatience remains – but I read this morning the first chapter of Augustine's *Confessions* – and the book, I believe, is way up with the *Bible*, as a source of comfort and patience. It rings clear, like a bell, "Great art thou, O Lord, and truly worthy to be praised, great is thy strength, and there is no measure of thy wisdom – lend man wishes to praise thee – such is but the nature of thy creatures and man casts about and sees his own mortality, and the proof of his own sin, and proof that thou resistest the haughty; and nevertheless man wishes to praise thee – another aspect of why creature. Then stirrest him, that it delights him to praise thee; for thou hast made us to thy self, and our heart is restless until it shall rest in thee. - - -" and so forth – Rereading this I remember the excitement of the whole book, and shall read it more.

This I have been reading from a little book I bought in town the other day – called ~~Regin~~ *Religio Nova* – a selection of passages from church fathers – Minncuis, Lactantius, Ambrose, Jerome, Augustine. I had never heard of Minncuis – but he has a very beautiful and delightful passage, about resting and relaxing on the beach near Rome – watching children play – throwing balls into the water – and this companion drew a picture in the sand of an seraph, as vulgarly conceived, and put lips on it by pressing his own lips to the sand, as I understand the description. Minncius questions the propriety of this – what Caecilius draws in the sand, others, not appreciating his levity, may carve in marble – (I have been very free in my summary) Then the book continues the Edict of Milan – a famous edict now taken to have granted tolerance to Christianity, but which some have understood to grant tolerance to paganism – which it did equally, I suppose. I shall watch for an opportunity to talk about the Edict of Milan with some local priest

– my understanding is that it is thought of as a kind of Magna Carta of the Catholic Church. But I don't know.

I am well – the weather is fine – I have nothing of which to write – and it is difficult to write at all, for I have had no mail for a very long time – except a letter from Janet – she writes a miserable letter – but I suppose I should be thankful for small mercies -

I send my love -

Henry

January 29

Dear daddy -

I wonder if my letters are reaching home as irregularly (or are not reaching there so) as letters from home are reaching me. I have had none now for about ten days – except now and then some dribble, as a Christmas card, which only makes me hope and wish the more for a letter. Well – the batch to be delivered is growing – not nearly so fast in fact, I am sure, as in my imagination.

I am well – really with nothing at all of which to write – the weather here and the present climate are magnificent – while I am quite idle, I am still so bounded by conscience that I do not run around much – rarely leave camp. There are not many places to go anyway. I shall possibly take a walk tomorrow – or Monday – to see what can be found. The nearest town has nothing. Further ones probably have little more. Well – I have already written every thing possible to mama – and doubtless you read those letters.

What is happening at home and at the office?

There is about to be started a drive here for the sale of US bonds – I do not intend to buy any for several reasons, unless I am compelled to do so – my reasons – that the principal pleasure is buying things – or looking for them to buy – so I desire to keep enough money on hand to buy anything I find for sale and want to buy. I understand you are buying enough for me at home. If asked why I do not buy, I shall give the second reason.

My finances here are in good shape – I missed pay day last month, and so have 2 months pay coming day after tomorrow. In addition, I have plenty of cash in my pocket. It is a rare occasion when one can find anything to buy – but maybe if I can get to a city, I shall find something. Meanwhile, I am asking all the women who come soliciting laundry if they have any fabrics they would like to sell. I doubt if they understand what I want – when I talk about "just a little piece." They tell me that Italy is very poor after four years of war – and that is obviously true – and that the Germans have taken every-thing.

I send my love – write soon

Henry

P.S. I keep the addresses of Lts. Ravarino and Freschi – and shall look them up if ever I get near them. Ben Charles is also nearby – I have not seen him.

January 30

Dear mama -

Are you receiving any mail from me? That is an unreasonable question to ask – but I just wonder if you are as impatient for mail as I am – I suppose mine will come eventually – meanwhile there is nothing to do but wait. I could send you a telegram – with a choice of about 60 messages, none of which, I consider worth saying. So I don't intend to send one immediately.

I am well – and completely without anything to write about. My attempts so far to find some fabrics have been a complete failure. The laundresses whom I ask never mention the subject again. Well – I suppose if they have any, they do not want to sell it.

Well – I just received a very nice letter from Neal Wood – dated January 12 – which is slow for a V-mail – but these dribbles, I hope, indicated that yours will come through soon. Meanwhile, of course, I am very impatient -

The weather is fine – I am well – I shall just keep mailing letters in faith that they reach you – and keep on hoping that yours reach here soon.

Why should I try to fill these pages? I can't, anyway -

Love -

Henry

January 31

To Mrs. A. Lowenhaupt
6237 McPherson Ave.
Saint Louis
Missouri

Dear mama:

I write this V-mail letter in the hope that maybe it will reach you, if mail to you is failing to arrive as drastically as mail to me seems to be failing. I received a V-mail letter last night from Neal Wood – so maybe this kind of letter will get there. But alas , I have nothing whatsoever of which to write, and if it does get there, all you will learn is what, I suppose you know already, anyway – that I am well, and haven't anything at all to write about. I suppose that I shall not be able to stick my nose out of this place for a few days, now, for there is being operated a Rest Camp, to which a man went from here, leaving only one other here in this office. While there is substantially nothing to do, still there must be *[word crossed out]* someone here substantially all the time, because there is a telephone. Well, it never rings, and maybe I shall begin taking chances – I do not know. The Rest Camp is said by those who run it to be very lovely – abundance of recreation, as ping pong and the like, and so forth and so on. De gustibu non est disputandum[118] – and next to me, Polyanna should be considered a carping critic. if standards are good, are not double standards better?

---

[118] Latin for "In matters of taste, there can be no disputes."
https://en.wikipedia.org/wiki/De_gustibus_non_est_disputandum

Well, I very much hope to receive mail this evening – this afternoon as every afternoon I build my hopes, but there is every reason to expect a big pile now. Presumably, I am so completely written out of things to say that I cannot even make up my mind to ask you to send me something – I think I have written plenty of requests to last a long time – mostly or entirely for things like candy, which of course I do not need.

I send my love

Henry

31 January

Dear mama

My last act of the month – to spoil a piece of paper which has the potentialities of bearing an interesting letter. Oh, well.

I received a letter from Craig Clark today – brother of Bill Clark, here, with whom I spent a little time in New York once. He is now living in Omaha, Nebraska – an artist – from New York.

So I answered it – raving a little bit -

There's not a bit to write about – I've done nothing all day -

I am well, and send my love. Write often – letters will possibly reach me tomorrow

Henry.

February 1

Mrs. A. Lowenhaupt
6237 McPherson Ave.
Saint Louis,
Missouri
U. S. A.

Dear mama -

I have a typewriter out and nothing whatsoever to say – but still feel that I should write now and then, just to do what I can to keep letters coming. I try this V mail again in despair that regular letters will come through at all – for I have been receiving substantially no regular mail. Maybe the situation is different there – and if it is this will be a kind of disappointment, I suppose, for it will be expected to be a letter than then will not be.

You see, the last letter I have from you is one dated December 24, except for a V mail note dated January 3. But I have an air mail letter from Craig Clark, Omaha, Nebraska, dated January 18 – and I do not understand the situation at all. Perhaps it surpasses human understanding altogether anyway. But I am sure that you are writing now and then – maybe you have taken a vacation in Tennessee in connection with the lecture daddy was to give there, and that might account for a lack of mail. I hope that you are all well.

I am well. Today is a cloudy day, but not raining, and yesterday was a beautiful sunny one – so I hope that by tomorrow the sun will be out again. It is chilly, but not cold – and my little kerosene stove, which I have burning on the hope of a wick and a pair of socks, does satisfactorily. I wrote to Sears Roebuck & Co for a wick December 27 – I wonder if they are sending it. The letter was somewhat experimental – I told them to send the wick by air mail, and to send a bill for it to Hy. I also wrote Hy that I was doing so. The whole time, I was satisfied that by the time it came, the weather would be warm anyway– and I suppose it will be. Meanwhile, wicks can be made, each of which will last a week or so, out of socks, string, rags, blotting paper, and anything else that will tangle up together and *[word crossed out]* stick into the stove. The wick burns consistently – but that does not matter.

It is a shame to have so little to write of – I have not been out as far as the road for a day or two – not because I am busy, but because I am under the necessity of being by the telephone most of the time. So I sit here – or stand outside, and watch the laundresses going around soliciting laundry. They do not seem able or else they are unwilling to get me a piece of material or fabric, although I should pay them a very splendid price for it. I shall ask them again – very likely they do not really believe I want it – or they think that the kind I want would be shiny rayon – which possibly they think is very beautiful – made into one of these piano-throws, in yellow and red and gold and green, either painted on or woven in very shiny threads. The kind which I think Mrs. Max Baron would like, but which I should consider too ugly to use even as a dust rag. Or maybe they actually have none, or having some are unwilling to sell it at any price. I have specified wool or linen – shall have to look up the word for cotton, so that I can include that – but after I ask, they never show up again. No harm done – the request is probably so strange and peculiar to them that they think there is some mystery to it. But there isn't.

How did daddy's lecture turn out? Did he enjoy it? Were you able to make him prepare it? Or was he too busy to do anything about it, or did he decide not to give it after all?

Still, what's the use of asking questions; unless you tell me, I shall have forgotten the questions before you can answer them specifically.

I send my love

Henry

February 2

Mrs. A Lowenhaupt
6237 McPherson Ave.
Saint Louis, Missouri
U. S. A.

Dear mama:

This is just a somewhat feeble attempt to keep mail coming to you – if that is possible. Now, as the evening comes on, I have built up all my hope very high of receiving at least one letter this evening, and if I do, I shall write a long hand letter. Presently, I just write another note, to let you know that I am well, and still hopeful. But I am becoming accustomed to not receiving mail – so if none comes this evening, I shall merely defer my hopes for tomorrow. But I have now finished writing about the mail situation – and shall not mention it again until I receive a letter. Then, I shall be so happy that I shall not be able to come any place near expressing my joy.

Captain Morris came up here to see me this afternoon, and I enjoyed his visit. We talked about nothing in particular – but it was a very great pleasure. He is intelligent.

The weather is beautiful – clear and sunny now – and after a few days I expect to take a walk to a nearby town. Right now, I may not because, being understaffed, I have to stay near the telephone a good part of the time myself – to see that it is answered if it rings, and I have no one to do the few little odds and ends of things which are to be done.

It is almost Ruth's birthday – I have written her a letter on the subject – and surely hope that you have some kind of celebration. Then Marian's comes next, and that calls for another celebration.

I send all my love,

Henry

February 3

Dear mama – I am ashamed that it has been so long since I have written a decent letter, and even now doubt that I can, since I have nothing to say and my mind is empty. I have been writing Vmails, because I have expected mail momentarily. But isn't that silly – suppose I do go for a month or six weeks without receiving mail – I suppose that is to be expected. That was impressed on me the other day by the family D'Alterio, who have a brother living in New York. ~~We~~ I wrote the brother a letter, saying that the family here was well and so forth – and he replied – sentimentally – that he was lighting candles for us in church, and so forth – Captain Morris delivered this letter to the D'Alterios here – and there was weeping and hysteria – for they had not heard of him for about four years.

Another funny thing – a lady sent Captain Morris some seeds – she was a garden club enthusiast, and in thanking her, he exaggerated a bit – about a farm family to whom he gave the seeds, how they were bundled over a few sticks of wood, barefoot, the doors of their house knocked down, and their furniture burned, windows broken, trees cut down, no crops, nothing – and they were so thankful for the seeds (zinnias, watermelons, radishes, carrots, tomatoes) because they could start their farm over again and have something to eat in the ~~spring~~ fall of next year. (A long wait, I say) The lady had the letter published in her garden club journal, which added an appealing editorial that everyone should send seeds to soldiers overseas. Maybe so – but I hope no friends of mine receive the editorials or send me seeds. I think that to give a hungry farmer a watermelon seed is a little worse than telling him to eat grass, or if he has no bread, to eat cake.

I am well – I received a V-mail letter from Janet Cerf last night – typed and disappointing. But she mentioned that she went to a movie with Marian and that Marian is working at a laboratory – so I infer that Marian is well – for which I am happy. She also says she intends to go out and see you and daddy – and I make the same inference. So possibly I am up to date on all the news there – I hope so.

Meanwhile – I send all my love -

Henry.

February 4

Dear mama -

I say every evening: "What a baby I am to feel so bad about not getting mail." And now I have myself steeled to the point where I really do not expect mail any more. But I still wait for evening, when it comes – partly for that, but largely to go to bed.

People lend me books sometimes, and I read them – and regret that they have been lent to me – as *The Prodigal Women*[119], which is a very uninteresting, rambling book. I have almost finished it – and shall be glad to get it out of the way.

I was just given a piece of excellent sausage – salami – and request, therefore, that you send me a sausage – about four pounds.

The weather is exciting today – rain for a while, and then the sun comes through, to the olive trees, which still hold their leaves, and beautiful green color – not at all like the color of wool called olive green.

I am writing this letter paragraph by paragraph, with hours between each paragraph. Shall mail it tonight,

Now it is evening – the mail is delivered – and I still have nothing of which to write. I am well – I shall telephone the post office and ask whether mail is coming through at all – but I do not know what I shall do with the answer.

---

[119] Best-selling novel by Nancy Hale about the lives of three women.
https://archive.org/details/prodigalwomen1988hale
Nancy Hale Wikipedia
https://en.wikipedia.org/wiki/Nancy_Hale

I am well – and send all my love – shall try to write a more nearly coherent letter tomorrow.

Henry

February 4

Dear Myron and Sonya[120]-

I have a recollection that I owe you letters – and I desire to write – although to begin with, I feel so dull and stale, since it is long that I have received mail, that I do not think I can write much. But I shall try – I have just finished what is considered an excellent dinner – steak, creamed peas, macaroni, and chocolate pie. "Better a dinner of herbs, and peace therewith , than a houseful of feasting and strife - - -" something like that – especially if the steak for the feasting is tough. But I enjoyed dinner and reflect that I have been eating extraordinarily well.

It would be nice to have a drink this evening – which led me to suggest a commercial venture, of which I have previously spoken to you, if the engineering business is slow. I have been offered good liquor once or twice – but have not been able to make up my mind to it. A bottle of Black & White, Scotch, at $40.00 a quart. A Bottle of "original" Italian brandy at $37.00 a litre – That indicates the prices – and if you should charter a little sail boat, load it with a few bottles of whisky or gin or rum, a few pounds of coffee, and a few chickens, you could make quite a killing in Italy. Your liquor you could sell at a bargain – say $35.00 a quart your coffee at about $40.00 a pound; your eggs – laid on the journey – at, say, $0.25 each. Then you could visit here for a while – and we should have a very jolly time. I'd entertain you on vino and walnuts and apples and oranges.

I'll advance the capital, or a share of it, for any such venture.

You may think I am not serious – but I am. You will recall the basic American fortunes were made just so – tea and silks and similar goods from China – many during the Napoleonic wars. For a small boat, the seas would be fairly safe. I am writing a letter to Hy, urging him to make such a venture – you might consolidate into one enterprise. There is not much you could carry back with you – but walnuts keep and might bring a good price -

Please contact Hy, to whom I am writing further details of the venture -

Kindest regards -

Henry

---

[120] The Glassbergs

February 5

Mrs. A. Lowenhaupt
6237 McPherson Ave.
Saint Louis
Missouri

Dear mama –

Just received your letters of January 6 and 8 – and write to tell you how delighted I am – and how I desire to revoke all my complaints about lack of mail -

Just took a very beautiful walk up the road -

Henry

February 5

Dear mama –

I am very anxious to write a decent letter, for it seems long since I have done so – and some day, when mail comes in, I shall have written, saying nothing. At the same time I go on from day to day, and nothing happens and I do nothing to write about. The weather changes a little – today, a heavy wind – last night, rain and hail – some sun now. My thoughts seem to remain perfectly static. So how can I write?

I am well. I took a shower yesterday – always enjoy showers, for as one stands in the hot water, one does not think of anything or try to, except whether to put more soap on; whether all the soap is off; how good the water feels – all one's thoughts become purely physical. The showers are quite an elaborate contraption – a water truck – and the hose leads ~~into two pep~~ first into a pump, which pumps the water into two pipes. One leads into a stove, and the other direct to the showers. I think the pump could be eliminated by driving the truck up a hill – but that would not be fancy. Then the heat of the water is adjusted by opening and closing the pipes with valves, regulating the relative amounts drawn through the stove and direct from the tank – you could make showers like that at Copperwood – setting them up down the hill a way, so that you would need to water pump – just two pipes from a tank, one leading through a fire.

So I have been taking about three showers a week – they are available every other day.

Food has improved enormously recently – Up to about a week ago we were eating what is called C rations daily for dinner. That consists of a canned stew of meat and vegetables or meat and beans or chili. For lunch, either what I call Spam (a prepared luncheon meat of mediocre quality – pork, I think), or corned beef. Breakfast is always, consistently my favorite meal – fruit juice (canned) cereal and ~~eith~~ hot cakes or French toast or powdered egg omelet. (I am now in the habit of speaking of "egg omelet" – is there any other kind?) But now we are getting some fresh meat – roast beef, and so forth, and they acquired some mustard and vinegar and other condiments (there has always been plenty of pepper) which add greatly to the taste. Last night – a kind of chocolate tapioca pie – even!

But I am a very skilled eater – I find that I can eat corned beef patties, and have no idea, unless someone asks me and makes me think of it, whether I am eating cod fish or sweet-breads or hamburger or anything else – and perfectly tasteless string beans – one doesn't know what one is eating unless one looks carefully. Why look carefully? Unless there is something good. It is always a surprise to eat a piece of bread, for that tastes very good -

Something just brought a matter into my mind concerning which I should like to write a note to daddy – so I'll write it with this -

All my love -

Henry

February 5

Dear daddy -

I have just closed a letter to mama – with which I send this – and therefore I have nothing to write about what I am doing or that I am well.

In that letter, however, I was interrupted by two boys who came in having family troubles at home, in which they were helpless and lost, and concerning which, of course, they felt terrible. I sent them to a man named Vogel, who is the local representative of the Red Cross – and he is able to give them satisfaction. So I remembered that I intended to write you about the work which Red Cross is doing here – and to express the opinion that of the agencies which I have seen attempting humanitarian work and so-called "morale" work, it is about the only mature one. USO, of course, does not exist here – The entertainers, for the most part, are juvenile – men go not so much because they enjoy it or get anything out of it as because it furnishes an excuse to get out for a while – and the more work there is to be done the more anxious they are to go. They all have a tendency, in fact, to, treat men like children at a boy's camp – but maybe that is right.

The Red Cross, it seems to me, is much more mature – it does not advertise itself so much – it allows for independence of thought and taste – and really simply holds itself available. It maintains places in the towns where men can go independently and has men in most units available to render services. The representatives here are excellent men, very quick to see what men want, and to the extent of possibility, to furnish it. They don't particularly render reports, which always make a tendency to talk in terms of sweetness and light, as of the beautiful games of ping pong and how popular the (Hobson's choice) game is. In other words, it seems to me that there is less of the social service mentality, as I call it, in Red Cross than in the other institutions I have seen – less of the selfish opportunism and going on a grand spree under the name of benevolence.

I decided to mention this opinion to you – because I do not know how much money I have or much else about any financial situation – but nevertheless should like to suggest that you give from whatever I have an amount which you consider reasonable. I think that Red Cross might well be the only war charity to which I give anything.

Maybe I have written only what is very well known – but I have decided to write it to you anyway.

Affectionately,

Henry.

P.S. From time to time I send checks to some charity or another – the total does not amount to anything, and I do not know if they clear -

H

February 6

Dear mama -

I just received your letters of January 6 and 8 – and it surely was a pleasure to hear from you – and now, with that beginning. I am sure I shall receive mail more regularly. I am glad you received the first plate I sent – and am glad you think it is pretty enough to keep out – I thought it quite magnificent – and hope you receive two others I sent. Also daddy's box should be there by now – I sent it about December 20 – and as I remember it, am not sure it was worth sending. But just wait till you receive – two more plates, a blue one and a yellow one, and two cups and saucers. My my – how that house will be littered with china – but Ruth can keep some of it in her corner cupboard, if you lack space.

I wrote a letter to Bunk White[121] last night, and enjoyed doing it, trying to describe the farming situation here. I do not know whether or not I succeeded – but I mailed my letter without rereading it, because I have learned that if I think too long about it, I never mail such a letter.

Right now – I am having a good time – it is required that someone be awake at all times – just why I don't know – so I am in another tent – I found they (the boys who usually use this tent) had some coffee and they also have some doughnuts. I adopted some of the coffee – and now have coffee brewing. So I shall have coffee and doughnuts –and imagine I am sitting at a trucker's restaurant.

I am well – without any news of which to write – the rain has ended –and the mud dried up – the weather is now lovely – I have even considered taking off my long underwear, 50% wool – but shall wait a month or so at least.

Please do not worry about my getting 50 or 60 letters at once – it would be a pleasure completely beyond imagination.

I took a walk yesterday afternoon – about a mile and a half up the road – it was lovely – the clear, snow-covered mountains in bright sun – this valley, turned quite green, and many fields covered with daisies – a few goats – little herds of 4 or 5 – three towns in sight on the hill.

This is the last sheet of paper I have here – I am borrowing these people blind – I think they won't care – and send my love -

Henry

---

[121] Bunk White was a farmer who was a neighbor in Silex (near Copperwood)

February 6

Dear mama -

I wrote a very short letter last night – telling you I have received letters from you. I have reread them today.

Now we are in a new place – and although I have not had opportunity to look around to any extent, I have seen that the natural beauty of the place is great – in a wild sense – We are on a mountainside – below us, a main road, and then opposite us, another mountain, making the place a perfect bowl – The mountain tops are covered with snow, but the lower reaches are still green – Ruins of buildings are visible on the mountains.

Then, close by, is a town – apparently once quite a large town – and seen from this distance, about a mile, it gives the beautiful appearance of Jerusalem in a medieval painting. But even here, if you look closely, you see that the standing walls are jagged, without roofs, and many of them have great holes through them. The church tower has no tops, and a side is missing. So I do not expect much interest in the town, even if I can get there.

Two children were wandering around here today. I asked if they could sell any chestnuts – "Niente," they said. Or any walnuts. "Niente." Or any apples – "Niente" they repeated - "Boom, boom! niente." I suppose that is the answer to every question.

This, again, is an olive grove, but here it is as if an enormous goose waddled through and ate the tops and parts of the trees – most of them are down. There are remains of two stone houses – just wrecks – but in the basements, you can see pieces of wine kegs, pitchers, and other things. An old worktable still stands on the first floor, but the floor is gone, except right under it – there is no second floor left.

But I shall walk a while tomorrow, if I can. This appears to be a terribly desolate valley – everything destroyed – and the towns were built so beautifully on the hills – on the rocks, out of rock, rising from rock – as if they should support the very keys to heaven. Mixing metaphors? Well -

It has turned cold – with a howling wind from the mountains – ~~one~~ but the sun when it shines is delightfully warm – and during the day one even perspires. Now, we have two tents put up together, and I am burning both kerosene stoves. I am holding my thumbs on the subject of wicks – Sears Roebuck should come through – soon!

I am well. It would be possible to go to see some grand opera some evening – but I do not like the idea of the drive – about forty miles each way – especially at night – I enjoy it during the day – and the opera – *[unclear]* at best – and the company had an excellent name – would not suit me – I don't think I could sit though *Carmen* or Rigoletto or any other. So I do not intend to go. It is not held in the regular opera house of the company, which is in a city to which we may no longer go. They have, instead, a small auditorium in a palace.

The move here today was relatively easy, for I found a trailer standing unloaded and hitched it on to the truck – So packing wasn't necessary, and everything could just be thrown in. But it is still quite a little work to put up tents and get straightened out again – and do various other things. Still, moving is the principal pleasure, for it gives variety.

I should like to tell you where I am, because you would be interested, and really my geographical location is of no significance except as a matter of curiosity – and it is rocky to restrain myself. But I'll just go along in the same old boat – near a nameless town on a stony hill, the town built of natural rock – they all are – anyway – if I should tell you I'd be elsewhere by the time this reached you.

I agree with Betty that Marian should have as much academic training as possible – and should continue in school – at least a master's degree – if possible, a doctor's. Right now is a tricky time, because, I suppose jobs are very easy to get. But later the demand will be less and the competition more severe. In usual times, I imagine Dr. Moore might get a good deal of even volunteer assistance, for the experience and contact and a recommendation – and I think Marian is lucky to have these.

I have not been <u>in</u> any snow in Italy – have only seen it on the mountain tops. I am glad Haymer received the little cards – they are of no value – except a joke – Particularly delighted that you agree with me – as I take it you do – that the plate (I assume it is the pink one) is a gem and masterpiece

Love

Henry

February 7

Dear mama -

It had been a very beautiful day today – cold and clear – and the sun on the mountains and in the valleys is lovely. This afternoon I walked up to the town – alas! there is no town left. It used to be on a steep hillside – with a cobbled street leading up in steps from a river, where women were washing clothes and other things. But the new road went by a bridge, over this street, which comes up a small canyon – the bridge was destroyed and blocked the street. Now one gets into the town, just walking in – and the town must have consisted of narrow, alley-like street, steep in steps, opening onto squares here and there – one can trace them by the jagged fragments of walls. One walks, not as through a town, but picking one's way over heaps of rubble – and I don't think there is a whole building left – Here and there a doorway stands, and someone sets up a barber shop in a corner of the ruins – a room may still be left – people live in it. But though the town looks as if it had about 7 or 8000 people, at one time, I don't think I saw more than about eight. One a barber – cutting hair among rocks – one little girl, holding a baby on her lap – and in back of her – in a little square, within a wall built of old stones, about two feet high, a woman with a charcoal fire.

Although there is no sign of fire – no clearing – I see no pieces of furniture, no pieces of cloth of clothing – either it was all removed long ago or the ruins have been very thoroughly searched for fuel and rags.

I may go back to the town – but I do not see how it can improve, now I suppose people will go back, for lack of any other place to go. I saw one old woman carrying rubble in a basket to the cliff, and throwing it over – cleaning up – but there were tons of it – and when she is all through, she'll have nothing there.

I came back and took a shower – using the last of the Fitch's shampoo Mrs. Max Myer sent me – it has proved quite enjoyable, for I have had opportunity to use it. But my hair is so short – I can wash it with any kind of soap very easily. So I do not need a luxurious shampoo.

That is all I have done today. I am well – without any complaints. Went to bed early last night, and slept substantially around the clock.

A Lt. Vallere here went a few days ago to a place where I spent a few days – I asked him to buy me an inlaid box, because I wanted to send a present to I've forgotten whom – I have the box – of course it is not nice, being poor workmanship, highly commercialized – but it is a sample of what is sold like hot cakes to souvenir buyers. I intend to send it to Myron and Sunny[122] – who sent me a rotten box of comestibles.

I am now out of edibles – chestnuts, apples and oranges being exhausted. I am doubtful that I shall be able to get more around here, for there are no people. But maybe I shall find an opportunity to go elsewhere.

February 8

Last night, there was a kind of party at the Rear Echelon – and I went back there – ate a recovered supper and drank some wine. I had a good time, because I had enough wine, and it was a very great pleasure to be with Lt. Clark & Claude Morris again for a while

[Letter incomplete.]

February 8 1944

Mrs. A Lowenhaupt
6237 McPherson Ave.
Saint Louis Missouri

Dear mama. I am writing this V mail because I am rather tired today, and at the same time want to write to you. I just received three letters – the latest of January 12 – and do not know whether it is because I am tired or what – I read into the letters that you are much worried about Ben. I wish I could suggest something to be done, but as far as I can see everything is just a matter of luck, Ben could ask for a furlough, but he knows, and I cannot know whether or not there is a possibility of its being granted. Of course he is wasting his time and doing nothing – and that is just about inevitable. Beyond just trusting to luck, the only thing is to go out feeling – and I think that if daddy should get to Washington or around military establishments, he might feel around and find out what could be wanted or what done. I should like to convey an idea of the caliber of the men he might expect to find with sufficient power to accomplish something. They are very able men, I believe, but that does not mean anything. To put them in the category of ability of men with whom daddy deals quite frequently, I name a few men from the Revenue Agent's Office – a man named Campbell, whom I remember, and one named Brown, and Beffa (I forget most of the names) Then among accountants, say, men like Boggiano and others. I think daddy may very generally have a tendency to miscalculate the ability and good qualities of people with whom he deals, considering appearance and self assurance as indicated of other than that of which they are indicative. But he knows very well how to deal with people, even of the calibre and quality of, say, Stix Friedman or Max Baron. If not, he ought to take a few lessons from Arthur Lindberg, say.[123]

Sometimes one gets quite impatient – and there is nothing which can be done about it. Time is so long – but I suppose one just cannot think much about it. I am sure that I cannot give long distance advice. Did I ever tell you that back in December of 1942 I was in very ill grace for a while – was told to go back after three weeks to learn if I would be forgiven a little imprudence I had not suppressed, During the period Mr. Ulmer telephoned me from an office in the Capitol, a secretary making the call and giving her employer's, a public official's name? The whole matter was promptly forgotten, and I had to insist upon being heard and told that I was forgiven because – well, there is no use surmising. So one can reflect on mental

---

[122] Glassbergs
[123] Stix Friedman was a close friend of Henry in later years. Max Baron and Arthur Lindberg were friends of Abe.

attitudes, and see that men are peculiar. I can imagine a game among little girls in which the President of the Wednesday Club would be such a great woman that her name would be spoken in whispers only. You can get special consideration and service from a newsboy if you say the name of the local Justice of the Peace or Policeman. The principle goes throughout. One hears and hears about the importance of a meeting which is to take place – and how one should prepare for weeks in advance. Then the meeting is moved up about three weeks – one is summoned hastily, and told to abbreviate the preparation by not putting on a clean shirt – just combing one's hair. So the preparation – well, it is all a matter of standards.

This is a rambling, senseless letter – the reason, I suppose, that I feel so strongly that I should like to be home, and cannot say anything which even shows up against the feeling. But I am well – sleepy, as I say, because I was up late last night, going to a kind of party, of which I wrote you this morning. The drive was thoroughly magnificent.

I have letters from Philip[124], Janet Cerfand Myron Glassberg – shall answer them.

All my love

Henry

February 9

Mrs. H. Lowenhaupt
~~La Playa Hotel~~
~~Carmel by the Sea~~
California, U.S.A.

Dear Aunt Sally -

Thank you so much for your letter. I cannot answer it now, because I am in a dull, stale mood – but it does arouse memories of an awfully good time I had at a rest place for two days about a month ago -

A beautiful place – and I spent a great deal of time wandering around, looking in shop windows, looking for, but not finding, of course, useful things, because, I suppose, there just are none left – there is so little left in this country -

And having a long talk with a woman whose name, as I understood it, was Gargiula – who ran a shop and told me about how hard it was to feed her eleven adopted daughters – how she woke in the morning, and thought about what she could give them, they needed at least a good soup – and finally got up with a headache. Then there was a woman – a nun – who had her 57 aged people to feed, and she had a can she had begged from a ration dump – (She hitch-hiked, and showed me how she thumbed a ride, with a full sweep of the arm in the bear Claudette Colbert manner) She asked me to translate the label, so she could tell what she had and how to purpose it. It was "Yankee bean soup, prepared from navy beans of the finest quality. Add the contents of this can to four gallons of water." How would you translate that into Latin? She knew the universal words of French – as soupe – Navy bean – haricot de marine? I doubt it. But I think before I was through, she at least knew she had soup – and I suggested she add water to the content, little by little, until it tasted good. I think that is better than to try to make an exact conversion of gallons to litres.

---

[124] Philip Moss, Henry's cousin

I wish I could tell you, my mother & others where I am and was – maybe later I shall be able to. I shall write again.

Henry

February 9

Dear mama –

Now and then it strikes me what piddling letters I write – refreshing to try to write what my mind wants to tell me, and what I refuse to hear – and I get kind of desperate to find some pleasant reality – seeing that things are so rotten. Well -

Right now I am a little worried – possibly I am going to get into some trouble, but not much, over an arrangement I have made for my own convenience – namely, that I am sleeping in the same tent with two men – and there is an insane idea that that destroys the proper distance and hauteur. I am of a contrary opinion – and it adds greatly to convenience, because I then have them around if there is something to be done – can keep them out of bed during the day – and use my space much better. Further convenience – that I think it is too cold to sleep in a pup tent, and I think there are lice in the big tents – so for my own protection I have to keep them here, and shall continue to do so until and unless someone steps on me for it. So that is not a very serious worry – my offense cannot be regarded as more than an error of judgment -

I am well. I cannot think of distant problems – they make for desperations – and I am kind of waiting things out, because everything has to end soon. It gets very long and very distressing and hopeless. But I am comfortable, meanwhile, and now and then can find a few things of interest.

I send my love – and should leave this letter unsealed till I see if I have mail this evening.

I have.

I am very sorry to learn that plates arrived broken – I considered them quite beautiful, and although I agree that in the cosmic scheme they are very unimportant, still I never think of the cosmic scheme and grow smaller and smaller. At any rate, I am glad the best one arrived intact – and if I can find any more shall see that they are packed better. But I have abandoned hope of getting back to a city. My little Capodimonte cups are on the way – and I hope they arrive safely.

Mama, your letters sound to me as if you are worrying a good deal, and about things which are temporary and which you can't help. Why not just give up – and let things pass and take it easy?

I gather that you did not go to Chattanooga or wherever it was daddy was going to be on January 21.

The motor of my power saw is probably alright– the connection very likely bad in the switch. I suggested the possibly if you turn an electric fan on it, and blow as much dust out of it as you can, and especially out of the switch (no oil), it will probably work with a little jiggling. Dust gets into it, especially saw dust, and breaks the electrical contact.

Now you get long-distance electric repair advice.

Cut-outs like pigeons, are best made of ply wood – because it doesn't split all the way through easily.

I hope you are able to have the plates repaired – they are, I think, colorful, and pretty.

I am well – and send all my love -

Henry

February 10

Dear mama -

No mail this evening – it is raining, and I am impatient to go to bed to hear the nice patter of the drops. First a quick note – with nothing to say for I have been close to this place all day.

I feel as if I am in an unfortunate period – my plates got home broken, and I considered them so beautiful! – and I learned of that last night. This morning, my watch was broken and it is just too much of an undertaking to try to have it fixed. I tried to fix it myself, and lost two hands of it now, it clearly is not worth trying here. So I shall send it home. Will you have it fixed and return it to me, if it seems worthwhile – or if anyone there needs a watch, let him keep it – letting me know?

So I feel that everything is getting broken – and it makes me sad – little things are so much more appreciable -

Add to that a stove – I sent it to an place to be repaired – and they lost a part – fine job of repairing, though.

I am well – and shall get over the unhappiness of this torrent of broken things. How small they are – but, as I say. I am not cosmic minded.

Love -

Henry

February 12

Dear mama -

I have great pleasure in your letter about spoiling Haymer on January 24 and shall read it again when I close this. You know that I am not in need of anything – when I mention comestibles, I name them as something I enjoy receiving. I have plenty of underwear and socks and handkerchiefs.

I sent home an ugly, inlaid box, which a man here got for me – I packed my broken wristwatch in it. It is a good watch – and if it can be repaired, possibly you will return it to me – or if daddy or Hy wants a watch, let me know and I shall look for another. I have become so dependent on time-pieces. The box – would you give it to Myron and Sonya or Heather and Forrest as a gift from me – or anyone else.

I wrote you, I believe, that I sent two Capodimonte cups and saucers – a friend went to the place where I got them, and I asked him to see if he could get me the third – If he can, I shall send it home too. I surely hope they arrive safely. I shall continue to look for plates to replace those broken. Let me see what I have on the way still – the cups & saucers – a large blue tablecloth; a bright colored tablecloth; a carved box; a piece of lace or linen (maybe for Betty?) a piece of brocade, and I think that is all. I suppose you have most of it by now, for the last was sent about January 2, and since that time I have seen nothing.

I walked up the mountain today – about two miles by road – as beautiful a walk as I have seen – looking out over the valley, to distant towns, and rivers spread out, through olive trees, which still have their leaves, although they are grown brittle and dry – but still a dull green. Just in sight a big building capping a hill – and way below it the town – a little mist in the air, but high, clear colors – Do you remember the stain glass window in a factory – I've forgotten just where – with a funny combination of angels and men in business suits? Well – I thought of it – I don't know why. On the other side – close by – the remnants of a town clinging to the mountain side.

I am well – the weather is cold – and tonight quite clear – after moonrise it will be bright as day. Now, it is pitch dark, with a howling cold wind, and I have both of my stoves going.

So I am warm.

Funny – I am not sure I should tell it – an officer here decided to set himself up beautifully. He put up his tent right at the base of a terrace – like this *[diagram]* - figuring he'd have much protection from wind – the back of the tent right against the bank. Then he dug a hole at the back of the tent – to play soldier, one digs fox-holes – a beauty, about two feet deep – just about six inches shorter than his cot, so that the ends rested about three inches beyond either end of the hole. The middle legs stood upon a board, placed across the hole, resting on about three inches on either side.

Then last night, it poured rain, with some wind for a while – the water drained from the ground above, filled the hole – and the walls began caving. The officer jumped out of bed – then the back pole of the ten washed out – the rivers flowed through the tent – and the front pole washed out, and the whole collapsed. Was he mad this morning – and cursing (almost) his orderly. Yesterday, he was beaming as he showed the set up with pride – his own design. But he is a dumb man – and his discomfiture amuses me a little bit.

Well – as they say, work and pray – ora et labor – and if there is less work there may be more pray – and I send my love -

Henry

February 13

Dear mama -

I have your letter of January 15 – You should not be sorry you mentioned materials – because they are a pleasant thing to keep in mind looking for – and I have not yet found any. Maybe I shall – Being in a new area, I shall ask the man who is gleaning olives – shriveled ones left on the ground. He had already told me he has no chestnuts or walnuts.

My, you cannot realize how exciting shopping on Delmar[125] sounded – I had not realized that grocery stores might be crowded – and crowds of civilians shopping and buying is something I have not seen or thought of for so long. You see, I really have not seen any civilians except a few isolated individuals – no crowds, which were not poor and unprosperous looking – for almost a year now. That is very strange to

---

[125] Street in St. Louis that had supermarkets

me, and I have no appreciation of whether your description indicates wild panic going on – shopping for dried onions – or whether Delmar is usually or normally crowded on Saturday morning.

Ah Things go on – without change – magnificent weather today, a warm sun. But the instant sun sets, it turns cold. Last night, it froze – ice on the puddles, and a crust over the ground.

I am very well contented. While frequently I become homesick, still if I am to be in the army, I much prefer it here. Presently, it is even fairly pleasant– as I lead a quiet, peaceful, remote life, without interruptions – and able to forget most of the notions and characteristics of the army, which flourish most there – and just go on, eating enough, sleeping enough – quite idle and comfortable.

I send my love -

Henry

February 14

Miss Marian Lowenhaupt
6237 McPherson Ave
Saint Louis
Missouri

Dear Marian:

I have written you one birthday letter. Now I have some forced waiting and shall write another. The mails are not certain, it seems. *[Word unclear]* to the contrary notwithstanding, and the time of arrival is highly speculative.

I should certainly like to have at least one birthday present reach you in good time. The bracelet was not intended as a birthday gift, but an incidental nothing, sent long before I even thought of your birthday. I hope you like it, as I understand now you have received it. It amounts to nothing, in my opinion. Recently, I've had no opportunity to look for anything, not having been to a town or city. It is long since I have been to a city, so long that no matter how I try, I cannot remember what building and streets and crowds look like. So mama's description of Delmar fascinated me.

Mama says that she likes unexpected packages, for no particular occasion, best, to remain unexpectant, which, on experience, ought to be too hard – and I hope I shall have opportunity to surprise you. I don't know what an "anscingo[126]" is, but expect or hope to be given one. Italy offers no finer one than I shall get – because the man's sister made it. But I fear that anscingoing *[sic]* may be to simply knit – I shall see.

So I wish you a very, very happy birthday – and very many returns – and send my love -

Affectionately -

Henry

---

[126] No such word in Italian exists. I assume this is a phonetic spelling.

February 14

Dear mama:

I cleaned out my suit case today and a barracks bag – partly to see what I had and to try to find out if I needed anything. It is a distressing inventory and one which makes me a little sad, for some reason. But first let me relate my incident of the morning. The man who owns the ground on which we are staying was gleaning olives – he came over, and I sent some laundry and got into a conversation about the beauties of Italy – and he about the beauties of the United States, to which he hopes to go after the war. I told him that Italy had such beautiful things made by hand – and in America there was nothing except factory made things. That I should like to show "mama mia" some of the beautiful things they had in Italy – and he volunteered that he would like to give an "ansciugo" (I don't know what that is – but he indicated a head cover, and I suppose it is a shawl) "Per ricordar" as a souvenir. I protested that I had nothing to give him in exchange, when he said he did not wish to sell it. So my purpose in going through my baggage was to see what I could give him if an "asciugo" is something I want. (I fear it may be just a knitted piece). I found – a cake of soap (I am low on private soap, but can get issue soap, which, however, I may not give away) a dirty comb, one pair of civilian socks (red) one tie (of the two you sent me), do you remember? The other] I gave to Jacques Peyrus in Algiers) and that is all. Well, I wish National Candy would come through with some candy – they do at intervals, and maybe I shall get some soon.

So you see, if you feel like sending me anything, how easy it is to find something – either practical or sentimental. Little religious cards, such as I am sure the store down on Broadway between Market and Chestnut would sell, would be of surprising and great sentimental value. Then I am always ashamed when I give away something poor, because it seems so condescending to give a man something possibly useful but not desirable – like giving toilet paper. But perfumed soap; thread, cigarettes, any pretty, small object, such as you might consider a curiosity if you got it from Italy, food of any kind (candy, of course), is *[sic]* so far, and I think I could not resist eating almost any I might receive. so candy is not in the class of barter-goods. But maybe things are not available there either.

This man told me about his sister, who lives in the neighboring town. Her brother-in-law, sent her from a city a fine Singer (pronounced Sinjer) sewing machine – a new one, just about five years old, and it was the finest thing in town. Nobody had anything like it, and the whole town knew of the machine, and was proud to have it in town, and when they had some fine sewing to do, would borrow his sister's machine. So the Germans knew about this fine machine, and before they left, they took the machine and carried it away, because it was the finest in town. It was terrible – they broke it, he is sure. What a moral! Lay up your treasures in heaven, where moths do not eat gold – is that right? – and wood does not rust.

Well, I enjoyed my conversation with the man – maybe he was friendly because when I sent laundry, I wrapped it with a few rolls of these terrible fruit drops, hard things with holes in the middle, in rolls, which are so abundant here. Also a cake of Woodbury's soap, in addition to enough laundry soap. He is a nice man, and from his manner and pleasant appearance, I should say that he once lived well. He owns land, which indicates wealth – not a peasant, but a kind of small-town tycoon. His father lived in Brooklyn for a long time, and, I suppose, when he came back invested his savings in this land. The land had a fine olive grove, and good buildings – stone houses. But the houses are destroyed, and the olive trees very much broken up. It is rocky – I suppose too rocky for annual crops, although there are parts of it where the soil is deep and rich. It is just below the town – I cannot see what the future of these towns is, they are so badly destroyed.

I am well. I send my love. This paper I found in my suit-case, for I had carried it since Caltanisetta[127], and now, I think, I may use it – curiosity. Do you remember that I wrote you about a palace in Sicily? With records of courts and trials and everything else strewn all over, and archives scattered to the four xxx winds? That was Caltanisetta.

Henry

15 February

Dear mama -

I am typing this letter because I am tired this evening, having been up very early this morning. Typing is less work than long-hand. Nevertheless, I have had such a pleasant day today that I am anxious to write this evening – one pleasant experience, and two distressing sights.

I have already written you about the man who was going to give me an "ansciuga" as a souvenir of the beautiful things that are made by hand in Italy. Well, much to my surprise and delight, he brought it with my laundry today. It is a towel – for which my dictionary gives "asciugamno" – I suppose a hand towel, but this is a bath towel, maybe an "asciuga". I am sending it to you, and I consider it a beautiful piece of materials – the kind I like particularly to see. It is of natural colored linen – home spun and home woven – quite big – and may be a dresser scarf, but I think it is a towel. It is very beautiful linen – no color, nor decoration, except a repetition of three heavy threads at each end, and tassels at each end. It is heavy linen, and if you decided to use it as a towel, I especially request that daddy be permitted to use it after his next bath. But I think it is lovely enough, just as plain, fine craftsmanlike work, to use just to look at. It is the example of fine work on fine material. But what a luxurious bath towel it would make – I put a drop of water on it and it spread and absorbed into the material – one could dry anything beautifully.

I suppose it is an expensive towel, if you consider the cost of what I gave in exchange; but if you consider its value to me – I am glad I gave it away; and should be glad even if I hadn't gotten very beautiful towel. I cleaned out my baggage, as I told you. I gave him the green and red tie – which I think he appreciated very much – a cake of soap, a few razor blades, a tooth brush. Then it all seemed so paltry, and I so enjoyed my success in getting a beautiful piece of material, such as I have really sought for a very long time and with pleasure, that I added a pair of civilian shoes which I had – a good pair of shoes, but I have two pairs left, and very rarely wear them. In addition to my two pairs of civilian shoes, I have two pairs of high, heavy shoes and one pair of boots, so that I am very well shod still.

I hope you enjoy the linen towel – it is really not fabric, for it can hardly be cut up and made into anything. It is completely made as is. Still, I consider it very pleasant to handle and touch. It is fine linen, I am sure.

So that was all on the side of pleasure. Then I walked up to the town and had a very interesting walk through the town. It is completely destroyed – not a whole building; only broken walls and rubble. One can see, however, that it once was a very charming and beautiful town. Not a whole thing in it – among the ruin, I saw one china cabinet, standing on a bit of floor which still clung to a wall. I saw one whole plate and one whole pot. Those were the only whole things I saw. Still, a few people are living among the ruins – children crying and fighting and mothers chasing children to catch them – running over the piles

---

[127] Town in central Sicily.
Via Wikipedia. https://en.wikipedia.org/wiki/Caltanissetta

of rubble. All barefoot, or in shreds of shoes, which is what really convinced me to give the man a pair of shoes. Fragments of the church tower still stand. A schoolhouse, with most of the walls out, and the textbooks strewn over the countryside. One page – parts of the notes and commentary on Dante. Another, the text of the third grade – with interesting miscellaneous facts – from December 21 until June 21 the days become longer and from June 21 until December 21 they become shorter. Then a page from a primer of Latin, with the conventional Tuba tubae tubae tubam tuba, and porto portas portat etc. It was kind of distressing to see, for the people look so ragged and dirty, and so many of them just sit hunched up, quite apathetic, that one forgets they study too.

Then I saw a hilltop landmark being put out of existence – on a remote hill, as planes went over it, it appeared that the whole mountain went up in smoke. I hope the spirit of the building and its tradition again achieved heaven in the column of dust, and the dust returning from heaven will carry back some of the idealism and service in the preservation of that which is good which are the tradition of the building. xxxx I really did not believe what I saw, and still do not, and I am sure that the people who were around the building still do not believe it and never will. One thinks of such irrelevant phrases under the circumstances, and imbues them with meaning which is not there at all – as "Magnus es tu, o domine, et laudabilis valde" – "Great art thou, o Lord, and truly worthy of praise", which is the exciting and apparently irrelevant beginning of St. Augustine's *Confessions*.

Do you ever read Boethius, *Consolations of Philosophy,* which we have there? I think you might enjoy the poetry at the beginnings of the chapters. Would you like to copy out one or two of the verses? I have quite forgotten them.

It has been a thoroughly magnificent day – bright sun and strong wind, clear air, so that one could see very far, to new and remote mountains and up long valleys.

While I was up early this morning, in the half light of sleepiness, I wrote Marian a letter wishing her a happy birthday. I did not half express my wishes, but shall not write again. Or maybe I shall,

The man who gave me the towel solicits laundry around here and has his womenfolk do it. They do beautiful work – get things white and iron them well, with a great charcoal iron. They use the wreck of a building here to iron in, so that they can be close to their business. The man owns the land on which we are staying. He is a very intelligent man – he is able to understand a great deal of what I say in Italian, and to make himself understood. I now see the meaning of his gesture as he said "asciuga" – he was drying his face. I thought he was illustrating a lady's shawl or head-dress – coming over her ears and temples. I never thought to look for towel in my dictionary, or I should have found a word very close to what I understood him to say.

I am well. No news, no changes, nothing special, except for no reason I feel cheerful this evening. I hope it lasts. Meanwhile I send my love.

Henry

February 16

Dear mama -

I have the feeling that I have much to write – although really I have nothing – because I still have the pleasure of the memory of acquisition of my very beautiful piece of linen – and I enjoyed that so very much. I hope you receive it in due time. But I have already told you about that.

Today, I went to see "Red" Doyle – who worked here, and is in the hospital with a slight case of dysentery (non-specific – cause, eating un *[word unclear]* apples; he has no sense) and enjoyed the drive – there, through the valley – all crowded with soldiers – and then onto a side road, where farmers were trimming their grape vines, and cleaning up their vineyards „trimming the olive groves, plowing the weedy fields. The country, even so close, is beginning to look beautiful again. And there have appeared from nowhere flocks of sheep and goats. A month ago, when one asked for cheese, the Germans had taken both cheese and goats. That was in the same place which is beginning now to look neat and fertile and productive. It is no longer so crowded with soldiers.

The country was beautiful – still midwinter – like a Missouri winter day – bitter cold driving – although it was not freezing – snow on the mountains, coming quite far down. Towns sit on the mountains beautifully – and there are many villages not destroyed, and many towns quite nearly intact – only a few buildings down – and when the debris is piled neatly, they look alright.

Came back over the mountain – a magnificent drive -

But I did not stop at any of the villages or towns – not having time – and the man with whom I was with not desiring to stop. Also it was cold.

I am well – have two kerosene stoves going now – and these keep very warm in here.

I am continually surprised at the fact that I can usually make myself understood in Italian – as with the man who gave me linen – and I understood his story – except the material word.

The officer who was going to get me a cup and saucer, whose location I know, did not do it. Well – that is one Capodimonte cup the less – unless I can make other arrangements. It is about seventy miles away.

I am reading "So Little Time[128]," because it was lent to me – and not enjoying it very much. But I shall finish it.

Now news, you know that the monastery at Cassino has been bombed[129] – as appeared in the papers. Previously destroyed by the Lombards – considered an act of Vandalism, I suppose; but I wonder if

---

[128] A New York Times bestselling novel by John P. Marquand
Preview Via GoogleBooks
https://www.google.com/books/edition/So_Little_Time/IXqrCQAAQBAJ?hl=en&gbpv=0
John P. Marquand Via Wikipedia
https://en.wikipedia.org/wiki/John_P._Marquand
[129] The historic Monte Cassino, was bombed by the Allies on February 15, 1944 during the Battle of Monte Cassino.
Monte Cassino Via Wikipedia https://en.wikipedia.org/wiki/Monte_Cassino
Battle of Monte Cassino Via Wikipedia
https://en.wikipedia.org/wiki/Battle_of_Monte_Cassino
"The Destruction of Monte Cassino," National WWII Museum
https://www.nationalww2museum.org/war/articles/destruction-of-monte-cassino-1944

possibly the Roman were using it as a defensive position – so that possibly Huns, Vandals, Lombards and all have had the same justification as we. But the Romans wrote the history. I think maybe many intelligent Italians are glad to see these ancient things destroyed – for they feel they want to start anew – that they are too heavily burdened with tradition – and think that if they could get rid of it, they could be like Americans. Maybe – I wrote you of Ciro Gallo's dissertation on the subject.

Love -

Henry

February 19

Mrs. A. Lowenhaupt
6237 McPherson Ave.
Saint Louis
Missouri

Dear mama -

I received two letters today – Jan. 9 & Jan. 25 – and enjoyed them. It is a pleasure to read descriptions of setting the table – who eats there, and the like, because then for the moment I imagine I am there.

I write this V mail because I have nothing to say. I have not done anything today – the weather is very windy, but not as cold as it sounds – and my mind keeps running to "There was a sound of reveling by night, and Belgium's capital - - -[130]" which is all I know. My memory is that the next deteriorates from these beginning lines – and I don't know why the lines are in my mind.

I was in a city yesterday but did not have opportunity even to look around. Not a bit of news – I am well – and send my love.

Henry

February 19

Mrs. A. Lowenhaupt
6237 McPherson Ave.
Saint Louis
Missouri

Dear mama -

I write to let you know that I am well – with nothing whatsoever to say – and in one of my blue moods, which I hope to get over soon.

Nothing is permanent (thank God) but changes always disturb me- because I am neither interested nor curious about what comes next. It would certainly be nice to get home out of the army – for one feels so

---

[130] From *The Eve of Waterloo* by Lord Byron.

completely futile and useless – nothing to do; nothing one wants to do. But time still passes, and I send my love. I think I shall not write for a few days or weeks.

Henry

February 21

Dear mama -

I find it excessively difficult to write now but not having written for a few days, feel that I must – at least to let you know that I am well. I am -

The reason I find it so hard to write is that I am unsettled, and somewhat sad – I suppose without sufficient reason – indeed without any particular reason.

I saw Ben Charles for a few minutes yesterday – and was amazed and shocked he is an old man – his hair is grey; he is thin and wiry – looking something like Dr. Larrimore. I did not recognize him at all. He does not even talk the same. I remembered him as having very black hair – being quite pink-cheeked and cherubic.

He saw I had changed – but I don't believe it – so I have a picture taken (with Lt. Clark) which I have sent to you. Unfortunately, the picture does not show my face – but at least my hair is not grey – but I don't care any more.

I have a very nice letter from Betty, which I shall answer.

I was in a city yesterday – but did not see or do anything. It was Sunday, and most shops were closed. But, as I say, I saw Ben Charles not far away from the city – and wandered around a little – bought some cookies and some glacé fruits, which were quite good. And had a picture taken on the outskirts of the town – by a man with a very ancient camera – a whole darkroom in the box.

I send my love -

Henry

February 21

Dear mama -

I have nothing I want to say today – but shall write some other time. I send some silly pictures -

All my love

Henry

The other one on the pictures is Bill Clark, whom I've mentioned.

H

February 22

Mrs. A. Lowenhaupt
6237 McPherson Ave.
Saint Louis, Missouri

Dear mama -

I expect that I shall not write for a few days – but maybe my letters arrive so irregularly that it will not be noticeable.

I am well – and have no news to write. Received a paper from daddy, which I have signed and returned.

I am running low on soap. Would you please send me, if it is available, several cakes of face or toilet soap, and several cakes of laundry soap.

Hope to hear soon -

Love -

Henry

February 22

Dear mama -

I am not writing often – and have nothing to say anyway – except that I am well. We are in a new area – it is raining and very muddy. That covers the whole situation.

I received letters from you – that you received a box – and I am glad that daddy likes it. I do not know why the letters AC are on the handkerchief – it is not new and probably AC stands for the former owner. I suppose they could be ripped out – but they make little difference.

Maybe it will clear soon – it will take a while to dry out the mud even after it clears!

You see how little I have of which to write. Partly because I am very mad at the world in general – just on general principles, like Wordsworth and Milton.

I wish I could write a decent letter. But there is nothing whatsoever to say.

I send my love – and shall try to write again.

Henry

the sun is coming out – no doubt before this letter is dispatched I shall be happy again -

February 23

Dear mama -

I received a very wonderful batch of letters from you and daddy yesterday – have written to daddy in answer to his. You do not ask me any questions. But you see how dangerous it is to write about health. I told you I had lost my voice. Then I told you I was regaining it. (I now have it back completely) But you received the letter that I was regaining it – and apparently missed the one in which I said I lost it.

Your letters, too – I hear that Ben likes his new location   and only now receive the letters previously written, that he had a new location. I enjoy the letters – like a continued story and jig saw puzzle, in addition to the great delight which comes just of hearing

Both you and daddy mention that you received the D'Alterio box – so I await the next installment, that the box has been opened. Maybe it is pure junk. The materials inside – I do not know what they are either.

I am well. It has begun to rain. I expect to have a new address and a new assignment soon – and shall write it as soon as I get it. Meanwhile, I must look forward to a long gap in mail – and so am particularly glad to have letters, one as late as February 5.

They say that Spring begins here about the 1st of March. I hope so.

Nothing new – the rain keeps me inside, so I don't see anything.

Love -

Henry

February 25

Dear mama -

A day has passed without my writing – and I might as well write. I am quite idle at the present – doing nothing, and really am contented to do nothing. I suppose I am getting lazy.

Am presently in a very beautiful area – an olive grove on a gradual hill-side, which slides down to a winding, flat river, whose course can be followed through devious convolutions for many miles. The ground is rich. The nearby peasants very friendly – and everything is serene.

The weather – cloudy – it may rain.

I am well – now back with ~~Lt. Cla~~ Bill Clark and Claude Morris – we share two tents, adjoined, so that one is our bedroom and one our sitting room. I do not know how long things will stay thus. Nor does it make much difference. Time passes -

I have been without mail for two days, for there's been no delivery – so may receive a pile this afternoon, or may not.

Received a stove wick from Scars Roebuck – complementary – and shall thank them. Guffaw! Spring is here!

My last letters said you had received (or daddy had received) a box, but hadn't opened it.

So I expect a letter saying that it has been opened. Funny that the order of arrival has no relation to the order of dispatch. ~~W I shal~~ I am impatient to know whether or not you have any pleasure of opening the box – and of the linen and brocade enclosed.

I am without anything to say – without news.

Well, possibly I shall go out and see if I can talk to some peasants about getting some hand-made materials – for fun. I am encouraged by my one success, and this territory here is in good shape – I see no physical damage to buildings – I have seen a few chickens – heard roosters crowing – seen about three cows and a number of small herds of sheep and goats. That suggests another quest – cheese – formaggio. Up to this time they have all had none – not even any goats.

I send my love. The valley below us must be very fertile. Nothing growing there now, but I suppose it is cultivated in wheat or some annual summer crop.

Henry

February 29

Mrs. A. Lowenhaupt
6237 McPherson Ave.
Saint Louis, Missouri

Dear mama -

I have been receiving mail well, and enjoying it. I received daddy's statements of income of business; acknowledgement of receipt of a box, and am very happy that you have some enthusiam about it – as I had. Do you consider the piece of brocade of any interest? I thought the handkerchief quite handsome, although I did not know what AC stood for. That leaves en route a linen towel, which I think you will enjoy as a fine piece of spinning and weaving, two cups, which are for me myself, a blue linen tablecloth, and an ugly box.

I am well – now and then badly in need of encouragement but hope I shall be able to refrain from folly, and continue in patience. I find nothing quite so encouraging as going to bed – so I have been going to bed early, and sleeping much. I have not a bit of news. I anticipated that I shall be transferred to some other unit at some time in the near future, and shall be very happy to go, for at least there will be variety in that, place where work is expected. I have learned to expend time very happily in idleness; but maybe I am not irremediably lazy. In the last analysis, I do not care very much if I am. To care, it seems to me, is like a chip worrying as it goes floating down the Mississippi. So I shall see what happens – and I am not taking matters very seriously, nor worrying, as I see some people doing, about opportunities and so forth.

There is the doctrine, much spoken of, called "Utilization of Manpower", which, of course, when one looks around is very amusing – as when one sees three Ordnance Battalions (for the repairs of vehicles and the like) engaged for six weeks (to exaggerate a little) on the making of a trailer for residence of one man, with indirect lighting and the like. But Congressional Investigations consist of words – and therefore dealt with by words. Do you know the summary Peripatetic Philosophy? "Solvendum est ambulando" (It ought to be resolved by walking around), paraphrased, "Solvendum est risu" (It ought to be resolved by laughing) So I am singing my little song: Solvendum est risu; solvendum est risu! and I suppose that most things are – if one can keep it up.

I hope to have an opportunity to drive someplace tomorrow – in another part of the peninsula; we shall see. I do not intend to stick around here any more than is necessary. Called a rest area – but rest areas tend to take on the appearance of xxx mad houses. Solvendum est ambulando, et risu.

I enjoy your letters very very much – and hope you will keep on writing frequently, notwithstanding that I can reply only so shabbily. I had a letter from Madame Peyrus of Algiers today – they have requisitioned one room of her apartment, so Algiers must still be crowded, leaving her with a bedroom, bath, dining room and parlor for herself and son. She gave a party for her son, Jacques, which the young people attended. She has changed jobs – although she is still in General Giraud's headquarters – and says she likes her job. All the men officers there (there are many women) are men who escaped France, most of them recently, although one xxx may not say how. In view of the numbers (even before I left Algiers, there were many) it cannot be so hard to get out. I am reminded of the Hollid House and its role.

Love,

Henry

March 1

Mrs. A. Lowenhaupt
6237 McPherson Ave.
Saint Louis
Missouri

Dear mama -

It is difficult to write   but I am anxious to let you know *[word cross out]* I am well. It is rainy – and things are somewhat in confusion, for I have not much of a regular place to sit and write. The job (?) I had is ended. and I have found other places. Agreed to take just about the first – and still have no reason to believe that it is not the best. It is in the Air Corps – administrative work, whose exact nature I do not know – so I shall have a change of address soon. Administrative difficulties have, I think, been cleared. I am not sure of the unit, and do not know what the address will be. But shall leave a forwarding address.

Under these circumstances, I cannot write of anything – what I should like to write of, I don't know anything about.

Beautiful country – I suppose I miss the opportunity of a three day vacation – of which I wrote – but there is no place to go anyway, the city being forbidden for the same old reason – or lack of reason.

So I hope you will excuse these mere notes. I am receiving letters now – and enjoying them. Numbering does no good – you forget to number some and others I forget to keep track of. It is turning warm – found a beautiful poppy in bloom today. Henry.

March 2

Dear mama -

It is some time since I have written a decent letter – and I shall now try to force myself to write something.

I was in the city for a few hours yesterday – more or less on business – and enjoyed it, although I did not have time to do anything – except buy a little candy. I should have liked to shop a little or something – but Ciro Gallo's place was closed – and I did not get anyplace else, except for a few minutes in an arcade there. No merchandise – except I saw a pretty shawl in a window – except cameos and tortoise shell and the like. I bought nothing – except a coca cola – which the men with whom I was were very anxious to have. Well – it is the first coca cola in well over a year.

But I enjoyed the visit – a bottle of wine with lunch, and I now have a bottle of brandy.

Today I have been walking around with an olive branch in my mouth – to denote that I have, I hope, found a place to set the sole of my foot. As I have written, I am leaving II Corps. While I dislike the idea of packing up and moving, I am not sorry to begin another environment. The place I have found to set the sole of my foot is 15th AFSC[131], which, I think, stand for 15th Air Force Service Command. I have no idea

---

[131] It is likely this could be referring to the 15th Air Force, which was stationed in the Mediterranean.
Via Wikipedia
https://en.wikipedia.org/wiki/Fifteenth_Air_Force

what it is – it is in Italy – that is all I know – and I shall leave tomorrow. Lt. Clark is going too. I have a flattering letter from this place, signed by the commanding General. Well – well -

Neil Wood's brother-in-law – or his wife's brother-in-law – named Staley is in the 15th AAF, I understand which is closely related to the 15th AFSC – although I do not know the exact relation.
So I am going into the Air Corps – a change, and I do not know whether it is more or less desirable than this. A place to set the sole of my foot.

Bill Clark reminded me of a quotation I have not thought of for a long time – "o soeii, o passi graviora, dabit deus his quoque finene" – o friends, o you who have suffered more serious things, God will give an end to these things also. So I have been reciting it.

Well – it is ironical – I shall, I think, forsake my stove. Now I have wick – from Hy & from Sears Roebuck and more on the way. I shall probably wear summer clothes – I gave many away in Algiers, and have more winter clothes on the way. Wasteful? Yes. But the future is completely uncertain – and I shall keep on going. It is time to go through my clothes, anyway and ~~pick~~ discard those worn out. I inherit your dislike of throwing a piece of wool away – even if it is in rags.

I am well. I must look forward to a period of about a month without mail, for the forwarding process is slow. I do not know my new address yet – but shall write it as soon as I have it – and possibly it will arrive before my letter -

Love -

Henry

                                                            Bari
March 5

Dear mama -

I am writing for a moment while I am in an unsettled state. I am now in a hotel – where I may stay and may not – being presently assigned to the 15th Air Force Service Command[132] – shall learn possibly something of my status this afternoon. Until I do, I shall not write my new address.

What a drive I had yesterday – first – the driver formerly drove a New York taxi! Wheee! But it was magnificent – an all day drive – through plains, over the mountains – magnificent country – and drive here, into fine, fertile, level country again. Fruit trees are in bloom – how Spring has sneaked up on me – and here there are fine, concrete roads, cities appearing to the eye undamaged. And such fine cities! This one (I have not seen much – it is Sunday, and places are closed) had, along the waterfront, heavy, fine buildings – magnificent, as Washington -

How strange it feels to be in a city – a dry floor – windows – running water – electric lights – no blackouts, even, to amount to anything. I have seen nothing like it since Algiers. And well-dressed civilians – wide, clean streets – much less interesting than the dirty alleys of my former favorite town –

---

[132] 15th Air Force had its headquarters during this time in Bari, Italy. Presumably, this is the city described.
15th Air Force Via American Air Museum
https://www.americanairmuseum.com/unit/5
Bari, Italy Via Wikipedia
https://en.wikipedia.org/wiki/Bari

which smelled so bad. This is like a colonial capital. Bars – with pretty good wine - I think there is regular communication with Cairo -

It is a cosmopolitan city – I was asking directions last night – the first man spoke only Yugoslavian – the next was an Indian who did not speak English – then an Italian who did not know – then a Scotsman, who did not know, and whom I couldn't understand anyway. Finally an American who knew.

I wish I could describe the magnificence of the drive yesterday – and the excitement of being in a city for a while. But I can't possibly – and feel that it won't last.

I am never going to write for anything again (I resolve, believing I shall break the resolution) for now I have things on the way I cannot possibly use. Well – I hate waste – but I shall nevertheless take the bull by the horns and throw stuff away. Blankets – woolen underwear – wool suits – alas! I am so overstocked!

I am well – curious as to what happens next. I am not sure I want to stay permanently in one place – it is bound to become boring, and in a city, there are many problems – as laundry, ~~etc.~~ pressing, and so forth. But I shall see what happens. I'm sure I don't know what I want.

All my love

Henry

March 6

Dear mama -

My day today has been so mixed between military matters, about which as a matter of policy, I do not usually write, and non-military, that it is difficult to write. But I shall try to begin chronologically. As you know, I am now assigned to Air Corps – although I am still in Adjutant General Department. Yesterday, I reported to 15th AFSC and was told to come back this morning between 8 and 8:30, since the personnel officer was not there. So I went back – he was sick, but they would see him, and I should come back again at 1:30.

He is the one to whom a cable was sent, saying that there was a vacancy for Clark and me elsewhere – did he need us urgently – and he replied "yes." But this is conventional, I suppose.

So we walked up to the headquarters of 15th AAF, along the sea wall – and called on Major Staley – whom daddy knows – and talked for about an hour – he was quite cordial. Then we visited the adjutant general of 15th AAF, and had lunch here at the hotel (Food is uninteresting – only messes are available)

Then back to 15th AFSC – where they still did not know anything – and the personnel officer was displeased, he said, that we had let it be known we were here – But that does not disturb me – he just wants to be sure that he controls our assignment – I do not care if he does not. Come back tomorrow -

So I spent the afternoon walking, especially through the old, walled town, which is completely charming – archways, close streets, or alleys, squares, crowds – people cooking on the streets – colors (in which

Italy excels) and a magnificent cathedral – St. Nicholas[133] – without carvings and statues – a cloister. All the windows have been taken out – I hope for safe-keeping.

I walked through the new town, too, which is largely government or public buildings all along the waterfront – like an enormous WPA project. Shops all closed and nothing much for sale. I rested while getting a shampoo.

So my status is indeterminate still. I have no address – do not use the one on the outside of the envelope, because I expect that it will change. Just as soon as I know, I shall write my new address.

Now I am tired. It quite amazes me how quickly I get used to beds, floors, and so forth.

Maj. Staley inquired about daddy – and St. Louis. He is the AP Green[134] Staley, not corn products.

I send my love – and cannot say "write soon." You must await a more nearly permanent address.

Henry

March 7

Mrs. A. Lowenhaupt
6237 McPherson Ave
Saint Louis
Missouri, U.S.A.

Dear mama -

This is just to keep mail coming to you – if that is possible – and to let you know that I am well. I do not yet know what my arrangement is, nor my best address. You might, if you like, try APO 520 – without more – but probably not worthwhile. Within a few days, I shall have, I believe, a more certain address – and shall write it. I am reconciled to receiving no mail for months to come – but maybe someday it will catch up with me.

I am in a very beautiful place – a city substantially undamaged – fine buildings, lovely cathedral – an old walled town – the new section outside the walls – with beautiful surroundings – combination Atlanta City, St. Malo, Washington and Algiers – I think I should like to stay here – but don't care if I go elsewhere. My address is now as *[word unclear]*

Love

Henry

APO 520
Hq 15th AAF

---

[133] Historic basilica in Bari, Italy.
Via Wikipedia
https://en.wikipedia.org/wiki/Basilica_di_San_Nicola
[134] A Missouri Company

March 7

Mrs. A. Lowenhaupt
6237 Mc Pherson Ave
St. Louis, Missouri

Dear mama -

My address is:

Hq 15th A.A.F., AG Sec
APO – 520
c/o Postmaster
New York, N. Y.

LOVE

Henry

March 8

Mrs. A. Lownhaupt
6237 McPherson Ave.
Saint Louis
Missouri

Dear[135] <u>mama,</u>

My correct address is:
<u>2d Lt. Henry C. Lowenhaupt 01001835</u>
Rank   Name   Serial No.

<u>HQ Squadron 15th Air Force</u>
Unit   Organization

APO <u>520</u> c/o Postmaster
New York, N.Y.

My cable address is <u>A7OCHA</u>.

Use V-Mail

Henry

---

[135] This is a formatted V-Mail letter. The underlined portions were filled in with the correct information.

March 9

Dear mama -

I am now installed again permanently for the present – but have an idea I shall not be able to write as often as I have in the past. My address – AG Section, Hq. Squadron, 15th Air Force, APO 520, c/o Postmaster, N.Y.

I do not yet know what work I am doing ~~yet~~ – maybe shall learn. Shall have one day a week off – and shall spend it wandering around in this resort.

I was billeted in a hotel – but desired to stay with Clark – hotels are uninteresting anyway. So we found a room in an apartment – surprising how quickly one gets used to inner spring mattresses; running water – a bath tub – good lights – dry floors – The family who occupy the apartment – a man, a woman and their son and daughter – are friendly; they come from another part of Italy, where they were bombed out. The apartment is on the seventh floor – with elevator. We visited with the family last night - I am learning Italian – but am far from fluent.

Also – I unpacked my baggage last night. What a mess! delving in historic remains – it is still not straightened out – never will be, I think. But that I will not think of.

So I am comfortable – even sheets on the bed.

I eat at a mess– which uses Italian cooks. So the cooking is different, and very pleasant. I suspect that the cooks steal about half – but that is alright with me. There is a coffee shop in the building – sandwiches, cookies and coffee – and it is a pleasant place to waste time.

Seems strange to attempt to write of a place – you have no idea where it is – but maybe someday I shall be able to write it.

Lots of fishing here – and along the wall, they sell shellfish which look like chestnut burrs, outside – inside, little red things. I am afraid of them, although the natives seem to eat them with pleasure.

Love -

Henry

March 10

Dear mama -

I am well – living comfortably – and in a special kind of Bedlam – which is very funny. I am forced back to my pseudo-peripatetic anxious about "solvendum est risu" – it is resolved by laughing – although walking is also a very satisfactory resolution. I walked last night, pretty well around town – a beautiful, moon-light night, over the sea -

Came back about 9:00 o'clock, and visited with the family Turetto, playing a kind of pseudo poker, and trying to talk Italian. One counts to three or four without difficulty. Quite a sociable crowd – Porzia, Antonia, another Antonio, an Ezio and Signor and Signora – so we played for match sticks – but not having enough the winner had to return them to the pot. That lasted until about 10:30 – when to bed.

Beds are very comfortable, and soft, and have clean sheets on them. I sent laundry this morning – giving the last of my laundry soap.

Therefore I make a request – could you please send me a few bars of laundry soap.

Another request – I originally had a cap – the peaked kind – but when I moved to Sicily, had no place to pack it – and gave it away. Now I could use one if I had one – so if they are available, should like for you to send me one – size 7 3/8.

That is all I can think of needed at the present.

Living is going to be more costly here – more laundry and cleaning. I pay $8.00 a month for room (an extravagance, but I don't care) and $10.00 a month extra for food – for which one gets table linen, service, and a little extra food. Really not extra – because the regular natives seem to disappear in part – But it is alright – fresh eggs sometimes (great luxury) cookies, some fresh vegetables, wine and so forth.

I've already said I'm in a mad house – or so it seems – Maybe I shall come to have an understanding of some method or system – it takes time for confusion to clear. Meanwhile, all is cleared by laughing – and I have learned to enjoy idleness, so that nothing disturbs me.

There are a number of middle westerners here – St. Louisans – of whom I have met one boy named Barad, who lives on Northwood drive someplace – a nice, friendly, puppy-type. There are others who will appear.

I send my love -

Henry

March 11

Dear mama -

I have started a quest – which may be silly – but I shall see if I can succeed. I am looking for a music teacher – and if I can find one shall take one or even two lessons a week, although I shall be unable to practice. I have my enthusiasm for it now – and shall be disappointed if I cannot succeed. I saw a little placard in a pastry ship (what a life I lead, you will say!) advertising a Prof. Toma – but when I went to the address given, was told he had moved to the country. Well – I shall look further. Bought an Italian newspaper today – to look at the advertisements – a little one sheet affair like a junior high school weekly – but the only noticed were death notices. No music teachers advertising. Oh, well -

So I asked my landlady – ah, yes, she says, they've all gone to the country. But she does not take me seriously. I think I shall go to the opera conductor, if there is one, or to some such person. But I'm afraid the opera is just a visiting one, from another city.

Meanwhile, I am watching for little cards and notices. Prof. Toma advertised so well – but did not take his signs down before he went away.

Weather is beautiful – the sea is bright blue and green – with ships on it – and many fishing boats – palms begin to look fresh – almond trees in bloom – fruit trees in large bud – All I need is piano lessons for the evening – although I may be told that the Germans took all the pianos with them. Maybe they did -

This town looks somewhat souvenir-less. It is too modern – the new part overwhelms the old – and no one seems to be attempting to capitalize on the willingness of soldiers to buy anything. All I have seen is souvenir picture post cards – which I cannot send because they would bare the location in which I find myself (it is around you are familiar with all landscape and buildings!)

I am well – no news – I send my love -

Henry

March 12

Dear mama -

No changes to report. I have not found a music teacher, and begin to fear I shall not. I am still appreciating the comforts of this beautiful city – in good health – and going to take Tuesday off. I do not know what I shall do – but very much enjoy wandering the streets – along the water front, through the old city, and elsewhere. I want to explore across the railroad tracks, where, I think, soldiers do not go so often. See what is there. But all that is anticipation. I expect to have a good time – indeed, may admit that I am now – not working much – solving my problems by walking and laughing. Ambition to find a music teacher consumes me.

The landlord's daughter wants to go to a Red Cross dance to be given soon. I hate that kind of entertainment – and to bring her requires an invitation from the Red Cross – and she wants her brother to go along and her cousin. Well – it is hard to combine an American dance, to which a girl can go, with Italian customs that a girl must not leave the house at night unchaperoned. That is the reason for the brother and cousin. My problem? Not particularly.

I have found a candy store which sells very delicious pink sugar coated almonds. So I eat about a nickel's worth a day, paying about a dime for them. Then good cookies – if you can steer clear of the ones made with a base of figs and dates, which are concealed to look like chocolate. The others – almonds, sometimes a kind of gooey cream, which particularly attracts me.

Movies in abundance here – I have seen one – alter hünde gleich and eggs is eggs – There is a mediocre symphony here, and will be a visiting opera from another city. I do not particularly anticipate going – partly inertia, partly I enjoy other things more.

Of course, I have received no mail recently. Maybe, if I'm lucky, it will catch up with me in a week or ten days.

I repeat my address, for no one knows what letter will reach you first.

Hq. Squadron,
15th Air Force (AG Section)
A.P.O. 520, c/o Postmaster
New York -

All my love

Henry

March 13

Dear mama -

Walking from breakfast to this place (about eight blocks) was very beautiful this morning – a wild, stormy morning, raining hard – thankful I'm not in the mud, but on nice, paved sidewalks and streets – along the sea. The wind is violent, a full gale with the fury of Sappho pushing it, ~~bud~~ it blows a mixture of rain and salt spray. The sea is rough, with breakers way out, and the waves break against the wall, along which the street runs. The wind is wet and very sweet smelling. This is not much of a harbor here – but I suppose it is enough for this sea – which even this morning was not as rough as Lake Michigan frequently used to be.

I am well. Still enjoying my soft beds and clean sheets. Without news. Food is good, and adequate. Last night, since it was raining, I stayed in, and went to bed early.

The landlady mystifies me – towel and wash rag disappear every morning, and reappear dry and clean two days later. Does she wash them every day? It is really quite unnecessary.

We eat in a hotel – a large room, with sky-light, which is lovely in sunny weather, but under this morning's east wind was leaking furiously. The waitresses are gaining weight fast.

Last night, when I came out, two women were standing at the door. The elder said that her daughter Rosita was working inside – could I find her and have her come out a moment – she had to tell her something. I looked cursorily for Rosita, but could not find her – and have no idea what the woman wanted to tell her. And that leaves such infinite play for imagination – these people are inclined to the dramatic anyway – and the whole gamut of coincidences is within possibility – how to cook artichokes, or please try to pick up a cake of soap – up and down. That was for "my daughter Rosita."

I have no luck in finding a piano teacher. Everywhere, Professor Toma is advertised; except on his own door, where there is a little sign that during his absence from the city, lessons are suspended. It is difficult to inquire after him, because if you ask his neighbors they think you want to put him in jail or something. Like a white man looking for a negro in a negro neighborhood – they all assume I wanted to collect a bill. So I asked the landlady – who is, unfortunately, a stranger in town – but maybe she'll find out.

I am beginning to be hopeful of receiving mail - but had better give up hope, for I have, doubtless, a long wait. At least two weeks more I should guess.

I may telephone to II Corps this evening – just to see what is going on. What a tricky thing memory is – I shall reread St. Augustine on the subject.

All my love -

Henry

March 14

Dear mama -

I am sitting down at noon on my day off – mostly to rest a while at the room before I go off wandering again. I have had a most magnificent time so far, with success everywhere.

First I walked across the railroad tracks – did not get beyond the town – and over there is the factory district, the warehouses (agricultural – figs, dates and so forth) I walked around a while – then bought a bottle of brandy and a bottle of Anisette. And walked back with them. It was beginning to rain, but the sidewalk had a double row of citron trees – which cover it close. I left my bottles here and went out on a double quest – not too determinedly. First, I stopped and got a hair cut and shave. Then I went to a music store and asked a recommendation of a piano teacher. They gave me a name and address. I had to look for it a while – first asked a man who showed me the direction. Then, after a while that way, a woman, who must have thought she was a beauty. She tossed her head into the air and ran. Then I came upon it – and rang the bell. No answer.

So I walked a while. I went to the church, and through it. It is not one of the finest examples – that is, not up to Monreale and Rouen and Notre Dame de Paris – but it is lovely – the tomb of St. Nicholas, they say, in cast silver, which I don't fully appreciate. Beautiful stairway on the tomb of the Queen of Poland. Beautiful columns, shape – one misses the color of stained glass windows – but I suppose it may be these southern churches never had them.

Then, after wandering through the old city – which is endlessly intriguing, with its archways, its narrow passages, and howling of babies, women calling, all kinds of noises and smells, its carpenter shops, nuns, priests, all pushing through – I decided to have lunch on the hoof. A delicious orange, at the market, some candy, a cream puff, and, as always, I tried something that looked like chocolate cake, but turned out to be figs and dates.

By this time, it was almost noon, and I went back to see my music teacher. Wonderful! a little man, who speaks a little French (as much as I speak Italian, so there's no advantage) and had a thoroughly magnificent studio – a big room, in the old quarter, with paneled walls, and fine hangings dark furniture, with red upholstery, a big window at one end – glass chandelier – a thoroughly magnificent room. I asked if he would give me lessons – telling him I could not practice – solely for the love of music, as he asked and I answered affirmatively, and 100 lire a lesson, if it could be in the evening – he said no – and it will be at noon on Tuesday – which is my day off. Too good to last – but why not shoot at the stars?

Maestro Nicola Costa[136], is his name, and his wife was calling him to lunch while I was there – and he was saying "Momento, Maria!" He is a little tiny man – not quite up to my shoulder – and has a very fine piano, in perfect tune – it is a long time since I have seen one like it.

So I have a music teacher – and he accepted me, after I played some scales, and read some for him. You may tell Janet and Heather that I shall be unbearable on the subject of my Italian musical education ~~before~~ when I get home.

Then I walked up to the sales store and bought my rations of a little cleaning fluid, cigarettes, etc., and here – to rest. Now the sun is out – and I am going out again. I am enjoying myself immensely today.

PS -   Love -

Henry

---

[136] There is a possibility this Nicola Costa is a piano teacher at the Conservatorio di Musica Niccolo Piccinni in Bario.
Conservatorio di Musica Niccolo Piccinni
https://www.consba.it/it/20/la-storia
Conservatorio di Musica Niccolo Piccinni, page 8
https://www.ic-sarnellidedonatorodari.edu.it/attachments/article/162/Conservatorio%20Piccinni%20-%20Brochure_Web.pdf

PS – I find I forgot to specify my other quests – a corkscrew, which I decided I needed for my bottles, and a glass. I bought the last corkscrew (cavaturaceiola) in the city – a handsome fine one – and some little cups, intended, I think, as ash trays. But they'll do. Cork-screw – $2.00. Music lesson: $1.00. There is no sense to it all!

Stopped in a church book store – for St. Augustine's *Confessions* – no. Only Latin book, was *Imitation of Christ*. But a priest was there, and we got into a conversation. I have a vague invitation to use the church's library – wherever it is – which I might be fine to do anyway. I shall see – and maybe look for it.

I said – I am having a very jolly time today -

H

March 14

Dear mama -

I am now waiting for a bottle of water to heat – I shall bathe in it – and that will be about the end of my *Pippa* Passes[137] day, for I walked around town again this afternoon, until about four o'clock - not doing anything in particular – except thinking how good a hot bath would feel. So I am about to have it.

What a set-up – hot baths and music lessons. But I fear it will not come to pass -

My water must be hot now – it has had fifteen minutes. But it's not.

The sun is out -

Now I've finished my bath – how wonderful! abundance of hot water in a tub (do you realize it is now one year and one week since I have been in a bathtub?) I bathed thoroughly – and now have put on all clean clothes – dressed up with cotton shirt and coat and dark pants – it is a wonderful sensation.

How shall I thank Signor Turetti for heating the water for me? Of course, he does not know what a delight I have had. I have said "Grazie "Grazie molto" and so forth. I have given him a cigar. I shall give him another tomorrow.

Shall I open my brandy and give him some? Tonight, maybe.

He is listening to the radio – *La Bohème* being broadcast very beautifully – it almost makes me want to go to opera. I think Signor Turetti likes to be useful – he hung my towel out in the sun this afternoon, after my bath. He usually hangs my towel out in the rain, but intentions are good.

The wind is coming up. I am going to wait here until six o'clock - and if Bill is back by that time, eat with him. If he is not – go alone.

I see Major Staley – daddy's friend – from time to time – and he inquires after daddy – the HP Green Staley. Ate with him the other evening. Neill Wood is responsible for my knowing he was here – and so I went to see him after I had job proposition settled.

---

[137] *Pippa Passes* is a verse drama by Robert Browning from 1841.

I had a letter from Mme. Peyrus just before I left the old station – Mme. Peyrus of Algiers, who is a bright woman, capitalizing to the utmost on her little knowledge of English ~~about~~ and quite a little personal charm, in General Geraud's headquarters.

Now I know how Pippa felt after she had passed. I am surely impatient for my music lesson – and expect to find Signor Nicola Costa, or Signor Costa Nicola – not sure which – a charming man – and a good teacher. It was fun to play even scales again, and he gave me a little Beethoven to read there at sight – between his "momentos" to Maria, who called him for dinner. But I've written of that -

Henry

15 March

Dear mama

I just received, much more promptly than I hoped, three letters from you, forwarded from my old address – the last written on the train from California.

As for me – what can I write? The weather is beautiful, and the sea intriguing. But today I have been more or less busy on routine. How remote interesting office work seems! I visited with the Turettis last night – mostly laughing about our Italian and their English. I tried to teach them about Theophilus Thistle, the Thistle thruster, who thrust the thorn of a thistle through the thick of his thumb – and Peter Piper picking pecks of pickled peppers.[138] We drank part of my anisette. Porzia T. has been in the country, trying to find food for the family – says things are so expensive, for a refugee family, as they are, from the north of Italy. Eggs – 15¢ a piece (or 15 lire) flour, or grain, 90 lire a kilo. No meat at all. But there are plenty of oranges, apples, nuts, lettuce, artichokes, and so forth. Also, here, they have olives and olive oil. They are much better off than in other places.

But how can I write of anything except my music lesson – 6 days away. For I look forward to that with such delight – Nicola Costa – a little man in frock coat – with a great big piano, in a very portentous room – heavy and magnificent with a little shrine in it and many articles of bigotry and virtue. Yesterday, he said he could not give lessons at night – I think he suspected and mistrusted me – for he had been warned that I was coming again (the first time no one answered, and I suspect all the neighbors came to tell him a soldier had rung his bell) He says the building is locked at night. Well – maybe I can arrange to come there one evening a week in addition to the one noon-time. I shall ply him with cigarettes – and I have one nickel cigar which I am saving to offer him. And I shall give him what else I can get – a cake of soap, if friendly relations are established

That is ~~so~~ Maestro Nicola Costa – he is a patient little man, I think. I write his name so often, partly to memorize it – 22 Via Vallisa[139] – just inside the old quarter. I should like to hear him play – He had quite a library of music.

---

[138] These are tongue twisters

[139] This exact address cannot be 100% accurately located in Google Streetview, but does still exist within the city of Bari, Italy. Via Vallisa via Google Streetview.
https://www.google.com/maps/@41.1275405,16.8704256,3a,75y,218.09h,86.37t/data=!3m7!1e1!3m5!1sDTIYhlMa-ch_qyDdYRCspw!2e0!6shttps:%2F%2Fstreetviewpixels-pa.googleapis.com%2Fv1%2Fthumbnail%3Fpanoid%3DDTIYhlMa-ch_qyDdYRCspw%26cb_client%3Dmaps_sv.tactile.gps%26w%3D203%26h%3D100%26yaw%3D158.87137%26pitch%3D0%26thumbfov%3D100!7i13312!8i6656

Unfortunate that the food situation is as it is – otherwise I should hope to have him ask me to eat there. But now I have no stove – so if you have sent me food to be cooked, I shall make him a gift of it – as coffee or tea or bouillon cubes. But – So you see what my mind is full of.

Love -

Henry

March 15

Dear daddy -

For a long time, of course, I have wanted to write to you – but I tell all my daily incidents and thoughts to mama – and do not want to write again to you. But I might as well write some of my introspections, prefacing them with the observation that I am now very comfortably situated, and hopeful that, through a music teacher, I can create some expanding interest. Fearful, too, that all things are tentative.

This evening, after supper, I walked a while – then stopped in at a bar of a hotel – rotten liquor – cognac – but there was an officer there whom I know I had seen before – so I spoke to him. His name was Gravely, and he used to work for Independent Packing Co. (St. Louis – Swift & Co?) and I had known him someplace. He is an aide to General Alexander – what a sinecure – and a drunkard. Well – he is the wiser for being so.

My present attempts are to try to find some interest for evening's entertainment – and I should really like to associate with civilians, because soldiers cannot possibly have much to say. Besides, I see them all day long. I hope for associations from my music lessons, as Maestro Costa seems quite a gentleman. I shall ply him with cigarettes, although I am afraid such actions are ostentatious, and make people just beggars. Maybe I can arrange to take two lessons a week – I shall see. I am hopeful. But language is a barrier.

And people (respectable, conservative people) are, I think, extremely suspicious and while not hostile, reserved – as is to be expected. In the first place, I suppose they have long been taught that Americans are strange barbarians. In the second place, I suppose they think they may be under suspicion and being investigated. Well – such attitudes and prejudices cannot be attacked directly – I shall just be naive.

They tell me that before December 2, this town was open and thriving and all the shops were filled. But after that day, everything went into safe keeping – and only gradually is the town opening. That may be. It looks very whole and intact to me.

Civilians are horror stricken at the thought of air raids – but in one raid, really little damage, proportionately is ever done. One or two buildings, maybe, but a city has a lot of buildings.

I hear you are going to give another lecture or two. Will you send me copies? But I hope you do not intend to reform anybody. It can't be done – But I shall not go into a discussion of that.

There are an awful lot of crying babies in this town – and I always imagine they are crying because of some deep suffering – they cry so pitifully. Until this evening – one stopped crying very suddenly when it got a top, which an older child had taken away. So I suppose they are not crying more passionately than American children.

Well, I warned mama that I should be writing about nothing but my piano lessons – for I anticipate that ~~sono~~ fervently that I am bound to be disappointed. This is Thursday – I go there Tuesday. Still a long way off. And, of course, I do not practice.

[Letter incomplete.]

March 17

Dear mama –

I received a package from you today which I think contains items of uniform. ~~Irony~~ So I haven't opened it, but wait until I get back to the apartment. Irony of fate! Yesterday the general gave a speech, saying that we are required to wear coats – which means also dark trousers and cotton shirts. Alas! But most of my other clothes are worn out – so that I shall discard some – and can use those I have received at one time or ~~the~~ another. So I thank you very much – and hope you learn not to take my requests seriously. Freight is so impossible. Presently I can ~~use~~ get everything I need.

I wrote to daddy last night – and have little or nothing to add.

There is a tea shop here in the building, run by a Viennese refugee woman. She serves her tea and cookies in very handsome pottery – and I have been admiring it. So I asked her where she got it – and she told me it is of local manufacture – but not made any more – and she has bought all of it. She will not sell me any. So I am mad at her – but I shall not therefore avoid her coffee shop, because her cookies are excellent.

We had an exceptionally fine lunch today – including a fresh lettuce salad and fish in oil.

The weather has turned very beautiful – the days warm, but the nights and evenings cold. So I debate whether or not to take off my winter underwear. I shall do so soon.

My mind is still full of ~~Sig~~ Maestro Nicola Costa and music lessons. I shall make an effort to take more than one a week. He does not even know my name - I think maybe he does not expect me back.

I am well. The sea looks very beautiful.

I hope to hear soon about your expedition to California – having received letters day before yesterday that you were going.

I just remembered – the package you sent may be the one with cheese in it. It is well that I have not opened it if it does, for the cheese would be eaten in no time. That makes me eager to get back and open it, however.

The days are becoming perceptibly longer. It is now bright daylight when I get up – and soon I suppose we shall have daylight savings time – frightens me - I shall have been here a year, and last summer I thought I should never be here so long. The sunny olive grove near Tunis, where I used to find potshards, and the shop is Relizane where I bought a rug, having it shipped "on the reputation of the house" – and Oran, with sidewalk cafés, and I watched figs growing in Algiers. Then the first rains in Sicily, and Cefalu, with its fancy sewing, and the first nights of autumn in Italy – they have no fixed placed in time. All the time, idle and all the time hoping that maybe there might be something to do. Now I have given that up. But there had always been very much of beauty. I remember watching a city called Troina[140], on a hill top, and shells were landing in it – little puffs of dust went up, and mushrooms, and gradually the city just melted down into the mountain.

Algiers was the most cosmopolitan place I've been, I think. The French make any place seen cosmopolitan. Air raids seemed like fourth of July celebrations, and everyone went out on balconies to watch them.

Well, well -

Henry

March 18

Dear mama -

I shall write more of the life of Riley – but first:

I received a package – and am delighted to have chocolate, cheese and gum drops. I shall share them with the Turetti's, who are having a hard time getting enough to eat – including the little grand-son or grandnephew, about 2 yrs. old – who lisps "grazie" in exchange for caramelli. Of course, they have plenty of fruit, vegetables, oil and nuts – but no flour or such other staples.

Last night I saw the opera, *Madame Butterfly* – with a prima donna who sang magnificently. Enjoyed it immensely.

Of course, all opera is ridiculous in plot – and it is an advantage not to understand the words – as when they sing in the most heroic style, "I have a letter for you," and she replies "Thank you"

This opera was interesting – I think they were making a political satire of it, for they worked into the orchestration, repeatedly, the themes of *Star Spangled Banner* and *God Save the King*. If so – it was a very sad satire, and to a large extent true, I suppose – but very pitiful. The music is so very lovely, in the second act, where the prima donna sings almost the whole thing – and one forgets that she had just played the Bull in Carmen (or is fit to have) I can see how, if one went to opera frequently, it would become habitual. I enclose the program – which conceals the name of the singers and company, lest it be known where the company comes from. It is from another city – an old favorite city of mine -

I also enclose a picture of myself, a snap shot, because I don't know how else to get rid of it. It is a ridiculous picture - I think I shall have a picture drawn or painted, as I know I can have done here, to see if I can get something I like better. This is a snapshot by a doctor – amateur of photography. Burn it.

So I am well – the weather is lovely and mild. I shall take off my woolen underwear tomorrow – although it does keep my cotton sheets clean.

I have your note from California – Betty's apartment sounds nice – my apartment faces the wrong way – over the roof tops, instead of over the sea. But it is a sunny room, in the evening, as is desirable in this cool weather.

---

[140] Troina, Sicily was the site of a battle July 31 – August 6, 1943.
Via Wikipedia
https://en.wikipedia.org/wiki/Troina

All my love -

Henry

[Madame Butterfly Conducted by Maestro Gioacchino Ligonzo[141]]

March 19

To Mrs. A. Lowenhaupt
6237 McPherson Ave.
Saint Louis
Missouri, U. S. A.

Dear mama

I write a V mail letter for a change assuming it will probably reach you before the ordinary letters which I have been writing currently. My mail situation has been excellent for the past two days, and I have learned that you are (or have been) in California and visiting Betty. I await more.

I am well, and living in the lap of luxury, the life of Riley – still sleeping on a bed with springs and a good mattress, in a room of the apartment of the family Turetti – mother, father, daughter and son. Try to talk with them in the evening. Seeing opera – Madame Butterfly, with a very fine prima donna, which is here for a few days from elsewhere – about to begin piano lessons from Maestro Nicola Costa, a dapper little man who wears striped trousers and morning coat, and has an enormously big piano and an enormously bigger wife – in a studio which is magnificent. I am well – the weather is fine and the sea, city and whole surroundings magnificent too. I am working like hell – a sentence whose punctuation I leave to you. Eating sugar coated almonds, oranges, fancy pastries, of which I try all designs seeking some which are not a paste of figs and dates and nuts looking like chocolate. I have found a few cream puffs, which are good and a few pastry rolls, filled with a custard of some kind.

Day after tomorrow is my music lesson. I am bound to be disappointed, because I anticipate too much – and when I get time shall be reticent, for fear of attempting too much cordiality. I may bring him a piece of cheese – although it seems better to wait a while. Well – I suppose I am in for a failure. But it won't be serious.

I send all my love -

Henry

---

[141] Gioacchino Ligonzo was an Italian conductor and musician. A street in Bari, Italy is named for him.
Via Vocidi Banda
https://www.vocidibanda.it/gioacchino-ligonzo-storica-figura-delle-bande-pugliesi/
Via GoogleMaps
https://www.google.com/maps/place/Via+Gioacchino+Ligonzo,+70132+Bari+BA,+Italy/@41.1302074,16.8333825,17z/data=!3 m1!4b1!4m5!3m4!1s0x1347e8bed4b216af:0xa5bae391feac4091!8m2!3d41.1302034!4d16.8355712

March 19

Dear mama -

(Green ink is not so much from choice as from necessity – it is the only color, except red, which my stationer– cartolleria – had)

Nothing new – weather continues splendid with bright sun and pleasant air. I have been given occasion to worry about my Tuesday music lesson – for I was put on a board, and I am afraid it will decide to meet Tuesday. But I hope not. Will see – if I cannot keep my first appointment with Signor Costa, I shall have to start all over. As exciting as horse racing!

I am well – with little of which to write – all being peace and tranquility. The city is still beautiful – and I have been seeing quite lovely inexpensive pottery. Problem – is it worth packing for shipment? I shall reach a conclusion.

I enjoy walking in this town. There is a main street – six or eight blocks long, running from a corner of the old town and the sea – with a boulevard – and on the sidewalks double rows of trees which I think are lemon trees. Then in the boulevard larger trees. This is lined with fine buildings. Another main street runs along the land side of the old town, at right angles to the first, and then drives along the shore, around the old city. The streets are heavily travelled with army trucks – But today, they were quite crowded with carriages – which are of all kinds. Many for hire – serve as taxis – then apparently many privately owned. Light little ones, the formal black ones – driving along the sea. And quite pretty horses. It makes the drive look much like a painting of the French painter whose name I've long tried to recall, who painted in spots.

People dress up on Sunday and take walks – and it makes the sea-side walk look stylish and haute monde-ish with ladies and men and children all strolling along. Quite interesting – that is the new city. I haven't been in the old town on Sunday.

I left my Record of Immunizations at the Surgeon's office today – so I expect soon to be called in and punched full of holes – how I hate it! – against typhus and smallpox and tetanus – there is no end to the list – I should rather be a Christian Scientist than a sieve.

I am now about to go to supper with Bill. As I missed my mid-morning coffee and cookies and my mid afternoon tea and cake today, I am quite hungry. A bite of cheese? Ah yes! as an appetizer.

I send my love. There is so much paper left that I shall leave this letter open – to be continued.

Henry

Now it is morning – and I had better fill up this paper quickly – so I can mail it today. I went to bed early last night – about 8:30 – and slept well all night. Before 8:30 – I took a walk – it does not get dark now until about 7. Walking is always pleasant.

Last night I ate dinner with Bill Clark – at his mess hall – which is a former yacht club out at the end of a pier – very elaborate and very fancy – salad (lettuce, onions and canned salmon, with olive oil and vinegar) soup (bean) meat loaf and mashed potatoes and string beans – a kind of tart-like crisp sponge cake filled with apples and raisins. Wine and coffee So you see I am in no danger of starvation.

Then on my walk, a Yugoslavian officer asked me directions to a theatre – I showed him – the theatre was closed – so we had a conversation. He is from Sarajevo – and says Belgrade is the most beautiful place in the world – a little Paris. And Sarajevo is so lovely – this town, he says, is uninteresting. It is, possibly, comparatively. His wandering from Yugoslavia to get to this part of Italy – I thought of Ulysses Africannus or Odysseus Africannus – whatever it was called.

I am well -

Love

Henry

March 20

Dear mama -

I write you my trials and tribulations – that which I feared has occurred – I must laugh at it – at hope defeated. Tomorrow is my day off – my music lesson day and it is decided that a board on which I must sit, is to sit tomorrow afternoon. So I shall have to rush my music lesson – and miss lunch – and shall not be able to proceed slowly and leisurely with Maestro Costa, as I intended. Deferred a week. Well, it is ordained in God's counsel, that one must part from that which one desires most.

I gave Porzia some cheese today – in appreciation of her kindness – she is keeping my clothes pressed and will not accept money – taking care of laundry – collecting, listing etc. – and I pay only for the laundry. In other words – being very helpful in a most intelligent way. She says she always did it for her brother.

I am well – without news. At any rate I shall take tomorrow morning off, and wander around the town. Do you want some cheap, pretty pottery? I may get some and ignore the absurdity of packaging a 10¢ piece as if it were much better.

I send my love -

Henry

March 22

Dear mama -

Yesterday was my day off – but, as I wrote, there was a board meeting in the afternoon, so I had only a half day off – and enjoyed it. (I postpone writing about music lesson –)

I spent the morning walking – the old city and the new are endlessly interesting. Sat down for a shave at a barber shop – a way of resting. Then I came into a street, about 9 00 o'clock which was jam packed solid with people. They were pushing and crowding, filling the whole block. I asked what it was – a store was going to sell some materials, cloth. There was a regular mob for it. I asked Porzia about it – she left most of her clothes in the city from which she came, has only the clothes she wears – and is knitting some more. She says there is no material – it is impossible to get. So she can't make any. I gave her a pair of pants which is too small to wear without leggings – she will make a shirt of it.

I walked through markets – where they sell oranges and vegetables, and a very delicious orange – saw the standard rayon tablecloths being sold at high prices.

Then it rained. So I got a shampoo. One can't get two shaves in one morning. Then to ~~the~~ another market – lunch on the hoof of dried olives and an orange – and to see Signor Costa. His prior pupil and her mother were there – very different looking people from those one sees on the streets. Then my music lesson – which I enjoyed more than anything I have done for a very long time. Signor Costa is putting me to work on Czerny – and is a stickler for fingering and technique. His own is magnificent, and he is an excellent teacher. Some Mozart and Haydn – I doubt that I shall be able to accomplish much, without practice, but it is a very rare and great pleasure – not only to go into his very beautiful studio, to touch his fine piano. He is a gentleman – and I am anxious to get acquainted with him. I am learning to understand Italian a little.

Then back to this place – to finish some work – and I stayed late to get it out of the way. I am completely out of the habit of having any work to leave to the next day.

Now I wait another week for another music lesson.

I send my love -

Henry

March 22

Dear mama -

I am not sure whether or not I have written to you today – but no harm if I write again.

I telephoned to Claude Morris last night – across the country – he is now near the D'Alterios again – and may get me another box. If I get one, I shall send it, but that is very tentative.

Meanwhile, you should have received a few tablecloths and cups – but I shall await letters, which ought to begin overtaking me with some regularity soon.

I am well – the weather has turned very lovely – although yesterday it rained, as I suppose it will every Tuesday.

Such conflicting reports! Yesterday, I saw women and men mobbing a place, and filling the whole block – said they were there to get materials and cloth. Today I saw a shop with a number of bolts of silk. Maybe the crowded place was a "government monopoly" place, where they may set at pre-war prices. I did not price the silk – but if it is, say $ 300 or 400 lire a yard, at pre-war exchanges, that would be to these people about $60.00 a yard – which no one would pay for dress material. So the government monopoly of spaghetti sells it at, I think, 1 ½ lire a pound. But free flour from farmers costs about 50¢ a pound. So all is confusion – and I cannot understand it.

I am now appointed "assistant defense counsel" for a general court martial here. It may give me opportunity to wand around a little bit – and I shall sing "pink-a-pink, pink-a-pink," to accompany the spiritual.

I skipped lunch today – and left my watch to be repaired. I am not sure but that I eat more when I skip lunch than when I don't. Today, an orange and some little cookies and a few sugar coated almonds, of which I am very fond.

A man here, whom I met this morning, said he used to work for Carter and Company, and to get leases called on a woman – a widow – who lived all alone in Mt. Vernon. Her name was Rosenbaum[142] – (we were talking about Vandenburg County[143] leases) I wondered who she was. I thought that was funny.

I found yesterday that my description of Maestro Costa's studio was all wrong – it is not paneled– but papered in dark red. The chandelier is not glass, but iron – and quite handsome. But the room is as pretty as I remembered it.

Write often. I send my love.

Henry

March 23

Dear mama -

An interesting natural phenomenon is now occurring – it is raining out, and the rain as it falls is a thick mud. If one holds a piece of paper out, it is spotted with mud. I did not imagine that the dust would carry this far. For the sea outside had quite changed color – the mud floating on the surface. Even the breakers are yellow instead of white.

I suppose it is fortunate that it is raining – the dust, otherwise, would be quite nearly unbearable. It would be interesting to see the lava flow, but I haven't a chance of getting over there – and even if I had, wouldn't waste my time looking at natural phenomena. Vesuvius can be seen for many many miles, and I have seen it frequently, for a long time constantly. A kind of beacon at night. Aetna was never active when I was near it – and the days were too long to stay up to see it at night often. How long ago that is! now the days are getting longer again.

I just walked to lunch – and back – stopping for 200 gms. of sugar coated almonds, of which I am fond. So now I am more or less coated with mud – my eyes, ears, nose, etc. It is quite a remarkable phenomenon.

I am well – I know nothing either new or interesting. So I wrote a letter to Haymer this morning. How is he? Is he talking or walking yet? Write soon.

Babies here are dressed in what I suppose to be swaddling clothes – and it looks very funny – a baby wrapped up stiff – just its head sticking out – The mother carries it, and if she had to use her hands or wants to rest, she just stands the baby down, leaned up in a corner of a wall. It is so stiff that it stands here, leaning against the wall. The baby leans there crying or cooing and doesn't seem to mind it a bit.

I ought to have a batch of letters on the way – they will catch up probably in about two weeks.

---

[142] Abe's mother's maiden name was Rosenbaum and she came from Mt. Vernon.
[143] Mt. Vernon is in Posey County.

Write often. I had a good lunch today – including a lettuce salad with oil and vinegar and celery and onions – of which I am very fond.

All my love -

Henry.

I think I'm writing too often – I'll cut down a little.

March 24

Dear mama:

Today is clear – and the wind from the sea. It carries little dust – until it gets back a block, where yesterday's mud stream is drying. It will blow this way and that, I suppose, for months to come.

Last night I had a good time – it was Bill's birthday – so I bought a bottle of Vermouth to give him with which he might celebrate. But when I got back from supper with it, he was not there. And Porzia and her friend Ida asked me to go with them to their or Porzia's aunt's house for a cup of tea. I accepted – and Ida was getting dressed. But Porzia cannot get dressed – she had only one dress – a knitted affair which she made. So she just washes and combs her hair. I lent her my rain coat, because it was cold. She is very witty, and insists on being called "Sotto Tenante Porzia[144]" when she has my raincoat on.

So while they were doing that I talked to Signora Turetti – who is weeping most of the time now. Really can't blame her – but she would be more sensible if she didn't. She lost all she has (except one dress) when her house was bombed. Her son was home – but now has gone, she says, to the front. She thinks he does not get enough to eat – but I think she is mistaken, because the Italian troops have American rations, with extra flour for pasta (spaghetti, etc.) and it is cold, and he has no clothes. I suppose he hasn't. It really is quite sad.

But withal, they asked me to dinner on my birthday - I accepted on the condition that they would serve only fresh vegetables and fruits – of which I expressed myself inordinately fond, because we have only dried and canned ones, and too much to eat. So I said artichokes are the greatest delicacy in America, and I expect a dinner of artichokes, which will satisfy me.

Then Porzia and Ida were ready – so we walked over to the aunt's – about a block – and had tea. It was much fun – the tea was a tasteless herb tea, but with lots of lemon made a good hot lemonade. And we talked away. Ida is easy to understand. The other more difficult – The aunt had a room she wants to rent to soldiers – so I said I would give the information to the billeting officer – as I have. Billets are in great demand – and it is a fine, big, airy room. Better than ours, but I should be afraid of the aunts. One – a great big woman, whose solicitations to do you kindness would leave you no peace.

These are rather fine people – all with quite a little character and individuality. I like them and enjoy their company.

Signor Turetti had brothers in America – I said I should write to them for him, and shall.

---

[144] Likely meant to be "Sotto Tenente" or "Sottotenente," which translates to second lieutenant.

Back to the room after tea – where Signor T. was busily engaged with an interpreter composing letters to his brothers. I said they had to be in English.

All my love -

Henry

March 25 1944

Mrs. A. Lowenhaupt
6237 McPherson Ave.
Saint Louis, Missouri

Dear mama:

I am writing a V mail letter just to let you know that I continue well – that I am now receiving mail somewhat irregularly – but receiving it nevertheless, as a January 5 letter on the same day with a February 25 one. So I am thankful.

I am also well, with nothing new of which to write. But I have decided that in view of the uncertainty of the mails, I might as well repeat my address

Headquarters, Fifteenth Air Force
APO 520, c/o Postmaster
New York, N.Y.

I had a music lesson last Tuesday. And enjoyed it more than anything I have done for a very long time. So I shall have another next Tuesday. But I have written of those things frequently already.

I accepted an engagement for supper for my giorno natale – with the condition that nothing will be served but artichokes, oranges, and other fruits and vegetables, which are in abundance here. Well, I have written a request for tea or coffee – and if it comes in time, shall furnish that for with the dinner. I expect the dinner to be good, for I have eaten samples of their home cured olives and pickles, which are excellent. Also, cooking here is generally good, like the French. Witness the almond paste cookies, of which I am inordinately fond. I haven't got up my nerve yet to try fish, and probably shall not.

A wild stormy, windy day today, with great surf on the sea.

Love

Henry

[March (Not Dated), postmarked March 25 1944]

 I have no doubt (or I hope) that I shall get to the point where I desire to give him a token of esteem. What would you think of a pound of coffee or tea? I should like to receive it anyway, and therefore, request that you send me 2 pounds of coffee and 2 pounds of tea, if it is convenient.

My understanding is that coffee is worth about $20 to $30 a pound here. I have not seen any genuine tea, although I have seen some herb tea – artificial, Italian tea, ersatz.

I have no news – I am well – I think frequently of the office there, and wonder what is going on. The distance is too great, however, and it is so long since I have even thought of a legal problem.

How is Haymer?

My regards to all there -

I am ignoring here the amount of money I spend – and shall know I am spending too much only when my purse is empty. But that may not be for a long time, because for the past year, I have not had opportunity to spend. But here things are very expensive – I buy about a nickel's worth of sugar coated almonds for 30¢. Now and then a bottle of cognac (I have some good now) for which they charge the fancy price of $7.00. It does not last long, because I drink it with the landlord and his son and family – Then I bought a raincoat, since mine was stolen in a city where they'll steal your eye teeth. I left it in the vehicle – the driver in the front seat – a crowd surrounded the vehicle and a man ran away with the rain coat – the driver couldn't chase him, because if he did someone would have stolen the vehicle or/and the other things, which he was sitting on.

I also bought a coat – now required to wear them again, and I abandoned one to lighten baggage. Cookies – now and then. Mess plus club dues (which are paid because everybody else does – and being there, one buys a drink now and then – rotten stuff) – So I have given up all attempts to count. One gets robbed for haircuts and laundry, shoe shines, everything else.

There is a coffee shop in the office building, where I now go for coffee or tea and cookies about twice a day. The woman who runs it, a refugee from Vienna has collected all the hand-painted pottery in town for her coffee shop, and really serves beautifully – with good cookies. Her husband, they say, was a designer of pottery decorations in Vienna. I shall attempt to make their acquittance – but it is difficult, because she is always busy at the place. She has some kind of arrangement by which she gets her materials from the United States army – the charge is for her service.

You see - I am living in the lap of luxury.

Write soon and ~~for~~ often -

Henry

March 25

Dear mama -

Nothing new – it is cold here, but we have central heat in the office – delightful, warm beds. Last night, I came back here (office) after eating dinner with Bill at the Adriatic Restaurant – and tried to telephone Claude Morris – but he wasn't in. So we talked here for a while, then went back to the apartment where Signora and Porzia were busy ironing – they send our laundry out to be washed – take it back wet – and dry it and iron it there. When we came in, they quit – and we talked – signora brought out olives, which she had cured – very delicious – and told me the recipe – which seems to be just to soak them. As I have written, they are quite unfit to eat fresh.

What did we talk about? Really, nothing. Question was asked: Was I Catholic? Was Bill Catholic? I answered no – and Bill tried to tell them what he was. But it was impossible – they have never heard of anything except catholicism – so it ended that we believed in God and maybe in the madonna – we weren't quite sure – and we proceeded to give an English lesson. They wrote down phrases phonetically, so that they could learn them today – and their spelling was hilarious. I becomes Ai. "Raining" becomes "Urenengh" and so forth. "I like" = "Ai Laich." "Quiet" becomes "cuaied." They like phrases - "Go take a walk," "Keep your shirt on." And the reason for "You like" and "Do you like" is mysterious.

But having olives and gin and vermouth, we decided to make a martini. No ice – water instead – but the vermouth was sweet and it came out something terrible.

I received a message that the aunts would like for me to call on them. I think I shall do so. It is somewhat mysterious – introductions do not seem to be in vogue, and either no one cares about names or everyone assumes you know them. I do not know the aunts' names – they are Mrs. Turetti's sisters – and could be named anything – from Jones to [scribble]. They call me Henrico – which I consider funny. I've quite given up on Lowenhaupt.

I gave my music teacher a calling card – being out since he had not asked my name, and could not possibly know it. Which reminds me that I am out of cards- and if yo convenient, you might send me 100 or 15 – they are in a drawer someplace. I noticed my music teacher had your habit – he runs his thumb over the card – to see if it is printed or engraved.

No news – hard to write - I am not reading anything except a little Lucretius – of whom the first two pages are so far the best that I read them over and over, rather than going on.

My biblical references are never very serious – they are allusions, subjective and otherwise. The Bible offers so many -

Love -

Henry

March 26

Mrs. A. Lowenhaupt
6237 McPherson Ave
Saint Louis
Missouri

Dear mama –

I must mention again the beautiful surf today – great waves, breaking high over the light house and the pier and the road – so the spray flies all the way to the buildings on the landwards side of the road. And a wonderful stiff wind.

There is a Lt. Stern in the office with me – he got a cable this morning, saying "Mother very worried. W Cable at once." Signed – somebody with a different name. I decided to answer it for him – he being absent today – and cabled his mother. Now conscience begins to twinge – whose mother was very much worried? Well – a mistake would not be serious – but I stuck my neck out. I'll let you know about the blunder if I made one – it will be funny. It won't hurt for his mother to receive a cable that he is well and writing anyway.

I am well. Mail is coming in in dribbles – maybe I'm just too hard to satisfy – a letter from Janet today. Thanking me for an ugly box I sent her. Made me ashamed. Henry.

March 26

Dear mama -

A beautiful wild stormy day – cloudy – with a gale from the East building up great waves, so the ships on the horizon are seen to rock and roll above the swell. And waves come pouring over the breakwater into the basin, and crash against the wall of the boulevard by the sea. Such a wind that to walk you must push into it. It looked very cold – so I put my long woolen underwear back on – but it is not that cold, and I shall not put it on tomorrow. I know you will say there is danger of catching cold – but remember, it will be mid-June before your letter reaches me.

A little deviltry – not much – Last night, after supper, I went into the bar at The Miraware Hotel and had a glass of vermouth. There came in two officers with II Corps patches on their sleeves – so I spoke to them. They had taken 3 days off – and were driving – this was the end of the first day – to see how things were. So I talked to them – told them to look up some of the worst leeches and sycophants – telling them they were particular friends of mine – and asked them to come to the officer's club with me. So we spent the evening, drinking a few cocktails, and watching a floor show – imitation New York – a singer and a dancer and a jazz band. They think I do it every night, and I showed them as many splendors and luxuries as possible. Then asked them to come to dinner with me tonight – intending to bring them to the Adriatic They agreed that if they were still in town, they would be here at five o'clock. So I shall see if they turn up.

I am well – without news - I am receiving some mail now. A minute ago, a letter from Janet Cerf – V mail of 2 March – pretty good time, all things considered. So I'll intersperse a V-mail letter now and then.

Just returned from the coffee shop, where I had a cup of coffee and an almond cookie - I envy them their china principally – and shall skip lunch and take a walk, which I enjoy more – maybe supplementing my coffee and cookie with on orange and some olives. I think I could live for a long time on oranges and olives – maybe because I've never tried to.

The sun is out now, and it is much warmer. There are lots of cabinet makers here, and I may look for one and have him make me an inlaid box. So far I have not seen any whose designing I admire. It all had a decidedly Grand Rapids look – a look which the D'Alterios avoided.

The mails are now open to North Africa – if it would give you pleasure – write a letter to Mme. Peyrus, 8 Rue Lys du Pac, Algiers, Algeria. She reads English. Her son graduates from high school this June. I do not know if packages can go through, nor whether eor essential commodities are still so rare there.

All my love -

Henry

March 27

Dear mama -

Cold again this morning – and the gale continues. But the sun is shining and I am inclined to the opinion that it will be warm by noon.

Last evening I went on with my little deviltry spree – and brought the two officers from II Corps to dinner – or Bill did – at the Adriatic Club. Then we had a glass of cognac downstairs at the sumptuous yacht club bar, and saw a bum movie in the lounge – but in comfortable over-stuffed chairs. I think it is desperately funny to live the life of Riley in that manner in a town which reporters call bomb town. (But I am reminded of <u>Time's</u> apologia – explaining how they get the news – how their reporters always just <u>happen</u> to be present. The fact is, of course, that a pebble shot from a sling shot, landing within 20 feet of a reporter, is a bigger event than the bombing of Berlin. Hence, wherever there are comforts and good bars, you have, according to the press, terrible activity. A few windows were broken – the reporters saw it, because they were inside at the bars, and the news eclipses the complete destruction of a city where there were no bars still open. So they have their stories. But I digress)

Then, in order that Lt. Terrell and Capt. Green should be able to give complete description of our milieu, we brought them to the apartment. There, Signora Turetti was very cordial – and Porzia called in her neighbor, Ida, we turned on the phonograph – Ida's mother came in (a perfectly square woman – so solid on the ground – clean as a pin and polished all over, but you have to look close, because her square shape is suggestive of a peasant cleaning streets) and we danced. Then Captain Le Blanc came in – and we continued – with a bottle of good vermouth – not Cingano, but Cora, which, everyone tells me, is second only to vermouth.

The family desired to hear all about the other parts of Italy – and they were told – laboriously.

That is why I rather like to go to the transient officer's hotel. With transportation and communication out, it is like a mediaeval cross-roads town in spirit. You always run into people who have been other places – and tell tales of the wonders – of London and Casa Blanca, Oran, Algiers, Tunis, Alexandria, Cairo (which seems to be a kind of capital of the world, with Shepherd's Hotel – and highballs, and clean people on the streets, plenty of food and drink, steaks, eggs – the descriptions sound like Marco Polo descriptions of another world) Palermo – I have found one officer who talked about Belgrade – (he spoke German, Ach! ein klein Paris, ein kleine Paris! so schöne![145]) and Sarajevo, which sounded interesting.

So we passed the evening – trying to tell how people lived in other parts of Italy, what they had to eat, to wear, and so forth, dancing and drinking vermouth.

Then they left – going back, having promised to see various people – and we went to bed.

Tomorrow is my day off – and music lesson – I hold my thumbs.

Love -

Henry

---

[145] Translates to "a little Paris, a little Paris! so beautiful!"

March 28

Dear mama -

My day off, and I have had a very wonderful time, so far – and sit down to rest a while – and write.

I left the room shortly after seven – a windy morning, and ate breakfast – tomato juice, cereal, eggs, bacon, toast and coffee. Then walked out across the railroad tracks, and out of town – The day meanwhile having become cloudy. Magnificent! A farm road, between high stone walls, over which the olive trees and fruit trees crowded. Here and there, open to a field – or through an open fence to a villa – as the Re David villino – which is a great house, in a grove of pines, with formal, paved gardens, statuary of cupids and gods – the Italians work with stone so naturally that the garden statuettes even are handsome. Then the almond trees in bloom – and the petals blooming, like snow – the gentlest fragrance! Peasants plowing – carts going to town with artichokes and the like – quite fine horses – and gentlemen driving in carriages. Children running along the road in wooden shoes, strapped on, one carrying a flask of milk – looked like goat's milk.

How I wished you had been with me on that walk -

Then back – getting back to town at about 9:30 or a quarter of ten, and sat in a barber chair and was shaved while I rested.

Then I walked through town – stopped to buy some wine to have a birthday celebration on, and they had me sampling their liqueurs – chocolate and something bitter, but good. But not strong, and samples were restrained. A kind of nice man. He is across the railroad tracks too.

Town is opening up somewhat. I think after a few more weeks, there will be much for sale. To the present, I have found nothing.

Then I walked through the old city - which I find endlessly delightful.

Next, it was time for my music lesson. The preceding pupil and her mama were there. The pupil is going to ask her papa if I may come over to practice on their piano. I may be getting into difficulties – but I shall see - I do not like the idea of practicing with the family watching. But – intentions are of the best.

Music lesson was fine – a little Beethoven – some more Czerny exercises – in Maestro Costa's magnificent studio – the loveliest I have ever been in.

Then a hundred grams of macaroons for lunch – walked a little longer – and came back here. I am scheduled to take Porzia and Ida to an Italian movie this afternoon. Well – it may be fun.

That is about all I know – that's all I've done today.

Now to thank you for a box of candy, soap, needles and thread – wonderful. My thread left is rotten and not worth sewing with because it breaks all the time – so the thread is needed. So is the washing, and I gave my last cake of soap for last week's laundry. And the candy! What a delight! I have been eating it – have passed it among the Turettis – it is their first soft candy in five years – and am still enjoying it. It is agreed that we shall have the bouillon for supper when I have supper with them here.

The sea is rough – flurries of snow now and then – so you see it is still quite cold.

I had my watch cleaned – at a recommended jeweler's . Got it back today - I hope still in good shape. The watchmaker offered to buy it from me for 50000 lire – I thought that was interesting – but not wanting 50000 lire decided I would not sell it at any price. I will keep it – and if after the war I have a chance and desire to stay in Europe for a few months, shall sell it to defray expenses. 50000 lire is, for civilians, an awful lot of money, and prior to the war would have been about $10,000, I think.

I am well. I send my love. I wonder if I have mail at the office – I am not going there to find out.

Henry

Forgot to mention – during another rest, I got a shampoo, and could not stop the barber – my best "asciugie[146], asciugie" went unnoticed, while he told me about the English espionage system prior to the invasion of Italy, and poured oil and perfume on my head. So I need another shampoo.

March 28

Dear mama -

What a lot I have to write – it seems. First, a lot of mail, which I have put into my desk to reread at because – for it came just before I left on a trip I am about to mention. And also first, two magnificent packages – one, I think, from Ruth, but I have all the content mixed up, and know only that I have a magnificent supply of edibles – cheese, crackers, toast, candy, things which delight me. I have started to eat them – wonderful! -

Now I have just finished a hot bath, and am about to go to bed. Yesterday I left town to talk to some witnesses. Went by plane, a B-24, converted, and watched the country and sea go past like a rare show – cities scattered here and there, square fields, orchards and all. Then from the holding field, drove about twenty miles and that was far more interesting – through the towns which down there look more like Arab towns than European – white stucco houses; byzantine towers and domes – but always the magnificent Italian color.

Well – the interviewing of witnesses was quite inconsequential. I feel so sorry for people who get themselves in trouble – and I am so unable to help them – especially when they cry "peccari, peccari, de profundis clamari!"[147] and talk about how they've gotten nearer to God now and have learned by their crimes and they still have punishment coming. They are not really bad – they are just weak, and punishing them will not make them otherwise. Well – the ignorant get so self-righteous. "Judge not lest you be judged." But that is out of my mind now – I see no triumph in sending a poor, ignorant, weak boy to jail for stealing – but others will see in it a triumph of justice.

But that part took only about two hours out of the two days I spent. Ah, inefficiency!

I was with a Captain White (extremely pedestrian mentality) and we then drove back to the air-port where we were to spend the night. He proposed a game of ping pong, and I a walk. Ping pong won; I played

---

[146] Translates to "dry"
[147] "Peccari" is likely a misspelling of "peccare," or "to commit a sin." "Clamari" is not an Italian word and I am uncertain of a proper spelling.

three points – all his – because I couldn't hit the ball with the paddle, and he found a better player. So he played ping pong and I took a short walk – it was then after five, for we had gotten settled in our quarters – a barracks with cots and five blankets each. A little pack of orange vendors on the road and I ate about six oranges, which are very delicious and sweet. They were also selling eggs at 16¢ each – or ten for a package of American cigarettes – and had a rooster and some almond candy and cookies. I was tempted to buy eggs and the rooster – and fancied myself going back on the plane with a musette bag (a little overnight bag) a rooster and a basket of eggs. I think if ever I want a disguise, I shall get a cape, dirty, a basket of straw and eggs and a chicken, I refrained from the purchases. The poor rooster – legs tied together – was taking a lot of abuse. But again – the colors in Italy – you must imagine them – big hand woven baskets, filled with oranges – a pair of copper scales – an olive grove – a field of white and green – a stone wall covered with lichen, in the low sun a red mud road – a yellow rooster in the air – horses and wagons in the background. Then supper – read a little – Life and the first pages of Lucretius again – and to bed early. I was glad for my five blankets – needed them all. They were dusty and dirty – but I slept well.

Up and to breakfast, eating one orange, which I had left over in advance. We were told the plane was to leave at 10:30 – so I walked toward another town – which appeared on the highest part of a low ridge of hills – with ball-topped towers, and big buildings, beautifully. I did not get there – but the road was lovely – through olive groves, which are fresh again, between stone fences. The soil was poor – with rocks protruding in many places. Almond trees in full blooms, and fig trees, the branches of which, a beautiful pink-gray, bend to the ground, budding in green – the fields a brilliant emerald in some squares, elsewhere white with small daises, or yellow with a little flower I don't know. Then along the road, brilliant purple poppies and asters of some kind. And colts foot in great profusion – white and purple, like crocus. I got fairly close to the town – and then started back. Another orange on the way.

Got back and waited. At about 11:30 the plane not having arrived, we telephoned and found it was not going to arrive – there would be one down there at 2:30. So to lunch – spam and string beans – and Captain White to ping pong. I – another walk – this time up a dirt side road – through the fields, past many tiny stone houses, little olive presses, and beside stone walls, dividing the fields into squares. Plowing in progress – and hauling of olive twigs. The trees have been trimmed to perfect shape, and are beautiful. Apple blossoms – fragrance of almonds -

Beside a stone wall, a crowd of boys – 5 or 6 to 13 or 14 – had built a fire, over which they were heating a gallon can of food – kitchen waste – mixture of hash and beans and fruit and all – They offered me a bottle of cognac – and asked for cigarettes. Refused.

On my way back I talked to them – one of the biggest, a ragged, long-haired, bare-footed boy, seemed to be the spokesman. He said their food was good and they were all going to get fat. That since their parents (apparently referring to all – they did not look like brothers) had died or gone away, it was easy to get food from the soldier's kitchens. They offered me a drink of cognac – and I noticed the bottle was almost empty. The littlest boy was rubbing his eyes, and unsteady. I think the whole crowd was drunk. They seemed happy.

So I walked back to the airport – and waited. The plane came at about 3:00 o'clock – an old B-17, without usable windows, so I came back here as in a box. To the apartment – and to the office, feeling dirty – too dirty to go to bed.

So I have put all my clothes in my laundry bag – a kettle of hot water and a luxurious hot bath. A few pieces of candy – a cheese sandwich – this letter – and bed.

I shall review your letters tomorrow, and answer some of them.

All my love -

Henry

I shall write Ruth to thank her for whichever box she sent – but this is too long a letter to repeat the substance -

March 28

Dear Betty -

I suppose I ought to admit I am having a good time, in an idle, vacationing sort of way – irresponsible – when not interrupted by the petty and unsignificant details.

At the moment, for example, I am eating very delicious artichoke fritters, which Signora Turetti saved for me from their dinner – and an orange. I may be getting myself in much too thick – but I do not know what they can expect of me – a little soap - I share candy with them when I get it, and so forth, and it is all very funny.

Then, today being my day off, I took a walk into the country. Beautiful! Villas, with formal gardens – olive groves, turning a fresh green again; almond trees in bloom – petals being scattered by the wind – the loveliest, faint fragrance – and the road crowed with horse drawn traffic – gentlemen in flies and carriages, farmers with carts loaded with artichokes, cauliflower and the like.

Then on the way back, I stopped to buy a bottle of wine – and the merchant had me sampling his liqueurs. He charged me enough for the wine to pay for the samples – but I have the affectionate feeling that I had a hospitable treat – two or three kinds of cordials. Then I wandered through the town – resting to have a shampoo (or rather, having a shampoo to rest) I could not stop the talkative barber – and he covered my head with olive oil and perfume - I am scheduled to take Porzia and Ida to the movies this afternoon (funny!) and they think I perfumed my head on that account. I was going to take just Porzia – but that would have to be concealed from Ida, lest Ida resent it and fight with Porzia – we are common property. So I decided it was much easier to take both.

Then my music lessons – one this noon, with the inimitable little Maestro Nicola Costa – who is outdoing himself on my lessons. Quite fun – although I do not practice. So one of his students is going to ask her papa if I can come to their house to use their piano. I shall soon have to begin keeping a date book – what with, in addition, the aunts of the landlady inviting me over to tea. It is all very, very funny, and I frequently feel very much ashamed of myself, as if I am imposing, and cannot possibly live up to expectations. So I give away lots of cigarettes. I am afraid they want me to give them shoes and clothes. Ah, well!

The place here is beautiful – on the sea, with lots of surf today and quite cold. I go to a transient's bar – which is like a mediaeval roadhouse for traveler's tales – people who just come from London, New York, Baltimore, Palermo, Casa Blanca, Algiers, Oran, Tunis Alexandria, Cairo, the Holy Land, and all places. Quite wonderful.

I am well – have nothing new of which to write – note the new address.

Do you have any use for a stop-watch? I have one, which seems to be working alright, which I have been carrying around for a while. I never use the stop feature, although they are very fancy.

Note a new address – as is obvious from allusions to living conditions.

Write now and then, Betty; I enjoy your letters. Tell me about mama's visit, of which I have just heard.

Your devoted brother -

Henry.

March 29

Dear daddy -

By this time you should have the signed slip concerning redemption of excess bonds. I have read your first speech – and found it interesting. Your second I have put aside (received it yesterday) to read at leisure. I received a great batch of mail yesterday – and am enjoying it. Do not try to send me eggs. While it would be nice to have them, I think by the time they were packed and sent, they would be more expensive than locally purchased ones – I can buy eggs at about 18¢ each – or trade cigarettes for them at 3 or 4 or better eggs per package. The price of eggs is not exorbitant in comparison with the price of other commodities. So you see, in sending, things should be chosen which are easier to ship.

My trouble is always that I cannot resist giving things away to people who are kind to me – candy, cheese, soap, everything else. But maybe they need it worse than I, and there is no harm.

I am now assistant counsel in a general court martial. I am stringing, in the present case, the trial judge advocate along on the hope that I will plead guilty. Maybe I should – but I do not see what I can gain. I have no witnesses – and can't find any, not even character witnesses, who all say they liked the man until they learned he had rolled a drunk in Atlantic City for $50.00 and searched the pockets of sleeping men for money – crimes with which he is not charged. So I don't think they'd do me much good. And the accused himself would make a poor witness – having confessed several times already, and so I can do nothing except heckle the prosecution and see what happens. So I intend to confuse the issue – and urge that the charge should be embezzlement, not larceny (much gained, if I prevail.) and exclude all the evidence I can, and see what happens. A sad case – the man repents and has gotten religion. Like *Moll Flanders*[148].

I am well – the weather is beautiful – spring here – flowers out – everything. I am busy today and shall be tomorrow.

I am living in a room in an apartment – not a very larger room, but clean and with good beds and a balcony over a court-yard. No hot running water – but the people make up for it – for they are extremely anxious to do everything I might want. A mere hint that I want to bathe – and presto! there is a bottle of boiling water, a bath mat, a chair and a knock on the door – my bath is ready. So I do not intend to look

---

[148] Novel published in 1722.
Via Wikipedia
https://en.wikipedia.org/wiki/Moll_Flanders
I had always heard that Moll Flanders was Henry's father's favorite book.

for better accommodation. Maybe I am too easily satisfied, but I think not. They give us the use of the living room, whenever we want it.

Spring is here - I have been writing just about every day.

Affectionately -

Henry

April 1 1944

Mr. A. Lowenhaupt
408 Pine St,
Saint Louis, MO
USA

Dear daddy -

You should have received by this time the form on redemption of bonds purchased in excess of limitation, signed etc.

If not please send me another -

Henry

I'm well -

April 1

Dear mama -

Time passes and spring is here – showers, sun, alternating (I hope, because now it is a shower) It is warm – I've taken off my woolen underwear for good, and shall I think abandon it – with the hope of being able to get more if necessary. Wasteful? Yes.

There is no news – except I have been receiving mail beautifully, and enjoying it.

Last night, I went to the apartment of a Fran and Herr Weigher, refugees from Vienna – she runs the coffee shop here – he used to be a porcelain decorator. They served cookies, beer, and wine – collected from all corners. Quite pleasant people, but extremely confusing to vacillate from German to English to Italian and then mix them all together. I can do fairly now in Italian <u>or</u> German but not in both at once. Viennese German is much easier to understand than Prussian. They said they knew Mr. and Mrs. Schlesinger[149]- I do not know how adequately I understood them.

I am well – my birthday is coming soon and I am saving a bottle of wine, cheese and crackers for a celebration. I suppose with the Turettis – who have invited me to dinner. So I shall add my cheese and crackers to their artichoke and cabbage and so forth. She cooks artichoke in a way which is good, but not nearly as good as plain boiled with olive oil and vinegar – Using only the hearts, she makes fritters out of it – so you bite through first a layer of crust – like pie crust, but not crisp, and then an artichoke heart. The taste of artichoke is much concealed.

Please take my complete assurances that I am well. You must gather that I am from my walks and activates. Such is the fact – It delights me to read your letter that in the photograph I sent I look thin. My conscience hurts a little when I eat pastries, cookies, olives and the like. But no more! If I look thin – well, if necessary I shall use a rope for a belt - I cannot get one longer than 40 inches – or I shall sew two of them together. Bill has a friend who is a sergeant near here – a man named Thomas, who entertained me once in New York. He may come to this city for a visit for a while – and I propose if he does to have

---

[149] St. Louis friends of Henry's parents - refugees

Mrs. Turetti cook at least dinner for us, because there is no place where he and Bill can eat together – and I should enjoy the change in cuisine. So I should like (and think of trying) to furnish food – raw – and have Signora Turetti cook it; in exchange for which they may eat of it. For that, I should ask her to procure the food, and I should give her cigarettes, soap and the like for barter. A chicken can be bought, for example, at about $6.00 - a rooster. But maybe it could be had for about a carton of cigarettes, or a few cakes of soap. If so, the rooster would not be expensive. So also eggs; there are sheep around here; and therefore must be lambs. But all is in the planning stage. Shall let you know. Maybe, we can draw some rations in kind – consisting of canned hash and the like. No use writing what you think of the proposals – because before then, action one plans will be complete (ly abandoned) – (strike out part not applicable – I've been reading forms.)

I send my love – how is Haymer?

Henry

April 1

Dear Marian -

By extraordinary luck I received today your birthday letter of 24 March – illustrated – and am delighted. How your illustrations amuse me – they are completely recognizable – and you make Haymer look like quite a big boy – I suppose his is.

Spring is upon us. The sea today is wild, blustering rough – with white caps way out.

I think I have been a little lazy and lax recently in my package sending campaign, having got nothing at all for a long time. That, because my standards became too high in other places. So I shall stimulate my determination and see what I can find – costume jewelry if nothing else. Little cups – anything.

I am now committed to a box at the symphony here for Saturday nights – and shall go sometime. My trouble is, I am getting too much entertainment. But I do not have to go.

I am well – mama urges me to write, so I quite exhaust myself on letters to her. But I trust you read them.

This is poor stationery – and I have a huge quantity – so I shall have to write big to exhaust it – as I now do.

I wish I could draw pictures – but the censor wouldn't pass them, and besides, I haven't a horse. So I had a photograph taken and shall send it to you.

Write again -

Henry

April 2

Dear mama -

I received a very splendid illustrated birthday letter from Marian today – or rather yesterday evening – and have written her thanking her for it. It was really a great delight.

Tomorrow is my birthday – but I intend to celebrate it day after tomorrow, which will be my day off, if all goes well – a day I always look forward to with pleasure. My trouble is, I am accumulating too much for pleasure -

Last night I went to the symphony – a short but very pleasant concert – by a competent orchestra – just good craftsman on their instruments. They played Mozart's *Overture to Marriage of Figaro*; Mussorgsky – *Night on Bald Mountain*; Franck, Gershwin *Rhapsody in Blue* and so forth. Lasted about two hours. We had a box, which three of us have taken for the month of April – will accommodate eight – and so we filled it up. The audience consisted almost entirely of soldiers – possibly the prices – 50 lire – are prohibitive for civilians. Programs printed in English – and funny. They have terrible trouble with spelling.

So after the concert we went to the Club Adriatico, where there was a dance in progress, with only ~~two~~ three girls – two nurses and one civilian – a kind of devil-may-care looking woman who is probably a refugee from some place, because native girls are afraid for their reputations if they are seen after dark.

Now we have daylight savings time – so I missed an hour's sleep last night, and am sleepy – shall catch up tonight.

I am well. The weather today is magnificent, with a light sea breeze, but without news. I walked this noon, instead of eating lunch – having fortified myself with a cup of coffee and a sandwich – finding an orange on my walk, and upon return, another visit to the coffee shop with three cream puffs and a cup of tea. So some would say I did not miss lunch. I just hate to spend the time to sit down at noon – would rather wander around.

Especially on Sunday – all the world is dressed up and out walking, making the streets crowded and I enjoy it. ~~I see~~

I see some very pretty costume jewelry here – and may send Marian some - I am inclined to the opinion that she gets more pleasure of it than anyone else. So if she becomes overburdened, she can give it away.

I enjoyed Marian's picture (drawn) of Haymer – he looks like quite a big boy. How is he? What is his progress?

Had another photograph taken yesterday, and when (if) I get it, shall send it to you.

Last Easter, I went to the cathedral in Oran. It seems so long ago. The cities I have been in in North Africa? I think I can mention them now – Oran, Algiers, Relizane, Tunis, Bizerte, Carthage – and in Sicily – Gela, Caltanisetta (Royal Prefecture), Gangi (mummies) Palermo, with the cloister nearby, Cefalu, city of fancy sewing, Termini Immeresi[150], Nicosia, and so forth. Oh yes, Campo Felice for a long time. Italian cities will have to be named later.

Henry.

April 3

Dear daddy -

I expected to be in a court martial proceeding all day today – ~~but~~ as defense counsel – but it ended quickly, for today, with me as a witness rather than counsel – for I moved for postponement and examination by a psychiatrist on the grounds that the man was not capable of conducting his defense. I was afraid not to make the motion – and once it was made, I testified. My testimony was true and the motion was granted. But I am inclined to the opinion that the man will not get over it, because it is nervousness for fear of the trial. But what can you do, when a man doesn't answer questions, but goes into a religious tirade instead? And, with the obvious possibility of a number of years in jail before him, keeps asking you to get him a job in another headquarters? And how could he get everything cleared up if he were free to disclose things which he is under oath not to disclose? Well – it will come up again next week, and we'll see what the doctors say.

I received your letter enclosing copy of income tax return. Thank you very much. I shall try to understand it this evening.

I celebrate my birthday tomorrow, a day late, with an invitation to dinner at the Turettis. A little embarrassing – they feed me, when they have anything – as cheese from her brother in another part of the country and wine – and then I give them my jelly and candy and crackers. I get the better of the bargain – but part with things I like.

Funny – the principal witness in the case I was about to try (against me) was in the same law office as Bill Clark. I think, of course, that he is a scoundrel, but Bill assures me he has the rudiments of integrity. He looks like a scoundrel.

I am well. Even a scoundrel can happen to tell the truth on occasion – and there is nothing to be done.

There is no news. I am busy in sprints. And idle in sprints. Tomorrow is my day off and I shall take it. Music lesson – with the possibility of being invited to use a piano in my preceding pupil's house.

Affectionately -

Henry

---

[150] Likely a misspelling of Termini Imerese, Sicily.

April 3

Dear mama -

I received your letter (Henrysson included) that you were sending me two boxes. I have received one box of candy – and am not sure but that is the one you sent. I look forward eagerly to the receipt of salami.

I am well. The weather is beautiful and now on daylight savings time, it is light until about eight o'clock. So I took a walk last night. There was a huge crowd watching a little corner of the harbor – enclosed and calm, where two English ~~soldiers~~ sailors, quite drunk, had got into a row-boat, and were tugging away. I don't know how they had gotten in – it was anchored, and they weren't getting anyplace at all. They had apparently gone to the boat in another, released the other, and let it drift away. They almost fell overboard several times – and the crowd gasped with anticipation that they might. Quite funny.

So I shall walk again tonight.

Today is my birthday – but I am celebrating it tomorrow – with dinner with the Turettis - I look forward to the occasion. Mrs. Turetti is nice, but there are certain times and occasions when she weeps and weeps – holidays, she says, which are hard, because her son is away (in the Italian army) and everything is gone, and her husband has lost his health, and he doesn't know how to do anything except write. So he is not working.

They go out to her brother's farm, about seven miles away, almost every Sunday, to bring back food – principally artichokes and cabbage – for flour has now gone up to 120 lire a kilo. Almonds, oranges and the like.

Then also I have my music lesson tomorrow – so I shall have a full day – and my preceding pupil was going to inquire whether or not it would be permissible for me to come there and practice on her piano. Ha ha!

No news - I am well. Wrote to daddy today – and this letter is very largely repetitious of what I have written to him.

Love

Henry

April 5

Dear mama -

I celebrated my birthday yesterday – quite a big day – full of "Augurii[151], augurii," from the ~~Turret~~ Turettis. It was my day off – and I spent the morning walking, over into new parts of the city and all around. Then to my music lesson, which I enjoyed – Czerny and Beethoven – but there is no reply yet on the use of a piano for practicing. Nevertheless, I enjoy the lessons, even without progress.

---

[151] Translates to "wish."

Then back to the apartment for dinner – and what a dinner! First pasta, called orecchiette, because it is shaped like little ears of shells. With tomato sauce and a little cheese. A big soup bowl of it. Then cauliflower (which by description I had thought was artichokes) in fritters, and a few fried potatoes and fried clams – then oranges and nuts and cheese (my contribution) and then a kind of custard. So I was very full. Then I walked a while again – and that evening dancing in the parlor. So it was quite a celebration – with Ida, Porzia and the cousin Adelina – as big as a house.
We talked about everything – these people are treating me very royally – they are somewhat of beggars, but why not? So I give them my rations of hard candies, which I do not like anyway.

Oh yes – we had wine too.

I am well - I ate so much yesterday that I think I shall never again be hungry.

Major Morris is sending me another carved box from the D'Alterios. To whom shall I give it? Keep it for myself? I shall send it home, and you may make disposition of it. But I'm counting chickens before they hatch.

The weather today is very beautiful – although it started out rainy. Spring is here – and the sun begins to take on the summer colors.

The old town yesterday was as beautiful as ever. One place was selling hemp (I think it was that) and everywhere, old women had gotten out their spindles and distaffs – and were spinning thread – quite a pretty process, although it is a very slow way of making thread. A spinning wheel is a modern, efficient method by comparison. They attach a little of the stuff to a bobbin, give the bobbin a whirl, and it spins and twists a thread. Then they wind the thread on the bobbin, and spin it again, making more. I have not seen any weaving here.

The town is full of Italianate table clothes of rayon or some similar stuff. That is all I see for sale and I consider them very ugly. So I haven't gotten anything, although I become impatient – maybe costume jewelry, although I dislike that even more.

I have been receiving mail beautifully – yesterday a letter of March 23, which is really good time – a Vmail letter.

No news. I am well. Need nothing – but if you enjoy sending packages, shall ask for things to enable you to send them. I surely enjoy receiving them – anything. Am now well stocked on clothes and the like. But they change uniform so often that I may not be so long.

I send my love.

Henry

April 6

Dear mama -

Last night I took a walk – quite exciting – it is light so late now, and more or less a favorite entertainment seems to be to promenade along the sea of an evening – so the street is thronged with people out walking slowly.

Then suddenly there came a black cloud from the north, with lightning and thunder and hail – a violent hail storm, which Sr. Turetti tells me will much damage the almond trees, knocking the flowers off. I went under the porte cochere of the building now used as a Red Cross Club, and watched the hail, which lasted about 15 minutes.

Then walked on, making detours around flooded streets. Watched about three different English soldiers, who get into fights when they are drunk – sadistic entertainment!

And walked through a street of the old town before dark – looked in a window, where a man was carving wooden plaques – heads of saints, copied from pictures – apparently quite skillfully. He saw me watching him and asked me to come in – so I did – gave him a cigarette, and he told me about how he was going to New York as soon as he could get there; that he could not make a living any more, because bread cost 100 lire a kilo, and his plaques – a week's worth – brought only 1000 lire. I asked him if he could design a small box – while his plaques are very fine, the subjects are all too saintly – and he brought out his folio of designs and pictures. He wants to make a carved chest – large – which would of course be an extremely handsome thing to have. But too bulky. He has splendid designs – keeping the patterns of everything he has previously designed or made – So he is going to design a box and show me the design, if I go back, and I think I shall ask him to make me something, although maybe not a box. He seems to me to do a kind of portrait carving very well – copying pictures of saints and the like – his plaques intrigued me with the detail of hands and expressions, and the intricate patterns of robes and halos – flowered halos seem to be in fashion.

So I walked back to the room, and went to bed early. But Bill came in then, and we talked until late – after 10 o'clock. Nevertheless, I caught up on sleep.

I am well – was rather busy yesterday, although I really can't say what I did – just confusion and running around. I have no news of which to write. Weather now beautiful and calm after last night's storm.

I am to get some photographs of myself today, and shall send them to you.

Write often – my mail is now coming through well – and I am receiving even fairly recent mail as a March 23 V-mail – together with some old mail – December and January, which is catching up.

I send my love -

Henry

April 6

Dear mama -

I wrote once today – now write to enclose a picture of myself.

Received delightful pictures of Haymer, and consider them a rare, fine and delightful birthday present -

Have your V-mail of March 15 – Time varies enormously.

Please send me a few pounds of coffee and tea.

I send my love -

Henry.

April 7

Dear Haymer -

I received some very beautiful pictures of you yesterday, and certainly enjoyed getting them. I showed them to Porzia and her mother, and they said: "Bello bambino! quell' bello bambino. E vostro nepote? Filio de vostra sorella? Bello bambino!^152" They asked why you had the basket on the back of your bicycle, and I told them to carry packages home from the grocery store for your mama. They think it is a good idea. So I am sending you a picture of myself. It is not as interesting as your pictures.

Yesterday, I looked out of the window of the coffee shop, at the sea, and a little dock, and there were children swimming. My, it looked cold.

Then last evening – it stays light now until 8:30, for we have daylight savings time - I went for a walk through the old city. Crowds of children running and playing in the streets – dressed so funny – in little dresses, with nothing else, and when they run, the dresses get all tangled up around their shoulders – many of them without shoes – and many with wooden shoes, which keep falling off, and they have to go back to put them back on. Some with little fur jackets, made from old fur coats. The little girls wear long hair, and they pull each other around by their hair.

I went to see a wood-carver, who makes pictures out of wood. He said he could not make boxes because he could not get hinges and locks and keys. He has a little boy, about your age, who helps him, sandpapering things and helping to sharpen tools by turning the handle of a grindstone.

Then I stood on the wall of the town – which had a street on top of it – and watched some English soldiers practicing with an anti-aircraft gun. They sat on little seats, and turned handles, which made the gun go around, and one of them stamped his foot to make a noise, to imitate shooting. Then another one gave commands in a loud voice.

A fish-woman was standing near me – very big, and greasy and dirty, and a little fisherman stood near her. She mimicked and mocked the English soldiers – making noises which she thought sounded like the English soldiers. "Ho! Ha! Hohaho," she said, in a loud voice. The little man told her to stop, and she began scolding him – starting soft, and getting louder and louder, as she scolded him. Then the man began talking at the same time. What a racket they made! Finally, the little man ran away.

Then I walked through the town some more – stone streets, with ruts worn into the stones from carriages passing over.

Write soon – Tell me about yourself – how is Kim?

I am well. There is no news here – except that the Signora tells me that the Easter rabbit will not come here this year with colored eggs. I hope he comes here. Next Sunday – day after tomorrow – is Easter.

---

^152 Roughly translates to "Beautiful baby! that beautiful child. And your nephew? Son of your sister? Beautiful baby!"

Remember me to your mama and daddy – your grandma, grandpa, ~~unel~~ aunt Marian, Irma, and George and Kim and everyone else. Also to your chicken.

Love -

Henry

April 7

Dear mama -

I just received your letter of March 19. In it you say you wonder where I am, and I hope at sometime to be able to tell you "Be patient," one can only say, a little easier, I suppose, then being so. Well, I chafe against the restrictions on what I may say, but try to abide 'em, and since the restrictions are few, technical and irrational, don't have to try hard to succeed. I hope. It is now forbidden, as I understand it, to mention any place in Italy, as the names of towns.

I am well and the weather is beautiful. Yesterday I received three pictures – snapshots – of Haymer in one envelope. How I enjoy them! I showed them to Signora Turetti last night. She exclaimed even too enthusiastically, confusing the sex, as I understood her, "Bella bambina" – with all the trimmings. They were particularly curious about the basket on the back of his tricycle – and I tried to laboriously explain - I think I got the idea across, that it was to carry his mama's groceries home.

So I wrote a letter to Haymer, thanking him – and in it said, really, everything I have to say. I hope you read it – if you have any pleasure of letters such as these.

I enclose another picture of myself – you see I send them one at a time – even though they will probably all come in a batch anyway.

Weather beautiful – I shall take another walk tonight.

I send my love -

Henry

My requests are never very serious. I have received some soap – and now have enough for a few weeks or months. Wearing cotton shirts may take more soap, for they must be laundered more often.

Edibles are indeed always delightful - I think I have some on the way.

H

April 8

Dear mama -

I am enjoying now the very beautiful, long evenings, which I usually spend walking, sometimes along the sea – which is, curiously, and without intended humor, called "The Board Walk." It is not board, but a wide street, without a sidewalk and a concrete balustrade along the sea. And into the old town, again, last night, where the streets were jam-packed with people going into and coming out of the churches, of which there must be seven or eight. The weather is now fine, although I note that it is clouding up a bit – for Tuesday, no doubt, my day off.

I woke early this morning, to a new sound – having become accustomed to the crowing of roosters from all windows and balconies – like Algiers. This was the vigorous bleating of a lamb – which was on a balcony across the courtyard. Someone's easter dinner, no doubt, or I hope. I can't blame it for bleating – because it stood on a balcony, and right next to it, a lamb just its size, skinned and dressed and strung up by the hind legs. So I got up and got dressed myself -

Dinner hour is changed – 6:00 to 7:30, instead of 5:30 to 7:00 – which makes it hard to get to shows or anyplace else, for they all begin at 6:00 o'clock. To bed with the roosters – the Turettis tell me that is my habit – and I've been getting up with them too.

I am well. Complete lack of news still. The sea remains lovely. Not too much work to do – which is quite alright with me, for I am quite completely lazy. My Italian is not progressing very fast, for I lent my book to Ida to learn English from – but gradually I pick up new phrases. I ought to study the conjunction of verbs – but I am content to make myself understood, without too many refinements, as the past perfect and the past definite and the subjective and so forth. I am gradually learning words for everyday things, as keys and boxes and baths and the like. For the time I have now been in Italy, I know very little Italian – but most of the time, I have not had opportunity to speak to Italians more than once every two or three weeks. Maybe I shall progress a little faster now – although I fear getting on too friendly terms with the Turettis – they would become very possessive – and take all time – They are somewhat of beggars – they all are.

I shall have this letter open to see if I get mail today.

Love -

Henry

I just walked out for lunch – on the hoof – one little piece of pastry – disappointing – one cream puff and one dish of ice cream – very good. Oranges seem to have disappeared from the market – the one cart of oranges I saw was being mobbed by women. How they paw and fight to get anything which at the moment is not common! A week ago oranges were piled high, and nobody seemed to care about them. Lemons still abundant. These civilians, in the course of my walking, asked me how to say "Buono Pasquale[153]" in English – "Come se dice in Inglese "Buono Pasquale"?" I replied "Happy Easter" to all, and hope that is good, idiomatic English. It sounds rather funny to me – like "Happy Christmas" or "Merry New Year." What would you say?

No mail delivered yet – maybe I shall get none today. I received mail yesterday. -

H

Later -

I did receive mail! With two pictures of Haymer standing up way out in the middle of a yard – quite without help. He could not do that, last time I saw him – but some development is to be expected in a year. Is he walking? Talking?

---

[153] Translates to "Happy Easter"

I am thinking of having my portrait painted – what would you think of that?

April 9

Dear mama -

Last night I went to the symphony – in our box – with Lt. Clark and Lt. Stern – which latter is quite a fool – with very little sense about anything. I have no complaints in particular, except that it is funny – he likes to talk German – and so seeks out the German refugees to associate with – and most of them here are a rather low order. One or two exceptions. He is trying to rent an apartment – and goes to see people where, he had been told, there is an apartment – then speaks to them so rudely that they put him out, denying they have an apartment.

But the concert was really quite excellent – and the orchestra surprised me. In the past, I've only heard them play the nice tickling things, as Mozart and overtures to opera. Last night, they added Tchaikovsky's *Symphony Pathetique* – and did very well at it – with all the swells and fortes and all else. The man who played the cymbals and drums really had me worried – he almost came in in the wrong place several times.

Then an excellent clarinet solo – the kind which impresses me with the thorough competence of the musician – no genius, but he knows what his instrument can do, and makes it do it. That is Mozart – and I particularly like it. Inspiration and genius in a soloist are just pretense in the Oscar Wilde, long haired tradition, for the trade, and they are no more necessary in a musician than in a plumber.

So I enclose a program (me), with the name of the city cut out.

The concerts are short. Her Weigler was with us; (from Vienna) his wife had stayed at home with a sore knee (pretended, I think, when she learned that a Fraulein Tritski, or some such name, and a Miss or Signorina Torina were to be there. The latter, an Albanian refugee. You see what a mixed up place this is – and language confusion is something desperate – with Stern trying to speak German, and the Viennese replying in English, and a few Italian side remarks, so I never know whether to say "Si," "Ja," "Yes," or "Oui" or even "Doch" can come in now and then. We went to the apartment of Fraulein Tritski. I think her reputation is not of the best. She served coffee – an ostentatious display – and kept asking for things, as transportation or an automobile, and promising things – as the use of a beautiful villa on the shore, with lovely gardens and a fine beach, I picture a Merrimack River shack. The fuses kept blowing out, what with the electric stove and possible defective wiring – she had three extra fuses – and three fuses were blown.

So I did not stay long. Walked after I left, for it was a beautiful, moon-light night.

Now today is Easter. And I was greeted this morning with enthusiastic "Buon' Pasquale" and "Augurii." "Augurii" seems to be the word for all occasions – birthday and easter and so far.

Claude Morris sent me a present of a very, very ugly vase. I can't make up my mind whether to send it to you, poorly packed, to throw it out of the window; to send it to Myron and Sonja – it is of a low order. Raised fishes, on an ugly, blue-green shiny glaze. Poor shape, with fancy curlicues . It would solve my problem if it would break.

I am well -

Henry

April 10

Dear mama -

It is a drizzly, rainy day today. Maybe it will clear by tomorrow – my day off – which I always enjoy. Tomorrow, I plan to continue to wander the streets – looking around; to take my music lesson; to go to see my woodcarver; to look in shop windows – so to spend the day. I am well.

Yesterday evening I walked – since I find walking constantly pleasant and interesting – crowded streets; people all dressed up – children playing – rolling hoops, which seems to be a favorite pastime.

People do not seem to have adequate cooking facilities here – for it seems to be the custom to send things out to be cooked. So Children wander through the streets carrying pans of unbaked cookies – pieces of meat, all salted and peppered – and so forth – and then running home with them baked. I suppose they bring them to the baker – who rents his oven or something.

That only during the day - I have not seen it at night.

I am well.

People were all dressed up for Easter – children's clothes very interesting because they have such an obvious home made look – and children run to their mamas with heart breaking tears, to point out that they have gotten their shoes muddy. The policemen with red-lined uniforms on – lots of flowers around.

Signora Turetti gave us four of her easter cakes – very nourishing, heavy, bread rolls, with a slight suggestion of sweetness. I ate one with cheese – I suppose a culinary sin – but the rolls are quite tasteless. Maybe we are used to tastier things – and these ancient recipes are disappointing.

I have not yet resolved the problem of what to do with the vase Claude Morris sent me – send it home? Terrible waste of shipping space, but I suppose there is plenty of space going that way. Or break it? Well – I shall do something.

I hope for mail this afternoon – that is because I have been receiving so much so well that I am spoiled.

So having nothing to say, I'll hold this letter and see. Did you ever receive a linen towel I sent?

Love, Henry

Today I ate lunch on the hoof – always the same – soup, Vienna sausage (called tube steak, no bone, no fat, and tender) beets, potatoes and a slice of pineapple – too much lunch, and now I am sleepy. One would think that they could get excellent trades – canned vegetables for fresh, which would be much better.

So I have now bought my rations for the week – one cake of Palmolive soap; one tube of shaving cream; one tube of tooth paste; two 5¢ Hershey bars; one Tootsie Roll; 5 packages of cigarettes; one cigar; one can of orange and grapefruit juice, blended and sweetened, and one bottle of coca cola – to be drunk only on the premises, to secure the bottle. Coca cola – so long thought of as one of the unobtainables; I am told they now have a bottling plant in a city in Italy -

I could have gotten, but declined, playing cards, talcum powder and brass polish and shoe polish. Shoe polishing becomes a pleasure – an excuse for sitting down on my walks.

I suppose I'd better close this letter, for it appears there will be no mail today. It is clearing. I intend to leave early, on the reason (excuse) of going to the jail to see my client. He should trade his lawyer for a witness – or the Divine – he needs some kind of help I can't give him.

All my love -

Henry

April 11

Dear mama -

This is a quick note before I go to dinner thus polishing off my giorno de permisso[154] – Tuesday. I have walked almost all day – first going to the PX and getting to two little things (that's after a shave and some walking), having my watch adjusted, for it was losing time – then to see my woodcarver, but he was not there. So I walked to the end of the pier and around the old city – then back. They had seen me trying to get in the first time – or it had been reported to the wood carver. His little boy was there when I came back – and told me to wait – he would run and get his papa. So he did – and his mama – and I found that the wood carver had not been able to get any hinges or lock to satisfy him. So he is designing me something without hinges or lock – which he says he can do, and I am to see his design tomorrow evening. If I do not like it, I am going to ask him to make me a plaque of St. Nicholas. He carves hands beautifully – with rings and all. Eyes in wood carving – flat – look rather strange.

Then I walked some more – out to the railroad stations and back, stopping at one place and having a cookie, at another and having some poor ice cream – then to the market. Oranges are almost gone – and the places which have them are mobbed by women fighting for them. One place had four or five baskets, and was emptying them fast – nice, woven baskets, with lids. A farmer selling them. He emptied one basket, took off the lid of another – a surprised look came over his face – the women around gasped, and I caught sight of a little boy in the basket – rubbing his eyes. He got out, and the farmer took him by the ear, and words flew – among which the principal seem to be "città[155]." So I guess the boy had sneaked into the city with his father in an orange basket. He must have been awfully sleepy to sleep so long.

Then to my music lesson – which consists of reading under supervision. I enjoy it. Maestro Nicola (Costa) is very skilled. The local symphony is going to play one of his symphonies next month – with him as piano soloist. I am, of course, very anxious to hear it. All the musicians here seem to have studied together.

Then I walked down to the office and did about 20 minutes work I had left – and ate a cake and drank a cup of chocolate.

---

[154] Roughly translates to "day off."
[155] Translates to "city."

Then walked some more – seeing an exhibition of mediocre paintings and pricing costume jewelry. Good stationery is getting scarce, and I may soon have to forego this means of varying letters.

Then I went over to the jail and saw the prisoner whom I am to represent in a few days – whose case was postponed because he was incapable of making defense, because, I said, he was crazy with nervousness. He seemed alright now – I feel so sorry for the poor fool!

My music teacher told me about his son who is in Russia – he hasn't heard from him since Christmas, 1942. He is a nice little man. It is very hard to think that his son, if he is still on either side, is on the other side, fighting against the Russians. Or I suppose he must be.

Then I came back here – no one at home, so I took a cold bath. The weather is warm enough for that. Put on clean clothes, and began to write this letter, which I now finish.

That brings me to date. I am flirting with the idea of having a portrait painted. There is one artist here, whose work is mediocre. That is fair. There are many cartoonists – a likeness is 15 minutes – but I may look around, because there is some good, craftsmanlike painting in exhibition, and I think it must be by local painters.

I am well. Send my love.

Henry

I am encouraged by your letter saying photographs show so little. In the one of Bill and me, the trees are big sycamore trees. In the one with one man cut out, the trees are olive trees.

April 12

Dear mama -

I received a letter from you today. I suppose, if my letters reach you in batches, it is partly the fault of the mails – and partly my fault – because I sometimes carry them around in my pockets for two or three days – or leave them in a desk drawer, or something else – and then mail them three or four at once.

I have not done or thought about much today – until this evening, when, before supper, I wandered around for half an hour – and went in to see my woodcarver, a cheerful little man, who has a design for a box he wants to make – not a "scottola[156]," he says, but a "coffera[157]," which I take to mean "jewel box," and he says he wants to make it, and if I do not buy it from him, he will bring it to New York with him when he goes. He refused to name a price – he says he is going to have to run around town and look for wood which is good enough: walnut, he says, is the only wood - I suggested oak – no, too coarse. I think I suggested oak – using the Latin word, and he seemed to understand.

I am not sure that I am sorry he could not get hinges and lock to suit him – although if he had, they would probably have been nice – he was looking for handmade ones, small, from the jeweller's . His design is a lead effect, and he plans little carved feet. He says it will take him at least 15 days. His first idea was a true miniature carved chest – he is very proud of the large chests he has made – but he had to abandon that – and his present is quite a fine idea in shape – abandoning the straight lines entirely – being quite

---

[156] Likely means "scatola," or "box."

[157] I am uncertain what this phonetic spelling translates to, but "coffa" or "basket" is somewhat close.

Queen Anne ish in shape. So of course I am very much interested – and afraid I shall buy it quite regardless of his price. I am just afraid of leading him to think – he is a naïve little man – that all Americans want carved boxes, and I can build up a thriving trade for him. That would not be fair, would it? So, while it is quite true that if I like his work, I shall show it to a few people, I have no doubt that everyone I show it to will say it's fine – and he would like to have one at $1.50 or $2.00. He plans to spend two weeks on it – and I shall be prepared to pay at least $10.00, and maybe more, if I want it.

He has a beautiful little shop – a work bench with a high char, in a tiny room – under an arch in an old building, just at the curve of a very narrow street – a few feet from the place where it opens into a paved place – with a public fountain, where people are always filling their jugs and buckets, and a stone lion[158] – Egyptian in appearance – lying on a stone platform – up a few steps; inscribed to "justice" in mediaeval Latin – "Esto justicie." Then a building, as intricate as lace, with statues on top – not a church, but possibly a castle, now with shops and dwellings. In his shop, just off the lacy square, the walls are covered with pictures of saints, which serve as models for his plaques – which he does in great detail.

Now I have spent a number of intervening hours – with a Capt. and a major who are witnesses against me tomorrow – drinking beer and talking. So now it is bedtime.

Love -

Henry

Now it is morning of the next day - I enjoyed being with Capt. Sessa last night. He speaks Italian fluently – and almost understandably to me. He's spent much time in Italy – used to practice law in New York – with many Italian clients – with a firm named Wuigate & Cullen – the same as that with which Bill was.

I am well -

Henry

April 13

Dear daddy -

Now I sit in a former Fascist court room – a fine, simple room with a noble motto: "La legge è uguale per tutti[159]" – with fancy chairs and all. Which proves nothing anyway. The case I have is desperate, so I intend just to bark at the heels of the prosecution, and see if they will make a mistake – they won't; the court won't let ~~one~~ them – and I have a fragmentary quotation from each book available (three) and shall see which books they bring. If they forget any, I shall read the quotation from the forgotten one. I can't make up citations, because everybody knows I have no books available.

---

[158] This location is likely the Piazza Mercantile in Bari.
Via GoogleMaps
https://www.google.com/maps/@41.12805,16.8720088,3a,56.3y,85.55h,81.64t/data=!3m6!1e1!3m4!1sTEzOaeSsmV_Yb-a1cEjvlg!2e0!7i16384!8i8192
Via Trip Advisor
https://www.tripadvisor.com/Attraction_Review-g187874-d7050197-Reviews-Piazza_Mercantile-Bari_Province_of_Bari_Puglia.html
[159] Translates to "the law is the same for everyone."

It is a beautiful day – I am early, as always, but did not want to go first to the place I usually spend my time – would just get started in confusion.

Last night, I spent with the prosecution's two principal witnesses – one of them used to be in Wuigate & Cullen's office in New York – so did Bill Clark. So they are friends – but far from Bill shaking ~~any~~ the witness, the witness shook Bill, who now says only: "What the hell, you're not being paid for it, are you?" So I am afraid to testify for a conversation last night that the witnesses said "I hate his guts; we're going to get him – I don't like his looks – we'll hang him" and so forth. They didn't – I could be successfully contradicted. Oh well – the accused will come in playing with his rosary and bible, and dropping 'em all the time, and unable to sit still. That's alright – I'd just as soon he appeared a little weak minded, because I've already raised the issue of his competency to conduct his defense. Decided against me – and time will not make him more capable.

You see I have no news of which to write. I am beginning another adventure with a woodcarver – and shall send what, if anything, turns out.

I am well. Write soon – I have been writing so often that I have no material for any letter. So I try to accomplish variety by stationery – buying it in little envelopes – small quantities.

How are the people in the office? I have not had one of Miss Thompson's news summaries for a long time – which I always enjoy when I get them.

Did you ever receive the papers about overpurchase of bonds?

I send my love -

Henry

April 14

Dear mama –

I received a letter from daddy yesterday, acknowledging receipt of papers I sent him – mail takes a long time.

Weather is beautiful – I am well. Last night I walked around the walls of the town, and through the old city – it grows more surprisingly beautiful every time I go through it – narrow alleys and streets, crowded with people, children playing, peddlers, everyone – big buildings – with arches over the streets to support the walls of the buildings – archways, where the streets go under the buildings. All the streets paved in flag stones, with ruts worn in the wider ones – worn right into the stone from the wheels of carriages – columns remaining, apparently, from some very ancient church or temple –

(I can't decide whether it is picturesque – a woman sitting in the doorway combing children's hair, and picking the bugs out – if you don't know what she's doing, it is picturesque.) The children are ingenious in their games – and play quite beautifully – one, which looks like ring a round the rosy – but they chant something, having one child in the circle, about the chicken is encircled and can't escape – so I suppose the one in the center is trying to get out in some way – Then they chase each other all over. Of course, there is an awful lot of crying going on – little children being abused by bigger ones – taking their balls away, and so forth – and mama's calling loud and furious for "Giovanni" and "Nicola" and begging for candy and chewing gum and what not.

Then I went with Bill to the Adriatic Club – and drank a bottle of beer – and then to bed. The elevator in the building is broken – a tender subject with all – the inhabitants saying that English soldiers kicked in the door, and thinking that it should be a pleasure, therefore, to walk up; and I not caring how it was broken, but not liking to walk up, although it does no harm – only 6 flights, and I go up only once or twice a day.

I am well – and without anything of which to write. A Captain, who speaks Italian and is stationed about forty miles or more away, visited with us and the Turettis night before last – and it is now understood that next time he comes to town he will bring a supply of fish – and the Turettis will furnish the salt and pepper – and we shall have a feast. So I look forward to his return. Not with any confidence that it will ever come about, but it may.

Write often – I expect mail today – but shall not hold this letter for that anticipation. Instead shall write again.

For the sake of your records, if any, I mention that I did not write yesterday. No letter dated 13 April.

Love -

Henry

April 15

Dear Myron -

I was much pleased to receive your news letter yesterday – with the advices of the prospering chicken ranch. One ought to send chickens here – with eggs at 20¢ each - a hen is a valuable piece of capital. Regret that you will not undertake the venture suggested – coffee, tea, etc. would bring handsome prices – $20 a pound for coffee and the like.

But my real reason for writing is that I now have some sealing wax to make up for the deficiency of glue on most of the envelopes I get. Also – to lend variety. And next market day, I shall get some ribbon to complete my seals.

No news here. I have found me a woodcarver, whom I now visit every evening or so, give him a cigarette, and stay about half hour, watching him work – and maybe he will make me a carved object of some kind. Then the big event is coming off next month, to wit: Maestro Costa will render the world première of his own piano solo, with symphony accompaniment here. I am inclined to fear it may also be the world dernière too. I shall bear it, God willing.

The weather continues fine – spring is upon us –

I am impatient to use my seal – and send my kindest regards.

Signor T. – my landlord, went to the country today – to visit a friend about 30 miles away – by horse and wagon, he expects to make it in one day. I equipped him with a present for his friend – three packages of American cigarettes. He expects to bring back fresh fruit and vegetables – maybe eggs and even cheese and flour. On a small scale, this is the venture I planned for you.

The country now is beautiful – cherries will be ripe in a few weeks – apricots will be coming in – and all luxuries. Now is the mid-season – oranges going out – but there are vegetables – cauliflower, artichokes, and peas and beans beginning to come in.

Sincerely yours -

Henry

April 15

Dear mama -

I am getting very spoiled in respect of mail – so if hereafter I complain on the subject, don't pay any attention – a letter almost every day. Last night the one with the verse from Boethius – who gets his analogy and tugs it out of the ground as if it was a worm. But I like the nice naiveté of it. So obviously moral. The letter was delightful – even perfumed, I think with talcum powder.

So I grow ambitious for more – although my sense tells me not to expect any.

Last night I walked – first to the Red Cross – which has taken over a fine house – more or less Victorian – and has card rooms and comfortable chairs and a "snack bar" with sandwiches cookies and ice cream – so I ate again – and did not stay long. Balconies over small formal gardens of lemon trees and bushes. Then walked down and saw the woodcarver – who is getting busier and busier. I am afraid he will rush on the job. He is now just finishing a plaque copied from a portrait – a style of expression with which I am out of sympathy – plaques for portraits. He showed me the wood he had gotten for my box – a good pieces, about three inches thick, but needing planing down. So I smoked a cigarette with him – he is a happy little man.

Then I walked up the main street – the one with a don three double rows of trees along it – one on either side and one in the middle – little, solid trees – lemon, possibly – and noticing a shop open, went in. They were setting up a display of paintings – about four artists – hanging their own pictures, each being allotted a portion of the shop. I thought much of the work was very good – some with the nice simplicity of line and color, and clarity – which I think is the best part of futuristic stuff – or whatever it is called – and a few very interesting portraits – self portraits, I was told by one of the artists, who kept steering me away from what I was looking at to his own section of the room. He showed me paintings – "Do you like that?" landscapes, very confused with little splotches – and I told him I liked greater simplicity. So he brought out his simplest – a small landscape with a cow – and a very tiny patch of sky, complicated with billowy clouds – I told him that I like the tiny patch of sky then he told me he was really a sculptor, and we decided that sculpture was a more powerful medium, then they were closing and I agreed to come back in a few days, maybe.

Then I walked a little further – and back to the apartment and went to bed. Signora Turetti giving me a very delicious orange to eat before I went to bed.

That brings me to date – except that I got up this morning at about six thirty – washed and took a cold bath – dressed – left money on the dresser for laundry – $1.55; they had added it to $1.49, but were wrong – which is one week's laundry, without sheets, and we furnishing soap. They use so much soap, and complain that the soap available – palmolive and lux and sometimes a kind of very dry, grainy Armour & Co. Soap – is both insufficient and of too poor quality. So I had to give them my fine laundry soap, which you sent, and which I have been saving for I don't know what. Well – sufficient unto the day – I still have one cake of laundry soap left, and after that they will have to use Palmolive or Lux. I am afraid I am furnishing soap for the whole city of _____ (I almost slipped and named it) Don't care much. Maybe they use it to launder my sheets – they are always very white and clean.

Then to breakfast – tomato juice, cream of wheat, toast, pork sausage and coffee. Quantity is small here – because I believe, again, they are feeding the whole town at the back door. But I have plenty to eat – and enjoy supplementing with oranges and olives and figs and dates and other things in abundance here -

Which reminds me of the evening I walked in Sicily, picking ripe fresh figs – and eating them fresh from the trees. Were they good! milky and juicy and sweet and syrupy– have you ever eaten them? – big white ones.

I send my love -

Henry

April 15

Dear Marian -

I received a letter from you today – and a Vmail from mama. Also a ------- package containing soap and Shakespeare. I think that probably you have no appreciation of the tremendous value of soap in a place like this. If I wanted money, I could sell it for a dollar or more a cake. That would, however, seem like profiteering; and besides, I need soap. So now, for a while, I can be somewhat generous – and build up good will towards dinners and pastries and oranges from The D͟r Turettis -

Signor Turetti is going today to visit with a friend in the country – about 30 miles away – by horse and buggy, that being the only transportation. He thinks he can make it in a day – and maybe he can. He desired to bring a present to his friend, and I furnished him with three packages of cigarettes – which he says is a very handsome gift. He anticipates bringing back fruit and vegetables, and maybe some eggs, even some flour – and if he does, I shall <u>probably</u> be invited to a dinner (as I have been once) which will be very wonderful for variety. I wrote about my last one – with pasta (little ears) with cheese and tomatoes, and fried clams and cauliflower fritters, and all else – quite wonderful. So I feel indebted still – one cannot pay for such a dinner in exact terms of soap and cigarettes. Besides, I get all my pressing and ironing done free – as well as dry cleaning, where I get cleaning fluid. So I get service and bargains which could not be bought.

In view of the fact that you like costume jewelry, I am watching for some. But prices in cash become outrageous here – as $40.00 for a silver bracelet of some beauty but no value. So I let those go – and I do not know how to go into an established shop and offer cigarettes for a bracelet. Since cigarettes are worth about 60¢ - $1.00 a pack, that would be, say, 40 packs of cigarettes – still expensive – but it could be got, I think, for, say, 10 bars of laundry soap. But I don't know how to initiate such a trade with a jeweler] – and I don't want to, anyway. Until I need something, I shall stay on an intangible basis.

I am now in process of acquiring a coffreta, or jewel box or something – having it made. Unfortunately, my woodcarver gets orders to make carved plaques from photographs – which I consider low. Carving should be decorative, not illustrative – and portraits require greater depth, as in sculpture, in order to portray things like eyes and ears and nose – or color, foreign to carving, or else can be only a silhouette, which is decorative and not illustrative any way *[sic]*. Do you concur in the theory? To my way of looking, there is nothing worse than a carved portrait – maximum depth about half an inch – it looks like Bette Davis – eyes popping out, suffering from some kind of thyroid trouble, and so forth. Now a religious plaque – as of a saint is different, because it can be somewhat Egyptian looking in style. But if you want a wooden plaque of yourself, send me a photograph and I'll see what happens.

I frequently think of what a very interesting and good time you could have here, if you could get here – without a job, because that hurts the conscience. One thinks one should be doing something, and isn't. For these areas, living would be easy and comfortable – with a bicycle for transportation and living out of the crowded towns, and in towns the enemy hasn't taken over. The people are so completely friendly and nice – most of them so scrupulously clean. But that is all out of the question, because of passports and transportation, unless you will just get yourself a sailboat and come. But that is fanciful.

I have Shakespeare now – with a clean, soapy smell.

I admired the two cups very much and am happy that they arrived safe.

Write again, Marian -

I send my love -

Henry

April 16

To Mrs. A. Lowenhaupt
6237 McPherson Ave.
Saint Louis, Missouri
U.S.A.

Dear mama -

I am writing a V mail letter because I have nothing to say and might as well keep you posted on my state of health, the weather and so forth with a little more expedition than ordinary mail receives, if this does in fact get there any faster. I am well and the weather is spring like and magnificent.

Last night, I went to the symphony, and enjoyed it very much – Beethoven's Third, *Heroica*, Respighi's *Fountains of Rome*, and an overture from Wagner. All were completely played, although the Beethoven seemed in passages a little too difficult for the orchestra, especially the conductor, who was one of the hissing kind, and filled the hall with noises like a cat sneezing. Maybe I wrong him – maybe there was a cat sneezing.

Night before last, in my walking, I stopped in a store where about five or six artists are displaying their own work for sale. Some of the painting is very competent, or seems so to me, and I expect to go back. A very nice man, who speaks about as much English as I speak Italian, took it upon himself to show me the paintings, and to keep steering me away from the ones I liked best to his own – which were mostly very complicated and intricate landscapes, all broken up into little pieces and complications. He explained that he was principally a sculptor – but still kept pointing out his own paintings. But he was nice about it – I told him they did not conform to my taste – that I liked greater simplicity. He asked me to come back – and I decided to take it as a personal invitation to come back, and not as the invitation of every shopkeeper, as saying "au revoir" (here a riverdila *[sic]*), instead of good bye. So I shall go back, for the ostensible purpose of talking to him. I think he enjoys practice in speaking English, which he speaks very poorly, anyway. The business venture had just started – they were just hanging the pictures – and there was no indication that they were going to do a land-office business. But a lot of people stop in to look around.

I believe (hopefully, as in every place I've been so far) that the quality of merchandise is improving, although very slowly. I believe also that the English are in large part responsible that it does not improve more quickly, for they drive prices down too far, and sometimes even insist upon purchasing at their own price, regardless of whether or not it is agreeable to the merchant. So, I believe, merchants are afraid to display much merchandise, for fear they will be forced to sell it below the price they believe to be fair. For my part, I see no justification for insisting upon
buying a non-necessity at anything other than an agreed price, for you can just decline to buy it at all.

I am going to walk out and see if I can find something to eat on the hoof . Although it is lunch time, I am not hungry, for I ate a big breakfast. Also the coffee shop will be open this afternoon, and I intend to drink a cup of chocolate and eat some cookies, which are very excellent. The Red Cross furnishes the materials, and a local pastry maker makes the cookies.

Love:

Henry

April 16

Dear mama -

I went to symphony last night and enjoyed it. They played Beethoven's Third (Heroic) and the Beethoven part is so very magnificent that the performance could not spoil it. Then Respighi's *Fountains of Rome* – a favorite around here – and Wagner – an overture, I've forgotten which one. The performance begins early – about six o'clock – and ends about eight. So afterwards, I walked for a while – stopped in a new bar and cocktail room – ridiculous imitation of New York or Indianapolis – and drank a, poor bottle of champagne – a bottle of poor champagne. You see what a hard life I'm leading? Good champagne is hardly available.

Then upstairs to bed. The elevator in the apartment is broken – so we walked up about six flights. They'd better get it fixed, or they're going to lose some tenants.

The manager of the building asked me if, since the apartment was really being run for the benefit of soldiers, the army shouldn't furnish the materials to repair the elevator. I don't think they will – but he would like to have his building put in complete new order. No harm in his asking. If I were he, I might ask for the same thing.

I am well. The weather is beautiful. I really have nothing of which to write now. Maybe I'll try again later.

Love -

Henry

April 17

Dear mama -

The day begins beautiful – and I think I mentioned that I received a very fine box of soap – with Shakespeare – and am much enjoying the embarras des riches – planning a bath this evening and trying to make up my mind what kind of soap I shall use. There is some soap – color of laundry soap, but I think it is castile. Not sure – so I gave half a cake to Porzia and told her it was the very finest face soap there was. I shall receive her comment – and accept it. If no comment, I shall try it as face soap.

I had a good time last night. First ate dinner with Bill – at my place, the Grand Allegro Oriente – a supper of boiled beef, fresh cabbage (excellent!) and canned string beans – ice cream and cake. Then we walked down the main street, and stopped at a picture galley – now open – and the appearance of the complicated landscapes has improved.

We walked on down into the old town – and looked at the leaning pillar with a ball on top, and a lion by it – a fantastic, flat faced lion, which children pet – and they have polished parts of it highly with years of petting. I have quite an affection for the lion and pillar – with the motto on its collar "Esto justicie." Maybe it is a dog and not a lion – it is so docile and smiling.

As we looked at it, the little wood carver (Sunday – he is all polished and dressed) comes running out, saluting and bowing as he runs – So we greet him, and he asks us to come to his house and have a drink – his room is just across the way, up a blind alley a little way – we go in – a big room, on the level of the ground, flag-stone floor – one side is mostly door, with an outer door of wood. In the corner, his wife, who was sitting with neighbors at the corner, joins us. In the room is one enormous bed – one table, a wardrobe thing and a few niches with a big piece of hand-woven and embroidered linen hanging in front of it. The wood carver apologizes – it is big enough for the two of them. The baby on the bed is his nephew – a little tiny baby – maybe six or eight months old – all wrapped up in blankets. There is excess of hospitality, in pulling up chairs – and we sit down at the table. He brings out (or has his wife bring out) a bottle of "grappa" – which he says is, in English "Vischi" (whiskey? it wasn't) and pours each of us a big glass. Then, for the event we do not like that, each a big glass of white wine. He and his wife take red wine – vin ordinaire – which comes from a pitcher – quite a beautiful old pottery pitcher. Pretty soon the baby begins to cry – and the wife shakes the bed; the baby goes back to sleep. Then his brother comes – a talkative man, all polished and dressed clean, with his wife, and four of his children in addition to the one on the bed. He has eight children – the oldest 11 years, and one on the way. The children are all polished and clean – the boys with little velvet hats – the girl in a green velvet upholstery dress, embodied. The children stand, beautifully behaved and quiet – apparently instructed not to laugh, they answer questions as best they can. Then another sister comes in – and the father – an old man of 70, who has been to Paris. The sister nurses one baby, while she holds another on her lap. Then three more brothers come in – add them up, if you can, I never did get count of them. And such politeness! Of course we had to keep our hands over the glasses, so keep them from filling them – but conversation flew – mostly about prices, by the tailor with eight children – the prices of food, and his own suit, of which he is very proud – the cloth is pre-war – but the lining cost more than all the rest of the suit, except the buttons. The old man worked on a short railroad in France – and did not work hard – spent most of his time in Paris where wine is so good. The cabinet maker expects to go to New York – what a surprise the naive little man will have if he ever gets there. He says a captain told him he knew where he could get a job as a wood carver, so it won't be hard, because he'll be expected, and be able to go right to work at high wages.

It really had cocktail parties beaten about three thousand miles.

We left, just after dark, and he showed us the way out of the old town – such deferential courtesy as I have never seen – and lots of fun. He would not accept matches – I forgot a package of cigarettes – leaving them on the table. The children's eyes bulged when they saw their father decline a cigarette.

I send my love -

Henry

April 17

Dear mama -

Monday night – I plan a bath – and tomorrow free. My plans for tomorrow – possibly it is ridiculous, but I take pleasure – and am now dabbling in the arts, head over heels – arts and instrumentalism. So my plans include – (besides shaving and the like):

   This evening I went to the exhibition of arts – show of paintings by artists around here – and concluded that a painting to be worth owning must be a masterpiece, unless the subject is interesting. Interest of subject makes up for a great deal. Landscapes – still lifes and the like are alright, may be interesting to see, but the thought of owning one that is not just a tiny nothing is displeasing. Unless it is the Rembrandt or what not, it would grow very shabby and boring. So, thinking the painting was good, and being interested in buying something, I inquired first of Steffani, who paints landscapes and speaks a little English, whether he knew of anyone interested in painting a portrait. He said he was a sculptor, and could do sculptured portraiture – but I said that was too heavy. So he said that he would inquire. Then I saw him this evening – and he introduced me to Signorina Emma Cusano Siciliani – There are two painters there whose work seems to me interesting as portraiture. She is one. Her paintings on display include a still life and two portraits – rather boldly done in strong color and big effect. The other is a De Belli, whose are most conventional, with a very smooth technique, and reserved color – style of the English – is it not Rayburn or some such name? Blue Boy, with pink eyelids – and rabbits? But Emma Cusano Siciliani has such a beautiful name – and having gone so far – and having decided that a portrait of myself would present an interesting subject at least to you, and also to me, because I am conceited, I made an appointment to see her tomorrow at 10:30, and go to her studio – see more of her work and talk about it. Talk about it, I say, in an unfortunate combination of French and Italian, with many "Si sis" and "oui ouis".

Well – I am thinking of size – and have no idea of price – shall consider about $10.00 to $15.00, and will insist on its being, say, at least 18" by 24" – that is, say, 45 cm. by 60 cm.

That is, as I say, dabbling in the arts with a vengeance. Would it be fair to agree to pay for it with a pound of coffee? I don't know, and I do not have the coffee yet, although daddy says two pounds of coffee and two of tea are on the way. In cash, that is worth about $100.00, I think.

Then at noon my music lesson – the greatest pleasure of my week – and a call on the wood carver. Those are my plans to about one o'clock. Afternoon – see what develops – maybe ask Porzia or Ida to come with me to the Red Cross and eat ice cream – first checking if that is permissible.

A wind is rising. I venture to guess that it will rain,

I send my love -

Henry

P. S. I venture to guess I shall not get a good portrait, if I get any. Pshaw! my sealing wax is all at the office! H.

P. S. There is another artist here who calls himself Prof. Curatelli – said to be a refugee from Rome. I have seen one portrait he painted – and I thought it very poor – without character or craftsmanship or style. So I do not intend to make any inquiries of him. De Bellis would be interesting, but I like to gamble – and fancy the idea a little bit. Shall see – and decide tomorrow.

No news – write often -

H

Porzia or Ida to the Red Cross is extremely free of being artistic – they have as much abstract appreciation as, well, a puppy or an egg or a cow or Uncle Sam – but like cooking and entertainment and pleasures -

H

I've finished this letter finally now -

H

April 19

Dear mama -

I am afraid my letters recently have been rather unsatisfactory – repetitious, little information, and all else. But I try to fill 'em up – and can do it only by repetition. So repeat. I can't even attempt to reform.

Yesterday I walked again. My usual Tuesday morning visit to barber shop – shave & shampoo – and 10 10:30, I went to the "Artistical Exhibition" – and fortunately (I think) was told that Emma Cusano Siciliani was too busy to take on new customers. Then walked some more. At noon – to my music lesson, where I played Mozart – for an hour – and I always enjoy that as more or less the high point of the week. Maybe sometimes I shall still find a piano to practice on. A few cookies, then, and continued walking. I bought four plates, which I considered interesting in a primitive way and mailed to Haymer. I hope they arrive for him to eat off of. Also, one modernistic tile, which I presently intend not to send home, but to someone else – I am not sure whom – walked some more – bought a book, in Italian, about a saint. I have read a few pages, and am amazed. So pious was he, and precocious, from birth, that when at the age of three days he was taken to be baptized, he leapt from his nurse's arms, into the basin of water, and stood there for his baptism. Illustrated with a photograph of a picture of his doing so. And more than that! Before he was weaned, he consistently refused to nurse on fast days, much to his mother's worry, for he did not appreciate the reason. It must be quite a problem to be the mother of a saint. I fancy her consulting Dr. Zaborsky – even he might be baffled in an attempt to diagnose the malady – or has he had experience with saint babies? You can recognize them by their halos.

Then I had my hair cut. Bill had had his cut the preceding day – and the barber had cut it too short to please him. So he has been raging ever since about Italian barbers and all Italians – taking it very ill. So I decided to give him company – and had mine cut very short. Further, knowing (or hoping), I had a bath coming, I did not say ~~know~~ "no" to anything – but just said "yes" to every bottle they held over my head – to find out. I came out of there perfumed to the gills – eau de cologne, bay rum, olive oil, perfumed petroleum, I had to shade my nose from my hair to breathe – the scents were so strong.

When I came back, the table was set – and the family T. told me they had saved dinner for me. But first I bathed – luxuriously – and put on clean clothes. Then ate – orecchiette and much else. Signora is going to give me to recipe for her pasta so you can make it (if you want to. A large part of the making is shaping it.) Lots of wine – and I did not finish until about a quarter of six. So I was not hungry for supper – and just walked over to meet Bill and show him my hair cut – he is now in good humour.

Oh yes – my box is progressing – four little feet almost done. It will be weeks before it is finished. Also, I got a lamp, which did not work at first. I fiddled, and decided it must be the socket – so stuck safety pins into the socket and blew a fuse. Decided, then, it was not the socket. What commotion! the family, playing cards, fetching candles, Bill in the bathtub hollering bloody murder where's the light and me, all helpful innocence, lending flashlights. There is nothing which makes me feel guiltier than blowing a fuse in some such foolish way – and I have confessed to no-one. So I fixed the fuse – stretching the wire a little – they are repairable fuses, and went on with the lamp on the assumption that it was not the socket which was bad. It wasn't – it was the connection between the bulb and its socket so I fixed that – and now we have fine reading light. Really do not need the lamp, but could not buy a bulb – none left – until I bought a lamp, and then the merchant gave me one of his bulbs, because he was about to lose the sale of the lamp. A precious bulb! So I read in bed.

Then this morning we paid our rent for two weeks – we pay $8.00 a month each – which is very expensive, but we are not looking for other arrangements. Advantages – scrupulously clean, and pleasant surroundings.

Elevator not yet working – but in process of repair. Doctor Rinaldi is a fraud – he implied to me that they could not repair the elevator without iron, and I should get him iron. He needs the iron to put the gates and so forth in like-new condition. Well - I am ready for him to ask me what I was able to do for him – shall give him the name of a general contractor, who does that kind of work (and whom he doubtless knows) and tell him he may go see the Engineers – let them kick him out – he is a round man, and will roll down the steps bouncing.

There is no news. I am using the soap I have received – bathed with the castile, and it was extremely luxurious. I expect the package with shampoo in it very soon, because I have substantially no hair. But I'll fool them, and keep the shampoo till my hair grows long again – or let a barber do a job on it again, so that even the little I have will need washing as if it were more.

Oranges are now out of season. Cherries are expected in a few weeks – then apples, apricots, green almonds, (if the hail hasn't destroyed them) peaches, grapes, all kinds of fruit. After the wheat crops, food ought to be abundant here, because this is farming country, and there is no transportation to carry it away. A little merchandise gets carried away by personal means from a city about 75 miles away – comes by people who get over here by horse, a-foot, or almost any other way. There is a railroad, little used, because there is no coal for it except that furnished by the army – so the railroad must be exclusively military transportation.

Shops are improving slowly. Prices are outrageously high.

Two page letters are an extravagance – it gives me an extra envelope – of which I have a great superabundance. Hate to buy just paper, because the envelopes are usually the prettiest part – with lining and so forth. But for a while I shall try to get just the paper – although the better qualities come only with envelopes.

All my love -

Henry

April 20

Dear mama -

I do not know where to begin writing. I am well, and the weather is beautiful. I am somewhat sleepy today having stayed up too late last night. At supper, Bill, who was required to stay at his place of work last night, telephoned me that his friend, a man named Thomas (whom I met in New York) was going to be here – and would like a place to sleep. I was very happy – he is using Bill's bed – so I spent the evening at the apartment, reading about St. Nicholas, in Italian, until he came – at about 10:00. I had just given him up. So I opened a bottle of Vermouth, which I had for the occasion, and drank it with him. We talked until about 1:00 or 1:30, and then went to sleep.

He is a pleasant man – from New York – used to be in the tire business – his wife an artist, now in New Mexico painting. An intelligent man – with the universal analysis and resignation – that there is only "piddling" to be done – and therefore one should make as much free leisure as possible, and use it for pleasure. "Quod omnio non bene, celeriter faciendum est" – a "quotation" I attribute to Cicero[160], and by which I mean that what's not worth doing well, ought at the least be done quickly. A sound maxim, I say.

Because I enjoy his company – and know he is a good friend of Bill's, in Bill's absence I completed arrangements for him to stay at the apartment as long as he is here. The duty of hospitality is about the most pleasant there is – and one which seems neglected and despised here – clubs, with little enough to offer, try to be exclusive – so that the 15th Air Force officers Club is open only to 15th Air Force officers – thereby excluding 15th Air Force officers from all the other clubs, and destroying the possibility of variety of company, which would be the principal interest of any such place.

In order to be able to eat with Thomas, I asked Signora Turetti if she would serve us dinner this evening – and gave her $10.00. She said she would. I do not know whether or not she will give me any change – but gave her that much to enable her to buy on the black market if she wants to. Emphasizing that we are very fond of artichokes, salads and cauliflower – as I at least am. So I shall fortify myself with a good lunch.

What luck! Here is a package, which I immediately opened, with two handsome sausages! Great Scott! I could never have imagined such perfection in timing! And a box of candy. I shall share them for dinner –

---

[160] As he got older Henry always attributed this to Benjamin Franklin not Cicero but never used the Latin.

and we shall have such a feast as has not been seen in years! This is wonderful – and delightful beyond any imagination! I'll write you about the party – and maybe skip lunch for it.

Love -

Henry!

(A gold seal occasion)

April 20

Dear mama -

I have to thank you again and more particularly for two sausages, more Shakespeare, and a box of candy – the sausages and candy come in such magnificent time that I have felt all day that happy feeling, as if I were lucky as I suppose I am -

They come in time for a kind of dinner which Signora Turetti is cooking for us – to provide for a Sgt. Thomas, whom I knew in New York before he came into the army, and at whose apartment I had dinner and drinks on or about March 29, 1943. It is a pleasure to be able to give him something to eat in pleasant surroundings, rather than to send him down with a mess-kit, to stand in line – even though food might be more abundant and better there.

So we shall eat, probably, half a sausage tonight – and save the rest for another similar occasion. Candy for dessert, too!

Love -

Henry

April 21

Dear mama -

What a feast last night! (I'll mention first that I went out and got a bottle of Italian Benedictine called Domenicus) – and then at 6:30, Bill and Thomas and I sat to eat – Signora and Porzia sitting with us, except when they were bringing more food and filling glasses with wine (we had about a gallon of it to drink). The meal began with orecchiette– pasta in the shape of little ears, with tomato sauce and grated cheese. Poor Tommy! He received express direction that he had to empty his plate – (He had eaten dinner at noon) and Signora sits by and beams. The pasta is served in plates the size of my big soup bowls – piled high – and is quite filling – but apparently considered no more than a light bouillon or broth. Followed with an omelet – aux fines herbes – such as I haven't eaten since I was in France, with a lettuce salad, oil and vinegar. Just imagine that! The sweetness of the omelet, and the pleasure of the lettuce which tasted so fresh and green – like an early morning. The vinegar, I think, is different from most – it is more like a spice, not just sour, but very fragrant. I think it is grape vinegar, instead of cider vinegar – and olive oil of a light, fine quality.

Well, that would have been enough, but then come the artichoke and cauliflower fritters – about my favorite food – and a small piece of salami – which was all we could take. Excellent! The salami is really wonderful – and I wish I could describe to you the delights of cauliflower and artichokes. I think the vegetables are fresher than any I have eaten in so very long – and in a very thin batter of some kind. And in great quantity! and at this point, whenever you begin to slow down, signora says "verdura - verdura non fa male – mangiate, mangiate." Vegetables – vegetables. They won't hurt you – you can't overeat on them. Eat, eat." So you go on – and when you remove your hand from your glass, the glass is filled with wine. Well – we went through a platter of cauliflower and artichokes.

Then came a little custard roll – very delicious – yellow outside, soft, not a crust, white filling – kind of creamy and slightly sweet.

Then almonds and dried figs and hazel nuts – with Signora urging you to eat, and you can always down one more hazel nut.

By this time, I was more delightfully near bursting than I have ever been – and drawing my consolation from Signora proverb – simple food, vegetables, they won't make you too full.

So we drank more liqueur – elixir coca de Brazil – left over from pre-war, and coming from Branca, of Milan, and some Domenicus of Stock, also of Milan.

Dinner lasted about two hours – and then we just sat around and talked – some in Italian – some in English. The cuzina Adeline (big as a house – and dancing with her is like swinging on a gate – but we did not dance) came in – and helped polish off my candy. And the neighbor Ida. We get flattered – or maybe should appreciate that we're dupes – Adeline had a vacant room, and asks us to find someone to stay in it – not to ask the billeting officer, but to find some friends of ours – like ourselves. And Ida's family is losing their tenant, by transfer, and Ida wants someone to take the room – someone nice, she says, like us. Well – I suppose most people do not want entanglements – but truthfully, I enjoy them and I think get the long end of the bargain   now I am told of an apartment – private – which I could have – but when I think of the details – as taking care of my own laundry arrangements, having someone to clean – and probably getting a dirty woman – and other details, rather think I prefer the present arrangements. Cleanliness is valuable here, for fleas and all such things are common, and to be infested with lice is an accepted state among the poor, from whose midst a cleaning woman would have to come.

So – "Tommy" being still here, he stayed with us last night – again by courtesy of the family Turetti – we shall eat ~~wet~~ at the apartment again ~~to~~ tonight. I asked them to confine themselves to fresh vegetables – with a little salami – and to eat with us -

I hope we do not have so much again, because it is always so good. I cannot help eating all I can bear.

Love

Henry

April 22

Dear mama -

Tommy "having left, I feel like the end of a celebration – for during his stay, we have eaten so well and so much and with such pleasure. Last night again – dinner with the Turettis and again an excellent excellent dinner. Pasta (noodles)and good ones! A stew of shell fish (octopus, I think, with potatoes and carrots) fried clams, fritters of artichokes and cauliflower, salad of lettuce, Boston, and artichoke hearts and peppers preserved in oil, and olives, and nuts and figs, and "apostles' fingers" How I enjoy the change in eating!

Apostles' fingers (Deti degali apostoli) are delicious as a dessert, and since I think both daddy and Haymer would be very fond the them, I write you the recipe, as Signora Turetti gives it to me. Some ingredients I am not completely sure of – as "ricotta," which my dictionary gives as buttermilk curds. But "ricotta" is sweet, not sour, and I suppose must be sweet cottage cheese. So I'll just call it buttermilk curds, and let you make up your mind what it is. So for Diti degali Apostoli – take some eggs, and beat them, white and yellow together. Have a small frying pan, with a very little oil in it – they say very, very little, and put a spoonful of the egg into the pan, hot. Spread it thin, but not too thin, and when it is done – set and solid, take it out and put in on a plate or piece of brown paper. Do this with all your egg – a large table-spoon full at a time.

Take some _fresh_ buttermilk curds. Add sugar and a little vanilla, and stir it well. Roll this mixture up inside the egg cakes made as aforesaid – the whole roll should be about an inch in diameter. Serve cold.

That is simple food – and you would be surprised how very good they are. You do not cook the buttermilk curds. Also, they are very pretty – bright yellow, sometimes fading to a little edge of brown, like yellow iris, with a clear white center. So you can just eat them almost indefinitely, unless you have just eaten fish, pasta, potatoes, more first, nuts, raisins, artichokes, cauliflower, lettuce, more artichokes and peppers. So I suggest you try 'em, and write me how they come out.

Then this morning, having eaten so much last night, I intended to skip breakfast – but the Turettis fed us some leftovers – "crema," which is a pudding, very good, but unconventional at 7:00 AM.

I am going to symphony tonight, and to bed early.

You see, on the whole, I am having a ridiculously comfortable time. I do not feel ashamed of it – I reason.

Went with Lt. Stern to look at an apartment, into which he considers moving, *[word unclear]* it is a nice apartment – on the main street – lots of room, little furniture. I don't see the use of it, and although it was suggested we take it with him, I refused. We are too well off where we are. Things like kitchens are a snare and a delusion. They don't have gas, but use wood, and I know I would never carry wood and go to all the other trouble to use it. But I suppose it is better than the Hotel. I consider that I am just plain lucky, to have a place with the intangible advantages I most enjoy.

First class mail has lapsed of late – none has come in for four days – but it will pick up, I suppose – may be today.

I send my love -

Henry

P.S. Mention again – since I am not sure how to when my letters arrive, that I have sent to Haymer some plates, which I hope reach him intact (doubtful) and in due time.

H

April 23

Dear mama -

I went to the symphony last night – and enjoyed it. Programme is herewith. The conductor really was not excellent, and I am not sufficiently modern or sophisticated to enjoy Brahms symphonies as much as the more feelingful Beethoven, Mozart and the like. I nevertheless enjoyed the concert.

After the concert we first went up to Lt. Stern's new apartment – a two room affair with great expanses of floor. I do not know whether or not I am a little jealous of it – but this now, because so much space is unnecessary and useless, and the pleasures and interests of living with civilians are great. I spend so little time awake in the bed room anyway, and in any event so firmly beholden to the Turettis' that I couldn't possibly move out. So we went next to Herr and Frau Weigler's apartment, where a company was assembled, and we drank mulled wine. I did not leave till after I had drunk it. It was made in a vessel intended as a chamber pot. Cookies and sandwiches – Frau Weigler runs the coffee shop. Much talk – which began to bore me, so I did the talking and enjoyed it. It was a trick I had quite forgotten – I shall have to begin using it again, because I am never bored in any company while I am talking.

Then back to the room and to bed, where I slept very soundly. I now think of the advantages of our apartment. Certainly not price – we are paying $8 a month each – that's $16.00 a month, for quite a small room with balcony over a court – get linen (sheets) water, light and service. Lt. Stern pays $13 a month for two big rooms – even bigger – over a street (without elevator) I do not know whether or not he had maid service or pays extra – or light or water or what – but think he may have a quarrel on his hands before long – you see how I justify my room. Others tell of being served tea in bed in the morning. Well – I shall cease comparing – it is much too funny and ridiculous. I am well content – and the difference between $5.00 a month and $8.00 is completely immaterial.

I am well. Without news – I hope to receive mail soon – we are in a period of suspense when no one is receiving it – I suppose just none coming in. The weather is very beautiful – and I shall take a walk this evening.

I suppose I might as well request a package – very hopeful that you will not send it unless you would like it. That is the stipulation with regard to all my requests. My pajamas are wearing out. I think I have some silk ones at home, which I might as well use for summer – or others. Pajamas are a luxury to which I still cling. Therefore -

Please send me a few pairs of pajamas. Pack the interstices with candy or other trinkets.

I send my love -

Henry

April 24

Dear mama -

This will be a short letter. I am well. I took a walk last night – around and through the old town. What a variety of games the children play – from the very beautiful singing games – they are really square dances – going to and fro to meet each other – and part as they sing, and going around in a circle singing about the chicken being caught – the only words I could understand – and fighting and throwing stones at each other, and chasing each other with clubs.

Then I saw a real fight – in a narrow street a crowd was gathered – the balconies outside each window were packed, and the women proceeded to yell at each other – and, I suppose, curse. All took sides, and it was a regular bedlam of yelling and finger pointing and making devil's horns and shrieking. I tried to find out what the fight was about – one man told me the children had had a fight, and the others took sides. And then told me that an English soldier had given one a pair of shoes, and another had taken it. Another said that one woman had taken another's shoes, and while they were disporting whose they were, an English soldier had broken each shoe in half, and given each one half. So I suppose there was an English soldier in the picture someplace, and a pair of shoes – maybe the children's shoes. But the fight was really raging, in grand opera style.

I find I forgot to send the symphony program I said I was sending with my last letter. So it is with this – if I can find it.

I hope to get tomorrow off.

Love -

Henry

April 25

Dear mama -

I consider this a day of misfortune – it should be my day off, but I have to be here – so I cancelled my music lesson – and shall get away if I can.

I saw my cabinet maker last night – box almost done – and well done, so far – but not as well designed as it should be. I think he got tired of the details. But maybe when it is finished I shall send it to you – it is very handsome but, I think, not quite up to the other box.

With what shall I fill it when I send it? I shall look for something.

I must begin going around more actively looking for interests – the place will get dull otherwise, as it is whenever I am not at leisure.

Last night, I walked – visited Lt. Stern's apartment – that is what I mean by getting dull – for he is a jackass and a bore -

I am well -

But Lt. Stern has some chocolates – so I ate them -

I am well -

Received pictures of Haymer yesterday and enjoyed them – still do. I send my love

Henry

April 25

Dear mama -

Here, for further variety, begins variety of ink – this being Indiana ink, the only black ink I could find – made in Hamburg, so I suppose it is antique.

Today was supposed to be my day off, but there being a court martial case, I had to be there all morning. So I took the afternoon off – and walked in familiar territory – in town. I stopped in to see my wood carver. He will have finished my box tomorrow evening, and I think it is going to be quite interesting – although the designing could be better. I hope that when it is through, it is well finished – he complained that shellac is not available – and I told him to finish it just natural.

So I am more or less looking around for something to put in it when I send it. I can't find anything. Well, maybe a scarf I bought in Sicily – and decided was not worth sending home – as it isn't. The box is too small to put a tile in – would hold a cup and saucer if I could find one – but I can't. Costume jewelry while pretty available here is so expensive that I won't buy it – well, maybe I can find some kitchen type pottery – which might be interesting there, though not worth packaging alone. Or I could get my vase in, by breaking it up into little pieces, and it would be worth as much so as it is whole.

I wrapped my tile today – and addressed it to Ruth, on the chance she may like it, because, at the last minute, I decided I thought it had a little character. If she doesn't like it, she may give it away, I shall mail it, I have mailed some plates to Haymer – on a compromise; because they were not very nice. I did not wrap them very well – which I suppose is foolish – like putting a decimal point in just slightly the wrong place.

I missed my music lesson – having left a note last night that I should. Then this afternoon, I saw Maestro Nicola Costa on the street – he said he had received my nota– and I said I should see him next Tuesday.

Walked some more – had a shampoo, because I couldn't stand a haircut yet and didn't need a shave and wanted to sit down. Then walked by the harbor, and came back to the room, where I had a cold bath, no one being home to heat the water. I then went out again -

I am still flirting with the idea of having a portrait painted – but think I shall not.

I am well – the weather is much too windy, with dust blowing very heavy and thick down some streets in gusts. There is no news – one sometimes has a tendency to get bored – but I restrain it, because I've learned that everyplace is boring – and I enjoy my days off.

This ink isn't so hot for writing – Now for supper -

Henry

April 26

To Mrs. A. Lowenhaupt
6237 McPherson Ave
Saint Louis, Missouri

Dear mama -

These letters seem to reach you more promptly than others – so I write that I am well – and completely without news. My box is to be done this evening, and I am impatient to see it in it finished form.

Things go on from day to day – I suppose Ben will have finished his school soon – he ought to get home for a little while at some time – although I am satisfied that if one is in the army anyway, it is better to be overseas than at home – you can ignore the war so much better – and have more freedom. But maybe Hawaii is just like the states.

Love -

Henry

April 26

Dear mama -

I wrote last night, and since that time have done nothing except eat dinner, walk a short distance and go to bed. I slept well. Got up this morning at about a quarter to seven, ~~bathed~~ shaved and washed – walked to breakfast and then here, where I am now. So I have nothing of which to write. The weather is lovely – the sea bright – there is no mail – except I have three photographs of Haymer and enjoy looking at them.

I saw my box again last night – and must reserve judgement until it is finished, because it looks much finer now that the top is carved – it gives the top enough weight, which it lacked when it was just a board. I suppose I shall take the box – hoping he does not ask an outrageous price. I am well.

I just received your letter of 24 March – and was awfully glad to hear. I have a suggestion for shabby, old worthless furniture – just burn it – even without getting new. Then ~~when~~ you can start fresh. But I suppose that is intensely radical. I have been noticing furniture here – and all I see is very, very poor – both in shops and in apartments. A lot of jerry-built modern – that is all I see being made, with its only virtue matched grain in veneer. That is not enough. But I surely think I could have very handsome carved chests made – and the like – except for the impossibility of shipping anything too big to go through the mails. I come more and more, as I see other makers, to appreciate the skill and ability of the family D'Alterio as cabinet makers.

Since you say you want more which I am permitted to name – I think I've already named Monreale, near Palermo – and written of the church and the cloisters there – the orange groves of Sicily, and dusty Campo Felice – about watching Troina, one a mountain top, and the church in Gangi when the former priests were strung up around the walls, by wires through their necks, preserved in wax. How that delighted the children – but the current priest had a worried look. Then Bizerta – of which little or nothing remained – and Carthage, Caltanisetta had the palace where we stayed a few days.

But I may not mention towns in Italy. I ~~won~~ am permitted to say that I saw the eruption of Vesuvius – but I didn't when it was on the rampage. So where censorship does not restrict me, honesty does – and between the towns, I am in a dilemma. When I get the rare privilege of naming the mountains, I can't use it! My place names have to stop at Messina – which I remember for its rows of modern walls of buildings in jagged ruins – with fragmentary mottos – parts of "Combattere, obbedire credire[161]" and "Vincereino[162]" and "Tireino diritto[163]" and the like.

Now it is beginning to rain.

Write often – I send my love -

Henry.

27 April

Dear mama -

Last night I got my box – the wood carver did not want to part with it, and I stood and watched him carving for about an hour before I could get to the subject. When I did get there, he finally came around – and refused to name a price. "Whatever I wanted." So I decided to overpay him rather than risk underpaying him. And I did.

The box is a masterpiece. It is far superior to the other one, and so delightful that I cannot resolve to do anything with it but send it home for myself or you or Marian or Ruth – maybe as a kind of taking Aurus proposition[164]. The finish – fine. The wood, beautiful – The design – well it had the intricacy of a fountain – and the weight and texture of the finest Italian Renaissance refectory table. In other words, it is a <u>piece</u>, which could be stood on the floor in a room, with nothing else table, and it would make the room beautifully furnished. Walnut – no hardware – vaulted top – shape – the ~~so~~ corners convex – so it is like this: *[drawing of carved box]* The feet very intricately carved – the top plain, except for the border, which fits it into the box itself. It is the most genuine delight! So I got myself a wooden box to ship it in – and shall send it in a few days. Meanwhile, I shall look at it on all occasions. It is an object worthy of note.

The tile I said I was sending to Ruth – I shall put it in the same box – and it can be disposed of as desired. When you receive the box, write me if you think it is as fine as I do. I can get another, but the wood carver says the work is too close – it will take him a month to six weeks to make another.

When I returned to the apartment, there were a lot of visitors – so I talked to them for about half an hour – with a glass of wine – but one of them spoke bad English and bored me, so I went for a walk in a slight rain. It was very pleasant – the rain so gentle and warm that you really would not know it was raining. Then back to the apartment and to bed early, where I slept well. They have given me ~~a~~ different bed springs, because the other squeaked. These are silent, therefore preferable.

Then this morning – they gave me an orange – which I enjoyed. These people are very studious for my comfort and pleasure.

---

[161] "Combattere, obbedire, credere" translating to "Fight, obey, believe"
[162] "Vinceremo" translating to "we will win"
[163] "Tireremo Diritto" translating to "we will keep a straight course"
[164] Uncertain of what he means

I am well – despite the pleasure of sealing letters, I shall leave this one open until I see if I receive any mail this morning. Maybe I shall, but all mail is coming through irregularly and slowly at the moment.

I send my love -

Henry

On further thought – I shall seal this letter and write again if I receive mail -

H

April 28

Dear mama -

Since mail has not been coming through to this place (one gets accustomed to the good service and forgets the hazards through which mail goes – perils of the sea and so forth) I feel that I have nothing about which to write.

Last night I took a walk with a Captain Le Blanc – an awfully stupid man – and ended up at a movie, where I left him on the excuse that my eyes were tired. So there is nothing about which to write there. I came back to the room and packed my box for mailing - I shall mail it this afternoon, or sometime in the future. It contains – a tile, which is more or less pretty. Such are available easily and in abundance – and don't amount to much. A box – about which no further comment, from this quarter. Inside the box, a small scarf on which I got stung in Sicily – the first time I went to Palermo, when I desired to buy anything I could lay hands on. My judgement was bad, but I paid very little for it – about 25¢, and have carried it around unable to make up my mind to throw it away or send it. So now I use it as filler for the box – there is not even enough material in it to make a handkerchief. So it can be thrown away there – or anything else.

I ate a big breakfast this morning. The more I eat, the more I desire to eat – and walked to this place. I wore my raincoat, because it looked like rain – so the sun came out. It absolutely never rains when I have a raincoat with me.

Last night the Turettis gave us a big plate of olives. I stayed awake far into the night (10:30) eating olives in bed – quite a delight. Then an orange this morning. Oranges are just about out of season and there are no longer many on the market. Cherries are almost in. Then apricots and green almonds – what pleasures are in store!

Love -

Henry

Write often -

April 28

Dear mama -

I just received three letters – March 26 and 27 and April 20. How do you like that for variety in time? No reason – but am delighted to hear. It is the first I have heard that you received a blue tablecloth. I hope Ruth received the napkins and you have consolidated one way or another. I have written once today but write again in view of your letters.

In one letter, you mention your preference for portraits over photographs – and I think I shall try again to find a painter to paint a portrait of me – conceited as that may sound. For I see many paintings for sale here, which I like – except when I consider how uninteresting the subjects are – street scene, landscapes and still lifes – and then they are just not worthwhile. They are for sale very cheap – $5.00 and up – and it therefore seems to be desirable to try to overcome their one deficiency by furnishing a subject which would be interesting – and there is only one within my capacity to furnish. Is that logic? Add to that, that it might be fun to sit for an hour or so and see what developed. My first try was a failure for two reasons – first, Signora Casina Siciliani said she was too busy, and second, I was not very enthusiastic about her peak painting, with much too big blocks of solid color without detail of texture. But that is just one attempt, and I can, if I try, find others.

No news. It is lunch time – I am skipping lunch but desire to go to the apartment and get my box for mailing. I wrote of the contents this morning. Now, during the usual lunch period, I have fetched the box, and upon opening of the APO shall mail it.

Tell daddy – if Mr. Dave Wohl[165] writes a letter of inquiry to The Adjutant General, Washington, he <u>may</u> get some additional information. There is a department, as I understand it, set up to answer such inquires, and give all available information. Many people write all the way to the unit overseas – and the answer and inquiry go all the way back to Washington for dispatch – takes so long it is hardly worthwhile. It is a Red Cross function to ascertain who are prisoners of war, and the time it takes for information to reach its destination varies between such great limits that you just can't say any time. One month seems unusually prompt. Six months I think is not unusual. Writing all the way to the unit rarely yields more information than is available in Washington. Usually there is no material information, no definitive information which is not sent promptly. There may be information that a certain number of parachutes were seen to open, or the like, which means something, but not conclusive of anything.

I suppose my advice on whether <u>or not</u> to set a hen on eggs from the ice box would be supererogatory. Why not try, though, setting her on deviled eggs, of which I'm very fond, and see if you can't hatch chickens à la King or chicken mincemeat or something.

I hesitate to make a request for cookies from Mrs. Schlesinger[166]– I think I shan't – we eat them so fast that I hate to think of their being individually and carefully baked. Besides, with summer heat, they might well be spoiled. The thing to do is to send materials only – as cocoa, sugar and the like – but that isn't worthwhile.

I send my love -

Henry -

---

[165] A St. Louis businessman and philanthropist.
[166] A friend of Henry's mother.

P.S. I don't overeat – no opportunity except on rare occasions, when it is worth being groggy for the pleasure of overeating. Much less drink too much, for the liquor is generally pretty bad.

April 29

Dear Marian -

I've written to mama today – and suppose you will read the letter. But for variety, and because I enjoy writing to and hearing from you, I address this letter to you. The weather here has turned lovely – it is balmy, between summer and spring, and I am inclined to believe that I am the same. But let that pass.

I have a surplus of envelopes – so I am writing on scratch paper to use them up. Paper is sold here – at least good paper – in "buste" – which hold an equal number of sheets of paper and envelopes. Now and then I write a two-page letter – and so envelopes are left over.

I sent a carved box – addressed to mama – yesterday. Please write a comment on it – for I considered it a masterpiece and hated to part with it, but could not keep it here conveniently.

I received from mama some clothes – socks, tie and hat – and shall use them. Unfortunately, the hat lacked essential insignia – which I haven't been able to get here yet – tried to have it embroidered on – but there is no thread of the right color. So I shall look for someone who has an extra one – and if I fail write for one. It seems to me that I can buy here everything except what I want – with the result that I accumulate terrible quantities of junk. I shall have to go through things – as baggage – and throw away wholesale a year's accumulation.

It seems to me that I write all the requests for things there – and enjoy getting the things sent. But it would be nice if you would write and ask for something you think I might be able to get here – this can be in the nature of costume jewelry, wood carving (any item – can be made to order) embroidery or fancy serving can be done if materials are furnished, I think. Some pottery, ask for something, and it will at least give me a quest to see if I can find it.

Meanwhile, I am spending much time wandering the streets of the city – especially the old city, and enjoying it, for it is always interesting and the streets always crowded. The harbor is beautiful – filled with small fishing boats, and lined with men repairing nets, I imagine as it was in ancient times, for Horace refers to the place in one of his satires as "fishy."

I am well – write often

Henry

April 30

Dear mama -

I am still enjoying my fine haul of three letters yesterday, which, of course, makes me hope for three more today. But they won't come -

I have renewed my subscription to symphony for the month of May – first concert tonight – for I enjoy the concerts.

Of recent evenings, I have been somewhat bored – so I am looking around for new amusements – whatever I can find. Visiting the exhibition of paintings for sale, where I may still be taken as a sucker. I am reading a life of St. Nicholas, about half hour an evening, in Italian, and getting some sense out of it. This I use my new bed-light. I still enjoy walking through the town – a pastime I shall not tire of, for the old city is very, very beautiful – with its arches, and crowded, complicated paths and streets and churches. I may buy some watercolors of it, which I have seen, although they are only mediocre, they are pictorial, and the subject is interesting – my lion and pillar and other "views."

The weather had turned very lovely. I am inclined to the opinion that substantial Italians are unfriendly to Americans – that they are still fascists at heart, and those who are here are the ones who were unable to escape to the north. They consider that the Americans are just the dupes of the English (a sentiment in which I believe the English concur) but I do not mind their sentiments. Those who are friendly are so because that's the side their bread is buttered on. But I usually am inclined to believe that if I had been an Italian I should have been fascist too, and that the only mistake they made was one of judgement in getting into the war – and maybe they had no choice.

I

Just received a package – containing – candy, of which I now eat a nougat – and enjoy it beyond expression. A cap – which I am glad to have – since the peaked kind keeps sun out of my eyes, so I can look at the sea in the morning – and tie and socks. The cap lacks the insignia without which I may not wear it – and I shall scout around to see if I can find it. If I can't I shall write for it – Vmail.

I am well – and quite without news – I am flirting with the idea of having a portrait painted again – but probably shall not.

I send my love -

Henry

April 30

Dear mama -

I have already written to Haymer enough about my concert last night – and Signora ~~Elepha~~ Elefante – and completing my hat, as I have now done. Nothing to add on that score -

The day is wild and windy, with lots of surf and spray and sea gulls flying in over the land. There is no news.

I walked to the finance office this noon, to be paid, and when I got there (2 minutes after 12) found that it was closed from 12 to one. So I walked for an hour – stopping to get a hair cut – the barber shops seem to flourish on Sundays, and stopping at a pastry shop called Stoppani[167]. There, as I looked at the meagre display, they beckoned me to a back room – where I bought one "etto" (100 grs.) of little pastries – like

---

[167] There was a historic cafe named Stoppani's in Bari, Italy.
Cafe in Bari Via Aiello
https://www.caffeaiello.it/en/blog-en/world/cafes-in-bari-the-historical-cafes/
Blog Post Via Elizabeth Minchilli
https://www.elizabethminchilli.com/2012/04/pastries-coffee-at-stoppani-bari/

petit fours – little cream puffs, with caramel and chocolate, and other icings, thick, and jelly tarts and cookies and all things in variety. They had two trays of them. I ate my "etto" – about 1/5 of a pound – and decided that it was a shame to ~~eat~~ let the rest go. So I bought a half kilo – about a pound – to take out, and brought them back here with me. I said it was my birthday[168] I was celebrating as I always do when there is anything with which to celebrate. My little pastries were a very great celebration - I only wish I had got two or three kilos.

The concert was very enjoyable last night. I liked the simple style of playing – without being intellectual about it. Brahms – they played him so well, you wouldn't know it was Brahms if the programs did not say so.

I am well. I hate to have so little of which to write. Have you ever received a linen towel I sent you?

It seems that mail is not delivered here on Sunday either – so I expect none today, But I still hope so, although I got three yesterday – one of which was only a week old.

Love,

Henry

---

[168] His birthday was April 3

May 1

Dear mama -

It frightens me again to write a new month – but I've just about lost track of time – and see no reason why I should try to remember it – May, June or July or December make little difference.

Last night I took a walk again – which I find pleasant because I don't think of anything while I'm walking – out past the railroad station, the Palace of Justice, the parks with fountains,

Since it was Sunday night, everyone was all dressed up, returning from his Sunday afternoon stroll. The strolling was scattered because the usual promenade, along the sea, had spray flying over it from the surf in very numerous places. The children were tired and cross and most of them were crying about something – many of them being carried – others just crying to be. It does not get dark until close to nine o'clock.

I am well. Tomorrow is my day off. I surely hope I can take it, for I missed it last week. I am holding my thumbs today, that no one tells me of something I have to do tomorrow. My present plans do not go beyond a music lesson – but I am still (or again) playing with the idea of having a portrait painted – although it is bound to be rotten; it may be more interesting than a photograph. This time with a man named Roberto de Robertis[169]. He had enough Roberts in his name!

This letter looks longer than it is, being written so big.

Love -

Henry

May 1

Dear mama -

I am delighted today to have received three letters from you and one from Betty. Betty tells me that Haymer performed a great work, having written her a letter, a sheet of paper with the letters KMI. I can't fancy what they might mean. I am collecting his incidents in my memory – his desire for a goat; his loathing to sleep in a crib; his writing letters. He ought to be talking soon – he certainly has plenty to say.

I suppose my letters are very confusing, arriving as they do without order. I suppose some of them may not reach you – and therefore have less hesitancy about repeating. If only I had more to repeat!

I sent you a box not long ago, containing three items – one worthless craft, which I have carried around since Sicily, unable to make up my mind to do anything with it, and not having definite incentive to throw it away. One tile, rather pretty, and one carved walnut box, which I am inclined to consider less sophisticated than the first, but more beautiful – a masterpiece of the local woodcarver. I am inclined to wonder if possibly Betty would enjoy having it – as something very beautiful to have around – to keep handkerchiefs or cosmetics (guffaw!) or any other little things in? But the retention or disposal is yours -

---

[169] Roberto De Robertis Via Wikipedia
https://it.wikipedia.org/wiki/Roberto_De_Robertis

Sooner or later, I shall buy a painting - I look at them often – and say how silly it would be to buy one – and eventually for just one minute shall be of another notion. That's all it takes.

What a flock of chickens[170] you have! Sixty! As baby chickens, maybe they won't take up much room – but when they grow up, they will pack your chicken yard tight. If they are all hens – you will have more eggs than you can use; and if they're all roosters, most of them will be old and tough before you can get around to eating them. Ruth is an extremist. But I suppose some of them have died already.

I have no news. The town continues interesting and extremely cosmopolitan with people from all over the world on the streets. A pleasure to walk anyplace. Post Exchange rations today – one Hershey bar – some Walnettos; a Clark bar. One cake of soap; cigarettes and a can of orange and grapefruit juice. The last makes me furious! To use canned juice where fresh fruits are abundant! But – maybe in Alaska or someplace else a can of orange juice is a great delicacy. Of course I took it – shall save it until oranges are completely out of season – but even then – apricots, peaches cherries and the like are better.

In one of your letters were the calling cards. It surprises my understanding how some things arrive so quickly!

I have received the hat.

Love -

Henry

May 4

Dear mama -

Today having been, so far, a day full of interruptions, I do not feel much like writing. But I shall anyway.

I had my day off yesterday – and spent it – my music lesson with Mozart and Chopin. I may abandon music lessons just on the principle that without practice it isn't worthwhile – as I suppose it isn't. But I enjoy them – And walking my feet off – and having tea with a man named Robertis, who is an artist and soliciting business – and pleasant enough company except that my Italian is still very poor. Since Ida has borrowed my Italian book, I can't read it – but I shall get it back.

May 8 is St. Nicholas day[171] – and I am told there is usually a big celebration – a fiesta – and all the trimmings. I look forward to seeing some of it.

Then I found a woman who desires to serve dinners to parties of ten or more. It sounds to me like a good idea. She says she has to have at least a week's notice – so she can dress the meat. May try it – although I have no definite plans.

I am well. As I say – I am still playing with the idea of having a sketch of myself made in some form – see if it means more than a photograph – and shall not mention it to you again.

---

[170] Henry's parents raised chickens in their yard in the suburb of Parkview for a while.
[171] The Festa di San Nicola is held on May 7-9 and is of particular importance in Bari, as St. Nicholas is the city's patron saint. Via Wikipedia
https://en.wikipedia.org/wiki/Saint_Nicholas_Day#Italy

The weather is magnificent – turning quite warm – there is no news.

I am receiving mail nicely now – yesterday a letter. Today a letter from Janet Cerf. She writes very uninterestingly. Also this Julian Miller publication "Upon Friends" which clutters up the mails.

I had a letter from Betty too, and have written her.

I send my love – shall write more, when I feel at ease -

Henry

May 4

Dear mama -

I just received a very interesting letter from you – and have read it several times. You mention Mr. Gusdorf's French cabinet, and it sounds interesting. I shall write him a letter – but unfortunately his replies are so completely illegible – his hand as well as his language. Sometimes he types, however.

I looked yesterday for Barney's[172] complete address – APO 520 covers a vast territory – and "a bombardment unit" covers almost all units. I shall wait a week or ten days, and then see if possibly the postal delivery system has his name. Meanwhile, I've written to Edith, asking for his address. He may be either near or far.

I received yesterday two pounds of tea and two pounds of coffee from daddy, and intend to put them to good use. One pound I intend for my music teacher, who, although he is a somewhat futile little man, is very pleasant and nice. So I hope next Tuesday to give him a package of tea – and see how he receives it. He wants to be friendly, I think.

Then I shall keep the coffee for the most urgent occasions. Maybe to drink for myself – or if the Turettis give us more dinners, to provide part. Lt. Clark says I spoil people. I think I do.

Well – my conscience hurts me - I shall confess, and you may laugh. My folly is in large part the result of casting about for interests, and finding officers' clubs and movies without merit. I said in my last letter I would not confess. But the damage is not material.

I found a painter whose work I liked well – and am now in process – and committed up to my ears – of getting a sketch made, a little better than the 10 minutes caricatures. It will be a white elephant – and I shall send it to you for your amusement – if you will not take it as a serious blunder or more than a little folly – not the greatest I've ever been guilty of. I see your point – it will be better and more interesting than a photograph. Also more expensive – but the expense makes no difference because my pockets are full of money, and I don't know what to do with it. If I refrain from drinking for a month, I shall pay the cost – which will be about 10 times as much as a photo – I shall write you what I pay – I can still back out, but know that I shan't.

So look forward with fear to a white elephant tramping up your front steps! When I wrote of lack of interesting subjects in paintings I omitted consideration of lack of paintable subjects.

---

[172] Bernard and Edith Barenholtz were friends from St. Louis.

There are faint prospects of five day vacations – and if any opportunity materializes, I shall have to make up my mind where to go. Cairo, I am told, is out of the question. Also, I have no particular desire to go to Cairo – which always sounds to me like another swank edition of Toronto or Montreal. Algiers? A beautiful city! and I should be welcomed to visit Mme. Peyrus or Col. Alibert, who would put me up. But it is a military establishment, and I should enjoy more someplace where I could more easily ignore such things. They exist in Italy – one such place I have visited. Would not go back to the same place, but would look for another. I could even arrange, I think, to visit with the Uncle of Porzia on a farm for a few days. That would seem strange to them – to choose a local farm in preference to the capitals of the world – as Algiers, Tunis, Cairo, and the like!

I am well.

I send my love -

Henry

May 5

I received two letters today – one in part about Ben – who, I think is alright, and will very likely receive some assignment which is agreeable. But by this time, I suppose he is assigned – and you know about it.

I don't know why I started writing this letter – I have nothing of which to write. But having started it, I shall ramble on for a while.

May 8 is a holiday – a religious celebration with parades and carrying the statue of Saint N. through the streets and so forth. I hope to see some of it.

I keep being urged by my desires to tell you where I am – but shall not because it would be silly. Further, I suppose – and this supposition I indulge to suppress desire – that you already know. So why mention it?

I am well. Feeling a little dull – which is not unusual.

Do not worry about my drinking too much – that is one thing of which there is no danger. I drink wine now and then. Not much else is available. The wine is weak and not very good. I would overeat if I could.

The weather is lovely still. I suppose we shall change to summer uniforms soon, and I shall better get mine out. They are all rolled up – and dirty from being carried around all winter. I shall send them to the laundry.

Love -

Henry

P.S. Have a letter from Bill Charles in which he said he received a letter of mine with part cut out. If you receive any so cut, I wish you would write me the words around the cut – so I can tell what is deemed objectionable – and what I have ~~failed~~ tried to say, but have not been permitted.

H

May 5

Dear mama -

The subject which I said I would not mention again fills my mind – and I laugh at myself, for it is ridiculous – but that makes it hard to write.

I was occupied all day today – just barely had time to read the letters I received, and not to enjoy them fully, so I put them away and shall reread them tomorrow. Mail is coming in strange orders. The letter saying you were sending a hat reached me after the hat. And Haymer is blowing bubbles! I can appreciate what an accomplishment that is, because I can remember trying to teach Marian, I think it was, to do it, and was utterly unable to appreciate why she wouldn't do a thing so simple. She talked before she could blow, I remember.

Last night I had tea with a crowd of Italians – and enjoyed it – they talked about music and the like, and I was quite amazed at the extent to which I could follow their conversation. I ought, it is fine, be able to do much better – but really have very little occasion or opportunity to speak with natives, all day, one speaks English, and in the evening at dinner and so forth, English almost exclusively. The waitresses don't count – to say "please" and "seconds on meat" doesn't count as talking Italian.

But I can – thanks much to Mrs. Meyer's book – make myself understood. Amazing lacks in vocabulary which stump me – but generalizations are not hard.

I am well. There is no news. Did you ever receive a linen towel I sent you – must have sent it about the middle of February.

Beautiful weather – here on the coast the breeze is steady and fine and cool. The days long. I have canvassed the malaria situation, and am most reliably informed that there is none here. Mosquitoes do not come this high – and indeed I have felt none. Singularly free of flies, too, considering that there are no screens.

For the past few days, there has been shortage of water – I suppose just ~~was~~ not enough pressure to get this high. So in the morning when it runs, we fill the bath tub, which furnishes water for evening washing.

Strange how quickly I get used to certain things – I was just thinking of the barrage balloons over the harbor, and it twisted my imagination to think that there were some harbors without them. They are beautiful – like silver dirigibles – and I think of them as part of a harbor as much as ships or buoys or docks or anything else.

I now wait for Bill – if he comes in before six, I shall eat with him. Otherwise I shall not.

I send my love

Henry

May 7

Dear mama -

This is a quick note to keep mail coming – for I did not write yesterday – and shall be sitting around a court martial all day today. So I let you know I am well – and if I have time to write further, I shall.

Heard an excellent concert last night – Mozart's Eine Kleine Nachtmusik – Chopin Concerto and Rimsky-Korsakov's Scheherazade. I particularly enjoy Mozart as a kind of specialist in violins, and Chopin as specialist in piano.

Now news – Lt. Little is considering renting a sailboat with me – which would be fun and he says he knows of one. I doubt that it will materialize.

Also under discussion is moving into an apartment. Bill is mad at the Turetti's because they beg for his PPX rations – I think they are just teasing him for and that it makes no difference. Of course, I abuse him – when they ask for it, I say it is Bill's. This he doesn't know.

I send my love -

Henry

May 8

Dear mama -

I was busy yesterday – and more or less enjoyed it – but it lasted too late – until about 10 o'clock – and the result is that I am somewhat tired today. I shall enjoy my day off tomorrow, during which I shall wander around town – maybe to the country. Music lesson at noon. That is if all goes well. If it goes otherwise, I shall be disappointed.

Weather now very beautiful.

When I got back to the apartment last night, the family had saved bites of their dinner delicacies for me. A fried fresh sardine and artichoke fritters [Also, some fresh, raw peas, which tasted very good. They seem almost always to eat peas raw – and do not consider cooking them. I think that is because long boiling is difficult – and fuel consuming – pasta would be an exception.

I received yesterday a letter from Stix Friedman and one from Philip. I shall answer them.

I reviewed my summer clothes situation, and find I am adequately prepared.

Ha ha! A man is proposing that we rent a 17 room villa about 5 miles out – with swimming pool and formal gardens and the like. I do not think the comfort would be worth the trouble – although the swimming pool would be nice – one would be there so little. But it is fun to think of it – and go out to see the villa and so forth. The same is true of a sailboat. I have no doubt that as soon as I acquired any such things, I should be transferred elsewhere. I was just about to acquire a sailboat when I left Algiers. Maybe just about – I had found one.

It is easy to take to luxuries – as a duck to water! All the world is crazy – and the very thought of these things is ridiculous. One says: "it is silly not to be as comfortable as possible." That is logically true, but morally false.

Now I have two letters from you – April 30 and May 1, which is really excellent service! And good to get such fine letters – they make me happier than 17 room villas with swimming pools.

You speak of rumors concerning Ben's assignment. They are false. I do not know exactly what one learns in an electronics school – but it does not qualify one for duty on a pursuit plane, which usually carried only a pilot anyway. So if Ben writes and believes that, he is being "kidded." My impression has always been that detection of planes involves electronics – and so I assumed that Ben's assignment would involve anti-aircraft – he would be stationed near something which it was desired to protect from hostile aircraft – which means anything from a field or bridge or road to a city.

That Haymer is a nice boy, with gentle disposition and kind, is to be expected – he learns it from his mother, and no one could be around Ruth very much without learning gentleness of disposition and kindness and bigness of character. (You may tell her I said so)

Henry

May 9

Dear mama -

I've had a good time today – and am now tired. So I sit down and write for a few minutes before going to bed.

I got up at the usual time, and, as is my Tuesday custom, went to breakfast without shaving. After breakfast, a shoeshine and the barber shop – and then walked a while. At a little after noon, I found myself in a great crowd – and that the parade for St. Nicholas was forming. So I followed it for a while – a parade of embroidered banners, of each church in town, and then to statue of St. Nicholas, with the pedestal covered with flowers, was carried by about eight men, a white canopy was carried alongside him – and baskets of flowers on long poles. The statue was dressed in magnificently embroidered cloth of gold. All along the street, people had hung from their windows their best laces and linens, and colored table clothes and bedspreads. It was really both beautiful and interesting. I understand there is usually much more – This morning there were two bands, playing sweet, soft music. The day celebrates the bringing of the bones of St. Nicholas hither.

After I had had enough parade, I went out to the university, and out of curiosity spoke to a boy standing at the door with books in his arm. In view of my bad Italian, he proposed to speak German. But it is completely impossible to speak two languages at once – so I stuck to Italian. I asked him if the school had a library – and he said they had two excellent ones – what book did I want? I could see it there. I had to think hard to think of a book – and asked for a book on the common law of England. So we went in and looked for it. Lots of books on Roman law and German law – and finally, in the Faculty of Arts and Sciences we found a book on the English criminal law – by a man named Havers – ~~copied~~ translated into Italian. So I said that was exactly what I wanted – and sat down at a table with it, diligently copying the title and thanking them. I am told that I am welcome to use the university library – which is a good library, although, of course, most of the books are in Italian.

Tell daddy – just wait for the next court martial case I have to try – I am really going to have fun, citing books existent and nonexistent in the Biblioteca Consorziale Sagarriga Visconti Volpi de[173] ---. I'll cite them by bookcase, shelf, and number! But they'll be obscure ones!

Then I walked to my music lesson – stopping on the way at Mme Stoppani's pastry shop, where I struck it lucky – and had a hundred grams of cream puffs.

And my music lesson – where my preceding pupil has learned one phrase of English – "good night" – and when she said it at high noon, I failed to understand it. That was a fault – but when I did understand it, she and her mother laughed. The fault was not with the English – it was with the time of day.

I enjoyed my music lesson – with Chopin nocturnes and Beethoven. Maestro Costa is himself a magnificent pianist. He says, in fear of bombardment he brought most of his library to the country – left the piano because it was too heavy, And in the country, he had only a small upright piano. So his music and his piano are separated.

Then this afternoon I walked some more, along the harbor – and stopped and saw Bill. He had been out to the 17 room villa – says it is magnificent – with fine hedges, a beautiful building. But there is no running water and not a stick of furniture in it. So there is an additional reason for not moving into it – I like my soft bed – and see no reason to have the inconvenience of travel every morning in order to sleep on a cot.

In the meantime I had eaten lunch. I walked back, then, through the old town and via the railroad station – arriving here at about five, I lay down – read a little more of the Life of St. Nicholas – a discussion whether or not he attended the Council of Nicaea – and fell asleep. It was six-thirty before I awoke, so I rushed to dinner, to get there before seven. Ate – and walked back slowly. That brings me to the immediate present.

I enclose a post-card I got at the parade this morning. Children and women were getting rapturous over this card – kissing it and weeping. I think St. Nicholas is as a saint particularly interested in purity – hence children – and seafarers, and in fires, for when he was being consecrated bishop, a house burned down. The lady of the house was at the ceremony, and her children burned. St. Nicholas brought them back to life. So, I suppose, by transfer, he becomes an important personage when people fear air raids and consequent fires – as they do here, having read of them.

I am well – and send my love -

Henry

---

[173] Biblioteca Consorziale Sagarriga Visconti Volpi di Bari or the National Library Sagarriga Visconti Volpi in Bari.
Via Internet Culturale, in Italian
https://www.internetculturale.it/it/64/partner/27795/biblioteca-nazionale-sagarriga-visconti-volpi-bari
Via GoogleMaps
https://www.google.com/maps/uv?pb=!1s0x1347e85e62156eef%3A0x7e11ccca0d31d957!3m1!7e115!4shttps%3A%2F%2Flh5.g
oogleusercontent.com%2Fp%2FAF1QipOuEq7Vdm6Sh1YjJlkGasAsLmgFX8HJEEPabRZ5%3Dw266-h200-k-
no!5sBiblioteca%20Consorziale%20Sagarriga%20Visconti%20Volpi

May 10

Dear mama -

I have already written everything I have up to the time I went to sleep last night – since that, a little of which to write -

I just received a box of soap from you and am now supplied for a while at least. Thank you very much.

The weather is lovely – and I stood in the sun for about an hour today while the General was presented a medal.

Vanity, vanity, sayeth the Preacher, son of David King in Jerusalem.

The sun is lovely.

Then I had the rare treat today of having Tom Smith Jr. – who is in Italy and was spending a few hours in this city – come in to see me. It was a pleasure, for he is agreeable, and I urged him to come over here when he can stay a day or two – and let me know in advance, he stayed only a few minutes – having flown over, and having to fly back tonight. I believe that daddy knows him. So we had coffee and cookies.

I am well. I think I told you yesterday of the library I found which is available to me. So maybe I shall go on with reading a little Roman law – in which this library ought to be good – and I find I can read Italian without too much difficulty. (Shaw! I dipped my pen into the wrong bottle!)

This is my new ink.

I am well. The weather is magnificent – and I intend to take a walk this evening. No news. I am enjoying smelling the soap.

Oh yes! I gave my music teacher a half pound of tea yesterday, just for fun, and he says he will enjoy it.

M

Love

Henry

May 10

Dear daddy -

A note, because for a long time I have not written directly to you – and I have no idea how my letters arrive.

There is no news. I have found an interesting library here – part of the university, and intend to read in it now and then – a law library, including mostly Roman law and codes, but quite interesting – and a good general library. So you see what a civilized place I am in.

Tom Smith, Jr., came in to see me today – and I had a very, very pleasant visit. I do not know him well – he is stationed far from here.

I am well -

I see WG Staley almost daily – Hear from Ben Charles now and then – so you see this is a St. Louis center.

I received the tea and coffee you sent – and have given ½ pound to my music teacher – who will have me to his house to drink it, he says. But I've already written you thanking you for that. I am hoarding the balance for a propitious occasion -

Affectionately -

Henry

May 11

Dear mama -

Last night, I ate dinner with Bill at the fine Service Command Mess – we are both fortunate in being able to get variety by eating at each other's messes.

Then, Bill having a jeep available, we drove to a town about ten miles down the coast. Lovely! Big, red poppy fields – wheat standing high, fruit forming on the trees. The sea, close by, with a shelving, rocky, low shore, and in the distance the sun setting behind a low line of hills. Quite a few little villages and houses.

The new town – new towns are always interesting to me. This one – narrow streets out of a square with a big statue in it, and an old town, crowded with children just getting out of school. The town extends on a narrow spit of rock or a mole, out into the sea – and on either side the fishing boats are anchored. It is really very beautiful.

We got back before dark – and went first to the 15th Air Force Officer's Club – which was dismal and empty. Then to the Allied Officers Club, which was fun, because it was crowded with utterly uninhibited Englishmen – singing as loud as they could and standing on the tables to conduct each other, and merchant marines, who are the lowest of God's creatures, crawling around on the floor and dancing Irish jigs. What a racket!

Thence to the apartment, where I read a little more of St. Nicholas and went to bed.

I believe I wrote you yesterday that Tom Smith, Jr., came in here – brought a message from Ben Charles that he may come over here soon – so I sent a message back that if he did, I should like to see him, and make arrangements for his staying here. Maybe I can.

I am well. The weather continues very beautiful. This evening I am going with Lt. Little up the coast, and see what kinds of boats there are. Isn't that nonsense?

All my love

Henry.

(P.S. My pajama supply is dwindling. Could you send me about three pairs? This is no emergency – I can sleep in underwear.

H

May 12

Dear mama -

I send a masterpiece of sycomancy. (? hypocrisy) If you concur, will you dispatch it?

Received letters this morning. About apostle's fingers – and remember how good they were. Can you make them roll up nicely? So, they make a very pretty dish – one which I think Haymer would enjoy as well as daddy. Mrs. Turetti's are cooked in olive oil, but I think butter might be better.

I am well. Yesterday I went to a town north of here – and looked at boats, called on the Port Commander, and generally had fun. The nice boat – no one knows the owner. Which may be fortunate. Some say it belongs to a Yugoslavian colonel – others to an Italian lawyer and so forth.

Now I must go.

Love

Henry

May 13

Dear mama -

No news. I intend to mail you a white elephant today. I am well. The weather is beautiful.

Last night I walked through the old town, and along the water front. After I have not been there for a few days, I forget how very beautiful it is. Visited the wood carver – who is busy carving plaques and boxes. When you receive his box, let me know what you think of it as a sample of craftsmanship. I considered it fine. So fine that I am tempted to get another. But when one begins to repeat, one is stale. So I must watch for something else. Embroidery here is out of the question, for all embroiders are engaged in making insignia, which brings very fancy prices. So the simple art is lost, at least for the present.

I have already said that I am well and have no news. I told Signora Turetti last night that you had made apostle's fingers and enjoyed them – and she was enthusiastic and delighted taking personal pride. I think she fancies that from now on you will spend all your time making them for Haymer and daddy.

After I finished my walk I passed the Iruramar*[?]* Hotel – and saw an officer I knew in Tunis. He asked me where the Allied Officer's Club was – and I said I'd show them, so I showed 'em all, and went in with them. No sooner in, than a ship's engineer and steward (very fat – little tiny arms and legs and feet) began talking – and urged us to come to his ship and have coca colas and steak. I think I shall do it. Food is traditionally very good on the ships – especially the stewards' food, and it might be worth trying, although one likes to think of eating and dinner invitations as more idealistic with more intangible pleasure than mere eating. Still, there is pleasure in eating.

You will note a slight change in return address -

Love -

Henry

May 13

Dear mama -

I have been receiving mail very beautiful – and am so satisfied that I can hardly write. But there is nothing new of which to write – but of the future – I intend to go to a concert tonight – six o'clock – and after the concert, to a club where there will be dancing. What a life! But I've really quite given up – I'll go along and see what happens.

I dispatched a box to you today, containing something very funny – I sent it contrary to my better judgment – you can burn it as well as I can, and I am told that the ships going west are not particularly burdened. So – well -

I enjoy your letters. Last night I wandered through the old town – and old cathedral – very, very lovely, dating back to 1035, and a church founded in 1087. Dates like that give a sense of security. Hence I write them. An old castle – 1170 or 69 or so – with cobbles in front, where children play dancing and singing games beautifully.

Almonds still abound – and are they delicious! If I could describe them adequately, they would be the world's most famous. Maybe they are anyway.

The Sergeant here is going home (contrary to my recommendation) means that one gets a short furlough and then reassigned. I expressed the opinion to him that if one had a good assignment it was unwise to gamble and jeopardize it for a short furlough. But he wants to go home – as everyone does – and lives in Chicago. I suggested he might go to see Uncle Jesse[174], if he wants to – I write this just to avoid complete surprise.

I am well. The reason I told him he might go see Uncle Jesse is that he was the only one I could think of in Chicago, and I love flattery. The Sergeant gives every indication to me that if he talks about me, he will do so in terms which ought to be reserved for God Almighty. So why not give him opportunity to talk?

The harbor is crowded with fishing boats – row boats – and some bigger, which the English soldiers like to use – crowding about eight men into a small boat, so that it sinks to the gunwales.

---

[174] Jesse Lowenhaupt, Abe's brother and a lawyer in Chicago.

I received a letter from Alma Myer – and answered it. Also one from Sonja. I am afraid I have exaggerated the beauties too much in my letters to her – she asks me to try to select a breakfast set for her. If I could find any nice pottery, I should get it for myself. A whole set? No such thing.

All my love -

Henry

May 14

Dear daddy -

I have a letter from you stating that you have placed me in a partnership with Joe Newman and others to buy surplus government supplies. I write to tell you that I approve, and to commit myself, and ratify.

The business booming here is the court martial business – in which I am somewhat engaged at the present time. I am glad to be on the side of the defense – even though most of the clients are not much good, and need ~~m~~witnesses far more than lawyers.

I think I wrote you I have found a library, with a few very esoteric books on the law of England – and I intend to cite them as well as others not on that subject, which can be done by a little mis-translation.

Well – I have no news. I received the excellent and fine package of tea and coffee – and have not had time to make use of it yet.

I am well. With absolutely nothing of which to write. I was up too late last night – celebrating by dancing – and so am sleepy today.

I was promoted to 1st Lieutenant – that was the nominal reason for celebrating.

Affectionately -

Henry

May 16

Dear mama -

I have been receiving mail so very beautifully that I think I may be getting indolent about writing. But I shall try to write -

Today being my day off, I have done intensive loafing all day – walking through the town, old and new, looking in ship windows, watching children and what not, with my music lesson at noon – which is still the high point of my week. I enjoy it very much, I went into the cathedral - I do not find it as inspiring or as beautiful as I expect – maybe because I do not understand this conservative, solid architecture – and am come to expect vaults and gothic windows. Still, it is unquestionably a solid piece of stone building, with many delicate details of stone carving. The tomb itself – a great piece of silver, with scenes from the life of the saint I cannot understand at all as a thing of beauty.

But I believe it is generally fine that beautiful Italian things are usually much less striking than French or Greek – and I have come to think of fine Italians as much more conservative than the English even, and with feeling very deep – and self-contained. Not at all like Spanish or others, with superficial decoration. I believe it may take quite a little time for the merit of a thing like this cathedral to grow on you. It is enormously quiet and heavy and dignified – very little color – but that there is (some ceiling paintings and a few others) very modern in its contrast and the natural color is everywhere so high, that the old gray-green of the stone is restful. It is so completely far from tawdry and decorated. I think the more often I go there, the more I shall enjoy it.

The same is true of the whole old town   the walls, the old castle – heavy and plain – but they grow very interesting as you watch them, and very dignified – way beyond the dignity of the inhabitants and naked pa babies squawking in the streets. I come to think from this especially that fine Italian people are something superfine – but most you see are poor dirty beggars.

Cherries are ripe – but I postponed getting any, and then they were all sold. They will be more abundant later. there is now the most magnificent profusion of fresh vegetables I've ever seen – peas, beans, artichokes, spinach, cabbage – and all else -

Love

Henry

Not worth starting a new page – I sent you a white elephant yesterday – a picture of myself which you may find more interesting than a photograph – maybe it will not arrive. H.

I find I have a little more I write. I have been working recently a little with a man named Coleman. He is going home on so-called <u>rotation,</u> and expects to spend four or five days in St. Louis, where his wife will meet him. I gave him your and the office telephone number – and told him that if he wanted to talk to someone interesting he should call you or daddy. He may call before this letter arrives – or not at all – I don't know. Since it is prohibited to send messages by other than the usual means, I gave him no message – and after all, what message is there to give? I am well – and so forth.

Now having space left – I can mention further what I squeezed on the preceding page – my picture sent. I consider it a quick sketch – too big and clumsy . Hence the name white elephant. But fun – because I had tea with the painter – and now visit him from time to time. He speaks French somewhat better than I speak Italian – so we get along alright.

I have also sent a <u>second</u> carved box (two altogether) – which I think more interesting than the first. I would get another – except it is a mistake to repeat.

I suppose there may be mail at the office this evening. But if I go there, I will find something to disturb me. So I shan't go.

Henry

May 17

Dear mama -

Mail has been coming through so beautifully that I can hardly write – I so enjoy reading new letters.

With reference to Ben – I do not think there is much to regret in his staying in Hawaii – all places are the same, after a few months – but Ben might talk to his commander about the possibility of getting home for a furlough of a few weeks -

Of course, it is silly for Ben to be wasting his time as he is – but if he is fairly comfortable – so many people are just wasting time. Ben ought to be promoted – maybe will be – though policies differ radically in different places. But I just don't know anything about it. I think Ben is probably fairly well situated. But I am so comfortable helpless even to think about it.

I go on from day to day.

Your letters sound as if you are working too hard, and need a vacation.

I am well – rather tired this evening and being constantly interrupted all day. But I shall maintain my equilibrium. I have a Latin letter from Dr. Duffy which I am trying to answer in kind – just for fun – but compared to his nice Latin style, my sentences come out so short – as they must to avoid the subjunctives I've forgotten.

I shall write again. Now it is almost going home time. I think I shall move into an apartment soon – mostly because Bill wants to. He is intolerant of the foibles of the Turettis – and frets.

So this evening we shall look at another villa.

Love

Henry

(This is poor paper – I must get better -)

May 18

Dear mama -

I received your letter about Kim – and think that Haymer alone is likely to miss the dog. He was very old – and Haymer's memory is short.

Also – I <u>did</u> have a portrait painted for fun – and it can be burned. I enjoyed it – because it gave me an opportunity to sit with some rather interesting people, and sent it home because I wanted to tell them I had. As far as expense or spending is concerned – the silly things as a picture cost nothing – I paid $5.00 for the picture. Photographs are expensive, because of lack of film. Boxes, wood carving and the like are very cheap. So the pleasure of buying now and then is worth the cost – not the commodity. Prices of things in demand are very high – liquor, silk, cloth (here) and food.   But in order that you may get an idea of the little value of the things I send home, I'll tell you some of the prices – The carved box (last one) was $3.50. But the tile with it was $5.00. The plates I sent to Haymer were 80¢. The box I sent first was $10.00. The table linen I sent ran about $8.00 a tablecloth, on the average. Prices go up when people discover soldiers will buy such things.

Compare them: whiskey, for example, sells if at all, at about $35.00 a quart. Poor champagne at $6.00. Wine - $2.00. My stationary is an extravagance. So the fact that I send these things, while I have the sensation of wildness, does not indicate very much. It is just as kind of lark, to try to keep life at home interesting. My extravagances are in waste of things, as clothes, of which I have too many – a raincoat, for which I had to pay $40.00 and the like. and the policy is to buy things only which no one else wants. One doesn't find much – but now and then one is lucky – as with the naive wood carver.

So I sent home a very terrible picture. You may be thankful for a capacious third floor – and if you open the package at all, the contents may be burned. The cost I charge to pleasure -

The same thing is true of music lessons.

The whole thing is very perplexing. One should be working – but when one finds oneself in these thoroughly ridiculous surroundings, one just has to go along and play with ideas. For these circumstances are thoroughly incongruous, and are bound to be so – with children playing a game – one now and then had an urge to try to get into something else, a little more serious. It is a foolish impulse, because it can't be done. So pretense continues and one gets lazier and lazier and more and more hypocritical and cynical.

But I did not intend to sound bitter. All continues sweetness and light – or one pretends it does – and has the most interesting time possible.

A long time ago, I decided that being in a ridiculous situation, I was fortunate in being able to ignore money as long as I had any in my pocket – and that to the extent that trying a new attitude toward spending money could be interesting, I would try it. So I do – and it is, truly, self indulgent. But there is nothing to do, and I like to be able to spend money if I want to. I could send some home – but don't know what I'd do with it after I got it there. So I just go on as best I can, being as little bored as possible – and I suppose foolish by many standards. But most people I see look like such complete fools too.

I send my love. Do not worry about my character – fundamentally it is still alright – but I am still too much of an idealist. That is your fault.

Henry

May 18

Dear mama -

I had fun last night – Lt. Little (who has a sense humor) and Lt. Clark and I went out to look for a villa – with Tom, the interpreter, who said he knew where there were some. We went north, along the coast, looking for villas – and came into a little village, something like Hooverville[175], with villas galore – little 3 room villas, along dusty paths, piled with garbage and refuse – overlooking a rocky shore, covered with kelp and decaying fish. What villas – we went into six or seven of them, all piled high with rubbish, without water or light – and each empty one, the natives said, was owned by wealthy people living in the city.

One woman talked to us a long time – a woman of about 40 years of age, dressed in a single, sleezy cotton dress, and barefoot, but with quite an athletic stride – who had lived for years on the Côte d'Azure of France. She talked well – French, English and Italian. I wonder how she got there – All are anxious to rent their "villas" – I think "hovels" is a better word.

---

[175] Homeless encampments during the Great Depression in the 1930s. Named "Hooverville" after the President Hoover whom many considered responsible for the depression. St. Louis was home to one of the largest Hoovervilles

But I know where there are finer ones – the Villino Davido and others – and we shall go out and look at them tonight. You know, there is no danger whatsoever of my getting a villa. But I think it is funny – I shall call it, if I get it, "Villino Vino." I want one with statuary in the garden – on a high bluff over the sea, with electric lights and running water. There <u>are</u> some with statuary; but there are no bluffs over the sea – it is a low shore – and so I argue with Tom the interpreter much as the lady argued that she wanted a sandy beach north of Le Havre. Poor Tom desires so hard to pleasure – I suppose he will begin looking for a bluff overlooking the sea first.

So I have postponed my quest for a boat, until I find a villa on a bluff over the sea, with stone cupids in the garden and mathematical hedges, and orchards and vineyards

When we got back, we ate dinner – I had a hot bath and went to bed – first reading a little about St. Nicholas and "huius loci moenia pesconi[176]."

I send my love -

Henry

May 19

Dear mama -

I shall have to get some more paper this afternoon, because I am now writing on my last sheet – or next to last. I've about exhausted the variety in stationary and may therefore become conservative.

Last night we went out into the country again – for our humorous quest, looking for villas – and found a perfect one – the Villina Re David – set in about two acres of formal gardens, with fine terraces and porches – looked inside – a big, formal dining room, all glass on one side – and an enormous living room, furnished in oak and plush and heavy drapes – lovely windows. But it was not available. A Fascist had owned it, so, in justice, the AOC (which is British for Air Officer Commanding) took it over, incidentally making himself very, very comfortable. The British surely install themselves tight – and if they once get an inch, never under any circumstances give it up. So they accumulate – I envy them their suavité *[sic]*. And Englishman can get anything for a cup of tea and a kind remark to an American or Canadian – on much the same principle as that on which an American matron would give anything she had for an introduction to the Queen – which is cheap for the Queen. Good business!

How silly my letters are getting! I feel much the same about my activities. I suppose it is necessary to go out and find something interesting and put a definite end to this stupid attempt at entertainment consisting of going to places and listening to American orchestras playing jazz and movies and attempted entertainment with stupid, uninterested people. Or else begin writing V-mail – which might not be a bad idea anyway.

I think maybe this time of year is dull. The weather is too lovely – it makes one lazy.

There is talk now of requiring us all to move back into the Hotel. That would be no hardship, although it would be less interesting than present living. Also Lts. Clark & Little speak of getting an apartment, and if they do, I shall go with them – that would be less interesting too, but I do not want to leave them – appreciating their company. I make friends too slowly and find too many people obnoxious. I was living

---

[176] Translates roughly from Latin to "the walls of this place."

strictly alone for about five months at II Corps – and liked it – now for a while I shall like more communally. But I have about enough -

I am watching for something to volunteer for – just to see what happens – because I think unless I do, I shall stay indefinitely in this Washington atmosphere. But I see no opportunities at present. And probably – almost certainly – shall do nothing. Just Thinking – and playing with ideas – I ought to know when I am well off.

I walked out during lunch time – skipping lunch, as is now my habit – and got some paper. So I must end this letter – and start on new. I owe a letter to Chris Peper[177]. I got a very lovely Latin letter from Dr. Duffy, which is fun to read -

Henry

May 19

Dear mama –

This is a sample of my new conservative stationary. And I write again today because I have in mind that I wrote an introspective letter this morning. The result of being somewhat bored. But I am no longer bored, having just finished a cup of tea and a sandwich, which is a satisfactory lunch.

Also I just read a note *[sic]* circular which permits me to mention my "battle experiences" at Casino – so I might as well write now of a period past – the time when I was still living in a tent. I now remember the weather as always sunny, although my intellect tells me it wasn't. One day, particularly, I stood on a stone wall and watched through a gap in the olive trees, the abbey at Monte Casino being bombed, with flashes jumping up all around it, and then dust smoke rising in a column to the clouds. Each time the column blew away, there would be a little less remaining of the abbey – but after they were all through, there were still walls standing. That was also the place where there was a big gun – one or more – about a mile behind, and every few minutes, a shell would pass overhead, making a whishing noise, and then an instant later, one would hear the shot – so I concluded that shells travel faster than sound – I never could quite satisfy myself of the order in which one should hear the various noises at various points along the path of the projectile, which I suppose slows down to go more slowly than sound at some point. One gets so accustomed to the noises one misses them. A city seems so very quiet.

There was also the telephone call one night from a Negro[178] company running shower baths and giving clean clothes out – asking what some flashes were, because they were almost having a riot – the place was filled with soldiers covered with soap under hot showers – and every time the Negroes saw a flash, they shut off the motor which ran the water, and rushed out to their fox holes – leaving about fifty men soapy and cold. Under those circumstances, I told them the flashes were practice firing beyond a range of mountains. I have no idea what they were.

We had a perfect location from which to watch the road the Germans were shooting at – but they didn't seem to hit it very often – just around it – and only once did I see a truck – a gasoline truck, which just wasn't there any more when the smoke cleared.

---

[177] A St. Louis lawyer
[178] Black soldiers served in segregated companies in the War.

It is all very different here –

Love

Henry

May 19

Dear Aunt Sally –

You see I try to lend variety to my letters by variety of stationary – having long since abandoned any attempt at variety of content.

I have your letter about a tomato garden. You may be sure we are getting plenty of canned vegetables – but I have a kind of twinge of conscience at eating canned vegetables when fresh are in season – and the worst culinary crime in the calendar of atrocities is to drink canned orange juice when fresh oranges are piled high – next comes eating canned string beans when fresh artichokes and peas are wasting in the streets. I suppose I omit from consideration the labor situation.

My greatest pleasure in a garden was always in putting the seeds in the ground – and with each seed planted, looking at the illustration on the package of how it should come out. What potentialities there are then! But soon after sprouting, my plants began to scraggle, and I abandoned hope of approaching the catalogue illustration.

The weather here is as lovely as California's. I have quite forgotten that it was even rainy, and remember even the past winter as clear and sunny. My knowledge tells me that it rained almost constantly – but memory is a happier thing than knowledge – one seems to have the power of choosing things from memory, like pulling books from shelves, and those which don't seem pleasant, one just puts back – or phonograph records from an album. So I remember only the sunny days of the Italian winter.

I am now living very comfortably – in a town – spending my leisure wandering around the old, walled city – with its churches, cathedral, narrow streets and alleys, and filth in the streets – children playing all kinds of games – from charming dancing and singing games in the nature of square dances, and the like, to dragging each other around by the hair and throwing stones at each other and wrestling in the gutters.

I am not too busy – in fact, live in hopes of getting a week off sometime and going to one of the capitals I hear described by men passing through here – Cairo, Jerusalem, Palermo, Alexandria – where not. But the hope is remote. From all descriptions, Cairo is now the liveliest and wildest city in the world, and Jerusalem runs a close second. Palermo has become a sleepy village, and Algiers is a center of politics and high statesmanship comparable to Paris or London in former times – the capital of existing France.

Affectionately –

Henry

[Post script sentence unclear.]

May 20

Dear mama -

This morning it is raining for a change – which is refreshing – a gentle summer rain which makes everything look clean again, and bright, as I remembered it when I first came here.

I went to bed early last night – which is a delight – about eight thirty – with the result that I woke early, and got to the hotel before the dining room was open – a habit I must not cultivate. For breakfast, then, orange juice (canned) oat meal, boiled eggs, toast, butter, and coffee. and orange marmalade. The waitresses call anything that comes in a soup dish, apparently, suppe *[sic]*, and since all food except coffee is served in soup dishes, all things are called suppe. So if you want more of anything, you ask for more of the <u>first</u> suppe or more of the second suppe, and so forth.

Then, since it was raining, I got a ride down here – rather regret it because it would have been a pleasant walk, even with rain. But I shall walk this noon.

The plans – sponsored principally by Lts. Clark and Little – to procure an apartment – proceed. They describe the place, which there is no reason to believe we shall procure – as an apartment on a third floor, with three bed rooms, a living room, a bath with hot water heater and a kitchen. Being on the top floor, it opens on all sides, and the living room, an interior room, had a skylight. Each bedroom opens onto a terrace, which surrounds the apartment. It is furnished, they say, very comfortably, with modern furniture, soft chairs, and so forth.

I surely hope you have learned not to take me too seriously on these subjects of luxury. "Better a meal of peas and herbs, and quiet therewith, than a house full of feasting with strife." Is that a proper quotation? But if there are no peas or herbs?

I am well – when I get to writing that, I am just about out of things to say. Your letters are arriving beautifully, and it is very wonderful to feel so nearly current, as I do when I receive a letter only a few days or a week old – as I have on several occasions. I wonder if mine are coming through equally well?

Do you enjoy sending packages? If so, I need pajamas (light weight) fearing to wear my good woolen ones, for fear of wearing them out before next winter. Maybe that is too long range vision. I am now down to wearing my silk ones – another luxury – and my last pair. Also my billfold is wearing out – but I can possibly find someone going to North Africa who will get me one. So I request ju pajamas – hoping you understand that I can get along comfortably without them. My present burden is too many woolen clothes – which I'm not allowed to give away, and am loathe to burn. This variety of required uniform is distressingly wasteful.

I send my love -

Henry

May 2

Dear mama -

Beautiful weather had returned.

Last night I went to the concert – was late, since I went to dinner first, but heard a very very beautiful Grieg piano concerto – then a Brahms symphony (no 4) which I did not much enjoy, Brahms seems a little too difficult for this orchestra.

After the concert, I went with Lts. Clark and Little to the Service Command Officers Club, where there was a party – Saturday night – and what a party! Floor show, with local talent singers, who sing Italian translations of American songs in throaty, over rich voices. And a chorus of danseuses. What a riot they would have caused on the Chicago market! They shook the building, which stands in the harbor.

Then Lt. Sterns and Capt Jones came in   they had found two young ladies, Rosa and Frieda Gallo of Turin – quiet girls who have lived here three or four years, and run a small <u>Mode</u> Shop. They speak in whispers, and refuse even to attempt to learn English. So conversation is extremely halting – partly because they cannot be heard above the orchestra. They know no French, no German, nothing except Italian, which they speak only very quietly, without gesticulation.

I left before the rest, being tired, and went to bed.

So you see I have no news – and little or nothing of which to write. I am well. I had originally planned for next Tuesday to go to a town about 30 miles away with Lt. Little – but he is taking today off, instead, ~~and~~ since he had a ride ~~on~~ to both Corsica and Sardinia, which places he wants to see. From all descriptions, Corsica is completely fantastic at the present time. So I shall spend Tuesday in something not far from routine – library for a while in the morning – music lesson – walking through town, or into the country in the afternoon. Unless I have to work – which can never be foreseen.

Discussion of getting an apartment still goes on – and descriptions of one available – a matter of which I am purely passive.

How is Haymer? Did you ever receive a linen towel I sent you – which was interesting to me.

I send my love -

Henry.

PS – I did receive my Algerian watch – and it is serving me well. Thank you very much

H

May 23

Dear mama

Yesterday – my day off – I spent in routine – The morning passed very quickly, with a walk along the harbor and through the old town - I am coming to enjoy the cathedral more and more, especially as I learn to ignore the little boys who volunteer to show you through – ignore them, or reduce them to courteous sense. They all (even the priests) say "Hey Joe, Santa Nicola?" and in such a manner that it is hard to appreciate they are not bums. Yesterday, a boy who looked better cared for than most addressed me: "Hey, Joe, Santa Nicola? basilica? *[sic]*" and I decided not to get mad at him. So I carefully explained to him that I had already been shown through five or six times, and that is pleased me to go into the church alone. He acquiesced very nicely – surprisingly! Then an old man robbed me – he came trotting out, pointing to his unlit pipe, and saying "match," so I handed him a book of matches, and held out my hand to accept return of matches. Then he took his pipe out of his mouth and asked for a cigarette. I refused. He ran away with my matches – my last package. So I had to get some more.

Then I bought a nickel's worth of very wonderful fresh cherries, and, was buying them at a public fountain, ate them. I do not like cherries – but now they taste so fresh and good for you that I am very fond of eating them and spitting out the seeds. Ciliege is the name. Then 100 gms. of almond cookies – and to my music lesson, where I played Beethoven and Chopin preludes.

Then I met Lt. Clark and Lt. Little – we first went out to a hospital where we were told a man we used to know was – but he wasn't in his bed, and we couldn't find him. I guess he had come to town. Then we started to another town, but it began to rain, and we came back. We looked at another room – Bill wants an improvement – a beautiful room with fine views – big – handsome crystal chandelier – comfortable chairs – and a bath in the apartment of pink tile. But of the beds – one without springs, one without mattress and the lady had no linen, and there is no closet or wardrobe arrangement – I think that sheets are worth more than glass chandeliers. A Dutch consular representative lives in the house – and had two mattresses. We could steal one from him – it would be almost worth moving in to see what he did. But I oppose the move.

Then we spent the rest of the afternoon talking – and drinking a bottle of Cinzano Vermouth, which has been given to Little. After supper to bed early, being tired.

I have a letter from daddy – mentioning Lt. Freschi at P.B.S. I have no prospect of going to his city soon – but intend to look him up if I get there. Who knows – maybe I shall. PBS means Peninsular Base Section. I shall write him a note, suggesting he look for me if he gets over here.

I am well – and send my love -

Henry

May 26

Dear mama –

I've not written yet today – and have little of which to write. I received your letter about shopping on Delmar[179] – in which you say it is foolish to be homesick. Well – I remember Delmar as being very beautiful – and am shocked now and then to appreciate that this town is probably much more beautiful. And even just as comfortable. So I am forced to the conclusion that I shall never be satisfied – and I am now reconciled to that.

So I have the most interesting possible time.

I am well – today a man came in whom I formerly knew – being nearby for a few days – and told me the latest gossip of the place I formerly was – which I cannot repeat of course – but it sounds like the same old confusion continues.

Last night, after supper, I walked a while – the city grows more beautiful every time I look at it – and boxes of cherries, piled high, were so beautiful that I bought a pound – cherries are about the most beautiful fruit there is – and carried them up to the room, where Signora Turetti washed

---

[179] Delmar: A shopping street in St. Louis

them for me, and put them on a plate – and I got out my *Taming of the Shrew* - set my chair on the terrace, put my cherries and feet on another chair and ate cherries – a pound of them – and read *Taming of the Shrew*. Wonderfully refreshing fruit – I do not know why they tasted so good – sweet and wet and cool – and with the wit of *Taming of the Shrew*!

It stays light late – but at about 8:30 it becomes too dusky to read on the terrace, and Signior Turetti came out and we discussed two subjects: 1) the war situation, in which he is extremely optimistic, that the war in Italy is almost over, and is enthusiastic on the news broadcasts. The situation in Rome, where his brother is and where he has kind of grape-vine reports, as I understand (or misunderstand) him. What kind of city Milan is, where he used to run a small hotel. (He is a skilled host) Then he proceeded to the second subject 2) Peas, which are now abundant and delicious here (I've eaten them only raw). I told him how they were cooked in America – boiled in water, with a little bit of flour and butter. Is that right? Like they come in cans – and up went his hands in horror. You must a *[sic]* And he brought me a delicious piece of meat pie – and told me that you cook peas as follows: cut up an onion in olive oil, and brown it; then put in the peas and cook them a short time. What do you think of that recipe? So you begin to cook peas by cutting up an onion – a principle in so much Italian cookery. You begin to cook spaghetti by cutting up a tomato. I conclude that food is my favorite subject of discussion, and eating my favorite pastime. Oh! The hardships of war in ------ ! *[sic]* Signior T. said as soon as Signora came back, she would cook some peas for me – but she was visiting the neighbors – but at 9:00 she had not come, and I went to bed. She will cook some peas for me tonight. When you eat good things, you must stroke your throat with your forefinger and say "Lish, lish!" That is the high fashion in Milan.

Love

Henry

May 27

Dear mama –

The weather is magnificent today. But first I shall get off my chest my remorse for folly – this time possibly for folly not entirely within my control. Major Morris sent me a present of a carved box – just like the one I previously sent home with pleasure. So I have sent the second one – if one is good, are not two better? So they must be. I hope you receive it – and this one can be given away – to almost anyone – or kept. Possibly Edith and Bernard Barenholtz would appreciate it as a gift without reason. Barney is near here – I haven't seen him yet, but hope that I shall at some time soon. It is up to him to come to see me – if I got away from here, I do not intend to spend time wandering around military installations.

I am well. Nothing of which to write, so I shall continue in the morning, when I may be able to write about peas cooked in the Italian style – of which I am tentatively promised a dish for this evening. Nothing is known, however.

Henry

May 28

I cannot write of peas cooked in the Italian style. On the way home last night, I met Porzia – all dressed up – walking over to see a friend of hers. She told me her brother was home. So I went up to see him – he was there for about a week when I first arrived – he is in the Italian army – and he's just returned from the other side of Italy – having about a week. For the past month he has been in a hospital. The family was not restraining itself – Signora Turetti weeping full blast, partly because she was glad he was back but in larger part because he had to leave again in a week. He is a very nice boy, and a very intelligent boy. After supper, I came back, the storm had subsided, and all were talking. So I read until dark (finishing *Taming of the Shrew*) and then sat with them, talking too. I weakened, and contrary to my resolve, gave Signora Turetti half a pound of coffee deciding maybe I could get more, and I would never know the most favorable reason to use it anyway. With all the talking it was eleven o'clock before I got to bed.

This morning I had my first breakfast with them – consisting of coffee. I then went over to the hotel and had my regular breakfast consisting of cereal *([word unclear]*, called suppe) and fried egg toast and coffee – marmalade. Meals are good – improving, I think. Last night we had fresh asparagus (overcooked). The Turettis asked me to come up and eat Italian peas with them this evening – but I can't since I am going to the symphony.

There is talk of going on a six day week – with Sunday off – that I shouldn't like, because I should have to abandon music lesson. But that will be as it may.

I send my love -

Henry

May 28

Dear mama -

I received letters from you today of May 5 and 6 – and am more or less at home in my imagination, for I should so much like to see everyone there – and especially with Betty there. Yes – the time I have been away is so long that I am afraid to think of it – but day to day takes care of itself. And your principle that on the rocky hillsides I write of Augustine and here of food proves only this – that one must make the best of a situation – and if on the rocky hillside Augustine is the best that offers, then Augustine it is – but given a choice between food and the saint – the choice is easy. In fact, I have little doubt that most virtues exist because of necessity – not preference – or at least out of expediency.

I am well – and shall continue this letter in the morning – since it is now time to get out of here -

Love – Henry

Having written the above, I went to dinner with Bill Clark and Lt. Stern, at the Oriente Hotel, for I learned that they were having the chicken which the Service Command had had the preceding night. So chicken two nights running! St. Augustine offers no pleasure like that!

Then I left Bill & Lt. Stern, who went to a movie, and I went back to the room, where Porzia and her brother were just leaving for a ciné. And Signora was setting the table – with a beautiful, shining white linen napkin as a doily ,a folded napkin for use as such, and a big bottle of red wine. So I sat down to a dish of peas milanaise – which were not as different as I expected them to be, but were, even after dinner, very very delicious. I can't give you the exact recipe – but they were flavored with a little onion and olive oil, quite juicy, with egg beat up in them – the style of the egg you put in soup. I ate a soup dish of them. Then (to my surprise) came fritters – artichoke hearts and a kind of squash fritter – like a cucumber, but not so seedy, and very sweet, something like egg-plant. Well, I suppose it was Italian squash. Next – a big bowl of cherries, cool and refreshing, with a dish of freshly roasted almonds. Signora sits by and says "mangiate, tenente, mangiate. Non fa male – sono verdure[180]" Her theory is that meat and cheese and eggs may make you sick – but you can eat an indefinite quantity of fruit and vegetables. But you must never drink water with cherries or with figs – if you do, they act as a purgative. Full of wise *[unclear]* on the subject of eating – on which they are quite expert.

Then Captain Le-Blanc (who is no good) came in – and a man named Vincentis who lives next door – and we sat on the terrace and talked until dark. Then came Porzia and her brother – and we moved inside and talked until bed time – which was soon for me.

Then this morning I bathed, had breakfast, and came down here, stopping at the stationers on the way – to get a pen and pen points (with which I now write) and some paper, my supply being low.

Lt. Little showed me an apartment yesterday – a nice place, but without beds or sheets. I am inclined to prefer a smaller room with those things to more space with cots. So it goes.

Henry

May 29

Dear mama -

This is the paper I purchased this morning – it is the best available in ---, and therefore I do not object to using it until the supply is exhausted – which will not be long hence, for the stationer had only three or four envelopes of it left.

I am rereading your letters – about Betty coming home – which, I say, makes me feel as if I were at home drinking root beer in the kitchen – and that you are filling my request for pajamas – and your running two households. I think you ought to quit it, for it seems to me you are going too steadily and too hard. But I've abandoned all hope of giving advice from this distance – and just piddle along.

I am really never bored – except when I think of the future – and that there is really nothing I intend to do, nothing I am planning to do – which is laziness and lack of initiative – For example, sooner or later I shall, I think, have an opportunity to go to a place which, for lack of a name, I shall call the Island of The Zodiac, a name without relation to the place, but just a word which pops into my head. Most people rave about the place – its beauty and its luxury – and I suppose it had them. But it seems so much bother to pick up and go places; and what if I do see landscapes and grottos and mountains?

And now I have just finished an expedition which I found quite disgusting – at the ostentation, megalomanic Lt. S's instigation. I had lunch with him, and afterwards, he wanted to stop at a hospital to see a girl who is there with some kind of injury – a friend of a man named Marx. That was alright – about 3 minutes chat – but then he went into the children's ward and gave each baby a piece of hard candy - I left – because it seemed to me such an ostentatious display over so little. He gave the candy he didn't like.

The day is beautiful – warm and clear and fresh. There is not a bit of news, and no hope or prospect of acquiring any.

---

[180] Translates to "eat, lieutenant, eat. It doesn't hurt – it's vegetables."

A play here – called *Cicero* – in Italian. I expect not to see it. Arturo Rubinstein[181] played here, but the Special Service Section forgot to announce it, and nobody came – except, I am told, about 2 men who wandered in by mistake and thought there was just someone practicing on a piano. That I suppose is rather funny.

I am well – and send my love.

Henry.

May 31

Dear mama -

I did not write yesterday – and beginning this enormous sheet of paper frightens me, because I can't possibly fill it.

Yesterday was my day off. After breakfast, and my day-off barber shop shave – I went to the University, and got out a book on Roman Law – in Italian – but was soon interrupted by two young students, who said they would like to talk to me (in bad English) and I suggested we walk outside. So we did, and sat in the park, while they fed me blood oranges from their brief case. (Everybody goes around looking like a clerk or lawyer carrying papers – but every case I have seen opened contains principally oranges, cherries, or other fruit or vegetables) They were medical students, about to finish the study of medicine, and wanted to talk about the practice of medicine. Both intended to go into private practice, and had opportunity to do so – one the son of a pharmacist, the other of a doctor, in a city not very far away. But they were interested in California and New Jersey (why New Jersey? I don't know) to practice medicine. So I told them that Italian medical education was not sufficient to permit them to practice in the United States – that they would probably have to study another year and then intern in a hospital for one or two years. But that if they did that, and were good doctors , they could doubtless practice successfully in America, especially since they were Italians and Italians in America would like to have Italian doctors, especially those who did not speak English very well. Is that true? For the rest, we just talked about the glories of medicine and what a fine profession it was, the climate and Geography of California and New Jersey, and similar subjects. But I did not read Roman law.

Then I walked through the old town – and at a little before noon ran into Lt. Stern, who was walking back to his apartment. I went with him – and saw Captain Marx – an English officer – who considers himself sick, but likes to say he isn't to make other people say he is. I disappointed him by agreeing with him that he was well and should get to work.

Then down to my music teacher – who had left a note that he was unable to be there, but I should use his piano at any time until his return. A note in bad French. Then to lunch, and back to his piano, which I played until about two-thirty. Then walked some more – the cathedral, castle, harbor and old town. The Px Sales store (flints, wicks, hair oil (and lighter fluid, which I use as cleaning fluid) And walked some more.

(Hooray – I just received a package. Tea – coffee – wrapped in clothes – what fun I shall have. Did I tell you the Turetis are serving me coffee in bed every morning – since I gave them a pound of coffee?)

---

[181] Acclaimed pianist.
Via Wikipedia
https://en.wikipedia.org/wiki/Arthur_Rubinstein

I called Lt. Little later – and got myself invited to dinner at the Service Command – and to a movie afterwards – with Clark and Lt. King of the MRU – which stands for Machine Records Unit – but when they want something there, they call themselves the Mobile Reconnaissance Unit – and people hop, saying "operational priority!" The movie - "See here, Private Hargrove[182]," which was rather funny.

Then we learned Lt. Sasse and Lt. Fields, a pilot for General Keyes' airplane, were in town, and went looking for them. We finally found them – and stayed with them for two hours. They are going back to II Corps this morning – Lt. Sasse being now discharged from the hospital – so I had breakfast with them – and asked them to greet a few people there for me. They are as much amazed at the ridiculousness of this place as I was at first – and I had forgotten I was originally so amazed.

I am well. I send my love.

Henry

---

[182] 1944 MGM comedy
Via Wikipedia
https://en.wikipedia.org/wiki/See_Here%2C_Private_Hargrove_(film)

June 1

Dear daddy -

I have your letter – May 9 – and yes my client was convicted. They all are, although I have had two whose convictions were set aside and reversed.

I think I had better give you this information for any records which may be being kept for me – my pay (gross cash received) up to May 7 1944 was $165.$\frac{00}{}$ per month. For the month of May, it was $178.87. So I guess my pay is $185.$\frac{00}{}$ a month.

I am well – and completely without news. I have not been busy – but just interrupted very often – and you know how confusing that is. Add to it that there is constant confusion and nothing ever gets done.

This letter is too short. I shall write again soon.

Henry

June 1

Dear mama -

It is intended that we move tonight, having an apartment, which may be pleasant, and may afford privacy, which Lt. Clark says he desires. It is farther from my place of work, but since I enjoy walking, I take that on the side of advantage. Parting with the Turettis? A hard break, but I shall try to make it cordial.

June 2

I am beginning too many letters – and not finishing most of them. I just completed one, and dispatched it, before I found this beginning of yesterday. So I'll try to save this for tomorrow's letter, or this afternoon's.

It is now afternoon. I am well. There is no news. I have agreed to meet Lt. Little and Clark for dinner tonight at the hotel at which I am supposed to eat. That is at 6 o'clock. If I get away from here at 5, I shall call on the Turettis on the way. I do not know what my relation with them is – I think they believe that Lt. Little and Lt. Clark persuaded me to leave, which is not far from the truth. But not as bad as they would think. They dislike Lt. Little, who employed civilian workers, and fired Mr. Turetti's brother, for alleged stealing. They liked me, because I gave them cigarettes and laughed. Clark is inclined to be over-serious, and intolerant, and think he should be severe with former fascists, and resents giving them chocolate and cigarettes. But I don't care much. So I shall call on them. Signora Turetti's Onomastico or Saint's Day is June 13 – St. Anthony – and I shall reserve a carton of cigarettes for the occasion. But I cannot wait so long to call on them. I like them, as pleasant people and excellent hosts. Most people prefer to stay clear of Italian connections. It's quite true, we were played for suckers – overpaid them, ga and so forth. $16.$\frac{00}{}$ a month for one room! But when they had it, they did everything they could to earn it. For that reason, I do not wholly agree with the advice you give about overpaying – one can afford to drive a bargain only when one knows exactly what one's getting. In other instances, one must leave the price to the vendor, who can make the value.

Have you received my second carved box? Do you think it is a masterpiece too? I have an idea the plates I sent Haymer will arrive broken. Little matter – they were ordinary. But only when I see photographs or pictures of things at home, or of North Africa or Sicily do I appreciate how different in character this country is from other places – and it takes a distinct effort of memory to recall Sicily and painted carts – and the feeling of getting out of the manifest colonialism of North Africa – with the native characteristics all suppressed.

So I wrote both sides of a page, with nothing whatsoever to say.

Love

Henry

June 2

Dear mama -

Well, well well! I am now installed in an apartment. I like it. I also liked the Turettis – but there was little space, and Clark wanted to move – and Little wanted to move in with us. So we picked up and moved.

What an accumulation! Barracks bags of underwear, sheets, trousers, blankets, helmets, canteens (someplace, I've acquired four – I used to be in dread of having none – conservation) pistols. We got a truck – and two Italian soldiers and about 20 Italian children, and threw everything into mattress covers, barracks bags and so forth – then they proceeded, like a swarm of locusts, to haul it to the truck – to swarm on the truck, and then haul it off.

The apartment is very fine – new and clean – with a dining room, kitchens, three bedrooms a living room, a bath, (with shower) gas hot water heater, one extra toilet, three extra wash basins – skylights in the living room; terrace off the dining room. Good light and good air. Third floor – and so far no mosquitos. I shall become very lazy. Alas! St. Augustine!

But it is 20 minutes walk to breakfast. That is alright too.

Telephone, radio, phonograph, comfortable chairs. (Beds lacking – we used cots, but possibly shall acquire beds)

Coffee, tea; wine – the first two, thanks to you and daddy.

The owner lives next door – and volunteers to keep the place clean, to take care of laundry and such other things.

To get the place, we put out a sullen, one-eyed Italian officer, who kept complaining, where shall I sleep (he wanted to stay <u>with</u> us) and finally we just put him out and told him to go find himself a place to sleep. He did, without difficulty.

I am well – writing early, since I am up against my ~~old~~ habits of early rising. A hot bath this morning – a cup of coffee – and it is now almost seven o'clock. The weather is magnificent.

Got no work at all done yesterday – for the typist did not show up. I shall say nothing of it if he shows up this morning – except to him – and to him I shall say all I can – it will go in one ear and out the other, so I might as well enjoy it. So will he.

Now I have written all the news. A Dr. Guido asks the privilege of visiting us – says he wants to talk English – and we may talk Italian with him. He lives with the proprietor in the villas of the proprietor about five or six miles out of town.

What things turn up when I repack! 20 pairs of shoe strings! About 500 razor blades – six tooth brushes. But I accomplish nothing by abandoning such little things!

All my love -

Henry

June 2

Dear mama -

I now embark upon a new style of living – equivalent of Algiers – with the pleasure of wandering from room to room, and sitting in comfortable chairs. I am inclined to believe it will not last long – nothing does. But I shall enjoy it while it does last.

My trouble is that I have always taken luxuries so much for granted that I do not appreciate them as much as I should.

A strange odor pervades the town today – as it has for several days – as of stagnant water or rotting fish. It seems to come from the harbor. The natives seem to accept it, as if it always existed, and although it is quite noxious, I am becoming accustomed to it.

There is no news, other than what I have already written.

What would you think of sending me some raisins and the like? Which would taste awfully good. In any event, I request them, and you will, I hope, do as you like.

The weather continues very beautiful – and there is no news, as I have said before. I am well.

There is a Dr. Guido who says he wants to visit us now and then and talk English – and help us talk Italian. He is a "Commercialist" – and I do not know just what a commercialist does.

I found a bottle of Cinzano Vermouth (tell Dr. Schlesinger) and bought it. I know where there are two more – it is white vermouth, and very, very excellent. I guess there is still plenty around, not offered for sale – partly because people can't quite realize that they can sell for 300 lire what they have always thought worth 3 or 4 lire.

I cannot get over what a mess my baggage is in. I really ought to spend a day putting it in order and making out a card index of it. Random discarding does no good, because I find after I've finished I've discarded only a few pins or something similar. But I shall gradually get rid of more. Thinking of discarding an overcoat – which I've carried for a year and worn about three times. But the situation is hopeless.

I send my love -

Henry

June 3

Dear mama –

I continue in the lap of luxury.

Last night, or evening, I called on the Turettis – and talked to them for quite a while – to learn whether they were mad – they weren't. Then went to dinner at the Oriente; and there met Captain Sessa; with whom we returned to the apartment. Then called on the Gallo sisters of Turin, where there was the cousin, with whom they live, and about four or five Italian officers, who spoke French. So we spent the evening talking. But I am becoming dull – with little to talk of. I am resolved to get out of that state promptly. It results in part from seeing too much of Lt. Stern, who is a very stupid and ignorant man – jejune and immature. I am constantly mad at him for no other reason than what he is – he does not do anything in particular.

Mail is rare these days – but today, I got your letter – about Betty's visit and it surely must be fun to be with Betty. I hope Haymer does not monopolize her from you completely.

I am well. As I say, I must find something to be alert and enthusiastic about.

Write often. The weather here continues beautiful. The English have taken to running a barge out into the harbor for swimming. I think it is a good idea – the water near shore is kind of stinking – but out further I see no reason why it should not be clear and fresh.

Love

Henry

P.S. I have a letter from Ben Charles – that Bill is someplace else now. But I don't know where. Possibly I shall hear from him soon.

H

June 4

Dear mama –

This is Sunday – which does not make any difference. Tuesday is my marked day. But last night I went to the symphony – it now begins at eight o'clock – an improvement over the old six o'clock beginning, for it gives a chance to eat dinner. I enjoyed the concert. Unfortunately, they played Beethoven's Fifth first, and that is so magnificent and new and refreshing that the rest was just a jumble – Strauss, Tod and Verklärung, Wagner's *Dance of Valkürie* or something of the kind, Mendelsohn's *Calm Sea*.

After the concert, we went to the apartment – we, being Lt. Stern (an ignorant, coarse, noisy fellow!) Capt. Marx – an Englishman of charming manner, but a beggar always on the receiving end, Lt. Clark – alright – Lt. Gregorien – a Russian who said not one word all evening. He speaks English, maybe doesn't understand it. Stern is overwhelming! Herr Weigler, who is a gentleman. So we drank the bottle of Cenzano Vermouth and ate chocolates (which Bill had received) and a can of lobster – quite a combination.

Then all left – and we went to bed – that ought to be the end of this letter, because nothing else had happened. This morning I got up early – and had a cup of coffee. I gave one pound to the landlady – for two week's laundry. Not an exchange, but a gift of coffee. She is not charging for laundry. I think she wants to do it for the soap she can recover that way.

I intend to go to Sr. Turetti's Onomastico party on 13 June – since I am on good terms with them – and make him a present of some cigarettes or a pound of tea.

I am beginning again on a campaign for more interest. It is too easy to sit back and settle into a routine of boring company. So I shall go out and visit people – or talk to strangers – or begin a quest.

My first quest must be for a mouse trap – "una trappola" – for I saw a mouse last night. I think I am likely to be able to get a very fancy one – like a birdcage, of wood, with a falling door. I shall let you know my success – first in buying a mouse trap and next in catching the mouse. A pretty little black furry mouse, which, last night, sat behind a chair and watched.

I send my love -

Henry

June 5

Dear mama -

I am now writing early in the morning – yesterday evening I left work at about 4:30 – meeting Little and Clark first, and having a dish of ice cream at the coffee shop! Then went to a movie with them, for we were not hungry for supper – small wonder. The movie was no good, of course. Thence to supper – and then walked. Walking is always exciting – crowds and people doing all kinds of things – up and down the boulevards, under the trees – through the parks and along the harbor. The night was very lovely – with full moon, and cool and pleasant. I hear many saying it is so very hot here – but I have not felt it at all – it seems to me very pleasant and cool.

Did a Major Coleman ever call you or come to see you? Maybe he isn't home yet – but he intended to spend a week or ten days in St. Louis – and I suggested he might enjoy calling you or daddy or both. He intended to meet his wife in St. Louis – stay at the Chase and celebrate for a week there – then go home for the rest of his time – in Oklahoma. It sounded like a strange decision to me. Why meet in St. Louis instead of Chicago or New York? But maybe he had a reason.

The principal occupation of leisure here seems to be writing letters. I do not understand that either, because in fifteen minutes a day I can write more than I have to write. But I think most of the time is usually taken in settling down to write – which takes a long time. I am enjoying the luxury of this apartment. While it lasts. Walking from room to room, hot water at the turn of a spigot faucet – coffee – tea – and today I intend to buy asparagus and artichokes – the luxuries of the land.

I am well – and send all my love. Mail has been rare these days – I expect a big batch today -

Henry

June 5

Dear mama -

I wrote you a letter early this morning – but left it at the apartment. So it will not be mailed today – and I might as well write another. But there is nothing left to say – because I shall mail the letter tomorrow, and had nothing whatsoever to say in it either.

~~Sor~~ A freak accident happened yesterday – ~~do~~ I was a passenger in a jeep. A man stepped off the sidewalk, while looking the wrong way, and absent mindedly walked into the jeep – not the front, but the side – his head coming in just behind the windshield, and hitting me in the nose with his head. I did not know until then what a strong weapon the nose is – it raised a goose-egg on his head, but my nose is alright – so slight a bruise that it hasn't even turned black and blue. But what a mob collects – all talking at once – you can hardly push through to see if the man is hurt. He wasn't – there was an ambulance right behind us, and he refused to get medical treatment, and wrote his own name for me, so he wasn't hurt.

Then I have a small campaign – all children, when begging for chewing gum, candy and the like begin "Hey, Joe." I am trying to teach them that "Hey" is not a courteous form of salutation, and "Joe" is not everybody's name. I have no firm decision as to what they should say, but that suggested: "If you please, sir" and "Hear me, I beg you, sir." Those I have tried to teach have abandoned their quest for chewing gum and run away – which is also a desirable event.

The stores are full of fresh vegetables and fruits – and I intend this evening to buy a bunch of asparagus and some artichokes, and eat them just boiled before I go to bed. Maybe I shall try to get some salt and olive oil to put on them – but I have no container with me for the olive oil and salt is ~~vo~~ quite rare. I do not know how to use salt in big crystals – about as big as a robin's egg – but possibly can grind it up for use or eat a bite then lick the crystal. There must be a solution to the problem.

I am well. The weather is magnificent, the bluest sky I have ever seen – and everything scintillating and bright. It is the kind of sun which sneaks up on you and sun burns you while you aren't noticing. So I am surprised, when, in a mirror, I see a white line across my forehead from the shadow of my hair.

Now Rome is fallen[183] – the papers say – and I faintly hope I shall have opportunity to go there some day – but with indolence such as mine I probably shan't – and cities are extremely psychopathic under such circumstances. But it would be more interesting to see Rome than not to. However, it would be a hard trip there – and all the world will be trying to go. Well – I'll see. It is presently premature to think of it – and I can survive happily without seeing Rome – provided I don't go to movies as I did last night. Rome must be a very big city – the rumor among the natives here being that it has about 3,000,000 people – swollen from a normal population of about 1,000,000 – who have had no established supply of food or other necessities for ten days or two weeks now – that is, no markets and no transportation and no accessibility to the country and farms. I don't know how such a multitude of people can survive such a period.

I send my love -

Henry

---

[183] Rome was liberated by the Allies on June 4, 1944 during the Allied Italian Campaign.
Via Wikipedia
https://en.wikipedia.org/wiki/Italian_campaign_(World_War_II)#Allied_advance_on_Rome

June 7

Dear daddy -

I have a letter from you which I cannot answer directly. You have no idea how remote I am from international politics – and how completely I have abandoned any attempt to say what should be and what should not be in the future. There is no doubt that the English can get substantially anything they want – on the basis of the institution of tea. I think it works all the way up and down – as here, if an Englishman invites a billeting officer to tea, he can, for speaking to him in an English accent, get himself a villa. It was even more pronounced in Algiers, where a cup of tea and an English accent were worth medals and citations for heroism in battle.

The English are firmly installed, without opposition, in all strategic places – and have a way of never being dislodged from any place they are. The observation gives rise to speculation – whether they get it for tea or by agreement previously worked out. The tea agreement – we give you tea, you give us Europe – is one that takes advantage of American officers clamoring for culture. The English do invite them to tea, and English tea may be a very real factor in international affairs. But the possibility also exists (and this I mention in ignorance of the Pacific situation) that there is an understanding for English domination of Europe and Africa; American domination of the far East. This rather leaves Russia and China out of the picture; and I think Russia and China know they are intended to be out of the picture pretty completely. The implications of the De-Gaulle, Giraud controversy[184]; of the Russia recognition of Italy, and her apparent attitude that she will take care of her own interests as best she can. But this is speculation – I cannot completely believe that England will give up her classic Singapore and Canton – with Australia there, for Churchill once said that England had no intention of giving up her colonies. So that may be the key to what lines peace ~~will~~ negotiations will take.

My notion is that the trouble with European countries, as far as government is concerned, is that they are too small – that most people are not touched by government, which consists of a very few people – a kind of parlor government – or ten or twelve men, a brain trust, so to speak. That makes government unstable and irresponsible, and a league of such governments is not worth having. To maintain them, takes some external force.

But your letter is more idealistic. I do not know how to think of the proposition of an American Court of arbitration. But it seems at first blush that if England and Russia dictate the peace terms in Europe, they will do it sufficiently in their interest that, if they maintain force sufficient to furnish sanctions, no court would be necessary. Because they would have everything they wanted, and would leave and keep the other nations powerless. The only possibility would be a conflict between Russia and England which I think is (1) unlikely and (2) could not be presented by a court. So a court would be inactive – at least so long that it would be moribund before it would be called upon to act.

I have a better idea for the peace – one also which will not be adopted. Its fundamental thesis would be abolition of a trade and travel barriers and compulsory education in a ~~force~~ common language – as English – so that all college courses would come to be taught in English, and as many people as possible would know English. It could be contemplated that a license would be required to carry on any business, except possibly agriculture and manual trades – a prerequisite of the issuance of which would be proficiency in English. Further, free transportation, possibly abundant scholarships, should be furnished students to study in foreign schools. In twenty or thirty years the nationalism which makes European wars should cease.

---

[184] Henri Giraud was a French military officer who led the French resistance. Ultimately he had a falling out with De Gaulle and was removed as co-President in November of 1943.

Add to this – a government monopoly on the manufacture of one or two essential war commodities – an arsenal under joint control. The commodities would have to be well selected. But my thoughts are very tentative.

Affectionately -

Henry

June 7

Dear mama -

My day off – and I expect to be very busy today – a great list of things to be done: as get my hair cut; buy a mouse trap; see if I can get a bed spring; buy cherries and asparagus; and artichoke and olive oil and salt; first I shall get a haircut – then go after a mouse trap – I don't know what next – probably shall not get around to everything.

I am well – the day fair. Last night I walked – in fact I do a great deal of walking. To be continued. Henry.

Now it is evening – and I am tired. I got myself a haircut and bought a mouse trap of a fancy Rube-Goldberg kind – the mouse (they say) gnaws a string, to get at the bait which is behind the string, and breaks the string which releases a spring, which ~~catch~~ raises a wire which catches the mouse. Does it? I shall let you know. I set it with candy, being the only bait I had, except cherries. If nothing happens by tomorrow morning, I shall bring a piece of bacon from the breakfast table. Asparagus is gone. I walked my feet off – found several bed springs – did not feel like buying from the six year old children. Then I heard that the invasion of Europe had begun[185] – and forgot my bedsprings.

After supper – on the way home – I saw a crowd gathered outside the governor's palace – being harangued from the balconies by Italians, with great gesticulation. All I could understand was that "Allora," which means "Then" or "Next" and Rome is liberated, and all Italy would be free – and we should work. The most beautiful thing was the clergyman who stood on the balcony in scarlet robes and lace, nodding his benevolence. There were a few English officers – a few (one) American officer, a lot of Italian officers and civilians. But the most conspicuous man on the balcony (except the cardinal or bishop – who wears scarlet?) was a press correspondent, very drunk, who kept waving from behind the cardinal, in funny antics, and reclining around. The crowd got impatient toward the end – so I suppose the speeches were not very good. I asked what was being said – was told "A little of everything" and such, I suppose, was the case.

My music lesson I enjoyed very much. I'm going back tomorrow night to practice. Bravo! The maestro's son an Italian captain, will be there to let me in.

Love,

Henry

---

[185] D-Day occurred on June 6, 1944.
Normandy Landings Via Wikipedia
https://en.wikipedia.org/wiki/Normandy_landings

June 8

Dear mama -

A few lines before leaving the apartment – Nothing worth mentioning happened yesterday, until evening, when, as per schedule and on invitation I went to my music teacher's studio. He was not there, but as per schedule his son's orderly, an Italian soldier, let me in. I talked to the orderly for a while and there practiced – Czerny, Mozart and Chopin, and enjoyed myself more than I have for a very long time – a fine piano, as fine as the one there – except Italian style – Later the son came in, and when I was through I talked with him for a while – Shakespeare the musical classes and New York – the Jerusalem of the modern world, to which all hope to arrive.

So I am going again – having assurances that I am welcome – I shall go this evening or tomorrow.

I am well – and send my love.

Henry

P.S. Please send me a package, containing some candy, some food, and some raisins.

June 8

Dear mama -

This paper is quite discouraging – being so large that one should really write a book! But I like it nevertheless. I have letters from you – about Betty's visiting – and your being resolved not to worry about my buying a sailboat. Wise resolution - because there never was any possibility of my acquiring one. It was just an exciting joking quest, which brought one to neighboring towns and harbors and shipyards – in which I went on board many fishing boats, and tried to talk about sailing; and visited port commanders. I thought it was ridiculous and therefore enjoyed it. On the same principle – my quest for a country villa – which brought me into the villas already occupied by commanding generals and discussions with their orderlies and aids of how we could take them away from the generals – we couldn't.

My quest for a bed with springs – I have decided that my cot with a good mattress is plenty comfortable.

But the most exciting news – we caught a mouse in the Rube Goldburg trap of which I wrote – and it is a trap so simple – I could make one. I saw the mouse – friendly little creature – as I was reading, stick his head into the hold, gnaw the string to reach the candy; snap! squeal! Here is the trap: a block of wood with a large hole bored into it – not all the way through. A slit in the top of the block through which a wire ring slides, the size of the hole, so that it makes the circumference of the role – this attached to a wire and spring which holds it up; and a string goes over the wire, through little holes in the block, to hold the ring down. The bait is behind the string, which the mouse gnaws in two, releasing the spring. Thus: *[drawing of mouse trap]* A very poor illustration.

I am well. Last night, after supper, I went to Maestro Costa's studio – his son, an Italian officer, ~~bu~~ (another one – not the same who is in Russia) was there later – but first I had the studio alone for about an hour and a half, and enjoyed myself immensely. I made him a gift of some razor blades – which he said he needed. The most surprising things seem to be unavailable here – or of great value.

I am well. I am now prosecuting attorney (called Trial Judge Advocate) on one court martial and assistant defense counsel on another.

Tell daddy: the Bar Association ought to take an interest in General Courts Martial – their personnel, especially for such a court had power to impose the most severe penalties, without any judicial review – and if men should be appointed to the Supreme Court of any state, or even to a court of general jurisdiction, someone would inquire into their qualifications – whether they were learned in the law or had any qualification to entitle them to exercise judgment in such matters. But military courts are made up with 21 yr. old boys sitting on them – approximately – and doctors of medicine and the like.

Now I've had a long interruption in which I heard a summary of news, which I should like to parody – "about the X Unit attacking the Y Bridge with n000 tons of bombs – very accurate bombing, and all fell within a 500 yd. Radius of The Bridge. Strike charts and visual reports indicated complete demolition. Reconnaissance photos showed traffic still moving over the bridge. However, three haystacks were set afire and 7 cows and 3 pigs were killed." that, of course, is an untrue summary of the announcements. But I have no understanding of them anyway.

There is a new club opening this evening. I have no understanding of that, either. There prevails a fancy idea about clubs being exclusive – which makes them very stuffy. My idea is that they should be wide open. But it won't prevail.

What a surprise – I've filled up this big page!

Henry

June 9

Dear mama -

I am well. There is no news – except club news -

1. I had a letter from Edith Friedman Barenholtz yesterday, giving me Barney's address and telling me Westwood[186] burned. My thoughts remind me of the undertaker calling on the widow. "My dear Mrs. Smith – I'm so sorry – did the deceased carry insurance?"
2. A new club – Allied Officers' Club – opened. Its development, I believe, was this: A hotel operator had a stock of liquor. He tried a little club, and it was such a wild success – he found he could sell anything at any price. So he decided on a bigger venture. And what a venture – kew *[sic]*! He took over an old convent or nunnery – about ½ mile out of town, quite an enormous building, set in a big garden, with terraces overlooking the garden, honey suckle piling upon the building with the complete fragrance of its flowers – big trees in squares, and rose gardens. The building – long halls, with windows onto terraces and gardens – downstairs dining rooms, set up with his hotel equipment. And here we had a dinner of impeccable service, with heavy silver and linen tablecloths – The dinner itself delicious – a pasta affair, filled with cheese, called cancellara *[sic]* romana or some such name – a patty, potatoes and a stuffed pepper – roast veal, with abundance of this excellent Italian squash – a little bread – and cheese. The meat, cheese and flour were American – the cooking very excellent Italian. Wonderful!

---

[186] Westwood is a St. Louis Country Club to which his parents belonged.

Then upstairs – the front of the building is opened into one hall about 200 feet long, with bar at one end, dancing in the middle, and lounge at the other end. Then outside the long wall (filled with doors, on the other side of the building, are many small sitting rooms, opening onto the balcony and terrace. A veritable Westwood! Phoenix, I might say – What a war, what a war. It is a good thing that I come upon these places gradually, for if I had walked straight from II Corps into that, I should have fainted dead away. But – even so, what would Augustine think? And what are the ghosts of the nuns saying? "Tolerara jubes ea, non amari?" (Thon orderest these things to be borne, not to be loved?) And plain living with high thinking. What the hell!

Well   having acccss to thc place, I shall seek out people to bring there. I am still on friendly terms with the Turettis – and might bring them there for dinner in exchange for the dinner o expect from them on the 13ᵗʰ. But Sgr. and Signora would be very much out of place and disturbed – and Porzia and Ida would not go without chaperonage. But there is the son of the Maestro – an Italian officer – and his town sisters – Red Cross workers. Still – why interrupt their high thinking? The place is too amazing. I no longer have any opinion on taste. The place – lovely old building – with stone archives and old grey walls – newly plastered and with fantastic new murals – a kind of Velma's or Aunt Sadie's dream, or someone else's nightmare. My sympathy all goes to the nuns, who, whoever, I suppose, have an interest in the business be true. Drinks – 15¢ (wine) to 60¢ (cocktails) – high prices even here. Dinner – $1.00. Service, 10%. Strictly for the carriage trade – and any native would reflect that it wasn't worth that much.

I send my love. Do not worry about my character – because I do that for both of us.

Henry

June 10

Dear mama -

I have just one thing of which to write this morning – that is the very exceptionally delicious orange I had this morning. I bought a pound of cherries last night – and we ate them before going to bed. Also a pound of oranges – and those I saved. The first I ate this morning – and it was a blood orange, the best I've ever tasted, unbelievably sweet, with a slight, refreshing tang to it. So I looked at all the others – they were just plain oranges. I now have a quest – red oranges. The oranges still on the market are few – and very ripe. I like them that way. What a fruit season – oranges from December to June! Almonds – green in July – and August – ripe the rest of the year. Now abundant cherries. I hear of strawberries, but haven't found any yet. That fruit called "Nef" is here – we ate them in Algiers last year and they are poor, tasteless things – like a haw – very mealy and flat.

Last night, after supper, we went to the Adriatic Club, and drank a glass of beer. Then we sat on the balcony over the sea – as the sun went low – and we watched fishing boats – ~~seize~~ scinning *[sic]* for sardines or minnows, and a radio from a ship was playing very loud music from BBC – a horrible example of how a broadcasting station should not be. Then, about dusk, we walked around the quay and mole *[sic]* and looked at the ships and boats – talked to some people from some of them – all English and quite uninspired.

Then back to the apartment, where we tried to telephone to the old unit II Corps, but could not get a connection – or when we did, could not hear well enough to understand. It leads me to wonder, if I should try to telephone home some day, and see if by some miraculous accident I got through. $100,000^{100000000000}$ to $1/10000000^{1000000^{100000}}$ I wouldn't. But there might be a miracle, if I prayed to the god of communications while I tried.

Tonight – symphony. The hour is now postponed to eight o'clock – which makes it much easier. The former hour of six – with dinner at six made it impossible to do both – to eat and to listen to symphony. But there was some pleasure in scraping around for food after the symphony at Red Cross and the fruit markets. But I prefer the later hour.

No news.

Mail is not arriving – I expect a batch, say, next Monday. Or some other time. The weather continues magnificent – with cool air and hot sun. Everyone says it will be very hot in July and August, but I do not believe it. I have little desire to go swimming because the sea here is filled with algae and sea-weed growths, which stink, and the shores are generally slow – it looks dirty, although I suppose it is alright if one goes a few miles from town.

I am well. I wrote a request for cookies to Mrs. Schlesinger and shall enjoy receiving them if she sends them.

Write often. I send my love -

Henry

Sunday, June 11

Dear mama -

The sun is hot today – but the air still cool and fresh. I think it may be quite warm by the end of the month.

Last night, to celebrate no particular occasion, we had dinner at the Allied Officer's Cub, which is wonderful, being almost like a civilian restaurant. And such well prepared food! Like French. First, ravioli (taken in preference to soup. When I saw the soup, I wished I had had both) Then a boiled fish – cold – with potatoes. And the sauce for the fish well worth attempting to imitate. It had some olive oil – with orange and lemon peel grated in it very fine, and a little (very little) lemon juice – I think it also had w̶ olives grated or cut up into it – the whole being the consistency of thick mint sauce – mostly solid. Maybe you can imagine it! With a bottle of wine – and a pickle. What an entrée – my mouth waters to think of it. Next a very small steak, but well flavored, with fresh string beans, lightly cooked. They surely tasted good – Then cucumbers and lettuce, *[word unclear]*, cream puffs and coffee. How does that sound for a meal? The portions were small -

Then to the symphony, where there was a very interesting program from Bach to Borodin – with Haydn, Mendelssohn, and Wagner in between. We t̶h̶e̶n̶ were joined there by a Herr Weigler, a man named Darlow (an Englishman – and it takes a long time to get used to him) and a man named Schaeffer – a Pole who had just arrived from the north of Italy – by small boat. He just barely speaks English – so we got along in a strange mixture of French, German, Italian and English. We spent the evening talking and r̶e̶a̶ drinking coffee of my making. I am not a good coffee maker – I made four cups – and then discovered there was enough in the grounds to make eight more. So I have coffee left over – (a little)

So it was late before I got to bed -

Then this morning on the way to breakfast, ~~we~~ I met Signor Turetti. I am going to his birthday party Tuesday (if I can) his giorno onomastico or Saint's Day – Saint Anthony. He is enthusiastic – expecting to be able to go to his home in Milan very soon. I hope he can.

That is the news to date – I am in an avid news hungry stage again – reading Stars & Stripes and listening to news broadcasts too often. I shall stop it – wait a week before I read any news – and then hear it all at once,

Love -

Henry

June 12

Dear mama -

Tomorrow is my day off. Presently, my mind is cluttered with thoughts – I am so conservative that it is most difficult to accept change in my surroundings. I say that with your letter in mind that Marian and Al[187] wanted to marry during his furlough. I rather believed they might and suppose it is to be accepted – and is acceptable and alright – I am inclined to think selfishly that I hate to be away when Marian marries – but that is certainly no reason against it. So I just wish more happiness than I can possibly mention.

I do not know Al at all – having met him just once.

I am well.

There is nothing of which to write. I intend in a few days to send a telegram just for fun – although the choice of things to say is very uninteresting.

I am so far away – or feel so now – that I must just go on thinking about myself, and ignoring most other things.

Bill is back – and I go to supper now with him.

Love -

Henry

June 13

Dear mama -

I just finished my day off – and feel as if I have been off a week – such a sense of accomplishment. Let's see if I can review what I did – it will sound like mostly eating.

First, I overslept this morning and did not get to breakfast until about a quarter after eight. A light breakfast. Then to the barber shop for a shave, and I let him put "tonic" on my hair – which is perfumed

---

[187] His sister Marian and Al Klein. They did marry and had two sons.

water. Then I began a quest for an extra key to the apartment, everyplace was out of the blank keys – and told me to despair. So I began going door to door and shop to shop up one street and down the next. I found a lot of sympathy and willing helpers – but no key – until I came to a stationer's shop – office supplies – and he said he would show me where – off we started on a dog trot, to the first shop I had tried – and when I saw our destination, I told him I had already tried there – and we went back to his shop, where he rummaged through his old keys and found one which he said would do as a blank – and trotted back to the first place, where they said they could make it. So I left the blank, came back to the apartment and got out the cigarettes for a purpose to be mentioned, and brought my key back and left it.

By this time it was almost noon and I went to see my music teacher. I always have a good time there. I am going back Friday night to practice – and can arrange for the soldier orderly to be there anytime I want to come. A package of cigarettes will grease the way – although I think he would stay at home without this inducement, I should rather overpay than accept so many favors.

After music lesson, to Turettis, where a crowd assembled to celebrate his giorno onomastico – and I gave him cigarettes saying "Augurii, augurii!" I think he will sell them – 5 packages, about three dollars to him. The crowd was the family (Signora, Signor & Porzia Turetti) Eugenio – a friend – Signor's brother (a shiny wretch) and his wife. The brother speaks English fairly (Brooklyn) but is very stupid, and the wife is hypochondriac Then an Italian officer on furlough and his wife – intelligent and nice. Then, at 1:30 sharp begins the celebration of St. Anthony's day, with food. An enormous soup dish of pasta – like noodles – in layers – with meat sauce – it alone would have been plenty – washed down with abundant, good wine. I soon learned to spread my fingers when I put them over the glass to indicate no more – otherwise you get your hand full of wine. Next a lettuce salad (oil and vinegar) with three charcoal broiled lamb chops – the best things I have tasted since I left home. Then two kinds of fish – fried red-snapper (small ones – I ate two) and octopus, which tastes like fried clams. I began to warn them that I have the longest belt in *[word scratched out]* – and it would soon be too short. No avail. More fish. Then cherries and cucumbers – which they eat as dessert– just sliced fresh – and they are good. They called them citroni – and I thought they would be citrus. Said I had never eaten them – and so was stuffed. Meanwhile wine and more wine. I was a little drunk, I think. Next cake and coffee. By this time it was four o'clock.

Conversation was vigorous all the while – having come to an ecclesiastical discussion of Protestants, and miracles. It seems the most inexcusable part of Protestantism is that the priests may marry – they are not married to the Virgin Mary and the church. I am in agreement with their point of view – but discussion raged – and Signor Turetti tried to act as my interpreter – but could not understand my English. He kept translating "customs" and "clothes, costumes," until I gave up and did my best in Italian. "Customs, habits" – all became tailored suits in his translations.

At 4:30 I left – and walked over and (to my surprise) got my key and a new one. It has been an expensive day in cigarettes. I gave one package to the man who gave me the blank key. I paid for the making in cash – but smoked a cigarette with the key maker for good will. I visited my wood carver – he will sell me another box if I will buy it. But I wait your opinion of the one.

Then back to the apartment – and walked to supper with Bill. I could not eat much, but began to feel my excess of wine creeping up on me, so we walked this evening to the end of town. A crowd of happy American soldiers had a tub of water and a cake of soap – they saw a dirty child and caught him – the child was screaming, but they gave him a bath. A crowd gathered – and all thought it was hilariously funny. When they were through, the bathed child went out and helped them catch the next – who likewise screamed, hollered, was bathed and helped with the next. On the way back, they had five clean children helping and were still going strong – the water cold – from the nearby fire plug.

I taught one child (or tried to) not to call me "Hey Joe!" but to say "If you please, sir," which he learned fairly well. He'll really surprise the next.

So I am well – and ready for bed. I send all my love.

Henry

June 14

Dear mama -

I wrote last night giving complete details of all I had done until that time – and now have nothing to add. Except that I am still well – and the weather is turning warmer and warmer. That won't go on forever.

I am told today that cable service was available and consider sending a cable – but have absolutely nothing to say. I am not sure that cable service is unlimited – maybe it is still a choice of certain selected messages. But even if it weren't – to say that I've been well – or any such thing – what's the use?

Mail just had not been arriving lately. So it becomes harder and harder to write – and I have less and less to say. Except a continuing, unsatisfied curiosity about what is going on and what developments there are at home. That is rather futile. One gets tired of wondering, and determines to forget it all and just wander around here for whatever interests can be found.

Not much yet. My wood carver had made another box – on his own initiative – and is not selling it – but, as he says, is offering it only to selected customers, because he is afraid to show it, lest someone come in and say it is worth only $1.00 and he must therefore sell it for $1.00. He wants (and is entitled to) more. Do you want it? Or Marian? or anyone else?

They now serve ice cream in the coffee shop – not very good, but unusual – and so I can eat it now and then.

You see, I am hard up for anything of which to write – I am particularly curious about Marian – what she is thinking and how she is and so forth. But it is just worrying to think of any such thing.

The nights are cool – which I appreciate – and time passes very slowly. But it passes. It gets dark so late that it is very difficult to get to bed before 10:30 or eleven.

Tonight I plan to bathe. We have gas from 7 to 9 AM and PM – and hence those are the bathing hours – with our gas geyser. That determines the times for baths.

Love

Henry

June 15

Dear mama -

I think of the last letter I wrote you – yesterday – and how little I have to add to it. But here goes my daily effort.

Last night I intended to go to bed early – and at about 7 started out for a walk – to return at eight and go to bed. But I met Herr Weigler, also walking, and spoke to him. Then I asked him to come to the apartment and he came – We talked until eleven o'clock, so I did not get to bed after all. The subject was pottery and faience – he used to be a painter of pottery and manufacturer . Says there is much fine pottery in other parts of Italy – and there really ought to be some here. So far I've not found any – although I do see peasant type vases and bowls which are pretty in a plain way. The best I have found so far I sent to Haymer – and I hope it has arrived safely – triumph of hope over experience because it was poorly packed. I dislike to have a heavy wooden box made for cheap pottery – but may have a rather large one made and then gradually fill it up. Most of the pottery I see is psychopathic – like fish plates and pottery soup ladles or moustache cups. But I let Herr Weigler know I was interested, and I think he may tell me about some if I find it.

I have under consideration beginning to take Italian lessons.

I have an appointment for Friday evening at the Maestro's to use his piano. I hope I am able to keep it – and shall arrange then to go another time – perhaps Monday.

The weather continues very lovely – although it is turning much warmer the nights remain cool. Apricots are coming into season, and night before last I bought a kilo – small, and not quite as ripe as I like them. I think they will improve as the season progresses. Cherries are still abundant – and so I feast on cherries and apricots – a good combination.

Mail has not been coming through at all here recently – that is true of everyone here. So I have received only about two letters in the past two weeks – but still look forward day by day to a big batch to catch up.

I am well. My news is so far behind times – maybe by this time you are in Maine – but I cannot appreciate it, because I think of letters as being recent.

The old town continues lovely – and I have to pinch myself now and then to open my eyes and see it – the intricate stone carving, into round windows and stone lattices – the round towers – the narrow streets and arches – the vast grey walls – the town itself in very somber colors – which emphasizes the brilliance of the sky and the sea and the trees outside the walls. The old castle is an enormous, intricate building, with ships-prow corner on one side – a moat, now a garden. It sounds (and looks) beautiful – but how it stinks!

All my love -

Henry

June 15

Dear mama -

I received a letter today from you – June 6 – which is good time, and indicates to me that mail is piled up and sorted from the top. I was very glad to hear that you are well – and that things go on quietly.

I also received a letter from the Gusdorfs, telling that Marian was married in New York. I suppose another letter telling me so is on the way – but I really knew it long ago, because I believed that she and Al would desire to marry when Al came home, and saw no sufficient reason against it.

So, being sure of the fact, I sent a cable this afternoon – or a radio – and am curious to know how long it takes to reach you.

It is difficult to keep going sometimes – except that there really is no choice from moment to moment – and one must have some interest or standard which does not change. Things keep changing around one – and one can never settle down to comfort and peace of mind – except for the moment.

I am well. I can appreciate (it so seems to me from your letter too) that you feel somewhat distraught and unsettled. I do too – and should like better than anything I can imagine to be home for a while. Maybe in six months or so I shall be – and the future seems to drag by so slowly.

I send all my love -

Henry

Now it is the next day – Last night I walked – and that is all. I am well. It is always a pleasure to see the church of St. Theresa – such lovely stone carving, that every time I look at it, it becomes more lovely. There is great solace and comfort in beautiful things – which soar so far above the dirty people swarming around them, and yet so related – like a halo on a saint, maybe.

I have been speculating recently on the corruption of the people here. They are like real estate dealers, and I really believe they do not know what honesty or integrity is. I have no specific examples, but think of the hotel operators and the crowd more or less in power – they, I believe, are just out to fleece everybody they can. I frequently wonder just how much cooperation they find among the Americans, for they are shrewd enough to pick out the people with whom they can deal.

Henry

June 16

Dear mama -

I write this evening thinking that I may not have time to write tomorrow – just why I may not I do not know. I feel constantly that I desire to urge you to take things easy, and not press so hard and to be more indifferent – but then I cannot, because you know how you want to go along, and can exercise choice without my urging.

So I'll see what factual I can write about. Not much.

This evening, I agreed to meet Bill in the lobby of the hotel – and then as I started walking there, I met daddy's friend, ~~Wal~~ Mr. Staley – and went to his apartment with him. We talked and drank a glass of brandy and walked to supper – it was 6:30 before we got there and Bill was not there. I assume he left. I ate with Staley – brother-in-law of Neill Wood. Then he was going to take an Italian lesson – and I left him. I went down to the old town and called on the wood carver – still a very pleasant little man, working very hard. Presently on chair and couch legs. He has made another box like mine – but omitting some of the details, as the vaulted inside of the lid.

Can you think of any carved pieces you would like? I can have them made well, I think, and inexpensive. I dislike bookends; have plenty of boxes, I think, and can think of nothing else. His specialty is plaques of St. Nicholas – quite beautiful – but still just plaques.

Then I walked to the Maestro's studio but they had someone else there and the evening was not convenient. Another time.

Then walked over town – bought cherries (8¢ a pound) and this poor paper. Home – where I write -

Sending all my love -

Henry

PS.

Daddy – what goes on in the office?

18 June

Dear mama -

I am much pleased to have an abundance of mail – three letters – this morning – I too am a mail hound, and wait for the deliveries. I have cabled my best wishes to Marian, sending through you, because I did not know where it would reach Marian.

I should like to give Marian some present – but of course do not know how to buy much other than junk here. I have an idea that a well carved silver chest might be interesting, and if I remembered the size and general design, and the fitting inside, I might be able to have quite a fine one made here. If you think the latest box I sent ~~is~~ (I mean the one without hinges) is good enough in design and workmanship to be worth giving the wood carver the job of making a box for silverware, would you like to make a mechanical drawing of a chest for silverware – showing the sizes necessary. Possibly I could then have one designed and made here – including inside fitting. Or that might not be interesting, I do not know. I think of the shapes of the ones in the Art Museum – and remember them as quite pleasing, and possibly lending themselves to carving rather than inlay – although my wood carver knows his trade well, and I think had good judgement in designs for carving. Inlay is the specialty of another part of Italy, and is highly commercialized. I do not like it. Once sent Janet a fair sample. Maybe she had showed it to you.

There is little opportunity here to get anything already made – pottery – some of the rude variety, rather pretty, but not fine. I wish Herr Weigler would help me find some – but his wife wants all he can find. However, if Ruth likes the type I have sent, I shall send more. It is not available in any quantities – 4 of a kind usually being the limit. I saw a woman working on some linen, but hardly know how to go about finding any. However, the search will continue.

I am well. Last night, I went to the symphony and enjoyed the concert. I met two men who had just come back here from north of Rome, and enjoyed talking to them about what was going on in Rome and other cities. I should like to go there – but for some reason have difficulty in making up my mind to get into a struggle and all the confusion of equivocation necessary. I could try a straightforward naive request – and I think it would be refused. Also, then if I tried to make a circuitous disintegral one, it would be transparent. So I'll see how opportunities go. All reports are that Rome is beautiful and interesting – St. Peter's, colosseum etc. It may remain on my list for after the war – someday. Meanwhile, I can have a very interesting time in this provincial town - which is completely magnificent to look at, too. I never get over the beauty of the old town – more lovely and exciting to me than the splendor of broad streets and formal statuary. But I like fine buildings, of which there are only a few here – the castle, the fortifications, the churches. The modern churches surpass my understanding. With the models of St. Nicholas and St. Theresa and other just a few blocks away, they build in the new town yellow brick or stone things just like suburban Chicago.

Well – you see I have no news.

I am well. I met Mr. Turetti on the street this morning – he is profuse in his avowals of friendship – and holds my hand, shaking it, while we labor through a conversation of mutual enjoyment of each other's company. I like him – he is a cordial and skillful host.

Mail is coming through again – and I enjoy it. The usual course is that the newest letters come first – then older ones, and then packages. I think I have some packages on the way.

All my love -

Henry

June 21

Dear mama -

I have been receiving delightful and splendid mail for which I am more than duly grateful – since it makes a high spot in any day. I started a letter this evening at the office – and covered fairly yesterday. So I shall continue that tomorrow – and meanwhile write of other things.

This evening two boys came to see me – one a boy named Fenn, who lives in Cambridge where his father is a Presbyterian minister at whose house I once had tea by some mistake. I met him here before – and remembered him then by his name – he was only about seven years old when I saw him.

He has the nice, naive manner so characteristic of minister's sons, for some reason.

He brings me the Harvard Alumni Bulletins, which I do not particularly enjoy, but I encouraged him to do so because I enjoy seeing him. He was in town for the day – and I suggested walks to him, and did what I could, which is always distressingly little. But I hope he comes again.

Major Coleman could hardly have been at the Chase Hotel in April – or does time pass that fast? Maybe. And how does Craig Clark happen to be calling? Clark is a sophisticate – Coleman a baby – what extremes!

We are now permitted to name places in Italy we have visited – but not places we have been stationed. So I'll give you some names. (Just some we may mention – so I can't tell you where I met the priest, who got $10.00 from me for the relief of the poor).

But Sorrento I may name – as among the loveliest of places I have even seen – with Vesuvius in the distance and the sea and all else. I did not have a chance to go to Capri. Naples used to be my favorite city.

That's all I've seen and may name -

I am well – and hope you too are so -

Love,

Henry

June 21

Dear mama -

A bright spot in my day – and I need a bright spot because I am very reproachful of myself today for being reticent and holding back and not going ahead full of initiative and doing what I feel like doing – and sticking so tight and worrying that so much is done wrong and I am helpless to do anything about it. But I'll get over it – the truth, I believe, is that I do not desire to do the things I should have to scramble to do – but I do not know whether I really don't want to or really don't want to do the politicking necessary to get to do them.

I rather enjoy some other things – as last evening, when I went to dinner (a mediocre dinner) at the Allied Officer's Club of which I have previously written, with a Russian lieutenant named Igor Gregoriev, and a Yugoslavian girl named Darya Klamaunsk – from the Island of Vis, which all say has such excellent wine. Travelers tales – which excite the imagination more than the seeing of the places, which are still only brick and stone and soil – ratiocinations [That is the heart of my self reproach – should I be galivanting [around more? gathering souvenirs of battles, as enemy rifles – when I had opportunity, I studiously avoided it – but when one gets to these base sections, all the world thinks a fox hole or slit trench the most exciting adventure in the world, and a German rifle or helmet, such as used to lie in heaps, a rare trophy – and he has not lived until he's visited battlefields. But particularly – to try to finagle a pass to Rome? Hard – and would be distressing. So far, reports are only of bars and women, the museums closed – but St. Peter's open. Can't get there and back in one day.

So I come to the bright spot in my day – the receipt of a package, with blue silk pajamas; a pound of coffee – in good order and time – will you write me directions for making boiled coffee? – and a splendid piece of sausage, which will afford me very great pleasure.

I am all confused mentally – and do not see much opportunity of getting straightened out – It delights me to speak a foreign language, and I find if I drink a little I can speak French quite fluently – because my thoughts must be simply to express them. So we spoke French last night, which is a musical language – the one the Russian, the Yugoslavian and I had somewhat in common.

Write often – your letters make many bright spots in days which are beginning to be dull. I must've let them. It is opportunity which makes dissatisfaction.

All my love -

Henry

June 21

Dear mama -

Now today is almost finished, and I have forgotten about yesterday, of which I intended to write. I walked just about all day. With music lesson, visiting the wood carver, and wandered around all day. A supply of fruit – which I enjoy enormously – beautiful fresh figs, apricots, peaches, cherries. One big round green thing – I had never seen the like – so I bought it. It is a cucumber!

Tonight – engaged to bring Dr. Guido to dinner. We'll see what comes of it. He seems to desire to be friendly, and one cannot know without trying whether he will just ask for a pair of shoes or be interesting. He seems a pleasant, somewhat bashful man – speaks English.

I am well – shall continue tomorrow.

Love -

Henry

June 22

We had dinner last night with Dr. Giordano. (Guido, as above named, is his first name, which they write last on their calling cards and all). Ate at the Allied Officer's Club, which serves interesting food – last night rice with tomato sauce, an egg patty or frittata of some kind with cheese and onions, beef ala mode with spinach and potatoes, and a peach tart. Coffee – wine. Then we returned to the apartment, and I ~~drank~~ made coffee, in which we perforce used cointreau (Sicilian) instead of sugar or/and cream. We talked – an economic discussion – in which the purchase of tangibles was discussed – it being agreed that it was now too late to purchase them – and we agreed that it was prudent now to hold lire because the value will probably increase.

Dr. Giordano is a resident of Rome – here for the present with his wife and small child, but his parents are still in Rome. He says if we go to Rome as we hope to do, but probably shall not, he would like to go along as a guide – to see his parents – and if he could get a permit to travel, it would indeed be an advantage for him as well as for us. But those things do not often occur.

I am well.

Tonight I have an appointment to go to my music teacher's. You see, life is just a round of entertainment – or sounds so – with long, boring days between. But they pass.

Last night I saw my wood carver again – He is working on frames for mirrors, for above two dressers – and they are going to be quite beauties. I wish I could think of some more carved objects to ask him to make for me. Am thinking of a box for nuts – such as is used here – in this general ~~des~~ pattern: *[drawing of a box]* with a mallet and block on which to cracks the nuts. But that amounts to very little. What else is there? Is a small mirror frame – say one foot or 18 inches on the outside worthwhile? I think not, because it is so much mirror and so little carving. And a carved plaque of St. Nicholas – I do not know – I consider it beautiful, but rather peculiar, and I don't know where it could possibly be placed.

I send my love -

Henry

June 23

Dear mama -

I received your letter about daddy's speech in Dallas – and am very happy to hear of the enthusiastic reception it received. I hope to receive a copy of the speech, if available. Maybe it is on its way now. I told W. G. Staley about it, who offers his congratulations and felicitations.

Last night, after supper (meals are getting rotten here – I am glad to have fresh fruit to help out – as it does, figs, peaches, apricots, and much else) I went down to Maestro Costa's studio and practiced. I enjoyed it very much, and stayed for about an hour and a half.

Then to Herr Weigler's apartment – where we had cookies (almond paste) and vermouth and talked. He showed me a series of pottery coins from Meissen, which were quite curious, and pictures of his pottery work – figurines and statuettes, ~~of~~ which I am not enthusiastic about – the kind is ridiculous to me. So, at about 10:30 home and to bed. We have a wise old mouse in the apartment ~~which~~ who has learned to get the bait from my trap without gnawing the string. I shall have to devise a way of fooling him. He is getting very fat on the bait. (sausage skin)

I have no news of which to write – time passes slowly; we are engaged to visit Doctor Giordano Sunday Evening – may be interesting. He does not speak English as well as he thinks he does – and his meaning is frequently problematical.

I am glad to learn you are sending nice packages, because I enjoy receiving them very much. I am looking, without success, for something to send home – may get some more pottery next Tuesday, or another box carved. I can't think of anything else to have a wood carver make. Maybe a different box. The pottery does not look very fine here, but might look better when it reached home.

Did Craig Clark ever reach you? Was he in St. Louis or calling from Omaha, where he now lives?

Write often – I send my love.

Henry

June 24 1944

Mrs. A. Lowenhaupt
6237 McPherson Ave.
Saint Louis
Missouri

Dear Janet -

You see the result of receiving fine long hand letters from you is that I write V-mail in reply – not that I desire to encourage you to do likewise, because I think such letters lack character and personality. Do you not think so?

I visited my wood carver last night, hoping to be able to get him to make me something else; but, alas, he complains that he is so busy making furniture that he cannot do it. Why are the furniture makers so busy? That has been the subject of diligent inquiry, and I conclude, from the advice of Dr. Giordano and the wood carver that the following factors enter in: 1) There are many people making money hand over fist in the sale of wine and souvenirs. They are making money so fast that they cannot believe it has any value they can get. 2) There are many marriages, since, after years of war, Italians are coming home and settling down. The new homes (heaven knows where they are) are to be furnished. 3) Considerable furniture has been lost or destroyed as a result of moving to the country or where not, or of enemy action – in other places, and has been replaced by relatives and friends, who now purchase new.

Or course, there is very great beauty in dressers, mirrors, tables and the like intricately xx *[sic]* carved by this skillful artisan – and I wish I could know how to get any such things home. But they are just too bulky. I have been flirting with the idea of having a piece of furniture made, as a coffee table or something similar, and sending it home in pieces, requiring only to be glued together there. Or a mirror frame in pieces, or possibly the carved parts of a cabinet – the fronts of drawers and a frame for the top. But hesitate, because probably it would be difficult to put it together after it got there. So I think I shall not. Any suggestions?

Tonight I am engaged to go to symphony – which should be quite a party, for we have a crowd coming – not only Lts. Little and Clark and myself, but Lt. Igor Gregorovitch (Russian lieutenants wear little stars, and he is always taken for a brigadier general when he leaves his hat lying someplace – I mean his hat is taken for a bg's) one Darya Klamaunsk, until recently of Lisa (Vis) a lady of culture who speaks English not at all, but if I have a few drinks I shall be able to do fairly well in French or Italian, a lady of a neighboring town, with her mother to act as chaperone (Customs! Customs! O tempora, o mores!) I do not know what the music will be.

Sunday night I am engaged to call on Dr. Giordano Guido, who desired to be friendly and whose friendship I desire to accept in every way possible. His home is in Rome, and I should love to be able to negotiate a pass and transportation to Rome for myself, and a permit to travel for him, and then go to Rome with him and let him put me up in his parents' house. But that is too good to transpire. Well, well, Roma may have to get along without my presence, although I am sure the Pope does not know what he is missing. And Cicero and Ceasar will turn over in their graves if it appears after these centuries of patient waiting in their graves preordination that they should walk where I was thereafter] to tread, that they were making footsteps in which I might tread, was merely meretricious. But they will have suffered perhaps even greater indignities and disappointments than my omission to walk over their graves and walking places.

My best regards. How is your mother?

Henry

June 24

Dear mama -

One problem solved. Yesterday evening I went to see my wood carver and asked him if he would be interested to design and execute another box for me – entirely different from the first. He said he was so busy he could not get at it – but maybe in a week or two – so I shall go back to see him in a few weeks. My trouble is I have no appreciation of the passage of time – weeks, months, days – all these shreds of the whole piece of Time I'm waiting to get out from under are the same. Then I had supper with Lts. Clark and Little – walked a while, and then drove to a neighboring town – lovely, lovely evening, with the olive trees taking a feathery, black texture; and bright flowers – stone walls of pink and grey – white towers – The road lined with high-wheeled carts – most of them with a sheep, a goat or a dog running along behind – and loaded with bright burdens – one with a brilliant orange cask – another with boxes of cherries and apricots. I cannot get over the high, magnificent color which is everywhere.

We are not supposed to eat fresh fruit. Nonsense, say I! fruit which is peeled is perfectly safe – and anyone should have enough sense to wash cherries and apricots and peaches and the like. They are not safe at home unwashed – and I do not see the difference. Lettuce seems to be considered alright at the mess – washed – and I think I can wash fruit as well as they can wash lettuce. But my favorites do not need washing – fresh figs (peeled – the skin has an extreme laxative effect, washed or unwashed) peaches . And I begin to see green almonds. Bravo! Apricots, which I do not particularly like, need washing. Cherries are about gone. Green apples come in. Oh! for an apple pie! I could make one if I had flour, sugar, shortening, cinnamon. In other words, I have apples.

The town itself – a fishing town – with great moles into the sea, and the basins filled with ships hung with nets – more color, and narrow cobbled streets crowded with children – a very intricate rose window of a church is a landmark of the town, and you see it from everywhere. Few soldiers in the town which makes it particularly lovely.

Symphony tonight – we expect Igor Gregoriev and Darya Klamaunsk and diverse others to join us – we shall have a crowd – and afterwards, if they will come up here, I shall give them coffee to drink, which others than Americans seem to prefer even to wine and liqueurs. I have a coffee pot – quite fancy – boil the water in one end – then turn the whole upside down – and the water drains through the coffee. Would be an improvement if you could reserve the process to put it through a second time – but the coffee turns out a spout if you try.

I send my love -

Henry

June 26

Dear mama -

I wrote a letter to Marian last night, but left it this morning on the table in the apartment. I shall mail it tonight or tomorrow. Meanwhile – write again – in that letter I had nothing of which to write except my plans for the future. In this – nothing further – except a few hours of those plans have become past – as the concert last night. It was while waiting for that that I wrote the letter to Marian. So since that time:

I heard a very excellent concert   with a crowd consisting of the following – Lts. Clark and Little and myself. A Lt. Wade – (who does not talk) Igor Gregoriev, (Lt. Stern came in, foolish ass, with a civilian employee of somebody – a janitor, I think, and while I am not snobbish, I just don't see the use) Signora Patrono– an old woman, wife of a Professor of Latin and Greek at the local university, with her daughter – Ilena; Darya Klamaunsk and that's all. Ilena is diplomé in music – but unfortunately all live so "provisoramente" that they have no piano where they live – about 10 miles out in the country – But she comes into town 3 times a week for English lessons – and in their town apartment they have a piano – so I am invited to play duets – ha! ha! Her father comes to town with her – and I look forward to meeting the Latin professor. I sent him a gift of a volume of Lucretius and one of St. Augustine – *De Civitate Dei.*

(There is a man here now named Dickerson, very likely a friend of daddy's – used to be with Thompson, Mitchell, Thompson & Young[188]– and Shell Oil Company in St. Louis. He is defense counsel in a case which I am to assist. (which means do all the work – not much –) This is an interlude.

After the concert, we (neglecting Lt. Stern & his friend) went to the apartment, intending to have coffee. I had made it in advance – but unfortunately the gas was off and I could not heat it. So we drank cold coffee – Then all left – I I accompanied the Patronos to their home about 10 miles away – talking steadily. It amazed me. If only I could be limited to Italian for about a week, I should be in good shape in the language. We talked about how beautiful Italy is, about food, wine and other similar subject. I find I can talk Italian fast and they understand it better if I repeat a word until I am ready for the next – thus my conversation is padded with "bene bene bene bene" and "molto molto molto molto" and "poco poco poco"

Thus it was eleven o'clock before I got to bed.

I am well – intend to ask about a vacation soon – and am gradually convincing myself that I need one.

I send my love -

Henry

June 27

Dear mama -

I did not write you yesterday, being quite tied up all day with a Major Dickerson – who is defense counsel (I being assistant) and he is inexperienced and is an incentive to try to do the work thoroughly – which makes it interesting. So yesterday was spent interviewing negro witnesses most of whom are so hopelessly stupid that I can't get a straight story from them. One of them tells a story – and then says –

---

[188] A St. Louis law firm.

"or I could tell it this way" – and tells an entirely different one. Which one is true? for they conflict completely – "Well, I just don't know."

So I have also visited psychiatrists *[sic]*. (Just noticed – I'm writing on the back page first – maybe I should visit more) But it doesn't help to have them tell you a man is a high grade moron. But one man they helped on more – and told me he might be crazy – so I was a witness yesterday, to the effect that there were reasonable grounds to doubt the sanity of the accused man – and the Court referred him to doctors for an opinion. That was fun – I love to be a witness – but it is very difficult not to argue. That daddy knows – because as a witness he behaves terribly – arguing and asking his own questions. But I hid behind "privilege" on cross examination and refused to tell about specific instances and statements that the accused made to me. That is fun too. Confuse 'em, I say!

So today I have to do about the same thing – but I am all mixed up and confused because all the witnesses – negroes – are so dumb and look just alike and are named similar names – Smith, Jones, Bradley, Vaughn, and so forth – I can't keep them straight. Then too they all have inferior motives and are afraid they might disclose ~~pee~~ their own sins – I think they don't have any idea of truth, and have no ability whatsoever to distinguish between what they saw and what somebody told them they saw. I wish there were a more learned court. But that is beyond control.

I am well. Look forward to receipt of packages – but figs are coals to Newcastle – as are almonds. (Fresh green almonds on the market again – my favorite food) I missed my day off this week – but shall take a few hours off Thursday – Played the piano for an hour and a half last night – the most pleasant thing I do. It costs me cigarettes to the Orderly of the Captain. Also sailed for about an hour – childish paddling. But I sailed -

All my love

Henry

June 28

Dear mama -

I haven't written for a few days, but have received and enjoyed mail. And there is nothing new of which to write. Monday night I practiced piano at the Maestro's studio, and enjoyed it as I always do. Tuesday – yesterday – I had to work, and so did not get either my holiday or my music lesson. I doubt that I shall be able to make it up.

Then last night on the way home I bought a pound of peaches (small and hard – not particularly good) a pound of sickle pears – excellent! – and a pound of apricots, fair. I intend to get some figs tonight. The things in greatest abundance here are almonds and figs.

Oh yes – Monday night I also went for a sailboat ride – sailing out into the sea, and back again. There was very little wind, and we therefore went very slowly.

For daddy, I'll write about a trial. ~~A~~ I ~~poor~~ had a good time of it – confusing things and getting the prosecution excited very successfully. A man was accused of (1) discharging a pistol on April 20, (2) of threatening to shoot a man on May 20 and of going to sleep on guard post on June 5. a poor, ignorant negro – but all the witnesses were against him. The charge of ~~Ma~~ April 20 was dropped as of no consequence. Then the accused took the stand (he had to, because everything was so thoroughly proved he couldn't hurt himself) So I asked him when he was arrested, and he said April 20, and everybody except him and me thought he meant May 20. But he repeated it twice, and still no one seemed to notice or care and the matter wasn't mentioned again until argument, when I remarked that it was obvious that a man under arrest could not be placed on guard (sound? I don't know) Then the Court and TJA all jumped up and hollered that he had said May 20, but the reporter read April 20 and the TJA got mad and began hollering, and they let him reopen the case and present contradictory evidence – hearsay, I think, because he was not prepared on the point. But the Court was disturbed too, although I had asked the question 3 times and got the same answer, which wasn't then contradicted. An interesting commentary, I think, on how closely courts listen to evidence. So they convicted him – I suppose should have, but still doubt several points of criminal law – as a charge of "attempting to strike" – which I believe should be "assault" – and under the provision making "assault" a crime. It was under the provision making "all other disorders" a crime – which it seems to me can be sustained only if "attempting to strike" is not "assault" – that is, if there is a crime like, but less than, assault. I don't know – there are no books available here. The question is now academic.

They ought to get rid of me as defense counsel – I enjoy the technicalities too much – and to that end am uncooperative. Maybe a shyster. It doesn't do any good – but what else can you do without witnesses?

I am well – I send my love.

Henry

June 28

Dear mama -

Here it is almost the end of the month again – and I can't say I'm sorry, because the more time passes the less remains. I am well – did not write yesterday because I was occupied all day and tired in the evening. Now however it is morning – and there is little about which to write. Monday night I went to Maestro Costa's studio and practiced the same things – Czerny Mozart , Beethoven and Chopin – and gave the orderly a package of cigarettes for which he thanked me. I enjoyed the evening very much – the room is so very lovely, and the piano is exceptionally fine.

I told you that green almonds were in season – and day before yesterday I bought a kilo. They are about gone now. Then yesterday on the way back I got a pound (demi kilo) of peaches, a pound of pears, a pound of apricots. So you can infer that fruit is very abundant right now – and I enjoyed it to the utmost. Peaches are not very good, being small and hard, but the pears and apricots are the best I have ever eaten.

Now it is the next day. Last night I went to the studio of Maestro Costa for about an hour and a half. This time I gave the orderly a cigar, and he seemed well pleased. Played my usual Czerny, Mozart, Beethoven and Chopin and enjoyed it. Then I took a walk. It has been very warm here – no warmer than it is there, I am sure, and always during the day a pleasant breeze. But usually for about an hour in thee evening, just after sunset, it is quite hot and without breeze

Then today I expect to go to the house of Patrono, and see the Doctor, Professor of Latin and Greek at the University of_____ and where the daughter, diplomee in music, says I may use their piano. She comes into town on Tuesday, Thursday and Saturday with her father to take a lesson in English. So far all she can say is Good Night, Good morning, and similar phrases. In other words I speak Italian better than she speaks English. But that will not last long.

Now I must go to breakfast.

June 30

So yesterday noon I did go to see Dr. Patrono – and he is delightfully hospitable – gave me his own work a pamphlet about the mistakes of history of art of a Byzantine chronicler – extremely full of foot notes. I shall glance through it. Then played the piano with the daughter, who is an excellent pianist – but her duets were baby pieces – like melody from Aida – and left soon.

Then last night, after supper with Bill and Robert I went to a movie – rotten, and I shan't mention it further. Afterwards, it being still early, we went to see Dr. Giordano – he was not at home, but expected in 15 minutes – and we walked to the public square. Like an Arab town – enormously picturesque – the square with palms and thronged with people talking and walking – the streets, lined with low white buildings – here and there a tower – very dusty, and naked children running about everywhere. I desire a picture of some of these streets – they would be unbelievable if I were not used to them.

Then we walked back – and as we neared Giordano's house, a lady came up to us, and asked, in stuttering but enthusiastic English if we were looking for Dr. Giordano because he was expecting us – and had been so disappointed when we hadn't come Sunday night. She was Mrs. Giordano -

And I shall continue about the visit in a later letter -

Breakfast time

Henry

June 30

Dear mama -

My last letter ended with a̶ ̶u̶ my having left Signora Giordano on the dusty street, with an agreement to be back at her house in 15 minutes to visit, by which time her husband, Dr. Giordano, would be there. So we returned – and went in, had a cup of coffee, and visited. According to my notion they are very fine people. The baby – about 2 years old – was, unfortunately, teething, and so cross, and would not stay with his nurse without crying and hollering. The fellow speaks Italian. You say to him. "Come stai[189]?" and he lisps "Bene." Mrs. Giordano is a Romanian by birth – speaks English well, as does Dr. Giordano – a professional pianist, but living "provisionally" without a piano. We sat on a terrace, above the palms, olives, almonds – overlooking extensive groves of fruit and nut trees – the road concealed, and it got dark and the moon rose. I have not, for a long time, spent a more pleasant evening.

Here are the plans now brewing: Dr. Giordano desires to go to Rome, where he has a house, and parents. He has no transportation. He can possibly get permission to travel. Lt. Little can get transportation. We could go to Rome, if there were a place to stay – but there are just 3 rooms available for this whole headquarters, so each person is limited to 3 nights. So – we shall try to resolve the ifs one at a time – 1. Permission to go to Rome for a week; 2) Permission for Dr. Giordano to travel. Then we shall stay at his house. The ifs look numerous. He is anxious – it would give him a chance to see his family. I hope it works.

---

[189] Translates to "How are you?"

It is very hot here – sweltering during the days – except in the shade, of which there is little, it is somewhat cooler. I am well. I do not know how a drive to Rome would be – the roads probably crowded and dusty, and one must follow main roads, for elsewhere all bridges are out. The main roads have temporary bridges. Slow truck convoys, and so forth. I still think driving is preferable to flying.

No news of which to write. Maybe I shall have some soon.

I send my love -

Henry

July 1

Dear mama -

I have a few little details to add to yesterday's letter about visiting Dr. Giordano – as a commentary on the maid problem, which must be terrible – a girl of about 18 is the maid – she brings in the coffee – and as she puts it down asks me for a cigarette, please. I ignored the request. What does Emily Post say you should do under the circumstances?

Weather is warm – we are proceeding with plans to go to Rome – with Dr. Giordano – and so far have not hit a snag – but have hardly begun. Dr. Giordano still needs permission to be obtained from Allied Military Government. Dates must be specified etc.

Last night I ~~was~~ got my hair cut – the barber offered me an Italian pistol for sale – they are souvenirs in great demand – but I do not want one – I shall help him seek a purchaser. His asking price is expensive – $80.$\underline{^{00}}$. But I should not be interested at 1/10th the price.

I am well – quiet without news of any kind.

I send my love

Henry

July 2

Dear mama -

I suppose I'd better try to write a long letter, because, beginning very soon, I expect there will be a period of about a week when I shall not write at all.

Deeds: nothing new. I went to the symphony last night and heard a fair concert. After symphony, it being a cool, fresh moonlit night – full summer – I walked for about an hour. Then to bed.

It is quite hot here, and all say it will be hotter – but I do not need salt, because it is easily available here – salty bacon for breakfast, and I eat a good deal of salt with meals.

I have written of my plans to go to Rome – and they proceed apace. I cannot write the details of what may or may not be done – because I may plan a few things I cannot or ought not execute. Presently intend to leave Tuesday, 4 July – and from there on, all is a mystery.

My health leaves nothing to be desired. I seem to thrive on hot weather – and when it comes to the cool part of the evening feel refreshed and cool. Also the cool part of the morning – although as soon as the sun rises, it beats down with an intense heat such as I do not remember having felt. However, the air stays cool – I suppose from the sea.

Last night I bought myself a small knife – and had a visit with the shopkeeper, who returned to civilian life from the Russian front at the end of 1942. He says he is a great admirer of the Russians, who did so well at hiding their bread, that they always had bread, although it was black.

I bought a pound of apricots last night – the best and sweetest I have ever eaten – juicy and moist – quite a different fruit from the usual mealy apricot. Now I am watching for good peaches. The figs are also very good – the natives have taught me how to eat them. It is the peeling, they say, and experience confirms this, which has a laxative effect. And if they are peeled thick – taking off a great deal of the pulp and eating principally the seeds, they are fine. Something like pomegranates, except syrupy and soft. The big green or white figs are now about my favorite fruit. Now, also, green almonds in great abundance. They tell me these are hard to digest, but I have not found them so.

I wish I had more of which to write.

This evening, I intend to go to see Dr. Prof. Patrono– with the goatee . I am not yet prepared to discuss his book on the solecisms of history of Byzantine Art. I—, what a book! (I find myself tempted to swear – that's what the blank represents) But I must try again to read my autographed copy.

Mail has not reached me for three days now. I expect a batch today or tomorrow. Shall write again when I can – which I say may be a week off.

Love

Henry

July 3

Dear mama -

I had a very delightful time last night – first visiting the Giordanos. Dr. Giordano cannot go with us to Rome because he cannot get a pass – at least not in time. He is conservative and doesn't want to take a chance on being caught without a pass and shipped back – as he might be – as a prisoner of war. But we are told to stay at his house with his parents – and intend to try. Shall bring an introduction and possibly some foodstuffs. True[?] all say that oil is worth $14.00 a quart in Rome – $1.50 here.

We are to go back there this evening. Only Mrs. Giordano was at home and Frank – a cute baby who insists he does not want to go home with us and be our little boy – wonderful! I think he understood the question.

I also saw the Turettis – out of abundance of caution – his brother is in Rome, and I shall tell him that his wife, brother and so forth are well – he too had a place to stay.

Then we visited the Patrono's and were overwhelmed by their very cordial hospitality – with wine, apricots, figs, plums and so forth. Mrs. Patrono wants us to see her grandson – a boy of 2 years – whom she hasn't seen or heard of since he was 20 days old. So I shall report that he resembles his aunt or his grandfather or somebody. They have us a present of oil to deliver to the son – a doctor of medicine – and he too has a place to stay– And the brother of the Doctor has a daughter who has a place to stay – we have her address.

So I think we are very well fixed – with good security. Maybe shall look first for a hotel, but failing that, shall have plenty to fall back on. Doctor Patrono would like to show me around Rome – and I wish he could – he is a scholar of antiquities – and maybe at a later phase travel will be freer. He knows, he says,

Dr. Hedsitz[190], your uncle, from the time he taught in Rome – and brought up his name in connection with Philadelphia, where Lt. Little lives. I told him he was my uncle, – limitation of vocabulary! – and we are now fast friends.

So I expect much pleasure – starting tomorrow morning – a long drive and I propose to start early -

Love

Henry

July 3

Dear Ruth -

I am sending this letter home, since I think you may be in Maine – I received a letter from you and am still enjoying reading it.

What plans I have! But I shall not write about them because everything future is provisional. And if one commits oneself too definitely to plans, there may be the disappointment. So I had better call it hopes instead of plans – and arrangements are made as securely as I can make them.

Last night I visited – first to see the Turettis – who fed me fried cucumbers and apricots. I have a reputation for liking to eat, and I can't go anyplace but that they feed me. I am anxious to see these people – then if I get to the city, and find their relatives, I shall be able to tell about them.

Then, after dinner, to see Dr. Giordano for the same purpose. Mrs. Giordano was at home – a Romanian by birth, and a very charming lady – a pretty little boy – 2 years old – kept clean and polished and combed. He lisps beautifully – and it amazes me that I can ask him how he is, and he says, "bene," and if he wants to come to America with me and be my little boy, and he says "Non – resto con mama." Then he shakes hands and says "Ciao," which is a slang "good-bye." Her parents are in the city – living "provisoramente," having been bombed out of their apartment. His family lives in a house which, he says, has lots of room. So we shall possibly tell the family about the baby.

Then to see Professor Doctor Patrono – a teacher of Latin, who now resides in a village a few miles away. There we had wine, apricots, figs, plums and conversation. The old man, of course, speaks French – but I now get all mixed up between French and Italian.

A magnificent drive to the town – the H roads thronged with religious processions (celebrating the end of June, which seems to be a month connected to the Virgin). All the shrines were covered with flowers – bedspreads of lace, silk and what not hanging from all windows, to make color, the shrines illuminated (on the way back, after dark) with candles. The roads were solid with people, singing, walking, generally celebrating – and all dressed up. In the towns, you could hardly get through the streets and squares.

Doctor Patrono is an interesting old man – goatee and all. His son lives in Rome – and we shall visit him – tell him about his father – and have promised, when we come back, to tell Mrs. Patrono about her grandson – a child two years old whom she hasn't seen since he was 20 days old. She hasn't heard from them for about a year.

---

[190] No idea who this is.

So I expect to have a good time in the city – the visiting will take some time but I enjoy it, and desire the security, because we have no very definite place to stay. Patrono is a doctor of medicine – teaching in some Polyclinial Institute[191]. I do not know what Giordano's parents do.

Thus I have written anyway more of my <u>plans</u> than I intended.

I stopped to see my wood carver – he does not want to make another box, but says, if he gets time, he will draw another design for me. I hope he does.

Love -

Henry

P.S. Barney Barenholtz just called – will visit this afternoon -

H

July 5

Mrs. A. Lowenhaupt
6237 McPherson Ave
Saint Louis
Mo

Dear mama -

Here I am in a city with five days[192]– and having the best time of my life – without having started sightseeing yet – but intend to begin tomorrow – Today was going to see people – who are fun – and a boy (Roberto Giordano) who is having the time of his life as our guide

Am staying in a fine apartment – in the lap of luxury – in the world's most magnificent city – Am "well" – will not write much for a while -

Henry

---

[191] Policlinico Umberto I is a university hospital located in Rome. It's a highly specialized hospital and the largest in Europe. Several specialty outpatient clinics and more than 1200 impatient beds provide state-of-the-art patient care.
[192] Rome on July 5, 1944. Rome was liberated by the allies on June 5, one month earlier. Here is an excerpt from the National World War II Museum:
June 2 With Allied forces nearing Rome, Pope Pius XII declares over the radio that "Whosoever raises his hand against Rome will be guilty of matricide before the civilized world and the eternal judgment of God."
June 5 Following the German evacuation of the city, Allied troops, under the command of General Mark Clark, enter Rome in the afternoon, liberating the ancient city. It is the first capital of the Axis Powers to fall. Thousands cheer Clark's men and shower them with flowers. Addressing a crowd of some 100,000 people, Pope Pius XII thanks the Germans and the Allies for their restraint and calls for the populace to not seek vengeance.

July 5

Dear mama -

Without intending to finish this letter – I shall nevertheless begin it.

We arrived in Rome last night, and after much inquiry came to Via Taro[193] – where we stopped to see Signora Giordano. No one at home. Then down to Corso Trieste[194], where we looked for Signor Gallo – son-in-law of Signora Giordano. No one at home. We went to dinner, then, being very hungry, since we had missed lunch, Bill and I taking turns, since one had to watch the car.

What a magnificent street to walk on! An avenue of trees, fine buildings – an ancient wall at the top, a square with a fountain at the bottom. People well dressed and clean – I've seen nothing like it since New York, and compared to this New York is flat and dull.

Then back to Via Taro – Signora not yet home – and down to Via Trieste – There we met Signora Gallo – and told her our purpose – that we had come from her brother's with his greetings, and so forth, and sought a place to stay. She suggested her mother's and we said "yes, yes!"

So after a while we came back and found the old lady making beds for us.

What an apartment! But I won't describe it – These Romans (rich) live like kings!

And then to bed.

This morning, then, we went into town, having slept late, and to the Colosseum – where we wandered around for a few hours. We walked around town – the shops look so very modern and magnificent – that I keep thinking of the song – "Oh, Uncle John, since I've been to Boston - - life on the farm's too dull for me[195]!"

At two o'clock, we picked up Roberto, grandson of our hostess – who I think is having the glory of his career – and he showed us our way around town to see the various people we were asked to see – Dr. Patrono – living in a magnificent penthouse – to a family of six who having been bombed out, live in one small, confused room. Wine and cognac at each place – and we are to have dinner with Dr. Patrono (now it is July 6) this noon. (Roberto comes along)

Of course, I cannot describe the beauty of this city – it almost knocks me over – the fountains, trees, buildings, squares – the Palace of Justice, the ruins – all of it – you'll just have to get a series of 50 views 50 of Rome – It is unquestionably the most beautiful city I have ever seen.

---

[193] Via Taro, Rome, Italy
Via GoogleMaps
https://www.google.com/maps/place/Via+Taro,+00199+Roma+RM,+Italy/@41.9205381,12.5039233,17z/data=!4m5!3m4!1s0x1
32f6115205d3fe5:0xed45dacebcf72a7b!8m2!3d41.922474!4d12.5058545
[194] Corso Trieste, Rome, Italy
Via GoogleMaps
https://www.google.com/maps/place/Corso+Trieste,+Roma+RM,+Italy/@41.9204435,12.5072347,17z/data=!3m1!4b1!4m5!3m4
!1s0x132f616c76f8f69f:0x50125c8071414df5!8m2!3d41.9204395!4d12.5094234
[195] *Oh! Uncle John*
Via New York Public Library
https://digitalcollections.nypl.org/items/510d47de-1619-a3d9-e040-e00a18064a99

This morning – the Vatican City – where I may try to find Dr. Kuttner's brother – why not? But I didn't -

Henry

July 8

I am still completely amazed at the magnificence of this city – the newness & the brilliance – and can't describe it. Yesterday I spent walking (Bill drove to the front to see ~~ase~~ former unit – is not back yet) wandering through Piazza de Spagua and Piazza de Venetzia and around the Coliseum and everyplace else. ~~The~~ I have not had so much pleasure within my memory. Rome is whole – and very wonderful. Today I intend to shop for souvenirs -

Henry

July 7

Dear mama -

Here am I still – and having walking my feet off sit down for a while and write. I cannot pretend to describe the city – not ever attempt to. It has everything – modern, clean, beautiful beyond any possible description. Shops filled with modern merchandise.

I intended to buy something – but have concluded not to – looked first for linen – and found some so very fine that I can't look at anything else. But the prices range from \$350.$\frac{00}{}$ to \$750.$\frac{00}{}$ and - - - - -

Pottery in abundance – and I may get some -

But among my pleasures has been – 1) strings, for stringed instruments, which do not exist in my city – so I am bringing a few back for some people there – and cloth by the yard, which is expensive and of poor quality – but I'm still bringing about eight yards back, because it is better than nothing – and it seems a shame not to increase values when it can be done so easily.

So coming up here – oil was worth \$1.50 a quart. Here it is worth about \$18.00 a quart. We brought as presents about 20 quarts. Salt there is cheap. Here, about \$3.00 a kilo – \$1.50 a pound. So about 10 kilos of salt. I think that is interesting.

What a setup there is here! Red Cross Palaces – hotels for rest camps – parks – palaces. It completely staggers the imagination. And people on the streets look clean and well dressed. I've never seen anything like it. It makes even New York seem dull and lifeless, as I remember it.

Add to that, that we are receiving royal treatment – dinner with Dr. Patrono (dr. of medicine) room with Signora Giordano, whose husband has fled to Milan - - but I'm not interested in politics – if there are any politics involved.

Love -

Henry

July 9

I am still having a very good time – walking the streets and all else -

Last evening I saw Signor Turetti's brother – not quite a gentleman – and I let myself be imposed upon, although not seriously, agreeing to carry a few things back to his wife. He gives me an enormous package – funny – a big empty can (hint to send him olive oil if she can) and three pairs of shoes. I told him the risk of theft was his – and may leave them in the car for a few minutes. They will be stolen if I do.

But on the other hand, I should kind of like to bring them – I like the Turettis and there will be at least a dinner in it for me – as well as this – He has a room here in town, and I shall be enabled to send anyone to stay there, who will bring a few quarts of oil or a few nuts – The room is alright, and he will take anyone in. There are a number of men whom I should like to help who have asked me to try to find if they could get a place to stay in Rome. Well, by conveying the can, I shall be able to do it.

Then there is also an Italian soldier who wants a ride back – son of farmers – both parents died recently, and he wants to see his sisters and brothers. Maybe it is an opportunity – maybe just a burden, and maybe I am being lied to unconscionably. I really don't mind – he can be crowded into the back seat with the oil cans.

Signor Turetti's brother gave me a bottle of good wine – to bring along.

Yesterday I bought a little inexpensive pottery. I left it in the car. It was stolen. The loss is not great, and I am resolved not to be concerned about these things.

July 10

Yesterday drove up to an old unit – and secretly am thankful I'm not still there, although of course upon a visit everyone is so friendly that one enjoys it. Major Morris came back with us (and two other officers) and I shall see much of them today – my last in the City. Dinner last night at Hotel Excelsior – turned into an officer's rest camp – and very elaborate and good food.

This city is so very beautiful! I cannot possibly write about it.

18 July

I find I forgot to mail this letter – and therefore do so now -

Henry

July 12

Dear mama -

"Oh, uncle John, since I've been to Boston, oh, uncle John, since I've been to town, Life on the farm's too dull for me."

So you see I've been to Rome – and I cannot pretend to describe the magnificence of it – St. Peter's and the Vatican and new city. No merchandise for sale – and Romans were hungry – but clean and well dressed. We stayed with Signora Giordano, 35 Via Taro[196] – and enjoyed hospitality of a little circle of people with relatives in this city. Son Roberto guided us.

What a city! Like New York – but more magnificent, if possible. Of course, museums and so forth are closed, but fountains, streets, parks, all things. And modern! But I said I can't describe the delights of the place – and I can't.

We drove – and it is an interesting drive – through much country where reconstruction has already begun – women rebuilding the bridges. On the way back – in the midst of a ruined town (and I tell you this because I expect someone to come in and hit me in the jaw someday) we got a flat tire – Brought it to a civilian in the neighborhood who looked and found the innertube torn to shreds. No tire available. So Clark hitchhiked on to see what he could find – and I just tried honest methods – trying to trade a tire obviously no good for a spare tire – urging them they could salvage the old. no luck. "A bird in the hand is worth two etc." So, after about an hour or more, Lt. Clark not having returned and being pessimistic about his chances, I had the tire put back together, the innertube shreds stuffed inside, and the valve sticking through. The next jeep stop, I told the driver that I had gone for a walk and upon returning, found the tire flat – a nail – and I showed him a nail – that it could doubtless be repaired – and if we could borrow his spare tire, which was quite worn, he could have this one repaired. I gave him (such is conscience still) my true name and address, but I think he does not remember it. He traded – and there was a crowd of about 30 Italians around to do the changing so that he did not get near the tire – and about 10 more children asking for candy, so he left us promptly as he could – and I followed on, until I picked up Bill. So I reflect that necessity be stronger than my integrity.

Returned last night – and this morning found a package (sausage and pajamas) – which I shall put to good use.

My trip to Rome did me much good – and I find myself now with new enthusiasms and desires (to return to Rome, that is) I hope you are enjoying Maine. I was unable to buy anything in Rome – and the few trinkets and gadgets I did get (one interesting book among them) were stolen from the vehicle.

People are hungry in Rome, I think. The olive oil we carried was accepted as a godsend. A few tomato vendors – mobbed – and their tomatoes gone very early.

All my love,

Henry

P.S. You see, now, food is the most valuable thing to send. I shall request some in my next letter. Coffee – infinite value -

---

[196] 35 Via Taro, Rome, Italy
Via GoogleMaps
https://www.google.com/maps/@41.9218146,12.507043,3a,75y,38.42h,95.77t/data=!3m6!1e1!3m4!1smocAkLLAAr-5FNw97MDE8A!2e0!7i16384!8i8192

July 14

Dear mama -

Beautiful cool weather here – after a rainy day – and I do not know whether to address you in Maine or at home. I received a package of pajamas and sausage – in good shape – and now am well supplied with pajamas – Sausage is a wonderful thing to have – I intend to save about half to send to Mrs. Giordano in Rome when I find someone going to Rome. Meanwhile I hope to receive coffee, of which I believe I have some on the way.

I am now out of coffee. I therefore request some, if it is ~~on the way~~ available. Coffee is quite unavailable (legitimately) here. So also sugar.

When we went to Rome we brought 4 pounds of salt. It's amazing what enthusiasm it caused. Apparently salt in Rome, if available at all, is worth about four dollars a pound or kilo. Here it is not expensive, for small boats go to Sicily for it. Still – about 75¢ a pound for fine table salt. The natives, however, stand sea water out in the sun in flat pans, and make a coarse but usable salt.

I saw my cabinet maker last night. He is making more boxes - of which I shall get one, if they are nice. An entirely different design, and I don't think they will be as fine as the first – which he considered his masterpiece. He saved labor on his second – for another man – by not carving out the inside of the lid. Makes it, to my judgment, inferior. I broached the subject of mirror frames – but he has too much work to do. I should like to get a good frame – possibly for Marian, but if I insist and rush him, I am afraid it will not be good. So I shall wait.

This town seems to me to be opening up somewhat. But I have not been into any of the shops recently. Enterprising people could still do a great deal – as by trading with Sicily – a few days journey by sailboat, and I understand from travelers that Sicily is now flourishing. I believe natives could even trade with the north of Italy, and no one would stop them – but of course I don't know. Illegitimate trading – as if they should bring the allied military currency or United States money – as gold seal bills – I have an idea they could do very well.

Lt. Little intends to go to Rome about the first of August. I hope I have some coffee or something to send by that time.

I am well. Write often (I have no doubt you do.) I send all my love -

Henry

I wrote to Ben yesterday. It is awfully hard to write, but if he answers, it will be easier.

I suppose I am too sentimental with Italian natives. Maybe I ought to try to kick them around – but it would be so much less interesting.

In Rome, I bought a few yards of material – rather flimsy – but intend to give it to Mrs. Giordano and Mrs. Patrono– who may need it.

H

July 15

Dear mama -

No news of which to write – except last night I drove out to see Prof. Dr. Patrono, and give him the news of his son in Rome – and tell Mrs. Patrono of her grandson who calls all men in uniform "Ja, Ja!" I think it's funny – and his parents have sense enough to treat it as a joke – it can't be concealed, but tells quite a story. We had one dinner at Dr. Patrono's house. At the Professor's last night (after a beautiful evening drive through groves of almonds, olives, figs and vineyards [– with old stone walls – flat country and lovely) I was stuffed with delicious fresh figs (they call them ficaroni – a large, early fig, green, white or purple) apricots and plums. How I enjoy this fresh fruit! Maddaline Patrono is learning English – my Italian progresses – and all goes well. They have a maid – and the tradition seems to be that she stays in the room with the company, listening intently, and jumping and running for wine and apricots – extremely disconcerting if you're not used to it. Like a footman, I suppose, waiting for orders. The Giordano's maid asks for cigarettes now and then.

Which reminds me of a few things to ask for. Please send me some flints for cigarette lighter – the more the merrier – some soap – (having given four bars to Signora Giordano in Rome I am almost out) and any food available (except raisins, almonds, figs and dates)

Listing things nice to receive – it always comes down to food. I now have ample clothing.

While I was in Rome, a directive came saying that people were urgently needed to negotiate and draw agreements for termination of contracts, and all qualified and desirous should submit their names before a certain date – prior to my expected return. A man here submitted my name, believing that I should like it done. I approve, of course. That work would be in Washington, which is a reason for not wanting it, because this is much more interesting and pleasant than Washington could be. But, of course, "urgently needed" and so forth doesn't mean anything, as all things are urgent in the beginning and once begin drag on interminably. So I really expect never to hear from it, and do not care. The enormous advantage of its going through, would be that I should get home for a few days. The disadvantages – that I should be stuck in Washington or some similar place. But it is awfully nice not to have to decide – not to be able, even, to make an effective decision. But how brilliant New York would look.

I had a letter from Mme. Peyrus, acknowledging receipt of a pen for Jacques. I think she cannot write to the United States. My letters to her require French stamps, which are of course unavailable.

I shall go to symphony tonight.

Love -

Henry

July 16

Dear mama -

I heard a good concert last night – including a Mozart's *Jupiter* which particularly pleases me. Signora and Maddaline Patrono were with us – and after the concert, came to the apartment where we ate some beautiful, ripe peaches and large plums and drank canned grapefruit juice. There is now a piano in the apartment, and I have a volume of Mozart and one of Beethoven.

Signora Patrono was all perturbed – there are two girls in town – sisters – she says, whose father died about three months ago. They were friends of theirs, and the mother is stupid. They are no longer friends and won't speak to ~~as~~ the girls, who have become very bad, and go out without their mother and gamble and drink and smoke, and play cards for thousands of lire. She saw them as she was coming in, and is afraid they would come to see us and tell us they were friends of the Patronos. So I assured her we should not accept their statement to that effect. They are the daughters of an Italian colonel, and from her description sounded like wild ladies of Louis XIV's court.

The best peaches I have ever tasted – soft and juicy – you need a spoon to eat them – and sweet and rich in flavor. And plums. Fresh figs, however, remain my particular delight.

I gave Signora Patrono a few yards of cloth which I got in Rome – not of particularly good quality, but there is none at all here. It was not worth sending home – a material they called Bemberg or Bamberg or something like that, which is more like rayon than anything else. I also have a few yards of a cotton print which is not worth sending home – I shall give it away too. In Rome it was $1.00 a meter . Here it is worth (if one desired to sell it) about $20 a meter, because there is none available.

I am well. The weather is magnificent. I expect to see my wood carver Tuesday, he is now too busy to be worth much – but maybe not permanently spoiled. I shall also seek more pottery similar to that I sent Haymer. I consider it rather mediocre.

Tonight – a buffet supper instead of usual style – which is a change at any rate.

I send my love -

Henry

July 17

Dear mama -

This is very poor paper – I shall have to finish it up. And that is hard with so little to say.

Last night there was a buffet supper command performance, in honor of the General, at $2.00. So I went. Unfortunately, the food was very tasteless and poor. So I finished up in the apartment with some of my particularly good peaches and plums. Also I was not bad off, for dinner was not until 7:30. I took advantage of the extra time to go over to the Turreti's – to bring them some things sent down from Rome by my agency – big packages, but light. (I think they contained empty cans – a plea to send olive oil) S. T got me a horse and carriage and trolled over there. I am used to horse drawn vehicles – and no longer feel so sorry for the poor horse which must pull.

Mrs. Turreti knows the word I understand best – mangiate – eat – and so I had a plate of fish and eggplant and plums and peaches and a glass of wine.

I now feel in a position to get easy and good accommodation in Rome on a purely business basis – for myself and others – by carrying about two quarts of olive oil up there. Signor Russi has an extra room – he is an apartment manager of a big apartment building in the modern section of town, about 20 minutes to half hour's walk from the main part of the city. Maybe I could do better – but that is security – for my private rest camp. I am well. The weather here continues very fresh and cool and pleasant – and I am enjoying it. Everyone said it would be so hot in July and August – but it isn't yet. Maybe they do not know what hot weather is.

I am very careful with respect to food – my fresh fruit is always both washed and peeled – peaches, plums, figs and the like are easy to peel. Good housekeepers here are meticulous with respect to cleanliness, as they must be – for the streets are filthy and there are many dirty people – with lice and other infestations.

Tomorrow is my day off (I hope) and it will be the first for a long time in this city. I expect to review the shopping situation – to see my music teacher, who had probably forgotten my existence or given me up for lost. He is a good friend of the Patrono family – was Maddaline's music teacher. I shall so mention.

I send my love -

Henry

July 19

Mr. Abraham Lowenhaupt
408 Pine Street
Saint Louis, Missouri

Dear daddy -

I have a letter from Ben this morning which I intend to answer when I finish this which I write with Ben's letter in mind.

Ben says he would like a furlough. I think he has been away long enough that he ought to have one. He has asked for it, and been disappointed. I suggest, as offering a hope, and not possibly doing any harm, that you write a true letter to The Adjutant General, Washington D. C., requesting that Ben be given a furlough, for the reason that he has been away from family and friends for more than two years. That they desire very strongly to see him again. Further, a furlough would be for the benefit of the services, since it would give Ben new energy and enthusiasm. You are informed that he is not rendering indispensable or difficult or specialized service, and that his absence will not be felt in his unit. The letter should give his name, rank, serial number and address. It might ask not specifically for a furlough, but for return to the United States either on furlough or to a new assignment. The letter might be of some effect – it could not do any harm anyway, and the worst that could happen would be that it would be ineffective and you might get a snide answer about nobility and sacrifice – true but not worth saying. The latter should be written on office stationery. You would be surprised how clerks are impressed with engraved letterheads. If you want to be tough, state that you know of people who have received furloughs and opportunities to come home – that you request a statement of explicit reasons if a contrary policy is to be applied in this case. (I think that Randolph Paul could probably tell you how to be more effective. He is, I have always thought, more a politician than a lawyer.)

I am well – and send my love.

Henry

July 19 1944

Dear mama

Yesterday I took my holiday, and as usual, walked my feet off – it was a beautiful cool day. I saw my ~~cab~~ wood carver, who had two boxes almost finished, and I may try to get one. He thinks they will be sold like hot cakes – and I think he is mistaken, but fear he may be right. I found one very beautiful piece of pottery and bought it – a sugar bowl – and if I get a box, intend to send the bowl home inside the box. I also saw more china like that I sent Haymer – but it is all in big plates and platter. I was tempted, but did not succumb.

Places open only in the ~~aftern~~ morning – so during the afternoon I just walked – the old town and other places. Then took a bath and changed my clothes – a cleanup celebration. What I must do is get all I have together and find out what I have. That will be an evening's work sometime.

The last sausage you sent – I left it on the kitchen table. The De Cagno's took half of it – and since that time have been supplying me with fresh fruit – peaches, plums and apricots – the best I've ever tasted.

My music lesson yesterday – dear Maestro had, I think given me up as a bad job departed. But I turned up again – and told him I had been to Rome. "Bella Roma" they all say.

You see, there is no news. We now have beds in the apartment – which come as follows – There is a hotel in town used for transient soldiers. The surgeon ordered all beds taken out – because they require mattresses, which offer danger of infestation. So we got beds and mattresses, which have now been fumigated and are in use. Also a piano – well, well! the hardships of war!

I am told there are 2400 bags of mail here now for distribution. I count on some letters. Lt. Little intends to go to Rome on the 25th and if I get something, as a package, of which there must be two or three on the way, shall send it to the Giordanos by him. I intended to send part of the sausage – but after the DeCagnos had eaten part, I did not (I ate part) have much left.

I received a letter from Ben today – in which he seems contented. I wish he could get a furlough – but long-distance advice is impossible.

I am well. The sea, which I look at from my window is very beautiful and blue and restful. Food in this town is becoming abundant – fish, potatoes, vegetables, cheese. And other merchandise is appearing. For fun, yesterday, I asked a shop keeper in town if it would be possible to find a linen tablecloth of finest quality. She said she would have one in three days – and I may look at it. I should like to send something to Marian – but won't unless I can get something which is nice.

I send my love. I do not know whether to address letters to you in Maine or at home – but do not have sufficient Maine address anyway -

Henry

July 20

Dear mama -

What a haul today – three packages, which arrive in great time – some peanuts and cheese and the like (I wait to bring it home before I open it) some candy, with tempting looking figs and other things. Also some coffee – of which I shall send a pound to Signora Giordano.

Also letters. You must stop writing to me, because it scatters your thoughts too widely. I can get along very happily without letters – just get a supply of postcards and let Ruth write them.

Now I have eaten some prunes and figs – and they are excellent. Superior to Italian – I had just forgotten how good such things could be.

Last night I went to see my woodcarver– his boxes will be finished this evening. I find that I really want one – and shall try to get it. While in the neighborhood I revisited the old town – the cathedral which has enormous dignity. I think that in this country, where there is so much light and color, builders did not appreciate them so much as they did in France where there is less. The cathedral is built on heavy arches inside, of ~~ear~~ stone, with carved intricate capitals to pillars and supports – of coal gray colors – small windows, high up, now without glass – possibly always so, I don't know. One stained glass widow – dull colors – and the paintings high on the ceiling, are dull compared to Titian and the like – reds and golds. But the whole cathedral is of magnificent dignity – even with the temporary scaffolding supports. Then to the castle – the same style, with the beauty of stone and shape – quite windowless. The most intricate carving is in the church of St. Theresa – carved round windows – very delicate.

Then to the apartment, where I talked with Bill and read a little and played piano – Czerny – we now have a piano.

Dr. Patrono and his wife and daughter were there for a while – brought me a present of pears and plums, which I accepted with pleasure. I do not much care for the plums – but the sugar pears are excellent. I like old Dr. Patrono.

They are hard up for little things – as matches. They have a cigarette lighter, and can pick up enough gasoline for fuel for it – but the flints cost about $4.00 each. At home, I think they are about three for a nickel. So if you would like to drop a few in the next package you send – fine!

I believe there is now plenty of food in this city. Fruit, as I have said, in abundance, and vegetables. I see cheese beginning to appear, and lamb and mutton at about 150 lire a kilo. Fish everywhere – mostly of rather disgusting kinds, as octopus and squid and little minnows. I have eaten them at the Turettis and really octopus strew is very good – with carrots and the like – similar to a clam stew. And eggplant with tomatoes – I am sure not as good as what one eats at home, but it is different and interesting.

I hope Haymer is well now. And that you are finding the place restful. Ruth, I know, enjoys antiquing – I wish her luck at it. I am considering getting a piece of fine furniture – telling them to ship it after the war – a gamble like my Relizane rug. A carved chest? Well – I suppose not. Furniture here is in extremes – the conventional is the ugliest I have ever seen – veneered curves and the like. But the primitive and naively made is beautiful.

I send all my love.

Henry

July 20

Dear mama -

I have to use up this poor paper – I am glad it comes in small quantities. My objection to it is that the ink spreads.

I am well – last night I walked again all over town – and enjoyed it. There is no news. I am well. Had a letter from Mr. Gusdorf yesterday, from Copperwood and one from Ben, which I've answered.

No news I know – where I can get some pretty little pieces of pottery – one cup, one saucer, etc., and may send some home just as junk. Why not? This evening I intend to see about getting another box.

I look forward to receipt of mail – those 2400 sacks I hear of should begin trickling around.

Love -

Henry

July 21

Mrs. A. Lowenhaupt
Moody
Maine
USA

Dear mama -

Your letters sound too distraught – I think you need a lively vacation – and write with the single purpose of urging you, as soon as Haymer is on an even keel (nautical terms for seashore use) to go to New York for a week and sleep all day and stay up all night, and lead an exciting life. You know how – and I think it is not a long trip from Moody[197] to New York in terms of miles – although in other terms the distance may be infinite.

And if when you go to New York have one celebration à la Ronald Bates for me – with dinner at the Waldorf and waiters hovering around with big white napkins. The hardships of war! We use paper napkins.

Henry

---

[197] Moody is north of Ogunquit in Maine.

July 21

Mrs. A. Lowenhaupt
Moody
Maine

Dear mama -

I'm trying this address -

I just received three (3) packages yesterday. What a jackpot! and how they please me. Prunes – (excellent – I soaked six of them overnight and eat them now) and figs – better than the dried ones here – and sausage and cheese, which always please me immensely as a supplement to meals – tasty & good. Then Bissingers[198] – enough is said! Also four pounds of coffee – which comes in excellent time to pay a debt in Rome – since Lt. Little is going there Tuesday. So I am very happy -

But you must stop writing to me if it makes you feel too scattered and distraught. I'll holler a little about lack of mail – but that won't do any harm. You know by now that I begin bellowing promptly, long before it hurts.

I am well. Without news – except to visit my wood carver again this evening – boxes were not finished last night.

All my love -

Henry

July 22

Dear daddy -

The world is full of rumors this morning – about revolution in Germany and the like – such very good rumors that it is hard to sit still and one hopes they are founded and fears they are not and wonder, if they are, what complications are to follow. So the only thing to do is to forget them all and keep on waiting.

I received your V-mail letter – and it is always delightful to hear from you, even though you say your letters are formal. They have character, all their own. And I am happy to hear that you are busy. It would be interesting to read of specific cases, but I appreciate that you really don't want to write about them. Why not send me copies of briefs you write now and then – and of decisions when published? I feel very completely out of touch with such matters.

For my part, I have no news. I have a few pleasures – yesterday two men I knew in New York came to town – they are staying in the apartment – and today a man I used to know at II Corps – he is moving in with us for a few days – fortunately the weather is warm so there is no blanket problem. We are running a summer resort – and this is a good location for one. The swimming is excellent – one can rent a rowboat – go out about a mile and swim from the boat. Or a sailboat.

I got another carved box yesterday – and intend to send it home shortly.

---

[198] Chocolate shop in St. Louis

I received four pounds of coffee day before yesterday, with your return address on it – and thank you. But Hy tells me he sent it – so I thank him too. As they say – "one gives thanks to the Madonna." So, a lady said who had given me road directions once – the implication being that she wanted something more tangible. The coffee comes in the nick of time. Lt. Little is going to Rome soon – and I owe Signora Giordano something. A pound of coffee will discharge my obligation for a week's rent. As coffee is unobtainable, its value is either nothing or infinite. When a price like $30.^{00} a pound is mentioned, it means that coffee is of no value at all, it seems to me.

I am well and without news. This city is opening up – abundance of food now – fruits vegetables and the like of excellent quality. Last night I bought a watermelon but it was not ripe enough. We are only the heart. I think the farmers pick their fruit green to rush for the early market, or because they are in the habit of shipping it. So it is hard to buy ripe fruit. However, it ripens with keeping for a few days.

I am sorry I did not see Capt. Freschi when I was in Rome – if he is there, which I doubt, for Rome is being kept an open city, as is proper, without troops other than for civil administration and the like. But I was very busy there – with too much to do. Everyone I formerly knew turned up – Major Morris, Capt. Palmblad, Lt. Wheelock, and so forth – there for "rests," as I was.

Lighter flints are a rarity here. If you write again, will you drop a few in the envelope? They are about 3 for a nickel there, aren't they?

Tonight there is a concert – which I expect to attend with Captain Baker. What a life! I shall never get over my idleness. This afternoon a court martial. (I am assistant to defense counsel) The defense counsel has already pleaded the man guilty (which I think is always a mistake – what's the use?) and so there is not much assistance to be rendered. Another one coming up – where I have already testified that I thought there were reasons to doubt the man's sanity – I enjoying being a witness – and it is now in the hands of doctors. If they find him sane, I suppose I shall have to seek out a doctor to testify he's crazy. Maybe he is.

I send my love -

Henry

July 23

Dear mama -

I am well – although somewhat tired, having been up too late for the preceding two nights. Shall try to catch up tonight. Although I am not sure I can because Maddaline Patrono is having an onomastico party which I shall attend. There is no news.

Last night, I heard a good concert including Beethoven.

A man named Thomas and one Vaut were in town yesterday – and said they were hungry. They were on pass – and had missed breakfast by sleeping too late and lunch by forgetting or something. They were staying with us in the apartment – So we went out and bought six eggs (we were robbed – 25¢ each egg) and brought them to the Turettis, who cooked them for Thomas and Vaut – and added bread, tomatoes and fruit. The Turettis are alright – they like to do anything they can for us – and I think they are hard up. I am going to give them a present of tea or coffee or material or something, although I've already given them a great deal from time to time.

The weather here is very warm.

A man named Baker is also staying with us now – visiting for a few days – he is from II Corps – and is ~~eho~~ leaving – on his way to England, I think.

I have a new carved box – a very great beauty – I think as pretty as the other one from the local wood carver of this city. I intend to dispatch it within the next few days. It is especially for Marian – unless you are of the opinion that it is not a masterpiece. I am now through with carved boxes from this wood carver, unless I change my mind, but I may ultimately succumb to his plaque of St. Nicolas, which Ruth would enjoy, I believe. Not soon, however.

I have written that many people are now having plaques carved from photographs, and there is no doubt that this man does a fine job. But I do not like the genre – and it tends to spoil St. Nicholas for me, because I see that the perspective is a little false and so forth. Originally, in the St. Nicholas plaque, that did not disturb me – but the crookedness does disturb me in a haut relief of a girl with beads on.

I have made inquiries for linen – since things are opening up, I desire to see if any is becoming available. The woman said that if I would come back Monday, she would be able to show me some. I shall see what she shows me. She intends plain white – but that may be fine too – I suppose better than all cut up or embroidered. Well – that is just to satisfy curiosity.

I send my love -

Henry

July 24

Dear mama -

I intend to spend the next few nights catching up on sleep, since the past several I have been up rather late. As last night – with Captain Baker, Lt. Little, & Lt. Clark – I first went to dinner at the Allied Officer's Club – a good dinner – with a bottle of good wine. It is quite a luxurious place – dinner on a terrace by a musical fountain – a grove of figs and olive trees, profusion of blooming Bougainvillea or whatever it is called – paper-like purple flower – and a rose garden off to one side. Waiters in white jackets, white tablecloths and tasty food.

Then we went to see Dr. Patrono and his family – Maddaline's birthday – and she had baked with her own hands little pastries which were very good – with apricots and sweet red wine. So we said "Augurii, augurii" and talked fast and furious. Captain Baker used to teach German – so a new language was added to the confusion – German, English, French, Italian and a little Latin.

It is always a lovely drive out there – and the town – a village – the most crowded I have ever seen – the streets thronged in the evening, so you have to elbow your way through. Quite a beautiful town – with its square and church and all else. Filled now with Yugoslavians – women and men dressed in similar uniform – and most of the women as hefty as oxen.

Which reminds me of a man who returned from Moscow and described a drinking party on Vodka there – about eight men at a table and eight strong women around the room. Each drank as fast as he could, until he fell off his chair – a woman then came and took him under her arm, like a sack of potatoes, and hauled him off – revived him with cold water and massaging – until he could sit at the table again – where the process would be repeated – and so on until the women could no longer revive him. These Yugoslav women would make good attendants at such a party.

I am well. The weather is very warm – and the sun furious and intense – but the air remains cool, and the shade is always very comfortable. Yesterday I took a sun bath on our terrace (luxuriously) for about 3 minutes – that was enough.

This morning Captain Baker left – going back to the other coast.

There is now, I am told, civilian transportation – railroads running from *[word scratched out]* Naples *[word scratched out]* to Rome and so forth. Hence, the Turetti say, the price of olive oil in Rome has fallen to $3.50 a litre. It is about 80¢ to $1.00 a litre here. I shall send coffee to Signora Giordano in Rome – from the supply I have.

I told you of my receipt of packages from you – and how much I am enjoying them. Keep up the good work!

So I shall request – coffee is a very fine present. So also is sausage – and I even enjoy the prunes and figs.

So I'll request a few more raisins, and almonds and whatever else you can find. You can fill the interstices with, say, cigarettes and flints for lighters. How about canned lobster? And similar delicacies?

You see how great my need is!

All my love -

Henry

July 25

Dear mama -

I mailed a package to you today – and I hope it arrives safely. It contains: a masterpiece of a box – I suggest for Marian. One rather pretty piece of pottery – a sugar bowl – neo possibly for Haymer or Ruth or you (or Marian, if she wants it) And one cup. It also contains a piece of cloth, which is of poor quality, and used principally for packing. Do with it as you like. I got it in Rome – intending to give it away – and decided it was too valuable for anyone I know here – being rare here – and I was mad because I thought the laundress had stolen my best brown silk pajamas. But she hadn't – I had forgotten to send them – and found them after I sent the box – cleaning up this afternoon. (Bits of laundry in every bag and corner – I've just barely begun – and shall continue some evening.)

I haven't done much else today – except walk my blooming feet off. This morning I filled the bathtub (the water goes off at noon) and so was able to take a cold bath this afternoon. Left the water in the tub and expect to take another in a few minutes. The water will be back on at six.

I am well.

This morning I ate breakfast here – having prepared myself with three fresh eggs. So I had sausage and fried eggs and coffee and prunes and pears. The eggs and sausage surely tasted good!

I met Dr. Patrono on the street today – and later Maddaline.

Lt. Little left for Rome this morning – with a Lt. Schmelzer. What a cargo he brought! He carried rations for a week – to be independent of established eating places – for two people. That is in itself a load. And olive oil, as a present, and other food (potatoes and the like, as a gift for Dr. Patrono, Jr.)

It must be hard to become accustomed to change in value of money. Dr. Patrono sent his son a present of 40,000 lire. Pre war, that is a present of $10,000. Now – about $400. I don't think he knows how well off his son is – he is the best fed man in Rome, so far as I can see.[199]

I send my love. Let me know if you think this second box is up to the first – I would be inclined to say – not quite.

Henry

July 28

Dear mama -

Another month almost gone – and I wrote early in the morning (having gone to bed too early last night, and so awaking too early this morning). I am well – and put to new feelings of hope and fear by the news I now read – hope that this will be over soon – doubt that there is any veracity in the news – fear of changes which come and interludes when things go on of which I have no imagination whatsoever. But there is one overwhelming end – to get home – and everything leads to that end.

The weather here is completely magnificent, with hot sun and cool air, and breeze from the sea. The town seems to be opening up a good deal, with new shops and merchandise, and one sees many things appearing which up to now were considered impossible to obtain. As drinking glasses. Formerly, places advertised that they would cut bottles to make glasses – but bottles were as much in demand as glasses. Now there are real genuine glasses available. Ten cent store glasses, it is true, at about 40¢ each – but they are there, and an illustration of my economic theory that price control does not prevent inflation, because money is of less value if you can't buy anything at all than if you can buy only at a high price.

Now I have shaved, bathed and dressed. The maid came in – and told me she had walked all the way because the street cars were broken; she wanted to get here early to do the laundry. She left a 4 o'clock, she said. I sometimes suspect her of being a psychopathic liar – although it is hard to judge in Italian. They all talk so very much. So I told her to drink coffee.

I shall have to go out in search of things to write about. My letters must be getting very, very dull. Signor Turetti wants me to go to the country with him – I do not think I shall. I should be absolutely stuffed on figs and ~~da~~ nuts – and I do not know what else – and that is about all. It would be to Mrs. Russi's farm. Then Dr. Patrono wants to escort us to the great monument of the neighborhood, an ancient castle about 50 miles away. Oh well – that might be interesting. Maybe we shall be able to go there some day.

Mail comes sporadically. But I neither complain nor expect mail, because you are busy, and I think you may find it distracting to write to so many. So don't write. Let Ruth drop a post card now and then.

---

[199] This was a story I heard often. The Dr. father was sending much of his life savings to his son- a big box of lire. When Henry gave it to the son, the son laughed and said it was practically worthless and he didn't need it. This is probably the same story.

I repeat: I sent another box – and I remember it now as a beauty. Would Marian like it? I am looking for linen for Marian – and a friend of mine promised that when he got into Florence he would get me some. I do not stand a chance of going to Florence – even after it is captured.

Love -

Henry

July 28

Dear mama -

I've written you a few letters to Moody, Maine – which I feel is just a toss in the dark, because I really have no very definite knowledge that there is such a place, or how mail gets there or anything else – so this one I'll address conservatively – and the luck would be that this arrived – in which I have nothing whatsoever to write – and the others, in which I had very little to write, should not arrive at all. I must repeat, or just end this letter.

I sent a box to you about three days ago – last Tuesday, in fact, one which I considered a gem of the second order. I am anxious to have your opinion – I know it is not as well made as the first. But I thought it was still good. Inside the box are two pieces of pottery – a sugar bowl and a cup. Sent because I was sending the box anyway, and I liked the sugar bowl.

I am well. Things go on with nothing new.

I find that it would be possible to get almost the pick of the Italian army to serve as orderly – and keep the room straight and the like. The bed for him would be easy, but the feeding problem would be severe. So I intend not to do it. The present arrangement is satisfactory – a woman comes in every day except Sunday and Tuesday. She is funny – always has an abused look about her. But she is a zealous laundress – and very clean. I think she is a liar of the first rank, but she does not steal, so far as I have been able to discover. Except she eats whatever she finds, and I do not consider that stealing. She eats only what she finds in the kitchen – so I now keep the little cheese I have left in a bedroom – where she does not know it is cheese, I suppose. She cannot read even Italian –much less English – and American packaging is not familiar to her. I think she has a strange sense of values – she will not drink coffee, because it is too valuable; but she will eat meat or cheese, which is less valuable.

The weather continues very lovely. I intend to go to see the Turetti's this evening, although I do not know why. Still, why not.

I suppose I might as well request a package of food, since, I believe, all my requests are not fulfilled, and I have some outstanding. Will you please send me some?

I suggest: Baker's chocolate – if it is not milk chocolate, it might ship well. How about canned things – are they still rationed? If so, don't send them. As shrimp, lobster, sardines, ham and the like.

You know, of course, that I do not need any of these things. Would it be efficient, do you think to send the ingredients for fudge? Cocoa and sugar, an ampule of vanilla – butter is unnecessary? I am just thinking out loud. Maybe I could get these things here, but I don't know where to ask.

I received a letter from Betty – including a statement she had acquired a cat. I hope she has got rid of it by this time.

Love -

Henry

July 29

Dear mama -

I have nothing new of which I write since yesterday – nevertheless I try. I ate supper last night – first going to Lt. Stern's room, where his landlady gave us some freshly baked breads and sweet butter. I had forgotten how good that was.

Then after supper, I went home – and played my Czerny and a little Beethoven and a little Mozart for a while – and then to bed early. That brings me to date.

The weather continues beautiful, clear and fresh. This hot weather, of which everyone had been warning me, has completely failed to materialize – although it is true that the sun is baking hot during the day. Natives seem to sleep all afternoon – and then the streets begin to be noisy and crowded at about eight o'clock. They stay crowded then until close to midnight. But, then, it is light until almost ten o'clock – what with double or triple daylight savings time – I have never gotten straight just what kind of time we do have.

News looks so good, that I again get impatient for the next paper to read or broadcast to hear – and there is a great variety (more than you have in St. Louis) There is *Stars & Stripes*, which boys shout for sale as Staws and Steeps, and Union Jack (pronounced Onion Jock or Gioca) and the Noonday Journal, *Italia Liberata* and all others, with their little announcements of first communions and the like. Few or so advertisements. But there is only vexation in writing. We have maps all over, and stick pins in them. Then by hanging a colored thread, with weights on each end, over the pins, you get quite an effect – as good as the local Bureau of Notices, which had display windows of such maps. They have tassels on the ends of their strings – and so do better than we can. But it is only a vexation of spirit.

Mail is irregular again – and since I assume that mine arrives there irregularly too, I'll write a few things again.

I sent a box home last Tuesday – a masterpiece with a bunch of flowers on top. Do you want another? I am inclined to think there may be enough there already.

Then requests – may I suggest chocolate – as Baker's sweet chocolate? And anything unrationed in the form of canned goods, as lobster and shrimp. Edibles are the best things to receive. So I request that you send me a box of food. I believe that liquids cannot be sent through the mails.

Coffee is always splendid – I now have a one pound reserve, having had three pounds reserve, sent one to Rome, and opened one for use. Usually there is no gas when I want coffee.

I send all my love. This evening I shall go out and see if I can find something about which to write.

I hope you get to New York for a vacation, because I really believe you need one and need it badly.

Henry

July 30

Mrs. A. Lowenhaupt
Moody
Maine

Dear mama -

V Mail letter because I really have nothing to say anyway. I received your letter from Maine – the first intimation I have that Marian is not in New York – so I imagine I have more letters on the way. I hope so, and ought to receive them today or tomorrow.

I think I shall begin looking around for an Italian teacher. I am not progressing much by myself. But maybe I have progressed far enough. The trouble is that everyone tries to teach Italian and most of them do not know enough English to do so. However, that is still vague and indefinite. If I should begin getting more among Italians, it would help. So I shall see.

Last night I took a walk which, however, was quite without incident. A lovely evening, preparing to rain, and eventually – about nine o'clock, – it did rain, a thunderstorm, with such lightning and thunder, and only a few drops of rain. I stood under a balcony and kept dry for the ten or fifteen minutes that it rained, and then continued my walk home. I bought two eggs and fried them, using the last bit of my sausage as grease. They came out very excellent and a great pleasure. So I may from time to time get more eggs, although the current price is 25¢ each. Maybe I could do better if I shopped for them.

I intend next Tuesday to shop for food a little bit – going to the big market here, where last Tuesday I saw some cheese which looked good, in addition to the great variety of fruits and vegetables. Also I see meat for sale now, especially lamb and the like. There is a Madame Stoppeni, a Swiss woman here, who runs a pastry shop, and would like to serve dinners to anyone who orders in advance. I think it might be fun to try one of her dinners, for she has access to farms, and describes her own menus so that they sound very good. Or induce the Turitti's to ask me again – which can be done quite easily

Love

Henry

July 31

Mrs. A. Lowenhaupt
Moody
Maine

Dear mama -

This is a rumor with sufficient foundation to justify some action – and sufficient to tear me between the extremes of not knowing what I want. I may be coming home in a week or two. But would be on the way for a month or two. So maybe it would be as well not to send any more packages until you hear further, and if you don't feel like writing, don't. If I came home, I should probably be in Washington.

I fear the hard living of the States – and think of Florence and Milan and all the pleasures and interests here. But I shall take no action to influence fate, because there is much there too.

Henry

Here are two more photographs. I am cleaning out my desk drawers, which accumulate junk so very fast.

Henry

I've written one letter today – this will be enough, therefore, till tomorrow, when I shall be writing again

How's Marian?

Henry

August 2

Mrs. A. Lowenhaupt
6237 McPherson Ave.
Saint Louis
Missouri

Dear mama -

One letter to Moody – and one to St. Louis – not knowing which will reach you – that it seems likely I shall start home in about ten days.

Time of arrival – ? Two weeks from Aug. 15 to Three months – so you see I have no idea whatsoever.

Henry

August 2

Mrs. A. Lowenhaupt
Moody
Maine
USA

Dear mama -

I think that I shall probably be home in about 10 days – but whether it will take two weeks (the minimum, I think) or two months to arrive, I have no idea whatsoever. So I merely suggest that you quit writing to me until further notice – and when I arrive anyplace in US, you may be sure I shall telephone.

Yesterday evening, we went with the Patronos to the loveliest farm I have ever seen – just outside a town – so the wall of buildings, with church dome, formed the edge of the farm – all of old, grey stone. The farm's buildings of rock – and the fields tiny, closely cultivated in egg plant and cucumber and squash; fig trees between. We picked a cucumber and ate it. A spring in the middle of the farm – used for irrigation. (Mosquitos so thick you could cut 'em with a knife) Eggplants are beautiful. They told us of a 12th Century church in the neighborhood – we may go to see it.

You see – I do not want to come home – except to see you – but the choice isn't mine.

Henry

August 3

Dear mama -

I have not written often lately – partly because of the uncertain feeling one had when one is told unofficially and hears rumors that one is going home very soon – but that is still as uncertain as ever, and I shall ignore it.

But when I think of it, I realize what an interesting time I am in fact having in my leisure here, I fear going home. So I am glad things are out of my control. As night before last, we brought the Patronos home – stopping at one of Mrs. Patrono's farms on the way. What a night! The tight, little, patriarchal institution – the old grandmother taking care of one little baby (wrapped up right in swaddling clothes) and two older ones, running around – and all the rest working the land, closely cultivated. It lies right below the solid stone bank of buildings – the town – from which the church bells ring. Beautiful cultivation – eggplants very heavy, and profusion of cucumber, squash, melons, figs not yet ripe, and all else. A well, and a spring used to irrigate the land. We carried away a huge basket of produce. It is hard to remember a Kansas farm, when one sees such a place – the people so tight in it. The country people do not speak Italian – they speak a dialect[200], which is much more classical than Italian, much more like Latin and Greek. The joke of the language is the word "Cra." (like Latin "Cras") for tomorrow; that is also the word for the call of a crow – like our "caw." So when you get mad at someone for procrastination (as you always do if you wany anything done) you say "'Cra, cra' diceva lo corbaccio" – "'Tomorrow, tomorrow,' said the crow." It doesn't make sense in English. But everyone thinks it is an enormously funny joke. I suppose it is very ancient.

So, after our visit to the farm – the quietest place I have ever been – we went out to the Patrono's house for a short time. Dr. Patrono – a professor of Latin – is also a judge in criminal cases. He had just finished convicting a man of cutting down a living olive tree – and discussed the provision of the Code, which makes an olive tree sacred, like a human being, and one may not cut down even ~~his~~ one's own tree. Posterity has a vested interest in such a thing, because the tree lives for centuries, and becomes more productive with time. It is part of the wealth of the nation, and not merely of the owner, who had only the right to the fruit while he lives. So many communities are much incensed that Americans and English do not appreciate the tree – and clear a grove in order to use the tract for storage of supplies for a few months. That is terrible vandalism, they say (and I agree) because the trees cannot be replaced for centuries. It would be better to tear down buildings, which can be replaced with labor alone. But an olive tree must grow. The discussion was exciting – a combination of religion, economy and law.

I am well – send my love -

Henry

August 4

Mrs. A. Lowenhaupt
Moody
Maine

Dear mama -

This is the last note I write. I suggested that you keep some people in New York informed of your address – and gave you the name John D Clark – as one I should call. But the address given was incomplete – so I repeat it:

---

[200] This could potentially be referring to the Neapolitan language.
Via Wikipedia
https://en.wikipedia.org/wiki/Neapolitan_language
Languages of Italy Via Wikipedia
https://en.wikipedia.org/wiki/Languages_of_Italy

John D. Clark
New York Telephone Co.
101 Willoughby Street
Brooklyn. NY.

A bientôt!

Henry

August 6

Dear mama -

I have decided for the moment that I might as well keep on writing as if I were not coming home, because maybe I shan't, and by not writing, I become too impatient and get too great a sense of urgency.

August 11

Well – I have been so busy with details that I have not written anyway, for five days now. The Patronos have called and bid me farewell – a kiss on each cheek from the bewhiskered old doctor – and a basket of fruit and cakes from Maddaline – they are very nice to me. I called on Turettis – Porzia is sick in bed with a fever; so I did not stay, and on Dr. Giordano .

Other than that, nothing. I have mailed home two boxes of clothes – which I hope arrive in fairly decent shape. And may mail more. The less I have to carry the better off I am – and I intend to abandon more or less wholesale.

I am well -

Last night – a party was given by a lot of men in my honor (quite flattering) They saved their beer rations for three weeks and had them all at once. Added bread and tomatoes and onions -

I But I hope it is futile to write all this – all I am instructed to inform my correspondents (you) not to write to me until they receive a new address.

Henry

August 6

Mrs. A. Lowenhaupt
6237 McPherson
Saint Louis
Missouri

Dear mama -

I really cannot write any more – and said that you would not hear from me for a long time. Well – just consider each letter my last – for I still have no idea when I shall leave. So many things begin as "urgent" and then you begin waiting. So it goes.

I am well – and send my love -

Henry

PS – no use writing any more – as I shall not receive the letters.

BARI DURING THE ALLIED OCCUPATION (1943-1945)

HISTORICAL RESEARCH

Including observations by Henry Cronbach Lowenhaupt from the Letters

Storie di Famiglia
RICERCHE GENEALOGICHE

The city

Bari in 1943-1945 is a very different city from the one we know today. It was already the second largest urban center in southern Italy (after Naples, excluding the islands), with a population of about 200,000. The extent of the urban center was also limited to the old town, the nineteenth-century center (Murat) and the neighborhoods to the east (Umbertino, Madonnella, and monumental waterfront built during the Fascist period) and west (Libertà). However, in the 1941 map provided by the U.S. War Department, the city's early development can be glimpsed to the south, beyond the train station and the railroad tracks, toward the great center of the Policlinico hospital. But the coastal hamlets of Palese-Santo Spirito (to the north) and Torre a Mare (to the south) were still far from the city.

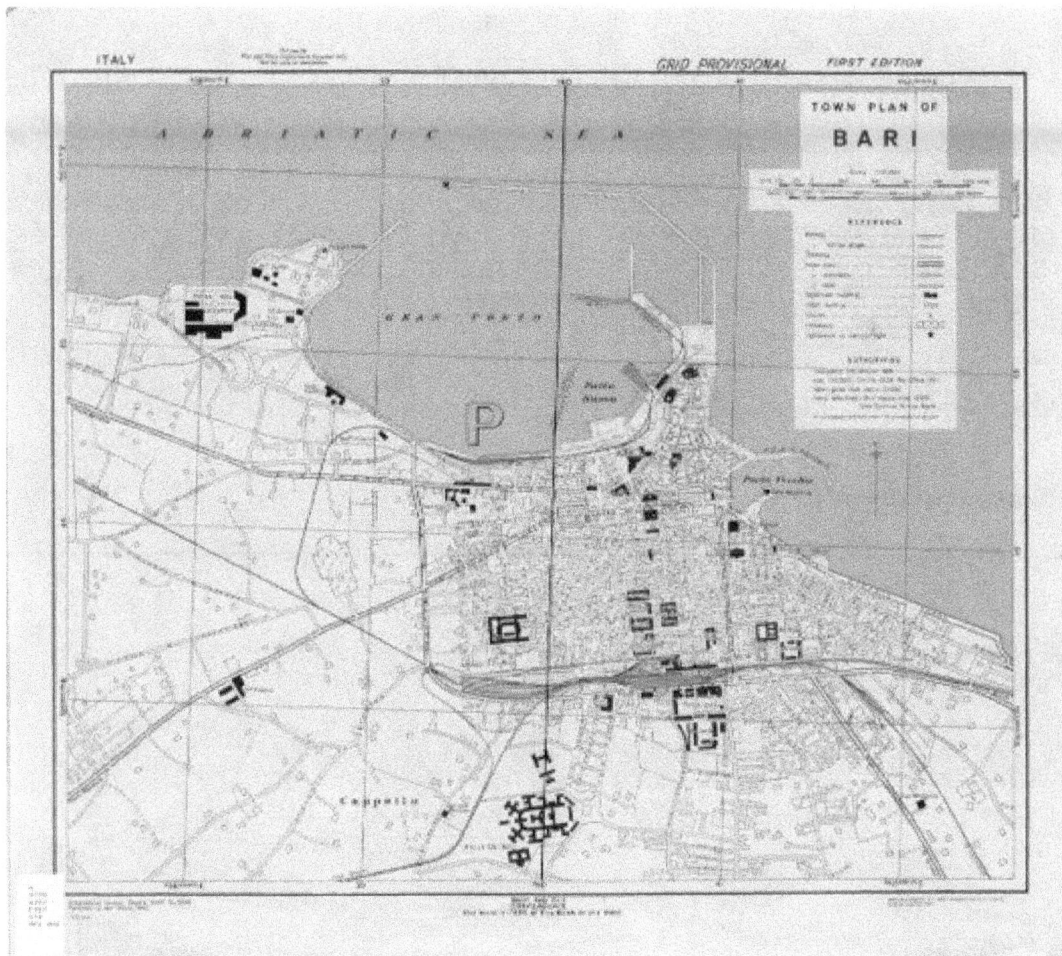

Figure 1. Town plan of Bari (War Office, 1942)

Figure 2. Bari. Aerial view of the city (1937)

The old town

Bari Vecchia occupies a triangle of land jutting out into the sea. A ferry terminal monopolizes the western side with two levels of seafront promenade on the eastern edge. One of these levels are the old walls, which until the early 1900s directly overlooked the sea. But by the 1940s the lower level, the promenade that today runs along the peninsula, had already been built. As with most medieval towns, there's no pattern to the streets, but the district isn't big enough to get lost in for long.

Mappa di Bari
Incisore Giambattista Albrizzi, 1761

Figure 3. Map of Bari, corresponding to the old city (1761)

It has long been one of the most popular and populous areas of the city, as beautiful as it is dangerous. Beginning in the 2000s, a gradual revaluation took the old town from a fiefdom of crime to a place of first nightlife and then massive tourism. Today the narrow streets are saturated with B&Bs, but you can still breathe that air of authenticity that has characterized it to this day.

I spent the afternoon walking, especially through the old, walled town, which is completely charming – archways, close streets, or alleys, squares, crowds – people cooking on the streets – colors (in which Italy excels) and a magnificent cathedral – St. Nicholas – without carvings and statues – a cloister. All the windows have been taken out – I hope for safe-keeping. [6 March]

Then, after wandering through the old city – which is endlessly intriguing, with its archways, its narrow passages, and howling of babies, women calling, all kinds of noises and smells, its carpenter shops, nuns, priests, all pushing through – I decided to have lunch on the hoof. A delicious orange, at the market, some candy, a cream puff, and, as always, I tried something that looked like chocolate cake, but turned out to be figs and dates. [14 March]

Figure 4. Arco Meraviglia in the old town (1940s)

Lots of fishing here – and along the wall, they sell shellfish which look like chestnut burrs, outside – inside, little red things. I am afraid of them, although the natives seem to eat them with pleasure. [9 March]

Figure 5. Fishermen at the Mercato del Pesce (fish market) in piazza del Ferrarese (1920s)

Figure 6. Fishermen at the Mercato del Pesce (fish market) in piazza del Ferrarese (1910s)

Figure 7. Elderly woman on via Tresca Vecchia (1940s)

The old town yesterday was as beautiful as ever. One place was selling hemp (I think it was that) and everywhere, old women had gotten out their spindles and distaffs – and were spinning thread – quite a pretty process, although it is a very slow way of making thread. A spinning wheel is a modern, efficient method by comparison. They attach a little of the stuff to a bobbin, give the bobbin a whirl, and it spins and twists a thread. Then they wind the thread on the bobbin, and spin it again, making more. I have not seen any weaving here. [5 April]

Figure 8. Via Venezia in the 1920s The ancient city walls directly on the sea, before the waterfront was built

Weather is beautiful – I am well. Last night I walked around the walls of the town, and through the old city – it grows more surprisingly beautiful every time I go through it – narrow alleys and streets, crowded with people, children playing, peddlers, everyone – big buildings – with arches over the streets to support the walls of the buildings – archways, where the streets go under the buildings. All the streets paved in flag stones, with ruts worn in the wider ones – worn right into the stone from the wheels of carriages – columns remaining, apparently, from some very ancient church or temple. [14 April]

Figure 9. Fishermen's boats repairing nets in the old harbor (1948)

Meanwhile, I am spending much time wandering the streets of the city – especially the old city, and enjoying it, for it is always interesting and the streets always crowded. The harbor is beautiful – filled with small fishing boats, and lined with men repairing nets, I imagine as it was in ancient times, for Horace refers to the place in one of his satires as "fishy." [29 April]

Figure 10. Norman Swabian castle (1950s)

The old town continues lovely – and I have to pinch myself now and then to open my eyes and see it – the intricate stone carving, into round windows and stone lattices – the round towers – the narrow streets and arches – the vast grey walls – the town itself in very somber colors – which emphasizes the brilliance of the sky and the sea and the trees outside the walls. The old castle is an enormous, intricate building, with ships-prow corner on one side – a moat, now a garden. It sounds (and looks) beautiful – but how it stinks! [15 June]

I revisited the old town – the cathedral which has enormous dignity. I think that in this country, where there is so much light and color, builders did not appreciate them so much as they did in France where there is less. The cathedral is built on heavy arches inside, of car stone, with carved intricate capitals to pillars and supports – of coal gray colors – small windows, high up, now without glass – possibly always so, I don't know. One stained glass widow – dull colors – and the paintings high on the ceiling, are dull compared to Titian and the like – reds and golds. But the whole cathedral is of magnificent dignity – even with the temporary scaffolding supports. Then to the castle – the same style, with the beauty of stone and shape – quite windowless. The most intricate carving is in the church of St. Theresa – carved round windows – very delicate. [20 July]

Figure 11. Santa Teresa dei Maschi in the old town

People do not seem to have adequate cooking facilities here – for it seems to be the custom to send things out to be cooked. So Children wander through the streets carrying pans of unbaked cookies – pieces of meat, all salted and peppered – and so forth – and then running home with them baked. I suppose they bring them to the baker – who rents his oven or something. [10 April]

Figure 12. Ancient wood-fired oven where people brought food to be cooked

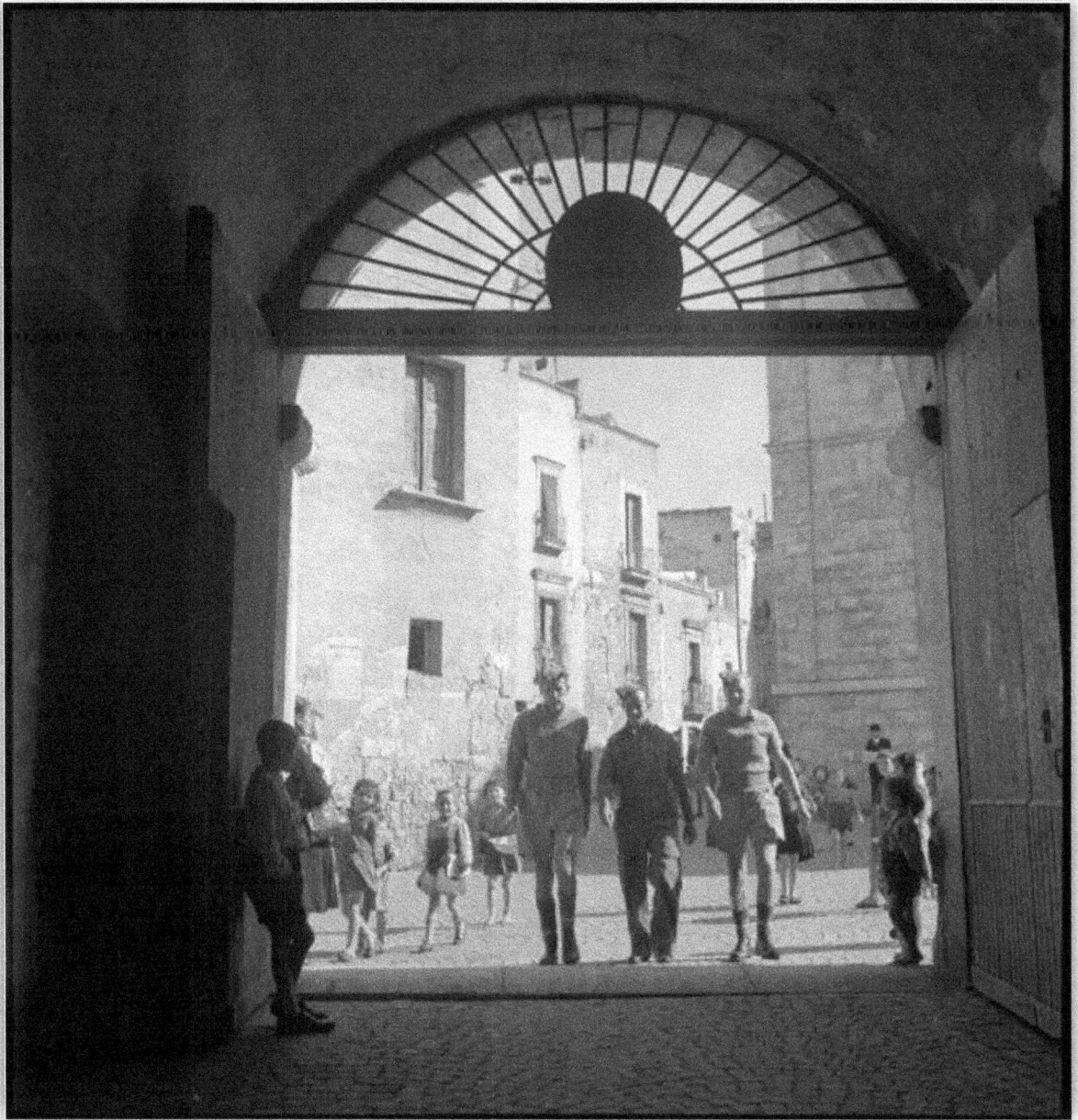

Figure 13. New Zealand soldiers explore the byways of old Bari (1943). Photograph taken by George Kaye from inside the archdiocesan seminary, near the Cathedral.

San Nicola

I walked a while. I went to the church, and through it. It is not one of the finest examples – that is, not up to Monreale and Rouen and Notre Dame de Paris – but it is lovely – the tomb of St. Nicholas, they say, in cast silver, which I don't fully appreciate. Beautiful stairway on the tomb of the Queen of Poland. Beautiful columns, shape – one misses the color of stained glass windows – but I suppose it may be these southern churches never had them. [14 March]

Today being my day off, I have done intensive loafing all day – walking through the town, old and new, looking in ship windows, watching children and what not, with my music lesson at noon – which is still the high point of my week. I enjoy it very much, I went into the cathedral - I do not find it as inspiring or as beautiful as I expect – maybe because I do not understand this conservative, solid architecture – and am come to expect vaults and gothic windows. Still, it is unquestionably a solid piece of stone building, with many delicate details of stone carving. The tomb itself – a great piece of silver, with scenes from the life of the saint I cannot understand at all as a thing of beauty. [16 May]

But I believe it is generally fine that beautiful Italian things are usually much less striking than French or Greek – and I have come to think of fine Italians as much more conservative than the English even, and with feeling very deep – and self-contained. Not at all like Spanish or others, with superficial decoration. I believe it may take quite a little time for the merit of a thing like this cathedral to grow on you. It is enormously quiet and heavy and dignified – very little color – but that there is (some ceiling paintings and a few others) very modern in its contrast and the natural color is everywhere so high, that the old gray-green of the stone is restful. It is so completely far from tawdry and decorated. I think the more often I go there, the more I shall enjoy it.

The same is true of the whole old town – the walls, the old castle – heavy and plain – but they grow very interesting as you watch them, and very dignified – way beyond the dignity of the inhabitants and naked pa babies squawking in the streets. I come to think from this especially that fine Italian people are something superfine – but most you see are poor dirty beggars.

Figura 14. Basilica of San Nicola (early 1900s)

Borgo murattiano

The new city begins with the Muratti suburb, which arose from the early 19th century outside the walls of the old city and is bounded by the city's two main streets: corso Vittorio Emanuele and corso Cavour. Here are also the commercial streets, such as via Sparano, now a place for strolling and shopping.

And such fine cities! This one (I have not seen much – it is Sunday, and places are closed) had, along the waterfront, heavy, fine buildings – magnificent, as Washington (5 march)

I walked through the new town, too, which is largely government or public buildings all along the waterfront – like an enormous WPA project. Shops all closed and nothing much for sale. I rested while getting a shampoo." [6 march]

I am in a very beautiful place – a city substantially undamaged – fine buildings, lovely cathedral – an old walled town – the new section outside the walls – with beautiful surroundings – combination Atlanta City, St. Malo, Washington and Algiers – I think I should like to stay here – but don't care if I go elsewhere. My address is now as [word unclear] [7 March]

Figure 15. Corso Vittorio Emanuele (1920s)

I enjoy walking in this town. There is a main street [CORSO CAVOUR] – six or eight blocks long, running from a corner of the old town and the sea – with a boulevard – and on the sidewalks double rows of trees which I think are lemon trees. Then in the boulevard larger trees. This is lined with fine buildings. Another main street [CORSO VITTORIO EMANUELE] runs along the land side of the old town, at right angles to the first, and then drives along the shore, around the old city. The streets are heavily travelled with army trucks – But today, they were quite crowded with carriages – which are of all kinds. Many for hire – serve as taxis – then apparently many privately owned. Light little ones, the formal black ones – driving along the sea. And quite pretty horses. It makes the drive look much like a painting of the French painter whose name I've long tried to recall, who painted in spots." [19 March]

Figure 16. View down the Via Cavour, one of the principal streets of Bari, Italy, during World War II. Taken circa November 1943 by an official photographer.

Figure 17. Corso Vittorio Emanuele from palazzo Fizzarotti. Elevated view of one of the main streets of Bari, Italy, during World War II. Taken circa November 1943 by George Frederick Kaye.

People dress up on Sunday and take walks – and it makes the sea-side walk look stylish and haute monde-ish with ladies and men and children all strolling along. Quite interesting – that is the new city. I haven't been in the old town on Sunday. [19 March]

This town looks somewhat souvenir-less. It is too modern – the new part overwhelms the old – and no one seems to be attempting to capitalize on the willingness of soldiers to buy anything. All I have seen is souvenir picture post cards – which I cannot send because they would bare the location in which I find myself (it is around you are familiar with all landscape and buildings!) [11 March]

I can have a very interesting time in this provincial town - which is completely magnificent to look at, too. I never get over the beauty of the old town – more lovely and exciting to me than the splendor of broad streets and formal statuary. But I like fine buildings, of which there are only a few here – the castle, the fortifications, the churches. The modern churches surpass my understanding. With the models of St. Nicholas and St. Theresa and other just a few blocks away, they build in the new town yellow brick or stone things just like suburban Chicago. [18 June]

Figure 18. the church of San Ferdinando in via Sparano (1930s)

Lungomare

Beyond the old city and the Murattian center, the city spreads eastward along the sea, with the Lungomare (waterfront promenade) that starts from the San Nicola pier (where the Barion club is located) and skirts the late 19th-century Umbertino district with its elegant buildings to the monumental Lungomare built during the Fascist period.

I am enjoying now the very beautiful, long evenings, which I usually spend walking, sometimes along the sea – which is, curiously, and without intended humor, called "The Board Walk." It is not board, but a wide street, without a sidewalk and a concrete balustrade along the sea. And into the old town, again, last night, where the streets were jam-packed with people going into and coming out of the churches, of which there must be seven or eight. The weather is now fine, although I note that it is clouding up a bit – for Tuesday, no doubt, my day off. [8 April]

Baritantotempofa

Figura 19. The monumental Lungomare with the characteristic lampposts, absent during the war period. In the background is the old city (end of 1940s)

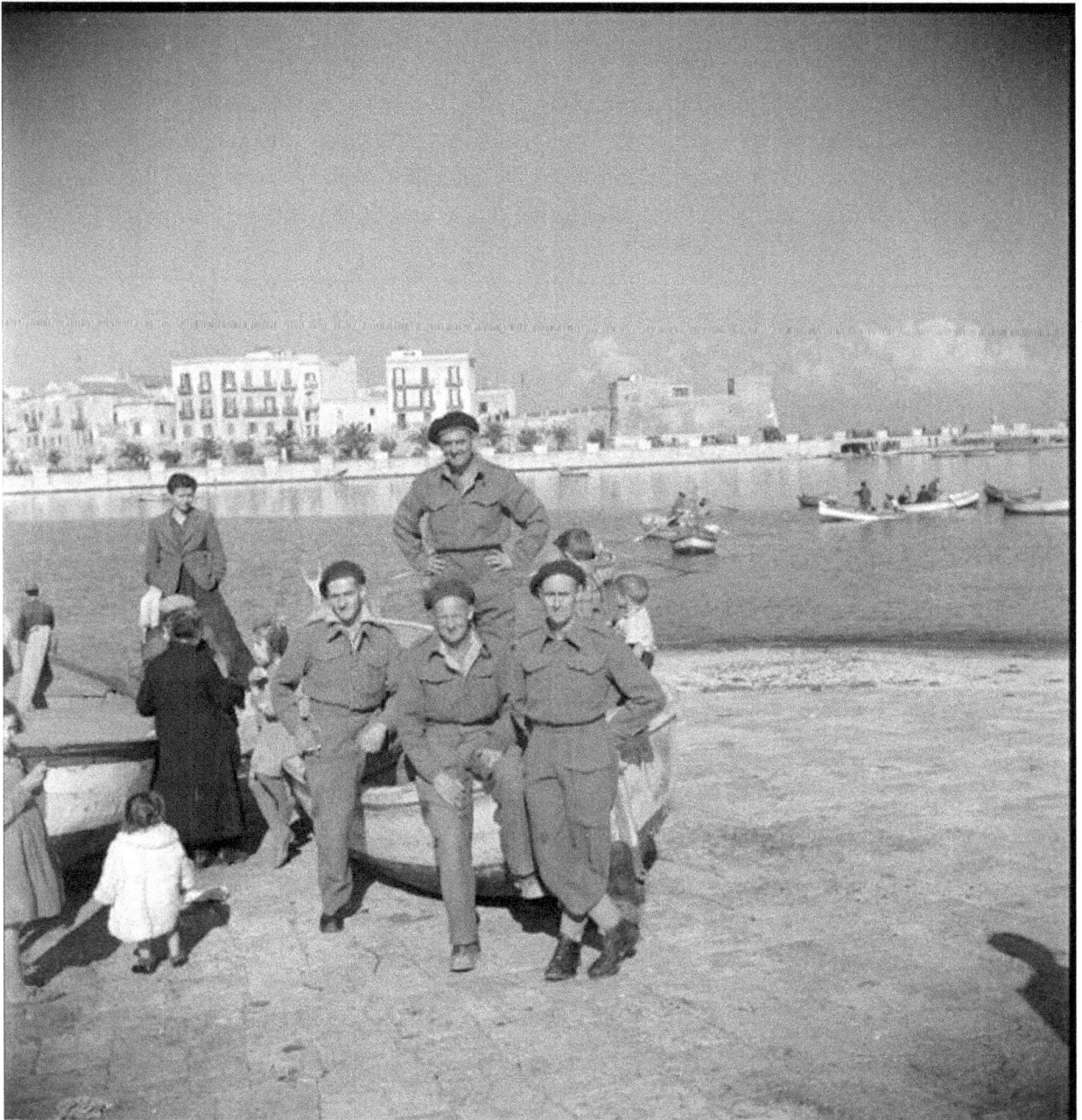

Figure 20. New Zealand soldiers on the *molo San Nicola*, near the Barion club (1944) Photograph taken by George Kaye, circa 1944.

Beyond the railroad

Beyond the station and the customary belt (today "via Capruzzi") began what was for a long time the city's industrial zone, with the first factories in the late 19th century. By the 1940s, (mostly working-class) neighborhoods were already developing. Going further, on the routes leading to the towns of the province, the countryside began, dotted with the majestic villas of wealthy families, mostly gone with urban development, or incorporated into the chaos of today's city.

Prominent among these residences were Re David and De Filippis villas, which were adjacent and united by the marriage union between their heirs, but were destroyed after the war to make way for modern residences.

Although the buildings no longer exist, statues and remnants of the gardens are still preserved within the residential complexes.

First I walked across the railroad tracks – did not get beyond the town – and over there is the factory district, the warehouses (agricultural – figs, dates and so forth) I walked around a while – then bought a bottle of brandy and a bottle of Anisette. And walked back with them. It was beginning to rain, but the sidewalk had a double row of citron trees – which cover it close. I left my bottles here and went out on a double quest – not too determinedly. First, I stopped and got a hair cut and shave. Then I went to a music store and asked a recommendation of a piano teacher. They gave me a name and address. I had to look for it a while – first asked a man who showed me the direction. Then, after a while that way, a woman, who must have thought she was a beauty. She tossed her head into the air and ran. Then I came upon it – and rang the bell. No answer. [14 March]

I left the room shortly after seven – a windy morning, and ate breakfast – tomato juice, cereal, eggs, bacon, toast and coffee. Then walked out across the railroad tracks, and out of town – The day meanwhile having become cloudy. Magnificent! A farm road, between high stone walls, over which the olive trees and fruit trees crowded. Here and there, open to a field – or through an open fence to a villa – as the Re David villino – which is a great house, in a grove of pines, with formal, paved gardens, statuary of cupids and gods – the Italians work with stone so naturally that the garden statuettes even are handsome. Then the almond trees in bloom – and the petals blooming, like snow – the gentlest fragrance! Peasants plowing – carts going to town with artichokes and the like – quite fine horses – and gentlemen driving in carriages. Children running along the road in wooden shoes, strapped on, one carrying a flask of milk – looked like goat's milk. [28 March]

Last night we went out into the country again – for our humorous quest, looking for villas – and found a perfect one – the Villina Re David – set in about two acres of formal gardens, with fine terraces and porches – looked inside – a big, formal dining room, all glass on one side – and an enormous living room, furnished in oak and plush and heavy drapes – lovely windows. But it was not available. A Fascist had owned it, so, in justice, the AOC (which is British for Air Officer Commanding) took it over, incidentally making himself very, very comfortable. The British surely install themselves tight – and if they once get an inch, never under any circumstances give it up. So they accumulate – I envy them their suavité [sic]. And Englishman can get anything for a cup of tea and a kind remark to an American or Canadian – on much the same principle as that on which an American matron would give anything she had for an introduction to the Queen – which is cheap for the Queen. Good business! [19 May]

Figure 21. Villa Re David

Figura 22. Villa De Filippis

Figure 23. Via di Carbonara, now Corso Alcide De Gasperi, in 1933. Here it was still in the countryside with its residential villas

Places of interest

During the wartime period under the fascist regime (June 1940-September 1943) Bari was spared from the most deadly effects of the conflict. Of course, activities were curtailed and curfews were in force, food was scarce, but the city was spared from the heavy bombing that hit nearby cities such as Taranto or Foggia. After the armistice of September 8, 1943 - by which the Italian government headed by General Badoglio ceased all hostilities against the Anglo-American allies - Bari and other southern cities had to face German troops who were in large numbers in the territory.

Bloody clashes occurred in Bari, and troops of the Italian army, flanked by the civilian population, successfully confronted Wehrmacht units that wanted to destroy the port and other infrastructure, forcing them to retreat.

Starting on September 18, Allied troops landed in the city, taking over the port and Palese Airport. The port was filled with Allied ships and was the main target of the massive German air raid on the city on December 2, which resulted in the sinking of numerous military ships and the deaths of thousands of soldiers and civilians, partly due to the dispersal of mustard gas stored in the American ship Harvey.[1]

From the earliest days, various government buildings were occupied to establish commands and other major infrastructure. The *15th Air Force Service Command* - to whose service Henry was assigned as soon as he arrived in the city - settled in the *Comando III Regione aerea italiana* building on the monumental waterfront.

"When the Fifteenth was activated its headquarters was in the Lycee Carnot in Tunis, where the headquarters of the XII Bomber Command had been located. But an advance echelon had already been established at Bari, and on 22 November orders were issued for the entire headquarters to move there, beginning 30 November. The movement, except for motor vehicles, was handled by planes of Mediterranean Air Transport Service; it was completed on 3 December, except for a rear echelon of fifty troops who did not complete their move until 18 December. **On 1 December, the headquarters officially closed at Tunis and opened in Bari, where it remained until the end of the Italian campaign**" (Source: www.ibiblio.org/hyperwar/AAF/II/AAF-II-16.html)

Figure 24. Maj. Gen. Nate Twinning and 15th AF Wing Commanders

Headquarters Adriatic Depot found its headquarters in the Camera di Commercio building on Corso Cavour:

> "The development of air bases in Italy not only created problems of airfield construction and of moving gasoline but also of handling supplies for the air forces, a problem which proved to be a peculiar one in eastern Italy. That area was to be a great base for the USAAF, the Mediterranean home of its heavy bombers. But eastern Italy was under the jurisdiction of the British because their Eighth Army was operating there; consequently, the American Services of Supply would not establish a base section for handling supplies common to ground and air, although British common items were altogether unsatisfactory to the American air units. The problem was solved by **establishing the Adriatic Depot at Bari, a depot that operated under the control of XII AFSC but was staffed largely by ground forces service personnel**. It got under way late in October and by the end of the year was supplying American air units with common items from numerous offices, warehouses, and dumps in and around Bari. Few operations in the Mediterranean were more unique - or more successful - than the depot, in which the American air forces ran a ground force activity in a British-controlled area." (Source: www.ibiblio.org/hyperwar/AAF/II/AAF-II-16.html)

In Bari, one of the first Allied objectives was the control of the main news media-Radio Bari and the local newspaper *la Gazzetta del Mezzogiorno* - whose activities from that time began to be subordinated to the directives of the *Allied Military Government of Occupied Territories.*

Allied troops also organize their own hospitals, in the Policlinico but not only. The ***26th US General Hospital*** was located at the military Hospital in Corso Sicilia (today Corso Alcide De Gasperi).

To enable the daily life of the troops, numerous hotels, restaurants and even theaters were also requisitioned, where shows and concerts were given to entertain the soldiers. In Bari, for example, the ***teatro Margherita*** became a Garrison Theatre (theaters run by ENSA - *Entertainments National Service Association*), but the **Petruzzelli** and **Piccinni** theaters were also used for the purpose.

At the ***circolo Barion*** (at the beginning of the waterfront, *molo San Nicola*) the Officers' Club (inter-force?) was established, while New Zealand troops placed the **NZ Forces Club building** in the Riunione Adriatica di Sicurtà building on Corso Cavour. Other clubs sprang up in other parts of the city, such as on the premises of the *circolo Unione* at the Petruzzelli Theater. Sports centers were also requisitioned, such as the Tennis club.

Allied officers also frequented many restaurants in the city. Among them was the *ristorante Adriatico*, which always stood on the San Nicola pier next to the officers' club (Barion). A reception hall and restaurant still exists there today (called sala Zonno).

Numerous private homes were requisitioned for officers' residences, especially in the suburbs of Torre a Mare, Palese-Santo Spirito and Carbonara.

City hotels were also occupied, starting with the *Hotel delle Nazioni* on the waterfront, called **Hotel Imperiale**.

Figure 25. New Zealand soldier in a wayside shrine in Bari (1943) [14] **Photograph taken circa November 1943 by George Frederick Kaye.**

15th Air Force Service Command

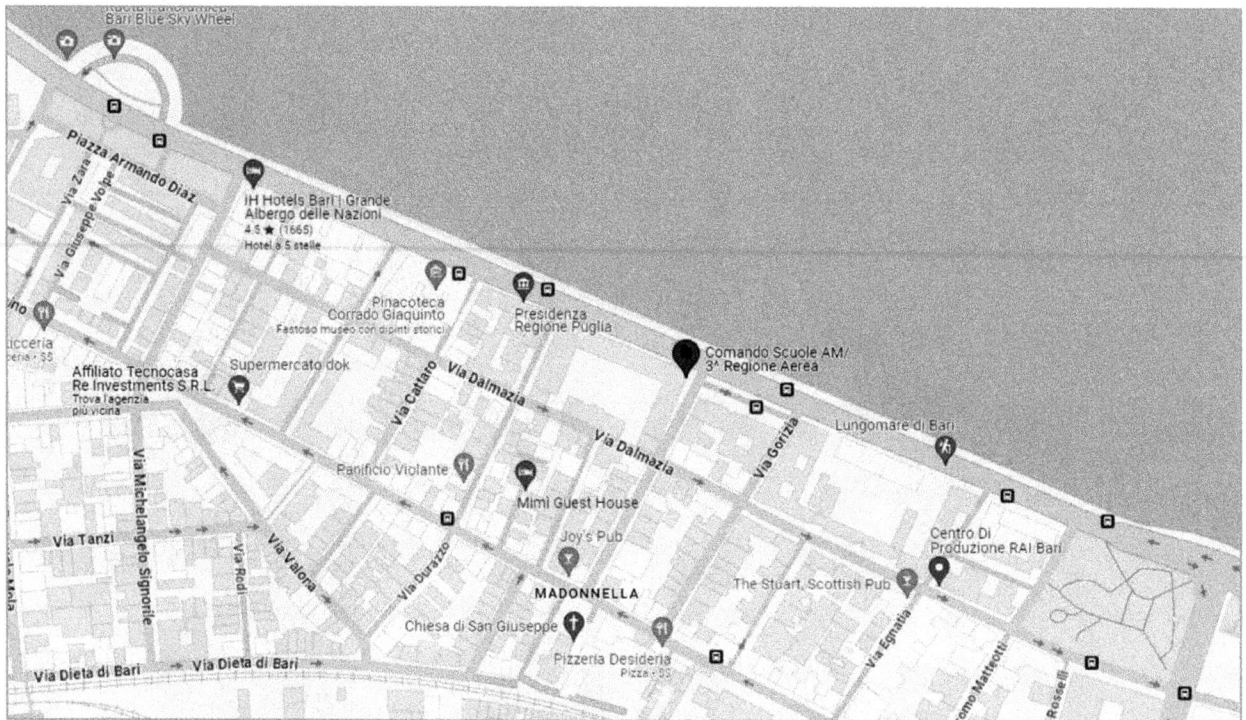

Figure 26. Lungomare Nazario Sauro, 39, 70121 Bari BA

BARI - Palazzo dell'Aeronautica (Lungomare Nazario Sauro)

Figure 27. Bari. Palazzo dell'Aeronautica home of the *15th Air Force Service Command*

Figure 28. Anti-aircraft station defending the 15th Air Force Service Command (photo by W. Pugh)

---

[15] P. Marturano, V. Raimondo, Bari 1940-1950, Adda Editore, p. 54

Headquarters Adriatic Depot

Figure 29: Corso Cavour, 2, 70121 Bari BA

Figure 30. Adriatic Depot headquarters in the Camera di commercio building

Figure 31. Corso Cavour. The last building is the Headquarters Adriatic Depot (1943). The view is from the NZ Forces Club looking along the Via Cavour in Bari, Italy, during World War II. Taken circa November 1943 by an official photographer, probably George Frederick Kaye.

General Hospital USA

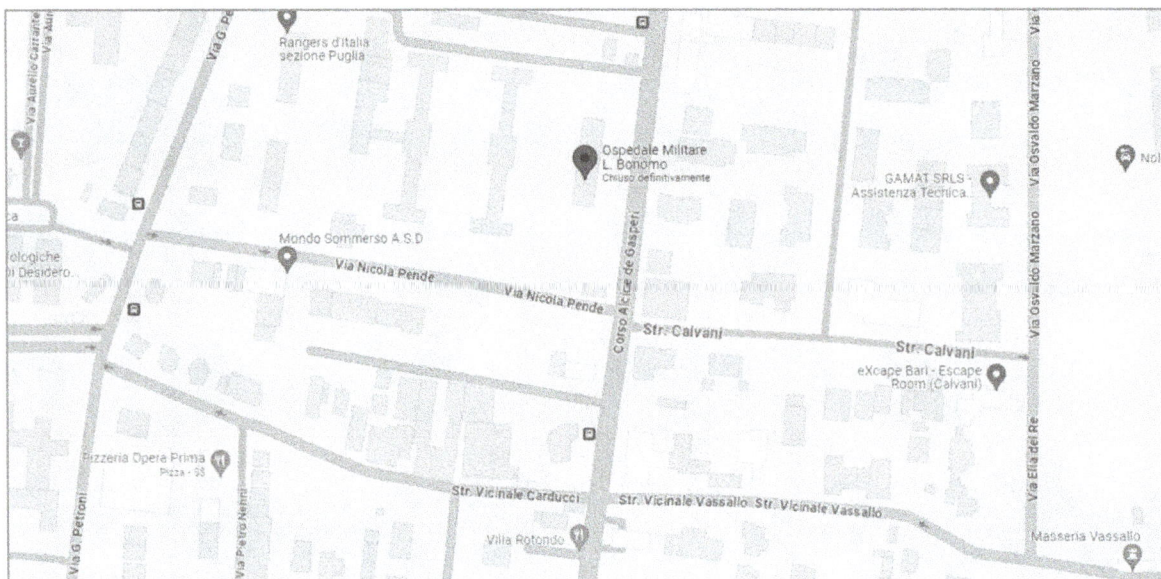

Figure 32. Corso Alcide de Gasperi, 79, 70124 Bari BA

Figure 33. U.S. General Hospital is located at the *Ospedale militare* in corso Sicilia

Teatro Margherita - Garrison Theatre

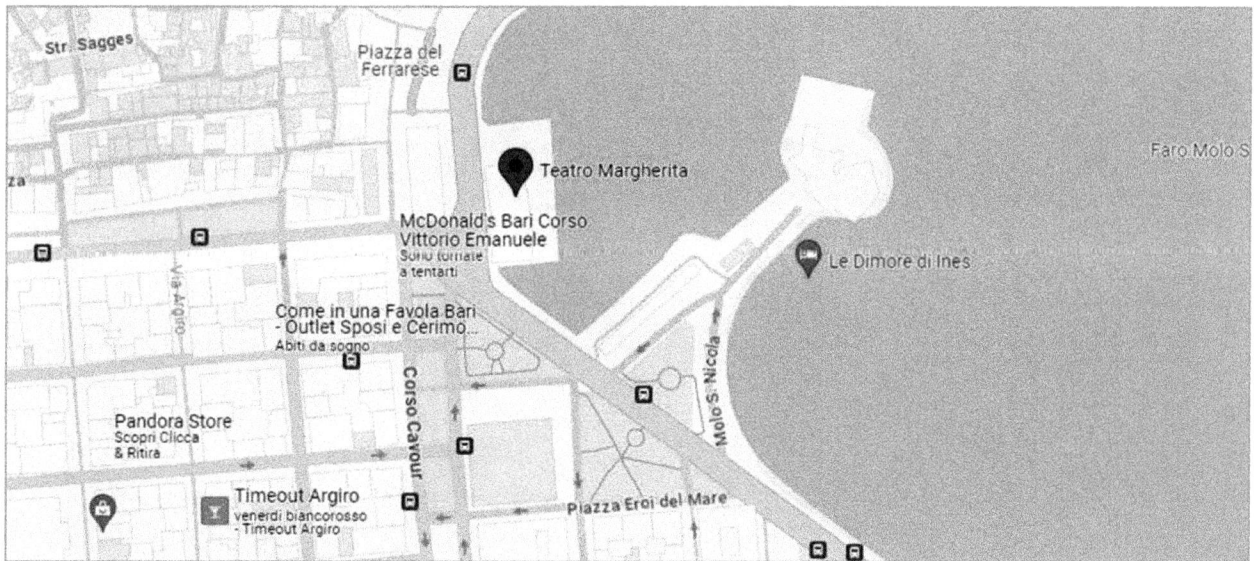

Figure 34: Teatro Margherita, Piazza IV Novembre, 70122 Bari BA

Figure 35. Teatro Margherita (1952)

Teatro Petruzzelli

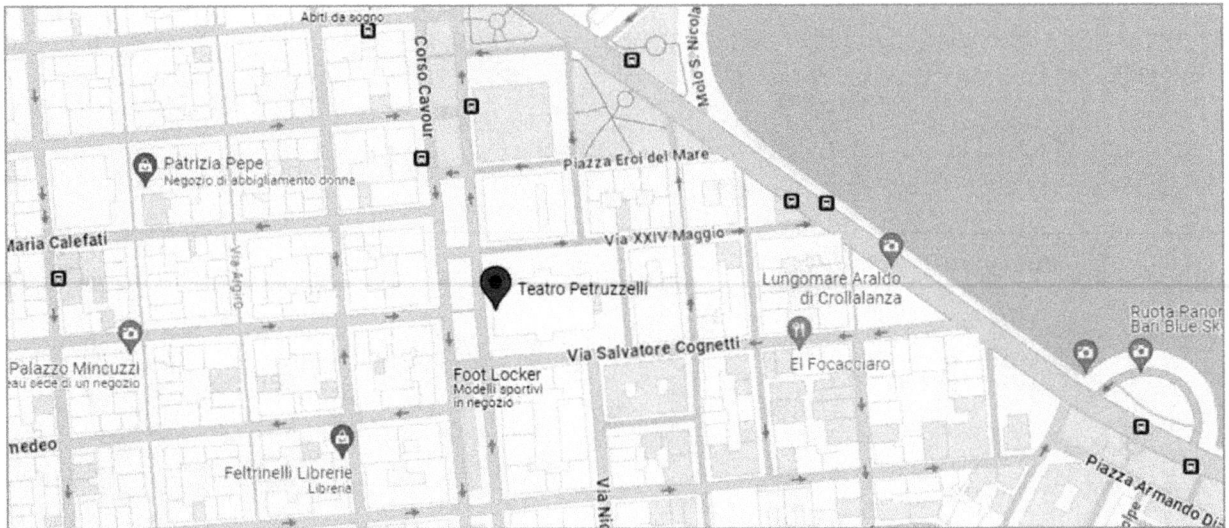

Figure 36. Corso Cavour, 12, 70122 Bari BA

Figure 37. Playbills from the Garrison Theatre of Barletta and the Petruzzelli Theatre of Bari

Figure 38. Teatro Petruzzelli (1943) Teatro Petruzzelli, opposite NZ Forces Club, in Bari, Italy -
Photograph taken by George Kaye

Figure 40. U.S. soldiers use a urinal near the Petruzzelli

Figure 41. Allied officers dance

Figure 42. RAF Malcolm club (indefinite location)

Teatro Piccinni

Figure 43. Corso Vittorio Emanuele II, 84, 70122 Bari BA

Figure 44. The Piccinni theater on Corso Vittorio Emanuele

Heard an excellent concert last night – Mozart's Eine Kleine Nachtmusik – Chopin Concerto and Rimsky-Korsakov's Scheherazade. I particularly enjoy Mozart as a kind of specialist in violins, and Chopin as specialist in piano. [7 May]

CINEMA E TEATRI

Il concerto odierno al Piccinni

Oggi, alle 18, si darà al Teatro Piccinni il 19. Concerto sinfonico degli Amici della Musica, che sarà diretto dal maestro Lav Mirski con la partecipazione del pianista Ladislav Sternberg. Saranno eseguite musiche di Mozart, Chopin, Rimski Korsakoff.

Figure 45. May 7, 1944 symphony concert in the local newspaper

Hotel Imperiale (Hotel delle Nazioni)

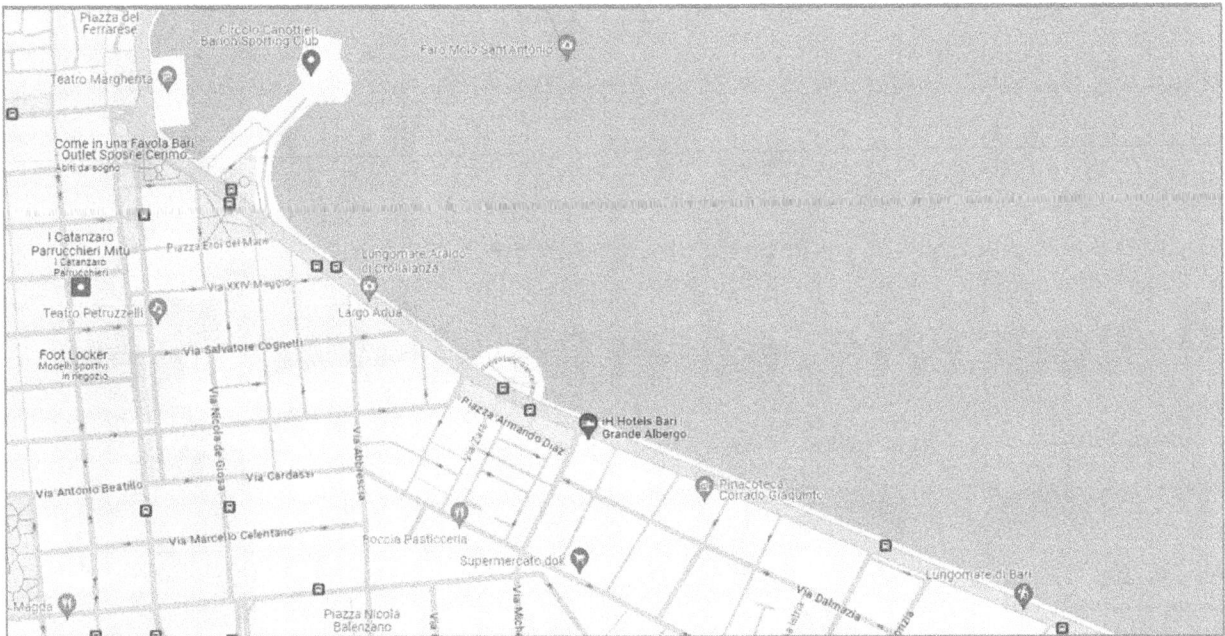

Figure 46. Lungomare Nazario Sauro, 7, 70121 Bari BA

Figure 47. Hotel Imperiale (archives George Frederick Kaye)

Figure 48. General view of the waterfront at Bari, Italy, taken from roof of Hotel Imperia. Photograph taken by George Kaye.

Officers' Club (circolo Barion)

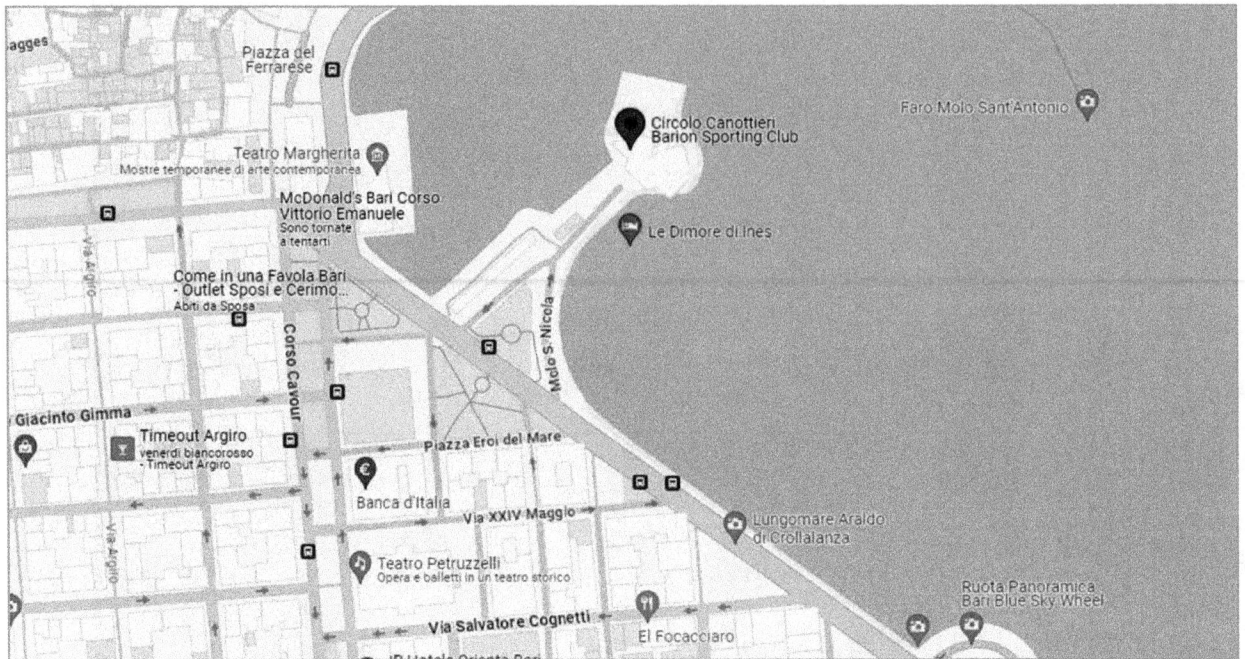

Figure 49. Molo S. Nicola, 5, 70121 Bari BA

Figura 41. Allied soldiers on the San Nicola pier. In the background the officers' club (Barion) and the Adriatico restaurant on the right

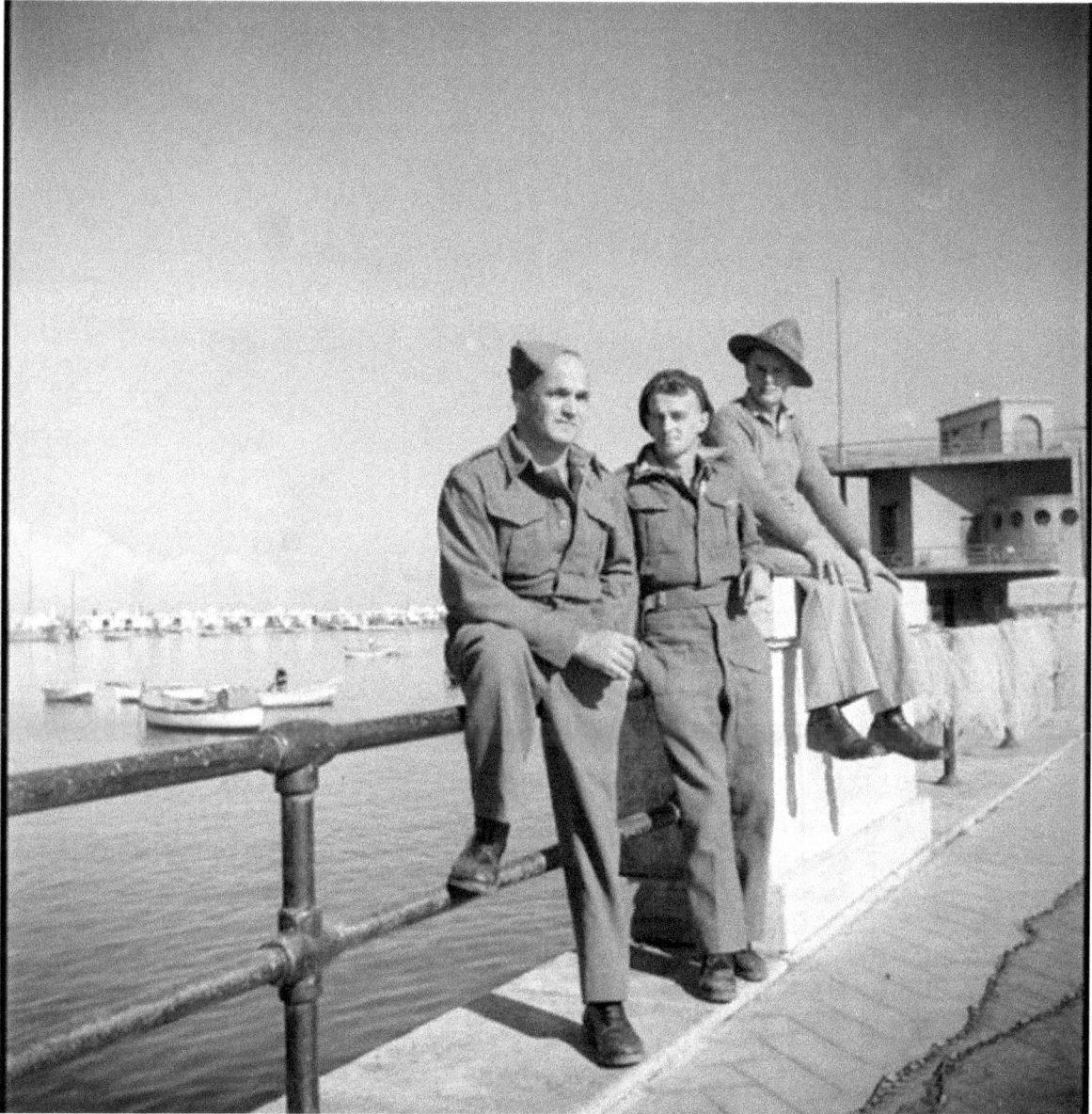

Figura 42. New Zealand soldiers on the San Nicola pier. In the background the officers' club (Barion)

Ristorante Adriatico

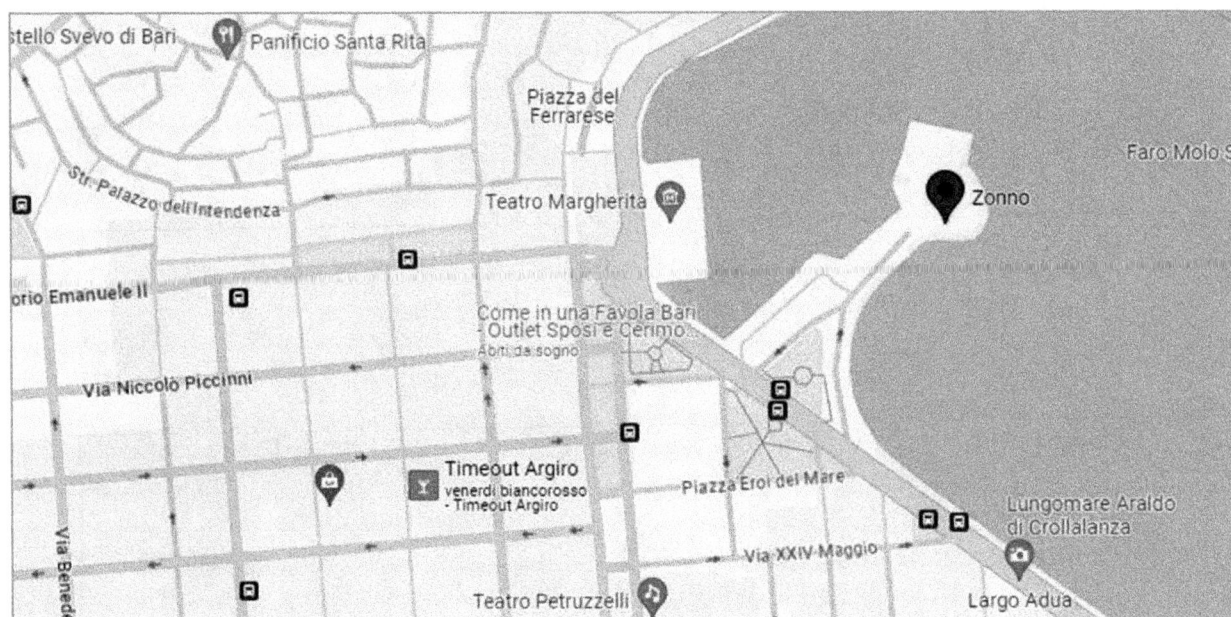

Figure 52. Molo S. Nicola, 3, 70121 Bari BA

Figure 53. Ristorante Adriatico advertisement in the 1930s

Figure 54. Circolo Barion (left) and Ristorante Adriatico (right) in 1930s

Last night I ate dinner with Bill Clark – at his mess hall – which is a former yacht club out at the end of a pier – very elaborate and very fancy – salad (lettuce, onions and canned salmon, with olive oil and vinegar) soup (bean) meat loaf and mashed potatoes and string beans – a kind of tart-like crisp sponge cake filled with apples and raisins. Wine and coffee So you see I am in no danger of starvation. [19 March]

Then asked them to come to dinner with me tonight – intending to bring them to the Adriatic They agreed that if they were still in town, they would be here at five o'clock. So I shall see if they turn up. [26 March]

Last evening I went on with my little deviltry spree – and brought the two officers from II Corps to dinner – or Bill did – at the Adriatic Club. Then we had a glass of cognac downstairs at the sumptuous yacht club bar, and saw a bum movie in the lounge – but in comfortable over-stuffed chairs. [26 March]

So after the concert we went to the Club Adriatico, where there was a dance in progress, with only two three girls – two nurses and one civilian – a kind of devil-may-care looking woman who is probably a refugee from some place, because native girls are afraid for their reputations if they are seen after dark. [2 April]

NZ Forces Club building (Riunione adriatica di sicurtà)

Figure 55. Corso Cavour, 83, 70121 Bari BA

Figure 56. Building entrance at 12/A Putignani Street today

Figure 57. NZ Forces Club building in corso Cavour. Photograph taken by George Kaye.

Biblioteca consorziale Sagarriga Visconti Volpi

Figure 58. Piazza Umberto I, 1, 70121 Bari BA

Figura 59. The Ateneo building, home of the Biblioteca consorziale (then Nazionale) Sagarriga Visconti Volpi from 1927 to 2006

After I had had enough parade, I went out to the university, and out of curiosity spoke to a boy standing at the door with books in his arm. In view of my bad Italian, he proposed to speak German. But it is completely impossible to speak two languages at once – so I stuck to Italian. I asked him if the school had a library – and he said they had two excellent ones – what book did I want? I could see it there. I had to think hard to think of a book – and asked for a book on the common law of England. So we went in and looked for it. Lots of books on Roman law and German law – and finally, in the Faculty of Arts and Sciences we found a book on the English criminal law – by a man named Havers – copied translated into Italian. So I said that was exactly what I wanted – and sat down at a table with it, diligently copying the title and thanking them. I am told that I am welcome to use the university library – which is a good library, although, of course, most of the books are in Italian. [9 May]

Tell daddy – just wait for the next court martial case I have to try – I am really going to have fun, citing books existent and nonexistent in the Biblioteca Consorziale Sagarriga Visconti Volpi de ---. I'll cite them by bookcase, shelf, and number! But they'll be obscure ones.

I enclose a post-card I got at the parade this morning. Children and women were getting rapturous over this card – kissing it and weeping. I think St. Nicholas is as a saint particularly interested in purity – hence children – and seafarers, and in fires, for when he was being consecrated bishop, a house burned down. The lady of the house was at the ceremony, and her children burned. St. Nicholas brought them back to life. So, I suppose, by transfer, he becomes an important personage when people fear air raids and consequent fires – as they do here, having read of them.

Figure 60. U.S. soldier posing with Bari children in front of the Ateneo

Relations with civilians

"It happened exactly as we had predicted in our crazy plans. Only the conclusion was different but by then everything was different.

The first Allied tracked truck came clattering from Corso Vittorio Emanuele. It skidded on a crawler in facing the curve of Giardino Garibaldi toward the Istituto Borea and paused for a moment. On board were two soldiers. Armed with stones, my friends and I looked at them with the same incredulity with which one takes note that something long awaited has been accomplished. To tell the truth at that moment we thought nothing of it. Time only to see a handful of cigarettes thrown at us, Victory's from the blond tobacco that tingled in the throat to smoke several. Dazed and perhaps even a little unfazed in our unconscious by the gesture, we remained a few moments undecided and dumbfounded by the surprise. Then, after a very quick glance, with simultaneous gesture we threw ourselves into the fray to contend for cigarettes with more determined groups of boys who had arrived from the old city. We managed to seize a couple of cigarettes, no more.

- They are cigarettes ...

- Give it here, let me see ...

- What if they're poisoned?

- Don't talk nonsense ... Can't you see they're fine cigarettes? Smell them. Other than ours.

Blond, plump, they seemed delicious to us because of the novelty of the taste and perhaps because of all they represented. And echoed for the first time the cry, the call, the invocation that for years would mark the time of our whirlwind adolescence: *Hey, Joe!* The allies had arrived.

Everything was new, different, interesting, fantastic, as some of us said. We began to stay out of the house more and more. Curiosity and interest stretched our days. And we soon learned with the pliability of the busy, of those who needed everything, to distinguish between the aloof and disdainful British and the friendly and childlike Americans, between the Canadians always ready to settle arguments with their fists and the religious Poles who came to Mass at St. Francis framed and disciplined.

The most generous were the Americans, and we found that they could afford it. They thus became the most sought after by the people of Bari, who with unerring business instincts understood that one could get as much as possible out of these allies full of <<Am- lires," tins of meat and a desire for <<segnorine>>." (Source: Michele Campione, Ehy Joe. Gli alleati a Bari tra cronaca e romanzo, Levante Editori Bari, pp. 49-50)

This is how Bari journalist Michele Campione (1928-2003), then just 15 years old, recounts his first impact with the Allied soldiers. It was a shocking and wonderful encounter for him and for all Italians, who had come from years of suffering and deprivation, and decades of imposition by the fascist regime.

Campione immediately mentions the nickname by which all American soldiers were called by the locals, that famous "Hey Joe" that also gives his book its title. An appellation that after months in Bari must have irritated Henry in no small measure:

> *Then I have a small campaign – all children, when begging for chewing gum, candy and the like begin "Hey, Joe." I am trying to teach them that "Hey" is not a courteous form of salutation, and "Joe" is not everybody's name. I have no firm decision as to what they should say, but that suggested: "If you please, sir" and "Hear me, I beg you, sir." Those I have tried to teach have abandoned their quest for chewing gum and run away – which is also a desirable event. "[5 June]*

Figure 61. Bari. Children play in the street in the old town (1950s)

Certainly there was no shortage of problems between those who were occupied and occupiers, problems related on the one hand to the freedoms young soldiers were taking while at war away from home (alcohol, relationships with women, etc.), and on the other hand to the sometimes borderline criminal resourcefulness that the local population could have when faced with so many opportunities for enrichment after years of misery. For many it was worth risking a few weeks in jail to get their hands on a case of canned meat, useful for feeding the family and reselling on the black market. More generally we can imagine a culture shock in the meeting of such diverse populations (just think that with the allies there were also New Zealanders, Australians, Indians, Africans, etc.).

Speaking of theft, Henry recalls this incident:

Then I bought a raincoat, since mine was stolen in a city where they'll steal your eye teeth. I left it in the vehicle – the driver in the front seat – a crowd surrounded the vehicle and a man ran away with the rain coat – the driver couldn't chase him, because if he did someone would have stolen the vehicle or/and the other things, which he was sitting on. [25 March]

In some of the letters, Henry also emphasizes the distrust of allies from people in the wealthier classes.

And people (respectable, conservative people) are, I think, extremely suspicious and while not hostile, reserved – as is to be expected. In the first place, I suppose they have long been taught that Americans are strange barbarians. In the second place, I suppose they think they may be under suspicion and being investigated. Well – such attitudes and prejudices cannot be attacked directly – I shall just be naïve. [15 March]

It should not be forgotten that the requisitions of buildings affected them (their homes, their places of recreation and culture, restaurants, clubs, theaters, etc.) more than the working classes, who saw in the Allied soldiers opportunities to improve their condition:

I am inclined to the opinion that substantial Italians are unfriendly to Americans – that they are still fascists at heart, and those who are here are the ones who were unable to escape to the north. They consider that the Americans are just the dupes of the English (a sentiment in which I believe the English concur) but I do not mind their sentiments. Those who are friendly are so because that's the side their bread is buttered on. [30 April]

About the commercial advantages that enterprising Barians could gain from newcomers, again Michele Campione:

"With these simple directions that were later applied to everything <<Made in USA,>> from clothes to shoes to entire truckloads and liquor, an incredible trade flourished that lasted for years. Since then the commercial soul of Bari never knew such resounding splendor and renewed Levantine sweetnesses that seemed dormant for centuries.

Another prodigy was the rapid and immediate birth of a special language between occupants and occupied. By one of those miraculous events that no historian will ever be able to penetrate in all the folds and details the most elementary words of Italian and English with mispronunciations and transformations difficult to imagine ended up becoming an extraordinary instrument of communication between victors and vanquished. And everything worked perfectly. Time was in charge of smoothing out angularities and remedying initial difficulties.

- Hey, Joe, wont wine? Good... Very good... Very good.

- Oh, yes. You, sister?... Segnorina?

Typically, this point in the dialogue was followed by an expletive from the Bari side, directed at the deceased ancestors of the Anglo-Saxon interlocutor. The response was not long in coming.

But these occasional verbal disagreements did not spoil relations at all between a hungry city like Bari, between helpful and well-disposed people like the Baresi, and the allies. And business prospered. The most lucrative initially were the bars and cafes.

The thirst of the British, the Americans, the New Zealanders, seemed unquenchable and limitless. First all the liqueurs that figured in the display cases and in the shelves were given over. Then it was the turn of vermouths but the most in demand were the strong liquors. The factories, however, did not produce them and the people of Bari set about making them themselves. In the homes, mothers, aunts, sisters-in-law became expert alchemists in making *Fuoco di Russia, Latte di Vecchia, Caffè Sport, Doppio Kummel* with less and less sugar and increasing amounts of alcohol made from grape stems or dried figs. When pure alcohol began to become scarce some bartender without excessive scruples, after all, how could anyone get any at a time when only money was being chased? began to mix sugar and essences with elongated burning alcohol. The drunkenness of the unwary drinkers became hospital hangovers. A few others did not hesitate to make terrible mixtures even with the use of bleach. For a while this deadly concoction also worked and found enthusiastic customers.

The days of American Prohibition were small and pale in the face of the ingenious and destructive resourcefulness of the bartenders at our house." (Source: Michele Campione, Ehy Joe. Gli alleati a Bari tra cronaca e romanzo, Levante Editori Bari, pp. 51-52)

On the local population, it is clear from the letters how impressed Henry was with Bari's children, a childhood that was at times complicated and wild, especially in those difficult times. Here are some passages from his letters:

There are an awful lot of crying babies in this town – and I always imagine they are crying because of some deep suffering – they cry so pitifully. Until this evening – one stopped crying very suddenly when it got a top, which an older child had taken away. So I suppose they are not crying more passionately than American children. [15 March]

Babies here are dressed in what I suppose to be swaddling clothes – and it looks very funny – a baby wrapped up stiff – just its head sticking out – The mother carries it, and if she had to use her hands or wants to rest, she just stands the baby down, leaned up in a corner of a wall. It is so stiff that it stands here, leaning against the wall. The baby leans there crying or cooing and doesn't seem to mind it a bit. [15 March]

Yesterday, I looked out of the window of the coffee shop, at the sea, and a little dock, and there were children swimming. My, it looked cold. [7 April]

Figure 62. Children bathe near the old port (early 1900s)

Then last evening – it stays light now until 8:30, for we have daylight savings time - I went for a walk through the old city. Crowds of children running and playing in the streets – dressed so funny – in little dresses, with nothing else, and when they run, the dresses get all tangled up around their shoulders – many of them without shoes – and many with wooden shoes, which keep falling off, and they have to go back to put them back on. Some with little fur jackets, made from old fur coats. The little girls wear long hair, and they pull each other around by their hair.

Figura 63. A group of Bari children near the Castle (1913)

I took a walk last night – around and through the old town. What a variety of games the children play – from the very beautiful singing games – they are really square dances – going to and fro to meet each other – and part as they sing, and going around in a circle singing about the chicken being caught – the only words I could understand – and fighting and throwing stones at each other, and chasing each other with clubs. [24 April]

(I can't decide whether it is picturesque – a woman sitting in the doorway combing children's hair, and picking the bugs out – if you don't know what she's doing, it is picturesque.) The children are ingenious in their games – and play quite beautifully – one, which looks like ring a round the rosy – but they chant something, having one child in the circle, about the chicken is encircled and can't escape – so I suppose the one in the center is trying to get out in some way – Then they chase each other all over. Of course, there is an awful lot of crying going on – little children being abused by bigger ones – taking their balls away, and so forth – and mama's calling loud and furious for "Giovanni" and "Nicola" and begging for candy and chewing gum and what not. [14 April]

Figure 64. Scenes of daily life in the San Triggiano court in the old city. On the left, a woman cleans a little girl (1930s)

Figure 65. Bari, Palese airport. U.S. female soldier teaches military salute to a little girl

The maestro Nicola Costa

Nicola Costa (Naples 1879 – Rome 1963) was a musician and composer who lived for many years in Bari. A full biographical profile is available online.

I DUE CONCERTI DI IERI A BARI

Ricordo di Nicola Costa
il vecchietto dal cuore d'oro

La manifestazione, organizzata dalla Polifonica, era dedicata alle sue musiche vocali e a brani dall'opera « Margot » -- La figura dell'artista rievocata da Donato Marrone

Il m° Nicola Costa

Ad un anno dalla morte, la Polifonica ha dedicato ieri un concerto a Nicola Costa, musicista fra i più nobili e generosi di Puglia, il vecchietto dal cuore d'oro, musicista autentico diremmo, nel senso più lato dell'espressione, perché la sua attività spaziò proficua e copiosa in tutti i campi, dalla composizione al concertismo, dallo studio profondo e meditato all'insegnamento più fertile, sì che la scuola pianistica barese gli deve, al di là della retorica, un vero monumento di gratitudine. Il programma di ieri era interamente dedicato alle sue musiche vocali. La manifestazione, ha spiegato Donato Marrone prima del concerto, era un doveroso omaggio all'artista e un tributo di affetto, un grato sentimento per tutto ciò che Nicola Costa ha compiuto per la formazione e l'elevazione del nostro ambiente musicale. Tanto più significativa l'iniziativa della Polifonica, poiché Costa, sin dal sorgere dell'istituzione, la seguì con entusiasmo e fu largo di incoraggiamenti per la fervida attività di Biagio Grimaldi. D'altronde, come previsto nel programma generale della stagione, la Polifonica commemorerà prossimamente anche Pasquale La Rotella e don Cesare Franco, rispettivamente nel primo e nel ventesimo anniversario della morte; l'insieme delle tre manifestazioni serve appunto a dare l'opportuno rilievo al contributo offerto da questi indimenticabili artisti pugliesi allo sviluppo della nostra cultura musicale.

Le pagine contenute nel programma di ieri sera non sono indubbiamente le più impegnative di Nicola Costa, autore di

Figure 66. Homage to Nicola Costa on the pages of La Gazzetta del Mezzogiorno one year after his death

Nicola Costa's house stood in via Vallisa 22, near Piazza del Ferrarese, at the entrance to the old city. The house should still be there, as can be deduced from the initials NC present on the entrance door of the building.

Figure 67. The entrance door of Nicola Costa's house

By this time, it was almost noon, and I went back to see my music teacher. Wonderful! a little man, who speaks a little French (as much as I speak Italian, so there's no advantage) and had a thoroughly magnificent studio – a big room, in the old quarter, with paneled walls, and fine hangings dark furniture, with red upholstery, a big window at one end – glass chandelier – a thoroughly magnificent room. I asked if he would give me lessons – telling him I could not practice – solely for the love of music, as he asked and I answered affirmatively, and 100 lire a lesson, if it could be in the evening – he said no – and it will be at noon on Tuesday – which is my day off. Too good to last – but why not shoot at the stars?

Maestro Nicola Costa, is his name, and his wife was calling him to lunch while I was there – and he was saying "Momento, Maria!" He is a little tiny man – not quite up to my shoulder – and has a very fine piano, in perfect tune – it is a long time since I have seen one like it.

So I have a music teacher – and he accepted me, after I played some scales, and read some for him. You may tell Janet and Heather that I shall be unbearable on the subject of my Italian musical education before when I get home. [14 March]

But how can I write of anything except my music lesson – 6 days away. For I look forward to that with such delight – Nicola Costa – a little man in frock coat – with a great big piano, in a very portentous room – heavy and magnificent with a little shrine in it and many articles of bigotry and virtue. Yesterday, he said he could not give lessons at night – I think he suspected and mistrusted me – for he had been warned that I was coming again (the first time no one answered, and I suspect all the neighbors came to tell him a soldier had rung his bell) He says the building is locked at night. Well – maybe I can arrange to come there one evening a week in addition to the one noon-time. I shall ply him with cigarettes – and I have one nickel cigar which I am saving to offer him. And I shall give him what else I can get – a cake of soap, if friendly relations are established.

That is so Maestro Nicola Costa – he is a patient little man, I think. I write his name so often, partly to memorize it – 22 Via Vallisa – just inside the old quarter. I should like to hear him play – He had quite a library of music. [15 March]

I found yesterday that my description of Maestro Costa's studio was all wrong – it is not paneled– but papered in dark red. The chandelier is not glass, but iron – and quite handsome. But the room is as pretty as I remembered it. [22 March]

The Turetti's

From an initial search it was not possible to identify the place where this family, not originally from Bari, lived, nor any particular information about them.

I was billeted in a hotel – but desired to stay with Clark – hotels are uninteresting anyway. So we found a room in an apartment – surprising how quickly one gets used to inner spring mattresses; running water – a bath tub – good lights – dry floors – The family who occupy the apartment – a man, a woman and their son and daughter – are friendly; they come from another part of Italy, where they were bombed out. The apartment is on the seventh floor – with elevator. We visited with the family last night - I am learning Italian – but am far from fluent. [9 March]

The landlady mystifies me – towel and wash rag disappear every morning, and reappear dry and clean two days later. Does she wash them every day? It is really quite unnecessary. [13 March]

The wood-carver

The figure of this carver emerges in Henry's letters, also due to the relationship of esteem that was created between the two. Unfortunately, the research carried out also with local residents has not allowed - at present - to precisely identify this person and locate his laboratory and his home.

From Henry's descriptions we can hypothesize that the carver was near the column of justice in Piazza Mercantile. Two streets are suspected: Corte Sant'Agostino, a closed alley that begins with an arch, and Strada Manfredi, at the end of which there was a carpenter near a big arch.

Figure 68. Column of justice in Piazza Mercantile (1908)

And walked through a street of the old town before dark – looked in a window, where a man was carving wooden plaques – heads of saints, copied from pictures – apparently quite skillfully. He saw me watching him and asked me to come in – so I did – gave him a cigarette, and he told me about how he was going to New York as soon as he could get there; that he could not make a living any more, because bread cost 100 lire a kilo, and his plaques – a week's worth – brought only 1000 lire. I asked him if he could design a small box – while his plaques are very fine, the subjects are all too saintly – and he brought out his folio of designs and pictures. He wants to make a carved chest – large – which would of course be an extremely handsome thing to have. But too bulky. He has splendid designs – keeping the patterns of everything he has previously designed or made – So he is going to design a box and show me the design, if I go back, and I think I shall ask him to make me something, although maybe not a box. He seems to me to do a kind of portrait carving very well – copying pictures of saints and the like – his plaques intrigued me with the detail of hands and expressions, and the intricate patterns of robes and halos – flowered halos seem to be in fashion. [6 April]

I went to see a wood-carver, who makes pictures out of wood. He said he could not make boxes because he could not get hinges and locks and keys. He has a little boy, about your age, who helps him, sandpapering things and helping to sharpen tools by turning the handle of a grindstone. [7 April]

He has a beautiful little shop – a work bench with a high char, in a tiny room – under an arch in an old building, just at the curve of a very narrow street – a few feet from the place where it opens into a paved place – with a public fountain, where people are always filling their jugs and buckets, and a stone lion – Egyptian in appearance – lying on a stone platform – up a few steps; inscribed to "justice" in mediaeval Latin – "Esto justicie." Then a building, as intricate as lace, with statues on top – not a church, but possibly a castle, now with shops and dwellings. In his shop, just off the lacy square, the walls are covered with pictures of saints, which serve as models for his plaques – which he does in great detail. [12 April]

We walked on down into the old town – and looked at the leaning pillar with a ball on top, and a lion by it – a fantastic, flat faced lion, which children pet – and they have polished parts of it highly with years of petting. I have quite an affection for the lion and pillar – with the motto on its collar "Esto justicie." Maybe it is a dog and not a lion – it is so docile and smiling.

As we looked at it, the little wood carver (Sunday – he is all polished and dressed) comes running out, saluting and bowing as he runs – So we greet him, and he asks us to come to his house and have a drink – his room is just across the way, up a blind alley a little way – we go in – a big room, on the level of the ground, flag-stone floor – one side is mostly door, with an outer door of wood. In the corner, his wife, who was sitting with neighbors at the corner, joins us. In the room is one enormous bed – one table, a wardrobe thing and a few niches with a big piece of hand-woven and embroidered linen hanging in front of it. The wood carver apologizes – it is big enough for the two of them. The baby on the bed is his nephew – a little tiny baby – maybe six or eight months old – all wrapped up in blankets. There is excess of hospitality, in pulling up chairs – and we sit down at the table. He brings out (or has his wife bring out) a bottle of "grappa" – which he says is, in English "Vischi" (whiskey? it wasn't) and pours each of us a big glass. Then, for the event we do not like that, each a big glass of white wine. He and his wife take red wine – vin ordinaire – which comes from a pitcher – quite a beautiful old pottery pitcher. Pretty soon the baby begins to cry – and the wife shakes the bed; the baby goes back to sleep. Then his brother comes – a talkative man, all polished and dressed clean, with his wife, and four of his children in addition to the one on the bed. He has eight children – the oldest 11 years, and one on the way. The children are all polished and clean – the boys with little velvet hats – the girl in a green velvet upholstery dress, embodied. The children stand, beautifully behaved and quiet – apparently instructed not to laugh, they answer questions as best they can. Then another sister comes in – and the father – an old man of 70, who has been to Paris. The sister nurses one baby, while she holds another on her lap. Then three more brothers come in – add them up, if you can, I never did get count of them. And such politeness! Of course we had to keep our hands over the glasses, so keep them from filling them – but conversation flew – mostly about prices, by the tailor with eight children – the prices of food, and his own suit, of which he is very proud – the cloth is pre-war – but the lining cost more than all the rest of the suit, except the buttons. The old man worked on a short railroad in France – and did not work hard – spent most of his time in Paris where wine is so good. The cabinet maker expects to go to New York – what a surprise the naive little man will have if he ever gets there. He says a captain told him he knew where he could get a job as a wood carver, so it won't be hard, because he'll be expected, and be able to go right to work at high wages. [17 April]

Eruption of Vesuvius

On March 18, 1944 there was a powerful eruption of Vesuvius. The ash dispersed for hundreds of kilometers, reaching even distant locations such as Bari.

The eruption occurred during the Second World War, in the midst of the Italian campaign. The eruption caused damage not only to civilian homes in the surrounding municipalities, but also to the US and British military structures, still present in the Neapolitan area after the liberation from the occupation of the Wehrmacht forces. Thanks to the presence of foreign operators in the city to document the war, the 1944 eruption of Vesuvius was documented with video images taken in real time. Furthermore, there are numerous testimonies from American soldiers or reporters who described the eruptive activity.

This is how Henry recounts the effects of the eruption in his letters:

"An interesting natural phenomenon is now occurring – it is raining out, and the rain as it falls is a thick mud. If one holds a piece of paper out, it is spotted with mud. I did not imagine that the dust would carry this far. For the sea outside had quite changed color – the mud floating on the surface. Even the breakers are yellow instead of white.

I suppose it is fortunate that it is raining – the dust, otherwise, would be quite nearly unbearable. It would be interesting to see the lava flow, but I haven't a chance of getting over there – and even if I had, wouldn't waste my time looking at natural phenomena. Vesuvius can be seen for many many miles, and I have seen it frequently, for a long time constantly. A kind of beacon at night. Aetna was never active when I was near it – and the days were too long to stay up to see it at night often. How long ago that is! now the days are getting longer again.

I just walked to lunch – and back – stopping for 200 gms. of sugar coated almonds, of which I am fond. So now I am more or less coated with mud – my eyes, ears, nose, etc. It is quite a remarkable phenomenon." [23 march]

Figura 69. Eruption of Vesuvius (1944)

Feast of Saint Nicholas

On May 7th, 8th and 9th of each year, the city of Bari celebrates its patron Saint Nicholas with three days of civil and religious celebrations, remembering the arrival of the relics in 1087. We can imagine that in times of war these celebrations were on a smaller scale , but no less felt by the population.

So those days in Henry's story:

May 8 is a holiday – a religious celebration with parades and carrying the statue of Saint N. through the streets and so forth. I hope to see some of it." [5 May]

I got up at the usual time, and, as is my Tuesday custom, went to breakfast without shaving. After breakfast, a shoeshine and the barber shop – and then walked a while. At a little after noon, I found myself in a great crowd – and that the parade for St. Nicholas was forming. So I followed it for a while – a parade of embroidered banners, of each church in town, and then to statue of St. Nicholas, with the pedestal covered with flowers, was carried by about eight men, a white canopy was carried alongside him – and baskets of flowers on long poles. The statue was dressed in magnificently embroidered cloth of gold. All along the street, people had hung from their windows their best laces and linens, and colored table clothes and bedspreads. It was really both beautiful and interesting. I understand there is usually much more – This morning there were two bands, playing sweet, soft music. The day celebrates the bringing of the bones of St. Nicholas hither. [9 May]

Figure 59. Procession of Saint Nicholas on May 8th

Allies entered Rome

On 7 June 1944 the Allies entered Rome, freeing it from the harsh months of Nazi occupation. Even in Bari the authorities held speeches for the occasion, speeches which evidently did not have to enthuse the citizens from what Henry says.

After supper – on the way home – I saw a crowd gathered outside the governor's palace – being harangued from the balconies by Italians, with great gesticulation. All I could understand was that "Allora," which means "Then" or "Next" and Rome is liberated, and all Italy would be free – and we should work. The most beautiful thing was the clergyman who stood on the balcony in scarlet robes and lace, nodding his benevolence. There were a few English officers – a few (one) American officer, a lot of Italian officers and civilians. But the most conspicuous man on the balcony (except the cardinal or bishop – who wears scarlet?) was a press correspondent, very drunk, who kept waving from behind the cardinal, in funny antics, and reclining around. The crowd got impatient toward the end – so I suppose the speeches were not very good. I asked what was being said – was told "A little of everything" and such, I suppose, was the case. [7 June]

Figure 71. Report of the demonstration for the liberation of Rome in the local newspaper

Storie di Famiglia

RICERCHE GENEALOGICHE